The New United Nations
International Organization in the Twenty-first Century

John Allphin Moore, Jr.
California State Polytechnic University

Jerry Pubantz
University of North Carolina at Greensboro

PEARSON
Prentice
Hall

Upper Saddle River, New Jersey 07458

Library of Congress Cataloging-in-Publication Data

Moore, John Allphin
    The new United Nations : international organization in the twenty-first
century / John Allphin Moore, Jr., Jerry Pubantz.
        p. cm.
    Includes bibliographical references and index.
    ISBN 0-13-184488-1
    1. United Nations.   2. International relations.   I. Pubantz, Jerry, 1947-   II. Title.
    JZ5005.M66 2006
    341.23—dc22

                                                    2005023179

Editorial Director: Charlyce Jones Owen
Director of Marketing: Heather Shelstad
Marketing Assistant: Jennifer Lang
Senior Managing Editor: Lisa Iarkowski
Production Liaison: Fran Russello
Manufacturing Buyer: Mary Ann Gloriande
Cover Design: Jayne Conte
Cover Illustration/Photo: Getty Images, Inc.
Composition/Full-Service Project Management: Kelly Ricci/GTS/TechBooks
Printer Binder: RR Donnelley & Sons Company

This book was set in Times by *TechBooks/GTS*, York, PA. It was printed and bound by RR Donnelley & Sons
Company. The cover was printed by RR Donnelley & Sons Company.

Credits and acknowledgments borrowed from other sources and reproduced, with permission, in this textbook
appear on appropriate page within text.

Note: Every effort has been made to provide accurate and current Internet information in this book. However,
the Internet and information posted on it are constantly changing, so it is inevitable that some of the Internet
addresses listed in this textbook will change.

Pearson Education LTD. London
Pearson Education Singapore, Pte. Ltd
Pearson Education, Canada, Ltd
Pearson Education–Japan
Pearson Education Australia PTY, Limited

Pearson Education North Asia Ltd
Pearson Educación de Mexico, S.A. de C.V.
Pearson Education Malaysia, Pte. Ltd
Pearson Education, Upper Saddle River, New Jersey

10 9 8 7 6 5 4 3 2 1
ISBN 0-13-184488-1

Dedicated to those who taught
us to understand and write about
the world, especially:

M. Margaret Ball
Charles S. Campbell, Jr.
Jeane J. Kirkpatrick
Myron Roberts

Brief Contents

INTRODUCTION: WAYS OF THINKING ABOUT THE UNITED NATIONS
AND INTERNATIONAL ORGANIZATIONS   1

Chapter 1   THE MANY PLACES OF THE UNITED NATIONS   10

Chapter 2   ORIGINS AND HISTORY OF THE UNITED NATIONS   36

Chapter 3   THE EVOLVING UN CHARTER   77

Chapter 4   EVOLVING INSTITUTIONS   118

Chapter 5   MAINTENANCE OF INTERNATIONAL PEACE AND SECURITY   161

Chapter 6   PEACEKEEPING AND NATION BUILDING   197

Chapter 7   MAKING GLOBAL PUBLIC POLICY: PROMOTING CIVIL SOCIETY,
HUMAN RIGHTS, AND WOMEN'S EMPOWERMENT   227

Chapter 8   ECONOMIC DEVELOPMENT, THE ENVIRONMENT,
AND HEALTH POLICY   254

EPILOGUE   286

APPENDICES

Appendix A   CHARTER OF THE UNITED NATIONS   289

Appendix B   UNIVERSAL DECLARATION OF HUMAN RIGHTS   313

Appendix C   UN MEMBER STATES   319

Appendix D   STATUTE OF THE INTERNATIONAL COURT OF JUSTICE   322

Appendix E   SECRETARIES-GENERAL OF THE UNITED NATIONS   335

Appendix F   SELECTED UN RESOLUTIONS   343

Appendix G   ACRONYMS AND ABBREVIATIONS   352

Index   359

Contents

List of Figures, Tables, and Photos   xi

Acknowledgments   xiii

INTRODUCTION: WAYS OF THINKING ABOUT THE UNITED NATIONS AND INTERNATIONAL ORGANIZATIONS   1

International Organizations   2

Theories of International Relations   2

    Realism   3

    Idealism   3

    Marxism   4

    Critical Theory and Constructivism   5

    Feminism   5

    Dependency Theory   6

    Postmodernism   6

    Other Theories   7

The United Nations   7

Notes   9

Chapter 1   THE MANY PLACES OF THE UNITED NATIONS   10

The UN System   10

    New York City   10

    Geneva, Switzerland   16

    Nairobi, Kenya   20

    Vienna, Austria   22

    The Hague, The Netherlands   23

    Montreal, Canada   24

    Rome, Italy   26

    Pristina, Serbia-Montenegro (Kosovo Province), and Dili,
        Timor-Leste   27

The New United Nations   29

Summary   33

Notes   33

Key Terms   34

Resources for Further Research   34

Chapter 2   ORIGINS AND HISTORY OF THE UNITED NATIONS   36

Overview of Early Historical Efforts to Establish
   International Organization   36

International Relations before the Twentieth Century   37

The Concert of Europe   38

The League of Nations and World War II   39
   The League of Nations   39
   Woodrow Wilson and the Elemental
      Weaknesses of the League   41

U.S. and Allied Visions of the Post–World War II
   Period   42
   Franklin D. Roosevelt (1882–1945)   43
   Winston Churchill (1874–1965)   46
   Joseph Stalin (1879–1953)   48

Three Wartime Conferences   50
   Dumbarton Oaks Conference   50
   Yalta Conference   51
   Bretton Woods Conference   53

UN Conference on International Organization   53

Eleanor's UN: Beyond International Peace and Security   59
   Specialized Agencies and Eleanor's UN   61
   Nongovernmental Organizations and Eleanor's UN   61
   Millennium Summit Goals and Eleanor's UN   62

The Cold War   63
   Korea   64
   Nuclear Weapons   65
   Persisting Tensions   65
   Waning of the Cold War   68

Iraq and the Post–Cold War United Nations   69
   September 11, 2001, and the Age of Terrorism   70

Summary   73

Notes   74

Key Terms   75

Resources for Further Research   76

Chapter 3   THE EVOLVING UN CHARTER   77

Contents of the Charter   77

Amendments to the Charter   79
  Informal Modifications of the Charter   80
  Chapter VI½ Provisions   81

The Cold War, Expanding Membership, and the Charter   81
  Membership   82
  North-South Relations and the United Nations   83
  National Liberation and the United Nations   84
  The Non-Aligned Movement and the United Nations   84

Evolution of International Law   85

Financial Crisis and the Impetus for Reform   91

The Continuing Budget Crisis   92
  Scale of Assessment and the Budget Process   93
  U.S. Nonpayment of UN Dues and the Demand for Reforms:
    Is the United Nations Worth It?   95

UN Reform   97
  Efforts by Pérez de Cuéllar and Boutros-Ghali to
    Accommodate U.S. Demands for Reform   97
  Kofi Annan and the Reform "Revolution"   100
  Scandal and the United Nations   112

Summary   113

Notes   114

Key Terms   116

Resources for Further Research   116

Chapter 4   EVOLVING INSTITUTIONS   118

Coordination of the UN System   118

Principal Organs   119
  General Assembly   119
  Security Council   126
  Economic and Social Council   133
  Trusteeship Council   136
  Secretariat   137
  International Court of Justice   139

Specialized Agencies, Programmes and Funds,
  and Other Groups   143
  Specialized Agencies   143
  Programmes and Funds   145
  Other Groups   146

New Structures on the Global Stage   148
 World Conferences   148
 The Global Compact   149
 Special Rapporteurs   150
 Human Rights Tribunals   150

Globalization, Bretton Woods Institutions, and the United Nations   150
 Bretton Woods Conference   151
 World Bank   152
 International Monetary Fund   153
 World Trade Organization   155

Summary   158

Notes   158

Key Terms   160

Resources for Further Research   160

Chapter 5   MAINTENANCE OF INTERNATIONAL PEACE AND SECURITY   161

Historical Perspective on International Peace and Security   161

The Concept of Collective Security   162

Collective Security Provisions of the UN Charter   166

Legal Authority for Collective Security: UN Charter Chapters VI and VII   168

Collective Security under Cold War Conditions   172
 Uniting for Peace Resolution   173
 Emergency Special Sessions of the General Assembly   173
 Peacekeeping and Military Observer Groups   176

Disarmament and Arms Control   176
 Changing Disarmament Priorities   180

Post–Cold War Collective Security   183
 Smart Sanctions   184

The UN's Longest Collective Security Crisis:
 The Arab-Israeli Dispute   187

Summary   193

Notes   194

Key Terms   195

Resources for Further Research   195

Chapter 6   PEACEKEEPING AND NATION BUILDING   197

The Origination of Peacekeeping in the United Nations   197

Important Cold War Peacekeeping Missions   198

UN Military Observer Group in India and Pakistan 198
UN Operation in the Congo 199
UN Peacekeeping Force in Cyprus 200
UN Disengagement Observer Force 201
UN Interim Force in Lebanon 202

Second-Generation Peacekeeping 203
UN Department of Peacekeeping Operations 204
Early Nation-Building Missions 205
Later Second-Generation Peacekeeping Missions 208
Brahimi Report 212
Peace Building 213

Africa 219
Somalia 219
The Congo 221
Sierra Leone and Liberia 222

Summary 224

Notes 225

Key Terms 226

Resources for Further Research 226

Chapter 7   MAKING GLOBAL PUBLIC POLICY: PROMOTING CIVIL SOCIETY, HUMAN RIGHTS, AND WOMEN'S EMPOWERMENT 227

The Emergence of Thematic Diplomacy 227

The Age of the Nongovernmental Organization 228

Special Rapporteurs 231

The Global Compact 232

Global Civil Society 234

Human Rights 235
The Policy Process 235
The Judicial Process 241

Women's Rights 246
Securing Group Rights through Public
Mobilization 246
Research on Women 249
Assistance to Women 250

Summary 251

Notes 251

Key Terms 252

Resources for Further Research 252

Chapter 8   ECONOMIC DEVELOPMENT, THE ENVIRONMENT, AND HEALTH POLICY   254

Backdrop to Economic Development Policy   254

UN Conference on Trade and Development   257

UN Development Programme   259

The Right to Development and the Least Developed Countries   261

The Environment and Sustainable Development   266

UN Environment Programme   268

Atmosphere and Climate Change   271

Water Pollution and Marine Resources   274

Biodiversity and Natural Resources   275

Desertification and Deforestation   276

International Financing   278

Sustainable *Human* Development: The Fight against HIV/AIDS   279

Summary   282

Notes   283

Key Terms   285

Resources for Further Research   285

EPILOGUE   286

APPENDICES

Appendix A   CHARTER OF THE UNITED NATIONS   289

Appendix B   UNIVERSAL DECLARATION OF HUMAN RIGHTS   313

Appendix C   UN MEMBER STATES   319

Appendix D   STATUTE OF THE INTERNATIONAL COURT OF JUSTICE   322

Appendix E   SECRETARIES-GENERAL OF THE UNITED NATIONS   335

Appendix F   SELECTED UN RESOLUTIONS   343

Appendix G   ACRONYMS AND ABBREVIATIONS   352

Index   359

List of Figures, Tables, and Photos

(Number in parentheses is the number of the chapter in which the element appears.)

FIGURES

UN Bodies in Geneva, Switzerland (1)   18
UN Specialized Agencies around the World (1)   25
Principal Offices of the UN System (1)   30
Important Moments in the Founding of the United Nations (2)   55
Quotation by U.S. Senator Jesse Helms (3)   100
Executive Committees of the United Nations (3)   102
Chronology of UN Reform (3)   109
UN System (July 2005) (4)   120
Chronology of General Assembly Special Sessions (4)   123
Economic and Social Council: Its Network of Commissions, Committees, Bodies, Funds, Programmes, and Experts (4)   135
UN Specialized Agency Locations around the World (4)   144
Legal Basis for Collective Security: The Covenant of the League of Nations (5)   163
Legal Basis for Collective Security: Charter of the United Nations (5)   169
Security Council Resolution 242 (5)   189
Ongoing Peacekeeping Missions (6)   204
Ongoing Political and Peace-Building Missions (6)   218
Nongovernmental Organization Participation in the UN System (7)   229
Landmarks in the Development of Human Rights International Law (7)   238
Chronology of UN Efforts on Behalf of Women (7)   247
UN Development Programme at a Glance (8)   260
Chronology of UN Policy on the Environment (8)   272

TABLES

Emergency Special Sessions of the UN General Assembly Authorized by the Uniting for Peace
Resolution (5)   174

Second-Generation Peacekeeping, Nation-Building, Political, and Peace-Building Operations in the
New Era (6)   214

Millennium Development Goals and Targets (8)   264

PHOTOS

UN Headquarters Building in New York City (1)   13

Palais des Nations, the UN Headquarters in Geneva, Switzerland (1)   17

Soviet Foreign Minister Molotov, U.S. Secretary of State Stettinius, and British Foreign Secretary
Eden Conferring in the San Francisco Opera House, Where the UN Conference on International
Organization was Meeting on May 1, 1945 (2)   56

The International Court of Justice (ICJ) in The Hague, The Netherlands (3)   88

General Assembly Hall at UN Headquarters in New York City (4)   119

Security Council Members Adopting the Brahimi Report, November 13, 2000
(Resolution 1327) (4)   127

U.S. Permanent Representative Richard Holbrooke, President of the Security Council,
Chairing a Debate on AIDS (the First Discussion of a Health Issue as a Threat to
Peace and Security) (5)   166

UN Transitional Administration in East Timor (UNTAET) (6)   209

Eleanor Roosevelt and *The Universal Declaration of Human Rights* (7)   236

Vaccination in the Congo (8)   280

Acknowledgments

This text is the third book about the United Nations that we have written together. Along the way we have published articles on the United Nations and world affairs, and we have participated together in a number of conferences both in the United States and overseas. Three meetings of special note have put us in the good company of colleagues whose reflections on our theories and propositions have honed our conception of what we think the UN's importance is to current times. At the University of Tartu in Estonia in 1999, as invited guests of the New World Order Forum at St. George's College at Windsor Castle in 2002, and at the University of the Aegean on the island of Rhodes, Greece, in 2003 we were compelled to clarify our thesis of a new United Nations. We have also attended several meetings in New York through the years. We extend our thanks for the intellectual challenges we have encountered especially to Peter Ashby, Simon Duke, Taina Järvinen, Elvira Osipova, Warren Kimball, Blanche Wiesen Cook, and Michael Eaton. Also, we have had the regular feedback of Cindy Combs (University of North Carolina, Charlotte) and Martin Slann (Pennsylvania State University, Wilkes-Barre) during recurring presentations to the International Studies Association, South.

In the following pages we have drawn on our earlier work, including the book *To Create a New World? American Presidents and the United Nations,* and, more often, our coedited *Encyclopedia of the United Nations.* Within the text readers will find citations to these volumes when appropriate. With that in mind we would like to acknowledge Facts on File, publisher of the *Encyclopedia,* and to thank, for his guidance and friendship, Owen Lancer, who was our editor on both these previous works.

We began our joint interest in the subject as young faculty advisers accompanying our students to the National Model UN annual conference in New York, the *Ur* simulation of the United Nations. During the nearly thirty years we have continued this activity, we have learned from our students and refined our understanding from contact with talented fellow advisers. The current text has benefited from their insights and help. Meaning to forget no one among the Model UN community who has assisted in our work, we could always seek out and receive extraordinary insight and critiques from Kenneth J. Grieb, University of Wisconsin, Oshkosh; Douglas Becker, Colgate University; Sean McMahon, University of Alberta; Robert McNamara, Sonoma State University; Donna Schlagheck, Wright State University; Thomas Weiler, University of Bonn; Shelly Williams, Austin College; and Karen Vogel, Hamline University.

The UN professional staff have been more than accommodating in our efforts. Our visits to the Dag Hammarskjöld Library, especially to the lush photographic unit there not only have been enjoyable, but also have resulted in our being able to make use of several official reproductions for this text. First and foremost among the many impressive individuals at the United Nations who have been receptive to our work and helped make this book possible is Anne Cunningham. From different posts in the Department of Public Information during the last five years, Ms. Cunningham guided us through the UN labyrinth to the proper sources as we worked not only on this, but also on our previous two books. We also thank Hiroshi Murakami, Chief of the Cartographic Section, and his staff, including Bernhard Wagner and Vladimir Bessarabov. Clara Gouy and others in the Photographic Unit guided us to the precise pictures that would bring this text alive for students. We are also in debt to Diane Poole and Renata Morteo in the External Publications Office for helping us with the necessary permissions to reprint UN materials.

As valuable as primary sources are to the successful presentation of an undergraduate text, this work owes nearly as much to the careful review of the manuscript by some fine scholars provided by our editors at Prentice Hall, whose criticisms and advice have saved us from avoidable errors, brought fresh information to our attention, and encouraged us to rethink some of our assumptions. We particularly thank Mark Amstutz of Wheaton College, Robert Blanton from the University of Memphis, Debra Delaet of Drake University, Radoslav Dimitrov at the University of Utah, and Bob Switky of the University of Nebraska at Kearney. Our editors at Prentice Hall— Glenn Johnston and Charlyce Jones-Owen—and their superb staff, including, most important, Suzanne Remore and John Ragozzine, as well as Linda Landis-Clark and Kelly Ricci from TechBooks/GTS, have been genial, exacting, and crucial in this enterprise. The thorough copy-editing of Kathleen Riley-King has brought to the text salutary tautness and cogency. We would be remiss if we did not mention Emily Cleary, our original Prentice Hall contact, who was sure to shepherd the idea for this book to just the right editors.

We want to pay our intellectual debt to our academic institutions and colleagues on our respective campuses. At California State Polytechnic University, which has always reinforced John Moore's scholarly work, understanding that it complements his larger task of teaching, several colleagues warrant recognition for their assistance: Barbara J. Way, Dean of the College of Letters, Arts, and Social Sciences; Mahmood Ibrahim, Daniel Lewis, Zuoyue Wang, Steve Englehart, John Lloyd, Joshua Sides, and Gayle Saverese, all of the History Department; political scientist Sid Silliman; and Kate Seifert, friend and mentor at the university's cutting-edge library. Jerry Pubantz is imminently taking up the post of professor of political science at the University of North Carolina at Greensboro, where he has taught sporadically for twenty years, and where he has developed an admiration for his colleagues and the intellectual community that abides at the university. Much of his work on this text has come with the insights of his colleagues at Salem College, where he has taught for the last twenty-nine years. At Salem the advice and steady counsel of Errol Clauss, senior member of the History Department, and the expert talents of reference librarian Susan Taylor have kept him focused on what needed to be included in the text and how it should be said.

As always, we tender our deep appreciation to our spouses—Linda and Gloria—who each have their own active careers but are somehow able to tolerate, even appreciate, their conjugal scribblers.

Fortunate as we are with the encouragement and assistance we have received, we remain fully apprised that any errors of omission or commission in the current text rest firmly on our shoulders.

John Allphin Moore, Jr.
Pomona, California

Jerry Pubantz
Winston-Salem, North Carolina
June 2005

Introduction: Ways of Thinking about the United Nations and International Organizations

This text is intended neither as a glorification of the United Nations nor as a reproof of its ineffectiveness or potential menace. Rather, we describe what the United Nations is and what it does. This task is not simple. Those of you who have examined your national government often find yourselves faced with a baffling array of institutions, bureaucracies, personalities, and long-term practices that make full understanding difficult. The United Nations, having existed and changed for more than half a century, presents a similar dilemma. The challenge is uniquely daunting in that the United Nations, although having every nation-state in the world as a member, is an international organization, not a national, sovereign government.

In the following pages we offer a thesis and a structure meant to help you grasp the full range and meaning of the United Nations. We present the history and functioning of the institution by looking at both the "old" United Nations—that is, the organization as its founders envisaged it in the 1940s and as the public often views it today—and, markedly, the "new" United Nations, by which we mean what it has become during the six decades of its evolution. The configuration of the text can be discerned by looking at the table of contents. However, given the complex organization that is the United Nations, the structure of the book will result in periodic overlapping of subject matter and themes. This parallelism cannot be avoided.

At times, you may find yourself—as you would while studying U.S. government and politics—in a state of bewilderment while trying to absorb a battery of information. We have tried to assist you in several ways: We have organized each chapter with sections and subsections around explicable themes. We have highlighted certain words or phrases in each chapter and then listed them at the end of the chapter to encourage you to focus on and distinguish specific institutions and ideas. Cross-references to other chapters covering similar topical material appear throughout the text. A brief and select list of books, articles, documents, and Web sites at the end of each chapter provides access to further information about the topics. Finally, the inclusion of graphics helps clarify textual comment.

INTERNATIONAL ORGANIZATIONS

The study of the United Nations falls conveniently within the larger academic field of *international organization*. Scholars who study international organizations come from a variety of academic fields, including political science, history, economics, geography, sociology, law, philosophy, and international relations. International organizations in the twenty-first century often bring together nation-states, nongovernmental organizations, academic associations, organizations with specific interests (such as the environment, international law, finance, and business), regional alignments (such as the European Union and the Organization of American States), and other groupings. The extensive UN System (described in Chapter 4) is the quintessential international organization of current times.

One other useful term to define is *intergovernmental organization*. Often this term is difficult to differentiate from *international organization*. We note a fine distinction: *Intergovernmental* organizations bring together *governments* for definable and agreed purposes. Examples are the organizations within the UN System; the various specialized agencies, such as the Food and Agriculture Organization or the Universal Postal Union (discussed in Chapter 4); and regional organizations such as the Caribbean Community (CARICOM) and the North Atlantic Treaty Organization (NATO). Intergovernmental organizations can be studied within the larger province of international organizations.

International organizations differ in many respects from other common social combinations, such as a family, a religion, or a nation. An individual's allegiance to a family, a religion, or a nation tends to be much firmer than his or her commitment to a more transcendent international organization like the United Nations. Thus, people are less inclined to forgive or overlook flaws in the United Nations than in the other groupings to which they belong. As individuals, we are close to our family, faithful to our religion, and patriotic to our country. Our connection to the United Nations is, understandably, more tenuous, particularly because *other*—less familiar—religions, nations, and cultures are also represented there. You should keep in mind this personal remoteness and the extraordinary diversity of the United Nations as you study it.

THEORIES OF INTERNATIONAL RELATIONS

International relations is a field of academic study often considered part of the discipline of political science, although some people would insist that it is also a field of public policy or even of history. In this field, academicians investigate and analyze the relationships among nation-states within what is frequently called the *international system*. Thus, they are interested in international organizations like the United Nations. However, how someone understands the role, importance, and possible merits of an international organization in the current global system depends on the theoretical framework he or she adopts concerning international relations in general. Many such frameworks exist; thus, you should become aware of those that are most familiar before continuing. We are not suggesting that you adopt a single or definitive schema for understanding current international relations. In fact, in the following pages, although we mention certain theoretical perspectives when doing so is appropriate, you will see that the main aim of this text is to explain the United Nations straightforwardly rather than theoretically.

Scholars often think of international relations as being either *positive* or *normative*. In this context the word *positive* refers to how things actually are, rather than how they should be. *Positivism* comes from a system of thought associated with nineteenth-century sociologist Auguste Comte that recognized only positive facts and observable phenomena. In contrast, *normative* refers to how things ought to be, at least in someone's eyes. It refers to standards or norms, which could originate from more metaphysical (beyond observable facts) prescriptions of proper behavior. These two perspectives have produced the two most prominent viewpoints on international relations: realism and idealism. Other viewpoints include Marxism, critical theory and constructivism, feminism, dependency theory, and postmodernism.

Realism

We associate realism with thinkers from Niccolò Machiavelli (1469–1527) through twentieth-century scholars like Hans Morgenthau and Kenneth Waltz (sometimes called a *neorealist*) and policymakers like Henry Kissinger. Realists insist that a person should look at world affairs as they really are and not as he or she might want them to be. Doing so, realists understand that the principal players in the international arena are nation-states, usually with significantly different cultural traditions and each acting in its rational self-interest within an environment of international anarchy. No sovereign authority over nations exists to control their relations; states must develop their interactions with other states on their own. International or multinational organizations may be useful but are not of primary consequence. A struggle for power is ongoing in world politics, and in pursuing the national interest above all, policymakers use various tools, including diplomacy, economic power, and, ultimately, military force, to try to attain their aims. A country's relative level of power, including economic and military power, determines its relations with other states. In summary, realists emphasize national interest, power, security, and the centrality of the nation-state. In the quest for security, nations try to build up resources. Realists do not encourage the use of international politics to try to force upon other nations and cultures specific patterns of "good" behavior. Nor do realists believe that changing human nature, which is constant and can be both good and evil, is possible.

Idealism

The term *idealism* has philosophical roots and, by historical standards, predates realism as a theory of international affairs. The term is associated with Plato, who taught that all properties and objects people could imagine have independent, "ideal" existence. Plato spoke of "higher truths" than what humans know in the material world. The eighteenth-century German philosopher Immanuel Kant elaborated the modern conception of idealism, placing politics at the service of morality. He postulated what was called a *transcendent idealism* beyond concrete reality, and he believed that by rigorous mental effort, people could come to understand it and profit by the understanding. Kant encouraged all republics (which he supposed were growing in number) to unite into a federation of peaceable nations. He was convinced that republics would not war against one another. He assumed that growing interdependence, in terms of both world trade and international communication, would eventually ensure the growth of republicanism, homogeneity, and peace. He hoped that standards of appropriate political behavior on the international stage could be measured by the world's public in terms of what rightly ought to be done, rather than by national leaders, who often act in secret according to their primary standards—power and self-interest. U.S. president Woodrow Wilson reformulated Kant's hopes. Wilson's principles were sometimes referred to as *liberal internationalism*.

Devoted followers of idealism can be found in the academy today, and among some policymakers. A whole body of scholarship (devoted to the so-called democratic peace thesis) has emerged to try to prove that the number of democracies expanded during the late twentieth century, that democracies will not war against one another, and that international regimes of law and cooperation can be developed and then studied as examples of human progress. Such liberalism covers a wide range of views and activities, from Wilsonian idealism, as reflected in the Fourteen Points of 1918 and the Covenant of the League of Nations (explained in Chapter 2), through contemporary so-called neoliberal theories, such as the advocacy of transparent and equitable trade and finance rules for the world community, and the democratic peace thesis just mentioned.

For liberal idealists, nation-states are only one set of actors in international affairs, and even they can cooperate by means of transnational institutions like the United Nations. In so doing, they can demonstrate that the world's peoples are able to rise above base interests and military aggression. Believing in higher, "idealistic," goals for humans beyond mere existence and security, idealists insist on the independent and significant role that multilateral organizations can play. Unlike realists, they tend to emphasize the goodness of human nature. Nevertheless, in some instances, idealists may justify military action to force reform on recalcitrant nation-states, such as in Bosnia in the late 1990s.

Marxism

Marxism derives from the historical studies and political and economic theories of Karl Marx, nineteenth-century philosopher and "father" of modern "scientific" socialism, or communism. Some scholars have refined Marx's notions and posited an approach to international relations shrewdly different from the more traditional realist and idealist attitudes. A number of terms characterize the complex theory of Marxism. Among the terms of interest are *economic determinism, class struggle, revolution,* and *historical materialism.* Although Marxism as a political program became a worry for much of the Western world during the twentieth century, you should bear in mind how students of history, politics, and international affairs have tried to use its insights for analytical purposes. Marx stressed that economics—not ideas or ideals or spiritual, religious, or cultural values—chiefly influenced the course of history. This "economic determinism" produced an inevitable historical process of class conflict between the oppressor and the oppressed. People, institutions, and forces in a society that control the means of production and the distribution of goods (the landed aristocracy in the Middle Ages, corporation capitalists in the modern world) not only represent the wealthiest members of society and its upper classes, but also determine the sources of information, the education, indeed the broad culture of a society (including its values), and dominate its social and political life to their own advantage.

Marxism differs from realism and idealism in asserting that class divisions are more important determinants in history than are national interest or ideals. Classes are determined by economic relationships; higher classes are those that dominate the economy. However, the prospect of a lower class's gaining the upper hand by taking advantage of innovative economic changes always exists. Inevitably, a revolutionary "leap" to a new stage of history occurs. Thus, the *bourgeoisie* (middle-class, profit-minded entrepreneurs living in cities) gained control of the new capitalist system of banks, money, and commerce, and by the nineteenth century replaced aristocratic landowners as the prevailing political and cultural force in the Western world. From the Marxist perspective, the world is dominated by this bourgeois class, which is intent on maintaining its ascendancy worldwide, and it uses the state to maintain its power. The dominant class is not necessarily crude, vicious, or overtly imperialistic. However, through foreign aid, international loans, grants, investment, trade agreements, cultural exchange programs, and participation in international organizations, the bourgeoisie attempts to draw into its orbit those outside who might represent a threat to its supremacy. The late U.S. historian William Appleman Williams described this kind of policy as an "informal empire."

International organizations like the United Nations can best be studied if you consider them as the settings in which an economic struggle takes place between the fortunate class and those representing an immediate challenge (such as the "Second World" of the Soviet region during the cold war), or those (such as the less fortunate in the "Third World") beneath it. In an era of globalization, the worldwide capitalist class uses international organizations, financial institutions, and competitive markets to maintain its dominance.

Critical Theory and Constructivism

Critical theorists also reject realism and idealism. They likewise deny the reasonableness of positivism, finding that humans simply cannot find abstract "objective" truths. For critical theorists, any premise, theory, or idea has a purpose and is designed for or useful to someone or some group. That is, a relationship exists between a person's knowledge and his or her actual practice—or, that is, between the knower and the known. Thus, separating fact from value is difficult, or impossible. Knowledge, then, is not impartial and obtained by objective study but is, rather, "constitutive" (i.e., a product and result) of existing values and interests. The comparable "constructivist" theory emphasizes that norms and culture, which produce (or "construct") a group's "identity" as a people or nation, play important roles in international affairs (although any one group must share the world stage with other "constructed" identities, and relations among different cultures, institutions, and norms can affect the way nations interact).

We as individuals can easily sense the force of these contentions because we all likely have preliminary views springing from our distinctive culture (American, Christian, liberal, conservative) that guide our interpretation of any international event, irrespective of what might be the independent facts of the event. According to critical theorists, for us to study international relations adequately, we must concede the predispositions of diplomatic actors, critique positivists' insistence on traditional objective problem solving, and emphasize new forms of international harmony that recognize plural perspectives and possibilities for cooperation among them. In this perspective, international organizations are "conveners" of diverse actors, are perceived differently by each participant, and have a changing value and importance depending on how international affairs are generally constructed at any given time.

Feminism

The international relations approach of feminism is couched in an emphasis on "gender." The terms *gender* and *sex* are not identical. Rather—with reference to the preceding discussion on constructivism—gender roles are "socially constructed," not a product of biological sex differences. Thus, at your college all department secretaries could be women, not because only women are genetically capable of being secretaries, but because the role of secretary has been "genderized" or "socially constructed" by U.S. culture so that only women perform the role. Whatever differences exist among feminists (and there are many), all agree that gender is significant in world affairs and that the fact that, for the most part, only men have composed the main theories about international relations—whether realist, idealist, or Marxist—has made a difference. For feminists, this fact means that a large segment of the academy is ignored at the peril of thorough exploration from as many perspectives as possible. Some feminists might argue that if the writing of international relations theory and the formulating and crafting of international diplomacy were infused with women's perspectives, much less violence would exist in the world. However, such an argument in itself posits a "genderized" notion of international affairs.

Moreover, mostly men have been in control of nation-state governments and state-state interactions. Even women may ignore the possible role of their sex when thinking about international relations, acceding to the common assumption that women necessarily find themselves in a "separate sphere" of domestic life, engaging in activities wholly separate from the large issues of world politics. Again, this disregard underscores the genderized notion that men, but not women, are competitive, rational, and power seeking. Particularly obvious to feminists is the male-oriented "realist" doctrines of an aggressive world of competitive nations in a state of international anarchy. Within this anarchic "jungle," international organizations have traditionally served male-oriented expectations by emphasizing diplomatic and military purposes and the adjustment of relations among states. A feminist sees the value of these organizations as serving broader communal interests and agendas.

Dependency Theory

A variant of Marxism, *dependency theory* became attractive to the developing world during the 1970s, although its popularity has diminished since then. Proponents of dependency theory maintain that the inadequate level of economic development in poor countries is caused chiefly by their asymmetrical dependence on the more dominant highly developed countries. Some dependency theorists believe that less affluent countries (most in the Southern Hemisphere) will remain poor because the developed countries will continue to use multinational corporations to siphon off whatever surpluses the impoverished countries produce. One damaging result is that no profit is left for the poor countries to use for reinvestment.

As a rule the countries ill affected by the current world economic order are former colonies of wealthier Northern Hemisphere nations. Even as these countries have become independent, they have remained poor. Some dependency theorists believe that poorer nations should discontinue economic ties with wealthier nations, protect their surplus production, and pursue more nationalist and protectionist—even socialist—policies to break the vicious cycle of underdevelopment. Other theorists, dismissing the neoliberal theories of economic growth through international markets, criticize capitalism as a system that perpetuates inequality. They find international institutions such as the World Trade Organization and the International Monetary Fund particularly noxious because, they charge, such institutions benefit only the rich. Thus, only a radical reform of the world economic system, including a fundamental redistribution of income and resources from the Northern Hemisphere to the Southern and the introduction of a world progressive tax system on foreign exchange transactions, will rectify inequalities and end poverty. Many dependency theorists favor complete elimination of Third World debt and the full funding, by means of grants (not loans), of large development projects. According to dependency theorists, the United Nations and its related international organizations can best be examined as the institutions most capable of forwarding a restructuring of world economic relations.

Postmodernism

Postmodernism (sometimes called *poststructuralism* to distinguish it from its predecessor, *structuralism*) first became fashionable in language studies. It has begun to make an impression on other humanities and on the social sciences, although its impact on international relations theory remains limited. Postmodernist theory is linked with a number of twentieth-century French philosophers, including Michel Foucault and Jacques Derrida. The term *postmodernism* can be understood by noting that the term *modernism* is associated with the Enlightenment, a period in

Western history in which science, empiricism, rationality, secularism, objective truth, and individualism were emphasized. According to "post" modernism (i.e., "after" modernism), the Enlightenment was a wholly inadequate guide to understanding the world. Objectivity, rationality, and the individual are critiqued. In this sense, postmodernism is related to critical theory, constructivism, and feminism, which were discussed previously.

Postmodernists make use of literary theory to dispute the possibility of an objective reality in world affairs. They jettison the "dominant discourses" in the field of international relations—realism, idealism, and Marxism—which are based on Enlightenment notions of objective reality, but are, in fact, according to postmodernists, simply reflections of a Western (and white male) culture that has sought to dominate the rest of the world. By insisting that the *words* of modernity (*liberty, freedom, rights, equality, written law, impartiality, individualism, economic entrepreneurship,* and so forth) are universally applicable, Western theorists of these schools of thought are simply exerting their command over other, equally valid opinions of reality (including communitarian, uncommon, and premodern notions of social order). Postmodernists urge a new and radical politics, in place of these imposed Western ideas, to give voice to groups and nations that have been marginalized by authoritarian discourses. International organizations must be open to these groups and their issues.

Postmodernists, in rejecting the Enlightenment, emphasize relativism rather than certainty, nihilism rather than optimism, and historical circumstance rather than the independent individual. They seek to "deconstruct" texts—such as treaties, constitutions, and charters (like that of the United Nations)—to find the real source of hierarchical power hidden behind the (only apparently benign) words that Western thinkers have put in the texts. In this way, postmodernism gives some sustenance to critical theory, feminism, and dependency theory.

Other Theories

Many more perspectives than those just mentioned have been adopted by various groups, but these give you a taste of how scholars tie theoretical frameworks to studies of international relations. We restate that this text does not require you to look at the United Nations through the eyes of any particular hypothesis. In fact, we prefer that you avoid speculative assumptions and instead concentrate on examining the United Nations with a clear eye and an inquiring, almost Socratic, demeanor.

THE UNITED NATIONS

With the preceding information in mind, we should utter just a few opening words about the subject of the text to provide you with a prologue to the study that follows. We note that the organization of the United Nations, which was initially something of a mystery to Soviet leader Joseph Stalin, rings familiar to citizens of the Western world or individuals conversant with presidential or Westminster-parliamentary systems of government. For example, the United Nations has legislative (the General Assembly), executive (the Secretariat combined with the Security Council), and judicial (the International Court of Justice) branches. The UN Charter also emphasizes equal trade and the "territorial and administrative integrity" of sovereign states (Article 2) and is supplemented by the Universal Declaration of Human Rights, with its commitment to individual freedoms.

All this notwithstanding, the United Nations is too often marginalized in discussions of world affairs. Part of this disregard is undoubtedly due to certain misconceptions about the organization. One useful point to remember is that the United Nations is a "confederation," not a unitary or a federally organized government. That is, it is made up of sovereign members; it has no overarching authority apart from these states, and it is then only what its members make of it. Thus, it acts effectively only by means of consensus, not by strict majority vote. Moreover, it cannot fulfill utopian notions of world peace and order because, as former Israeli representative Abba Eban said, it is an "international organization . . . a *mechanism,* not a policy or principle."[1] As Secretary-General Dag Hammarskjöld once explained: "The United Nations is not . . . a superstate, able to act outside the framework of decisions by its member governments. It is an instrument for negotiation. . . . [It] can serve, but not substitute itself for the efforts of its member governments."[2]

Another point to note is that, in the aftermath of the cold war, the United Nations is not alone on a pinnacle above all other institutions that connect the world. Rather, it is a consolidating axis for the organizations that link sovereign states into ever-widening and more closely knit international units. The intricate international order purposely crafted following World War II has proved durable and mature. By 2005 the General Agreement on Tariffs and Trade (GATT) had become the World Trade Organization (WTO); the World Bank and the International Monetary Fund (IMF) had extended their activities; at Vienna in 1993 human rights were proclaimed and accepted by most nations as "universal"; and regional groupings such as the North American Free Trade Association (NAFTA), the Association of Southeast Asian Nations (ASEAN), the Asian Pacific Economic Cooperation Organization (APEC), and the European Union (EU) were working in close coordination with the United Nations. Unlike any comparable multistate organization in history, the United Nations has remained operative for an unprecedented sixty years, expanding its membership to virtual universality. As this expansion continued beyond the turn of the millennium, the organization found itself at the forefront of some of the most significant international developments, many made evident on the front pages of newspapers or as a lead story from the world's major news outlets.

Apart from the oft-remarked activities of UN agencies, consider, just for example, the following eleven milestones associated with the UN's participation in world affairs:

1. Israel came into being by the Jewish Agency's unilateral implementation of a UN resolution, which initiated the modern Middle East quandary. The United Nations has been the central institution in defining, in international legal terms, the nature of the Middle East problem. From the establishment of Israel through the crisis of 1956, to UN Resolutions 242 and 338, through the Camp David Accords, to the handshake at the White House in 1993, to the impasse of 2001 and the continued violence that followed, the common perception remains that the internationally recognized legal basis for any possible resolution to this seemingly intractable dilemma rests in a long-term connection with the United Nations.

2. The remarkable developments in South Africa and Namibia during the last decade of the twentieth century—which resulted in the purging of apartheid, the introduction of a democratic government in South Africa, and the full independence of Namibia—were conditional on UN resolutions.

3. The 1993 elections in troubled Cambodia took place under the legal rubric of UN resolutions and with UN administration. In 1998 international monitors returned to watch over another election, and the United Nations remained involved as part of the international effort to establish a war crimes tribunal to address the forced deaths of some 1.5 million Cambodians during the 1970s.

4. The ongoing negotiations to settle the Cyprus problem are based in UN resolutions. In 2004 the "Annan Plan," named for its author, Secretary-General Kofi Annan, was put before Cypriot voters, which gave the island nation the best chance for peace in thirty years.

5. By the mid-1990s, the United Nations, by passing resolutions and establishing observer groups to provide supervision, guided the end of civil wars and the ultimate general elections in three beleaguered Central American countries: Nicaragua, El Salvador, and Guatemala.

6. The Gulf War in 1991, which removed Iraqi forces from Kuwait, was based on UN Security Council resolutions (particularly Resolution 678); thus, the war was a genuine "collective security" operation designed to uphold the sovereignty of a UN member.

7. The Dayton Accords of 1995 were U.S.-led impositions to implement the UN's insistence on ending the brutal fighting in the former Yugoslavia, and for the next seven years the UN Mission in Bosnia and Herzegovina (UNMIBH) coordinated a wide range of responsibilities, including provision of humanitarian and relief supplies, human rights enforcement, demining, monitoring of elections, and rebuilding infrastructure.

8. In Kosovo, the UN Kosovo Force (KFOR), starting in the spring of 1999, supervised the final peace settlement following the NATO war against Serbian domination of the province, and the UN Interim Administration for Kosovo, which monitored the relatively peaceful municipal elections in the province in October 2000, was considered an example of successful nation building by the United Nations. A new eruption of violence in 2004 did not diminish the UN's importance to peace in Kosovo, but only reaffirmed it.

9. In 1999 the United Nations took over administration in the embattled territory of East Timor, setting up a transitional authority in the area as it proceeded to separate from Indonesia. In late August 2001, UN monitors administered elections for East Timor, providing self-rule for its inhabitants for the first time since the Portuguese and the Dutch arrived four centuries earlier.

10. UN war crimes tribunals were, by 2001, active in The Hague, The Netherlands, and in Arusha, Tanzania, prosecuting and trying alleged war criminals from the Balkan and Rwandan civil wars.

11. By the summer of 2004, as we describe in some detail in the coming pages, even the United States had returned to the United Nations to seek help and legitimacy for the reconstruction of a fractured Iraq, a half year after the United States launched a largely unilateral preemptive strike without Security Council authorization.

Despite the criticisms so often directed at the United Nations, the institution seems to remain begrudgingly indispensable. It is worthy of study. Accordingly, we invite you to turn the page and enter the world of the "new" United Nations. We begin with a "snapshot" of the UN System scattered around the world in the fall of 2003.

NOTES

1. Abba Eban, "The U.N. Idea Revisited," *Foreign Affairs* 74, no. 5 (1995): 40.

2. Dag Hammarskjöld, "The Promise of the U.N.," *New York Times Magazine,* September 15, 1957, 21.

Chapter 1

The Many Places of the United Nations

Since its inception in 1945, the United Nations has grown from its New York City headquarters to a system of facilities addressing various issues around the world. In this chapter we provide you with a global snapshot of the UN System, especially in relation to its operations during the fall of 2003. Afterward, we discuss how the United Nations of the 1940s has been evolving through the years into a "new" United Nations.

THE UN SYSTEM

New York City

Saint Lucia is a Caribbean island nation of 163,000 people. Geographically it is only three and a half times the size of Washington, D.C. Granted independence in 1979, it joined the United Nations the same year, one of the smallest and newest members of the world body. Its role in the day-to-day affairs of international politics has been necessarily limited. However, on Tuesday, September 16, 2003, Julian Hunte, Saint Lucia's minister of external affairs, ascended the dais of the UN General Assembly Hall in New York City as the new president of the General Assembly. He opened the fifty-eighth session of the assembly and prepared to preside over its deliberations for the next year. His presidency was a personal honor for Hunte, but it also gave Saint Lucia a new importance in the United Nations and, therefore, world affairs. In his opening remarks Mr. Hunte drew the world body's attention to such a notable moment: when the presidency of the UN General Assembly passed to a representative of the smallest country ever to hold that office. By his election, the United Nations, in his view, reaffirmed its faith in the equal rights of nations large and small. President Hunte said that he would focus the work of the session on the fulfillment of UN development goals for the new millennium and in particular seek to address the issues of AIDS, poverty, and environmental challenges.

Before he could turn to his agenda, however, Hunte had to preside over the opening ceremonies and procedural matters. A week later, on September 23, he began **General Debate,** the yearly practice of allowing the UN member states to address the assembly on the important issues facing the world. Compared with most opening sessions, this one was particularly dramatic—a session that demonstrated the strengths and limitations of the United Nations in the contemporary international environment. With the world warily mindful of events in Iraq and the inability of the great powers to reach agreement within the UN Security Council on both the merits of the war just fought in Iraq and future policy in that occupied country, U.S. president George W. Bush and French president Jacques Chirac were among the world leaders to address the session. The French president had been the most vocal critic of the U.S. decision to overthrow Saddam Hussein without formal authorization from the world body.

President Bush was the fourth speaker during the morning session on September 23. Spiritedly defending U.S. actions, he called on the world community to step forward and assist in the reconstruction of Iraq. Separated only by the remarks of the fifth speaker—Alejandro Toledo Manrique, the president of Peru—President Chirac followed, standing at the same marble podium President Bush had vacated minutes before. Chirac acknowledged that the United Nations had just "weathered one of the gravest trials in its history" and charged that "the war, embarked on without Security Council approval, [had] undermined the multilateral system."[1] He obliquely chastised the United States for its actions and then acknowledged that events had called into question the vitality and viability of the 58-year-old institution. He told the 191 gathered nations,[2]

> In an open world, no one can live in isolation, no one can act alone in the name of all, and no one can accept the anarchy of a society without rules. There is no alternative to the United Nations. But in the face of today's challenges, this fundamental choice, as expressed in the [UN] Charter, calls for a far-reaching reform of our organization.

Despite their use of the General Debate to express their countries' divergent views on current events, Chirac and Bush met later in the day behind closed doors to try to narrow their differences. The United Nations thus provided a forum for the expression of continuing discord and a setting for traditional diplomacy in the pursuit of reconciling differences.

Prior to the speeches by the U.S. and French presidents, the seventh and current UN secretary-general, **Kofi Annan,** descended from his seat next to Julian Hunte on the upper dais overlooking the speaker's podium so that he might address the assembly. His remarks were sobering, reminding the world's representatives that they had gathered in the same place three years earlier for the Millennium Summit, at which time they expressed their optimism in "a shared vision, a vision of global solidarity." Now, he said, that vision was in question. Recognizing that countries have a right to defend themselves against new threats such as terrorism, for which the United Nations had not found as-yet reliable responses, he criticized states such as the United States for reserving the right to act unilaterally, or in ad hoc coalitions, even if they have not been attacked. He worried that the precedent of preemption by one state or a group of states, without UN Security Council authorization, would result "in the proliferation of the unilateral and lawless use of force, with or without justification."[3] He posited that the United Nations had reached a "fork in the road," a moment as fraught with uncertainty as the one in 1945 when the world created the organization.

Like Bush and Chirac, most foreign ministers, heads of government, and ambassadors who had gathered for the debate directed their remarks toward events then unfolding on the other side of the world in the Middle East. Alternatively, they spoke of the worrisome implications of such events for the future of the United Nations, the centerpiece of the post–World War II effort to sustain world peace through collective security. Just one month earlier, twenty-two people had lost their lives at the UN office in Baghdad as a result of a massive car bomb explosion. During its 58 years of existence, the United Nations had lost many employees in violent conflicts, but never had the numbers been so high on one occasion or the attack so blatantly meant to drive the United Nations from its assigned task. Headed by Secretary-General Annan's special representative, Sergio Vieira de Mello, the UN effort in Baghdad was designed to provide humanitarian and reconstruction activities in the wake of the occupation of Iraq by the United States, Great Britain, and their coalition partners. The decision by these countries to topple Saddam Hussein's regime by military force had divided the UN members the previous spring and had weakened the organization. Now, Vieira de Mello's death, along with the deaths of his many colleagues, lay like a pall on the proceedings.

The UN casualties in Baghdad reminded everyone in the Assembly Hall of the gruesome conditions under which the world had gathered only a little more than two years earlier. The opening session of the Fifty-sixth General Assembly, scheduled for September 11, 2001, had been postponed because of the terrorist attacks on the World Trade Center and the Pentagon. The avalanche of events since then, including war in Afghanistan and Iraq, seemed to have undermined the bright prospects for peace entertained at the end of the cold war. These events also undercut the renewed hope of the late 1990s that the United Nations was poised to manage the newfound peace with a new will and new authority.

Iraq and terrorism likewise dominated discussions in the UN Security Council throughout the summer and early fall of 2003. As the General Assembly moved toward its fifty-eighth session, the council was under U.S. pressure to approve the participation of military forces from other countries in an effort to secure postwar Iraq. Most of the other fourteen Security Council members were hesitant, given the unwillingness of the United States to relinquish coalition military and political control in Iraq. The bombing of the UN facility further diminished the interest of several governments in sending their national forces.

In addition to the situation in Iraq, violence in Liberia faced the council that September. Liberian president Charles Taylor had been forced from office, but a tentative peace accord between the government and rebels had not been secured. On September 19, council members approved a new peacekeeping mission (UN Mission in Liberia, or UNMIL), authorizing fifteen thousand troops, administrators, and police to begin arriving in the "failed" state October 1. On the council's plate were also simmering conflicts in Afghanistan, Congo, and Burundi. Meanwhile, members viewed with heightened anxiety the apparent unraveling of the "Road Map" for peace in the Israeli-Palestinian dispute, put together so painstakingly by the "Quartet" of the United States, the United Nations, Russia, and the European Union. A storm of mutual revenge attacks by both sides had once again soured hopes for any progress in this lengthy quarrel. Finally, the Security Council continued to monitor the work of the international tribunals for Rwanda and the former Yugoslavia, where individuals charged as war criminals stood trial for acts of genocide and crimes against humanity.

As a result of the numerous television and news images people have seen for the past half century, the lush Assembly Hall over which Hunte presided in the fall of 2003—with its magnificent seventy-five-foot-high dome and cascading rows of seats for the representatives of the world's nations, along with the more intimate Security Council Chamber within the imposing complex of buildings on the East River in New York City—*is* the United Nations. There, for better or worse, the member states bring the most serious challenges facing the world community, and with varying degrees of success or failure, the United Nations responds to these challenges with resolutions, programs, military force, funds, or negotiation. Its actions often lauded, many times criticized, the United Nations, since its creation in 1945, has rarely been ignored or avoided by the international community. Even the harshest critics of the United Nations may concede that there in New York City sits "the institution that comes closest to providing a forum for global governance."[4]

UN Headquarters Building in New York City (UN/DPI Photo. Reproduced by permission from the United Nations.)

However, the United Nations is far more than this—more than speeches, resolutions, and negotiations at world headquarters. It is also soldiers in blue helmets, aid workers in developing countries, civilian administrators in post–civil war states, police, doctors, engineers, volunteers, demining experts, agronomists, and an increasingly wide variety of professional and service workers. The *United Nations System* (*UN System*) is found in many more places than the photogenic buildings on the east side of Manhattan. UN operations are under way in other offices in New York and in special cities on every continent around the globe. Whereas other international organizations, alliances, and even states of the cold war era have vanished or have had to remake themselves wholly, the United Nations shows both the wear of changing times and the durability that makes it as potentially relevant today as when Franklin Roosevelt, Joseph Stalin, and Winston Churchill first agreed to have it replace the far more mortal League of Nations. With all its warts and weaknesses, the United Nations is simply an expected part of international reality and the epitome of international organization in the twenty-first century.

Vieira de Mello's death, the instability in Iraq, and the collapse of peace prospects in the Middle East may have moved to the head of the UN agenda on the assembly's opening day in 2003, but these issues far from monopolized the work of the organization. In the same marble-and-steel building where the world's ambassadors gathered, governments used the occasion to lobby for UN action on myriad other issues. They also consulted with their colleagues in their respective UN missions scattered across the city. Combining **parliamentary diplomacy**—in which using democratic legislative procedures, committees, and political persuasion, representatives of sovereign governments pass resolutions, usually by large majorities, in support of their national interests—with old-fashioned intergovernmental negotiation, the member delegations sought to commit the United Nations on matters of not only peace and war, but also human rights, economic development, humanitarian assistance, peacekeeping, environmental issues, social well-being, and gender equality.

To address such issues—issues that were not central to UN consideration in 1945—the United Nations developed a comprehensive bureaucratic and policymaking structure, much of it out of the view of world attention. Other principal organs of the world body created by the Charter of the United Nations (UN Charter) operate in the same political environment of UN headquarters as the General Assembly and the Security Council do, and may have even more impact on a day-to-day basis on the world's population. For instance, the Economic and Social Council (ECOSOC), charged with carrying out the Charter's instruction "to promote social progress and better standards of life in larger freedom,"[5] coordinates and recommends funding for the work of dozens of UN commissions, standing committees, programs, special funds, specialized agencies, and regional bodies. Its agenda each year includes compilation of reports from commissions that range in subject matter from the status of women, indigenous peoples, children, and political prisoners, to the vast economic and social needs of poverty-stricken parts of the globe. (Chapter 4 covers the extensive work and responsibilities of the fifty-four nations on ECOSOC.)

Looming over UN Plaza in New York City is the 544-foot-tall office building that houses seven thousand employees of the Secretariat. These civil servants provide administrative support for all UN activities in New York City and around the globe. Headed by the secretary-general and divided into departments for every aspect of international policymaking at the United Nations, Secretariat personnel are often the human face of the United Nations to the recipients of its activities. These personnel are the professional bureaucrats who are charged with carrying out the decisions the member nations make. However, they also help crystallize the agenda, the hopes, and the initiatives of the world organization. From this site the Department of Peacekeeping Operations (DPKO) oversaw more than thirty-six thousand peacekeepers serving around the world, operating in fifteen dangerous missions, as Julian Hunte took the dais in New York City in 2003. The new General Assembly president was undoubtedly pleased that the Secretariat was addressing the distinctive problems of small island nations like Saint Lucia in addition to well-publicized peacekeeping needs. From Room 900 of the Secretariat building, one of the newest UN programs (created in December 2001)—the Office of the High Representative for the Least Developed Countries, Landlocked Developing Countries and Small Island Developing States (OHRLLS)—was working out of the public's view to mobilize the international community's resources to assist particularly vulnerable, smaller countries.

The creation of this new office to assist small and poor countries reflects the reality that the issues before the United Nations are more comprehensive than, and sometimes dramatically different from, those its founders hoped to address in the ruins of World War II. The United Nations was founded as an intergovernmental organization (IGO) "to secure the maintenance of peace and security." In this endeavor, the Security Council was intended to play the central role within the organization, managed by its permanent members, who would act in concert, and endorsed by the plenary General Assembly. Currently, the institution is also expected to respond to ethnic and religious violence, AIDS, childhood diseases, disintegrating nations, demands for democracy, human rights violations, and sundry other "people problems." (Chapters 7 and 8 include discussions of UN policymaking on these issues.) As the work of the United Nations has expanded to areas of concern beyond those contemplated in the 1940s, so too has the organization grown in terms of both its institutional structure and what has been demanded of it.

As an evolving institution, the United Nations is an expanding organization, with offices beyond UN Plaza in New York City that reach into many cities of the world. The most important of these are Geneva, Switzerland; Nairobi, Kenya; Vienna, Austria; Rome, Italy; The Hague, The Netherlands; Paris, France; and Washington, D.C., in the United States. In addition, significant UN operations can be found in Addis Ababa, Ethiopia; Bangkok, Thailand; Tokyo, Japan; Santiago,

Chile; Beirut, Lebanon; and all the major cities in countries where a peacekeeping presence exists. During any given week the United Nations is active on every continent, and much of its work has a significant impact on both international and domestic affairs around the globe.

In New York, for example, if tourists walk west on Forty-second Street from UN headquarters on First Avenue, they will pass the offices of the **UN Population Fund (UNFPA).** A subsidiary organ of the General Assembly, UNFPA receives voluntary contributions, from ninety nations, amounting to $250 million annually. Its executive director since 2001, Thoraya Ahmed Obaid, from Saudi Arabia, and her nine hundred staff members set as their goals the provision of universal access to reproductive health services worldwide and the 75 percent reduction of maternal mortality by 2015. Since its founding in 1969, the agency has worked to make available family planning education, safe motherhood practices, gender equality, and the resources necessary for women to make their own fertility choices. As the Fifty-eighth General Assembly session convened, UNFPA was actively engaged in restoring health care to the people of Afghanistan in the aftermath of the 2001 overthrow of the Taliban regime. With the fund's support, nongovernmental organizations (NGOs) and other international agencies were rehabilitating hospitals, providing maternal and child health services, preparing for a national census, and creating women's education and training centers. The fund was particularly interested in reducing the Afghan maternal mortality rate, which stood at sixteen hundred for every one hundred thousand live births.[6] UNFPA was working closely with the Joint UN Programme on HIV/AIDS (UNAIDS) to lower the incidence of the disease not only in Afghanistan but throughout the developing world. It sought to reduce the HIV infection rate among pregnant women, which is a major factor contributing to the spread of the disease.

UNFPA shares an executive board with the UN Development Programme (UNDP), also located in New York City. As the General Assembly prepared to convene on September 16, 2003, the thirty-six UNDP/UNFPA board members were just reassessing the decisions made at their meeting, which concluded only the previous Friday.[7] The members had reviewed the agency's multiyear funding plan for 2004–2007, which laid out the core goals of the organization and elaborated the organizational strategies UNDP would use to achieve the ambitious development targets established following the UN Millennium Summit in 2000 (see Chapter 8). The board members' decisions were critical to hundreds of millions of human beings because UNDP is the largest and most comprehensive economic assistance organization in the world. With more than 130 offices in all geographic areas, UNDP has struck partnerships with other development agencies, environmental organizations, the World Bank, governments, and NGOs. It serves as the coordinator for nearly all UN initiatives in the developing world.

Having completed board activities for the year, UNDP administrators, with an eye on deliberations then under way in the General Assembly, turned their attention to the Tokyo International Conference for African Development (TICAD), which was scheduled to convene in less than two weeks. This meeting of the conference would be the third since 1993. UNDP served as its coorganizer along with Japan, the Global Coalition for Africa, the World Bank, and the UN Office of the Special Adviser on Africa. The TICAD process provided a framework for Asian-African collaboration on development projects. In prior sessions more than one thousand participants attended from more than one hundred countries and forty international organizations. UNDP staff now prepared to hold TICAD III, focusing its work on African agricultural and private sector development, HIV/AIDS and other infectious diseases, the water supply, and the African economic infrastructure. Through the conference, UNDP hoped to serve as a catalyst for increased Asian business and government investment on the African continent.

For many UN agencies and bodies other than the organization's principal organs, New York City provides the hub for their activities. Even as the world gathers in the UN General

Assembly Hall or urgently convenes in the Security Council, agencies such as UNDP and UNFPA are doing other critical work. The UN Children's Fund (UNICEF) headquarters is also in New York City and has been since its creation in 1946. So, too, the chief executives of the key agencies in the UN System fly regularly to New York to orchestrate plans for coordinated UN activities worldwide. Nevertheless, most UN initiatives occur beyond the borders of New York and the United States and define a large portion of all ongoing global diplomatic affairs.

Geneva, Switzerland

The Committee on the Rights of the Child, the monitoring group for the convention of the same name, held its second day of fall meetings on September 16, 2003, in the ground floor meeting room of the historic Palais Wilson in Geneva, Switzerland. Given the time difference between New York and Geneva, the committee had just completed the day's review of San Marino's report on its implementation of the convention as the General Assembly gathered at New York City headquarters. The eighteen-member panel of experts meets several times a year to review country reports by signatories of the Convention on the Rights of the Child and to discuss general problems facing the world's children. Wednesday, September 17, was allotted to reviewing the status of children's rights in Canada. Friday, September 19, the agenda called for a general discussion on the rights of indigenous children. According to the convention, an indigenous child "shall not be denied the right . . . to enjoy his or her own culture, to profess and practice his or her own religion, or to use his or her own language." The committee's discussion was part of the activities for the International Decade of the World's Indigenous People (1995–2004). The group also assessed progress on the convention's optional protocols barring the use of children in armed conflicts and prohibiting the sale of children, child prostitution, and child pornography.

The committee's meeting in the Palais Wilson raised interesting historical contrasts. This facility was built on the shore of Lake Geneva in 1875 as a grand hotel for the wealthy and famous. It was occupied in 1920 by the secretariat of the League of Nations, the ill-fated predecessor to the United Nations. Following a devastating fire in August 1987, the Palais was restored to its former brilliance and subsequently occupied by the offices of the UN High Commissioner for Human Rights (UNHCHR). The life of the building seemingly paralleled the history of international organization in the twentieth century. Now used to house meetings of UN bodies and specialized agencies predominantly committed to addressing economic, social, and cultural issues that were considered secondary concerns to the immediate pursuit of security and peace by the League and the original United Nations, the Palais reminds its visitors how dramatically the international agenda has changed.

The presence of the UNHCHR, one of the UN's newest creations, in the halls and offices of this magnificent grande dame on the Rue des Pâquis has brought new attention to the role of Geneva headquarters in UN global activities. The General Assembly created the post of UNHCHR in 1993. Its charge is to advocate human rights throughout the UN System and to draw the world's attention to particularly egregious violations of these rights. This body is authorized to coordinate all UN programs, agencies, and offices involved in the field of human rights. The visibility and prestige of the UNHCHR in world affairs led Secretary-General Annan to tap the High Commissioner for Human Rights, Sergio Vieira de Mello, as his special representative to occupied Iraq in 2003.

The vital center of UN activity in Geneva is at the Palais des Nations on the Avenue de la Paix, an extraordinarily spacious facility first opened in 1936 to house the League permanently. When the League was dissolved in 1946, the United Nations took over the Palais, with its large

Palais des Nations, the UN Headquarters in Geneva, Switzerland (UN/DPI Photo by P. Klee. Reproduced by permission from the United Nations.)

Assembly Hall; added new wings to the building in subsequent years; and used it for conferences and negotiations. Located in beautiful Ariana Park, overlooking Lake Geneva, with Mount Blanc beyond, the Palais des Nations houses the UN Office at Geneva (UNOG), which oversees more than three hundred international conferences a year and more than sixty-five hundred half-day meetings annually. Each year, more conferences are convened in Geneva than in New York City. Geneva is also the focal point for UN activities in social, humanitarian, and cultural fields. Many UN specialized agencies and treaty-monitoring committees have their headquarters there.

More than 140 governments maintain permanent missions in Geneva that are accredited to UNOG, as do several IGOs, including the European Union, the African Union, and The Arab League. Approximately nine thousand employees work for components of the UN System in Geneva, more than thirty-five hundred for UNOG directly.[8] Large staffs also serve the UN Conference on Trade and Development (UNCTAD—discussed at length in Chapter 8) and the Economic Commission for Europe. Specialized agencies, some predating the creation of the United Nations, are also located there. The oldest and most famous is the International Labour Organization (ILO), founded at the time of the League's creation. Attracted by the presence of the United Nations in Geneva, more than thirty thousand diplomats, international civil servants, and NGO representatives work in the city, which makes it the "most active center for multilateral diplomacy in the world."[9]

The Palais des Nations hosts ECOSOC biennially and every year serves as the venue for meetings of the UN Commission on Human Rights. From time to time the General Assembly

UN BODIES IN GENEVA, SWITZERLAND

International Trade Centre (ITC)
Joint Inspection Unit (JIU)
Office for the Coordination of Humanitarian Affairs (OCHA)
UN Commission on Human Rights (CHR)
UN Committee of Experts on the Transport of Dangerous Goods and on the Globally
    Harmonized System of Classification and Labelling of Chemicals (UNCETDG/GHS)
UN Compensation Fund
UN Conference on Trade and Development (UNCTAD)
UN Economic Commission for Europe (UNECE)
UN High Commissioner for Human Rights (UNHCHR)
UN High Commissioner for Refugees (UNHCR)
UN Institute for Disarmament Research (UNIDIR)
UN Institute for Training and Research (UNITAR)
UN Research Institute for Social Development (UNRISD)

Specialized Agencies

International Labour Organization (ILO)
International Telecommunication Union (ITU)
World Health Organization (WHO)
World Intellectual Property Organization (WIPO)
World Meteorological Organization (WMO)

Special Bodies Associated with the United Nations

Basel Convention on Transboundary Movement of Hazardous Wastes Secretariat
Conference on Disarmament (CD)
Convention on International Trade in Endangered Species (CITES) Secretariat
Global Resource Information Database (GRID)—Geneva
Intergovernmental Panel on Climate Change (IPCC)
International Bureau of Education (IBE)
International Union for the Protection of New Varieties of Plants (UPOV)
Joint UN Programme on HIV/AIDS (UNAIDS)

meets there in special session. The UN staff also provides administrative services for the autonomous **Conference on Disarmament (CD)**, the world's principal negotiating forum for disarmament issues. Likewise, the ILO and the World Health Organization (WHO) convene their annual plenary assemblies in the facility.

During the same week in September 2003 that the Committee on the Rights of the Child was meeting in the Palais Wilson, several high-level negotiating sessions were convening at the Palais des Nations. Even in this peaceful setting, the war in Iraq intruded. As the General Assembly convened in New York City on September 16, so, too, the **UN Compensation Commission (UNCC)** went into session in Geneva. The UNCC was created at the end of the 1991 Gulf War to pay compensation to governments, individuals, international organizations, and corporations that had suffered losses as a result of Iraq's aggression. By its September meeting the commission had resolved most of the 2.6 million claims submitted to it, awarding nearly $252 billion to the claimants.[10] The funds the commission distributed came from the export sales of Iraqi oil. During the next month the UNCC allocated another $18 billion to twenty-six governments and three international organizations; the largest amount—nearly $140 million—was given to Kuwait. More important to the future of Middle East peace than the work of the UNCC was Secretary-General Annan's cajoling the foreign ministers of the Security Council's five permanent members—the United States, the Russian Federation, China, France, and the United Kingdom—to convene in Geneva three days earlier (Saturday, September 13). He hoped to bridge the considerable differences among these governments over a draft of a U.S. resolution calling for more international assistance in postwar Iraq. This session ended after more than two hours of discussion. U.S. secretary of state Colin Powell reported afterward that differences had been narrowed on how and when to transfer power to a new sovereign Iraqi government, but on other issues the parties remained far apart. The foreign ministers agreed to continue the negotiations back in New York City.

Such high-level diplomatic contacts are common happenings in the Geneva office, which is often the first choice of parties seeking a venue for conflict negotiations, given its long history as the seat of diplomatic activity and its presence in hospitable, neutral Switzerland. In this regard, no issue area has been more persistently pursued in Geneva than has disarmament. Hours before the foreign ministers convened their Saturday meeting, the Conference on Disarmament (CD) closed its more-than-month-long third session of the year. The conference, created in 1978, is the latest institutional manifestation of Geneva-based multilateral disarmament negotiations, a process dating to the late 1950s. (See Chapter 5 for a thorough discussion of UN disarmament efforts.) The fall 2003 session proved particularly frustrating, marking the seventh consecutive year that the CD had been unable to agree on a program of work. Meeting in the Palais' council chamber, with its famous murals to human progress by José Maria Sert, the conference could not overcome differences between the United States and several other members over including weapons in space on the agenda. This topic was critical to the governments that hoped to halt U.S. efforts to build a ballistic missile defense system. A glimmer of hope did emerge when all parties signaled their support for the "Five Ambassadors" Proposal, which would establish ad hoc working groups on this issue and several others.[11] (The five ambassadors were from Algeria, Belgium, Chile, Sweden, and Colombia.) Hope remained that the conference would be able to end the stasis and make progress in its subsequent Geneva sessions. However, the impasse still remained as member states reconvened in January 2005. The president of the conference, Ambassador Chris Sanders of The Netherlands, stressed that if the current deadlock persisted, the conference might lose its relevance and have to be discontinued.[12]

Many specialized agencies and non-UN IGOs have also taken up residence in the city. The consequence is that while important and visible negotiations (such as the foreign ministers' meeting on Iraq) occur at UN headquarters, other important but more technical UN sessions are almost always in progress—each with long-term consequences for millions of people around the globe. For example, while the swirl of events associated with Iraq spun around them, experts from the Food and Agriculture Organization and the WHO met throughout the week to seek ways to limit pesticide residues in food and the environment. Also, even as the General Assembly convened in New York City, UNCTAD held discussions on its program budget and technical cooperation efforts in the Third World. The active use of Geneva for these disparate negotiations not only symbolized the emerging "new" United Nations—an institution increasingly centered on human beings' basic needs, in addition to the diplomacy of nation-states—but also gave new life to this old seat of international organization.

Nairobi, Kenya

On September 16, 2003, Conference Room 4 in the UN Gigiri compound in Nairobi, Kenya, began to fill up shortly before 9:00 a.m. with approximately fifty government representatives, all subcommittee members to the Committee of Permanent Representatives (CPR) of the UN Environment Programme (UNEP). Their work was in anticipation of the full committee's eighty-fourth session, scheduled for the next day. The CPRs for UNEP and **UN-HABITAT (UN Human Settlements Programme)** had been meeting in Nairobi since early September. The latter body is the UN agency dedicated to the promotion of socially and environmentally sustainable cities and towns with the goal of providing adequate shelter for everyone. The UN-HABITAT group spent September preparing for the Sustainable Cities Conference scheduled to convene in Alexandria, Egypt, on September 29, and for World Habitat Day (October 6), which was dedicated to the theme "Water for Cities." During the next month UN-HABITAT would also be an active participant, along with several NGOs (e.g., International Federation for Housing and Planning, International Society of City and Regional Planners), IGOs such as the WHO, and local communities (e.g., Weihai Municipality, China; Belfast, Northern Ireland), in a number of international meetings. The effectiveness of partnerships like these meant that 80 percent of UN-HABITAT's annual three-hundred-million-dollar budget would come from organizations other than the United Nations and national governments, organizations that believed UN-HABITAT could make a positive difference in addressing the housing needs of millions of people.

The General Assembly established the predecessor to UN-HABITAT, the UN Commission on Human Settlements, and its secretariat, the UN Centre for Human Settlements (UNCHS), in Nairobi in 1977.[13] The commission and the secretariat were collapsed into the current organization in 2001. That year UN-HABITAT had more than two hundred projects under way around the world. It was particularly concerned with urban management, housing, basic services, shelter conditions of the world's poor, and infrastructure improvements. Considering the UN prediction that by 2025 more than 60 percent of the world's people will live in urban areas, which will create enormous strains on prospective sources of services, housing, and health facilities, UN-HABITAT's work is all the more important.

UN-HABITAT is the central agency for implementing the Habitat Agenda, which was derived from the Declaration and Global Plan of Action adopted at the second UN Conference on Human Settlements (held in Istanbul, Turkey, in June 1996) and from the Millennium Development Goals the United Nations established in 2000. UN-HABITAT's work is directed by a governing council that meets every two years in Nairobi.

The UN Gigiri compound—with nature trails on twenty-seven acres that let the visitor wander past indigenous African trees; spot Egyptian geese, green pigeons, marsh mongooses, and olive baboons; and view a seasonal swamp—seems even farther than its 7,360 miles as the crow flies from UN headquarters in New York City. As one of the four UN headquarters worldwide, Nairobi feels like a place that none of the founders of the world body could have contemplated as a center of the organization's activities. Yet, the Nairobi office services many of the fifty-five UN funds, programs, and agencies operating in Kenya. The city is recognized as the capital of the UN global environmental effort and provides facilities for the work of many private and public international organizations that are addressing the overwhelming human challenges confronting the African people. As the diplomatic activity surrounding UNEP and UN-HABITAT demonstrates, Nairobi reflects the broadened mandate of the United Nations.

The UN Office in Nairobi (UNON) was officially created in 1996, but UN operations there date from the 1970s and the effort to solve the emerging issues then presented by environmental degradation and Third World development. In 1972 the United Nations convened the World Conference on the Human Environment in Stockholm, Sweden. The attending governments recommended that the world body create an agency to address the problems associated with environmental conservation. However, developing nations attending the Stockholm meeting worried that efforts to create environmentally friendly global policy would limit what national governments could do in terms of industrial growth and development. The General Assembly's placement of UNEP headquarters in Kenya sent a signal that the organization's mandate was not antithetical to Third World interests.

An executive director administers UNEP and oversees a significant number of departments, programs, and initiatives in many nations around the world. The 1997 Nairobi Declaration, which launched a new era of activism for UNEP, guides the agency's work in the new millennium. The declaration set a global agenda that includes developing international environmental law aimed at sustainable development, monitoring state compliance with environmental agreements and principles, and serving as a link between the scientific community and policymakers.

The UNEP secretariat provides extensive environmental information and communication to governments and NGOs. It operates several functional divisions, including these: Technology, Industry, and Economics; Early Warning and Assessment; Environmental Policy Development and Law; Environmental Policy Implementation; and Regional Cooperation. The last of these is serviced by UNEP offices in Africa, Asia, Europe, Latin and North America, and the Caribbean. UNEP also provides the secretariat for several international environmental conventions, including the Convention on Biological Diversity, the Convention on International Trade in Endangered Species of Wild Fauna and Flora, and the Convention on the Conservation of Migratory Species. Likewise, UNEP provides secretariats for conventions on climate change, desertification, and regional seas.

UNEP's success can be credited in significant part to its development of scientific and technical expertise, which it uses in a number of successful monitoring and information-sharing programs. UNEP coordinates or sponsors seven critical environmental network programs:

1. *Earthwatch* is a coordinating agency for UN systemwide environmental activities.
2. *Infoterra* is an information exchange network that operates through centers in more than 170 states. Each center provides a national environmental information service.
3. *Global Environment Outlook* provides a global network of regional multidisciplinary institutes that conduct assessments by using new methodologies to assess the state of the environment in any given region or nation.
4. More than a dozen *Global Resource Information Database (GRID)* centers from around the world gather information, paying attention to the atmosphere, oceans, the climate, transboundary pollution, and renewable resources. Employing the efforts of more than thirty thousand scientists, GRID provides a comprehensive database for further research and for policy action in more than 140 nations.
5. To provide data to both GRID and Earthwatch, UNEP operates GEMS, the *Global Environment Monitoring System,* through twenty-five sites around the world.
6. The *Environment and Natural Resources Information Networking* program promotes the development of national capacities in data and information management related to environmental issues.
7. Finally, UNEP's *Industry and Environment Office* in Paris promotes environmentally sound business practices through cooperation with international businesses.

In the 1970s UNEP was the sole UN organ primarily attentive to environmental matters. It became the catalyst and energizer for an international movement that gained public attention and support. UNEP officials focused much of their work on organizing the international bargaining process and promoting new ideas for international environmental cooperation. UNEP became an important negotiator in moving the world community toward pollution control, protection of the ozone layer, regulation of transboundary shipments of hazardous wastes, and protection of biodiversity.

UNEP also carved out areas of special expertise. Early efforts to protect the world's oceans resulted in a number of regional seas agreements. Nine were signed in the 1970s, beginning with an agreement among countries bordering the Mediterranean Sea. This agreement was followed in the 1980s with six more agreements, together covering many of the regional seas of the world. Since its inception, UNEP has also concerned itself with the movement of hazardous chemicals. In 1976 it established the International Register for Potentially Toxic Chemicals, and eight years later it created the Provisional Notification Scheme for Banned and Severely Restricted Chemicals. Its work in this area soon led scientific experts to refer to these substances as "UNEP Chemicals." Throughout the 1970s, 1980s, and 1990s, UNEP worked closely with the Food and Agriculture Organization (FAO) to develop the International Code of Conduct on the Distribution and Use of Pesticides. As we mentioned previously, UNEP representatives and their counterparts from the FAO met during September 2003 in Geneva to push forward on this initiative.

Vienna, Austria

The Viennese refer to it as "UNO-City." Its official name is the *Vienna International Centre,* and it is located on the Danube River not far from downtown Vienna, Austria. The center serves as the newest of the UN's four headquarters and home to several UN and treaty bodies, the most important of which is the International Atomic Energy Agency (IAEA). The agency's annual general conference convened on September 15, 2003, and continued through Friday, September 19. Its 136 member states concentrated on three suspected violators of the Treaty on the Non-Proliferation of Nuclear Weapons (Nuclear Non-Proliferation Treaty, or NPT): Iraq, Iran, and North Korea. Each was reputed to have developed a uranium-reprocessing ability that opened the door to nuclear weapons production. North Korea even claimed to have developed such weapons. Conference delegates and the agency's director general, Dr. Mohamed El Baradei, urged restraint by the North Korean government in Pyongyang. They also called on Iran to accept an enhanced IAEA inspection and verification program. The U.S. delegation pressed for a strong resolution requiring Iranian compliance and threatening Security Council action if Iran did not comply.

The IAEA's founding statute commits the agency "to accelerate and enlarge the contribution of atomic energy to peace, health and prosperity throughout the world." To that end, the agency, an independent IGO under the aegis of the United Nations, maintains a safeguards program first developed to implement the verification provisions of the 1968 NPT. By 2001 more than nine hundred nuclear facilities were under IAEA safeguards. IAEA members have also used the system to enforce the compliance terms of international treaties, including nuclear weapons–free zone agreements in Africa, Latin America, and the South Pacific. Following the 1991 Gulf War, IAEA safeguards inspectors enforced nuclear provisions of the armistice agreement imposed on Iraq. Ousted from Iraq in 1998, the inspectors returned in 2002 at the direction of the Security Council to verify whether Saddam Hussein's regime still had a nuclear program.

The September 2003 plenary session proved to be one of the most important meetings in the organization's forty-six-year history. The renewed international concern about weapons of mass destruction, their possible use by terrorist groups or aggressive states, and the proliferation of nuclear materials and technology since the end of the cold war elevated the agency's visibility. For the first time in a decade and a half, the major powers agreed to a significant increase in the IAEA's budget: from $230 million in 2001 to $245 million in 2003 and $255 million in 2007. The new concern also brought the agency criticism. Apparently it had not been aware of Iranian nuclear programs then under way. Once these programs were publicly acknowledged, the IAEA had not been able to force their cessation, which demonstrated the limits of an international organization's influence when it is confronted with a country's strongly held perceived national interests.

In addition to providing a headquarters for the IAEA, the Vienna International Centre is headquarters for the UN Industrial Development Organization (UNIDO), the Preparatory Commission for the Comprehensive Nuclear-Test-Ban Treaty Organization (CTBTO), the UN Commission for International Trade Law (UNCITRAL), and the Office for Drug Control and Crime Prevention (ODCCP). The ODCCP was created in 1997. It encourages international efforts to stop the production and trafficking of narcotics. Much of its effort is undertaken in cooperation with NGOs. UNIDO assists with the cultivation of industry in developing countries and states with economies in transition. It provides information, skills, and technology to its members to promote industrialization that will be economically sound and environmentally friendly. It is also one of four implementing agencies of the Montreal Protocol, which phases out the use of ozone-depleting substances in industrial production. UNIDO maintains field offices in thirty-six nations. UNCITRAL's mission is to harmonize national trade laws, to draft model laws and conventions on international trade law, and to encourage conformity among states to common standards that will lead to one worldwide commercial law. In light of accelerated globalization, the commission reflects a UN effort to play a more active role in reducing or removing obstacles to the free flow of international trade. Finally, the Preparatory Commission for the CTBTO, established in 1996, plans for the eventual implementation of the Comprehensive Nuclear-Test-Ban Treaty, once it comes into force, and undertakes preliminary tasks that will lead to the first conference of treaty members.

The Hague, The Netherlands

In contrast to the political swirl that surrounds UN activities in Vienna, Nairobi, Geneva, and New York City—where delegates and NGO representatives seek support for resolutions, reports, and individual agendas—the serious UN work conducted in The Hague has a sedate decorum. The only principal organ of the United Nations located outside New York City, the International Court of Justice (ICJ) can be found in this city. The court's fifteen judges continue a long tradition of applying international law to cases brought by sovereign states. The ICJ is the successor to the Permanent Court of International Justice (PCIJ), the judicial arm of the League of Nations. The seat of the court, like that of the PCIJ, is the Peace Palace, a gift from U.S. entrepreneur Andrew Carnegie. (Chapter 4 provides an introduction to the work of the court and its importance.)

In the fall of 2003, the court president was Shi Jiuyong from China. As is tradition, each permanent member of the Security Council had a representative on the court, although these judges served as independent jurists. They were joined by judges from Madagascar, Sierra Leone, Venezuela, The Netherlands, Brazil, Jordan, Egypt, Japan, Germany, and Slovakia. The court's docket was exceptionally full that autumn: twenty-three cases were pending. More than thirty nations had agreed to submit their disputes to the judgment of the court. As the UN General Assembly convened in New York City on September 16, the ICJ had just completed public hearings on a border dispute between El Salvador and Honduras and had taken the case under advisement.

The real courtroom drama in The Hague, however, was not in the stately chambers of the ICJ, but in the criminal proceedings at 1 Churchillplein, where the International Criminal Tribunal for the Former Yugoslavia (ICTY) was continuing its prosecution of alleged war criminals in the aftermath of the Balkan civil wars of the 1990s. These bloody conflicts, encompassing Serbia-Montenegro, Croatia, Kosovo Province, Bosnia, and Slovenia, produced the worst human atrocities Europe had witnessed since World War II. The world community was responding to the tragic events in the former Yugoslavia not only with peacekeeping operations in the area, but also with trials, at the ICTY, of war criminals charged with genocide and crimes against humanity. (Chapter 7 provides a full description of these judicial proceedings.)

On September 16, 2003, one of the scores of defendants charged at The Hague—Mitar Rasevic—made his first appearance before Judge Janu. Rasevic stood accused of crimes against humanity. He had been the commander of Serb forces that occupied the Bosnian town of Foca, just south of Sarajevo, in the spring of 1992. He allegedly presided over the torturing, beating, and killing of Muslim and non-Serb males in the city. These acts were carried out in the detention center Rasevic established, where men, nearly all civilians, who were 16 to 80 years old, were brought. These men included individuals who were mentally handicapped, physically disabled, and seriously ill. Reportedly, the commander personally selected specific detainees for beatings and inhuman treatment.

Rasevic's case was similar to many of the others before the tribunal. However, that of Slobodan Milosevic was not. For more than a year, the trial of Yugoslavia's former head of state had been under way. Charged with crimes against humanity, war crimes, and genocide, Milosevic challenged the authority of the international community to try him, the former leader of a sovereign state. He demonstrated his contempt for the proceedings by defending himself at trial. In the fall of 2003, his courtroom tactics had worn thin with prosecutors and judges, but he vigorously defended his decisions, blaming others for any excesses in the Balkan civil wars. Two years later the trial would be ongoing, with no resolution imminent, and with Milosevic so ill that the prospect that he might evade a final verdict was real.

Montreal, Canada

In addition to using the formal organs created by its Charter, the United Nations responds to the human challenges that confront the world community through a broad system of specialized agencies, programs, funds, and research and training institutes. Each specialized agency is an intergovernmental organization (IGO) with a contractual relationship to the United Nations. Some of these bodies were created long before the founding of the United Nations; others came about at the behest of the world organization. (Chapters 3 and 4 provide extensive information on these agencies.) An additional dozen "programmes" report to both the General Assembly and ECOSOC. Finally, five research and training organizations are part of the UN system.

In Montreal, Canada, the **International Civil Aviation Organization (ICAO)** serves as the primary agency for creating standardized rules and practices in the aviation industry worldwide. Created by the Chicago Convention of December 1944, the ICAO became a UN specialized agency in 1947. It is a good example of an IGO within the UN System that addresses an important functional task necessary for safe and effective travel and communication. Through negotiation among its nearly universal membership, the agency adopts standards that are then put into practice by its member states. Areas of standardization include the operation of aircraft, personnel licensing, air traffic services, navigation rules, aeronautical communications, search and rescue, accident investigation, airworthiness, and transport of dangerous goods. The ICAO is

UN SPECIALIZED AGENCIES AROUND THE WORLD

Vienna, Austria

UN Industrial Development Organization (UNIDO)

Montreal, Canada

International Civil Aviation Organization (ICAO)

Paris, France

UN Educational, Scientific and Cultural Organization (UNESCO)

Rome, Italy

Food and Agriculture Organization (FAO)
International Fund for Agricultural Development (IFAD)

Trieste, Italy

International Centre for Science and High Technology (ICS)

Turin, Italy

International Training Centre (ITC)

Berne, Switzerland

Universal Postal Union (UPU)

Geneva, Switzerland

International Bureau of Education (IBE)
International Labour Organization (ILO)
International Telecommunication Union (ITU)
World Health Organization (WHO)
World Intellectual Property Organization (WIPO)
World Meteorological Organization (WMO)

London, UK

International Maritime Organization (IMO)

Washington, D.C., USA

International Board of Reconstruction and Development (IBRD) [World Bank]
International Centre for the Settlement of Investment Disputes (ICSID)
International Development Association (IDA)
International Finance Corporation (IFC)
International Monetary Fund (IMF)
Multilateral Investment Guarantee Agency (MIGA)

also involved in the development of satellite-based navigation systems, regional planning, the facilitation of passenger movement through national terminals of entry and egress, and the development of international air law.

One service the ICAO provides is facilitation of negotiations among specific states over contentious bilateral aviation issues. On the eve of the Fifty-eighth General Assembly session, the ICAO announced that it had brought about a "historic" agreement between Greece and Turkey.[14] In the short term the agreement would facilitate air traffic services in the route network over the Aegean Sea during the anticipated 2004 Olympic Games in Greece. More important, the agreement marked another step in improving relations between two states that have regularly had tense relations resulting from territorial claims in the area.

While celebrating the conclusion of successful negotiations between Greece and Turkey, the ICAO secretariat also prepared for the Eleventh Air Navigation Conference, scheduled to convene in Montreal on September 22, 2003. This large membership meeting addressed many issues, but most were tied to enhancing security in the air; this concern was driven by the terrorists' use of civilian aircraft in the attacks of September 11, 2001. In particular, the ICAO planned to discuss how the air traffic management systems with new communication technologies might limit the terrorist dangers both to the flying public and to targets on the ground.

Rome, Italy

If Montreal is the world capital for the creation of aviation policy, Rome, Italy, is the world food policy capital. Two UN specialized agencies—the **Food and Agriculture Organization (FAO)** and the International Fund for Agricultural Development (IFAD)—and the UN's World Food Programme have their headquarters in Rome and work closely to feed the starving and malnourished peoples around the globe. The founding date of the FAO—October 16, 1945—is now observed as World Food Day. The FAO has operated from Rome since 1951. The World Food Programme was added in 1961, reporting to both the FAO and ECOSOC. IFAD commenced operations as an international financing institution in 1977. In 1996 the FAO hosted the World Food Summit in Rome, where 186 nations approved the Declaration and Plan of Action on World Food Security, outlining a set of commitments intended to achieve universal food security and halve hunger by 2015. Following the summit a concerted effort to coordinate the work of the three agencies was undertaken. This effort was reinforced by the UN's Millennium Development Goals announced in 2000, which committed the entire UN System to meeting the Food Summit's target on hunger.

More than thirty-seven hundred staff personnel worked for the FAO by 2000. The organization had five regional offices, five subregional offices, five liaison offices, and almost eighty country offices in addition to its Rome headquarters. At any given time it had about eighteen hundred field operations in place. Its budget was divided into a "Regular Programme" budget, which was $650 million in 2001, and a "Field Programme" budget, amounting to nearly $300 million in 1999.[15] The organization provides help to developing nations through assistance programs; it collects, analyzes, and disseminates information about nutrition, food production, agricultural issues, and forestry and fisheries matters; and it acts as a clearinghouse for farmers, scientists, and governments on food and agricultural issues. It encourages nations to seek its advice on strategies for rural development, food security, and poverty reduction, particularly in rural areas.

As we mentioned previously, the FAO also works with other specialized agencies on related issues. It met with the WHO in Geneva in September 2003 to address the problem of pesticide residues. While the General Assembly convened in New York City, the FAO held the ninetieth session of its programme committee in a joint meeting with its finance committee (September 15–19, 2003). The session took up, among other issues, the expanding cooperation between the organization and NGOs, the private sector, and civil society organizations. The FAO also looked at the UN response to food problems in the new, war-torn nation of Timor-Leste (East Timor).

The **World Food Programme (WFP)** is the largest international provider of food aid. At the close of the twentieth century, it expended, each year, more than $1 billion, supporting a field staff of more than five thousand that annually distributed more than 3.4 million tons of food. The organization is funded and receives food supplies from donor nations on a voluntary basis. In 2000 more than sixty nations supported the WFP's projects; the United States was the largest donor ($796 million), Japan was the second largest ($260 million), and the European Commission was the third largest ($118 million).

According to its mission statement, the WFP uses its food to meet emergency needs, support economic and social development, and provide logistical support necessary for food delivery. Its services include food distribution to people in emergency circumstances—natural or manufactured by humans, to poor people in developing countries, to communities where the food assistance will help with economic development projects, and to refugees in civil conflicts. In September 2003 the WFP was trying to feed the Afghan, Iraqi, East Timorese, and Liberian populations. Hunger, which was already a persistent problem in Afghanistan before the overthrow of the Taliban government in 2001, had to be addressed, along with the additional security threat of planned attacks by Taliban supporters on aid workers throughout the country. In Liberia, massive food shipments by the WFP in September 2003 reinforced the Security Council's decision to send peacekeeping forces. However, the most desperate situation the WFP had to address was in East Timor. By 2003 the aftermath of civil war and drought was forcing the population to find wild foods on which to survive. At its peak, the WFP was feeding more than four hundred thousand Timorese.

The changing nature of world politics has seriously affected UN food efforts. In 1990 two-thirds of all UN food aid went to development projects, which were attempts to make individuals self-reliant. By the end of the decade, 80 percent of the distributed food went to humanitarian relief for people in crisis. Far from Afghanistan, for example, in South America, the WFP fed several hundred thousand refugees who were displaced by civil war in Colombia. In 2002 the WFP fed seventy-two million people in eighty-two countries. It directed much of the relief aid to vulnerable populations such as women and children and provided food to excombatant soldiers. To get food efficiently to the people who needed it, the WFP maintained working agreements with several international nongovernmental organizations, including Catholic Relief Services, Save the Children, CARE, World Vision International, and Food for the Hungry.

IFAD (the other UN specialized agency besides the FAO) works with the World Bank, regional development banks, and UN agencies to cofinance projects in poor countries. These countries use the funds for rural agricultural projects and repay the loans, which usually have a term of forty years. From the time it began work in 1977 through 2001, IFAD financed more than 580 projects in 115 countries and territories. The cost of these projects was about seven billion dollars in grants and loans.

Pristina, Serbia-Montenegro (Kosovo Province), and Dili, Timor-Leste

Three days after Julian Hunte opened the Fifty-eighth UN General Assembly in New York City—September 19, 2003—former U.S. president Bill Clinton was in Pristina, Kosovo. He received cheers from a public throng, the likes of which any sitting president could only dream about on the campaign trail in the United States. Ethnic Albanian Kosovars turned out to thank President Clinton for his 1999 "liberation" of the province (through the use of North Atlantic Treaty Organization, or NATO, forces) from oppressive Serb domination under the former government of Slobodan Milosevic. Few ethnic Serbs probably joined in the celebratory welcome because most Kosovar Serbs saw the subsequent UN-managed administration as reversing ethnic fortunes in the province and thus diminishing Serb rights and political participation. Since 1999 Serbs had been both the targets and the perpetrators of persistent ethnic violence.

While in Pristina, President Clinton met privately with the UN secretary-general's special representative, Harri Holkeri, former prime minister of Finland, the man charged with overseeing the UN's ambitious program of civil administration in the province. Although not technically "nation building" because Kosovo remained an internal part of the larger Serbia and Montenegro, the UN Interim Administration Mission in Kosovo (UNMIK) had undertaken the invasive governance of all aspects of Kosovar life. Holkeri, like his four predecessors since 1999, sought to bring Serbs and Kosovar Albanians together in a peaceful multiethnic state—not an easy task in a place where ethnic hatred had a long history, many Serb residents sought full unification with the rest of the country, and Albanians wished for nothing less than an independent state. In every hamlet and town of Kosovo, government consisted of Serb-Albanian-UN committees that determined every detail of public policy, although the UN representative retained final authority. President Clinton gave his full endorsement to Holkeri and the UN effort.

UNMIK was created by Security Council Resolution 1244 in June 1999. It was charged with performing basic governmental functions, providing essential services to the population, facilitating a political process to determine Kosovo's future while in the meantime establishing autonomy and self-government in the province, providing humanitarian aid, maintaining law and order, repatriating more than one million refugees, and promoting human rights. In May 2001 UNMIK promulgated a draft of a democratic constitution for Kosovo that recognized individual rights and group power sharing. The long-term outcome the UN administration was seeking was a freely elected multiethnic government. In the interim, the secretary-general's special representative retained the right to override all local decisions.

By September 2003 supporters and critics of the UN peacekeeping operation in Kosovo could be heard. On the one hand, rampant death and destruction had been eliminated; on the other, the seeds of future Serb-Albanian violence had not been removed. Everyone agreed that a pullout of UN forces would eliminate any chance for continued domestic peace. If Holkeri was to make any progress in Kosovo, he would have to stem the cycle of enmity that was visible daily. Only a month before President Clinton's visit to Kosovo, a particularly heinous ambush of Serb children playing on a riverbank near the village of Zahac had injured four of the children and killed two. UNMIK officials had attempted to head off likely retribution and counterviolence. What was not at all clear, however, was whether the United Nations had the resources, strategy, or will to actually do so.

Actions by NATO in 1999 and the subsequent UN administration of Kosovo challenged a central tenet on which the United Nations was built—the inviolability of a sovereign state's domestic jurisdiction. The UN's administration represented a continuing expansion of UN peacekeeping efforts authorized by the Security Council. Neither the Kosovars nor the central government in Belgrade was left with the decision on the final status of the province. The world community, through UN procedures, decided that the province would be autonomous but that no new state would be added to the community of nations.

In the distant Pacific Island nation of Indonesia, the world's judgment was significantly different. There, the Security Council defended the East Timorese people's right to break the sovereign control of the central government and establish a new state, Timor-Leste. This state subsequently became a full member of the United Nations (September 27, 2002), albeit with continuing UN administration. East Timor's successful secession from Indonesia culminated a four-decade struggle following the end of Portuguese colonial control, a struggle marked by repression and rebel insurgency. Finally, in May 1999, an agreement brokered by the UN secretary-general was signed that called for a "popular consultation" of the Timorese people on the question of autonomy. The Security Council then created the first of two peacekeeping operations to facilitate the process. In the ensuing referendum more than 78 percent of the population voted for independence. Pro-Indonesian militias and security forces retaliated with random violence, looting, and arson. With the pressured consent of the Indonesian government, the Security Council authorized the military intervention of a multilateral force under Australian command to restore order and, as in Kosovo, to establish UN administration of the fledgling state. In this case, however, the goal was a stable, independent government, not self-governing autonomy.

Under UN leadership, East Timor, with its capital in Dili, crafted a constitution, convened national governmental organs, elected an assembly and a president, and took control of governmental affairs in May 2002. Nonetheless, the United Nations continued as a presence in Timor-Leste through UNMISET (UN Mission of Support in East Timor). Well into 2004 the operation maintained a police force comprising personnel from thirty countries along with an additional five thousand troops. Also, massive economic, food, and humanitarian aid was critical for simple survival in the poor, war-ravaged state. On the day the Fifty-eighth General Assembly convened in New York City and debated how to proceed with nation building in Iraq, the acting prime minister of East Timor, Ana Pessoa, accepted the handover of police functions in the Baucau District from the UN police administration. Only Dili proper remained under UN supervision.

The "success" or "failure" of the United Nations in the twenty-first century turns not only on the results of debates in New York City on the potential for nation building in places like Iraq and Afghanistan, but also on the "facts on the ground" in Kosovo, East Timor, and other conflict zones where more than thirty-five thousand UN peacekeepers in 2003 were challenging old principles of state sovereignty and trying to create or maintain viable and peaceful communities. (UN peacekeeping efforts are discussed in more detail in Chapter 6.) Even as slow progress was being made in Dili and Kosovo, the world body prepared to take on the financial, security, and political burden of new peacekeeping responsibilities in Liberia, and possibly in Iraq. Whether the organization has the ability to turn events in these out-of-the-way "places" of the United Nations decisively toward peace and stability remains unclear.

THE NEW UNITED NATIONS

The United Nations is an IGO that is more far reaching than a review of its Charter would suggest and more comprehensive than its founders contemplated. The history of its formation, Charter development, and unique evolution is outlined in the next three chapters. Today, the United Nations is a collective of specialized agencies, institutional structures, forums, programs, and funds scattered around the world that is increasingly addressing global and domestic issues that were previously not considered central to the maintenance of international peace and security.

Secretary-General Annan described a "new" United Nations in his Millennium Report, entitled *We The Peoples,* in September 2000. At the Millennium Summit—an extraordinary gathering of world leaders, NGOs, and private individuals in New York City—the secretary-general noted the diplomatic origins and purposes of the United Nations that made it a "forum for sharing information, conducting negotiations, elaborating norms and voicing expectations, coordinating

PRINCIPAL OFFICES OF THE UN SYSTEM (SEE APPENDIX G)

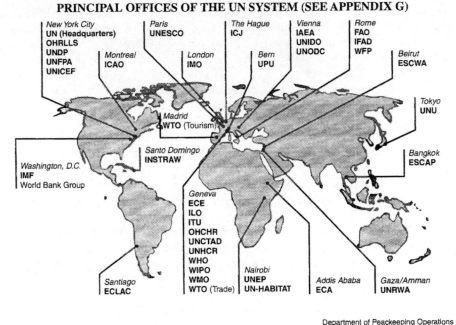

Department of Peackeeping Operations
Cartographic Section

(Map No. 4218(E), United Nations, April 2004. Reproduced by permission from the UN Cartographic Section.)

the behavior of states and other actors, and pursuing common plans of action." He also described it as something much more than a universal IGO committed to collective security. Noting that the Charter was written in the name of "We the Peoples," he called for a new emphasis on the rights of the person in both domestic and international life. He envisioned a United Nations that acknowledged state sovereignty but never let that principle stand in the way of defending individual rights or providing critical international humanitarian assistance.

What Annan was describing was an institution in the throes of change. An evolutionary process is occurring, changing the character and mission of the United Nations in at least five ways. First, the UN agenda early in the millennium includes a new interest in **thematic diplomacy,** a consideration of functional human problems that confront humankind on a global level and require for their solution not only the involvement of national governments but also the cooperation of international and subnational organizations. **Functionalism,** the belief that peace and security between nations may best be achieved through the "spillover" effect of expanding cooperation among peoples and through international organizations on the nonpolitical problems that confront the world community, has a rich two-century history of advocates and organizational experiments. However, the impetus to the UN's creation was the "high" politics of diplomatic relations on the questions of war and peace between states, with functional concerns such as economic development and human welfare relegated to the periphery of its work. Annan's promotion of thematic diplomacy moved functional world politics to center stage. By 2005 the United Nations was pursuing many areas of thematic diplomacy, but twelve topics of international cooperation predominated. They were the environment, women, the control of HIV/AIDS and other communicable diseases, disarmament, sustainable development, globalization, human rights, peacekeeping, poverty eradication (especially in Africa), population, democratization, and international law. Only slightly less attention was being given to human settlements, disease, migration, and the information revolution.

Each thematic policy area originated as a focus of UN attention at a particular point in the history of the organization. For example, concern for the environment can be dated, as we noted in the discussion about UNEP, from the 1972 Stockholm Conference. Each policy area developed through the adoption of declarations, conventions, and UN resolutions. In the field of human rights, the Universal Declaration of Human Rights laid out the principles to which the world community committed itself. These principles were subsequently codified in two international covenants in 1966. In the areas of peacekeeping and sustainable development, UN efforts created evolving definitions and international standards of behavior for nation-states and their leaders. In all these areas, world conferences, preparatory meetings, implemental programs, special funds, and intense multilateral negotiations were used to address perceived human problems.

Second, while the United Nations is an organization made up of sovereign states, increasingly nonstate actors play a role in its deliberations, in the formation of UN global policy, and in the success or failure of established UN programs. The growth in thematic diplomacy has accelerated this trend. Two groups of nonstate participants can easily be identified. The first is nongovernmental organizations. These organizations are associational members of international civil society. In effect, they are global interest groups or domestic groups that have international agendas. Welcomed in a peripheral way by the UN Charter to "consultative status" with ECOSOC, the NGO community now dominates much of the work of UN world conferences, formulates a global agenda that the world organization generally addresses, and serves as the most serious critic of UN programs. Since the early 1990s UN secretaries-general have courted the participation and goodwill of NGOs, hoping through them to mold public opinion and to implement UN initiatives more effectively than could be achieved solely through member governments. The second group of nonstate actors is the private for-profit sector of the world economy. Once viewed as the enemy of UN social, economic, and human rights policy, global corporations are now recruited as helpful financial supporters for UN activities. Beginning with Secretary-General Annan's Global Compact initiative in 1999 (discussed in Chapter 7), more than one thousand companies have voluntarily associated themselves with the work of the United Nations.

Third, the United Nations increasingly has been seeking to impose the rule of law on individuals within countries as much as it does among its member states. This trend is controversial because it is in obvious conflict with the Charter's admonition in Article 2: "Nothing contained in the present Charter shall authorize the United Nations to intervene in matters that are essentially within the domestic jurisdiction of any state." In domestic democratic society nothing is more central to its functioning than the rule of law. In the broader international community of states, the proclamation and enforcement of law have been extremely difficult given the sovereign nature of nation-states. International law allows for the voluntary adjudication of controversies among states but does not reach to individuals or carry the force of imposable sanctions. In the past, only in rare cases has the world community sought to apply legal standards and penalties to individuals who have been found to have violated standards of universal legal decency. The Nuremberg tribunals stand as an isolated example of that natural law tradition in the twentieth century.

The 1990s, however, witnessed a revival of this international legal trend with the establishment, under UN auspices, of the international criminal tribunals for the former Yugoslavia and Rwanda to try "war criminals." The experience of the Yugoslav and Rwandan ad hoc tribunals laid the basis for the creation of the International Criminal Court (ICC) in the Rome Statute of July 17, 1998. The ICC is intended as a permanent judicial body with universal jurisdiction over the crimes outlined in its founding document.

Intervention in the form of intrusive peacekeeping, a post–cold war evolution of an earlier relatively neutral monitoring process, also reflects the new concern for individual rights over state sovereignty. Decried by some people, and imposed with varying degrees of effectiveness, "nation building" and the defense of minorities clearly mark a move away from the letter of the UN Charter but may be a proper reinterpretation of its spirit in the context of the twenty-first century.

Fourth, the United Nations appears to be moving away from being solely an IGO of sovereign states primarily concerned with keeping the immediate peace among its members to becoming a member itself of international civil society. In 1997 Kofi Annan released his long-awaited reform program for the United Nations, entitled *Renewing the United Nations*. In it, he described the United Nations as the central institution of civil society, itself a product of irreversible globalization. He defined *civil society* as that "sphere in which social movements organize themselves around objectives, constituencies and thematic interests. These movements include specific groups such as women, youth and indigenous people. Other actors have also taken on an increasingly important role in shaping national and international agendas. They include local authorities, mass media, business and industry, professional associations, religious and cultural organizations and the intellectual and research communities."[16] Annan contended that international civil society was the product not only of globalization but also of "the quest for a more democratic, transparent, accountable and enabling governance." Annan warned that an "uncivil society" exists, made up of terrorists, drug traffickers, individuals engaged in organizing prostitution and in trafficking women and children, and others who have taken advantage of the processes of globalization. Only new multilateral partnerships between the United Nations and subnational levels of government and nonstate actors could provide a basis for UN success in countering these challenges. The UN System has increasingly sought these kinds of cooperative ties, thus enlarging its role beyond its traditional character as a forum for interstate negotiation and decision making.

Fifth, the United Nations has made an ideological choice, opting for democratization externally in new and troubled nation-states, internally in terms of its own reforms (discussed in Chapter 3), and substantively in terms of the issues that have moved to the head of its agenda. The United Nations was founded as an IGO for the maintenance of peace and security. To be sure, other concerns existed. These desires were reflected in Charter provisions for a trusteeship system, economic and social functions, decolonization, human rights, and specialized agencies to address the many functional issues shared by humans in all settings. This IGO was the first international organization that recognized women's rights in its originating document. These features of international attentiveness anticipated what we (the authors) call the *Other United Nations*. These concerns were primarily enshrined in the Universal Declaration of Human Rights, not in the UN Charter. The former document was crafted in the late 1940s by the Commission on Human Rights, chaired by Eleanor Roosevelt. Mrs. Roosevelt placed her faith in world public opinion and its ability to ultimately win the day and move governments and the United Nations to secure these rights for all individuals.[17] If the primary United Nations was Franklin Roosevelt's, the "Other United Nations" was Eleanor's. Increasingly, the United Nations of the post–cold war era is also Eleanor's UN. The "rebirth" of the United Nations has been characterized by its rapid "democratization," with the concomitant diminution of the claim of state sovereignty on the life of the institution. People's rights, people's participation, and the application of the rule of law all take up far more UN time, attention, and resources than was the case during its first 45 years of existence.

In late 1999 demonstrators gathered in the streets of Seattle, Washington, to protest the third ministerial meeting of the World Trade Organization (WTO), the successor to GATT (General Agreement on Tariffs and Trade), a Bretton Woods institution. Among other charges, the activist alliance criticized the WTO for its undemocratic nature. Like other post–World War II institutions, it was seen as unaccountable to the populations it affected, particularly in the developing world. Accused of being in the hands of corporate giants and government bureaucrats, WTO meetings were subsequently subjected to violent protests not only in Seattle, but also in Washington, D.C.; Prague, Czech Republic; and Genoa, Italy.

It is probably not without significance that the United Nations has so far avoided the popular fate of the Bretton Woods institutions. It has been able to do so in part because of a timely democratization that has provided for greater participation, accountability, and transparency. It has also changed its agenda, making the "Other United Nations" central to its work and thus implicitly recognizing that the maintenance of international peace and security depends in due course on fulfilling human needs.

SUMMARY

Far beyond the drama of global politics played out for all to see in UN facilities in New York City, the international organization, located in its many "homes" around the world, has created a web of agencies, programs, and initiatives that have been increasingly addressing human needs in the belief that these concerns underlie much of the conflict in the world. The UN System of the twenty-first century exceeds the breadth of the organization as it was conceived by its founders in 1945. Its aims have extended beyond the traditional interest in interstate diplomacy to the "sovereignty" of the individual, with all its concomitant implications for global UN efforts. Thus, we postulate a "new" United Nations, with not only new opportunities, but also new limitations and difficult if novel, challenges. Said in some quarters to be irrelevant, a leftover from the last era of international politics, the United Nations nonetheless remains the only truly universal international organization in the world. How this situation has evolved, what it means for the institution, and its impact on the global community and world affairs is laid out in the succeeding chapters.

NOTES

1. President Jacques Chirac, address to the fifty-eighth session of the UN General Assembly, September 23, 2003, http://www.un.org/webcast/ga/58/statements/fraeng030923.htm.
2. Ibid.
3. Secretary-General Kofi Annan, address to the fifty-eighth session of the UN General Assembly, September 23, 2003, http://www.un.org/webcast/ga/58/statements/sg2eng030923.htm.
4. Charles A. Kupchan, *The End of the American Era* (New York: Knopf, 2002), 114.
5. United Nations, "Preamble," in *Charter to the United Nations* (New York: United Nations, 1945), http://www.un.org/aboutun/charter/preamble.htm.
6. UN Population Fund, "UNFPA: Making a Difference in Afghanistan," news feature, August 22, 2003.
7. Executive Board of the United Nations Development Programme and of the United Nations Population Fund, "Provisional Agenda, Annotations, Lists of Documents and Tentative Work Plan," daily brief on the second regular session 2003, September 8–12, 2003, New York, DP/2003/L.3, http://www.unfpa.org/exbrd/2003/2003_second.htm.

8. Wendy Lubetkin, ed., *The Briefing Book on International Organizations in Geneva, 2000–2001* (Geneva: U.S. Mission to the United Nations in Geneva, 2000).

9. Eco'Diagnostic, *International Geneva Yearbook 2000–2001* (Geneva: United Nations, 2000), 74.

10. UN Office at Geneva, "Opening of the forty-ninth session of the UNCC Governing Council," press release, September 12, 2003.

11. UN Office at Geneva, "Conference on Disarmament Concludes 2003 session," press release, September 9, 2003.

12. "Conference on Disarmament Opens First Part of 2005 Session," CD press release DCF/446, January 27, 2005.

13. New Zealand Ministry of Foreign Affairs and Trade, *United Nations Handbook 2002* (Wellington: New Zealand Ministry of Foreign Affairs and Trade, 2002), 50.

14. International Civil Aviation Organization, "Historic Agreement on the Air Traffic Services Route Network in the Aegean Sea," press release, September 15, 2003.

15. John Allphin Moore, Jr., and Jerry Pubantz, *Encyclopedia of the United Nations* (New York: Facts on File, 2002), 114.

16. Secretary-General Kofi Annan, *Renewing the United Nations: A Programme for Reform,* UN agenda item 168, July 14, 1997.

17. Mary Ann Glendon, *A World Made New: Eleanor Roosevelt and the Universal Declaration of Human Rights* (New York: Random House, 2001), 69–72.

KEY TERMS

Kofi Annan (page 11)

Conference on Disarmament (CD) (page 18)

Food and Agriculture Organization (FAO) (page 26)

Functionalism (page 30)

General Debate (page 10)

International Civil Aviation Organization (ICAO) (page 24)

Parliamentary Diplomacy (page 13)

Thematic Diplomacy (page 30)

UN Compensation Commission (UNCC) (page 18)

UN-HABITAT (UN Human Settlements Programme) (page 20)

UN Population Fund (UNFPA) (page 15)

World Food Programme (WFP) (page 27)

RESOURCES FOR FURTHER RESEARCH
Relevant Web Sites

UN home page (www.un.org)

UN Office at Geneva (www.unog.ch/)

UN Office at Nairobi (www.unon.org)

UN Office at Vienna (www.unvienna.org/unov/index.html)

Web site locator for UN System bodies (www.unsystem.org)

Books, Articles, and Documents

Annan, Kofi. *Report of the Secretary-General on the Work of the Organization.* New York: United Nations, 2001.

United Nations. *Basic Facts about the United Nations.* New York: United Nations, published periodically.

Eco'Diagnostic. *International Geneva Yearbook 2000–2001*. Geneva: United Nations, 2000.

Glassner, Martin Ira, ed. *The United Nations at Work*. Westport, CT: Praeger, 1998.

Knight, W. Andy. *A Changing United Nations: Multilateral Evolution and the Quest for Global Governance*. Houndsmill, UK: Macmillan, 2000.

Moore, John Allphin, Jr., and Jerry Pubantz. *Encyclopedia of the United Nations*. New York: Facts on File, 2002.

New Zealand Ministry of Foreign Affairs and Trade. *United Nations Handbook*. Wellington: New Zealand Ministry of Foreign Affairs and Trade, published annually.

United Nations. *Report of the Secretary-General on the Work of the Organization*. New York: United Nations, published annually.

Ziring, Lawrence, Robert Riggs, and Jack Plano. *The United Nations: International Organization and World Politics*. Fort Worth, TX: Harcourt College, 2000.

Chapter 2

Origins and History of the United Nations

To understand the evolution of an organization, a person must first know its origins and early history. In this chapter, we cover the various attempts at establishing world peace and unity before the United Nations was formed. Then, we cover its beginnings, the setbacks it has faced, and the more recent challenge to one of its basic tenets: the principle of collective security.

OVERVIEW OF EARLY HISTORICAL EFFORTS TO ESTABLISH INTERNATIONAL ORGANIZATION

In their historical semblance, certain events foretold the founding of the United Nations. Among these events were the Peace Conference of Westphalia in 1648, which addressed the reorganization of Europe after the ruinous Thirty Years' War; the Vienna Conference of 1814–1815, which ended the Napoleonic Wars; and the Paris Peace Conference, where diplomats attempted to craft a peaceful international system following World War I. At Westphalia, the sovereign secular state became the prime actor in international affairs. The gathered emissaries hoped for peace among these states based on "the just equilibrium of power." At Vienna, for the first time, the architects of the new order sought to maintain the peace through succeeding regular meetings of the so-called great powers. A little more than a century later, at Paris in 1919, the world's leaders established the League of Nations, the immediate predecessor to the United Nations. Other historical examples of efforts to fashion fixed diplomatic relations and ongoing political international organizations exist, but they, like the three peace conferences just referenced, mostly failed. Whether in their failure they left sufficient lessons for the UN's founders that would result in an enduring international order remains patently uncertain. Nevertheless, the UN's existence for more than half a century suggests that something must have been learned.

INTERNATIONAL RELATIONS BEFORE THE TWENTIETH CENTURY

The so-called Enlightenment period of the eighteenth century brought modern rationality to learning while imposing on international affairs fresh notions that would eventually motivate world leaders and show the way, much later, to the United Nations. Eighteenth-century developments in politics, economics, international law, science, and conceptions of individual rights led to what some people have called *modern liberal democratic nationalism*.[1] In turn, influenced by liberals in the American and French revolutionary traditions, and by German philosopher Immanuel Kant, thinkers envisioned a peaceful world that would be characterized by democracy, economic interdependence, and international law and institutions.[2] Such notions may strike the twenty-first-century reader as commonplace examples of what the current age calls *globalization* and of normal contemporary international politics. However, nearly two centuries, bloody conflicts, and agonizing efforts would be necessary to effect a world organization that conformed to the prescriptions of enlightened notions of diplomacy.

Long before the eighteenth century, formal relations between and among nations, empires, and peoples characterized human activity.[3] The diffusion and ultimate availability of texts and treaties dealing with such relations suggest a pattern in world history of cross-cultural intercourse among political elites the world over that designed what might be called international relations. Basic principles and precedents emerged as different communities sought to impose order on their mutual relations and to resolve disagreements without resorting to force—unless those principles or their interests might allow or require such measures.

For most of history, public order was maintained by hierarchical imperial administrations whose dominance was punctuated by sporadic uprisings and dissolution that too often resulted in violence.[4] For example, the great periods of Chinese history are considered the times when powerful consolidating empires brought pervasive peace, some prosperity, Confucian (or later, Maoist) standards of conduct, artistic grandeur, and systematic rule to a society that nonetheless intermittently plunged into chaotic and disruptive civil strife. The Roman Empire is the prototypical administrative unit of the Western legacy. Rome brought stability, peace (the *Pax Romana*), law, infrastructure, a common language, and eventually Christianity to the known Western world. Byzantium was the imperial reflection of Rome in much of eastern Europe, and it lasted longer and left an impressive legacy of Slavic orthodox culture that was neither nationalist nor liberal in character. The Ottoman Empire imposed a flexible bureaucracy on a wide swath of land with an extremely diverse population. Likewise, great Russian empires, whether Romanov or Bolshevik, brought to heel the squabbling medley of ethnic groups covering their large landmass. As a rule, when the imperial power was challenged, the consequence was unwelcome disruption and sometimes anarchy. Empire, whether imposed willingly and brutally, or reluctantly and benignly, seemed the common solution to international disorder. In fact, as late as the turn into the twentieth century, international diplomacy was something characteristically conducted among empires (the Romanovs in Eurasia, the Manchus in China, the Ottomans in the Middle East, the Hapsburgs in south-central Europe, the Hohenzollerns in Germany and east-central Europe, and the British and French worldwide).

What might be termed the *postempire* era of political organization is more familiar to the modern world. The idea of *national sovereignty* provided nation-states the ultimate authority over populations within discernible boundaries. The nation-state, considered to have originated in Europe in the fifteenth and sixteenth centuries, heralded what some scholars have called *international anarchy*. Because no commanding sovereign authority rested above the nation, international order depended on the good faith of its individual sovereign members. In the West this phenomenon led to the development of modern international relations and international law. Scholars and practitioners such as Hugo Grotius (1583–1645) and Emmerich de Vattel (1714–1767) sought to codify rules of international behavior based on the understanding that each sovereign state would determine whether to abide by them. This "state of nature" in international matters presupposed an underlying possibility of conflict. An initial response to this problem was the **balance of power theory,** which suggested that if any one nation were to gain overwhelming power so as to represent a danger to other nations, the latter would unite to restrain—that is, balance—the powerful entity. In addition to introducing the balance of power theory, early European theorists proffered notions of what might now be called *international human rights law.* The earliest approaches to this issue came from alarm about the treatment of native populations in the new Spanish colonies of the sixteenth century, and then of civilians during the brutal religious wars, particularly the Thirty Years' War (1618–1648). Grotius and Vattel, and their readers in Europe and the United States, sought to codify into an embryonic international law accepted practices against what society currently calls *war crimes.*

By means of the Peace of Westphalia, which ended the Thirty Years' War, sovereignty became the criterion for authority in any political entity. For example, sovereign rulers were authorized to determine the religion within their state to prevent internal wars between competing religions, which had too often drawn in outside forces. Under the Westphalian settlement, Europe came to be characterized by sovereign nation-states theoretically abiding by an international law including the rules of war, but, first and foremost, defending their national power and interests. Following World War I, new nation-states appeared in central Europe. After World War II, India and Pakistan became independent of Great Britain, while various states emerged out of the former Ottoman Empire and the mandates administered there by Great Britain and France between the wars. From 1945 to 1970 many new states in the "developing world" gained independence. The nation-state had become the accepted mode of political organization.

THE CONCERT OF EUROPE

Meanwhile, the American and French Revolutions had brought to world politics the idea of universal principles applicable at all times and to all peoples. The idea that all human beings were, by nature, equal inspired but also disturbed existing politics. The French Revolution culminated in a long world war and the Age of Napoleon. The victorious allies who finally defeated the French general met at Vienna during 1814–1815 and restructured Europe and its diplomatic practices in an attempt to bring order to the continent and prevent another descent into violence. The Congress of Vienna crafted an arrangement—dubbed the **Concert of Europe**—to build a peaceful Europe. Diplomats settled on a new and transformed balance of power, complemented by territorial compromise among all the former belligerents; monarchical legitimacy and restoration; and an agreement to meet in the future to consult on actions to take to meet disruptive crises (which signaled the so-called congress system of European affairs).[5] Often considered a conservative settlement, the Vienna program was followed by a reasonably tranquil nineteenth century that experienced a creative expansion of international organizations. Early river commissions, such as the Central Rhine Commission (1815) and the European Danube Commission (1856), were examples. The International Red Cross was in place by the middle of the century, and the International Telegraphic Union (1865) and the Universal Postal Union (1874) paved the way for numerous future international agencies dealing with issues as diverse as narcotics, agriculture, health, weights and measures, railroads, time zones, and tariffs. The Paris Convention for the Protection of Industrial Property (1883) and the Berne Convention for the Protection of Literary and Artistic Works (1886) brought issues of protecting patents and copyrights into the larger realm of international law. In 1899 and 1907, The Hague Conferences marked a culminating phase in the arbitration movement, establishing the Permanent Court of Arbitration and expanding rules governing arbitral procedures.

THE LEAGUE OF NATIONS AND WORLD WAR II

Despite such progress, crises challenged both the arrangements of The Concert of Europe and the progress in international cooperation up to the plunge into the Great War of 1914–1918. When that disastrous war ended, a new participant—the United States—encroached into the club of the more traditional great powers to attempt a solution to the disorder that had caused the war.

The League of Nations

U.S. president Woodrow Wilson joined other leaders at the Paris Peace Conference. He brought with him positions he had articulated earlier in his liberal "Fourteen Points" speech, including an outline for a new worldwide organization—a **League of Nations**—committed to collective security and the elimination of war. The precursor to the United Nations, the League would be the first world organization intended to maintain peace and security, foster international cooperation, and develop international law on an ongoing basis.

     The League's initiation had resulted from the unrivaled bloodshed and carnage of World War I, which convinced many leaders of the necessity of a world organization to avert another such conflict. Eighteenth-century German philosopher Immanuel Kant had envisioned a global federation of republics, and the nineteenth century had witnessed the growth of numerous international cooperative ventures. The Hague Peace Conferences at the beginning of the twentieth century and the establishment of the Permanent Court of Arbitration gave further impetus to international cooperation. The war solidified opinion among an active group of diplomats, including South African Jan Smuts, Great Britain's Lord Robert Cecil, and Frenchman Léon Bourgeois, who all advocated a society of nations. As early as 1914 President Wilson had spoken with his closest adviser, Colonel Edward House, about the merits of forming a world association to avoid the kind of war just under way. The president may also have been influenced by the British writer Norman Angell, with whom he spoke before publicly articulating his ideas on a League. In 1917 the American Institute of International Law issued a recommendation in Havana, Cuba, calling for a world organization that dovetailed agreeably with Wilson's proposal.

     At the Paris Peace Conference in 1919, Wilson insisted on including the Covenant of the new League in the text of the Treaty of Versailles. The U.S. president headed a special committee at the conference that shaped the Covenant of the League and made it an "integral part of the General Peace Treaty." The Covenant, coming into force on January 10, 1920, included twenty-six articles, provided for an assembly composed of all members, a council to include permanent members from the great powers (at first the United Kingdom, France, Italy, and Japan, who were later joined by Germany and the Soviet Union), and a secretariat. Both the assembly and the council required unanimity on any decision. The Covenant called for disarmament, territorial integrity and political independence of nation-states, establishment of the Permanent Court of International Justice, a mandate system (whereby existing colonial administrators would prepare colonial areas for independence) that foreshadowed the end of colonialism, international cooperation in humanitarian affairs, and provisions for amending the Covenant. The most controversial provision of the Covenant, highlighted in Article 10, called for collective security to ensure nations League protection against aggression.[6]

The council's inaugural session took place in Paris in January 1920, but Geneva became the permanent home of the new League, which met at first in the Hôtel National (before construction of the Palais des Nations, which opened in 1936). By a two-thirds vote of the assembly, membership could be extended to any state, dominion, or even self-governing colony. The war's victors were the original members: Of the thirty-two winning Allies, twenty-nine joined the League initially. The largest victor not to join was the United States, because the Senate refused to ratify the Treaty of Versailles. In 1920 membership stood at forty-two states. The Soviet Union—isolated from world affairs during the Bolshevik Revolution—and several neutral nations did not become members in 1920. Germany, unhappy with the peace treaty, did not enter the League until 1926. Russia joined in 1934, just as the strains on the organization were becoming unbearable. The greatest number of members, achieved in 1937, was fifty-eight; by 1943 only ten remained. The League's secretaries-general were Sir James Eric Drummond of Great Britain (1920–1933), Joseph Avenol of France (1933–1940), and Seán Lester from Ireland (1940–1946).

The offices of the League's secretariat were in a building along Lake Geneva that in 1924 was renamed the *Palais Wilson*, following the death of the former U.S. president. Sir Drummond, the first and longest-serving secretary-general, assembled a genuinely international secretariat, and early on the League realized some successes. The League settled a Finnish-Swedish dispute over the Åland Islands in the Gulf of Bothnia (1920–1921), guaranteed the security of Albania (1921), aided Austria's economic reconstruction after the war, guided the peaceful division of Upper Silesia between Germany and Poland (1922), and helped prevent hostilities between Greece and Bulgaria in the Balkans (1925). The League also extended help to refugees, worked to suppress the white slave trade and to restrain the traffic in opium, and published surveys and data on a number of pressing international issues such as world health, labor conditions, and economics.

Nevertheless, intractable problems confronted the organization. For instance, without the United States as a member, the League lacked one of the influential players in world affairs. In addition, the problem of including the Soviet Union in international diplomacy was not resolved until late in the League's history. The nonparticipation of important nations, along with unwieldy rules of procedure, such as requiring unanimity in both the council and the League assembly, made effective enforcement impractical. Meanwhile, the worldwide depression that engulfed most countries by the 1930s made dealing with nations who were looking out for their own interests even more difficult. Then, as the dismantling of world order ensued, the League seemed destined to sit aside as aggressions proceeded. The League could do nothing as the French occupied the Ruhr Valley in 1923, the Japanese invaded Manchuria in 1931 (when the League accepted the U.S. policy—called the *Stimson Doctrine*—of simply not recognizing the occupation), the Japanese withdrew from League membership (1933), and Bolivia and Paraguay fought the Chaco War (1932–1935). In 1935 Italy invaded Ethiopia, and in the end all the League could do in response to the impassioned appeal from Ethiopia's leader, Haile Selassie, was to call for voluntary economic sanctions against Italy. Despite the seemingly automatic imposition of sanctions according to Article 16, many powerful nations, including the United States, ignored the League's request. Collective security was essentially dead as an effective instrument against the bellicose dictators of the time.

In 1935 the League completed a fifteen-year administration of the Saar Territory (in Germany) with a plebiscite, but Germany had already left the League (1933). Adolf Hitler's remilitarization of the Rhineland and repudiation of the Treaty of Versailles augured an ominous future for the organization. The Spanish Civil War (1936–1939); the Japanese invasion of mainland China (1937); the appeasement of Hitler at Munich, which allowed the dismemberment of Czechoslovakia (1938);

and German demands on Danzig, Poland—which a League commissioner in the city could not resist—culminated in the outbreak of World War II. The League's inconsequence became obvious when in 1939 the council—for the only time in the League's history—expelled a nation, the Soviet Union, for its attack on Finland following the German-Soviet Pact of August 23, 1939, by which the two totalitarian regimes agreed to divide eastern Europe. At the moment of the agreement, war became inevitable. This novel experiment in world cooperation virtually ceased to function with the outbreak of World War II, and in 1946 it officially dissolved itself. Several affiliated organizations and powerful ideas of international cooperation, however, did survive the crisis of World War II, and merged with the new United Nations after the conflict.

Woodrow Wilson and the Elemental Weaknesses of the League

The completed Versailles peace agreement had contained several compromises that troubled President Wilson's most resolute supporters. Almost no one seemed happy with the final national boundaries bequeathed by Versailles; many critics believed the final settlement had actually frustrated Wilson's bedrock principle of ethnic and national autonomy. Opponents in the United States complained that the president had made too many compromises in Paris and feared that he had overcommitted the country to international collective security. In September 1919, campaigning for Senate approval of the League, the president collapsed with a stroke in Colorado. His resulting illness removed the most ardent supporter of the League from the nationwide debate. Meanwhile, resistance to his plans mounted and partisan bickering between U.S. political parties made compromise in the Senate highly improbable. The Republicans had won a narrow majority in Senate elections in 1918, which elevated the Democratic president's most commanding opponent, Henry Cabot Lodge, to both majority leader and chairman of the crucial Senate Foreign Relations Committee. Combined, these troubles made the Senate's refusal to ratify the peace agreement inevitable and thus prevented U.S. entrance into the new League of Nations.

The Versailles settlement may have been doomed to failure irrespective of the U.S. snub. Diplomats at Paris had before them a dangerously disintegrating world. Most of the major organizing empires of the previous century were gone. The Manchu dynasty in China had collapsed in 1911, replaced by a weak republican government, and a disruptive civil war followed. In Russia a revolution ended the Romanovs' rule in March 1917, and by the end of the year the Bolsheviks found themselves in control of a truncated state because the former empire had lost considerable territory to the Germans months before the war concluded. By war's end, the Hohenzollerns in Germany and the Hapsburg rulers of the Austro-Hungarian Empire were likewise gone, as was the Ottoman Empire, now completely dissolved. Within the resulting vacuums in the center of Europe, in the Middle East, and elsewhere were a variety of religions and myriad ethnic entities that demanded sovereign independence along religious and ethnic lines. The Wilsonian principles of self-determination and internationalism, inherent in the treaty, were now put forward as the postwar formula to fill the vacuum and to promote communal peace. Nonetheless, the end of imperial rule left unsettled cleavages in many parts of the world. In one respect, world leaders have been trying since 1918 to restore order out of the chaos left by World War I.

Despite the U.S. rebuff, the League came into being and, as we discussed previously, functioned until the world descended into the next round of discord in the late 1930s. The three new permanent organs—an assembly with equal representation from all member states, a council with permanent and nonpermanent members, and a secretariat—signified innovative advances in the development of international institutions. Although earlier international conferences had made some use of secretariats, the League secretariat, providing centralized administration, expert advice, and day-to-day coordination, embodied a novel concept of a permanent international civil service. Outside the Covenant framework, but related to the League, were the Permanent Court of International Justice (the so-called World Court) and the International Labour Organization. Despite the ultimate failure of the League, its organizational structure and various activities provided a basis for its UN progeny.

Although the League, then, was a model for the later United Nations, five important discernible differences can be seen between the defunct League and the current organization. First, the League had been ensconced in the full Treaty of Versailles; thus, to reject the League, the U.S. Senate had to reject the entire peace agreement. Conversely, the United Nations was purposely separated from the terms of peace that ended World War II; U.S. president Franklin Roosevelt, informed by Wilson's lack of success, determined on a separate process of ratification in the United States. Second, the League Covenant had been a traditional agreement among governments, who were called in the Covenant "The High Contracting Parties." In contrast, the preamble of the UN Charter begins, "We the *Peoples* of the United Nations." Third, the League required unanimous votes in both the assembly and the council, but decision making in the United Nations is more flexible. Fourth, parties to a dispute before the League were prohibited from voting because of the obvious conflict of interest. In the United Nations, in a concession to the realities of power politics, member states have no such limitations. This freedom, coupled with the veto, means that a permanent member of the Security Council can block UN action. Fifth, and finally, in 1945 the United States, never a member of the League or the Permanent Court of International Justice, eagerly entered the United Nations and decided to play a major role in all post–World War II international organizations.

U.S. AND ALLIED VISIONS OF
THE POST–WORLD WAR II PERIOD

The challenges confronting the UN founders were not those that the world community would face in the twenty-first century, but they were no less momentous:

- Western leaders needed to assuage Russian suspicions of any Western-bred organization to which Moscow would be asked to commit.
- The United States was obliged to convince its people and the rest of the world that it would not again retreat from leadership in this postwar period.
- Great Britain required encouragement to complete the Wilsonian dream of dismantling worldwide empires, the largest of which was administered from London.
- The defeated nations needed to be reconstructed and fused into the new global framework.
- Urgent rebuilding and rehabilitation of a war-devastated world awaited action.
- Displaced persons and roaming refugees required immediate attention.
- The world economy demanded restitution and rational orderliness.
- The globe awaited a general, broad, and forceful commitment to the fundamental human rights so long promised by enlightened liberals and so clearly desecrated in the war years.

Whatever criticisms can be mounted against the early United Nations it—and its associated organs—met and resolved every one of these challenges within a few short years following the most destructive war in history. However, this accomplishment was not easy.

By the end of the 1930s, the League became effectively inoperative. Seeds for a new organization were planted in the Atlantic Charter of August 1941, issued by U.S. president Franklin

Roosevelt and Winston Churchill, the British prime minister. The document obliquely referred to a future international organization for "general security." On January 1, 1942, with the United States now in the war, twenty-six nations joined in a *Declaration by United Nations* (a term coined by Roosevelt), reaffirming the principles of the Atlantic Charter and committing themselves to defeating the Axis powers. At a meeting in Moscow in October 1943, the foreign ministers of the United States, Russia, Great Britain, and China signed the Moscow Declaration on General Security, explicitly recognizing "the necessity of establishing at the earliest practicable date a general international organization." Planning for the new body was centered in the U.S. State Department, where Secretary of State Cordell Hull organized a special committee of advisers to draft a proposal as the governing document of the new organization. The committee's draft charter became the outline eventually massaged into the final Charter of the United Nations (or UN Charter). Talks in August and September 1944, at Dumbarton Oaks, an estate in Washington, D.C., furthered planning. At the crucial Yalta Conference, held in the Russian Crimea in February 1945, Roosevelt, Churchill, and Joseph Stalin hammered out the final compromises that became the basis for the San Francisco Conference on International Organization. In June 1945, at the conference, attendees witnessed the signing of the completed Charter. With sufficient ratifications, the United Nations came into being at 4:50 p.m. on October 24, 1945. The history that preceded this event was intricate, was interesting, and involved the participation of three of the most compelling figures of the twentieth century—**Franklin Roosevelt, Winston Churchill, and Joseph Stalin.** These three men are often considered the most critical figures in initiating the United Nations. The birth of the organization is best told by following the intertwining biographies of these political giants.

Franklin D. Roosevelt (1882–1945)

Franklin Delano Roosevelt, the thirty-second president of the United States, was elected to the office four times (1933–1945). No one before or since has accomplished such a feat (and, with the Twenty-second Amendment to the U.S. Constitution, it will never happen again). Born into a family of wealth and connection in Hyde Park, New York, Roosevelt attended Harvard University and Columbia University School of Law. He was the fifth cousin of President Theodore Roosevelt, from whose enthusiasm for public service "FDR" developed a motivation to pursue politics and elective office. During his years at Harvard, he met, and then became engaged to, President Roosevelt's niece, Eleanor Roosevelt. They were married in 1905. President Wilson appointed FDR assistant secretary of the Navy in 1913. During World War I he was a strong advocate of military preparedness and of Wilson's internationalism. Running for vice president with the Democratic nominee James M. Cox in 1920, Roosevelt campaigned for ratification of the Treaty of Versailles, which would have brought the United States into the League of Nations. After the Democrats lost to Warren G. Harding, he returned to New York and a promising political future.

FDR's political fortunes received a severe blow in August 1921, when he contracted polio. Nonetheless, with the support of his wife, Eleanor, he kept his name before the public, and in 1928 New York elected him its governor. In 1932 he soundly defeated Republican incumbent—and former Wilson adviser—Herbert Hoover for the presidency, promising a "New Deal" to address the Great Depression. As president, Roosevelt faced not only the worst economic downturn in U.S. history, but also the rising threat of European dictatorships, an expanding Japanese empire, and then World War II.

We can accurately say that Roosevelt became the "architect" of the United Nations. Out of the ruins of World War II, he and his advisers—principally his first secretary of state, Cordell

Hull; Russian-American Leo Pasvolsky (a devoted internationalist in the State Department); diplomat Sumner Welles; and FDR's last secretary of state, Edward Stettinius—crafted a new world organization that they hoped would avoid all the League's weaknesses. The president convinced Winston Churchill and Joseph Stalin to accept U.S. plans for a postwar organization as the primary vehicle for maintaining peace and security. However, FDR's central role emerged only gradually as the war progressed.

When Churchill broached the idea of a postwar organization during the Atlantic Conference, off Newfoundland in 1941, before U.S. entrance into the war, the cautious president would concede only to "the establishment of a wider and permanent system of general security."[7] Roosevelt entered the war an advocate of great-power realism, believing former president Wilson's League had been too dependent on world public opinion and had not been adequately sensitive to the realities of power. Three weeks after the Japanese attack on Pearl Harbor, Roosevelt and Churchill drafted the Declaration by United Nations, presenting the Allies' war aims. Roosevelt decided that a signing ceremony would be held first for the representatives of the United States, the USSR, the United Kingdom, and China. The following day representatives of twenty-two "lesser" powers that were committed to defeating Germany in the war affixed their signatures. The president personally decided on the order of signatories, listing them on the basis of power differentials.

In 1942 Roosevelt assured Sumner Welles that when "the moment became ripe," he would push for a new world organization. His conception of it at the time was illustrated in his "Four Policemen" proposal, which emphasized the use of military power by the "Big Four" of the wartime Grand Alliance, who, he was convinced, needed to cooperate to ensure postwar peace. During 1943, Roosevelt shared his views of a great-power-dominated association of nations with Churchill (who at the time preferred the idea of regional security arrangements), and, at the Teheran Conference, with Stalin. In FDR's early view the Soviet Union, Great Britain, China, and the United States would have regional responsibilities for maintaining peace and would act together to enforce world stability, even forcibly carrying out the disarmament of smaller powers. At the State Department, a planning group proposed a "United Nations Authority" with a security commission consisting of the four great powers, thus incorporating Roosevelt's idea into a more general universal organization.

When the president floated his proposal in an interview in *The Saturday Evening Post* in April 1943, the public reaction was lukewarm. Moreover, practical problems with the concept were evident: It did not provide a place in the scheme for France, it did not envision how Great Britain and the USSR would disentangle their conflicting national interests in Europe, and it did not provide much enticement for smaller states to become part of the world organization.

While the president continued to proselytize for the Four Policemen as peacekeepers, his secretary of state, Cordell Hull, was moving in another direction. As early as July 1942, Hull mentioned to the president a growing sense in the State Department of the need for a postwar agency that could enforce the rule of law and the pacific settlement of international disputes. The secretary then set up a technical committee to draft plans for an international organization. This committee, largely under Leo Pasvolsky's leadership, worked until the end of the war to develop the ideas that would ultimately be the basis for the Dumbarton Oaks proposals (detailed subsequently) and for the UN Charter. In March 1943 Hull's committee forwarded a draft constitution to Roosevelt. The projected charter created a general conference, a secretariat, agencies for technical services, and, most important, an executive committee consisting of the Four Policemen and a council made up of the four powers plus seven other representatives of regional organizations. In a series of meetings during the spring and summer of 1943, Roosevelt informally gave his blessing to the effort to obtain British and Soviet assent to a new international organization, at least "in principle," along the lines of the draft charter.

As the Allies took the military offensive in 1943, concerns about maintaining cooperation among the great powers after the war were of growing importance to the president. Cordell Hull traveled to the Moscow Conference of Foreign Ministers in October. He hoped to convince Great Britain, Russia, and China that cooperation in a global organization would serve their interests after the war. The secretary made the necessary concessions to achieve the Joint Four-Nation Declaration, which supported the U.S. initiative. Following the conference, the Roosevelt administration found domestic public sentiment overwhelmingly supportive of a new institutional structure designed to maintain the peace. Even many Republicans, including the party's standard-bearer in 1940, Wendell Willkie, criticized Roosevelt only for not moving fast enough to put an organization in place by the end of hostilities.

After the Moscow Conference, the president became much more directly involved in the planning for the new organization and in the negotiation of its details. By the time the Teheran Conference convened in November 1943, Roosevelt's thinking about postwar arrangements had evolved to the point of combining Wilsonian organizational solutions with a hoped-for long-lasting friendship among the great powers. At Teheran FDR outlined his proposal for a world-wide assembly with an executive committee and a four-nation enforcement body. The president assured a perplexed, likely concerned Stalin that the new organization would not be able to impose its will on its members. Stalin and his emissaries would revisit this commitment during subsequent negotiations whenever proposals materialized that seemed to give the body some control over the great powers. In particular, Stalin would insist on an absolute veto for the Soviet Union. Stalin, in effect, demanded a fundamental revision of the earlier League of Nations voting procedure, which had not allowed states to vote on disputes in which they were involved.

Following his return from the meeting with Soviet and British leaders, Roosevelt approved the Plan for the Establishment of an International Organization for the Maintenance of International Peace and Security. According to the plan, not only would the new organization be responsible for international peace, it would have additional agencies for economic and social activities. It would also have trusteeship responsibilities, taking over the mandate system from the League of Nations and revising it to encourage decolonization. The U.S. government would now push for full self-determination. The future United Nations, through its Trusteeship Council (an explicit Charter-authorized entity endorsed by the wartime leaders at their Yalta meeting in February 1945 and finally approved at the San Francisco founding conference the following April), would provide the mechanism. Included in the president's plan for the United Nations, in addition to the Trusteeship Council, was a Security Council, a General Assembly, a Secretariat of international civil servants, and an International Court of Justice to replace the League's Permanent Court of International Justice. (A detailed description of each of these UN organs is provided in Chapter 4.)

The most serious Charter issue Roosevelt had to resolve in the final months of the war was the question of voting; from his perspective the issue was how to protect the traditional sovereignty of the nation-states that would be members of the world organization, yet not allow the United Nations to fall victim to the requirement of unanimity among the members that had so hampered the League. The administration addressed this issue in many settings, but not until the 1944 Dumbarton Oaks Conference and the **Yalta Conference** in February 1945 did Roosevelt bring the matter to conclusion.

These meetings are explained in detail in the next section. We note here only that Under Secretary of State Stettinius's recommendation that parties to a dispute before the Security

Council should not be allowed to vote on the matter, even if a party was one of the permanent members, was not accepted. Stettinius (who would succeed Cordell Hull shortly after the Dumbarton Oaks meeting) argued that while unanimity among the great powers was essential to the success of the new organization, if one of the powers could veto discussion of, much less action on, a dispute, the United Nations would become as moribund as the League of Nations. The president believed that U.S. public opinion would reject an organization that appeared unlikely to work because it suffered from the League's deficiencies. The Soviets rejected the proposal, insisting that all issues before the Security Council should be subject to the permanent members' unanimous agreement. Stalin believed this was the clear meaning of FDR's assurances at Teheran. This issue would remain unresolved until the Charter was completed in San Francisco in the early summer of 1945.

As the president prepared to travel to Yalta for his summit with Stalin and Churchill, his administration proposed a compromise on the voting procedure in the Security Council by limiting the requirement that a party to a dispute abstain from voting only on the questions of discussing the issue and recommending methods of pacific settlement. The unanimity rule for permanent members would still apply to decisions about enforcement when a breach of the peace had been determined. In essence, so that all the great powers would participate in the United Nations, Roosevelt conceded the political necessity of the veto in instances of forceful action by the world body. At the Yalta meeting, Stalin agreed to accept the U.S. formulation on voting in the Security Council.

The president spent the last two months of his life making plans for his address to the UN Conference on International Organization, which was scheduled for April 25; preparing the delegates to the conference; and fending off objections to the agreements made at Yalta. The administration made a concerted effort to sell the American people on the view that the United Nations marked a wholly new form of peaceful international relations in the history of world politics. According to *New York Times* correspondent Anne O'Hare McCormick, Roosevelt saw the United Nations as the crowning achievement of his political career, and in late March he opined to the reporter that when the war was over, he might consider resigning the presidency to become the UN's first secretary-general.[8] Many issues remained to be debated and settled at the San Francisco Conference. As late as April 9, Roosevelt told the State Department that on his return from Warm Springs, Georgia, the two weeks before the conference convened would be sufficient time to make final decisions about the trusteeship of non-self-governing territories under the United Nations and other outstanding issues. Three days later the architect of the United Nations was dead. A testament to his achievement was that his successor, Harry S Truman, within minutes of being sworn in as president of the United States, made his first presidential decision—to proceed with the San Francisco Conference to organize the United Nations.

Winston Churchill (1874–1965)

Winston Churchill served as British prime minister from 1940 to 1945 and again from 1951 to 1955. He had first gained the attention of the British public as a reporter covering foreign events. His capture and imprisonment by the Boers of South Africa while he was reporting the British-Boer conflict raised his visibility sufficiently to win him election to Parliament in 1900 as a Conservative. He switched to the Liberal Party during World War I and served in several capacities in the government. For much of the interwar period he was out of politics, but earlier than other people, he began to warn of the dangers of Adolf Hitler. He returned to Parliament (again a Conservative) as war broke out, replacing Neville Chamberlain as prime minister. As the leader of one of the "Big Three" wartime Allies—the United States, the United Kingdom, and the Soviet Union—he played a central role in crafting the United Nations. Churchill developed what he perceived to be a "special relationship" with President Roosevelt both before and during U.S. involvement in World War II. America's "nonbelligerent" relationship with war-beleaguered Great Britain reached a peak with the Atlantic Conference, when the two men met in August 1941 aboard the naval vessel *Prince of Wales* in Placentia Bay near the harbor of Argentia, Newfoundland. There, Churchill and Roosevelt discussed strategic issues and announced war aims and a joint vision of the postwar world. The most famous product of the meeting was the eight-point concluding statement called the *Atlantic Charter,* which contained a hazy reference to a postwar "system of general security," as discussed earlier.

When the United States entered the war in December 1941, Churchill journeyed to Washington, D.C., to coordinate Anglo-American strategy more formally. At U.S. secretary of state Cordell Hull's suggestion, the two leaders signed the Declaration by United Nations. The declaration created a wartime alliance against the Axis powers but failed to announce a postwar international organization as many people had hoped. Neither Churchill nor Roosevelt was yet committed to such a proposition, although key figures in both the British Foreign Office and the U.S. State Department were keen enthusiasts. The two leaders instead concentrated on winning the war in the desperate year of reverses, 1942.

When the tide of war turned more favorable for the Allies in late 1942 and early 1943, Churchill began to think of regional councils to stabilize the postwar world (and to protect the British Empire). Roosevelt, however, devised his concept of the Four Policemen to win the war and ensure the peace. Neither vision reflected the idealism of Woodrow Wilson's League of Nations.

The year 1943 was not only the turning point for the Allies' fortunes of war, but also the embryonic phase of the United Nations. In March, Churchill delivered an important radio address and at the same time sent an aide-mémoire to Washington, D.C., each outlining his vision of the postwar world. Dismissive of China and suspicious of the Soviet Union, the prime minister expressed the hope that the United States, Great Britain, and the USSR would create some sort of vague umbrella organization after victory, with the focus on a Council of Europe and a Council of Asia to ensure regional stability. Churchill's initiative compelled Roosevelt to begin focusing his attention on postwar issues, and by the time of the Quadrant Conference in Quebec in August, the president's advisers had devised a counterproposal to present to the British that combined elements of FDR's Four Policemen with Churchill's regional approach. British foreign secretary Anthony Eden was especially receptive of the U.S. proposal.

Stalin, however, was uninterested in any schemes that went beyond the wartime coalition against Germany. Churchill brilliantly suggested that the best approach to the Soviet leader was to present postwar plans as merely a continuation of wartime collaboration and to do so while the war was still ongoing. Attracted first by Churchill's regional approach and then Roosevelt's Four Policemen proposal, Stalin came to accept the concept of the United Nations at both the October 1943 Moscow Conference of Foreign Ministers and the Teheran Conference in December. During 1944 both Churchill and Stalin (both realists), and the American people began to realize that Franklin Roosevelt's United Nations, dominated by the Four Policemen, reflected the realism of Theodore Roosevelt rather than the idealism of Woodrow Wilson. Nevertheless, the Yalta Conference in February 1945 revealed a surprising divergence of opinion between the Anglo-American allies. Churchill agreed with Stalin that the Big Four should be granted an absolute veto power over the discussion of disputes presented to the Security Council. U.S. secretary of state Edward Stettinius and British foreign secretary Eden spent the first evening of the Yalta Conference attempting to change Churchill's mind. The prime minister finally accepted Eden's view that the small nations would refuse to participate in such an arrangement of raw power. On the third day of the conference, Churchill backed the U.S. proposal that the Security Council must accept the principle of free discussion in order to affirm great-power confidence in one another as well as in the sentiments of lesser nations. On February 12, 1945, Churchill, Roosevelt, and Stalin met for the last time and announced that all nations that had signed the Declaration by United Nations would be invited to a conference at San Francisco on April 12, 1945, to create a new world organization.

Still troubling Churchill, however, was American insistence on a role for the United Nations in the self-determination of colonial peoples. Ever an advocate of the civilizing role that Britain had played in the reaches of its empire, Churchill was concerned about the threat to British national interest if the United Nations promoted decolonization. As early as 1943 Roosevelt approved a State Department draft adding an "agency for trusteeship responsibilities" to the contemplated UN Charter. British objections postponed final acceptance of the UN's Trusteeship Council until the UN Conference on International Organization in 1945. In the final negotiations, Churchill's government accepted a UN commitment to "self-government," but not "independence," of colonial peoples. During the remainder of his time in office, he rebuffed efforts by U.S. presidents Truman and Eisenhower to soften his position on this issue.

Joseph Stalin (1879–1953)

In documents revealing early talks about the new emerging international organization, Stalin sometimes appeared to be mystified.[9] In part, this mystification can be attributed to his extremely different political and social background, as well as to his isolated personality and brutal style of rule.

Born to a peasant family in Gori, Georgia, Iosif Vissarionovich Dzhugashvili came to be known by his revolutionary pseudonym *Joseph Stalin.* Unlike Roosevelt and Churchill, he came from humble origins to lead one of the Big Three—the Communist Soviet Union—through the Second World War, establishing his country as one of the two superpowers at the conclusion of the war.

Attracted to Karl Marx's writings, Stalin joined the nascent Russian workers' movement at the turn of the century, and in 1903 he joined Vladimir Lenin's Bolshevik faction of the Russian Social Democratic Workers Party. He ascended to membership in the party's Central Committee and, in 1912, to editor of its newspaper, *Pravda.* Stalin was arrested a dozen times for revolutionary activity before the overthrow of the tsar in March 1917, after which he returned to Petrograd from his most recent internal exile. There he joined Lenin, Leon Trotsky, and a small group of Bolsheviks who ousted the provisional government in November (by the Western calendar at the time).

Stalin had not spent much time outside Russia before the revolution. Most of his colleagues in the new Bolshevik government had been in exile in western Europe during the preceding two decades. They were cosmopolitan, spoke Western languages, and debated the minute details of Marxist philosophy. By contrast, Stalin was parochial; he had no special oratorical skills or political following. His talents for organization, however, would serve him well, allowing him to defeat his rivals for power following Lenin's death in 1924. Two years earlier he had been appointed general secretary of the Central Committee, using the post to fill key bureaucratic positions with supporters and with others opposed to Trotsky, Stalin's chief competitor for leadership. Despite Lenin's admonition in his final testament that the Georgian could not be trusted to work well with other party leaders and should be removed as general secretary, Stalin managed to win the intraparty struggle for power and emerged as the uncontested leader of both the party and the state by 1929.

In the name of "socialism in one country," Stalin carried out the massive industrialization of the Soviet Union, the collectivization of agriculture, and the imposition of totalitarianism. Using the terror of the police state, he imposed centralized economic planning through "Five-Year Plans" that eliminated the vestiges of capitalism. Much of the hardship Stalin imposed—including the 1930s purges that wiped out Bolshevik revolutionary veterans, the high command of the Red Army, and millions of peasants as "enemies of the people"—was rationalized as the requirement of a socialist state facing inevitable future war with the imperialist capitalist states. The Soviet leader, now turned ardent Russian nationalist, saw the world divided into antagonistic ideological "camps," with the defense of the USSR dependent on the rapid development of the country and its military, the surreptitious encouragement of Communist parties in capitalist states, and the pursuit of a geopolitical, rather than a revolutionary, foreign policy.

The rise of Adolf Hitler in Germany in 1933 threatened Soviet security directly and led Stalin to ease his antipathy toward the capitalist countries. He sought and achieved U.S. recognition of the Soviet state. The USSR also joined the League of Nations, and Stalin directed European Communist parties to form a "common front" with democratic parties in their countries in an effort to find some common defense against the German danger. As the Nazi regime progressively violated the provisions of the Treaty of Versailles and moved against governments in central and eastern Europe, Stalin became convinced that Great Britain and France intended to goad Germany into a war with the Soviet Union. Particularly following the Western powers' appeasement of Hitler's demands on Czechoslovakia in 1938 (at the Munich Conference), Stalin concluded that an imperialist conspiracy was under way to destroy the socialist state through German aggression. Announcing that the Soviet Union would not be the country to "pull the chestnuts out of the fire" for Europe, Stalin secretly negotiated a nonaggression pact with the Third Reich. The Molotov-Ribbentrop agreement was signed in August 1939. Under its terms and secret protocols, Poland would be divided between Germany and the Soviet Union, and the USSR would be allowed to occupy the Baltic states.

Stalin was a powerbroker and realist. When Germany reneged on its agreement and invaded the Soviet Union in June 1941, the Soviet leader quickly forged an alliance with Great Britain, and after December 8, with the United States—not to create a new postwar global order as Churchill and Roosevelt had intimated in their 1941 Atlantic Charter, but to crush Germany and secure the future defense of the USSR through Soviet dominance of the region. The Soviet leader declined to attend early Allied summits, and his government played no role in initial planning for a postwar international organization. Only in the fall of 1943, following the August Quadrant Conference between Churchill and Roosevelt in Quebec, did Stalin receive from his allies a formal proposal for such an entity.

As we mentioned previously, Roosevelt and Churchill believed in the importance of obtaining Soviet concurrence on a postwar body while the war was still under way. The incentive to join as one of Roosevelt's Four Policemen in the maintenance of future world peace would be far greater while Stalin needed his Western allies. The first opportunity to gauge Soviet intentions came at the Moscow Conference of Foreign Ministers in late October 1943. Only after U.S. secretary of state Cordell Hull and his British counterpart agreed to open a second front from the West was Stalin ready to consider the idea of a general international organization. Throughout the negotiations in Moscow and later, the Soviet Union focused on the implications of such a body for Soviet geopolitical concerns.

Stalin had his first opportunity to discuss the proposed organization with Roosevelt at the Teheran Conference, which was held November 27–December 1, 1943. The president described how the United States, the Soviet Union, the United Kingdom, and China would have sole authority to enforce the peace and prevent aggression. He also outlined the likely organs that would be part of the organization, including an executive council. Stalin, apprehensive that the council might limit Soviet actions, asked FDR whether the proposed body would be able to make decisions binding on the great powers. The president said it would not. As we discussed previously, the issue of the veto was not raised directly at Teheran, but the Soviet leader and his representatives revisited this commitment by FDR many times during the next two years. By the end of the Moscow and Teheran meetings, however, Stalin indicated his willingness to support a postwar organization.

At the Dumbarton Oaks Conference in 1944, Stalin's representatives, led by Ambassador Andrei Gromyko, accepted nearly all the U.S. proposals for the expected Charter. Only on the matter of the veto in the Security Council did the Soviet delegation raise objections. As we noted before, the United States opposed the use of the veto by a permanent member to bar the council from hearing a dispute in which the member was involved. Yet Stalin always saw this veto power as an essential protection for Soviet freedom of action. The matter would remain unresolved until the Yalta Conference five months later. At Yalta a new matter, which Gromyko had raised at Dumbarton Oaks, would also have to be resolved. Faced with an overwhelmingly pro-American organization membership, Stalin sought to gain in effect sixteen votes for the Soviet Union by admitting each of the USSR's union republics to the world body. The other participants (the United States, the United Kingdom, and China) found this proposal completely unacceptable. Roosevelt and Stalin would, nevertheless, also settle this issue at Yalta.

When the final summit among Churchill, Roosevelt, and Stalin convened at Yalta in February 1945, the most important concerns for Stalin were the political and military arrangements in postwar Eastern Europe and the disposition of defeated Germany. Having lost more than thirty million Soviet citizens to German aggression in two world wars, Stalin placed his faith in controlling bordering regions to protect the Soviet Union. Instead of seeing collective security embodied in the United Nations as the formula for peace in the future, Stalin sought to protect his foreign policy options from any UN limitations. Only when matters concerning the future government of Poland and the occupation of Germany were resolved was he ready to make accommodations on the membership of the world body and the extent of the veto power. He reached a compromise with Roosevelt on the number of Soviet republics to be admitted—Byelorussia and Ukraine would be original members in addition to the USSR. He then conceded the position on when the veto could be used, agreeing that a permanent member could not block discussion of a dispute in which it was involved.

The Soviet Union served as a sponsor of the 1945 UN Conference on International Organization in San Francisco. Yet it sought significant changes in the Charter on matters supposedly resolved earlier. Stalin's delegation once again challenged the veto limitations but eventually accepted the earlier-agreed-upon formula.

THREE WARTIME CONFERENCES

We next take a look at three specific, late, wartime conferences, treating them in chronological order. Two were important in crafting the United Nations (and were discussed briefly in the foregoing paragraphs), and the third introduced the postwar financial and trade regime we have today, albeit much evolved by circumstance and the formal decisions of the major financial powers.

Dumbarton Oaks Conference

In 1944 two stages of diplomatic conversations took place in the elegant Music Room at **Dumbarton Oaks,** a nineteenth-century mansion in a bucolic wooded area of Georgetown in

Washington, D.C. (The mansion name derives from the Rock of Dumbarton in Scotland.) Representatives from the United States, the Soviet Union, and Great Britain met during the first stage, from August 21 to September 28, 1944. Then, from September 29 to October 7, Chinese envoys joined those from the United States and the United Kingdom. The conference convened while war continued to rage in Asia and Europe. Negotiations at this conference clarified earlier wartime discussions on a new international organization and thus represented a key step on the way to establishing the United Nations.[10]

The conference gave rise to the Dumbarton Oaks Proposals for the Establishment of a General International Organization. These proposals were in the form of twelve "chapters" and were important for four reasons. First, the proposals spelled out a structure for the evolving international organization. Chapter IV, for example, listed the General Assembly, the Security Council, the International Court of Justice, and the Secretariat as the principal organs of the United Nations; Chapter IX called for the formation of the Economic and Social Council, the functions of which would include the promotion of respect for human rights and fundamental freedoms. Second, the proposals assigned different responsibilities to each organ. Chapter VI gave the proposed Security Council responsibility for international peace and security, while Chapter V designated the General Assembly as the organ to be more involved in economic and social spheres and to supervise the overall operations of the organization. Third, Chapter III made membership open to "all peace-loving nations," which underscored what would become the principle of universal membership in a single organization—an idea that transcended the notion of dominant regional power arrangements like those broached earlier in wartime meetings. Fourth, the proposals articulated the idea that the permanent members of the Security Council—China, the United Kingdom, the United States, the USSR, and France (which was to become a permanent member "in due course," according to the language of the Dumbarton Oaks proposals)—should be able to veto any substantive (nonprocedural) matters before the body.[11]

The Dumbarton Oaks proposals, like the UN Charter, did not use the term *veto*. Rather, Chapter VI noted that an affirmative vote of the council would require the "concurring votes of the permanent members." A negative vote by any of the permanent members would then mean the failure of a proposed resolution. Although this idea contains the meat of the veto as it is known today, the Dumbarton Oaks Conference did not bring finality to the issue of the veto. At the Yalta Conference, Roosevelt, Churchill, and Stalin took up the matter again, and it arose a final time in San Francisco in the spring. Ultimately, the permanent members did receive veto power in the UN Charter. Signifying the transitional nature of the Dumbarton Oaks proposals, the conferees appended a "Note" at the end of the chapters, explaining, "In addition to the question of voting procedure in the Security Council referred to in Chapter VI, several other questions are still under consideration." Thus, while the Dumbarton Oaks Conference represented a significant step, more work remained.

Yalta Conference

Yalta, on the Crimea, was the site of the final meeting of the legendary Big Three personalities. There, at the Livadia Palace (built in 1911 as a summer residence for Tsar Nicholas II) overlooking the Black Sea harbor, the Allies resolved crucial post-war-era questions. These issues included arrangements for the occupation of Germany, for political settlements in East Asia and in liberated Eastern Europe, and for the organization and procedures of the United Nations. The meeting was held in secret at the chilly resort area during the week of February 4–11, 1945. The three heads of government met daily, often with only translators present, and planned the final stages of the war while addressing a range of postwar policies. As we pointed out, important steps regarding the United Nations had been taken before the meeting at Yalta, but various stumbling blocks still required resolution. In fact, Stalin had yet to consent fully to Soviet membership in the new organization.

At Yalta the three leaders refined their understanding about the UN's structure and membership and set the date of the San Francisco organizing conference. In several separate conversations, Roosevelt, Churchill, and Stalin intermingled discussions about the United Nations with negotiations on war issues. The leaders agreed that the United Nations would include an International Court of Justice (as provided at Dumbarton Oaks) and determined, for the first time, to create a separate trusteeship system to succeed the League of Nations' mandate system.

The Big Three also agreed on a definition of "peace-loving" and therefore on which nations would join the United Nations as original members. Stalin had insisted that only nations currently at war with the Axis be admitted as founding members. Roosevelt, responding to the concerns of Latin American nations, secured the Soviet leader's agreement that nations not yet in the war could, by entering no later than March 1, be defined as "peace-loving" and thus become members. This agreement allowed Argentina and Chile to enter the new organization and set the stage for a united Latin American bloc in the United Nations.

An awkward disagreement about the voting power of the Big Three was also resolved at Yalta. The USSR had persistently sought votes for each of its Soviet republics, contending that the nations of the British Empire gave the United Kingdom control of multiple votes. Roosevelt empathized with Stalin's concerns but insisted that to secure U.S. congressional agreement to this arrangement, he would need votes for each of the forty-eight U.S. states. Stalin backed down but insisted that in view of the huge wartime destruction in the Ukraine and Byelorussia, those two states must become members. Roosevelt conceded this much, since with the inclusion of a substantial, and assumed pro-U.S. Latin American contingent, plus the anticipated Western European support for the United States, Washington would appear to have an effective voting majority in the organization. In addition, Stalin finally acceded to some restrictions on the veto power in the Security Council. Retreating from his previous insistence on an absolute veto over all issues, he agreed that the veto would not apply to procedural matters and could not be invoked by a state that was a party to a dispute in order to prevent the Security Council from discussing the matter.

Roosevelt's apparent concessions on the use of the veto and on membership appear minor in retrospect. At that moment he needed Soviet help for the continuing war in Asia. Roosevelt achieved Stalin's promise to enter the war against the Japanese and to recognize the pro-U.S. government of Chiang Kai-shek in China. Moreover, the United States conceivably benefited even more in terms of membership in the new organization by the decision at Yalta to allow all nations at war with Germany by March 1, 1945, to be original members. This decision resulted in the membership of several Latin American countries friendly to the United States. A pro-U.S. China and France joined the Soviet Union, the United States, and Great Britain as permanent members on the Security Council. However, probably most important, when the USSR entered the U.S.-sponsored United Nations, it agreed to join an international organization that had the clear mark of an American enterprise, presided over by Roosevelt. Sitting in the well of the House of Representatives, Roosevelt reported to the legislators upon his return:[12]

> [Yalta] ought to spell the end of the system of unilateral action, the exclusive alliances, the spheres of influence, the balances of power, and all the other expedients that have been tried for centuries—and have always failed. We propose to substitute for all these, a universal organization in which all peace-loving Nations will finally have a chance to join.

Bretton Woods Conference

In addition to addressing issues of peace and security, Allied leaders determined to forge international cooperation in financial and economic realms, believing that trade barriers, monetary manipulations, and practices of economic nationalism had been factors dragging the interwar world into dangerous clashes. As in the case of UN negotiations, Americans took a leadership role in these financial negotiations.

The UN Monetary and Financial Conference convened in **Bretton Woods,** New Hampshire, from July 1 to 22, 1944. The conference members drafted agreements establishing three institutions meant to create a postwar global free trade system: the International Monetary Fund (IMF), the International Bank for Reconstruction and Development (IBRD)—better known as the World Bank, and the General Agreement on Tariffs and Trade (GATT). The last of these was supposed to be an "interim" agreement until an International Trade Organization (ITO)—which would provide a more ambitious regulatory framework for world trade—could be established. GATT, however, remained in place until January 1, 1995, when it was superseded by the World Trade Organization (WTO).

Sponsored by the United States, the Bretton Woods Conference and its ensuing agreements attempted to create a new international monetary and trade regime that was stable and predictable. Negotiators structured the IMF to limit the fluctuation of foreign-currency exchange rates while using the World Bank to pump needed capital investment into war-drained nations. U.S. planners hoped to avoid the economic nationalism of the interwar years by gradually removing protectionist barriers to free trade. Through "rounds" of negotiation, GATT members eliminated tariffs, quotas, and other impediments to international commerce. The success of the measures initiated at Bretton Woods depended, however, on the willingness of the United States—whose economy in 1944 accounted for more than half of the world domestic product—to fund these institutions and to maintain monetary policies conducive to world economic growth.

One point worth noting is that the Bretton Woods meeting was held during the latter stages of World War II while negotiations on a draft charter for the United Nations proceeded. The Roosevelt administration saw these courses of action as complementary. At Bretton Woods, delegates undertook the creation of a postwar international framework that would avoid the instability that had followed World War I. Soon after the Bretton Woods institutions came into being, Washington pegged the dollar to gold at thirty-five dollars an ounce, enacted large foreign aid programs to pump liquidity into the international economic system, and made the largest subscription of funds of any IBRD member to the assets of the World Bank.

The IMF and the IBRD both came into operating existence on December 27, 1945, when twenty-nine nations signed the IMF's Articles of Agreement that had been proposed at Bretton Woods, and twenty-one signed the IBRD's Articles of Agreement. By the end of the year, the World Bank had thirty members. GATT began operations when twenty-three countries signed the GATT treaty on April 10, 1947. Although independent institutions, these three Bretton Woods–initiated entities were considered part of the UN System.

UN CONFERENCE ON INTERNATIONAL ORGANIZATION

You can find a considerable amount of literature on the Treaty of Westphalia, which concluded the Thirty Years' War in 1648; the Congress of Vienna, which brought an end to the Napoleonic imperial period in 1814–1815; or the Treaty of Versailles negotiations following World War I.

Oddly, however, little information can be found on the conference that brought the United Nations to definitive birth, and, for at least a moment in mid-1945, engaged the world's attention. Between April 25 and June 25, 1945, about 5,000 people descended on San Francisco for this historically inimitable meeting. Some 850 delegates from fifty countries, 2,600 members of the media, 1,000 public servants of the nascent UN Secretariat, 300 security personnel, 120 translators, 37 foreign ministers, and 5 prime ministers, plus an untold number of local citizens, attended.[13] The conference also witnessed cameo appearances by a number of the famous or near famous, including a rookie journalist named John Kennedy, filmmaker Orson Welles, and future television host and historian Alistair Cooke. Yet, transcending the media hoopla at the gathering were the heroes (many were bipartisan Americans, reflecting the leadership role that the United States played in the whole enterprise). Russian-born Leo Pasvolsky's diligence in the State Department and at the conference was vital; Republican John Foster Dulles worked with Pasvolsky to resolve the most contentious challenges brought by, among others, smaller nations, as well as the Soviet Union. A central figure was U.S. delegation chair and secretary of state Edward Stettinius, whose steady diplomacy, constant attention to untested President Truman, and sensitivity to others' views proved indispensable at a conference that without him may have collapsed.

The Charter's basics, formulated in the U.S. State Department, had undergone diplomatic refinement during wartime meetings. However, San Francisco represented a decisive moment when the entire UN enterprise could have miscarried over touchy issues such as the great-power veto, the seating of Argentina, the situation in Poland, and more. Energetic diplomacy was crucial to ensure success.

The official sponsors—the United States, the United Kingdom, the USSR, and China—convened the formally titled **United Nations Conference on International Organization (UNCIO)** in the recently refurbished San Francisco Opera House. The conference invited as participants the "peace-loving nations" that had declared war on the Axis powers by March 1, 1945. The purpose of UNCIO was to consider the proposals drafted at Dumbarton Oaks the previous fall. The meeting concluded its work on June 26 when fifty "original members" signed the Charter. Poland, not in attendance because of the ongoing dispute between the Soviet Union and the Western powers over the makeup of its government, signed the document later as the fifty-first member.

Although the Big Three—the United States, the Soviet Union, and Great Britain—had already agreed on important decisions about the workings of the new United Nations, the participation of many other nations, with their own interests, made the San Francisco Conference a complex exercise in multilateral diplomacy. The great powers were often required to make meaningful alterations in the proposed Charter to achieve the necessary votes for passage of its provisions. At the opening session even the question of who could participate in the deliberations did not escape intense debate. Latin American nations (twenty-one of the participating fifty states) pressed for inclusion of Argentina in the conference, which both the United States and the Soviet Union opposed because of the Argentine government's friendly relations with the Axis powers during the war. The proposal to seat Argentina led to an angry counterrequest from Soviet foreign minister Vyacheslav I. Molotov that the Russian-backed Lublin government in Poland also be invited to participate, even though that government was not recognized by any Western state. He also reopened the matter of Byelorussia's and Ukraine's participation. Both were to be admitted to the United Nations under the terms of the Yalta agreement, but Washington had invited neither to San Francisco. After five days of argument, Byelorussia, Ukraine, and Argentina were admitted to the conference; Poland was not.

IMPORTANT MOMENTS IN THE FOUNDING OF THE UNITED NATIONS

August 14, 1941   U.S. president Franklin Delano Roosevelt and Winston Churchill, the British prime minister, issue the Atlantic Charter.

January 1, 1942   Twenty-six nations issue the Declaration by United Nations.

October 30, 1943   The Moscow Conference of Foreign Ministers meets, and China, the USSR, the United States, and the United Kingdom agree on the need for a postwar international organization.

July 1–22, 1944   The UN Monetary and Financial Conference convenes at Bretton Woods, New Hampshire.

August 21–October 7, 1944   The Dumbarton Oaks Conference convenes. The United States, Great Britain, the USSR, and China agree on the structure of the new United Nations.

February 4–11, 1945   The Yalta Conference convenes. The Big Three agree on the voting formula for the Security Council.

April 9–20, 1945   Jurists from forty-four nations meet to draft the Statute of the International Court of Justice.

April 25–June 25, 1945   The San Francisco Conference convenes. Fifty nations sign the UN Charter on June 26.

October 24, 1945   The UN Charter enters into force.

Plenary sessions of UNCIO were chaired on a rotating basis by the heads of the sponsoring countries' delegations—Stettinius (United States), Molotov (USSR), Foreign Secretary Anthony Eden (United Kingdom), and Premier T. V. Soong (China). Stettinius opened the conference as its temporary chairman, then chaired the Steering and Executive Committees, the most important bodies in the conference structure. The Steering Committee, comprising four sponsoring nations, decided important issues of policy and procedure. On April 27 it decided that the Dumbarton Oaks proposals and the supplementary decisions made at the Yalta Conference would serve as the agenda for the meeting. It also decided that decisions in all the working bodies dealing with the Charter draft must be made by a two-thirds majority. In so doing, the Steering Committee set aside the traditional rule of unanimity that had applied in diplomacy among sovereign states and had been the guiding principle during the drafting of the Covenant of the League of Nations. The Executive Committee, made up of the United States, the United Kingdom, the USSR, China, and ten additional states, made recommendations to the Steering Committee on critical and contentious issues. These structural and voting arrangements created a system of "parliamentary diplomacy" that gave smaller states a substantive role in the decision process at San Francisco.

The final drafting of the Charter was the responsibility of the Co-ordination Committee, chaired by Leo Pasvolsky. Recommended language for the Charter flowed into the Co-ordination Committee from four conference commissions and twelve technical committees. These bodies proposed dozens of amendments to the Dumbarton Oaks draft. Among their contributions was to elevate the Economic and Social Council (ECOSOC) and the Trusteeship Council to the status of principal organs of the United Nations, both of which would thus become coequal in the Charter with the General Assembly, Security Council, Secretariat, and International Court of Justice.

Soviet Foreign Minister Molotov (*wearing eyeglasses with no temples*), U.S. Secretary of State Stettinius (*center, holding pencil*), and British Foreign Secretary Eden (*sitting to Stettinius's left*) conferring in the San Francisco Opera House, where the UN Conference on International Organization was meeting on May 1, 1945. (UN/DPI Photo by Rosenberg. Reproduced by permission from the United Nations.)

The success of the conference turned on the resolution of several contentious issues. The most serious were matters related to the enforcement organ of the United Nations—the Security Council. An evolution of President Roosevelt's Four Policemen concept, the proposed Security Council was made up of five permanent members and six nonpermanent members and was authorized to impose mandatory enforcement measures against an aggressor. Several proposals were put forward at San Francisco to ensure that the nonpermanent seats were filled by states from certain regions of the world, or by states capable of contributing to international peace and security. Middle powers particularly emphasized this last point. Canada sponsored a proposal to hold seats on the council only for states with the means to carry out enforcement responsibilities. India recommended that only states representing a significant proportion of the world's population be elected to the council. From the outset Latin American representatives sought a greater role for Western Hemispheric states, including guaranteed representation on the Security Council. El Salvador recommended the addition of five more members to the council. Although the proposal gained support from small states in other regions, Brazil determined instead to seek a permanent seat on the Security Council for one Latin American country.

The sponsoring powers marshaled the votes to defeat all these proposals, successfully arguing that any attempt to alter the council's proposed composition would upset arduously worked out settlements and delay the establishment of the United Nations. They made known that any major change in the composition, powers, or responsibilities of the council would mean the end of great-power support for the organization. After intense negotiations among the four powers, the Steering Committee proposed language for the qualifications for election to the council that mollified some of the delegations. According to the draft, nonpermanent members would be elected by the General Assembly[14]

> [with] due regard being specially paid, in the first instance to the contribution of Members of the United Nations to the maintenance of international peace and security and to the other purposes of the Organization, and also to equitable geographical distribution.

Separate from the matter of council membership was the ongoing debate about the veto retained by the permanent members. Early in the conference, the Soviet delegation resurrected Stalin's persistent demand for an absolute veto on all matters before the council. The USSR had made this veto a condition of its participation in the United Nations on earlier occasions, but at Yalta, Stalin had agreed that procedural matters could be decided by an affirmative vote of seven council members and that the veto would not be allowed. He had also accepted the U.S. position that when permanent members were parties to a dispute, they could not veto a discussion of the dispute. To convince Stalin of America's resolve on this issue, President Truman sent a special envoy (former FDR confidant Harry Hopkins) to Moscow to explain that the Charter would not pass the U.S. Senate on the terms proposed by the Soviet Union. Stalin backed down and directed his delegation to accept the Yalta formula.[15]

The veto issue highlighted one general concern of smaller states at the conference: that the predominance of the great powers' control over peace and security issues would denigrate their role within the organization, diminish the competence of the General Assembly, and demote other purposes dear to weaker powers. For Latin American states in particular, one concern was that the use of the veto could limit the region's ability to deal with hemispheric threats. A lengthy history of cooperation in the Pan-American Union led hemispheric leaders to seek a major role for regional organizations on security matters, and greater autonomy from Security Council intervention. The U.S. delegation, however, feared that public support and U.S. Senate approval would be lost if the Security Council was not given absolute authority to address all threats to the peace. Facing an impasse, the United States orchestrated a compromise that recognized the authority of "regional arrangements" to manage local or regional affairs, provided their activities were "consistent with the Purposes and Principles of the United Nations" (Chapter VIII, Article 52). In addition, under Article 51 states were permitted to undertake "collective self-defense" until the Security Council had taken sufficient steps to restore peace. The new wording in the Charter, however, limited this grant of autonomy by asserting the right of the council to investigate and take action on any threat to the peace. It also allowed any state to bring any dispute directly to the council.

Also in response to small-state concerns, the competence of the General Assembly was expanded during the San Francisco negotiations. It was given control of the UN budget. The conference as well agreed that the assembly could discuss any issue, including security concerns and threats to the peace, at least until the Security Council was "seized" with the issue. Furthermore, the secretary-general, elected by the General Assembly, would be able to bring any matter that he or she believed threatened international peace and security to the council's attention (Article 99).

States from Latin America, Africa, and Asia envisioned an institution of universal membership with extensive activities in the economic, cultural, and human rights domains, beyond the initial security concerns of the great powers. In particular, they pressed for a UN role in the achievement of "independence" for existing colonial possessions. President Truman was likewise deeply concerned about the projected duties of the United Nations in the newly liberated territories of the enemy states and in the old colonial empires of the European powers. On this matter he found Churchill adamant in opposing any structure that might endanger the British Empire. So, too, the French delegation opposed Charter provisions that might limit France's policies in Indochina and Africa. During the Yalta meeting, where trusteeship was not on the formal agenda but was discussed, the Americans had devised a formulation that was acceptable to the British by limiting the jurisdiction of the UN's trusteeship system to territories still held under the League's mandate system, territories detached from the enemy states during World War II, and "territories voluntarily placed under the system by states responsible for their administration." This solution, however, had the unintended consequence of raising concerns by Syria and other former mandate regions that were independent states in the spring of 1945. The formulation could be interpreted to allow renewed administration by outside powers. Article 78 was added to the Charter to exclude this possibility by prohibiting the application of the trusteeship system to territories that had become UN members.

The more serious trusteeship challenge came from the states at San Francisco that wanted a Charter commitment to full independence and decolonization. Led by Carlos Romulo of the Philippine delegation, small states urged much stronger commitments in policy and structure on the question of ending imperial control. In the lengthy negotiations that ensued, the British and the French made clear that no reference to "independence" would be allowed in the Charter. Nevertheless, the sponsoring powers did accept a commitment to "self-government" and took the unusual step of allowing the placement of the Declaration Regarding Non-Self-Governing Territories into the Charter text (Chapter XI). The declaration called on administering states "to assist [these territories] in the progressive development of their free political institutions."

Even the United States, which generally supported a trusteeship system dedicated to ending colonial control, sought and obtained a limitation of the Trusteeship Council's authority with regard to "strategic" trust territories. As the U.S. armed forces liberated important Pacific islands from Japanese control toward the end of the war, the military expressed concern with plans to have the United Nations take these holdings into the trusteeship system. Shortly before his death, President Roosevelt approved dividing designated trusteeship areas into "strategic" and "nonstrategic" territories and limiting the role of the Trusteeship Council in the former areas. This step was accomplished in Articles 82 and 83, which allowed administering states to declare specific areas as "strategic" territories, then made those areas subject to the Security Council, where the United States had the veto.

Shortly before convening in San Francisco, Latin American governments met with a U.S. delegation in Mexico City. There they endorsed an enlarged role for the United Nations in social, economic, and human rights cooperation. At the San Francisco Conference, they were joined by other states on the Economic and Social Co-operation Committee in passing broadened objectives for the United Nations in these areas. The committee recommended that the new organization promote "universal respect for, and observance of, human rights and fundamental freedoms for all without distinction as to race, sex, language or religion." U.S. planners had earlier pushed for Charter provisions on human rights, but these efforts had been rebuffed by the other participants at Dumbarton Oaks. At San Francisco many proposals were made to incorporate the "protection" of human rights into the Charter obligations of the organization.

Much discussion, diligently covered by the media, centered on establishing in the Charter a Commission on Human Rights. Time constraints made drafting a Bill of Human Rights for

Charter inclusion impossible. However, a desire to meet public expectations for action in this area after the horrors of the Holocaust, and strong endorsement from a majority of the delegations, persuaded the sponsoring powers to agree to Article 68, authorizing ECOSOC to set up commissions "in economic and social fields and for the promotion of human rights." Thus a consequence of the deliberations was that ECOSOC, in February 1946, established the Commission on Human Rights, which proceeded, under Eleanor Roosevelt's leadership, to draft the Universal Declaration of Human Rights.

On June 25, two months to the day after the conference opened, the delegates to UNCIO adopted the Charter. The minutes of the session recorded, "At this point, the delegates and the entire audience rose and cheered." The following day President Truman addressed the closing session and congratulated the delegates on fulfilling their roles as, what he described two months earlier, "architects of a better world . . . a new world in which the eternal dignity of man is respected."

ELEANOR'S UN: BEYOND INTERNATIONAL PEACE AND SECURITY

As we just pointed out, smaller nations attending the San Francisco Conference, along with the United States, pressed for Charter commitments on decolonization, economic and social issues, and human rights. As a result of a serendipitous decision by the U.S. government, which was seeking to build public support for the United Nations, several unofficial "consultants" and other observers were invited to the San Francisco meeting and allowed to sit in on working sessions. These groups included representatives from the Council on Foreign Relations, the National Association for the Advancement of Colored People, the Catholic Welfare Conference, the National Education Association, the Congress of Industrial Organizations, and many more. Under the influence of these numerous organizations, the U.S. delegation acceded to Charter language regarding education, human rights, and the formal recognition of the consultative role of nongovernmental organizations (NGOs) at the United Nations. Article 71 led to the enduring collaboration between NGOs and the United Nations.[16] References to "education" and "human rights" appear early in the Charter (Article 13, paragraph 1b), and these words are sprinkled throughout the document. In addition, provisions empowering ECOSOC to make use of "specialized agencies" (Articles 57, 62, 64, and 67) augured a future of activities in the large province of economic, social, educational, and human rights policy.

This expanded thrust for the new organization was closely associated in its formative years with the work of Eleanor Roosevelt, the former first lady of the United States. Mrs. Roosevelt lived a long and fruitful life (1884–1962). Considered one of the most influential presidential spouses in U.S. history, she outlived her husband, Franklin Delano Roosevelt, by seventeen years, and during that time she served spiritedly in a number of important public service posts. In 1962 President John F. Kennedy appointed her to the first U.S. Commission on the Status of Women, and both Presidents Harry S. Truman and Kennedy made her a U.S. ambassador to the United Nations.

First appointed to a UN post by President Truman, serving from 1945 to 1953, Mrs. Roosevelt treasured her service at the United Nations, believing that forceful labors by dedicated and talented people from throughout the world were needed to launch this new organization that her late husband had envisaged. She once said of the United Nations that it was "a bridge upon which we can meet and talk."[17] Her prestige and personal qualities were key factors in developing the Universal Declaration of Human Rights. As she served, first as U.S. representative on the General Assembly Third Committee, and then as chair of the Commission on Human Rights, she became friends with, and was considered a leader by, some of the most significant thinkers and diplomats of the postwar period.

In early 1946 the newly formed Economic and Social Council (ECOSOC) asked her to serve on a "nuclear" commission that was to make recommendations regarding a permanent commission on human rights. This small committee convened at Hunter College in New York City that spring, where its first act was to elect Mrs. Roosevelt as its chair. The most important recommendation forwarded by this small committee was that the proposed Human Rights Commission write a bill of human rights. From the establishment of the commission in June 1946 until December 10, 1948, when the General Assembly approved the Universal Declaration of Human Rights, Mrs. Roosevelt was consumed with guiding the intricate negotiations and seeking broad public support for a UN role in nonsecurity issues. She convinced a reluctant U.S. State Department to accede to the inclusion in the declaration of social and economic rights along with more traditional political and civil rights. With skilled diplomacy she encouraged and cajoled powerful individuals from myriad philosophical and political backgrounds to come together and agree on the final composition of the document.

Her success warrants even more approbation, considering the environment in which she worked. Representatives from the Western nations; from the Soviet bloc; from Latin America; from the developing world; and from Christian, Islamic, Hindu, Buddhist, Confucianist, and secular traditions all converged to discuss a "universal" statement on rights. This discussion took place as the world plunged into new and difficult divisions caused by the onset of the cold war, serious divisions in South Asia as India and Pakistan gained independence, and the intractable dispute initiated with the partition of Palestine. Moreover, Mrs. Roosevelt had to guide the document through a drafting committee and the full commission, where serious disagreement occurred over the type of document to recommend to the General Assembly. Several small states wanted a binding covenant with methods of implementation. Others, particularly the great powers, wanted a nonbinding, vague declaration. The Soviet Union wanted no document at all.

Mrs. Roosevelt endorsed a process that divided the commission into three working groups. She chaired the First Working Group, which proceeded to draft a declaration with the persuasive "moral value" of past momentous proclamations, such as the U.S. Declaration of Independence and the French Declaration of the Rights of Man and Citizen. The other working groups focused on drafting binding covenants and implementation procedures. Having crafted the Universal Declaration of Human Rights through this procedure, Roosevelt then shepherded it through the debate in the Third Committee of the General Assembly (where each of the thirty articles was thrashed out in detail) and before the General Assembly. In the end the declaration passed without a negative vote. The final tally was forty-eight in favor, eight abstentions (Saudi Arabia and seven nations from the Soviet bloc), and none opposed. The president of the General Assembly, Herbert Evatt, closed the session with a tribute to Eleanor Roosevelt:[18]

> It is particularly fitting that there should be present on this occasion the person who, with the assistance of many others, has played a leading role in the work, a person who has raised to greater heights even so great a name—Mrs. Roosevelt, the representative of the United States of America.

The economic, social, and humanitarian tasks assigned by the Charter to the fledgling United Nations were perceived in the late 1940s as peripheral matters to the organization's central role in keeping the peace. However, as cold war politics increasingly paralyzed the world body, deadlocking the Security Council, and as UN membership grew, during the next two decades, to include states from the developing world, the United Nations found itself more often addressing the problems of human existence and social development that were of deep concern to Mrs. Roosevelt and her colleagues. With the close of the cold war in the late 1980s, the agenda of **Eleanor's UN** moved center stage, even within the Security Council and the global security strategies of the great powers. States recognized that the extraordinary human problems facing large portions of the world's population raised the real specter of global instability and regional war. In a number of ways, Eleanor's UN—in terms of both issues and UN policymaking— became the bedrock of the "new" United Nations we describe in this text.

Specialized Agencies and Eleanor's UN

Since 1945 the extensive activities of UN-related specialized agencies and nongovernmental organizations have furthered the more sprawling view of UN responsibilities suggested by Eleanor Roosevelt's diplomatic career. Article 57 of the UN Charter describes specialized agencies as separately chartered, independent organizations "having wide international responsibilities . . . in economic, cultural, educational, health and related fields." Each deals with a particular issue or problem that the international community has identified as requiring action or regulation. Specialized agencies are intergovernmental organizations (IGOs) composed of member states that have signed a treaty that has established the agency. They have their own governing hierarchy and their own separate budgets, funded through members' contributions. In many cases these contributions are voluntary, although some organizations have their own methods of assessing their members that differ from those used for the regular UN budget.

Some specialized agencies, such as the Universal Postal Union, date from the nineteenth century; others were established by the League of Nations and subsequently adopted by the United Nations. Most have been created since 1945, often urged into existence by the United Nations or by conferences it sponsored.

Articles 63 and 64 of the Charter authorize the Economic and Social Council to coordinate the work of the specialized agencies. Typically such coordination is accomplished through "consultation" and "recommendations" to independent organizations. Each agency retains its independence, and oversight is generally limited to broad issues and suggestions. In 2005 fifteen specialized agencies were in operation. Their activities spanned a wide swath of topical areas, from international finance (the World Bank Group and the International Monetary Fund) to the kinds of issues (education, development, and human rights) that attracted the attention of Mrs. Roosevelt and others of her perspective at the commencement of the United Nations. Among the agencies attending to the latter issues were the Food and Agriculture Organization (FAO); the International Fund for Agricultural Development (IFAD); the UN Educational, Scientific and Cultural Organization (UNESCO); the UN Industrial Development Organization (UNIDO); and the World Health Organization (WHO). Since the end of World War II, these UN-related agencies have carried forward mandates exterior to the more traditional concerns of maintaining peace and security. (Specialized agencies are covered in more detail in Chapter 4.)

Nongovernmental Organizations and Eleanor's UN

Also advancing an agenda outside traditional international diplomacy have been the nongovernmental organizations provided for in the UN system in Article 71 of the Charter. An NGO is any nonprofit, voluntary citizens' group. It may be organized on a local, a national, or an international level. NGOs perform a variety of services and humanitarian functions, bring citizens' concerns to governments and international institutions, monitor policies, and encourage public participation in local, national, and international affairs. An NGO may provide analysis and expertise on specific issues and help monitor and implement international agreements. Most are organized with specific issues in mind, such as human rights, environmental improvement, educational reform, women's or children's rights, labor conditions, health concerns, and more. Some of the best known are Amnesty International, Human Rights Watch, and the World Wildlife Fund. Other examples of NGOs are the World Young Women's Christian Association (with interest in children's and women's rights), the Institute of World Affairs (dedicated to conflict resolution), the Franklin and Eleanor Roosevelt Institute (promoting education), the National Collegiate Conference Association (which holds the largest collegiate simulation of the United Nations—the National Model United Nations—at the New York headquarters), and the International Campaign to Ban Land Mines. A full discussion of the role of NGOs in contemporary UN affairs can be found in Chapter 7.

According to Article 71 of the UN Charter, NGOs may attain consultative status with the Economic and Social Council (this is the so-called General Category consultative status). By ECOSOC Resolution 31, passed in 1996, the Economic and Social Council can qualify NGOs to engage in work promoting UN programs and goals. If so qualified, NGO representatives may serve as technical experts, advisers, and consultants to governments and to the Secretariat. Most NGOs are advocacy groups. Thus, they espouse UN themes of which they approve, and, in so doing, implement plans of action, programs, and declarations adopted by the United Nations. Therefore, they often participate in ECOSOC and its subsidiary bodies by attending meetings, making oral presentations, providing written reports and recommendations, and even offering fresh items for consideration. Qualifying NGOs are often invited to attend UN conferences, General Assembly special sessions, and other international meetings. By spring 2005, 2,531 NGOs had obtained consultative status with the Economic and Social Council, and, in a clear reflection of the "new" UN direction represented by these organizations, about 400 were accredited to an important subsidiary body of ECOSOC—the Commission on Sustainable Development. Some UN agencies actually require NGO consultation in their deliberations. The Joint UN Programme on HIV/AIDS (UNAIDS) was the first UN body to welcome NGO representatives to full membership on its coordinating board.

NGOs that distribute information may become associated with the UN Department of Public Information (DPI). In 1946 the General Assembly, in Resolution 13 (annex I), created the department and instructed it to "actively assist and encourage national information services, educational institutions and other governmental and non-governmental organizations of all kinds interested in spreading information about the United Nations." These NGOs typically disseminate information from DPI and other UN bodies to their membership, thereby building support for the organization at the grassroots level. Often, such information corresponds to the particular interest of the NGO and, depending on that interest, may include publicizing such matters as UN activities on issues of peace and security, economic and social development policies in less affluent countries, human rights activities, humanitarian affairs, international law, women's rights, educational reform, and much more. An elected eighteen-member DPI/NGO Executive Committee acts in an advisory and liaison capacity to represent the interests of the approximately fifteen hundred NGOs that work with DPI.

Millennium Summit Goals and Eleanor's UN

We should not leave the topic of Eleanor's UN without a brief look at the outcome of the Millennium Summit held at UN headquarters in New York in the fall of 2000. This meeting, which attracted the most prominent world leaders, concluded with the unanimous adoption of a list of goals that the representatives intended to be met by 2015. While the eight goals are general in tone, they represent the latest statement of "new," or "Eleanor," UN ambitions:

1. Eradicate extreme poverty and hunger.
2. Achieve universal primary education.
3. Promote global equality and empower women.
4. Reduce child malnutrition.
5. Improve maternal health.
6. Combat HIV/AIDS, malaria, and other diseases.
7. Ensure environmental sustainability.
8. Develop a global partnership for development.

These eight goals, accepted by all 191 members of the United Nations, expand considerably on the defined goals that the UN's founders anticipated for the organization they created at the end of the most destructive war in history. By the turn of the twenty-first century, the United Nations certainly continued to be burdened with pursuing the aims of the "old," or original, United Nations, but it had also taken on the much more expansive aspirations Eleanor Roosevelt had articulated.

THE COLD WAR

Unfortunately, the hopes of both the UN's originators and its innovators of the mid-1940s received an early and unwelcome setback at the end of the decade, as, concurrent with the debut of the United Nations, the world descended into something called a **cold war** that would hamper the anticipated functioning of the new organization. This term refers to the U.S.-USSR rivalry following World War II that lasted until about 1991. The two "superpowers," as they became known, engaged in a global competition with political, military, economic, ideological, and diplomatic dimensions that persisted as a "cold" confrontation, always with the potential to turn into a "hot," or shooting, war. Each side attracted allies, and the contest came to be seen as a struggle between the "West" (the United States and its allies) and the "East" (the Soviet Union and its allies). Other nations, declining to join either side, began calling themselves "nonaligned." Because the cold war shaped the global environment into a sharply divided "bipolar" arrangement, it significantly influenced the function and development of the United Nations. It differed sharply from earlier great-power conflicts in its intense ideological struggle, with single-party Communism on the one side and democracy and capitalism on the other, and further manifested itself in a conventional arms race as well as massive stockpiling of weapons of mass destruction (nuclear, biological, and chemical) by both sides. The rivalry was also waged within the United Nations.

When the United Nations began, because of the existence of the veto, the success of the organization seemed to depend on continuing the wartime cooperation among the permanent Security Council members. However, this apparent necessity evaporated as the United States disputed Soviet plans to impose a *cordon sanitaire,* or buffer zone, in Eastern Europe to defend against any future attack from Western European nations. Washington, instead, favored open, multiparty states and market economies in the center of Europe. Stalin, paranoid that U.S. insistence would result in anti-Soviet regimes at his border, reimposed iron-fisted control at home, subverted the provisional coalition governments in Eastern Europe, supported Communist movements in Greece and Turkey (though he later relented), hesitated in removing Soviet troops from

Iran and Austria (but, under Western pressure, eventually did), raided Russia's occupation zone in East Germany for industrial resources and personnel, and declined participation in the Marshall Plan. U.S.-Soviet cooperation turned to rivalry and hostile suspicion.

The United States declared its plan to "contain" Communism until the Soviet dictatorship would be forced to collapse or change, a policy recommended by diplomat George Kennan and initiated by President Harry S. Truman. Containment became the main aim of both the Truman Doctrine (1947) and the rebuilding of former World War II foes by means of the Marshall Plan (1947), and it found expression in military alliances, such as the North Atlantic Treaty Organization (NATO), initiated in 1949. The United States blocked the admission of pro-Soviet applicants to the United Nations, such as Albania, Bulgaria, Hungary, and Romania, and maintained that the Republic of China, seated in Taiwan—not the Communist regime in Beijing—was the "legitimate" representative of the Chinese people at the United Nations. Meanwhile, the USSR objected to the admission of pro-Western countries such as Austria, Italy, Ireland, and Japan. This deadlock was broken only in 1955, when several nation-states from each rival bloc were admitted to the organization. However, mainland China was not admitted until sixteen years later.

The cold war competition affected the working of the Security Council most intensely, beginning with its first session in 1946, which was called to address the failure of the USSR to remove its troops from Iran. During World War II both Great Britain and the Soviet Union had stationed troops in Iran to guard against a Nazi seizure of oil resources located there; British troops had withdrawn from the country, complying with an agreement with Stalin who, nonetheless, then refused to pull out Red Army forces occupying northern Iran. The Security Council struggled to find a viable role in mediating the conflict consistent with its charge in the Charter to "maintain international peace and security, and to that end: to take effective collective measures for the prevention and removal of threats to the peace" (Article 1). However, since the cold war had divided the UN members into competitive "East" and "West" camps, authentic collective action became difficult, if not impossible. In the end, only the threat of U.S. military action convinced Stalin to withdraw his forces. Because of the ideological divide and the superpower veto in later years, the Security Council was constrained from taking up serious matters such as the French, and then U.S., intrusions in Vietnam (1947–1974) and the Soviet dispatch of troops and tanks to Hungary (1956) and Czechoslovakia (1968) to suppress anti-Communist movements. Nor did the Soviets or Americans participate with significant troop deployments to UN peacekeeping operations.

Korea

Meanwhile, finding the Soviet Union "encircled" by the U.S. policy of containment, and outnumbered in the United Nations, Stalin used the veto regularly to block Western initiatives. Going even further, when Mao Zedong's revolutionary forces secured power in China in 1949, Stalin ordered a boycott of the Security Council to protest rejection of the Communist regime's taking the seat held by the Nationalist Chinese government. Shortly thereafter, Stalin gave his approval to a North Korean invasion of South Korea, which triggered a UN decision to use force to repel the attack. In June 1950 the Soviet leader found himself, by means of a surrogate, at war with the United Nations. When the Soviet delegate returned to the Security Council to block any further UN actions in Korea, the United States circumvented the council by pushing through the General Assembly the Uniting for Peace Resolution, which allowed the assembly to make recommendations on the restoration of peace and security when the council was deadlocked by the veto. (See Chapter 5 for a complete discussion of the resolution.) Stalin's government protested the maneuver as an unconstitutional revision of the Charter.

Korea was a prime early indication of the impact of the cold war on the United Nations. When Japan surrendered in 1945, which ended World War II, both U.S. and Soviet military forces occupied parts of the Korean peninsula. By agreement, the United States established a postwar occupation zone in the south, and the USSR controlled the north. The General Assembly had first considered the question of Korea at its session in 1947, with unsuccessful efforts to reestablish a unified country through elections. By 1948 two competing countries came into being, divided at the thirty-eighth parallel. The assembly called for the withdrawal of all foreign troops and established the UN Temporary Commission on Korea (UNTCOK). When, in June 1950, North Korean troops invaded the south, the Security Council, with staunch U.S. encouragement, recommended that member states furnish assistance to repel the attack. The UN Command in Korea (UNC) carried the UN flag, although it was not a UN peacekeeping operation under the secretary-general, but, in fact, a unified force under U.S. command. The Soviet Union, which was absent from Security Council meetings in protest of the continuing participation of the Republic of China delegation, declared the council's action illegal because it was adopted without the presence of two permanent members (the USSR and China). Moscow refused to provide any assessed funding for the operation, and, by all accounts, supported the North Koreans during the conflict. UN military operations became, in the eyes of the Russians, U.S. warfare against an ally, and a demonstration of the unwelcome control of the organization by their cold war enemy. Troops from the People's Republic of China also entered the war as allies of the North Koreans, and Americans (under a UN flag) found themselves in direct combat with these Chinese forces. Thus, the Korean War came to be seen as a "hot" war within the larger context of the global cold war. Fighting ended with an armistice in 1953, but the country remained—into the twenty-first century, long after the end of the cold war—the last divided country dating from the end of World War II.

Nuclear Weapons

One of Stalin's great concerns was the U.S. nuclear monopoly directly after the war. He had ordered the secret and rapid development of a Soviet atomic capability, but until a Soviet arsenal could be developed, the USSR was at a disadvantage in the cold war contest. At the United Nations, Stalin used disarmament talks to criticize U.S. nuclear intentions and policies and to call for large cuts in U.S. stockpiles. When the United States put forward the Baruch Plan in the UN Atomic Energy Commission in June 1946, calling for the creation of an International Atomic Development Authority (IADA) that would own and manage all aspects of atomic energy "potentially dangerous to world security," the Soviets rejected it as a clumsy move made to maintain the U.S. monopoly. The commission suspended its meetings on July 29, 1947, because of the deadlock between the United States and the Soviet Union. No further serious U.S.-Soviet disarmament discussions would occur until after Stalin's death. Then, when UN disarmament negotiations revived in the 1950s and 1960s—as described in Chapter 5—the most serious arms control issues were discussed bilaterally between the superpowers, which left secondary disarmament efforts to the multilateral UN machinery.

Persisting Tensions

Events from 1945 to 1953 in the United Nations reinforced Stalin's camp theory of international politics. He berated the institution and its first secretary-general, **Trygve Lie,** as tools of U.S. anti-Soviet policy. He responded largely by closing off the Soviet world behind what Winston Churchill in 1947 called an *Iron Curtain.* Within the Eastern European bloc, the USSR sustained Stalinist regimes, and in the Soviet Union the effort to root out bourgeois and capitalist influences was renewed. A cult of personality, which had begun during the terror of the 1930s, returned with new enthusiasm. In 1955, to counter NATO, Stalin's successor, Nikita Khrushchev, engineered an alliance—the Warsaw Pact—with the satellite states.

Stalin died on March 5, 1953. Despite initial hopes for a thaw as Dwight Eisenhower and Nikita Khrushchev assumed control of their respective governments, cold war tensions persisted. During the early days of President Eisenhower's administration, Secretary-General Trygve Lie, under pressure from Washington, allowed the Federal Bureau of Investigation (FBI) to finger-print and question all U.S. employees of the United Nations. McCarthy-era suspicions that Communist sympathizers had infiltrated UN headquarters led to the investigation. The practice continued until November 1953, when the new secretary-general, **Dag Hammarskjöld,** ordered the FBI to end it. The U.S. government then established the International Organizations Employees Loyalty Board to investigate all U.S. employees at the United Nations. Among those scrutinized was the highly respected Ralph Bunche, a senior member of the Secretariat.

Despite these political attacks on the institution, the United States took several cold war dis-putes to the United Nations during the Eisenhower presidency, or used the institution as a setting for propagandistic debates with the USSR. The Middle East Crisis of 1956 and the diplomatic pro-motion of Eisenhower's Open Skies Proposal for limiting weapons development were cases in point. (You can find extensive coverage of these events in Chapter 5.) Then, in 1960, U.S. spy planes (a U-2 surveillance craft piloted by Francis Gary Powers and an RB-47 lost over the Arctic) were shot down over Soviet territory, which sent the cold war into a deep freeze. Each side proceeded to use the United Nations for bombastic speeches about the perfidy of its opponent. Soviet leader Khrushchev appeared at that year's General Assembly session, where he banged his shoe on a desk to protest Western treachery, while in the Security Council U.S. ambassador Henry Cabot Lodge accused the Russians of planting secret microphones in the U.S. Embassy in Moscow. Television viewers were entranced. Nonaligned nations decried the inability of the United Nations to meet their needs or temper the contest between Moscow and Washington.

The Congo crisis of the early 1960s further underscored the challenge of the cold war to the United Nations. When the Congo became independent from Belgium in 1960, a complicated civil war broke out, in which one side was supported by the Soviet Union, one side was supported by Washington, and a third side was trying to secede. In the confusion, Secretary-General Dag Hammarskjöld tried to insert a UN presence to bring the disorder to an end. Believing Hammarskjöld to be carrying out the wishes of the United States and its cold war partners in the West, the Soviet Union demanded a reorganization of the office of secretary-general that would involve replacing the single secretary with a **troika**—a three-person executive with equal repre-sentation from the Western bloc, the Eastern bloc, and the neutral countries in the United Nations. The Soviets, along with the French, also refused to donate their assessment for the Congo oper-ation, claiming it to be illegal because the Security Council had not approved it. Their refusal to pay contributed to a serious financial crisis for the United Nations that would plague the orga-nization for the rest of the century.

Deflecting the Soviet challenge, Hammarskjöld persisted in his efforts, in the event dying in a plane crash in a remote part of Northern Rhodesia (now Zambia). The Congo dissolution persisted into the middle of the decade, after which the country was kept together but was left with an un-satisfactory dictatorship. The center of Africa continued to be a place where cold war differences disrupted any UN attempts at resolution. UN efforts in the Congo and elsewhere raised serious questions about the efficacy of UN peacekeeping, particularly in the era of cold war tension. Meanwhile, the Soviet troika proposal languished as U Thant of Burma succeeded the deceased

Hammarskjöld as secretary-general. In the wake of the Congolese fiasco, the Secretariat and the organization as a whole confronted new criticisms from its powerful member states.

Perhaps the most dangerous encounter between the superpower rivals occurred during the Cuban Missile Crisis in 1962. In October of that year, U.S. intelligence discovered that the Soviet Union was placing in Cuba intermediate-range missiles capable of carrying nuclear weapons. The Kennedy administration challenged the Soviets to remove the missiles under clear threat of military action against Cuba and, of necessity, against the Soviet Union. Adlai Stevenson, the U.S. Ambassador to the United Nations, argued with vigor the U.S. position in the Security Council and worked in private with Secretary-General U Thant in an effort to craft a liaison role for the secretary-general in ending the crisis. Soviet leader Khrushchev also suggested using the secretary-general as intermediary. The U.S. administration, imposing a naval quarantine on Cuba, hoped to incorporate the United Nations into its efforts to avoid war while ensuring the removal of the missiles. Meanwhile, urgent secret negotiations transpired in New York and in Washington to defuse the most serious threat of a possible nuclear exchange in the history of the cold war. The final resolution of the crisis, however, resulted from direct U.S.-Soviet negotiations, with almost no UN participation. By the end of October, the Russians agreed to remove the weapons, and the United States, in response, was poised to dismantle its nuclear weapons in Turkey. The incident seemed to have a deep impact on the rival leaders in the cold war—President Kennedy and Soviet leader Khrushchev—who, in mid-1963, agreed to sign a nuclear test ban treaty.

Following the Cuban Missile Crisis, relations between the cold war adversaries never reached such dire peril again, but within the United Nations the competition continued to have an effect. Each side was interested in using the United Nations to criticize the other in its foreign adventures—the United States in Vietnam, the Soviets in Afghanistan. The United Nations had virtually no impact on the U.S. involvement in Southeast Asia, but the United States and its allies were able to gain resolutions in the General Assembly criticizing the Russian involvement in Afghanistan.

In 1971, the United States witnessed an embarrassing reversal of its cold war China policy when, by an overwhelming vote in the General Assembly, the government in Beijing replaced the Republic of China in the organization, becoming an official permanent Security Council member. At first the United States had used its overwhelming support in the General Assembly to keep the seat for the government in Taiwan. Then, as the majority in the assembly shifted during the 1960s, Washington used the tactic of making any motion to replace Taiwan with a delegation from the People's Republic of China (PRC) an "Important Question." Under the Charter, Important Questions require a two-thirds majority to pass in the assembly. This strategy worked until 1971, when supporters of the PRC surmounted the two-thirds threshold, and the assembly not only seated Mao Zedong's government, but also humiliated the United States by removing Taiwan from the world body.

The international events that appeared on the front pages of major newspapers during the 1970s and 1980s rarely referenced the United Nations. In Vietnam, Afghanistan, Central America, and the Middle East, the cold war competitors frequently acted outside the framework of the world organization. On a few occasions, however, the United Nations was called into a major crisis. In 1967 the Security Council found itself sufficiently unified, despite the cold war, to pass Resolution 242, which became the legal basis of a future settlement of the Israeli-Palestinian standoff. Again, in 1973, the Security Council supplemented the earlier action with Resolution 338, reaffirming the essential principles of Resolution 242. (These Middle Eastern events are covered fully in Chapter 5.)

Waning of the Cold War

The 1980s witnessed the depths of U.S. cold war animosity toward the United Nations, followed by the first glimmer of a new respect, and even co-option of the world body. President Ronald Reagan withdrew the United States from the UN Educational, Scientific and Cultural Organization (UNESCO), which the administration accused of being too politicized. The U.S. withdrawal was a part of a general conservative attack on the United Nations. In 1985 the government also unilaterally cut its assessment payments to the world body from 25 percent of the UN's total budget to 20 percent, which made the United States one of the largest debtors to the United Nations by the end of the decade. The White House demanded significant UN reform before it would support repayment of its debt. (A full explanation of the UN reform movement and the U.S. role in it can be found in Chapter 3.) At the same time that it was harshly criticizing the UN's performance, it was also moving haltingly toward using UN mechanisms in new ways. The rise of Mikhail Gorbachev to power in the Soviet Union in 1985, and the Kremlin's rapid fashioning of a new, less antagonistic foreign policy, opened the door to possible cooperation with the USSR, under UN auspices, to address global conflicts. The most dramatic example was the collaboration of the United States and the Soviet Union to end the bloody seven-year Iran-Iraq war. For the first time in history, the superpowers jointly sponsored a UN resolution on the Middle East. On July 20, 1987, the Security Council unanimously passed Resolution 598, calling for a ceasefire in the war and threatening unspecified measures against either belligerent that did not accept the resolution.

At the United Nations in December 1988, Soviet leader Gorbachev made an important gesture toward ending the cold war. After a genial meeting on Governor's Island in New York with outgoing President Reagan, the Soviet president addressed the full General Assembly, insisting that it was now "high time to make use of the opportunities provided by this universal organization."[19] By the time of the Iraqi invasion of Kuwait in 1990 and the Gulf War in 1991, Gorbachev's anticipation of an effective United Nations seemed prescient as Moscow and Washington cooperated within the Security Council in ways that would have astonished earlier diplomats in both countries. Evidence of the end of the cold war was visible early in 1991, before the demise of the Soviet Union that year, when the Russian delegation did not veto a British-U.S. resolution before the Security Council authorizing the use of "any means necessary" (Resolution 678) against Iraq to restore the sovereignty of Kuwait. The action was all the more important because Iraq had previously been a Soviet ally.

With the demolition of the Berlin Wall in 1989 and then the dissolution of the Soviet Union in late 1991, the cold war was over. The impact rippled through the international system and within the United Nations. In 1991 the USSR's and Yugoslavia's dissolution into several new independent nations contributed to swelling UN membership. Joining the United Nations between 1991 and 1993 were Macedonia, the Czech Republic, Croatia, Slovakia, Bosnia and Herzegovina, Slovenia, Georgia, Estonia, Armenia, Azerbaijan, Latvia, Lithuania, Moldova, and the former central Asian Soviet republics of Tajikistan, Kazakhstan, Turkmenistan, Kyrgyzstan, and Uzbekistan. The Russians also joined a UN-sponsored multilateral peacekeeping operation in Bosnia in 1995 and helped end the NATO bombing of Yugoslavia in 1999 by convincing the government led by Slobodan Milosevic to withdraw its forces from Kosovo.

With the end of the cold war, peacekeeping and peacemaking became central concerns of the United Nations, as demand for UN intervention in conflicts continued to rise. The September 2000 summit of 150 heads of state at UN headquarters in New York (the Millennium Summit) affirmed the importance of peacekeeping operations, then no longer blocked by issues of superpower proxies and rivalry. The importance of arms control and weapons proliferation also moved to the forefront of the UN's agenda with the Comprehensive Nuclear-Test-Ban Treaty (CTBT) signed by the United States and Russian governments in 1996, and the extension of the Treaty on the Non-Proliferation of Nuclear Weapons (Nuclear Non-Proliferation Treaty, or NPT) in 1995.

IRAQ AND THE POST–COLD WAR UNITED NATIONS

The end of the cold war seemed to presage the rebirth of the founders' United Nations. Even as the Soviet Union suffered from the ills that would eventually destroy it, the Gorbachev government joined the United States in opposing the first real threat to international peace and security in the post–cold war era—Saddam Hussein's invasion of Kuwait in August 1990. Acting with alacrity never characteristic of the League of Nations, the Security Council unanimously passed tough resolutions condemning the invasion, demanding the withdrawal of Iraqi forces and the reestablishment of the sovereignty of Kuwait, and, by the close of the year, authorizing a coalition of forces under U.S. command to expel the invaders from Kuwait. In January 1991 an extraordinarily large coalition, including many Arab and European states, launched the first UN-authorized military action since the Korean War, driving Iraq out and restoring Kuwait's government and sovereignty. Hussein accepted all UN conditions, including recognition of an independent Kuwait and near-mandate postwar impositions by the world community, as the price for ending the war before coalition forces marched on Baghdad.

Following the termination of military hostilities in Iraq in 1991, the Security Council, under Chapter VII authority, imposed internal controls on many aspects of Iraqi life and politics. It affirmed Iraq's liability under international law "for any direct loss, damage, . . . or injury to foreign governments, nationals and corporations, as a result of Iraq's unlawful invasion and occupation of Kuwait." The Security Council created a compensation fund to pay claims by victims of Iraqi aggression, its assets coming from 30 percent of Iraqi oil export revenues. As noted in Chapter 1, the fund had paid more than three hundred billion dollars to satisfy 2.6 million claims by the fall of 2003. In addition, the council created the UN Special Commission on Iraq (UNSCOM) to verify Iraqi compliance with all UN resolutions and to carry out no-notice inspections inside Iraq for the purpose of finding and destroying all weapons of mass destruction (WMDs). UNSCOM was also charged with establishing a permanent system of monitoring and verification to ensure that Iraq could not rebuild nuclear, biological, or chemical weapon capabilities. UNSCOM conducted its work under continuing challenge and obstruction from the Baghdad government until Iraq ended all cooperation with the UN agency in 1998. During UNSCOM's seven years of operation, its demands on the regime were often buttressed with air reprisals, largely carried out by U.S. and British warplanes.

The rapid crumpling of Iraqi resistance to the UN-sanctioned coalition assault in 1991 sparked secessionist efforts by Shia and Kurds in southern and northern Iraq, respectively. President Hussein responded with air attacks against both groups. At the end of March 1991, the Iraqi army unleashed a massive attack against rebels in the northern part of the country. The attack produced more than two hundred thousand Kurdish refugees who fled to the region along Iraq's border with Turkey, and five hundred thousand crossed into Iran. On April 5 the Security Council condemned the attacks and called on "the Secretary-General to use all the resources at his disposal . . . to address urgently the critical needs of the refugees." The United States, with the assistance of Turkey, Great Britain, and France established "no-fly" zones in both the north and the south. The four powers launched Operation Provide Comfort, creating a massive humanitarian airdrop operation and protective "enclaves" for Kurds inside Iraq. Shortly thereafter the United Nations took control of the camps, imposing a near protectorate over large parts of the country, with military backup from coalition forces.

We should mention that during President Bill Clinton's days in the White House (1993–2001), the United States used what it called *assertive multilateralism*.[20] The administration sought to contain Iraq's development of WMDs, to defend minority communities, to encourage the collapse of the regime, and to limit Saddam's influence in the region through UN mechanisms. To give credence to UN resolutions and to back demands by UNSCOM inspectors, Washington regularly carried out air strikes against Iraqi military and radar installations. A critical moment came in 1998, however, when President Clinton ordered four days of bombing in retaliation for Iraqi unwillingness to allow inspectors into requested sites. The United Nations withdrew the inspectors for the duration, citing safety considerations. Baghdad then announced that it would not allow the return of UNSCOM, calling it an espionage vehicle for the United States. While both Washington and the United Nations condemned the Iraqi decision, no forceful means were used to reinsert the inspection teams. At the time, President Clinton faced impeachment proceedings that politically undercut any contemplated military action to enforce UN resolutions.

Unrecognized then, the 1998 events set in motion a slow erosion of U.S.-UN unanimity on Iraq. UNSCOM was soon replaced by the UN Monitoring, Verification and Inspection Commission (UNMOVIC),[21] an agency thought more acceptable in its personnel and leadership to Baghdad. The Swedish diplomat, Dr. Hans Blix, was appointed executive secretary; only one of UNMOVIC's sixteen commissioners was an American.[22] The Clinton administration, while it supported the creation of UNMOVIC and encouraged an expansion of programs to use Iraqi oil sale proceeds for humanitarian assistance, increasingly operated without reference to the UN Security Council to keep the Iraqi regime "in its box." In part, U.S. reticence was in response to growing criticism from UN members that the effort to isolate Saddam and penalize his government was imposing unacceptable pain on the Iraqi population. Having failed to topple Saddam Hussein, U.S. policy was criticized by many UN members as at least ineffective if not counterproductive.

September 11, 2001, and the Age of Terrorism

The crisis of 9/11 molded the Iraq policy of the George W. Bush administration and affected its bumpy relationship with the United Nations. The unconscionable terrorist attacks on the World Trade Center and the Pentagon required a forceful and calculated response. They also elicited considerable worldwide empathy. On September 12, 2001, the Security Council unanimously adopted Resolution 1368, denouncing the assault. Council members departed from tradition and stood during the resolution's adoption. In the text of the resolution, the council held that any act of international terrorism was a threat to international peace and security. Specifically, the resolution instructed the council to remain "seized" with the matter, meaning that, in a subtle shift from past policy, the council now viewed combating terrorism as a primary responsibility under the UN Charter. The General Assembly, convening the following day—September 13—also condemned the attack. On September 28 the Security Council passed Resolution 1373, calling on all states to "prevent and suppress the financing of terrorist acts." Council members invoked Chapter VII of the Charter, which made the provisions of the resolution mandatory on all member states. The council decided that all states should criminalize the provision or collection of funds for such acts. It called on states to freeze the assets of suspected terrorist groups and prohibit their nationals or organizations from making funds and financial assets available to potential terrorists. The resolution instructed states to deny safe haven to individuals or groups who financed, planned, supported, or committed terrorist acts. Finally, the council urged that states afford one another the greatest measure of assistance for criminal investigations and prosecution of terrorist groups.[23]

Washington received wide-ranging multilateral support to remove the Taliban from power in Afghanistan, curtail Al Qaeda activities there, and seek the reconstruction of the country. However, Afghanistan slipped from the front pages of U.S. newspapers as the Bush administration announced, with a virile combativeness, that nations were "either with us or against us," that some unwelcome nations made up an "axis of evil," and that one of them at least—Iraq—needed to be struck immediately, preemptively, even unilaterally, if the other Security Council members refused to accede to U.S. demands for military action. This posture merged with Washington's rejection of the laboriously negotiated Kyoto Protocol, its "unsigning" of the International Criminal Court agreement, and its withdrawal from the 1972 Anti-Ballistic Missile Treaty.

Meanwhile, Afghanistan, liberated from Taliban rule in early 2002 through a cooperative effort, faced deep problems of political instability and economic despair. Regional warlords remained and the drug trade persisted. In outlying areas the Taliban rematerialized as a threat to the government in Kabul. Still, with international encouragement, the Afghans, in a traditional *loya jirga,* or grand council, had, by early 2004, agreed to a constitution and to democratic elections. Abiding by a post-Taliban blueprint negotiated at an international conference in Bonn, Germany, in 2001, warlords began to turn in heavy weapons to the central government. A visible UN presence in the country, UN special representative Lakhdar Brahimi, along with the UN High Commissioner for Refugees and a variety of staff personnel, plied their trade with uncommon dedication. Hampered by a lack of money, the slow inflow of promised funds, and the diversion of attention to Iraq, the UN contingent worked to distribute an international aid disbursement, to increase security, to develop infrastructure, and to strengthen the government of President Hamid Karzai. Included in their efforts were plans to pay off, disarm, and disband about one hundred thousand militia. In August 2003 NATO took command of the International Security Assistance Force (the first time NATO had acted outside Europe). In October 2004 elections were held with international observers in attendance. That is, from late 2001 a multilateral approach had been used to try to solve the Afghan crisis.

Despite the challenge of Afghanistan, attention in Washington shifted to Iraq. President Bush seemed determined to attack, even without UN approval. During much of 2002 and into early 2003, disagreements within the Security Council on the reasonableness of war with Iraq became public. Washington began warning of the certain "irrelevancy" of the United Nations should the Security Council fail to accede to war, although, in fact, the United Nations, from a certain perspective, had proved fairly vibrant in addressing various serious problems like Iraqi aggression. In resolutions following the invasion of Kuwait in 1990, the Security Council had imposed on Iraq the most debilitating control regime imaginable. Arms inspectors roamed the country; "no-fly" zones in the north and south, legitimized at the behest of the United States, removed large portions of the land from Baghdad's political control; and, with Resolution 1441, pressed on Iraq in November 2002 by unanimous vote of the Security Council, arms inspectors with even more robust authority returned.

Still the crisis simmered into the late winter of 2003. At the Security Council meeting of February 14, 2003—after UNMOVIC executive-secretary Hans Blix and IAEA director-general Mohamed El Baradei issued their largely negative reports on Iraqi compliance with Security Council Resolution 1441, which had required immediate and complete WMD disarmament—each Security Council member responded, on live television, with careful, studied remarks.

As the drama unfolded, one fact became clear: A majority of the council, most of the world's population, and even the plurality of the American people—at least according to virtually all the public opinion polls at the time—favored military action against Iraq only with full UN consent.[24] This outcome resulted despite the efforts of a popular U.S. president during the previous ten months to paint Iraq as a member of the "axis of evil." Bush had also, in June 2002, asserted a new foreign policy of preemption, coupling fundamental U.S. security concerns with the need for "regime change" in Baghdad.

We must note, however, that the inability to generate broad public and coalition support for preemptive attack on Iraq had led the president back to the rostrum of the UN General Assembly in September 2002, where he announced a subtle change in U.S. Iraqi policy. Asserting that preventing the United Nations from going the way of the League of Nations was essential, he argued that the United States would seek to fulfill UN resolutions dating to the 1991 Gulf War that demanded Baghdad divest itself of all WMDs. Regime change (only for the moment it turned out) seemed a remnant policy of the recent past.

To see President Bush, no apparent friend of the United Nations during his first eighteen months in office, stand before the General Assembly and make his case for authorization to act in Iraq and to call the world to honor and enforce previous UN resolutions was an extraordinary assent to legitimizing the UN's role in Middle East affairs. Whatever his administration's short-term purposes or self-interested motivations, the appeal by the United States, the world's preeminent power, for UN enforcement of past Security Council resolutions encouraged the emergent global acceptance of the United Nations in Middle Eastern disputes. It also placed constraints even on the United States—that is, on actions that Washington would otherwise not sense—constraints taking the form of time limits, definition of goals in Iraq, continuing consultation with both allies and other Security Council members, and rising world antipathy for perceived violations of UN mandates. Having begun down this road, President Bush was forced into lengthy negotiations on the terms of Resolution 1441, delays brought on by the renewed inspection process, and effective restraint led by France and Germany. By the spring of 2003, the United States even faced the distasteful prospect of initiating military action against Iraq in the face of formal rejection of its proposed authorizing resolution.

Nonetheless, that is exactly what happened in March 2003, as the United States, with a "coalition of the willing," invaded Iraq. Although the United States seemed to "win" the 2003 war in Iraq, postwar challenges proved more intractable than originally thought. No WMDs were found. David Kay, who resigned in late January 2004 as head of the U.S. Iraq Survey Group trying to find weapons, declared before the Senate Armed Services Committee that no chemical, biological, or nuclear weapons existed in Iraq and no evidence that Baghdad had transferred any such weapons to Al Qaeda or any other terrorist group had been found.[25] As disquieting, the U.S. military and civilian administration of Iraq had not gone as hoped. By summer 2005, more than seventeen hundred Americans had been killed in the country since the U.S. invasion had begun on March 20, 2003. More than 80 percent of these deaths had occurred after President Bush announced the end of combat on May 1 (compared with many fewer American deaths in Afghanistan during a longer period of involvement). The usefulness of unilateral "preemption" outside UN sanction was at the least open to debate.

Evidence showed that the State Department had mounted an effort to move U.S. policy back to multinational cooperation (and at least to convince the U.S. public that it was succeeding). In an article published early in 2004, Secretary of State Colin Powell denied that the second Bush administration favored a unilateral, assertive foreign policy or that it had turned its back on the collaborative tradition dating from the UN's origins. The secretary stressed that Washington had continued to follow "a strategy of partnership," cooperation with other nations, and diplomatic regard for the United Nations.[26] Moreover, by early 2004, U.S. Iraqi policy had appeared to shift abruptly, as officials announced the U.S. intention to transfer sovereignty to an interim Iraqi government by June 30—a government selected by Secretary-General Annan's Special Representative Lahkdar Brahimi. To contain the certain confusion and possible instability that might result, Washington was now even making "urgent appeal[s]" to the United Nations to take an active role in restoring order in that country.[27] On June 1, 2004, Brahimi and President Bush acceded to decisions by Iraqi Governing Council members to appoint immediately their own selections for a new government, with authority to manage Iraqi affairs until scheduled elections in January 2005. The new leaders urged the UN Security Council to recognize the full sovereignty of Iraq and the government's complete control over the country's affairs and resources. President Bush accepted these recommendations and worked closely with other major powers on the Security Council to fashion multilateral reconstruction of Iraq. On January 30, 2005, Iraq held an election, and after long deliberation a government was formed by the end of April.

This instance would not be the first time in the post–World War II period that a U.S. administration, initially reversing the foreign policy of its immediate predecessor, reverted to continuity. That seemed to be the aim of Powell's State Department. However, the question lingered as to whether preference for going it alone, so forcefully articulated during President Bush's first term, or going together with others would win out in Washington. This issue had been one of the great questions of international politics in the twentieth century. When it faced U.S. policymakers in 1945, the trajectory of U.S. diplomacy at that time seemed fixed. However, by January 2005 Powell was gone from the State Department, replaced by former national security adviser Condoleezza Rice. Then, in March, the president announced his nomination of undersecretary of state for arms control John Bolton—a tough proponent of unilateralism and preemption, and a harsh critic—to become U.S. ambassador to the United Nations, which indicated that the United States would likely persist in its adversarial posture toward the organization.

President Bush's doctrine of unilateral preemption, if maintained, challenged the 1945 commitment to collective security embodied in the UN Charter. By acting without UN authorization, or early UN ratification after the fact, when no imminent threat to U.S. national security seemed to exist, the Bush administration circumvented the bedrock principles on which the United Nations was founded. Other major powers on the Security Council noted the grave precedent set by U.S. action and sought ways to constrain Washington's unilateral foreign policy. In the recent fog of history, even Secretary-General Kofi Annan expressed concern about the viability of the "old" UN formulations for maintaining international peace and security in a "new" age with both new and novel threats and a hyperpower finding itself unsafe and unable to ensure its security through current UN mechanisms.

SUMMARY

The United Nations originated out of a lush history of attempts to bring peace, stability, and regularity to international relations. Most immediately, its founders sought to craft an organization that would avoid the pitfalls of the predecessor League of Nations. At a number of wartime meetings, the leaders of the major Allied governments—Franklin Roosevelt, Winston Churchill, and Joseph Stalin—eventually agreed on the outline of the United Nations. The organizing conference at San Francisco in mid-1945 brought the organization to fruition, and early on, led by Eleanor Roosevelt, the United Nations came to be as interested in social, humanitarian, and human rights issues as it was with international peace and security. However, the simultaneous onset of the cold war hindered the new organization's ability to fulfill its hoped-for promise. Only in the post–cold war era did such promise seem possible. Nevertheless, as is too often true in human affairs, multiple troubling challenges arose even in the post–cold war period. Two of the most significant and divisive were the crisis over Iraq and the concomitant assertion by the UN's most important power—the United States—of a foreign policy doctrine inherently challenging to the principle of collective security, a principle ascribed to by the world community in the 1940s largely at the urging of the United States.

NOTES

1. Jack C. Plano and Robert E. Riggs, *Forging World Order* (New York: Macmillan, 1967), 7.

2. Bruce Russett and John R. O'Neal, *Triangulating Peace: Democracy, Interdependence, and International Organizations* (New York: Norton, 2001), 10, 29, 35.

3. See Raymond Cohen and Raymond Westbrook, eds., *Amarna Diplomacy: The Beginnings of International Relations* (Baltimore: Johns Hopkins, 2000); and James B. Pritchard, ed., *Ancient Near Eastern Texts Relating to the Old Testament* (Princeton, NJ: Princeton University Press, 1969), 199–206, 529–41.

4. Here and elsewhere in the early pages of this chapter, liberal use has been made of Chap. 1 of John Allphin Moore, Jr., and Jerry Pubantz, *To Create a New World? American Presidents and the United Nations* (New York: Peter Lang, 1999), and, by the same authors, the Introduction to *Encyclopedia of the United Nations* (New York: Facts on File, 2002).

5. Paul W. Schroeder, *The Transformation of European Politics, 1763–1848* (Oxford, UK: Clarendon Press, 1994); and Margaret Olwen MacMillan, *Paris 1919: Six Months that Changed the World* (New York: Random House, 2002).

6. John Milton Cooper, *Breaking the Heart of the World: Woodrow Wilson and the Fight for the League of Nations* (New York: Cambridge University Press, 2001).

7. Warren F. Kimball, ed., *Churchill and Roosevelt: The Complete Correspondence* (Princeton, NJ: Princeton University Press, 1984), 1:227–28.

8. Anne O'Hare McCormick, "His 'Unfinished Business'—and Ours," *New York Times Magazine,* April 22, 1945, 43–44.

9. See U.S. Department of State, *Foreign Relations of the United States: Diplomatic Papers: The Conferences at Cairo and Teheran, 1943* (Washington, D.C.: U.S. Government Printing Office, 1961), 530–32.

10. Robert Hildebrand, *Dumbarton Oaks: The Origins of the United Nations and the Search for Postwar Security* (Chapel Hill: University of North Carolina Press, 1990).

11. France had no representation at Dumbarton Oaks or at Yalta. Moreover, it was not considered one of Roosevelt's original Four Policemen, and it was occupied by Germany during the war. However, as the war drew to an end, both Churchill and Roosevelt (persuaded by planners in the Department of State), despite personal uneasiness with Charles DeGaulle, determined that a strong France was needed as a pro-West ally in a stable postwar world. By the time the Yalta agreement was written, Section 1.4 had elevated France (or the "Free" France of DeGaulle) to co-equal status with the United States, the USSR, and China. Thus, France, though dismissed as a second-rate power by Stalin, gained an occupation zone in Germany and a permanent seat on the Security Council. Secretary of State Stettinius, in a long advisory memorandum on all postwar plans, explained the matter to Truman less than one day after FDR's death: The French, he said, must be treated on the basis of "potential power and influence." Kimball, *Churchill and Roosevelt,* 3:633.

12. Franklin D. Roosevelt, "Address to Congress on the Yalta Conference, March 1, 1945," in *Public Papers of the Presidents of the United States: Franklin D. Roosevelt, 1933–1945* (Washington, D.C.: Office of the Federal Register, National Archives and Records Administration), http://www.presidency.ucsb.edu/ws/.

13. Stephen C. Schlesinger, *Act of Creation: The Founding of the United Nations* (Boulder, CO: Westview Press, 2003), 121. Schlesinger's well-received book and Ruth Russell's classic *A History of the United Nations' Charter: The Role of the United States, 1940–1945* (Washington, D.C.: Brookings Institution, 1958) are two of the few detailed renditions of the San Francisco Conference available to students.

14. United Nations, "Article 23," in *Charter of the United Nations* (New York: United Nations, 1945), http://www.un.org/aboutun/charter/index.html.

15. Schlesinger, *Act of Creation,* Chap. 13.

16. Ibid., 122–24; and Dorothy Robbins, *Experiment in Democracy: The Story of U.S. Citizen Organizations in Forging the Charter of the United Nations* (New York: Parkside Press, 1971).

17. Mary Ann Glendon, *A World Made New: Eleanor Roosevelt and the Universal Declaration of Human Rights* (New York: Random House, 2001), xix.

18. Ibid., 170.

19. Mikhail Gorbachev, *Memoirs* (New York: Doubleday, 1995), 442.

20. Madeleine Albright, President Clinton's first permanent representative to the United Nations and later secretary of state, coined this term to describe the overall approach of the new administration in 1993.

21. UN Security Council, *Resolution 1284 (1999),* S/RES/1284, December 17, 1999, http://www.un.org/Depts/unscom/Keyresolutions/sres99-1284.htm.

22. A full description of the work of UNMOVIC can be found at its Web site: http://www.unmovic.org.

23. For complete coverage of UN activities regarding terrorism, particularly with reference to the September 11, 2001, tragedy, see the relevant UN Web site: http://www.un.org/terrorism.

24. At the height of the war in Iraq, U.S. public opinion gravitated toward considerable support for U.S. unilateral military action. However, 50 percent of Americans believed the United Nations should lead reconstruction efforts, whereas 29 percent believed the United States alone should be responsible. See the opinion poll results in Ronald Brownstein, "Support Grows for Military Actions," *Los Angeles Times,* April 5, 2003.

25. Bob Drogin, "Iraq Weapons Data Flawed, Congress Told," *Los Angeles Times*, January 29, 2004, A1.

26. Colin L. Powell, "A Strategy of Partnerships," *Foreign Affairs* 83, no. 1 (2004): 22–34.

27. Steven R. Weisan and John H. Cushman, Jr., "U.S. Joins Iraq to Seek U.N. Role in Interim Rule," *New York Times,* January 16, 2004; and Edward Wong, "U.N. Aide Backs Cleric on Elections; Offers No Timetable," *New York Times,* February 12, 2004.

KEY TERMS

Balance of Power Theory (page 38)

Bretton Woods (page 53)

Winston Churchill (page 43)

Cold War (page 63)

Concert of Europe (page 38)

Dumbarton Oaks (page 50)

Eleanor's UN (page 61)

Dag Hammarskjöld (page 66)

League of Nations (page 39)

Trygve Lie (page 65)

Franklin Roosevelt (page 43)

Joseph Stalin (page 43)

Troika (page 66)

United Nations Conference on International Organization (UNCIO) (page 54)

Yalta Conference (page 45)

RESOURCES FOR FURTHER RESEARCH
Relevant Web Sites

The Avalon Project at Yale Law School: Twentieth-Century Documents (www.yale.edu/lawweb/avalon/20th.htm)

Cold War International History Project (http://wwics.si.edu/index.cfm?topic_id=1409&fuseaction=topics.home)

Foreign Relations of the United States Web site (www.state.gov/www/about_state/history/frus.html)

NGO-ECOSOC information (www.un.org/dpi/ngosection/)

UN Millennium Development Goals Web site www.un.org/millenniumgoals/)

Books, Articles, and Documents

Cook, Blanche Wiesen. *Eleanor Roosevelt.* New York: Viking Press, 1992.

Divine, Robert. *Second Chance: The Triumph of Internationalism in America during World War II.* New York: Atheneum, 1967.

Gaddis, John Lewis. *We Now Know: Rethinking Cold War History.* Oxford, UK: Clarendon Press, 1998.

Gilbert, Martin. *Churchill: A Life.* New York: Holt, 1991.

Glendon, Mary Ann. *A World Made New: Eleanor Roosevelt and the Universal Declaration of Human Rights.* New York: Random House, 2001.

Hoopes, Townsend, and Douglas Brinkley. *FDR and the Creation of the U.N.* New Haven, CT: Yale University Press, 1997.

Kimball, Warren. *Forged in War: Roosevelt, Churchill, and the Second World War.* New York: Morrow, 1997.

Krasno, Jean. "A Step along an Evolutionary Path: The Founding of the United Nations," *Global Dialogue* 12, no. 2 (Spring 2000): 9–18.

Medvedev, Roy. *Let History Judge: The Origins and Consequences of Stalinism.* New York: Columbia University Press, 1989.

Mingst, Karen, and Margaret Karns. *The United Nations in the Post–Cold War Era: Dilemmas in World Politics.* Boulder, CO: Westview Press, 2000.

Moore, John Allphin, Jr., and Jerry Pubantz. *To Create a New World? American Presidents and the United Nations.* New York: Peter Lang, 1999.

Northedge, Frederick Samuel. *The League of Nations: Its Life and Times, 1920–1946.* New York: Holmes & Meier, 1986.

Russell, Ruth B. *A History of the United Nations' Charter: The Role of the United States, 1940–1945.* Washington, D.C.: Brookings Institution, 1958.

Schlesinger, Stephen C. *Act of Creation: The Founding of the United Nations.* Boulder, CO: Westview Press, 2003.

Service, Robert. *A History of Twentieth-Century Russia.* Cambridge, MA: Harvard University Press, 1997.

U.S. Department of State. *Postwar Foreign Policy Preparation, 1939–1945.* Washington, D.C.: U.S. Government Printing Office, 1949.

Chapter 3

The Evolving UN Charter

Now that you have some background on the origins of the United Nations, examining the UN Charter and its evolution is a practical course to take. In this chapter, we cover the original provisions of the Charter, formal and informal amendments to it, the effects of various historical events (including the cold war) on it, the financial crises that beset it, and the various types of reforms the Charter underwent as a result of such crises and events.

CONTENTS OF THE CHARTER

The Charter of the United Nations (UN Charter) is the "constitution" of the organization. Member states agree to abide by its principles and procedures, which are laid out in a preamble and nineteen chapters containing 111 articles. The Charter was signed on June 26, 1945, at the San Francisco organizing conference and, sufficiently ratified, came into force on October 24, 1945. (The full Charter can be found in Appendix A.)

Chapter I of the Charter outlines the UN's purposes and principles, including the maintenance of international peace and security, respect for equal rights and self-determination, the encouragement of rights and freedoms, and the principle of sovereign equality of all member states. Chapter I establishes a collective security system among UN members, requiring them to "settle their international disputes by peaceful means." However, in the wake of the 2003 war in Iraq, some observers questioned whether the United Nations could live up to its purposes without fundamental reform, and others claimed collective security was no longer a relevant paradigm in an age of terrorism.

Chapter II deals with UN membership, the main qualification for which is to be a "peace-loving" state. The vagueness of this criterion has allowed the United Nations to become a "universal" international organization made up of states with significantly different political, cultural, and ideological systems. Admission into the United Nations requires a Security Council (SC) recommendation, followed by General Assembly (GA) approval by a two-thirds majority. Chapter II also allows for suspension of the membership of a state against which the United Nations has taken enforcement measures. Under the direst circumstances, the General Assembly may expel a state upon Security Council recommendation. Some critics have argued that the UN's universality has made the organization unwieldy and ineffective. Proposals have been put forward to establish weighted voting, to limit participation by "ministates" in UN bodies, and even to bar states from serving in UN organs to which they can contribute little.

Chapter III lists the five principal organs and explicitly mandates no restriction on "the eligibility of men and women to participate" in them. Chapters IV and V detail provisions for the General Assembly and the Security Council, including voting procedures for both bodies and the jurisdiction and actions each can take. General Assembly membership is based on the principle of sovereign equality: Each country, whatever its size, wealth, or power, has one vote. While a majority vote effects most actions, the GA also decides "Important Questions," which require a two-thirds vote of the members present and voting (Article 18). In the fifteen-member Security Council, nine votes are required to pass a procedural matter; "all other matters" require not only nine affirmative votes, but also concurrence of the five permanent members (the veto provision in Article 27). Probably no clause of the UN Charter has been criticized more than the grant of the veto power to these five states. Many amendments have been proposed to limit or revise this privilege.

Chapters VI and VII are the core of the historical development of UN peacekeeping policies and outline the collective security measures that the United Nations may use to restore peace. Chapter VI describes the procedures for dealing with the pacific settlement of disputes and threats to the peace. It lists the traditional international diplomacy methods that the parties should use to resolve their differences: negotiation, mediation, conciliation, arbitration, and judicial decisions. Chapter VII emphasizes the role of the Security Council under international law to "determine the existence of any threat to the peace, breach of the peace, or act of aggression" and to "decide what measures shall be taken" to halt the threat or punish the aggressor. In enabling the Security Council to take coercive measures to achieve these tasks, Chapter VII installs the United Nations as the international guarantor of peace and security.

Chapters VIII and IX define and sanction regional organizations to keep the peace and encourage economic and social cooperation. Article 57 encourages specialized agencies to develop a relationship with the United Nations in order to expedite the mandate of Article 55 to raise living standards, resolve economic and social problems, and enhance human rights. These chapters are followed by the related Chapter X, which defines and sets the parameters for Economic and Social Council (ECOSOC) action.

Chapters XI and XII deal with non-self-governing territories (typically colonies). The first of these two chapters is a declaration of the UN's intent to promote decolonization and the progressive development of "free political institutions." Chapter XIII establishes the Trusteeship Council and defines its membership (the states administering trust territories, the remaining permanent members of the Security Council that do not administer any territories in the system, and sufficient member states elected by the General Assembly to ensure an equal number of administering and nonadministering governments on the council). The Trusteeship Council is defunct because decolonization and self-determination ended the great colonial empires of the past five centuries. Suggestions abound for the transformation of the Trusteeship Council into a purposeful UN organ that could address some of the new challenges facing the world community. However, in March 2005 UN Secretary-General Kofi Annan recommended the complete elimination of the council.

Chapter XIV provides for the International Court of Justice (ICJ), the judicial arm of the United Nations. By stipulation of Article 92, the ICJ replaced the Permanent Court of International Justice, became an integral part of the United Nations, and gained its own statute, which was annexed to the UN Charter.

Chapter XV creates the Secretariat, headed by a secretary-general appointed by the General Assembly upon Security Council recommendation. In addition to being the chief administrative officer of the United Nations, the secretary-general plays an important political role. Article 99 allows him or her to bring to the Security Council's attention any matter that he or she believes threatens peace and security. The Secretariat is designed to be the administrative arm of the United Nations. Its members are "international officials responsible only to the Organization" (Article 100).

The "miscellaneous provisions" of Chapter XVI call for all treaties and international agreements to be registered with the Secretariat, establish the priority of the Charter over other international agreements, and extend to the United Nations (within all member states) privileges and immunities necessary to carry out its purposes. Chapter XVII, titled "Transitional Security Arrangements," sorts out specific matters that concluded World War II, and Chapter XVIII explicates the difficult method for amending the Charter (discussed in the next section), while the concluding Chapter XIX describes the time line and process of Charter ratification.

As we review the Charter, we find comparing it to the earlier Covenant of the League of Nations useful. Such comparison draws attention to certain new, or elaborated, principles of international law introduced by the later document. For example, the League's Covenant essentially suggested a voluntary commitment not to resort to force, whereas the Charter, in Article 2, paragraph 4, confirms the non-resort-to-war concept as an established principle: "All Members shall refrain in their international relations from the threat or use of force against the territorial integrity or political independence of any state, or in any other manner inconsistent with the Purposes of the United Nations." The preamble of the League's Covenant speaks of the dealings of "organized peoples with one another," as though "disorganized" or, perhaps, "less civilized" peoples existed in the world. The Charter disavows such distinctions with provisions devoted to decolonization (especially Chapters XI, XII, and XIII) and to the equal sovereignty of states (Article 2), and by its encouragement of universal membership (Chapter II).[1] Of equal significance is the principle of obligatory registration of treaties at a single, universally visible place and with a single institution—the United Nations—as provided in Article 102. This article also directs the Secretariat to accumulate and publicize all registered treaties.

AMENDMENTS TO THE CHARTER

Article 108, in Chapter XVIII, provides the method for **amending the Charter,** but as of summer 2005 it has been used on only five occasions. For an amendment to be added, it must be adopted by a vote of two-thirds of the General Assembly members and then ratified according to the respective constitutional processes of two-thirds of the member states, including all the permanent Security Council members. Amendments to the Charter include alterations to Articles 23, 27, and 61. The General Assembly adopted these amendments on December 17, 1963, and they came into force on August 31, 1965. An additional change in Article 61 was adopted on December 20, 1971, and it entered into force on September 24, 1973. The General Assembly amended Article 109 on December 20, 1965, and the amendment came into force on June 12, 1968. The amendment to Article 23 enlarged the Security Council membership from eleven to fifteen, and changes in Article 27 altered voting requirements in that body—increasing the number of affirmative votes needed to pass all resolutions from seven to nine. The veto for the five permanent members remained. The two revisions of Article 61 enlarged ECOSOC membership from eighteen to, first, twenty-seven, and then fifty-four states. The change in Article 109 increased the number of Security Council votes necessary to call a general conference to review the Charter from seven to nine. The two-thirds vote required of the General Assembly remained.

These Charter amendments resulted from the dramatic growth in UN membership in the 1950s and 1960s. Most of the new member states—products of the national liberation movements in Africa and Asia—clamored for representation, particularly in UN bodies where their security and economic development interests could be most affected. The great powers were willing to accept the enlargement of these organs so long as no amendment diminished the permanent members' ultimate check on Security Council actions or subjected them to mandatory resolutions in ECOSOC.

Otherwise, by mid-2005 the Charter remained as it was in 1945. Such little change does not mean, however, that serious proposals for Charter amendments have not surfaced repeatedly since 1945. Even at San Francisco, major proposed revisions were put forward that the "Big Three" rejected in the end. They argued that the Charter was a carefully negotiated document whose formula could not be adjusted without the loss of major-power participation. Charter amendment has always been a delicate balancing act among three phenomena: (1) the democratic legislative process inherent in parliamentary diplomacy; (2) the sovereign equality of each member state, which gives that state an equal vote with every other member as well as the equal right to ignore many UN decisions; and (3) the reality of power inequality among the UN's members, which allows the permanent members to "outvote" all other states in many circumstances. At one time or another, nearly every chapter of the Charter has been recommended for revision and subjected to the pressures of these three countervailing forces.

Informal Modifications of the Charter

Although the Charter has seldom been amended, the United Nations has evolved tremendously since 1945. This disparity is logically possible only because the interpretation of the UN's "constitution" has allowed informal "amendments" of the originally intended blueprint. Two of the Charter's accentuated themes have sometimes seemed at cross-purposes and have led to many informal adjustments of the Charter. First is the principle of the independence and sovereignty of equal member states (Article 2) and the concomitant principle of noninterference in the domestic or internal affairs of states, as explicated in Article 2, paragraph 7:

> Nothing contained in the present Charter shall authorize the United Nations to intervene in matters which are essentially within the domestic jurisdiction of any state or shall require the Members to submit such matters to settlement under the present Charter.

Second is the promotion of universal respect for human rights and fundamental freedoms, as found in Article 1, paragraph 3; in Article 13, paragraph 1; and in Article 55, section c—which, in succession, promote and encourage "respect for human rights," advocate "assisting in the realization of human rights," and call on the United Nations to promote "universal respect for, and observance of, human rights." On the one hand, sovereignty and noninterference appear to denote the right of a nation-state to enforce its own version of human rights. Yet, on the other hand, the Universal Declaration of Human Rights and several Charter provisions seem to proclaim rights as universal rather than culturally or nationally determined. In 1999 Secretary-General Kofi Annan maintained that such human rights could not be abridged in the name of state sovereignty. By the conclusion of the twentieth century, the proposition that sovereignty and the principle of noninterference deny any other nation, group of nations, or the United Nations, the right—even duty— to interfere in a state's domestic affairs came under increased challenge as the world community found itself dealing with human tragedies in collapsing and dysfunctional states in the former Yugoslavia, Indonesia, and areas of Africa. The Security Council, for example, authorized direct humanitarian intervention in Somalia, Rwanda, and East Timor, not always at the clear invitation of any central government. Moreover, the Brahimi Report—prepared by a special committee on peacekeeping operations (chaired by Lakhdar Brahimi) and available for international consideration at the Millennium Summit of 2000—underscored Annan's view. Its authors recommended strengthening UN peacekeeping and encouraged a more robust and offensive posture in danger-ous and out-of-control situations in disintegrating states.[2]

Chapter VI½ Provisions

Peacekeeping operations are not explicitly mentioned in the Charter. Through the decades, Charter responsibilities given to the General Assembly, and particularly the Security Council and the secretary-general, have been interpreted as providing legal bases for UN peacekeeping. Because Chapter VI calls for the pacific settlement of disputes and Chapter VII authorizes the Security Council to decide what actions must be taken to effect a peaceful resolution to conflict, diplo-mats and scholars have, by fusing these two UN responsibilities, invoked the term *Chapter VI½* to describe the guiding principles for peacekeeping operations. Chapter VI½ does not actually exist. Thus, individuals who cite it implicitly recognize the informal amendment of the Charter to meet changing demands. By the early twenty-first century, UN "Blue Helmets" (i.e., UN peacekeepers) found themselves in various parts of the world helping to "nation build," acting as a trip wire between contending factions, monitoring elections, and providing needed daily assistance. We discuss peacekeeping operations and Chapter VI½ extensively in Chapter 6.

The Charter's original authors may not have foreseen these recent developments. For the most part, as discussed in Chapter 2, the founders saw the new United Nations as an association of sovereign nations set up to prevent war and to deal with international security issues. Still, the preamble indicates that the Charter is an agreement not among "governments" or "states," but among the "peoples" of the world, a notion that caused considerable debate in San Francisco in 1945. Less deliberation was directed to the remaining paragraphs of the preamble, which deal with saving the future world from the "scourge of war," emphasize human rights and the legiti-macy of treaties and international law, and promote social progress and better standards of liv-ing. Thus, intimations that the United Nations might expand its functions beyond those constrained by the Charter's concession to traditional state sovereignty were present from the start.

THE COLD WAR, EXPANDING MEMBERSHIP, AND THE CHARTER

As described in Chapter 2, the onset of the cold war affected the UN's workings in ways the in-stitution's founders did not always foresee. For example, the United Nations was often used as an instrument of the cold war rivalry rather than as the tool to resolve international problems. The Congo Crisis of the early 1960s and the Cuban Missile Crisis of 1962 (discussed in Chapter 2) are illustrative; both superpowers used the United Nations as a forum to promote their views rather than as a negotiating agency. Likewise, arms-limitation talks were substantive only when the two main nuclear powers conducted them, which meant that the United Nations was not the initiating organization for issues of arms limitation or disarmament.

Perhaps the most obvious impact of the cold war was on the Security Council, which had been expected to deal with all major international security matters. However, the Council waned as an active institution. It held 130 meetings during the late 1940s, but by 1949 only 5. Moreover, between 1945 and 1975 the Soviet Union used its veto power 114 times, begetting frequent dead-lock in the Council.[3] One consequence was to elevate the activities of the General Assembly. An early example was the Uniting for Peace Resolution, passed by the GA on November 3, 1950 (see Chapter 5 for details). Through the resolution, the assembly granted itself SC-like authority to discuss a threat to the peace, a breach of the peace, or an act of aggression, and to make recommendations for collective measures whenever "the Security Council, because of lack of una-nimity of the permanent members, fails to exercise its primary responsibility for the mainte-nance of international peace and security." This authority allowed the GA to circumvent the Soviet veto in the Security Council and to recommend the use of UN forces in the Korean War. The provision was used sparingly, and usually ineffectively, during the cold war—first regard-ing conflict in Korea in the early 1950s, then in the Suez Crisis and the Soviet intervention in Hungary, both in 1956, and finally with reference to Moscow's invasion of Afghanistan in 1980.

Membership

The cold war also influenced—and was influenced by—the changing **membership** in the United Nations. Beginning with 51 member states in 1945, the United Nations grew to 191 nations by 2005. This growth was the product of cold war politics, decolonization, and the desire for uni-versality, and it transformed the operations and relationships of the principal organs of the in-stitution from those contemplated by the founding states. It also significantly affected internal UN politics and the agenda of the world body.

New members are admitted by GA vote, on the recommendation of the Security Council. As the cold war deepened, the USSR and the United States, both veto-wielding members of the Security Council, blocked the admission of members associated with the other bloc. Only nine states of thirty-one applicants became members between 1946 and 1955. A large pro-American majority in the original UN membership allowed the United States to muster the needed votes in the Security Council to block Eastern European candidates that Washington saw as satellite Communist regimes. Moscow, in turn, used its veto forty-seven times prior to 1955 to prevent states friendly to the United States from being admitted. The deadlock was resolved in December 1955 with what was known as a "package deal," which admitted sixteen nations from both the Soviet and Western camps and thus kept the voting balance little changed.

Separate from cold war politics, rapid decolonization in the 1950s and 1960s placed pres-sure on the organization for enlargement. Membership grew from 76 at the end of 1955 to 110 in 1962. Almost all the new members came from the developing world. With their admission, virtually all membership requirements, other than statehood, were set aside. Many of the new members were geographically small and poor, and each often represented only a minute por-tion of the world's population. By the turn of the century, more than thirty members had pop-ulations of less than one million people. Among the smallest, Tuvalu, admitted in 2000, had a population of ten thousand, and Nauru, admitted in 1999, had eleven thousand. These states' ability to fulfill Charter obligations was suspect. The General Assembly, however, was willing to accept their applications if they maintained friendly relations with other states and fulfilled other international obligations that they had made. After 1955 only a few "partitioned" states were initially barred from membership—East and West Germany, North and South Korea, and North and South Vietnam. The Germanies were admitted separately in 1973, and a unified Vietnam gained membership in 1977.

The growth in membership, coupled with the principle of sovereign equality that awarded an equal vote to each member, produced a new majority in the General Assembly capable of passing sweeping resolutions but without the power or resources to fulfill new UN commitments. This majority also could, and did, shift the agenda of the world body from peace and security in-terests among the great powers to economic development concerns. The enlarged size of the world body also led to the formation of caucus groups, the expansion of membership in UN bod-ies like the Economic and Social Council, and the proliferation of programs and funds for activities promoted by the new states.

North-South Relations and the United Nations

The growth in membership, particularly from formerly colonized areas, highlighted socioeconomic differences within the United Nations. Diplomats and scholars referred to these differences as those between the "North" and the "South." The designations **North** and **South** to indicate economic and political differences are comparable to the terms *First World* and *Third World.* Typically, nations north of the equator are considered those that historically were in the forefront of economic and political modernization and benefited most by the Industrial Revolution. Also, colonial powers usually came from the Northern Hemisphere. Conversely, Third World nations and peoples are often located south of the equator, are economically underdeveloped, and are often the countries and areas colonized prior to the last half of the twentieth century. Within the United Nations, observers and participants use the terms *developed,* and *less developed* or *least developed* to denote differences between nations of the North and nations of the South, although the labels *First World* and *Third World* continue to be widely used by the general public. (The designations *North* and *South* have not always been precisely accurate in describing the complete configuration of the world's countries. Some developing countries are found north of the equator, and some developed nations in the south—Australia and New Zealand, for example.) During the cold war the Soviet Union and its allies in the Soviet bloc were sometimes placed in yet another category, then called the *Second World.* Many of these states are now alluded to as *economies in transition.*

Within the United Nations the idea of different interests and aims between the North and the South came to have procedural meaning. Particularly in the General Assembly and ECOSOC, caucus groups were formed to promote common interests and highlight common concerns for the so-called South. For instance, the *Group of 77* was originally organized as a caucus bloc of Third World nations at the 1964 UN Conference on Trade and Development. The Group of 77 held its first ministerial meeting in 1977, and, as of the turn of the century, it counted more than one hundred countries, most from the Southern Hemisphere, in its membership. Several of the countries of the South were also nonaligned during the cold war, joining neither Western alliances of northern states nor Soviet-inspired alliances, such as the Warsaw Pact. These countries, becoming the majority from the 1960s on, often acted together as the largest bloc in UN organs, frequently frustrating the more powerful nations of the North who had instigated the United Nations in the 1940s and who found forming their own caucus group, the West European and Other States bloc, necessary.

During the 1970s, and with less vigor in later years, the countries of the South attempted in the United Nations to create international measures to provide for a significant transfer of economic resources from the North to the South. The Group of 77 proposed the **New International Economic Order** at the 1974 special session of the General Assembly, seeking a drastic revision of global trading rules and processes to replace the Bretton Woods system described in Chapter 2. The Group of 77 sought more favorable terms of trade for primary commodities and urged a revaluation of trade that would have constituted a global redistribution of wealth. The proposal was based on the *theory of dependency,* which charged that industrialized nations had rigged the rules of international trade to keep developing nations permanently impoverished and "dependent" on developed nations for goods, support, and markets for their underpriced exports. Specifically, the Group of 77, in cooperation with the UN Conference on Trade and Development, advocated commodity agreements, the transfer of technology to the developing world, a generalized system of preferences on tariffs for poorer countries, the establishment of producer cartels to negotiate with importing countries, and increased financial aid from the developed North to the South. By the mid-1980s, however, because withholding production had little effect on most commodity prices and the key to development was foreign direct investment, developing nations modified their objectives and adopted more pragmatic goals. The most radical ideas—the development of an entirely new trading system and a global redistribution of wealth—were abandoned and replaced with calls for debt reduction and debt forgiveness.

National Liberation and the United Nations

Contributing to the North-South division in the United Nations was the phenomenon of "national liberation." **National liberation** refers to the efforts of a people—sometimes an ethnic group, sometimes a self-defined "nation"—to free itself from colonial control or from any kind of oppressive rule. Wars of national liberation, then, are a means of seeking independence from outside or repressive regimes. The American and French Revolutions have often been considered the first successful "national liberation movements" of modern history in that the first event liberated thirteen colonies from an external, imperial overlord and the French upheaval freed a "people" from an internal, authoritarian monarchy. In the post–World War II period, national liberation struggles became common in world politics and succeeded in establishing the independence of several former colonial possessions in Africa and in Asia. Examples spanned the second half of the twentieth century and included ancient civilizations such as India (gaining independence from the United Kingdom in 1947); former French colony Vietnam, where national liberation guerrillas fought first the French and then the Americans; and many other polities that became new states and were usually located in the geographic South. In the 1950s and 1960s, newly liberated nations joined the United Nations, becoming the majority of the UN's membership. As a rule, the new states became members of the Group of 77 as well.

The Palestine Liberation Organization (PLO), founded in 1964 and led by Yasser Arafat from 1967 into the twenty-first century, represented several characteristics of national liberation movements. It sought to resist the intrusion of the state of Israel into territories it believed belonged to the Palestinian people. In effect the PLO defined an Arab population as "Palestinian" by virtue of its existing in the geographic area of Palestine, it organized a political infrastructure and a military arm for guerrilla resistance, and it led a diplomatic effort to convince the world of the legitimate national aspirations of the Palestinians. It signed international agreements and succeeded in receiving considerable support in the United Nations—particularly from nations recently successful in their own national liberation efforts—achieving observer status in the General Assembly in 1974.

The Non-Aligned Movement and the United Nations

With the expanding membership during the cold war, the **Non-Aligned Movement** became the most significant caucus group in the UN System. It was initiated at a summit conference in Belgrade, Yugoslavia, in 1961 so that newly independent former colonies could resist cold war pressures to affiliate with either of the two superpowers. Its summits continue to be held every three years, and foreign ministers meet in the interim. These nonaligned states have been held together informally and have included most of the Group of 77 countries. The United Nations became the main site of their diplomacy, their contact with other nations, and their involvement in global affairs. The movement transcended continental regional blocs, and the number and diversity of its member nations—in size, economies, governments, and ideologies—required it to adopt broad policies and concentrate on global issues. While seeking to balance itself between the East and West blocs, it also opposed colonialism and apartheid, supported the Palestinian cause, and called for development assistance, all of which underscored important shifts in the UN's emphases during the cold war. Because of the overlap in policy preference and the similarity of membership in the Group of 77 and the Non-Aligned Movement, the distinction between the two became blurred. As of 2004 the Non-Aligned Movement represented 105 member states and the PLO. Although critics often contended that no longer did anyone exist to be nonaligned with, given the end of the cold war, the movement grew stronger as the twentieth century came to a close. By emphasizing global rather than bilateral negotiations, the Non-Aligned Movement has tried to enhance the UN's role in international affairs.

EVOLUTION OF INTERNATIONAL LAW

In Chapter 4 the International Court of Justice (see Appendix C) is covered in detail. At this point we need note only that the court—and the progression of international law[4] that is part of the court's history—like the cold war, the emergence of Third World countries, and the specific amendments of the Charter, has rendered the UN's environment different, and in some respects more expansive, from what it was in 1945.

The Statute of the International Court of Justice, by containing the modern definition of *international law* (Article 38), codified world legal standards in the post–World War II era. Study of the United Nations (especially what we term the "new United Nations") requires at this stage of our text a recounting of the evolution of international law so that you can grasp the central connection between international law and the United Nations.

The rules and norms regulating activities between and among nation-states—often called *the law of nations*—was, according to tradition, termed *international law* by the English philosopher Jeremy Bentham (1748–1832). Bentham's term became preferred by the middle of the twentieth century, although it was often expanded to *public international law* to contrast it with *private international law* (also called the *conflict of laws*), which involves regulating private matters affected by more than one legal jurisdiction. By the beginning of the twenty-first century, in part because of the quickening developments in the international community, and particularly because of activities within the UN System, the province of international law expanded, in some instances including areas of jurisdiction once thought to be outside its realm. For example, the late twentieth century witnessed a development in the field of international economic law that is a mix of public and private. The expansion can also be seen in the recent war crimes tribunals in which individuals have been accused of violating human rights, even within their own country. Nonetheless, the new applicability of international law has not resulted in any comparable supranational means of enforcement. Whereas law within nations is enforced by means of what might be called the *police function* of the state, no such mechanism exists in an international community composed of sovereign nations.

Article 38 of the Statute of the ICJ names the sources of international law as international conventions, international custom, general principles of law recognized by civilized nations, judicial decisions, and teachings of the most qualified publicists on the topic. Of these, ratified international conventions and treaties carry the most weight. Some legal experts also consider arbitration awards as precedents for developing law in the international arena. International law is usually considered part of national or municipal law. For example, Article 6, paragraph 2, of the U.S. Constitution declares the following:

> All treaties made, or which shall be made, under the authority of the United States, shall be the supreme law of the land; and the Judges in every State shall be bound thereby, anything in the Constitution or laws of any State to the contrary notwithstanding.

Sometimes we (the current generation) think we have originated all the most progressive human procedures. However, the development of formal relations between and among nations, empires, and peoples has been a human activity since the millennia before the common era. In fact, scholars have seen a pattern in world history of cross-cultural intercourse among political elites the world over that has led to what might be called *international affairs* or even *international law*. Basic principles and precedents emerged as different political communities sought to impose order on their mutual relations and to resolve disagreements without resorting to force, except as those principles might allow or require it.

The modern concept of **international law** emerged at the end of the Middle Ages in European history. Typically, international law regulated diplomatic practices (i.e., protection of diplomatic personnel, rules of seniority among ambassadors to a specific country, and related diplomatic matters), maritime intercourse, restrictions on weapons, and the commencement and conduct of war among princely states. In 1625 the Dutch jurist **Hugo Grotius** (1583–1645) published his *De jure belli ac pacis (Concerning the Law of War and Peace)*, the first comprehensive text of international rules. His views were frequently studied and on occasion applied in international interactions. One point worth noting is that Grotius and many early publicists on international law—including Dutchman Cornelius van Bynkershoek (1673–1743), German philosopher Christian von Wolff (1679–1754), Swiss jurist Emmerich de Vattel (1714–1767), and German Georg Friedrich von Martens (1756–1821)—highlighted the sovereignty and legal equality of states, principles later placed in the UN Charter (Article 2, paragraph 1). The concept of the sovereign state was enshrined in the 1648 Treaty of Westphalia, which prohibited interference by outside powers in a state's internal affairs. In the Westphalian system, states took on obligations in the international community only by their voluntary commitments, which were made largely through treaties. By the late eighteenth century, the use of treaty agreements had advanced the course of international law.

Grotius developed many of his concepts of modern international law from an empirical study of what nations actually did in his time. However, the Dutch scholar also asserted that international law was a reflection of the law of nature based on reason. This assertion divorced his view from earlier theological conceptions of higher law. Accordingly, Grotius's 1625 work invigorated an already-existing "naturalist" school of international law. In the works of Francisco Vitoria (1480–1546), Father Suarez (1548–1617), and Samuel Pufendorf (1632–1694), these naturalists argued that international law should codify not simply what states do, but rather what states *should* do to conform to the principles of justice. The natural law tradition these scholars espoused remained a secondary thread of international law until the 1940s, when the horror of the Nazi era produced a new interest in using international law to defend human rights, protect values even if states had not officially agreed to them in treaties, and punish states for "crimes against humanity." In this spirit, the preamble of the UN Charter "reaffirm[ed] faith in fundamental human rights, in the dignity and worth of the human person, [and] in the equal rights of men and women."

The period of the Napoleonic Wars in the early nineteenth century witnessed a disregard for the law of nations. The Congress of Vienna (1814–1815), which concluded these wars, sought the restoration of traditional rules of diplomacy and introduced newer and more standardized legal principles, such as respect for the freedom of navigation on international waterways and more precise classification for and protection of diplomatic personnel. What had been "customary" international law—accepted practice—was clarified in legally binding international agreements. These changes in thought marked the beginning of the long era of "legal positivism." The Declaration of Paris (1856) following the Crimean War represented the first major attempt to codify the rules of maritime warfare and served as the accepted rule of law on the high seas until it became infeasible with the introduction of submarines in World War I. As the century proceeded, multilateral agreements were negotiated that established international rules for weights and measures, trademarks, copyrights, patents, and other matters for which legal uniformity was desirable. New technologies resulted in international conferences that established the International Telegraph Union (at Paris in 1865) and the Universal Postal Union (at Berne, Switzerland, in 1874). In the post–World War II period, these early unions became UN specialized agencies: the International Telecommunications Union and the Universal Postal Union.

Meanwhile, arbitration became fashionable as a means of settling disputes. With the Jay Treaty of 1794, the United States and Great Britain initiated the practice of setting up mixed commissions to settle disagreements unyielding to normal diplomacy. The post–U.S. Civil War *Alabama claims* arbitration in 1872 between the United Kingdom and the United States marked a decisive phase in the arbitration movement that culminated with the establishment of the Permanent Court of Arbitration at The Hague Conference of 1899. Subsequently, The Hague Conference of 1907 expanded rules governing arbitral procedures. Both Hague Conferences also issued a number of declarations and conventions dealing with the laws of war, including those banning aerial bombardment, submarine mines, and poison gas. In the meantime, Pan-American Congresses in the Western Hemisphere established several continentwide diplomatic practices. The onset of World War I brought this progress to a halt, however. Many provisions of international law were violated, and new problems arose (e.g., submarine warfare and the use of chemical weapons) for which existing standards of international behavior were inadequate.

The creation of the League of Nations and the Permanent Court of International Justice following the war were attempts to create multinational institutions that could subject disputes among nations to the rule of law. The League represented the first attempt in history to maintain a permanent organization committed to developing and codifying international law. League conferences brought forth more than 120 international understandings covering a range of subjects. Although many of these understandings fell short of full ratification, they became a model for the future United Nations, and some—such as those dealing with the control of narcotics, traffic in persons, economic statistics, and slavery—remained in force through UN amendments or further treaty action. Moreover, the UN secretary-general's office became responsible for the depository of extant League documents.

The rise of Fascism and Nazism in Europe and of militarism in Japan and then the collapse of international order in the 1930s wrought discredit to the effectiveness of international law and agreements, and destroyed the League of Nations. The advent of World War II tainted international law with the darkest of hues.

Yet, phoenixlike, out of the war rose the United Nations and the new International Court of Justice. In fact, during the post–World War II period, international law underwent considerable maturation. Although this momentum clearly did not and could not promise a world utopia, the crafting of such an international framework represented an extraordinary human achievement, and, from 1945 on, the United Nations was at the heart of these developments.

Since the end of World War II, differing opinions have been expressed about exactly what international law is and how it is to be executed. One straightforward view is that all nations should obey international law, just as individuals should obey domestic (or municipal) law. Yet, some lofty thinkers—Samuel Pufendorf and Thomas Hobbes in the seventeenth century, John Austin in the nineteenth, and Henry Kissinger in the twentieth—have challenged even the notion of an international "law," because no legitimate enforcer exists. Sociologists have emphasized the

The International Court of Justice (ICJ) in The Hague, The Netherlands. (UN/DPI Photo by A. Brizzi. Reproduced by permission from the United Nations.)

behavior of states rather than overarching principle and thus have argued that international law cannot shape international politics but merely adjust to it. Marxists have regarded international law as only an instrument of class oppression; Chinese scholars, whether or not followers of Mao Zedong, have described international law as a set of platitudes that have historically been ruinous to non-Western cultures. Many citizens of Third World nations have believed themselves victimized by Euro-centered notions of international law. Feminists have argued that "the rules of international law privilege men," that women are "marginalized," and that international law is "a thoroughly gendered system";[5] and postmodernists—emphasizing relativism, difference, and the problematic nature of language itself—have questioned any "universalist" assumption of a fundamental international law deriving from a narrow, elitist political tradition in the Western First World. Naturally, a common commitment to a single conception of legal principles is less likely when the core interests of one nation diverge from those of other nations. Yet, in practice, international law is widely recognized and most nations have participated in its evolution. The penalties for failing to comply, although less severe than in national cases, and often unenforceable, are economic sanctions, the constraint of public opinion, intervention by third states, international condemnation (e.g., by means of UN resolutions), and, as a last resort, war.

The wider reach of international law in the early twenty-first century is due in no small part to the activities of UN-related organizations. The International Court of Justice, which replaced the Permanent Court of International Justice after World War II and is popularly known as the *World Court*, has made modest but significant contributions to the development of international law. The ICJ has done so through judgments and advisory opinions that have affected maritime law, questions of diplomatic immunity, the legitimacy of mandates under the League of Nations, the competence of the United Nations, the jurisdiction of UN principal organs, and other matters. By virtue of Article 13, paragraph 1, of the Charter, the General Assembly acquired the obligation to initiate studies and make recommendations for "encouraging the progressive development of international law and its codification." In 1947 the assembly gave this Charter function to the International Law Commission, an auxiliary, autonomous organ of the assembly, which began the slow process of codification. The General Assembly Sixth Committee works closely with the International Law Commission; it reviews the work of the UN Commission on International Trade Law (UNCITRAL), negotiates relevant treaties and agreements to submit to the General Assembly Plenary (the Sixth Committee spent thirty years in intricate negotiations to determine an internationally acceptable definition of *aggression*), and deals with reports from all UN bodies on legal matters. UNCITRAL, created by the General Assembly in 1966, develops conventions, rules, and legal guides to harmonize international trade law. The UN Office of Legal Affairs, initiated in 1946, serves the Secretariat and provides legal advice to the secretary-general. The World Intellectual Property Organization (WIPO), established in 1970, promotes the protection of intellectual property worldwide, and the International Maritime Organization (IMO), begun in 1959, is the only UN agency solely involved with issues of shipping safety and environmentally sound oceans. The UN's efforts to internationalize outer space and bring it into the realm of recognized international law resulted in the 1966 Treaty on Principles Governing the Activities of States in the Exploration and Use of Outer Space, including the Moon and Other Celestial Bodies (Outer Space Treaty) and the 1979 Agreement Governing Activities of States on the Moon and Other Celestial Bodies (the so-called Moon Agreement). The Committee on the Peaceful Uses of Outer Space, set up by the General Assembly in 1959 to review and encourage international cooperation, has adopted several additional treaties and conventions to regulate outer space, and in 1974 the committee set up the Office for Outer Space Affairs, which maintains a registry of space objects.

Other important areas of developing international law that are less directly connected with the United Nations derived from various arms agreements (beginning with the Limited Test Ban Treaty of 1963), from the internationalization of Antarctica (1959), and from a number of agreements regarding international economic and financial relations. The General Agreement on Tariffs and Trade (GATT), a negotiating regime initiated in 1948 to encourage lowering trade barriers around the world, became the World Trade Organization (WTO) in 1995. GATT/WTO, along with related organizations (the International Monetary Fund and the World Bank) founded at the Bretton Woods Conference (the UN Monetary and Financial Conference) in 1944, sought to bring harmony and common rules to world trade and finance. The Bretton Woods institutions and the WTO became controversial in the late 1990s. These controversies are covered in Chapter 4.

One of the most comprehensive agreements affecting the development of international law was the UN Convention on the Law of the Sea (UNCLOS), which established a framework to deal with questions of sovereignty, jurisdiction, use, and national rights and obligations in ocean areas. The convention was opened for signature in 1982 and entered into force in 1994.

In addition, the United Nations has been involved in the growth of international environmental law. Usually the United Nations Environment Programme administers the many treaties brokered by the United Nations, including agreements on desertification, biological diversity, movement of hazardous wastes, protection of the ozone layer, and control of acid rain. The Kyoto

Protocol, negotiated at a UN conference in 1997, sets standards for states to use to curtail greenhouse emissions and thus combat global warming. In 2001 the protocol was renegotiated to meet some nations' concerns, and in 2002 the European Union and China ratified it. Following Russia's ratification, the protocol went into effect in spring 2005 (the United States has refused to ratify it).

Undoubtedly the most celebrated UN contribution to the creation of new international law is in the broad area of human rights. The contemporary development of international law as an expression of a higher law that governs all human activity found its first modern expression in the international war crimes trials following World War II at Nuremberg and for Japanese enemies in Tokyo. Nothing like the trials had happened before and nothing like them took place again until the late twentieth century. Captured German and Japanese leaders were not charged with violating any particular treaty commitment, or even with violating their own domestic laws. Rather, they were tried, convicted, and punished for crimes against humanity. Following the trials, with time, an abundance of international agreements and rules developed that seemed to proscribe the atrocities classified as human rights violations. In 1946 the General Assembly affirmed "the principles of international law recognized by the Charter of the Nuremberg Tribunal and the judgment of the Tribunal." At the same time, the assembly declared, "Genocide is a crime under international law," and in 1948 the GA approved the Genocide Convention (Convention on the Prevention and Punishment of the Crime of Genocide).

In 1946 ECOSOC established the UN Commission on Human Rights, which Eleanor Roosevelt chaired. This commission was given a mandate to compose a Universal Declaration of Human Rights. Working with a group of celebrated international legal minds from various cultures, Mrs. Roosevelt discovered that conceptualizing rights and fleshing out international law were multicultural, even multicivilizational, endeavors. Peng-chung Chang, a Chinese philosopher, brought an Asian and Confucianist perspective to the commission's discussions; Charles Habib Malik, a view from the Arab Middle East; Hernán Santa Cruz, from Chile, a Latin American political left perspective; and Hansa Mehta, an Indian outlook and an insistence that women's equality be clearly articulated. René Cassin, a French Jew, had a unique outlook, colored by the most recent, and appalling, example of human rights violations. When in late 1948 the General Assembly passed the Universal Declaration without a dissenting vote, no longer could anyone assert without challenge the notion that rights and the practice of international law were strictly Western conceits. René Cassin noted an extremely significant, if subtle, breakthrough in his 1968 acceptance speech upon receiving the Nobel Peace Prize: After the Universal Declaration, nations still retained jurisdiction over their citizens, he said, but it would "no longer be exclusive."[6] From the seventeenth century to 1948, absolute state sovereignty had been the underpinning of international law. With the ascension of the primacy of rights, international law entered a new, uncertain phase. Combined with the declaration, the International Covenant on Economic, Social and Cultural Rights, and the International Covenant on Civil and Political Rights—both opened for signature in 1966 and both brought into force in 1976—made up the *International Bill of Human Rights.*

UN organs passed other conventions and declarations announcing an assortment of human rights. Among these new rights were those of the child, indigenous people, women, refugees, stateless persons, migrant workers, and the disabled. The United Nations also defined rights to development, employment, and family life. In the summer of 1993, more than 170 nations met in Vienna and adopted a sweeping declaration affirming the principle that "all human rights are universal" and that "it is the duty of states, regardless of their political, economic and cultural systems, to promote and protect all human rights and fundamental freedoms." Add to this the establishment of war crimes tribunals (for Rwanda and the former Yugoslavia), which at the turn of the century were prosecuting individuals for crimes against humanity *in their own countries,* and the adoption in Rome in 1998 of a statute calling for an International Criminal Court to try individuals for genocide, crimes against humanity, war crimes, and aggression, and the implication Cassin discerned comes into fuller relief. As the third millennium began, international law was on a trajectory far beyond anything imaginable at its start.

FINANCIAL CRISIS AND THE IMPETUS FOR REFORM

The expansion of international law and human rights (as well as the UN's response to the demands of its new members in the developing world) is a reflection of the institution's continuing evolution. From the moment of the UN's creation, many governments have noted flaws in its structure and procedures and have recommended changes to make the organization more effective in the face of new challenges. Even at the founding San Francisco Conference, many delegates sought powers for the world body and greater participation for small states than the Big Three contemplated or the Dumbarton Oaks proposals spelled out. Acceptance of the Charter by several original members was predicated on their ability either under the amendment process or through normal diplomatic interchange within the United Nations to pursue future alterations in a decidedly imperfect organization. As you read previously in this chapter, the membership growth in the United Nations and the strains of the cold war only aggravated the weaknesses in the Charter, compelling the major powers, the secretary-general, and the General Assembly to make both formal and informal changes in how the United Nations operated. During the first twenty-five years, these changes included the expansion of membership of both the Security Council and ECOSOC. Such changes also included informal "amendments," like the Uniting for Peace Resolution and the creation of peacekeeping. Out of this last innovation—peacekeeping—a financial crisis emerged during the 1950s and 1960s that dramatically worsened during the ensuing thirty years and contributed to the most sweeping UN reforms in its history.

Responding to the British, French, and Israeli 1956 invasion of the Suez Canal, the General Assembly created the UN Emergency Force (UNEF)—the UN's first peacekeeping operation. The assembly, on the recommendation of Secretary-General Dag Hammarskjöld, determined that UNEF's costs were "expenses of the Organization" as defined by the UN Charter. Therefore, all members were required to pay their assessed share of the expenses. The Soviet Union, Eastern European states, and Arab governments balked at paying for the operation. They argued that these costs should be charged to the "aggressors."

The financial situation was aggravated further in the early 1960s by the huge expenditures required to deploy a UN force in the Congo. The General Assembly endorsed Hammarskjöld's initiative to put a UN operation into the midst of the Congolese civil war and use the force to protect and extend the authority of the central government. At its height, the UN effort cost more than the entire remaining budget of the world body. Making matters worse, not only the Soviet Union, but also France refused to pay for the operation. These states asserted that since the Security Council had not authorized the operation under Chapter VII of the Charter, the United Nations could not mandate assessments for it. Even a 1962 advisory opinion by the International Court of Justice upholding the General Assembly's position could not move the delinquent governments to meet their financial obligations to the organization.

Unable to raise the requisite funds through the normal budgeting process, the United Nations turned to unorthodox financing methods. The General Assembly authorized the sale of $169 million in bonds, effectively borrowing against future assessment income. The United Nations also postponed payment to countries that contributed troops and matériel to the Congolese and subsequent peacekeeping operations, in effect making these governments pay UN costs out of their national treasuries. In 1965 the assembly established a special account for sought-after voluntary contributions as a cushion against future unexpected expenses. In other words, the United Nations went hat in hand to its largest contributors, particularly the United States, to try to keep the organization financially solvent.

These measures were not popular with many governments that opposed UN actions on policy grounds. For example, the USSR, which saw the Congolese operation and Hammarskjöld's actions as little more than an extension of U.S. cold war foreign policy, refused to participate in any of these financing schemes. Other countries prorated their contributions or targeted their payments to avoid paying for UN activities with which they disagreed. These tactics became common practice and by the end of the century nearly one-third of the UN membership had not paid its assessments in full for the regular budget, amounting to $244.2 million.

Article 19 of the UN Charter states the following:

> A Member of the United Nations which is in arrears in the payment of its financial contributions to the Organization shall have no vote in the General Assembly if the amount of its arrears equals or exceeds the amount of the contributions due from it for the preceding two full years.

As the UN's deficit mounted during the Congo operation, the United States attempted to force the payment issue by threatening to invoke Article 19 against the Soviet Union. When the USSR said it would withdraw from the United Nations if it lost its vote in the General Assembly, the United States relented. In announcing his government's decision in 1965 to drop the matter, U.S. permanent representative Arthur Goldberg said.[7]

> If any member can insist on making an exception to the principle of collective financial responsibility with respect to certain activities of the United Nations, . . . the United States reserves the same option to make exceptions if, in our view, strong and compelling reasons exist to do so.

Known as the **Goldberg Reservation,** this statement appeared at the time to be just an expression of disgust and an admission of defeat, for the alternative to achieving full payment by all states in the United Nations was increased contributions by the United States. By the end of Lyndon Johnson's term as president of the United States, the U.S. government was paying nearly one-third of all UN bills. However, following the 1980 election of President Ronald Reagan, Washington willingly exercised the Goldberg Reservation, which produced an extraordinary financial crisis.

THE CONTINUING BUDGET CRISIS

The United Nations is a membership organization in which each member state pays a certain percentage of the budget. From the beginning, the General Assembly, which approves the scale of assessment triennially, has based the amount each nation is expected to contribute on its "capacity to pay." Therefore, the rich developed states pay a much larger percentage of the budget than developing countries do, although the desperate circumstances of the poorest countries often means that even the minimal contribution demanded of these states amounts to a high per capita payment and is often beyond the means of the government. Nearly all the nations that have lost their votes in the General Assembly at one time or another under Article 19 were among the poorest states with the lowest-percentage assessments. For example, in 2002 twenty nations, including Afghanistan, Kyrgyzstan, Tajikistan, Uzbekistan, Vanuatu, Dominica, and Haiti, fell so far behind in their payments that they were stripped of their vote for the year.[8] Also among the number were twelve nations from sub-Saharan Africa. Four additional states—Burundi, Comoros,

Moldova, and Georgia—gained a reprieve despite their not making their assessment contributions. These nonpayments occurred even though in some cases the assessment was as little as forty-six hundred dollars.[9]

To the extent that a country's share of world income determined the "capacity to pay," the United States would have had to pay 50 percent of UN expenses during the organization's early years. This situation would have been politically untenable for Americans, thus the "ceiling" set for any contributor was 40 percent of the budget. By the early 1970s the United States was paying approximately one-third of UN expenses but demanding that this amount be reduced. In 1973 the ceiling was set at 25 percent, at U.S. request, which remained the American assessment until radical revisions in the budgeting and assessment process occurred at the close of the century.

The growing unwillingness of the United States to pay its share of the budget as a result of consternation with UN policies or with specific UN agencies, coupled with the nonpayment of dues by other states, left the United Nations in a perennial funds shortfall. This deficit was particularly true in its peacekeeping budget, which along with the "regular" budget and the international criminal tribunals budget, compose the organization's expenses for which members have an obligation to pay. Even in the aftermath of the terrorist attacks of September 11, 2001, the United States moved slowly to make up its payments to these various budgets, owing in November of that year $265 million to the regular budget, $800 million to peacekeeping, and $14.6 million to the tribunals account.[10] The United States was not alone in its selective payments. Half the debt owed was held by members other than the United States. Between 1993 and 2004 the shortfall between actual payments and assessed contributions from all countries ranged between $200 million and $600 million annually.

Washington also continued to withhold funds from specialized agencies with which it disagreed, and it threatened other groups if they cooperated with those agencies. In March 2002 the Bush administration withheld thirty-four million dollars from the UN Population Fund (UNFPA) and additional funding in 2003 because the White House believed UNFPA's policies promoted abortion: a claim the agency denied. Then, in 2004, the United States pressured the UN Children's Fund (UNICEF) and the World Health Organization (WHO) to limit cooperation with UNFPA or have their financing cut. The State Department also cut financing to Marie Stopes International, a British nongovernmental organization that supports AIDS programs, because it worked with the Population Fund in China.[11] At the beginning of the new millennium, the UN System remained financially captive to its members' political and ideological goals, particularly those of the United States. By definition, international organizations are the creatures of the states that establish and maintain them. Thus, they cannot move far beyond their financiers' agendas.

Scale of Assessment and the Budget Process

The proposed UN budget for 2004–2005 was $2.92 billion, which reflected the first increase in nearly a decade (about $47 million more than a series of preceding no-growth budgets). Allocating required contributions would prove difficult given another decrease in the U.S. contribution, the large number of states with no realistic capacity to pay, and the General Assembly's decision to establish an additional $1.05 billion fund for capital repairs to UN headquarters in New York. The criterion of "capacity to pay" is subject to interpretation, debate, and political controversy. The General Assembly's Fifth Committee, supported by the Committee on Contributions and by the Advisory Committee on Administrative and Budgetary Questions (ACABQ), determines both the UN budget and the assessment each country contributes toward the budget.

The **scale of assessment** used to calculate the percentage of the budget each member state is to pay uses "ceilings" and "floors" above and below which no nation's dues may be set. These ceilings and floors were set in recognition that factors other than simply the capacity to pay are part of the triennial allocation of budget shares. The minimum assessment was initially .04 percent. It was lowered to .02 percent in 1973, .01 percent in 1978, and .001 percent in 1997. This downward shift has resulted from recognition of the economic challenges confronting the least developed and low-income states. The consequence is that the major industrialized nations pay the preponderance of the UN budget, particularly its peacekeeping budget. In December 2000 the U.S. contribution was lowered from 25 percent to 22 percent of the regular budget and from 31 percent to 27 percent of the peacekeeping budget, which effectively set the ceiling for the largest contributor. As of 2004, after the United States, Japan paid 19.5 percent of the UN budget; Germany, 9.8 percent; France, 6.5 percent; and Great Britain, 5.5 percent.

On the basis of each country's share of world income, a nation's contribution to the UN budget is "discounted" to account for the poverty level in the country. Thus, although two states may have the same share of world income, one will pay far less as a result of a per capita income that is considerably less than that of the other member state. A "scheme of limits" also arbitrarily prevents a state's assessment from rising or falling precipitously when its share of world income dramatically changes. This scheme sometimes benefits states that experience significant economic improvement, but it can also injure the same states when economic conditions worsen. For example, the oil-producing nations of the Middle East argued for this system when recognition of their increasing share of world revenues from oil sales would have driven their share of UN assessments higher, but then they found themselves with excessive payments when oil prices plummeted.

The upshot of these artificial restraints on the capacity to pay has been a financially strapped United Nations and many nations unhappy with the amounts they are required to pay for UN operations. Not only the United States, but also Japan and other large contributors have complained about their assessments. In 2004 Japan announced that it intended to cut its voluntary contribution to a number of UN agencies, including the UN Development Programme (UNDP), the UN Population Fund (UNFPA), and the UN Children's Fund (UNICEF).[12] A year earlier Japan threatened to cut its contribution to UN peacekeeping and UN regular operations by as much as 25 percent.[13] These cuts would have a dramatic impact on the United Nations because Japan's contribution amounted to more than that of Germany, France, Russia, and Great Britain combined. Within the UNDP and UNFPA budgets, Japan accounted for more than 15 percent and 11 percent of resources, respectively.

Japanese objection to its UN dues level was driven in part by the United States' ability to cut its contribution while Japan's rose. In 1994 Japan paid only 12.5 percent of the budget while the United States paid 25 percent. The U.S. diminution to 22 percent in 2000 coupled with a 19.5 percent assessment for Japan irked Japanese lawmakers at a time when Japan's economy accounted for 14.4 percent of the world's gross domestic product (compared with the United States' 30.3 percent share) and when Japan, under U.S. pressure, had forgiven sizable Iraqi loans owed to Tokyo. Japan was also unhappy that, despite long-standing commitments from major powers, it had not been able to secure a permanent seat on the Security Council, nor had it achieved what it considered "fair representation" in appointments to Secretariat positions.

The Japanese recalcitrance to pay its assessed dues demonstrated the financial frailty of the United Nations, dependent at all times on the economic largesse of its most important members. The financial crisis that set in during the 1960s had not been resolved by the new millennium, which limited the UN's ability to fulfill its commitments. In 2004, for example,

Secretary-General Kofi Annan worried aloud whether the UN's international tribunals would be able to even continue their work.[14] In fact, they had to borrow money from the peacekeeping budget to stay afloat. The United Nations regularly had to shift funds from one account to another to pay operating expenses. It also had to turn to outside donors—countries that were willing to make additional voluntary contributions, such as Canada, or private contributors, such as media mogul Ted Turner and Microsoft's Bill Gates—for funds to cover shortfalls or to pay for planned humanitarian programs.

The irony of the situation was that, given that in the 1960s the United States had led the effort to force the Soviet Union and others to pay their ascribed UN dues, the U.S. debt owed to the United Nations during the last two decades of the century—not the debt of Japan or the many other noncontributors—was the factor that most severely weakened the United Nations. By the close of the millennium, the United States, always the UN's largest creditor, had become its biggest debtor, owing the organization in excess of one billion dollars. The United States' unwillingness to pay generated questions about the survivability of the world organization.

U.S. Nonpayment of UN Dues and the Demand for Reforms: Is the United Nations Worth It?

Although broad support existed in the United States for the United Nations when it was founded, even then some political and foreign policy leaders believed that the organization provided little benefit to U.S. interests in the world and that it was based on a fundamental misconception of international politics. "Realists" like President Truman's secretary of state, Dean Acheson, rejected the vaunted merits of this Wilsonian edifice. One of the so-called Wise Men who constructed U.S. cold war policy after World War II, Acheson argued that the United Nations at best was a "modest aid to diplomacy" and that its Charter was "impracticable." He wrote of the latter that its "presentation to the American people as holy writ and with the evangelical enthusiasm of a major advertising campaign . . . raised hopes that could only lead to bitter disappointment."[15]

Acheson was a representative of an honored tradition known as *realism*. Other great figures in U.S. history have shared this perspective on the world, including John Quincy Adams, Theodore Roosevelt, Richard Nixon, and Henry Kissinger. This perspective is not a product of strictly American thought. In fact, as we noted in Chapter 2, both Joseph Stalin and Winston Churchill were "realists," so clearly this approach toward international politics can be found in most governments of the world. The realist believes a country acts in the world to protect its national interests. **Realism** emphasizes geopolitics, the acquisition of power, and the exercise of influence in the world community primarily to safeguard the state's sovereignty and freedom of action. As we noted in the Introduction, the realist claims to look at the world "as it really is" and to "calculate" policy on the basis of that analysis. For the realist, placing your hope and a country's fate in the promise of permanent international cooperation is usually considered folly.

Neither the League of Nations nor the United Nations was born out of the realist tradition. In the end they were the products of liberal internationalism and idealism. Presidents Wilson, Truman, and Carter reflected these traditions. **Idealism** is in some ways primarily, but not exclusively, a U.S. doctrine, built on the belief that universal values will ultimately triumph over power and interest. The idealist seeks a moral world based on self-evident virtues. Idealists posit that only in a world built on justice, law, cooperation, and democratic principles can humankind find peace, stability, and prosperity. U.S. idealists have sought these goals either unilaterally—Presidents Ronald Reagan and George W. Bush are good examples of leaders who adopted this approach—or in cooperation with a wide array of states. Idealism, when coupled with liberal multilateralism, denigrates the value of force and traditional diplomacy, substituting for them debate, the rule of law, the weight of public opinion, judicial proceedings, and global democratic institutions. Idealists tend to believe that the world need not be "as it is," but can be better in moral and absolute terms.

The UN's creation was part of the idealist and multilateralist traditions, and as such has found critics among U.S. realists, geopolitical advocates, and unilateral idealists since its founding. Their voices, however, were in the minority and limited in their impact on U.S. policy toward the United Nations until the early 1970s. Americans' "bitter disappointment" with the United Nations of which Dean Acheson prophesied emerged with the anti-U.S. tilt of the UN General Assembly in that era. The assembly's seating of the People's Republic of China (1971) and simultaneous removal of Taiwan (a U.S. ally), plus its shift to a decidedly pro-Palestinian posture in the Arab-Israeli standoff, undermined public support for the world organization. U.S. politicians asked aloud whether continuing to pay so many of the UN's bills made sense since the new Third World majority was using the platform of UN bodies to denounce Washington's policies and support friends of the Soviet Union. The Nixon administration (1969–1974), given its geopolitical outlook on world affairs, did little to dampen public hostility toward the organization.

The 1981 arrival of Ronald Reagan in the White House meant an even harsher approach to financial support of the United Nations. In the body politic, Reagan's conservative wing of the Republican Party had been the strongest critic of the United Nations. Under Reagan this philosophy translated into the administration's refusal to pay its assessments.

During Reagan's first term, the Heritage Foundation, a Washington-based conservative think tank, published an anthology entitled *A World Without a U.N.*[16] Its authors urged the president to rethink U.S. membership in the United Nations. They made the radical argument that U.S. interests could best be served by leaving the world body. This sentiment seemed reflective of the administration's general disdain toward the United Nations. The author of the foreword of the book was Charles M. Lichenstein, a former alternate U.S. representative to the United Nations, who, after sitting through a UN committee meeting in September 1983 at which several Third World delegates berated U.S. policy, advised the assembled diplomats to "seriously consider removing themselves and this organization from the soil of the United States." He continued, "We will put no impediment in your way and we will be at dockside bidding you a fond farewell as you set off into the sunset."[17] Other Reagan appointees joined the anti-UN campaign. Secretary of State Alexander Haig called the world body "with its vociferous anticolonialist coalition of Third World and Marxist members . . . ineffective."[18] Even the U.S. permanent representative Jeane Kirkpatrick, took an adversarial approach at the United Nations. Among the many speeches she gave as UN ambassador were those with the titles "Standing Alone" and "The Problem of the United Nations."[19] The president himself evaluated the United Nations as an institution that had diverged from the values and ideals that originally motivated its founders and was now "too often fraught with strife, division, and conflict."[20] However, his critics cited the president's UN policy as one of the sources of this strife and division.

Disillusioned with the "politicized" character of the UN Educational, Scientific and Cultural Organization (UNESCO), the administration withdrew its membership and canceled funding for the specialized agency. In 1985, twenty years after U.S. ambassador Goldberg suggested that the United States would exercise its right to halt payments to the United Nations if it believed its interests required the action, President Reagan signed congressional legislation unilaterally reducing the U.S. contribution to the UN regular budget from 25 percent to 20 percent and limiting its payments for peacekeeping operations until institutional reforms were made. The

Goldberg Reservation was reinforced with the *Kassebaum Amendment* (named for Kansas senator Nancy Kassebaum), which cut U.S. payments to UN organs until their staffs were reduced significantly and until these organs made revisions to their charters to allow weighted representation based on the size of the members' financial contributions. These actions led to a growing U.S. debt owed to the United Nations that by 2000 left the United States on the verge of losing its vote in the General Assembly. Only a last-minute compromise between Washington and the United Nations led to a payment of U.S. arrearages in 2001. The U.S. payment was made possible by the most extensive reform program in UN history.

UN REFORM

The departure of the United States and its funds from UNESCO produced a change in leadership at the agency and the introduction of a reformed system for staff appointments and promotions. The agency shifted resources to field operations more compatible with U.S. interests. Many delegations decried UNESCO's reaction as an inappropriate concession to the world's most important power. However, by 1993 the new Clinton administration was willing to tell Secretary-General Boutros Boutros-Ghali that "in principle" the United States would soon be willing to return to the agency. The lesson was not lost on Boutros-Ghali. The UNESCO episode was a harbinger of future change in the organization. U.S. financing was so critical to UN survival that reforms demanded by Washington would have to be accommodated in New York.

Efforts by Pérez de Cuéllar and Boutros-Ghali to Accommodate U.S. Demands for Reform

Responding to pressure from the U.S. government has been a recurring necessity for the United Nations and its secretaries-general. For example, Trygve Lie, the organization's first secretary-general, in the midst of Senator Joseph McCarthy's campaign to root out Communists in American life, allowed the U.S. Federal Bureau of Investigation (FBI) to investigate Secretariat members for possible ties to the Communist Party, even allowing an FBI office to be opened in UN headquarters. So, too, the mounting demands from Washington in the 1980s for changes in UN operations and policy led successive secretaries-general to look for some accommodation that would ease U.S. complaints and lead to U.S. payment of its arrearages.

Nothing in the UN Charter allows a national government to conduct an internal review of UN management. Yet, Secretary-General Javier Pérez de Cuéllar opened the records of the UN's Joint Inspection Unit (JIU), the auditing and evaluation arm of the General Assembly, to a full review by the U.S. General Accounting Office (GAO). Seeking to identify waste in UN agencies and operations, the GAO cited poor record keeping and little value to the reports the JIU had developed. The agency recommended to Congress that the UN office make significant reforms before new U.S. funds were sent to the organization.

To assuage U.S. criticism of UN administrative and financial systems, Pérez de Cuéllar's successor, Boutros Boutros-Ghali, launched a highly visible management review. In 1992 he appointed a former U.S. attorney general, Richard Thornburgh, as the new under-secretary-general (USG) for administration and management. Thornburgh was given a free hand to review the full UN administration and to make recommendations for dramatic reform. After a year's study he issued a stinging indictment of the Secretariat. In the **Thornburgh Report,** the former attorney general noted a high percentage of "deadwood" in the UN bureaucracy and called for a cut in staff.[21] Thornburgh proposed the creation of an inspector general's office that would root out fraud, waste, and abuse. The inspector general would have independent authority to conduct investigations and program evaluations.

Thornburgh also asked the Ford Foundation to fund its own study on UN administrative reform. The foundation appointed Paul Volcker, former chairman of the U.S. Federal Reserve System, and Shiguro Ogata, former deputy governor of the Japan Development Bank, to head the project. The final **Volcker-Ogata Report** focused primarily on UN financial operations. It called for a unified peacekeeping budget to be charged against the national defense budgets of the member states and for more efficient use of UN resources.

Washington embraced both reports. The Clinton administration indicated that it would not support any UN budget increases until these recommendations and other significant administrative reforms were undertaken. In November 1993 the U.S. delegation to the General Assembly's Fifth Committee formally submitted a proposal for the creation of the inspector general's office. After 1994 the administration's hard line was surpassed by the conservative Republican Congress, which also wanted to limit UN peacekeeping operations and U.S. participation in them. Senator Jesse Helms called the United Nations a "power-hungry and dysfunctional organization" and demanded a 50 percent cut in its staff.[22]

Boutros-Ghali responded to the many demands from Washington by freezing the UN budget and embracing the idea of an inspector general. His support led to the 1994 creation of the Office of Internal Oversight Services (OIOS), headed by a director with a five-year term and considerable independence from the secretary-general. The office was mandated to conduct internal audits and to search out mismanagement. OIOS claimed in 2004 to have identified waste and fraud totaling $290 million during its first ten years of existence[23] and to have made more than five thousand recommendations to improve organizational efficiency and effectiveness. OIOS established an investigative unit and a confidential hotline for whistle-blowers. However, coaxing UN staff members to report misconduct proved difficult. Many staff members feared punishment or retribution if they reported offenses. Secretary-General Annan pledged to enhance protection for individuals who came forward with information on waste and hidden scandal. OIOS also launched an ethics and integrity initiative, requiring all senior UN officials to participate in an executive program on corruption control.

Boutros-Ghali's efforts were clearly meant to allay U.S. criticisms of the institution and to reestablish U.S. funding. The secretary-general also hoped his reforms would allow the United Nations to take an expanded role in post–cold war security efforts. Following the Gulf War of 1991, both Presidents George H. W. Bush and Bill Clinton indicated that they hoped for a wider UN role in keeping world peace, particularly through the expansion of its peacekeeping functions. World leaders, including Bush, met in January 1992 in the first heads of government Security Council meeting to consider the future role of the United Nations; they directed the newly elected secretary-general to recommend ways to strengthen the United Nations and make it more efficient in "preventive diplomacy" and peacekeeping. In June, Boutros-Ghali published his recommendations. Entitled *An Agenda for Peace,* the report outlined the most ambitious UN program for peacekeeping in the organization's history. Boutros-Ghali recommended, among other things, that military forces be placed at the UN's disposal for rapid action in times of crisis.

Boutros-Ghali then became the prime mover in mobilizing the world community to deal with the collapse of order in the east African nation of Somalia. At his initiative, Security Council Resolution 751 (April 1992) created UNOSOM I (UN Operation in Somalia I), a small, unarmed peacekeeping force for Somalia. In November he then sought U.S. military assistance to restore order and to deliver food supplies to the starving population. The Americans soon became enmeshed in a nasty civil conflict between rival warlords. President Bush had fully expected a brief U.S. presence, but the new Clinton administration found itself drawn into a Somali state-building effort. In October 1993 eighteen U.S. soldiers were trapped in a firefight and killed. Lurid photographs and videos of one of them being dragged through the streets of Mogadishu appeared in the world press. U.S. support for more vigorous UN peacekeeping efforts waned, troops were home within the year, and criticism mounted that the United Nations was incapable of ordering the internal affairs of any country.

For Rwandans the shifting mood was particularly perilous because a brutal, genocidal civil conflict had broken out between the rival Tutsi and Hutu tribes. Although the Clinton administration had originally supported the UN Assistance Mission for Rwanda (UNAMIR), the outbreak of massacres in April 1994 caused it to propose cutting the number of peacekeepers in the region for fear of their safety. Even more important, in May, Clinton issued Presidential Decision Directive 25 (PDD-25), which severely limited U.S. involvement in UN peacekeeping operations and ended U.S. support for expanded UN missions. Using the language of realism, PDD-25 counseled that such efforts must be placed "in proper perspective among the instruments of U.S. foreign policy."[24] The administration set eighteen preconditions that would have to be met before the United States would support a peacekeeping operation. U.S. endorsement would hinge on, among other measuring sticks, whether the UN operation advanced U.S. interests, all parties consented to UN intervention, the proposed operation had "well-defined" goals, and the U.S. Congress and the American people supported the operation.[25]

PDD-25 also urged extensive reform of the peacekeeping process. It proposed a unified peacekeeping budget—in line with the Volcker-Ogata recommendations—funded by a single, annual peacekeeping assessment overseen by professional budget experts. It set as policy the goal of reducing the U.S. contribution to the peacekeeping budget from 31 percent to 25 percent. The directive called for an overhaul of the Department of Peacekeeping Operations as well.

The 1994 off-year congressional elections in the United States, bringing Republicans into a majority in both houses for the first time in almost half a century, brought the secretary-general and his ideas about an invigorated United Nations into direct conflict not only with a politically attuned White House, but also with a new legislative majority made up of senators and members of Congress who saw the United Nations as inefficient, inept, yet bent on gaining too much power at the expense of U.S. sovereignty. Conservatives even pointed to nongovernmental organizations with UN consultative status that held values different from theirs. In one telling case, the U.S. Senate voted to withhold millions of dollars in payments to the United Nations if the organization continued to recognize the International Lesbian and Gay Alliance. In the Senate the Congress's most severe UN critic, Senator Helms of North Carolina, became chairman of the Foreign Relations Committee. In this position he could block all U.S. funding earmarked for the United Nations. He made clear that only the most dramatic reform would lead to U.S. payments of its arrearages.

The secretary-general and Senator Helms then engaged in a public argument in the pages of the respected journal *Foreign Affairs*. In the spring of 1996, Boutros-Ghali penned a defense of his ideas about an active secretary-general at the head of a more vigorous, reformed United Nations committed to expanded peacekeeping and nation building. Five months later, in the same journal, Helms used highly blunt language to lambaste the United Nations and excoriate its leader. He accused Boutros-Ghali of resisting reform that "gets down to the fundamentals" and of protecting unqualified and unneeded UN bureaucrats. The senator charged the secretary-general with wasting U.S. funds on unnecessary world conferences and ineffective peacekeeping missions. Helms clearly stated that the U.S. Congress would not pay its debt to the United Nations unless Boutros-Ghali was replaced with a reformer acceptable in Washington, D.C.

"The time has come for the United States to deliver an ultimatum: Either the United Nations reforms, quickly and dramatically, or the United States will end its participation . . .

"I am convinced that without the threat of American withdrawal, nothing will change. . . .

"The United Nations has neither reformed nor died. The time has come for it to do one or the other."

—Senator Jesse Helms,
"Saving the U.N.: A Challenge to the
Next Secretary-General"
Foreign Affairs 75, no. 5 (1996): 2–7.

Although Boutros-Ghali had disavowed a second term when he entered office in 1992, a number of nations, including some of America's closest allies, strongly supported his reelection in 1997, and the secretary-general, having changed his mind, made a spirited campaign to save his job. However, the political climate in Washington, D.C. clearly made his continuance impossible. Boutros-Ghali, the object of unkind remarks during the presidential campaign of 1996, had become the lightning rod in the United States for displeasure at all that seemed wrong with the United Nations. Despite unprecedented diplomatic pressure on Washington from some of its major allies to reverse its position, the United States held to its decision to veto Boutros-Ghali's renomination in the Security Council. Having entered office at a high point of optimism within the United Nations, Boutros Boutros-Ghali, the victim of a spate of uncontrollable in-state collapses, a continuing decline in UN financing, and U.S. antipathy, left office after one tumultuous term.

Kofi Annan and the Reform "Revolution"

Four factors drove the UN reform process at the end of the millennium:

1. U.S. government demands for serious institutional changes
2. A long-term financial crisis brought on by many members' nonpayment of their UN assessments, most particularly the unwillingness of the United States to meet its financial obligations to the organization
3. The expansion of UN obligations, particularly for peacekeeping—the UN Administrative and Budgetary Committee approved $2.8 billion for peacekeeping in 2004–2005, with an expectation that the cost could rise by 60 percent in the following year—in the post–cold war world, including engaging in nation building, battling terrorism, and providing humanitarian assistance
4. The election of an activist secretary-general who made reform the hallmark of his tenure in office

In 1996, faced with implacable U.S. opposition to the reelection of Boutros-Ghali, the Security Council nominated and the General Assembly chose Kofi Annan of Ghana as the seventh secretary-general of the United Nations. He was clearly Washington's choice, immediately welcomed to the White House in January 1997. Annan promised the president and the U.S. Congress a reform program in the near future. On July 16 he delivered on his commitment, issuing **Renewing the United Nations,** the most sweeping set of administrative and financial reform proposals made in the institution's history. During the next six years, Annan pushed many of his proposals through the General Assembly and then undertook an effort to reform the programmatic direction of the world body and to address the growing demands for structural change in the half-century-old organization. This last area of reform came in response to the institutional crisis created in 2003 by the U.S.-led war in Iraq.

Administrative Reform

During his first month in office, Kofi Annan eliminated one thousand UN staff positions that were unfilled at the time. He also moved to consolidate more than two dozen departments, funds, and programs into four thematic groupings. A trusted aide of Annan's chaired the executive committee for each group and was later added to a "cabinet" for the secretary-general, known as the *Senior Management Group (SMG).* The thematic groups ensured coordination and lessened duplication among Secretariat offices, specialized agencies, and UN bodies that answered to the General Assembly. The largest was the Development Group, chaired by the head of the UN Development Programme, which brought together representatives of the five regional economic commissions, the UN Conference on Trade and Development, the UN Population Fund, the Food and Agriculture Organization, and nine other organizations.

These immediate coordination and streamlining measures sent a signal to Washington that Annan was serious about administrative reform and were pretext to the extensive proposals in *Renewing the United Nations.* In his reform package he recommended the creation of the Senior Management Group. The General Assembly approved the SMG in December 1997 as a strategic planning body to assist the secretary-general. This body included nearly three dozen senior UN officers—under-secretaries-general headquartered in New York; several directors general working out of Geneva, Rome, Vienna, and Nairobi; and key officers of UN programs and agencies. The most dramatic proposal was the appointment of a deputy secretary-general who would manage the Secretariat when the secretary-general was away from headquarters, would spearhead the reform movement within the organization, and would promote coherence in the efforts of the entire UN System. The General Assembly approved this post at the end of 1997, and Annan appointed Louise Fréchette of Canada, who became the highest-ranking woman in UN history.

As one of its concluding acts in 1997, the General Assembly approved *Renewing the United Nations.* Annan's reform program consolidated twelve Secretariat entities into five, cut UN personnel 25 percent below 1987 levels, reduced administrative costs by 33 percent, set up a development account in which cost-cutting savings could be held for development programs in poor countries, and decentralized "decision-making at the country level while [consolidating] the United Nations presence under 'one [UN] flag.'"[26] This last change reflected Annan's effort to enhance the role and authority of the UN resident coordinator in each country where the organization had programs and to bring together all in-country UN agencies into one "UN House." The approved reforms addressed the near-bankruptcy of the United Nations by shifting the organization to a "results-based budgeting" system, enhancing accountability requirements for all UN subdivisions and specialized agencies, calling for the creation of a revolving credit fund of one billion dollars, and establishing "sunset provisions" to guarantee that bodies no longer needed would be disbanded.[27]

Annan's reforms were sufficient to jar the U.S. Congress and executive branch into promises of final payment of the UN arrearages. Even Senator Helms noted the substantive changes being

EXECUTIVE COMMITTEES OF THE UNITED NATIONS

Peace and Security

Department of Political Affairs (Chair)

Department for Disarmament
Department of Peacekeeping Operations
Department of Public Information
Office for Humanitarian Affairs
Office of the High Commissioner for Human
   Rights
Office of the Special Representative for
   Children and Armed Conflict
Office for Legal Affairs
World Bank
UN Development Programme
UN High Commissioner for Refugees
UN Children's Fund
UN Security Coordinator

Economic and Social

Department of Economic and Social Affairs
   (Chair)

UN Conference on Trade and Development
UN Environment Programme
Office of Drug Control and Crime Prevention
UN High Commissioner for Human Rights
Five UN Regional Economic Commissions
UN Development Programme
UN Centre for Human Settlements
UN Institute for Training and Research
UN Research Institute for Social
   Development
UN Institute for the Advancement of Women
UN University
UN High Commissioner for Least Developed
   Countries
Department of Public Information

Development

UN Development Programme (Chair)

Departments of Economic and Social Affairs,
   and Public Information
Office of the High Commissioner for Human
   Rights
Office of the Special Representative for
   Children and Armed Conflict
Office for Project Services
Five UN Regional Economic Commissions
Food and Agriculture Organization
International Fund for Agricultural
   Development
UN Programmes on HIV/AIDS, Drug
   Control, and Human Settlements
UN Conference on Trade and Development
UN Educational, Scientific and Cultural
   Organization
UN Population Fund
UN Children's Fund
UN Fund for Women
World Food Programme
World Health Organization

Humanitarian Affairs

Office for the Coordination of Humanitarian
   Affairs (Chair)

Department of Political Affairs
Department of Peacekeeping Operations
Department of Public Information
Office of the High Commissioner for
   Human Rights
Office of the Special Representative for
   Children and Armed Conflict
UN Development Programme
UN Environment Programme
Food and Agriculture Organization
UN Conference on Trade and Development
UN High Commissioner for Refugees
UN Children's Fund
UN Relief and Work Agency for Palestine
   Refugees in the Near East
World Food Programme
World Health Organization

made in New York and urged U.S. funding. The secretary-general, for his part, continued to alter the UN's administrative structure. One of the oldest senior-level bodies of the United Nations was the Administrative Committee on Coordination (ACC)—founded in 1946—which was responsible for harmonizing the activities of UN agencies not tied to the Secretariat. In 2002 the ACC was converted into the UN System Chief Executives Board (CEB) for Coordination, which brought together twenty-eight key UN System organizations. Among them were the World Bank, the International Monetary Fund, and the World Trade Organization. Such consolidation furthered the process of integrating these Bretton Woods entities into the UN structure. Also included on the CEB were the heads of the WHO, World Food Programme, UN Environment and Development Programmes, International Civil Aviation Organization, Food and Agriculture Organization, UN Industrial Development Organization (UNIDO), International Atomic Energy Agency, and World Intellectual Property Organization. The new body also had high-level committees to ensure coordinated and thematic efforts among programs and management throughout the UN System, so that UN agencies would not waste or engage in contradictory efforts.

On April 26, 2002, the secretary-general appointed M. Patricia Durrant, Jamaica's permanent representative, the UN's first ombudsman. Her job was to provide impartial and independent service to staff members with employment-related problems. Completely independent of any UN organ or official, the **ombudsman** operates under strict confidentiality, hearing complaints from any staff member about work conditions, and advises the parties as well as the organization of conflict resolution options within the organization. The ombudsman cannot be dismissed, except by the secretary-general; serves a five-year nonrenewable term; and cannot be appointed to any other UN System post after service in the ombudsman's office. The General Assembly's creation of this office was meant to lessen infighting and formal administrative action with its concomitant lengthy appeals process.

Annan's appointment of Durrant as the first ombudsman reflected another major "reform" of the UN administration: the concerted effort to bring talented women into the Secretariat and other important UN offices. Notoriously male dominated, the United Nations sought a sea change in its personnel structure, work environment, and policy orientation that would reflect the importance of women to its work and vision. In addition to appointing Durrant, the secretary-general made several other highly visible female appointments; important among them were Louise Fréchette as deputy secretary-general; Mary Robinson, former president of Ireland, as UN High Commissioner for Human Rights; Catherine Bertini, former director of the World Food Programme, as under-secretary-general for management; and Carolyn McAskie as Annan's special representative to war-torn Burundi. This last appointment was particularly noteworthy because only one other woman had ever headed a UN peacekeeping mission: Margaret Joan Anstee of the United Kingdom, whom Secretary-General Boutros-Ghali appointed in 1987 to direct the operation in Angola.

Although women have found a voice and recognition in the work of the United Nations, the Louise Fréchettes and Eleanor Roosevelts have been in a distinct minority. Most female employees have served in gender-traditional and junior-level positions. Studies of the bureaucracy, professional ranks, and specialized agency staffs demonstrated at the end of the twentieth century that women were significantly underrepresented. Annan undertook a concerted effort to address the gender imbalance. In pursuit of gender parity, which the General Assembly set as a goal to be achieved by 2000, the secretary-general reported in 2001 that unfortunately women accounted for only 33.5 percent of the professional and higher-level staff of the UN System as a whole.[28] The percentages were slightly better in the Secretariat (40.2 percent as of July 2001). In Annan's SMG nearly one-quarter of the members were women. Nevertheless, much work needed to be done to attract and retain talented women. By the end of 2001, only one UN agency—the UN Population Fund—had a majority of women (50.4 percent) on its staff. At the slow rate of growth in female employment, parity was not likely to be reached until 2012. To address the imbalance, the secretary-general focused attention on the aspects of the workplace that might deter women from serving, including improving sexual harassment policies and gender-neutral promotion criteria. Many of these changes were encouraged by the organized activities of UN female workers, NGO lobbying, and diplomatic pressure from government delegations.

As a part of administrative reform, even paperwork and meeting time met with criticism from the secretary-general's office. Annan launched an effort to cut the "quantity, length, and frequency" of UN reports.[29] He noted that the General Assembly had entertained as many as five hundred reports, and that ECOSOC had been inundated with another one hundred. He contended that many countries, especially those with small delegations, had difficulty coping with the "mountains of paper." He said that the demands on the Secretariat for studies and reports requested by intergovernmental bodies were "drowning its ability to provide focused and value-added analysis."[30] Annan promised that, in the future, reports would be consolidated on related subjects and written more cogently and laconically. Besides being swamped in paperwork, countries had difficulty participating effectively in the meetings of UN organs. In the biennium of 2000–2001, 15,484 meetings of UN bodies were held worldwide. Even the largest and wealthiest nations had difficulty keeping track of and participating in all the work important to their governments.

Programmatic Reform

Administrative reform can make the United Nations more efficient and, therefore, more effective. At the turn of the millennium, such reform also made the United States more receptive to paying its bill to the organization. However, the legitimacy and usefulness of the United Nations in the eyes of its most important members in the post–cold war era turn more on the efficacy of its programs and the perceived relevance of its institutional structures. Is the organization still relevant? A creation of the 1940s, premised on collective security, the United Nations can make a meaningful contribution to peace and security in the twenty-first century only if, first, the major states of the world take it seriously and, second, its actions seem to respond effectively to the challenges of the new era.

While much of the publicity and praise for Secretary-General Annan's 1997 reform program was directed at the internal administrative and financial changes just described, he saw these reforms as prerequisite to UN programmatic and structural reforms, which would be qualitatively more important because they would position the world body to meet the new international challenges of a globalized community. Some of the program changes were already present in the first wave of reforms, but most of Annan's recommendations for fundamental change awaited the Millennium Summit of 2000 and his subsequent second term as secretary-general. The programmatic changes could be grouped into three categories: peacekeeping, development and democratization, and UN relations with international civil society.

In *Renewing the United Nations,* the secretary-general gave special attention to peacekeeping and the work of the Department of Peacekeeping Operations (DPKO). He had headed that department from 1993 to 1995, when the United Nations experienced its worst failures in nation building and peacemaking. After apparent peacekeeping successes in Angola (1988), Namibia (1989), and Cambodia (1992), confidence that the United Nations could intervene in disintegrating states and not only restore peace but also effectively encourage nation building was heightened. In this atmosphere of optimism, Boutros-Ghali had issued *An Agenda for Peace,* calling for more, not less, UN activism in conflict zones. In Somalia (1993), however, not only UN efforts to deal with the region's warlords, but also the inability of U.S. forces under UN mandate to restore national peace led to recrimination against Boutros-Ghali and demands from Washington that DPKO be overhauled. When ethnic tensions then rose dramatically in Rwanda (1994), Security Council members, particularly the United States, cautioned against UN intervention, and the genocide of nearly eight hundred thousand Tutsis ensued; even more Rwandans (Tutsi and Hutu) fled the country into makeshift refugee camps in the Congo and other surrounding states. After Somalia and Rwanda, many people questioned whether UN peacekeeping efforts were sufficient for the challenges of the time.

In his 1997 report Annan called for significant changes in how DPKO managed operations. He also picked up on Boutros-Ghali's earlier recommendation and proposed that the United Nations strengthen its capacity for nation building. He urged the creation of a High-Readiness Brigade that could establish a UN presence in the early stages of a conflict. He also recommended that the Security Council craft a model Status of Forces Agreement (SOFA) to be used when a peacekeeping operation was established. To give coherence and executive leadership to peacekeeping operations, Annan rapidly appointed his own special representative to take charge of each mission. The General Assembly responded positively to Annan's proposals and increased DPKO's staff by 50 percent. Then, in March 2000, as we noted previously, the secretary-general appointed the former Algerian foreign minister, Lahkdar Brahimi, to chair an expert panel on peacekeeping operations, with a view to making sweeping reform recommendations. In the weeks leading to the 2000 Millennium Summit, the panel issued a final document calling for a complete overhaul of the UN's peacekeeping function. (See Chapter 6 for a full discussion of the report.)

The Millennium Summit at world headquarters in New York City in September was a watershed moment in the evolution of the United Nations. It was, in part, recognition of the extraordinary leadership of Kofi Annan, who had personally proposed the gathering and convinced world leaders to convene in New York. Annan used the occasion to resurrect an old idea about the UN Charter, and about the organization it created. In his address to the gathering, and in his accompanying report, he reminded the world that the Charter opens with the words "We the *Peoples,*" not "We the *States.*" Kofi Annan acknowledged that the United Nations is a forum for coordinating the interests and behavior of states, but he asserted it is something more than this:[31]

> Even though the United Nations is an organization of states, the Charter is written in the name of "we the peoples." It reaffirms the dignity and worth of the human person, respect for human rights and the equal rights of men and women, and a commitment to social progress . . . in freedom from want and fear alike. Ultimately, then, the United Nations exists for, and must serve, the needs and hopes of people everywhere. . . . No shift in the way we think or act can be more critical than this: we must put people at the centre [*sic*] of everything we do.

The secretary-general called for a new understanding of the Charter's charge to "maintain international peace and security."

By the conclusion of the summit, Annan had convinced the assembled nations, often with divergent views about issues like development and human rights, to approve a declaration of the world's hopes for the twenty-first century. They agreed on six "fundamental values" essential to international relations: freedom, equality, solidarity, tolerance, respect for nature, and a sense of shared responsibility. These values were those of a new era in international politics, potentially inherent in the UN Charter but never at the heart of the day-to-day diplomacy within the international organization. The declaration set specific goals, including the following: to halve by 2015 the number of people living on less than one dollar a day, living in hunger, or having no access to clean water; to ensure by 2015 that all children complete primary school and that no gender inequality exists in education; to reduce maternal mortality by three-fourths and the deaths of children younger than five years old by two-thirds; to stop the spread of HIV/AIDS, malaria, and other infectious diseases; to achieve significant improvement in the lives of at least one hundred million slum dwellers; to promote gender equality and the empowerment of women; to encourage the pharmaceutical industry to make essential drugs more widely available; and to provide the benefits of new technologies to all the world's peoples.

These goals were a combination of both development and democratization targets. As world conflicts shifted from cold war causes to religious, ethnic, and economic origins in the developing world, Annan saw an opportunity to shift the focus of UN activity. Through the nexus of peacekeeping and nation building, the United Nations could address the overwhelming internal problems of states at risk, could raise the standard of living for millions of people, and could promote international stability by ending human rights abuses within countries. He wrote, "A new understanding of the concept of security is evolving. Once synonymous with the defense of territory from external attack, the requirements of security today have come to embrace the protection of communities and individuals from internal violence." He argued for the United Nations to defend "personal sovereignty." Upholding the new era of peacekeeping, humanitarian intervention, and nation building, he made this case: "Surely no legal principle—not even [state] sovereignty—can ever shield crimes against humanity." The United Nations has a "moral duty" to intervene on behalf of the individual.[32]

A concerted effort was made to promote democracy in each new peacekeeping and state-building operation. The United Nations sought to introduce democratic practices, most particularly regular elections and popular participation. This new approach was used in El Salvador, Mozambique, Cambodia, Guatemala, and Angola.[33] No longer was simply restoring peace between contending forces sufficient. The UN also needed to provide a transitional administration, overseeing the entire political process. According to Kofi Annan,[34]

> Inevitably that means political institutions. At the center of virtually every civil war is the issue of the state and its power—who controls it, and how it is used. No armed conflict can be resolved without responding to those questions. Nowadays the answers almost always have to be democratic ones."

The UN's state-building initiatives have included the protection of opposition factions, the political mobilization of often-marginalized groups such as women and indigenous peoples, and the restoration or creation of judicial institutions to ensure the rule of law and the defense of individual liberties. These activities have necessarily involved UN subsidiary bodies and agencies. In 2001 the UN Development Programme spent eight hundred million dollars on democratic governance projects in 145 countries. This expenditure included funds for national elections in Sierra Leone, enhanced public participation in Nigeria, and a judicial commission in Afghanistan to restore a justice system to that war-torn land.[35]

Annan's concept of personal sovereignty could only be inferred in the Charter, possibly in its provisions defending inalienable human rights. The usual purpose of intergovernmental organizations such as the United Nations does not include interfering in the internal affairs of states or trumpeting individual rights or protections over state interests. Yet, the Millennium Summit and ensuing General Assembly session did precisely that. The Millennium Development Goals

(MDGs) became the centerpiece of UN program initiatives and coordination. When the world's attention turned again to interstate war in the Gulf region in 2003, Annan noted the limited progress that had been made toward achieving these goals. One mantra of the United Nations and its agencies became that only by addressing these issues of personal sovereignty could interstate peace be maintained. Particularly within the General Assembly, with its large membership from the developing world, much disappointment was expressed that sufficient progress on the MDGs had not been made. The GA president in 2003–2004, Julian Hunte, accentuated this disappointment and encouraged renewed efforts toward development and democratization, as did his successor Jean Ping, the foreign minister of Gabon, who became assembly president in September 2004.

In Annan's view, the United Nations could achieve its goals only through partnerships with civil society on the international, national, and subnational levels. The United Nations must work not only with the governments that are its members but also with the nonstate actors that are so much a part of contemporary global affairs. He defined *civil society* as follows:[36]

> [The] sphere in which social movements organize themselves around objectives, constituencies and thematic interests. These movements include specific groups such as women, youth and indigenous people. Other actors have also taken on an increasingly important role in shaping national and international agendas. They include local authorities, mass media, business and industry, professional associations, religious and cultural organizations and the intellectual and research communities.

Early efforts by the secretary-general to engage civil society included the creation of the *Global Compact* in 1999, which invited corporations to establish formal relationships with the United Nations, the encouragement of NGO participation in world conferences and the work of UN agencies, and the cultivation of influential individuals in different countries.

In February 2003 the secretary-general appointed a panel of eminent persons, headed by Fernando Henrique Cardoso, the former president of Brazil, to look at UN–civil society relations and to make recommendations on how such relations might be deepened. The panel issued the **Cardoso Report** in June 2004.[37] It acknowledged that components of civil society had been among the prime innovators and motivators in global relations. As early as 1972, NGOs played a role in pushing the United Nations to address threats to human well-being, such as environmental problems, development issues, and human rights matters. The 1992 Earth Summit was a watershed as thousands of private citizens and groups gathered in Rio de Janeiro to publicize a global agenda for environmental protection. From that moment forward, excluding the private sector from UN deliberations became not only impossible, but also counterproductive.

The authors of the report encouraged the involvement of a wide range of civil society actors in UN affairs. The panel argued that these participants could serve as "a protection against further erosion of multilateralism,"[38] a veiled reference to the crisis the United Nations found itself in as a result of the U.S. decision to go to war in Iraq without UN endorsement. Panel members called for a "paradigm shift" in the work of the United Nations, with reforms based on four principles:

1. The United Nations should become an "outward-looking organization," serving as the "convener" of multiple constituencies, facilitating rather than "doing." It should put global issues rather than the institution at the center of its work.
2. The United Nations should include more, not fewer, actors in its deliberations, creating permanent partnerships whenever possible. Noting that critics often described NGOs as unelected, nondemocratic advocacy groups that speak for few more than their members and that are far less representative than sovereign states, the panel asserted that "politically active citizens now express their concerns through civil society mechanisms rather

than the traditional instruments of democracy."[39] The United Nations must recognize that "global civil society now wields real power in the name of citizens."

3. The United Nations must attempt to connect the global with the local, recognizing that in the process of globalization, the nation-state cannot always be the mediator between the citizen and the world. The United Nations will implement its programs effectively only if it has a working relationship with the subnational actors present in local communities.

4. "The United Nations should accept an explicit role in strengthening global governance and tackling the democratic deficits it is prone to, emphasizing participatory democracy and deeper accountability of institutions to the global public."[40] In other words, the United Nations needs to go beyond its intergovernmental nature and become an actor itself in civil society, promoting a particular political ideology and its supporting values and institutions.

Cardoso and his colleagues urged the creation of a new post: under-secretary-general for constituency engagement and partnerships. The USG would pull together in one office the Global Compact, civil society and partnership units, and several other projected and existing subdivisions of the Secretariat. The panel also urged a streamlining and unification of the accrediting process for nonstate actors at the United Nations. Cardoso and his colleagues called on the General Assembly to permit the carefully planned participation of actors besides governments in its meetings. The Security Council was also urged to engage civil society entities in its work. The authors of the report recommended an experimental series of "Security Council seminars" to discuss emerging issues. The panel suggested that the council pay the travel costs of NGOs and other private participants who would be asked to meet with council members and its president.

Structural Reform

As discussed in Chapter 1, September 23, 2003, marked the opening session of the Fifty-eighth General Assembly, and in his remarks to the gathered representatives, Secretary-General Annan expressed a level of pessimism about the future of the United Nations never in the past acknowledged by him or his predecessors. He called the moment "a fork in the road." For all the optimism generated by the Millennium Summit three years earlier and the reforms undertaken both before and after that event, UN organs had been through an acrimonious year. Particularly in the Security Council, the confrontation between the U.S.-UK coalition and the other permanent members over the war in Iraq raised doubts about the viability of the institution. President George W. Bush's doctrine of preemption, argued by the United States to be an essential tool in the battle against terrorism, challenged the long-held doctrines underlying the United Nations. Annan suggested that some route had to be found to reform the Charter, the Security Council, the General Assembly, and ECOSOC to meet the new threats to international peace and security, while continuing to improve people's living conditions through the fulfillment of the Millennium Development Goals.

In November 2003 the secretary-general appointed the High-level Panel on Threats, Challenges and Change, chaired by Anand Panyarachun, former prime minister of Thailand, to make recommendations on structural reforms that would ensure the effectiveness and relevance of the United Nations in the new era. Other members included Brent Scowcroft, national security adviser to President George H. W. Bush; Yevgeny Primakov, former Russian prime minister; and Amre Moussa, secretary-general of the League of Arab States. In his charge to the committee, Annan indicated that the past year had "shaken the foundations of collective security, and undermined

CHRONOLOGY OF UN REFORM

December 1985   The General Assembly creates the *Group of 18* to consider and make recommendations on the reform of UN administrative and financial operations.

August 1986   The Group of 18 makes seventy-one recommendations on UN reform to the secretary-general.

March 1993   The *Thornburgh Report* calls for the creation of an office of inspector general and other reforms.

July 1994   The General Assembly creates the *Office of Internal Oversight Services.*

January 1997   Secretary-General Annan creates *thematic executive committees* to coordinate policy in four broad areas.

March 1997   The secretary-general merges three departments into one *Department of Economic and Social Affairs.* He also announces his intention to cut administrative costs from 38 percent to 25 percent of the UN budget.

July 1997   UN secretary-general Annan issues *Renewing the United Nations: A Programme for Reform.*

December 1997   The General Assembly approves the first set of reform measures that Secretary-General Annan put forward.

March 1998   The post of *deputy secretary-general* is created and charged with overseeing reform.

January 1999   Kofi Annan proposes a *Global Compact* with corporations.

August 2000   The reform recommendations of the Panel on UN Peace Operations (*Brahimi Report*) are published.

September 2000   The *Millennium Declaration* is adopted.

December 2000   The General Assembly endorses *results-based budgeting.* It also lowers the "ceiling" in the scale of assessment to no more than 25 percent for any member.

July 2002   The *UN ombudsman* is appointed.

November 2003   The secretary-general appoints the *High-level Panel* to make recommendations on UN reforms to address world security challenges.

June 2004   The *Cardoso Report* recommends more active involvement of global civil society in UN affairs.

December 2004   The *High-level Panel* makes its recommendations on UN reforms to address security challenges in the world, calling for a broader interpretation of collective security.

March 2005   In his report *In Larger Freedom,* the secretary-general proposes enlargement of the Security Council, creation of a Peacebuilding Commission, replacement of the Commission on Human Rights with a smaller Human Rights Council elected by two-thirds vote of the General Assembly, and major Charter revisions.

confidence in the possibility of collective responses to our common problems." He gave the panel ten months to recommend "clear and practical measures" that would reform the UN's principal organs in such a way that the organization could respond to new threats effectively and collectively.

The High-level Panel reported its recommendations in late 2004 and called for "a new security consensus" and a broader interpretation of collective security in the UN Charter.[41] On the basis of the panel's recommendations and previous reform documents, Annan put forward structural reform proposals in March 2005. Entitled *In Larger Freedom,* the secretary-general's report called for an expansion of the Security Council to twenty-four members, either by adding six new permanent seats (none with the veto)[42] and three 2-year-term nonpermanent seats divided among the major regional groups, or by adding no new permanent seats but creating a new category of eight 4-year renewable-term seats and one new 2-year nonpermanent, nonrenewable seat. The secretary-general warned, however, that simply increasing the size of the council would be insufficient. Any changes would also need to enhance the Security Council's ability to take prompt and realistic action.

At various times in the past, the United States, Great Britain, and France had all indicated they would support the addition of Germany and Japan as permanent members to the council (without the veto).[43] However, Secretary-General Annan's proposed council expansion raised both membership expectations among important regional powers—among them India, Brazil, Nigeria, Argentina, and Egypt—and countervailing opposition to their permanent appointment. China, in particular, opposed Japan's selection and clearly indicated that the Beijing government was in no hurry to expand the Security Council. Thus, if an enlargement from fifteen to twenty-four members was to occur, some variation on Annan's second option seemed likely to emerge.

When the secretary-general appointed the High-level Panel, he charged it with finding some way to allow the United Nations to take preventive action, rather than simply responding to already-committed acts that violated international peace and security. Otherwise, the organization could become irrelevant to the decision-making processes of states that felt threatened by potential dangers. Critical for a more effective Security Council, in Annan's view, was the determination to use force before genocide or massive violations of human rights occurred in conflict situations. The U.S. military action against Iraq in 2003 without Security Council authorization also challenged the council's right to determine when force could be used. However, the panel, and the subsequent report by Annan, could find consensus only in a restatement of "just law theory" and a set of procedural standards for the council when it was deciding whether to use force. That decision, the secretary argued, should turn on the seriousness of the threat, the belief that the proposed action addressed the threat, the proportionality of the proposed action, the recognition that force should be used only as a last resort, and a calculation that the benefits of using force outweighed the costs of inaction.[44] None of these changed normal practice or moved the institution toward its own preemptive policy.

In addition to altering the makeup of the Security Council, the secretary-general recommended eliminating not only the Military Staff Committee (see Chapter 4 for a description of this body), which never functioned as intended, but also, and more important, one of the principal organs of the United Nations: the Trusteeship Council. When the former trust territory of Palau gained its independence in 1994, the trusteeship system accomplished its founders' goal of ending five hundred years of colonial rule and thus rendered the council's continued existence pointless.[45]

Annan also advised the creation of two new bodies and a revitalization of the Secretariat, ECOSOC, and the General Assembly. To address the growing challenges of peacekeeping and nation building, he urged the creation of a **Peacebuilding Commission.** He called the nonexistence of an agency to "help states with the transition from war to peace" a "gaping hole"[46] in the UN structure. This commission would focus on creating new national institutions, ensure necessary reconstruction financing, enhance coordination among international agencies, and review progress on postconflict recovery. The commission would comprise members from the Security Council and ECOSOC, from major troop-contributing states, and from states that contributed significantly to a proposed standing fund for peace building. Annan also recommended a dramatic replacement of the existing Commission on Human Rights with a new, smaller **Human Rights Council,** possibly as one of the principal organs of the United Nations. He argued that the current body had lost legitimacy, given its rotating membership, which often included states accused of human rights abuses, and therefore needed to be replaced with a council having "a status, authority, and capability" commensurate with its importance.[47] He urged that the new council be elected at large by a two-thirds vote in the General Assembly. He also recommended that the Economic and Social Council serve as a high-level development forum with more ministerial meetings. Finally, he asked the member states to give him authority to offer a one-time buyout of Secretariat staff in order to eliminate "deadwood" from the bureaucracy and to refresh the collective of personnel that serves the organization.

With regard to the General Assembly, Annan's proposals called for streamlining its work, speeding up its deliberative process, giving more authority to its president, restructuring its committee system, enhancing the role of civil society in its activities, and focusing on a far more substantive agenda than has traditionally been the case. In the assembly, increased membership put extraordinary pressures on its parliamentary process. Each country, caucus group, and regional bloc sought to put its important issues on the agenda, often repetitively for many years. The plenary body and its committees were ensnared in excessive meetings and paperwork, often concerning secondary issues. The need to reform the work and orderliness of the GA's bodies and to eliminate extraneous matters was clear. However, moving the unwieldy assembly—which for small and poor states serves as one of the few international platforms on which they can hope to sway world public opinion and where they have sufficient voting power to outvote the powerful and rich states—to reform itself along the lines suggested by the secretary-general appeared in the spring of 2005 to be exceedingly controversial and therefore unlikely.

Secretary-General Annan's initiative was the latest in a long history of efforts to improve the work of the major UN bodies, particularly that of the Security Council. The peculiar combination of sovereign equality, democratic voting procedures, and recognized great-power predominance in the council through the possession of the veto by the permanent members often resulted in frustration over the inability to exercise UN authority in times of international crisis. The end of the cold war renewed the hope that the council might be able to act as it was intended by the founding nations, and, in fact, for several years in the 1990s unanimity among the permanent members led to the regular exercise of Chapter VII enforcement measures in any number of hot spots. However, the changes in U.S. foreign policy following the terrorist attacks of September 11, 2001, and the preemptive, and largely unilateral, decision by Washington to go to war to drive the Iraqi regime from power undercut the council's consensus. They also led the secretary-general and major powers such as France, Germany, and the United Kingdom to look for revisions in the Charter that would restore the effectiveness of the council and the world body as a whole.

Some observers, believing the veto has constrained the Security Council's effectiveness and accorded too much influence to just a few superpowers, have proposed adding to the council new, veto-laden permanent members. Other people have recommended abolishing the privilege altogether or refining the use of the restraint by means of a "weighted" veto, by allowing only two or three members collectively to veto any given proposal. Still other individuals would amend the Charter to establish a requirement that a veto-wielding nation publicly explain the action. However, apart from the Uniting for Peace Resolution of 1950, which momentarily finessed the Soviet Union's veto authority during the Korean crisis, nothing has been done to curtail its use, and Annan's recommendations (just detailed) called for no change in current practice. In the early twenty-first century, the possibility that any current member would support amending the Charter to limit its own participation, cut its veto powers, or extend the veto to others seemed slim.

Kofi Annan and his staff contended that *In Larger Freedom* marked the most ambitious reform effort of the UN structure in sixty years. However, some of the reforms, such as the enlargement of the Security Council, which was meant to improve the "legitimacy" of the world body, seemed unlikely to enhance the legitimacy in the eyes of the U.S. government or other permanent members. In fact, this reform issue quickly became bogged down in squabbles over who the new members should be. Proposed revisions of the General Assembly's work seemed to run counter to the natural organizational tendencies of a forum made up of 191 sovereign states, each with its own desire to be relevant and visible in this global "parliament." Likewise, any effort to replace the Human Rights Commission with a smaller, select council was likely to be opposed by regions and states that feared a "moral imperialism" by major Western powers. Although Annan called for implementation of his recommendations by September 2005, the likelihood that any of them would be authorized by then was next to none. Only the suggested Peacebuilding Commission found broad support in the international community.

Scandal and the United Nations

The legitimacy of an institution, and the authority and power that flow from its legitimacy, depends significantly on its public image. Internal reforms mean little if the organization is perceived as corrupt or abusive of its power. Scandal can destroy an organization or be an impetus for reform. Given that large organizations, including corporations, governments, and international organizations, are likely to have some level of mismanagement, fraud, or scandal, an entity's ability to survive and maintain its legitimacy depends on how it responds to internal miscreant behavior. The United Nations, the largest international organization in history, is not immune to these forces.

The years 2004 and 2005 proved scandalous for the United Nations. The most significant outrage was the charge that its oil-for-food program, which it operated under Security Council authorization to provide humanitarian supplies (food, medicines, etc.) to the Iraqi population living under the dictatorial rule of Saddam Hussein and paid for with Iraqi oil revenues, had been fleeced for billions of dollars in kickback payments to Iraqi officials, in excessive payments to outside vendors, and in laundered funds to UN officials. Charges of sexual harassment were also lodged against Ruud Lubbers, UN High Commissioner for Refugees (UNHCR): A female staff officer said that Lubbers treated her improperly during a staff meeting.[48] The Office of Internal Oversight Services launched a broad investigation of the UNHCR, which led to Lubbers' eventual resignation. Then, three young staff members published *Emergency Sex and Other Desperate Measures: A True Story from Hell on Earth*,[49] detailing their demoralizing and even sordid experiences in UN operations in crisis areas around the world. The book left the impression that many individuals who serve in UN missions are unqualified and psychologically unfit for their positions. The publication described excessive alcohol use and sex parties among UN workers and underscored unremitting despair for some workers who saw UN efforts to assist people as ineffective, and even immoral, in some cases.

Emergency Sex appeared on bookshelves just as Secretary-General Annan was reporting to the Security Council about internal studies of UN staff in peacekeeping missions that found serious misconduct toward local populations and poor internal policing by the United Nations. The most serious seemed to be in the Democratic Republic of the Congo (DRC), where peacekeepers were reported to have traded food for sex with local women, to have had regular liaisons with prostitutes, and to have been involved in sexual exploitation of women and girls. The secretary-general announced a "zero tolerance" policy for such practices not only in the Congo but in any UN peacekeeping operation. The Security Council reaffirmed this policy in its reauthorization of the DRC operation,[50] calling on troop-contributing countries to prosecute offenses involving their personnel.

Of these scandals, the oil-for-food story dominated the world press. Driven in part by the extensive reporting of influential *New York Times* columnist William Safire, the U.S. Congress launched several committee investigations. Safire called the oil-for-food program a scam and a "great cash cow"[51] that milked ten billion dollars into the pockets of contractors, traders, banks, and UN inspectors, including Kofi Annan's son, Kojo Annan. The secretary-general sought to demonstrate that the United Nations took the charges seriously and would find the truth and punish anyone involved in wrongdoing. Sidestepping the normal UN investigative bodies (OIOS and the Joint Inspections Unit), Annan appointed Paul Volcker, mentioned previously in this chapter, to head an independent investigation. Volcker's primary targets were Benon Sevan, the former UN head of the program; his deputy, Teklay Afeworki; and the UN's contracted inspecting company, Cotecna, from Switzerland. Sevan denied all the charges, noting that the program was monitored by a Security Council committee of the whole. Therefore, representatives of all council members, including the permanent members, had reviewed all transactions and given their approval through the six-year life of the program. He accused these states of overlooking dubious contracts because the contracts benefited companies in their countries.

The Volcker panel issued several interim reports, the most scathing in March 2005. It found that Kojo Annan had concealed his continuing relationship with Cotecna, in which he received more than $150,000 subsequent to his departure from the company. He was also accused of lying to the committee and failing to cooperate with the investigation. Other individuals found culpable were Mr. Sevan; Dileep Nair, the under-secretary-general for the UN Office of Internal Oversight Services; and S. Iqbal Riza, the chief of cabinet for Kofi Annan.[52] The panel revealed that documents had been destroyed, and it criticized an unacceptably limited investigation by the Secretariat. Volcker faulted the secretary-general for lax governance and for not questioning his son's activities more carefully, but he said the panel found no evidence of wrongdoing or coverup by Annan. The secretary-general held an emotional press conference, maintaining that he had been exonerated by the report, saying he was saddened by his son's behavior, and insisting that he would not resign. The panel's findings did not put the scandal to rest. Calls were made for Annan to step down, and lead investigators for Volcker's group quit out of protest over how lightly the secretary-general had been admonished in the report.

In 2005 the UN's most important task was to address these scandals. The many reform efforts of the previous twenty years would amount to little if the organization lost its legitimacy in the eyes of the world's governments and populations. The investigations under way had to be used to press for truly qualitative changes in how the UN operates.

SUMMARY

The UN Charter provides a constitutional framework for the United Nations. Like any written foundational document, it lays out an organizational and functional arrangement that met its authors' needs but has required amendment and reinterpretation as times and conditions have changed. Although the Charter has been amended formally only five times in the UN's history, the majority of changes in the United Nations have resulted from informal revisions in UN practice. Most important, the growth in UN membership, cold war pressures, financial woes, U.S. discontent with the United Nations, and peacekeeping and new-era demands on the organization have forced concerted reform in the world body. The reform process has been closely associated with the secretary-generalship of Kofi Annan, who tried to refocus the organization on the challenges of human rights protection, development, democratization, and emerging international civil society. In this process, questions about the UN's relevance and structural change became paramount. The need to amend in fundamental ways how the United Nations operates seemed obvious to one and all, but the ability to bring about structural change seemed more difficult to achieve at the turn of the century than the desire to do so.

NOTES

1. See Nagendra Singh, "The UN and the Development of International Law," in *United Nations, Divided World: The UN's Roles in International Relations,* 2nd ed., ed. Adam Roberts and Benedict Kingsbury, 384–419 (Oxford, UK: Clarendon Press, 1993).

2. The full report can be found at http://www.un.org/peace/reports/peace_operations/.

3. Karen A. Mingst and Margaret P. Karns, *The United Nations in the Post–Cold War Era* (Boulder, CO: Westview Press, 1995), 23, 42.

4. What follows is based in large part on the entry for the term *international law* in John Allphin Moore, Jr., and Jerry Pubantz, *Encyclopedia of the United Nations* (New York: Facts on File, 2002), 175–79.

5. Robert J. Beck, Anthony Clark Arend, and Robert D. Vander Lugt, "Feminist Voices," in *International Rules: Approaches from International Law and International Relations,* ed. Robert J. Beck, Anthony Clark Arend, and Robert D. Vander Lugt, 253–55 (New York: Oxford University Press, 1996).

6. Quoted in Mary Ann Glendon, *A World Made New: Eleanor Roosevelt and the Universal Declaration of Human Rights* (New York: Random House, 2001), 114.

7. Thomas Franck, *Nation Against Nation* (New York: Oxford University Press, 1985), 85–86.

8. Reuters, "Afghanistan Loses UN Vote over $4,600 in Unpaid Dues," February 2, 2002, http://www.globalpolicy.org/finance/docs/2002/0201afgh.htm.

9. Ibid.

10. For extensive information on the UN financial crisis, see the Web site for the Global Policy Forum: http://www.globalpolicy.org.

11. Christopher Marquis, "U.S. Is Accused of Trying to Isolate U.N. Population Unit," *New York Times,* June 21, 2004, A3.

12. Thalif Deen (Reuters), "Squeezed Japan Threatens Cuts to UN Agencies," January 7, 2004, http://www.globalpolicy.org/finance/docs/2004/0107japan.htm.

13. David Pilling, "Japan May Cut Its United Nations Contribution," *Financial Times,* January 16, 2003.

14. Mark Turner, "UN Warns of Funds Shortfall for Tribunals," *New York Times,* November 21, 2003. Also see UN General Assembly, "UN financial status 'good, but only in parts,' under-secretary-general for management tells Budget Committee," press release, GA/AB/3614, May 4, 2004, http://www.un.org/News/Press/docs/2004/gaab3614.doc.htm.

15. Dean Acheson, *Present at the Creation: My Years at the State Department* (New York: Norton, 1969), 741.

16. Burton Yale Pines, ed., *A World without a U.N.: What Would Happen if the U.N. Shut Down?* (Washington, D.C.: Heritage Foundation, 1984).

17. Ibid., ix.

18. Alexander M. Haig, Jr., *Caveat: Realism, Reagan, and Foreign Policy* (New York: Macmillan, 1984), 270.

19. Jeane J. Kirkpatrick, *The Reagan Phenomenon— and Other Speeches on Foreign Policy* (Washington, D.C.: American Enterprise Institute, 1983), 79–91, 92–98.

20. Office of the Federal Register, National Archives and Records Administration, *Public Papers of the Presidents of the United States* (Washington, D.C.: U.S. Government Printing Office), 1981, 905–906; 1982, 2:1154.

21. House Committee on Foreign Affairs, *Management and Mismanagement at the United Nations: Hearing before the Subcommittee on International Security, International Organizations and Human Rights*, 103rd Cong., 1st sess., March 5, 1993.

22. Jesse Helms, "Saving the U.N.: A Challenge to the Next Secretary-General," *Foreign Affairs* 75, no. 5 (1996): 2–7.

23. UN Office of Internal Oversight Services, *Achievements*, June 18, 2004, http://www.un.org/Depts/oios/achievements.htm.

24. "Key Elements of the Clinton Administration's Policy on Reforming Multilateral Peace Operations" [U.S. Administration, Presidential Decision Directive 25, May 3, 1994], in *Documents on Reform of the United Nations*, ed. Paul Taylor, Sam Daws, and Ute Adamczick-Gerteis, 125 (Brookfield, VT: Dartmouth, 1996).

25. Ibid., 126.

26. Kofi Annan, *Renewing the United Nations: A Programme for Reform*, UN document A/51/950 (New York: United Nations, July 16, 1997).

27. The sunset provisions may have been a response to President Clinton's announcement, just weeks before, that the United States intended to withdraw from the UN Industrial Development Organization because UNIDO no longer served a useful purpose in the view of the United States.

28. Kofi Annan, *Improvement of the Status of Women in the United Nations System*, UN document A/56/472 (New York: United Nations, October 15, 2001).

29. Kofi Annan, *Strengthening of the United Nations: An Agenda for Further Change*, UN document A/57/387 (New York: United Nations, September 9, 2002), 17.

30. Ibid.

31. Kofi A. Annan, *We the Peoples: The Role of the United Nations in the 21st Century* (New York: United Nations, 2000), 6–7.

32. Ibid., 48.

33. For a discussion of UN activities in these states, see Gregory H. Fox, "International Law and Entitlement to Democracy after War," *Global Governance* 9, no. 2 (2003): 183–87.

34. Kofi A. Annan, "Democracy as an International Issue," *Global Governance* 8, no. 2 (2002): 137.

35. Mark Malloch Brown, "Democratic Governance: Toward a Framework for Sustainable Peace," *Global Governance* 9, no. 2 (2003): 143–44.

36. Annan, *Renewing the United Nations*.

37. Panel of Eminent Persons on United Nations–Civil Society Relations, *We the Peoples: Civil Society, the United Nations and Global Governance*, UN document A/58/817 (New York: United Nations, June 21, 2004).

38. Ibid., 7.

39. Ibid., 25.

40. Ibid., 9.

41. High-level Panel on Threats, Challenges and Change, *A More Secure World: Our Shared Responsibility*, UN document A/59/565 (New York: United Nations, December 2, 2004), 11.

42. The permanent seats would be distributed in the following way: two seats for Africa, two seats for Asia and the Pacific, one seat for Europe, and one seat for the Americas. See Kofi Annan, *In Larger Freedom: Towards Development, Security and Human Rights for All*, UN document A/59/2005 (New York: United Nations, March 21, 2005), 43.

43. See, for example, Robin Gedye, "Britain Seeks Radical Security Council Shake-Up," *Telegraph* (London), June 20, 2003. In late August 2003, French foreign minister Dominique de Villepin added his voice to the voices of other people publicly recommending the expansion of SC membership. See Tom Heneghan (Reuters), "France Urges International Force, Quick Vote in Iraq," August 28, 2003, http://www.lexpress.mu/display_article.php?news_id=3118.

44. Kofi Annan, "'In Larger Freedom': Decision Time at the UN," *Foreign Affairs* 84, no. 3 (2005): 69.

45. Annan, *In Larger Freedom*.

46. Ibid., 31.

47. United Nations, "Secretary-general outlines major proposals to reform UN human rights machinery, in address to Geneva Human Rights Commission," press release, SG/SM/9808, HR/CN/1108, April 7, 2005.

48. Colum Lynch, "U.N. Expanding Harassment Probe against UNHCR Chief," *Washington Post,* May 30, 2004. Reprinted in *UN Wire,* June 1, 2004.

49. For a review of the book, see Barbara Crossette, "When Peacekeeping Turns to Despair," *UN Wire,* June 14, 2004.

50. UN Security Council, *Resolution 1592 (2005),* S/RES/1592, March 30, 2005, http://www.un.org/Docs/sc/unsc_resolutions05.htm.

51. William Safire, "The Great Cash Cow," *New York Times,* June 23, 2004.

52. Independent Inquiry Committee into the United Nations Oil-for-Food Programme, *Second Interim Report: The 1998 Procurement of the Humanitarian Goods Inspection Contract, Other Conduct of United Nations Officials* (New York: Independent Inquiry Committee into the United Nations Oil-for-Food Programme, March 29, 2005).

KEY TERMS

Amending the Charter (page 79)
Article 19 (page 92)
Cardoso Report (page 107)
Goldberg Reservation (page 92)
Hugo Grotius (page 86)
Human Rights Council (page 111)
Idealism (page 95)
In Larger Freedom (page 110)
International Law (page 86)

Membership (page 82)
National Liberation (page 84)
New International Economic Order (page 83)
Non-Aligned Movement (page 84)
North (page 83)
Ombudsman (page 103)
Peacebuilding Commission (page 110)

Realism (page 95)
Renewing the United Nations (page 101)
Scale of Assessment (page 94)
South (page 83)
Thornburgh Report (page 97)
Volcker-Ogata Report (page 98)

RESOURCES FOR FURTHER RESEARCH
Relevant Web Sites

Global Policy Forum (www.globalpolicy.org)
Research on International Law Web site (www.lib.uchicago.edu/~llou/forintlaw)
UN Foundation (www.unfoundation.org)
UN International Law Web site (www.un.org/law)

UN Office of Internal Oversight Services (www.un.org/Depts/oios/)
UN Wire Web site (www.smartbrief.com/un_wire/index.jsp)

Books, Articles, and Documents

Annan, Kofi. "'In Larger Freedom': Decision Time at the UN." *Foreign Affairs* 84, no. 3 (2005): 63–74.
———*Renewing the United Nations: A Programme for Reform.* UN Document A/51/950. New York: United Nations, July 16, 1997.
Beck, Robert J., Anthony Clark Arend, and Robert D. Vander Lugt, eds. *International Rules: Approaches from International Law and International Relations.* New York: Oxford University Press, 1996.

Beigbeder, Yves. *The Internal Management of the United Nations Organizations.* New York: St. Martin's Press, 1997.
Drifte, Reinhard. *Japan's Quest for a Permanent Security Council Seat: A Matter of Pride or Justice?* New York: St. Martin's Press, 2000.
Fassbender, Bodo. *UN Security Council Reform and Right of Veto.* The Hague, The Netherlands: Kluwer Law International, 1998.

Gregg, Robert W. *About Face? The United States and the United Nations.* Boulder, CO: Lynne Reinner, 1993.

High-level Panel on Threats, Challenges and Changes. *A More Secure World: Our Shared Responsibility.* UN Document A/59/565. New York: United Nations, December 2, 2004.

Independent Advisory Group on U.N. Financing. *Financing an Effective United Nations.* New York: Ford Foundation, 1993.

Jackson, Richard L. *The Non-Aligned, the UN, and the Superpowers.* New York: Praeger, 1983.

McDermott, Anthony. *The New Politics of Financing the UN.* Basingstoke, UK: Macmillan, 2000.

Moore, John Allphin, Jr., and Jerry Pubantz. *To Create a World? American Presidents and the United Nations.* New York: Peter Lang, 1999.

Murphy, Craig. *The Emergence of the NIEO Ideology.* Boulder, CO: Westview Press, 1984.

Panel of Eminent Persons on the United Nations–Civil Society Relations. *We the Peoples: Civil Society, the United Nations and Global Governance.* UN Document A/58/817. New York: United Nations, June 21, 2004.

Simma, Bruno, ed. *The Charter of the United Nations: A Commentary.* New York: Oxford University Press, 1994.

Singh, Nagendra. "The UN and the Development of International Law." In *United Nations, Divided World: The UN's Roles in International Relations,* 2nd ed., edited by Adam Roberts and Benedict Kingsbury, 384–419. Oxford, UK: Clarendon Press, 1993.

Chapter 4

Evolving Institutions

Not only has the UN Charter evolved, but along with it, the various UN institutions—including the six principal organs of the United Nations—have evolved. In this chapter, we discuss the adaptations these institutions have undergone and continue to undergo. We also cover the new global structures that complement the work of the UN entities. Finally, we discuss the groups that emerged from the Bretton Woods Conference to effect global free trade and their role in and impact on the UN System.

COORDINATION OF THE UN SYSTEM

Because the United Nations is the umbrella organization for 191 member states and several non-governmental organizations, it can be said to be more than the sum of its parts. Although considering the United Nations in exactly this way is appropriate, remembering that it is also a collection of distinct institutions is important. Thus, while the UN's clichéd image in the public's mind is often unidimensional and reflects its early history, the evolving functions of its various parts suggest the protean nature of the organization and underscore the emergence of a "new" United Nations.

The **UN System** includes the full array of UN organizations, functions, programmes and funds, specialized agencies, and international bodies related to the United Nations. It is sometimes called the *UN family of organizations*. Some groups in the system act independently, but, as a rule, intrasystem communication is directed from the various wings to the six principal organs of the United Nations. Of these six organs, four—the General Assembly, the Security Council, the Economic and Social Council, and the Secretariat—provide guidance and communication for the full arrangement.

The secretary-general manages this sprawling system by means of the **Chief Executives Board (CEB) for Coordination**—the successor to the Administrative Committee on Coordination (ACC), which was initiated in 1946. The CEB comprises the heads of UN bodies and agencies. Whereas it had only four member organizations when it originated in the 1940s, by 2005 twenty-eight agency leaders met twice a year under the secretary-general's supervision. In the new millennium, the CEB has an increasingly important, yet complicated task: to mobilize the UN System coherently in its effort to address new and difficult world issues.

PRINCIPAL ORGANS

General Assembly

The General Assembly (GA) is the first of the main organs described in the UN Charter (Chapter IV). Articles 9 through 22 explain its composition, functions, powers, and procedures. Acting as the "legislative" branch of the United Nations, the GA meets in formal session every fall at UN headquarters in New York City. Some UN members think of the assembly as the most important of the six principal organs, given that it is the one forum in which all member states are represented and in which each member, no matter its size or population, has an equal vote. Smaller nations and former colonies, in particular, value these principles and thus consider the assembly the hub of the United Nations.

The GA's importance as a meeting place has grown through the years with the expansion of UN membership. Beginning with 51 nations at the end of World War II, the General Assembly comprised 191 members in 2005. This increase was a result of the end of colonialism in the 1950s and 1960s, which brought many nonaligned and developing countries into the organization. The end of the cold war also led to the addition of new states from Eastern Europe and the former Soviet Union. The admission of all internationally recognized states—with the single exception of the Vatican—made the United Nations by 2003 the first international organization in history to achieve virtually universal membership. Each member state may have five

General Assembly Hall at UN Headquarters in New York City. (UN/DPI Photo by E. Kanalstein. Reproduced by permission from the United Nations.)

UN SYSTEM (JULY 2005)

Principal Organs of the United Nations

International Court of Justice	Security Council	General Assembly	Economic and Social Council	Trusteeship Council	Secretariat

Military Staff Committee
Standing Committees
Ad hoc Bodies
International Criminal
Tribunal for the
Former Yugoslavia
International Criminal
Tribunal for Rwanda
Sanctions Committees
Peacekeeping Missions

Six Main Committees
Sessional Committees
Standing Committees
Subsidiary Organs

Other UN Entities
UN High Commissioner
for Human Rights
UN Centre for Human
Settlements
UN Office for Project
Services

**Research and Training
Institutes**
International Research
and Training Institute
for the Advancement
of Women
UN Interregional Crime
and Justice Research
Institute
UN Institute for Training
and Research
UN Research Institute for
Social Development

Programmes and Funds
UN Conference on Trade
and Development
-International Trade
Centre
UN Drug Control
Programme
UN Environment
Programme

Office of the Secretary-General

Senior Management Group | Ombudsman

Offices and Departments:
Internal Oversight Services
Legal Affairs
Political Affairs
Disarmament Affairs
Peacekeeping Operations
Coordination of Humanitarian
Affairs
Economic and Social Affairs
General Assembly Affairs and
Conference Services
Public Information
Management
UN Security Coordination
Drug Control and Crime
Prevention
UN Office at Geneva
UN Office at Vienna
UN Office at Nairobi

Functional Commissions
Commission for Social
  Development
Commission on Human Rights
Commission on Narcotic Drugs
Commission on Crime Prevention
  and Criminal Justice
Commission on Science and
  Technology for Development
Commission on Sustainable
  Development
Commission on the Status of
  Women
Commission on Population and
  Development
Statistical Commission

Regional Commissions
Economic Commission for Africa
Economic Commission for Europe
Economic Commission for Latin
  America and the Caribbean
Economic and Social Commission
  for Asia and the Pacific
Economic and Social Commission
  for Western Asia

Ad hoc and Other Committees
Expert and Standing Committees

UN Institute for
  Disarmament Research

UN Development
  Programme
  —UN Development
    Fund for Women
  —UN Volunteers
UN Population Fund
UN High Commissioner for
  Refugees
UN Children's Fund
World Food Programme
UN Relief and Works
  Agency for Palestine
  Refugees in the Near East

Related Organizations
International Atomic
  Energy Agency
World Trade Organization
Comprehensive Nuclear-
  Test-Ban Treaty
  Organization
Organization for the
  Prohibition of Chemical
  Weapons

Specialized Agencies
International Labour
  Organization
Food and Agriculture
  Organization
UN Educational, Scientific
  and Cultural
  Organization
World Health Organization
World Bank Group
International Monetary
  Fund
International Civil
  Aviation Organization
International Maritime
  Organization
International
  Telecommunication
  Union
Universal Postal Union
World Meteorological
  Organization
World Intellectual
  Property Organization
International Fund for
  Agricultural
  Development
UN Industrial
  Development
  Organization
World Tourism
  Organization

representatives and five alternates in the assembly. These representatives serve on the GA committees (explained subsequently) as well as in the assembly plenary.

Because three of the other principal organs—the Economic and Social Council, the Trusteeship Council, and the Secretariat—must consistently report to the General Assembly, it plays a role in most of the main UN activities. No specific requirement mandates that the Security Council and the International Court of Justice report their decisions to the GA for review, although Article 24 of the UN Charter commands the Security Council to submit "annual, and when necessary, special reports" to the General Assembly for the latter's "consideration." The language of this provision, however, underlines the authoritative rather than the subservient relationship of the Security Council to the larger body.

The General Assembly deals with a range of international topics. Like other legislative bodies, it employs a system of standing (i.e., permanent) committees to do specific initial work. Within these standing committees, delegates debate, review, and vote on issues, then, frequently, pass resolutions that are presented to the General Assembly plenary for consideration. The six main committees are as follows: The **GA First Committee**—the Political and International Security Committee—deals almost solely with disarmament issues, considered early in UN history to be such an important topic that it was consigned to a specific committee. The First Committee is now charged with addressing the larger category of "disarmament and international security." A separate Special Political Committee was established early in UN history to consider all other political questions. The other main committees are the **GA Second Committee** (the Economic and Financial Committee—or ECOFIN); the **GA Third Committee** (the Social, Humanitarian and Cultural Committee—SOCHUM); the **GA Fourth Committee** (the Trusteeship Committee), which in the late 1990s was merged with the Special Political Committee to become the Special Political and Decolonization Committee; the **GA Fifth Committee** (the Administrative and Budgetary Committee); and the **GA Sixth Committee** (the Legal Committee). Every member state is represented on each committee, which reflects the sovereign equality of all members in the assembly.

Characteristic of a legislative branch of government, the GA has also established special committees and working groups to deal with explicit and discrete questions, or to fulfill procedural and administrative tasks. The most important of these are the General Committee, the Credentials Committee, the Advisory Committee on Administrative and Budgetary Questions (with the unwieldy acronym ACABQ), and the Committee on Contributions, which, in sequential order, prepare the agenda, certify members' delegations, advise the assembly on budget issues, and establish each member's dues contribution.

The General Assembly may also call **special sessions** to deal with particular issues. Article 20 of the Charter authorizes the GA to convene such special sessions "as occasion may require." Often the Security Council, by means of a resolution, starts the process by requesting that the assembly call a session. Special sessions provide an opportunity for the United Nations to move into areas of concern by and large unrelated to international questions of the immediate post–World War II period. Since the 1970s, nations from the developing world, with little diplomatic sway but a majority status in the GA, have used special sessions as a way of arousing public attention to issues related to development, international economic exchange, women, children, human settlements, HIV/AIDS, apartheid, and several other topics. At the same time, special sessions have been called to address more traditional concerns, such as disarmament.

The annual meeting of the GA usually convenes on the second or third Tuesday each September and concludes by mid-December. This period of early fall into winter includes the most intense portion of the session, when the assembly considers the majority of agenda items. Less

CHRONOLOGY OF GENERAL ASSEMBLY SPECIAL SESSIONS

1947	Palestine
1948	Palestine
1961	Tunisia
1963	The Financial Situation of the United Nations
1967	South West Africa (Namibia)
1974	Raw Materials and Development
1975	Development and International Economic Cooperation
1978	(April) Financing the UN Interim Force in Lebanon
	(April–May) Namibia
	(May–July) Disarmament
1980	New International Economic Order
1982	Disarmament
1986	(May–June) Africa
	(September) Namibia
1988	Disarmament
1989	Apartheid
1990	(February) Drug Abuse
	(April) International Economic Cooperation
1997	Earth Summit +5
1998	World Drug Problem
1999	(June–July) Population and Development
	(September) Small Island Developing States
2000	(June) Women 2000: Gender Equality, Development and Peace for the Twenty-First Century
	(June) Social Development
2001	(June) Implementation of the Outcome of the United Nations Conference on Human Settlements (HABITAT II)
	(June) Problem of Human Immunodeficiency Virus/Acquired Immunodeficiency Syndrome (HIV/AIDS) in All Its Aspects
2002	World Summit for Children
2005	Commemoration of the Sixtieth Anniversary of the Liberation of the Nazi Concentration Camps

frequent meetings may resume in January and continue through April to deal with additional or lingering matters. As mentioned in Chapter 1, the September session begins with opening statements by each nation during two weeks of General Debate. These statements are member nations' formal policy declarations about current international affairs and articulate a nation's official stance on questions before the United Nations. Because these opening statements are usually the most comprehensive and widely broadcast of a nation's foreign policy position, each nation often sends its president, prime minister, or minister of foreign affairs to deliver the address.

The GA's agenda comprises subjects proposed by any member state as well as continuing items contained in previously adopted assembly resolutions. Although member states thus determine the agenda, the secretary-general may also recommend items for consideration.

Continuing items can come directly to the assembly without going through a committee, but most successful resolutions appear first in the appropriate committees, where they are meticulously discussed and then passed before being sent to the full assembly for a final vote. Because the standing committees also have a plenary membership, resolutions sent to the General Assembly are usually ensured passage, most of the time by consensus without a vote. However, the volume of agenda items—many of them repeated each year—and the many draft resolutions, for which the outcome is known in advance of the vote, have burdened the assembly with unnecessary work. Reformers have argued that the General Assembly's authority would be strengthened if the GA concentrated on fewer and more critical issues.

The leadership and committee structure of the General Assembly can seem as bewildering as it would for any legislative branch. Those of you who have examined the U.S. Congress, or a parliamentary system such as that in England, each with its elaborate leadership and committee arrangements, may appreciate the equally complex structure of the GA. A key difference, which adds to the perplexity, is that whereas in a national legislature the majority party assumes dominant positions and individuals could be in power for a long time, the GA has sought to establish leadership positions according to annual rotation and regional equity. The assembly elects its president—that is, its presiding officer—approximately equivalent to the Speaker of the U.S. House of Representatives. The presidency, however, is more honorific and persuasive than substantive. It is accorded generally to a respected diplomat from a middle-range or smaller nation; no representative from a permanent member of the Security Council has ever been elected.

In addition to electing the president, the GA elects twenty-one vice presidents. A new election is held at the beginning of each session in September. The assembly chooses the president on a rotating basis from five geographic groups—Africa, Asia, Eastern Europe, Latin America and the Caribbean, and Western European and Other States (which include Canada, Australia, New Zealand, the United States, and Israel)—and the vice presidents proportionally also according to geographic areas. For the 2003 session, as described in the Introduction, Julian Hunte of Saint Lucia became the new GA president. Assisting him were eleven vice presidents from Africa and Asia (including two from Middle Eastern countries), two from Latin America and the Caribbean, one from the Western European and Other States group, and one from Eastern Europe. Because Hunte was from the Caribbean, his region had one fewer vice president than would normally be the case. The five remaining vice presidencies are always allotted to the permanent members of the Security Council. The GA president, the vice presidents, and the elected chairs of each of the six standing committees make up the **General Committee,** one of the GA's so-called procedural committees. The General Committee acts as a steering committee and, as noted previously, sets the agenda for the assembly.

Although the assembly has passed some famous (perhaps infamous) resolutions by majority vote, as a rule, the General Assembly tries to act by consensus rather than by majority. The practical reason for this preferred modus operandi is that although a majority vote can ensure passage of a resolution, and it is all that is required by Article 18, paragraph 3, of the UN Charter, the United Nations—an *inter*governmental organization—is made up of individual sovereign nations and does not have police authority or any legitimate overweening power to impose its will on its members. GA resolutions are not binding but rather rely on the readiness of member states to implement them, much as would be required in a *confederation*. Consequently, resolutions passed by a majority vote are futile unless all member states—especially the most powerful—are willing to abide by their terms. Since the end of the cold war, more than 70 percent of all GA resolutions have been adopted by unanimous consent, usually without necessitating even a formal recorded vote.[1] During the fifty-eighth session, votes were taken on 76 of the 316 agenda items; in many of these cases, no negative votes and only a few abstentions were recorded. In about half the cases since the early 1990s, when votes have been taken, fewer than ten negative responses have been recorded per vote. The use of abstentions—more common than negative votes—has also increased.

Nations usually vote negatively only when their national interests or perceived national security is endangered, and, as mentioned, such negative votes are in decline. Nevertheless, on November 4, 2003, the assembly saw this rare situation occur for back-to-back agenda items. First, on a resolution criticizing the U.S. economic embargo of Cuba, three states voted against the measure: the United States and two of its closest allies in the United Nations—Israel and the Marshall Islands. Second, in a vote of 129 to 1, the General Assembly accepted the International Atomic Energy Agency report that criticized North Korea for not fulfilling its obligations under the Treaty on the Non-Proliferation of Nuclear Weapons. The North Korean delegate voted "no," objecting to the criticism on the grounds that his government had withdrawn from the treaty.[2]

Only a few exceptions to the general rule of consensus can be noted. For example, in 1971 a majority of the GA voted to accept the People's Republic of China in the UN seat formerly held by the Republic of China on Taiwan. The vote overrode strong opposition by the United States and several of its allies. To this day, Beijing is the official representative of China in the United Nations.[3]

The Charter further provides that GA decisions on "important questions shall be made by a two-thirds majority of the members present and voting."[4] Article 18 of the Charter identifies "Important Questions" as those involving international peace and security, the choice of non-permanent Security Council members and ECOSOC members, trusteeship, admission of new members, suspension of membership rights and privileges, expulsion of a member, and the budget. However, this Charter requirement has had a modest impact because resolutions have rarely been adopted with less than a two-thirds majority.

Because the GA uses parliamentary procedures and passes resolutions by large majorities or consensus, it is a hybrid, combining characteristics of a parliament and a global diplomatic conference. For sensible reasons, the General Assembly functions as a negotiating body rather than as a typical legislative body. Yet, delegates lobby participating nations to gain their votes and to ensure the broadest support for any resolution. To this end, legislative factions known as **caucus groups** have emerged in the assembly in hopes of guaranteeing sufficient votes for favored resolutions.

Caucus groups are organized by geographic proximity, national identification with internationally recognized political or economic issues, or shared interests. In the United Nations, these voting blocs perform the function provided by political parties in a legislative body. Such groups are formed, both formally and informally, according to a number of commonalities, which vary with any particular issue. The most influential caucus groups in the General Assembly are, first, the Nonaligned Movement, a cluster of states organized during the cold war that was not associated with either superpower and subsequently played a critical role in negotiations on trade issues, and, second, the Group of 77. The latter caucus grew out of UN negotiations on North-South issues in the setting of the 1964 UN Conference on Trade and Development. Other caucus groups parallel the recognized geographic blocs in the world body. In practice, these groups are also the points at which diplomatic negotiations begin on any given issue. Each group, agreeing on a common position, presents it to the body at large. Such groups are particularly important to small and midsize nations, which have difficulty exerting influence individually and, hence, are more likely to agree on a common position representing the entire group.

Some subgroups form within geographic groups (such as the Nordic Group). Other subgroups span geographic regions (such as the Middle Eastern Group). Specific groupings often emerge on a given issue, including the Group of 8 (G-8) on economic matters, the Nuclear Powers

Group on disarmament matters, the Organization of Petroleum Exporting Countries (OPEC), the Least Developed Countries, the Small Island Developing States, and many other special-issue groups formed by nations that share a particular concern with and usually a similar view-point on a given issue. While all nations are members of an officially recognized geographic group, most nations are also members of several caucuses, which at times overlap and vary with each issue under consideration.

The size of the General Assembly, its many voting blocs, its use of parliamentary methods among sovereign and equal members, and its domination by small and weak states in the inter-national system contribute to a recurring impression of GA dysfunction and ineffectiveness. Because each state has one vote in the assembly, nations with small populations and limited power can and have collectively dominated GA business. The great powers and rich nations often criticize the resolutions passed in this atmosphere; consequently, such resolutions have little chance of implementation. Through the cumbersome process of attempting to achieve consensus, often the resulting resolutions are overly long, broad in their assertions, and, as a result of the diplomatic language needed to obtain opposing states' support, open to differing interpretations. Assembly and standing committee negotiations customarily carry on until provisions of various initial proposals are juggled and intermixed to reach wide compromise on a single resolution for each agenda topic. Only when full agreement is reached or when a few holdouts remain is an item usually brought to a plenary vote. A resolution that cannot command overwhelming majority support may be withdrawn.

Beyond its legislative responsibilities, the GA has other duties. In addition to electing nonpermanent Security Council members and Economic and Social Council and Trusteeship Council members, the assembly, on the recommendation of the Security Council, selects the secretary-general and the judges of the International Court of Justice. The General Assembly can propose, by a two-thirds vote, amendments to the Charter, which then must be ratified by the governments of two-thirds of the member states, including all five permanent members. According to Article 109 of the Charter, the GA can also set a place and time for a general conference in which Charter amendments can be proposed, although such a conference has never been held. While the Security Council is authorized to deal with questions affecting international peace and security, the General Assembly may also consider such questions and make recommendations to the Security Council. Under the 1950 Uniting for Peace Resolution (explained in Chapter 2), the GA authorized itself to make recommendations in cases when a veto has prevented the Security Council from taking action.

Finally, you should note that the GA is a historically unique gathering place for, in effect, all the governments of the world. As such, it provides, in the heart of New York City, a constructive social environment for contact among significantly different nations—large and small, rich and poor, powerful and powerless. As a result, in the delegate lounge and the halls near the General Assembly Hall at the UN building, you can find representatives from friendly or antagonistic nations—some who even refuse to recognize one another—engaging in informal, behind-the-scenes diplomacy. The GA has evolved through the years to become, in fact, the world's first "town hall" meeting place.

Security Council

When issues of war and peace reach the United Nations—as in the case of the debate over war in Iraq in 2003 or the problems in Afghanistan in 2002—they are taken before the Security Council (SC). For many of the world's people, and for the world's media, the Security Council becomes the focus of UN news in such cases. The reason is because the council, according to

Security Council Members Adopting the Brahimi Report, November 13, 2000 (Resolution 1327). (UN/DPI Photo by Eskinder Debebe. Reproduced by permission from the United Nations.)

Article 39 of the UN Charter, carries the organization's responsibility "to maintain or restore international peace and security." At the council, the great powers, including those who originally founded the organization, play out international power politics, as they have done since the end of World War II.

Council Organization

The Security Council comprises fifteen members. Ten are nonpermanent members; the remaining five have permanent membership, accompanied by the right of veto. The United States, the United Kingdom, France, the Russian Federation (formerly the USSR), and the People's Republic of China are the five permanent members (the so-called **P5**). The General Assembly elects the nonpermanent members for two-year terms. In 1965 an amendment to Article 23 of the Charter enlarged the number of nonpermanent members from the original six to ten. Currently, the assembly elects nonpermanent members according to an equitable geographic distribution: five from Africa and Asia (including the Middle East), two each from Latin America and the Caribbean and Western European and Other States and one from Eastern Europe. Five new members are elected each year to serve overlapping terms, and no nonpermanent member can be reelected for a second continuous term.

In 1946, abiding by Article 30, which grants the Security Council authority to establish its own rules, it adopted "Provisional Rules of Procedure," which have been amended several times. We should note, however, that Article 27 specifies SC voting procedure. Each council member has one vote. Article 27 requires nine votes for a proposal to pass (raised from seven with the enlargement of the council in 1965) and distinguishes between "procedural" and "substantive" matters. All of the P5 must support (or abstain) for a substantive resolution to pass. This provision is often referred to as the principle of *great-power unanimity* or, more commonly, the *veto power* (the word *veto* does not appear in the Charter). Although the use of the veto has declined steadily, a proposal may fail because of the mere threat of a veto. By long practice, determination as to whether an issue is procedural or substantive is itself considered a substantive question, which thus gives the permanent members in effect a **double veto** on all matters before the council. In the history of the United Nations, each of the five permanent members has at one time or another exercised the veto. A permanent member may also abstain, thus officially not supporting a decision but not blocking it.

Theoretically, the Security Council is in continuous session at UN Headquarters in New York City, although it has occasionally met elsewhere. For instance, the council held its inaugural meeting on September 17, 1946, in London. Other meetings have been held in Addis Ababa, Ethiopia, in 1972, and in Panama City, Panama, the following year. In September 2003, to encourage preliminary discussion of a U.S.-requested resolution regarding Iraq, Secretary-General Annan summoned the foreign ministers of just the P5 to an unusual gathering in Geneva while the regular Security Council remained at UN headquarters. In November 2004, the council met in Nairobi, Kenya, to highlight its concern about the deteriorating situation in Sudan's Darfur region. SC members are expected to have representatives in New York continuously. At important times, heads of state may also attend meetings, as was the case in January 1992, when thirteen heads of state or government and two ministers of foreign affairs met at a summit meeting of the council, and again in September 2000, when heads of state represented SC member countries during the special session of the Millennium Summit. The SC presidency rotates monthly, following alphabetical order for the English names of each country.

The Security Council presidency is a demanding and politically sensitive position. Although a representative of a specific country, and in office for only a month at a time, an SC president is expected to seek consensus among council members and to speak for the council. Thus, "presidential statements" carry the imprimatur of the full council, not the views of a specific country. For example, following the attacks of September 11, 2001, and the bombing of UN headquarters in Baghdad on August 19, 2003, SC presidential statements transcended parochial positions. Of notable interest was President Fayssal Mekdad's statement responding to the Baghdad bombing. Syria had abstained in a 14–0 vote to authorize the UN mission that had been attacked. Yet, President Mekdad, the representative from Syria on the council, declared,[5]

> The United Nations mission in Iraq has been established by the Security Council to help the Iraqi people to achieve their objectives. The United Nations is in Iraq on a mission of peace, and for the reconstruction of the country and to support the Iraqi people.

Presidential statements, like resolutions, are often hammered out in private, and the SC president guides these negotiating sessions and is principally responsible for drafting SC documents. Unlike most other UN organs, the Security Council is small and can work efficiently as a committee of the whole, where members find negotiating directly and candidly with one another expedient. In this environment the president makes suggestions, arbitrates among the various members, and strives to find compromise so that a proposal, preferably with unanimous backing, can be composed and made public.

In the UN's early years, and during certain crisis moments, SC gatherings could be seen on television. Although the organization's founders may have expected sessions to be conducted openly (and some of the most legendary—such as the 1962 meeting on the Cuban Missile Crisis and the 2003 session regarding imminent war in Iraq—have been), when a member so requests, the council will convene in private. In fact, private meetings (sometimes called *consultations*) have become common practice. In some instances actual debate among SC representatives occurs in meeting rooms adjacent to the Security Council chamber and only official voting (and often careful explication of a country's vote) is conducted within the chamber. Articles 31 and 32 of the Charter provide that nonmembers who are affected by an SC decision may be invited to participate in the discussion. Such was the case in the televised sessions in late winter 2003, when the Iraqi ambassador to the United Nations sat with the council and issued an oral defense of his country during the deliberations on how best to compel Baghdad to comply with Security Council resolutions.

The Security Council has established two standing committees under Article 29: the Committee on Admission of New Members (described subsequently) and the Committee of Experts on Rules and Procedures, which provides advice on these and other technical matters. Article 47 provided for a Military Staff Committee, made up of the P5 chiefs of staff. The founders envisioned the committee somewhat as a "joint chiefs of staff," which would take responsibility for carrying out council decisions on the use of armed forces. However, because of the onset of the cold war and the consequent divisions among the permanent members regarding any number of international issues, the Military Staff Committee never materialized as the imagined potent tool of the Security council and has become, instead, like an archaic Latin phrase, a neglected contrivance, perhaps curious only to academic ruminators. In 2005 Secretary-General Annan proposed its abolition. The spirit of Article 47, however, rests in the policies, either by preference or by constitutional mandate, of some nations—India and Norway, for example—to commit armed forces outside their countries only with Security Council authorization.[6]

The Security Council can create ad hoc committees as needed. These committees are composed of all council members and meet in closed session. Recent examples include the Governing Council of the UN Compensation Commission, established by SC Resolution 692 in 1991, and the Counter-Terrorism Committee, created after the terrorist attacks of September 11, 2001.

Various sanctions committees and working groups are also set up to deal with SC-approved sanctions. Since 1990 such bodies have concentrated on Iraq (following the invasion of Kuwait), as well as fractious states like Libya, Afghanistan, Somalia, Angola, Rwanda, Liberia, Sierra Leone, and Ethiopia. The Security Council is also responsible for the operation of the two international war crimes tribunals—the International Criminal Tribunal for the Former Yugoslavia (ICTY), meeting at The Hague and established by SC Resolution 808 in 1993, and the International Criminal Tribunal for Rwanda (ICTR), convened at Arusha, Tanzania, and deriving from SC Resolution 955 in 1994.

Council Powers

Alone among UN organs, the Security Council has the authority to execute its mandates and to require all members to abide by its directives (Article 25) when it imposes enforcement measures against a state. Unlike GA resolutions, those passed by the council are legally binding under international law. This authority makes the Security Council's power greater than that belonging to any other UN organ or, for that matter, any international body in history.

When the council determines that a threat to international peace and security exists, it will act under Charter provisions in either Chapter VI or Chapter VII. A lengthy history and description of the council's use of these two Charter sections can be found in Chapter 5. For the current discussion, you need note only that under Chapter VI, entitled "Pacific Settlement of Disputes," the council can recommend that the parties in a dispute use traditional diplomatic methods. These methods include mediation, conciliation, arbitration, and submission of the dispute to judicial determination. The council is expected initially to recommend diplomacy if a complaint about a threat to the peace is placed before it. Increasingly, the SC has asked the secretary-general to appoint special representatives or to use "good offices" to resolve the dispute. Ultimately, the Security Council (provided all permanent members agree, abstain, or fail to vote) can determine to take military action against an aggressor. As of July 2005, the council had endorsed war on only two occasions: in 1950 to defend South Korea against North Korea, and in 1991 to remove invading Iraq from Kuwait.

Chapters VI and VII are powerful weapons in the hands of the Security Council. However, during the cold war, members came to recognize the need in some cases for more forceful tools than those stipulated in Chapter VI, yet they found superpower differences standing in the way of using Chapter VII enforcement measures. In these circumstances, the council frequently authorized "peacekeeping" operations, which scholars have placed under a non-Charter rubric of **Chapter VI½ provisions.** The Security Council found that peacekeeping actions—not explicitly anticipated by the UN's founders—are an evolving mission for the United Nations and a traversal between the instruction in Chapter VI to settle disputes peacefully and the concern in Chapter VII about potential breaches of the peace. Moreover, the term *Chapter VI½* recommends itself as a way of defining recent SC actions to seek resolution to conflicts *within* states as well as *between* states.[7] As discussed in Chapter 6, the council also sends, or authorizes specific countries to send, peacekeeping (or even what might be called *peacemaking*[8]) forces into troubled areas.

Issues of peace and security understandably consume much of the Security Council's time and attract more public attention than other issues the United Nations addresses. At the same time, the Security Council has some other duties that are of consequence. For example, it recommends to the GA the candidate for the post of secretary-general, as well as new members to be admitted to the United Nations. The council's Committee on Admission of New Members evaluates applicant countries and then reports to the full body, which forwards its recommendation to the General Assembly, where approval of admission requires a two-thirds vote. The Security Council also exercises all functions relating to "strategic" trust territories and upholding trusteeship agreements (Article 83), recommends to the GA terms of admission for non-UN states who want to join the Statute of the International Court of Justice (Article 93), and, jointly with the General Assembly, elects judges to the court.[9] Other SC duties described in the Charter include recommending suspension or expulsion of a member (Articles 5 and 6), investigating international disputes that may lead to conflict, recommending methods for adjudicating disputes, devising strategies to control armaments, determining whether a threat to the peace exists and proposing methods to defuse the threat, and directing UN members to place economic and trade sanctions against aggressor nations.

The Call for SC Reform

Since the 1960s, several proposals have been made to reform certain aspects of the Security Council. First, a number of critics have suggested finding ways to restrain the use of the veto. From 1945 through 2004, the veto had been used 257 times. The Soviet Union and its successor, the Russian Federation, had compiled 122 vetoes (although following the collapse of the Soviet Union, Russia had used the veto only three times). The second largest number—and most of the recent vetoes—have come from the United States (80 by the end of 2004), which usually wants to deflect resolutions aimed at Israel.

Given the nature of the United Nations, the likelihood that the most powerful members of the council (including the United States) would ever accede to limiting their unilateral, entrenched power of veto is practically nonexistent. Even with the use of the veto in decline, states are still willing to threaten its use, which forces other members to withdraw contemplated draft proposals from council consideration. For example, in 2003, France's asserted willingness to veto U.S. proposals seeking UN authorization for its actions in Iraq convinced the United States to act outside UN sanction when it invaded Iraq in the spring. During the fall, France, Russia, and China then forced the United States into extended negotiation on a resolution to encourage multilateral participation in the occupation and reconstruction of Iraq. From a certain perspective, as the scholar John Stoessinger has argued, the veto—by ensuring the great powers of their ultimate sovereignty (which thus attracts them to abjuring unilateral action and persevering with thorny negotiations in the council) and by causing the Security Council to move from the idea of majority rule to the more realistic principle of diplomacy and consensus among sovereign entities—has actually strengthened the United Nations,[10] even though the immediate appearance to the general public may suggest weakness or deadlock.

A second reform issue—SC membership—is more problematic. One recurring complaint is that the council is too small and, on the whole, unrepresentative. You should recall that UN membership grew from 51 in 1945 to 113 members at the time of the 1965 enlargement of the council, to 191 by 2005. Yet, no new council seats have been added since the increase in 1965. At the same time, the P5—representing logical power configurations at the end of World War II—includes neither an African nor a South American state, while three European countries are represented. Presenting further incongruity, the European Union, which contains within it two of the permanent members and has a total population and economic wealth exceeding that of the United States, is moving toward becoming a single federated union, yet it has no distinct, legitimate stature on the Security Council. In addition, Germany and Japan, the defeated nations of World War II, are both seen in the new millennium as equally influential, economically and politically, with some other P5 members. Thus, as we discussed in Chapter 3, advocacy for expanding SC membership, including granting permanent status to countries from overlooked geographic areas, is mounting. At the same time, the prospect of expanding membership raises issues of efficiency and effectiveness and leaves some doubters worried that future council consensus will be even more difficult to achieve.

The call for internal reform is only one feature of the disquiet routinely directed at the Security Council. For example, complaints from Washington escalated in the run-up to the Iraqi war of 2003 because the Security Council would not budge and endorse unwavering support for U.S. military intervention. The disappointed U.S. administration began dubbing the council (in fact, the whole United Nations) imminently "irrelevant" for its inability to confront Saddam Hussein's evil forcefully and thus predicted that the United Nations was headed to the same antiquarian dust heap of history inhabited by the ineffective League of Nations.

Although this characterization may seem excessively harsh, no one can deny that the council's historical record has been checkered. For example, at times the council has passed resolutions it knew had no chance of being implemented, and sometimes its resolutions have seemed out of touch with international realities. For instance, the so-called safe areas the council set up in Bosnia in the mid-1990s (during the devastating civil wars in the former Yugoslavia) were anything but "safe" for the Muslim populations who sought protection in them. The council also turned its gaze from the barbarous internal genocide that ravaged Rwanda in 1994. Then, on August 19, 2003, the Security Council, refusing heavy security, suffered one of its most mortifying and heartbreaking moments when a bomb exploded at the UN compound in Baghdad and killed twenty-two dedicated international public servants, including Sergio Vieira de Mello, the UN High Commissioner for Human Rights and the secretary-general's special representative to war-damaged Iraq. The UN mission had been authorized by a unanimous (14–0; Syria abstaining) council resolution (Resolution 1483) passed on May 22 of that year. The resolution empowered a UN presence to provide much-needed humanitarian relief and help in nation building after the war. The bomb attack undercut the UN effort in Iraq, and by the end of September, nearly all UN personnel were withdrawn from the country.

We must remark that, in each of these instances, the Security Council is no more or less than the determinations of its member states. That is, whatever disappointments we can document, they are not so much failures of an abstract and autonomous apparatus as the collective failure of all its members. Moreover, the apparent failures, circuitously, draw attention to the evolving, and extremely difficult, work of the Security Council. Intended as the commanding instrument of the United Nations—to be led by the most powerful members of the organization—the council was designed not only to combat traditional state aggressors such as those believed to have caused World War II, but also to check other states from accumulating the most dangerous weapons—tasks it has pursued with alacrity and by and large in harmony. Its dedication to these causes was demonstrated in the war against the aggressor Iraq in 1991 and through the myriad resolutions regarding Iraqi disarmament. However, by the end of the century, the council found itself, in the bargain, dealing with novel new crises such as unraveling dysfunctional states, ethnic and religious conflict, brutal civil wars, enduring boundary clashes, aspiring and potentially radicalizing nationalist movements (as in the Middle East, among the Kurds, and in the caucuses and Asia), and the specter of fanatical terrorism, along with much more than was anticipated in 1945.

Sergio Vieira de Mello's biography discloses in vivid profile the Security Council's changing and expanding role. This distinguished international diplomat had, under council direction, dealt with the riskiest situations in the nastiest trouble spots around the globe. He was best known as the head of the UN Transitional Administration in East Timor (UNTAET), which had adroitly guided East Timor to democratic elections and full independence after that tiny country's bloody separation from Indonesia. Success in East Timor, fittingly, was considered a major triumph for both the United Nations and the Security Council. Other council-authorized operations have included the missions in Bosnia, Kosovo, Afghanistan, and Liberia (the latter established by unanimous SC vote—Resolution 1509—in the midst of stormy and well-publicized SC negotiations during the fall of 2003 to craft a resolution bringing an international presence into Iraq). By council direction, each of these missions was to be the lead institution in stabilizing traumatized postwar societies.

Election-monitoring operations have perhaps been even more significant. During the 1990s, UN monitors—in groups established by Security Council resolutions—guided elections in Cambodia and in various Central American countries. As of 2005, these nations, previously beset by outside interference and gory civil conflict, were living in relative peace. In each of these mandates (and more), the Security Council usually found itself in unanimous accord. In fact, what deserves emphasis is that the council, especially since the end of the cold war, has performed for the most part with harmony and purpose. At the same time, its resolutions have addressed the ever-tougher issues facing the "new" United Nations while taking on the force of legitimacy in world affairs like no unilateral national decision could. Such legitimacy is one reason that even the United States made a genuine effort to elicit SC sanction for its invasion of Iraq and, after the war, sought council resolutions to bring a UN presence into the country.[11] Therefore, the Security Council did not appear "irrelevant" as of the first decade of the twenty-first century.

So, although prospects for achieving sweeping reform of the SC's structural and compositional inadequacies may languish for the moment, the council remains the main global organization that brings legitimacy to world affairs. It is, understandably, the focus of attention when we think of the United Nations.

Economic and Social Council

A great deal of UN activity occurs outside the more visible realms of peace and war and great-power rivalries. When you consider the beneficial works of the United Nations and the many emergent issues that have become the province of the "new" United Nations, you more often than not should think of the Economic and Social Council, or ECOSOC. One of the six principal organs of the United Nations, ECOSOC is charged by Chapter X, Articles 62–66, to supervise extensive activities in the economic and social sphere (about 70 percent of the UN's budget in 2003 funded ECOSOC-related activities). ECOSOC is the UN organ most associated with the worthy but elusive goals of raising standards of living; advancing full and useful employment; promoting economic and social progress; identifying and solving economic, social, and health problems; encouraging cultural and educational cooperation; and strengthening respect for human rights and fundamental freedoms.

The UN Charter has been amended twice to enlarge the size of ECOSOC. These two amendments represent 40 percent of the five Charter amendments that have been ratified, which reflects the importance many nations accord ECOSOC. When colonialism ended and UN membership grew, so did ECOSOC membership. The increased membership fulfilled the wishes of newly independent countries to be represented in this organ, which had responsibilities they deemed so indispensable. In 1965 membership rose from eighteen to twenty-seven, and in 1971 to fifty-four. Nations represented on ECOSOC serve three-year terms; one-third are elected annually by the General Assembly to overlapping terms, following a formula ensuring equitable geographic distribution (fourteen are allocated to African states, eleven to Asian states, six to Eastern European states, ten to Latin American and Caribbean states, and thirteen to Western European and Other States). Each member can have only one representative on ECOSOC, but unlike the proscription on nonpermanent Security Council members, retiring members of ECOSOC are eligible for immediate reelection. Each member country has one vote, and all decisions are made by a majority of members present and voting.

The Bureau of the Economic and Social Council, the executive arm of ECOSOC, is elected at the beginning of each annual session. The bureau, comprising a president and four vice presidents, is responsible for proposing the agenda, drawing up a program of work, and organizing annual sessions in cooperation with the UN Secretariat. ECOSOC parcels out work to five standing committees: the Committee for Programme and Coordination, the Commission on Human Settlements, the Committee on Non-Governmental Organizations, the Committee on Negotiations with Intergovernmental Agencies, and the Committee on Energy and Natural Resources.

According to Article 62, ECOSOC's responsibilities are wide ranging, at least in terms of subject matter. This council may "make or initiate studies and reports with respect to international economic, social, cultural, educational, health, and related matters." ECOSOC is expected to make recommendations to the General Assembly, to UN member nations, or to specialized agencies. It can prepare draft conventions that deal with its designated areas of competence, which may then be submitted to the GA, or even call international conferences to deal with topics falling within its orbit. ECOSOC regularly requests reports from specialized agencies and UN member states that explain how its recommendations are being carried out. In fact, ECOSOC's singular ability to exert influence in the international community rests for the most part in its monitoring and publicizing compliance. That is, ECOSOC's main exercise is to focus world attention on economic and social troubles. Deciding how best to address the issues thus raised then becomes the responsibility of the General Assembly or individual member states. The council often offers requesting nations assistance in composing legislation to meet ECOSOC benchmarks. ECOSOC's aims may also be met in a summit conference or, more potently, in a treaty.

Other council responsibilities include the following four:

1. Coordinating the activities of independent specialized agencies (in 2005 fifteen of these agencies were under ECOSOC purview; an explanation of *specialized agencies* appears subsequently)
2. Accrediting the many nongovernmental organizations—of which more than twenty-six hundred now have "consultative status" to the council and that with time have played a growing role in ECOSOC deliberations and specialized agencies' activities
3. Receiving reports from UN funds and programmes, eleven of which reported to ECOSOC in 2005
4. Establishing regional and functional commissions to deal with specific issues of concern to the council

In terms of this last council responsibility, the five regional economic commissions—for Africa, Europe, Latin America and the Caribbean, Asia and the Pacific, and Western Asia—encourage cooperation and coordination among governments in geographically proximate areas[12] and help finance economic development projects in their respective regions. In contrast, ECOSOC **functional commissions** deal with specific topics of global merit. ECOSOC established six of them in 1946: the Commission on Human Rights (one of the better known), the Commission for Social Development, the Commission on the Status of Women, the Statistical Commission, the Commission on Population (renamed in 1994 the "Commission on Population and Development"), and the Commission on Narcotic Drugs. The remaining three, established in later years, reflect ECOSOC's escalating concentration on issues affecting developing countries. In 1992 the council created commissions on Crime Prevention and Criminal Justice, and Science and Technology for Development; in 1993, on Sustainable Development. Each of these commissions is the principal UN agency in its field. They draft treaties, compose suitable rules, and monitor the fulfillment of previous agreements. In addition, the council and its commissions publish useful informational guides and model legislation in various relevant fields. ECOSOC and its commissions advertise and bolster existing agreements and encourage voluntary and normative international standards of behavior within the province of ECOSOC's charge.

Each July, ECOSOC convenes a month-long substantive session known as the *High-Level Segment.* These meetings alternate between the headquarters in New York City and that in Geneva and attract major government figures from the member states and the chiefs of international agencies. These sessions concentrate on a selected theme of global significance. (For example, in the summer of 2004 in New York the session addressed the theme of poverty eradication in the Least Developed Countries. In 2003 the session deliberated on "Promoting an integrated approach to rural development in developing countries for poverty eradication and sustainable development.") Usually, following the summer meeting, the council adopts a Ministerial Declaration forwarding recommendations for action. As an example, in 2002 the council endorsed the New Partnership for Africa's Development (NEPAD).

Because of the scope of the General Assembly's functions and because the GA has authority to deal with virtually any issue deemed appropriate for UN consideration, ECOSOC's role is less explicit than that of the other main organs. Also, given the expansive nature of ECOSOC's mandate, different member states often voice dissimilar views about what ECOSOC should be doing. The opening declaration of the UN Charter includes the aspiration "to promote social progress and better standards of life." Developing nations often view this injunction as important as the more traditional aims of preserving peace, enhancing human rights, and developing international law, which are also cataloged in the preamble. ECOSOC's dealing with the issue of economic and social development has pleased impoverished countries, which see such development

ECONOMIC AND SOCIAL COUNCIL: ITS NETWORK OF COMMISSIONS, COMMITTEES, BODIES, FUNDS, PROGRAMMES, AND EXPERTS

Functional Commissions
Statistical Commission
Commission on Population and Development
Commission for Social Development
Commission on Human Rights
Commission on the Status of Women
Commission on Narcotic Drugs
Commission on Crime Prevention and Criminal Justice
Commission on Science and Technology for Development
Commission on Sustainable Development

Regional Commissions
Economic Commission for Africa (ECA)
Economic and Social Commission for Asia and the Pacific (ESCAP)
Economic Commission for Europe (ECE)
Economic Commission for Latin America and the Caribbean (ECLAC)
Economic and Social Commission for Western Asia (ESCWA)

Standing Committees
Committee for Programme and Coordination
Commission on Human Settlements
Committee on Non-Governmental Organizations
Committee on Negotiations with Intergovernmental Agencies
Committee on Energy and Natural Resources

Ad hoc Bodies
Ad hoc Advisory Groups on African Countries Emerging from Conflicts
Ad hoc Advisory Group on Haiti
Information and Communications Technologies Task Force
Public-Private Alliance for Rural Development
Committee on Negotiations with Intergovernmental Agencies
UN Forum on Forests
Ad hoc open-ended intergovernment group of experts on energy and
    sustainable development
Ad hoc open-ended working group on informatics

Expert Bodies Composed of Governmental Experts
Committee of Experts on the Transport of Dangerous Goods and on the
    Globally Harmonized System of Classification and Labelling of
    Chemicals
UN Group of Experts on Geographical Names

**Expert Bodies Composed of Members Serving in
Their Personal Capacity**
Committee for Development Policy
Committee of Experts on Public Administration

(continued)

ECONOMIC AND SOCIAL COUNCIL
(*continued*)

> Ad hoc Group of Experts on International Cooperation in Tax Matters
> Committee on Economic, Social and Cultural Rights
> Permanent Forum on Indigenous Issues
>
> **Related Bodies**
> International Narcotics Control Board
> International Research and Training Institute for the Advancement of
>   Women (INSTRAW)
> Committee for the UN Population Award
> Programme Coordination Board of the Joint United Nations
>   Programme on HIV/AIDS
>
> **Funds and Programmes That Send Reports to ECOSOC**
> UN Children's Fund (UNICEF)
> UN Conference on Trade and Development (UNCTAD)
> UN Development Fund for Women (UNIFEM)
> UN Development Programme (UNDP)
> UN Environment Programme (UNEP)
> Office of the UN High Commissioner for Refugees (UNHCR)
> UN Population Fund (UNFPA)
> UN Relief and Works Agency for Palestine Refugees in the Near East
>   (UNRWA)
> Office for Drug Control and Crime Prevention (ODCCP)
> World Food Programme (WFP)
> UN Human Settlements Programme (UN-HABITAT)
> Board of Trustees of the International Research and Training Institute
>   for the Advancement of Women

as vital to their well-being.[13] Conversely, industrialized First World nations often regard development as secondary to the maintenance of international peace and security and see expanded trade and emergent globalization as the keys to lifting poorer nations into the economic mainstream. Nevertheless, so-called Third World countries use the word *development* to articulate what they believe to be the central purpose of the United Nations; poorer nations have, at times, even suggested that helping them with economic and social development constitutes a necessary precondition for the ultimate maintenance of international peace and security. So, when some nations talk about reforming the United Nations, they are hoping to strengthen ECOSOC rather than address the various complaints richer members voice. The debate about ECOSOC seems to mirror the debate over an "old" and a "new" United Nations, both of which, in fact, subsist.

Trusteeship Council

Of the six major UN organs, the Trusteeship Council most dramatically demonstrates the UN's evolution and, arguably, its success as a world organization. The Trusteeship Council is actually defunct, having accomplished the goals given it by the Charter in Chapter XIII. The Trusteeship Council suspended its operations on November 1, 1994, following the independence of Palau (October 1, 1994), the last remaining UN trust territory. All eleven trust territories identified at the end of World

War II had become self-governing, independent states or had merged with other neighboring independent nations. Early in his tenure, Secretary-General Kofi Annan suggested—in his 1997 reform proposal, *Renewing the United Nations*—that the council be reenergized and converted into a forum on global environmental issues and protection of common areas such as the oceans, the atmosphere, and outer space. By 2005 the secretary-general advocated terminating the council.

The Trusteeship Council had been assigned the responsibility of overseeing the territories placed under the UN's Trusteeship System and ensuring the advancement of these territories from colonial status to self-government. The council's membership consisted of states administering any trust territory, the Security Council's five permanent members (whether or not an administrating nation), and sufficient other states elected to ensure equal numbers of administering and nonadministering members on the council. Midway through the council's history, its membership reached fourteen, but by the late 1960s, rapid decolonization resulted in a membership of just the P5. By 1975 only the United States still administered holdings: the Federated States of Micronesia, the Marshall Islands, and Palau. In 1986 the first two approved a "free association" with the United States that allowed for complete domestic autonomy, and Palau gained independence following a plebiscite in 1994. Palau became the 185th member of the United Nations in 1995. The Trusteeship Council ceased operations, having supervised this transference of political authority, and all the new nations crafted from this feat became sovereign members of the United Nations.

Secretariat

The **Secretariat** is the main UN organ listed last in the Charter, but it is no less important than the other five. The Secretariat is the international civil service staff that administers the day-to-day operations of the United Nations. Provided for in Chapter XV, Articles 97–101, of the Charter, the Secretariat works for the United Nations at the headquarters in New York City and around the world, serves other principal organs of the United Nations, and administers the programs and policies determined by these organs. The job of the Secretariat is comparable, on the international stage, to the job carried out by the national bureaucracy of an individual nation. Besides performing other functions, these international civil servants administer SC-authorized peacekeeping operations; handle refugee problems; mediate international disputes; survey economic and social trends; prepare studies on human rights, economic development, and sustainable development; and undertake anything else commanded by any UN organ. The Secretariat provides information to the general public about the United Nations, organizes international conferences, monitors the implementation of UN directives, interprets speeches and translates documents into the UN's official languages, and more. Although its main headquarters is in New York, the Secretariat maintains an important presence in Geneva, Vienna, and Nairobi, and where related UN agencies are headquartered in yet other cities, such as The Hague and Rome.

The head of the Secretariat is the UN secretary-general. The General Assembly, on recommendation of the Security Council, appoints the secretary-general for a five-year term, and the occupant can be reelected.[14] Because the five permanent members of the security council retain a veto, a nominee could receive fourteen votes yet be unsuccessful. That is, all five permanent members must accede to any nomination. Tanzania's foreign minister, Salim Ahmed Salim, was a challenging candidate to Kurt Waldheim in 1981 and would have become the first sub-Saharan African to serve in the post. However, the new conservative Reagan administration in Washington, resistant to the recent tilt in the United Nations toward what it perceived as Third World radicalism, supported Waldheim, as did, interestingly, the Soviet Union, which ended Salim's candidacy.

The Secretariat consists of an assortment of offices and agencies, each headed by an under-secretary-general, an assistant secretary-general, or a senior official, all reporting to the secretary-general. These units are the Executive Office of the Secretary-General, the Office of Internal Oversight Services (OIOS), the Office of Legal Affairs (OLA), the Department of Political Affairs (DPA), the Department for Disarmament Affairs (DDA), the Department of Peacekeeping Operations (DPKO), the Office for the Coordination of Humanitarian Affairs (OCHA), the Department of Economic and Social Affairs (DESA), the Department for General Assembly Affairs and Conference Services (DGAACS), the Department of Public Information (DPI), and the Department of Management (DM). In 1997 the General Assembly established the Senior Management Group (SMG) as the central policy-planning body to ensure strategic coherence to UN activities. Chaired by the secretary-general, the SMG includes not only several under-secretaries-general stationed in New York City, but many agency heads and directors general head-quartered in Geneva, Nairobi, Vienna, and Rome. Originally twenty-three members were included, but by 2004 the number had grown to thirty-one. Secretary-General Annan expanded the group largely by adding several of the executive directors of the regional economic commissions and the heads of new offices created since 1997. In addition, the UN ombudsman, although largely independent of outside control, reports to and can be removed only by the secretary-general.

In 2004 almost nine thousand men and women, under the regular budget, from about 170 countries, made up the staff of the Secretariat (compared with more than 2.7 million U.S. federal government employees). Many more employees work for related agencies (like the World Health Organization and the World Bank). These workers are international civil servants and are not answerable to specific nations but to the United Nations alone. Secretariat employees take an oath not to seek or receive instructions from any government or outside authority. According to the Charter, member states must respect the exclusive international character and responsibilities of Secretariat personnel and not seek to influence their activities in an improper way. Although the public rarely hears about the day-to-day workers in the Secretariat—more likely aware of the current secretary-general or perhaps a highly visible appointee—these international public servants, working unassumingly within the Secretariat's many offices, in related agencies, and for the secretary-general's special representatives dealing with distinct challenges, are the most palpable UN presence in much of the world. The twenty-two individuals killed in the bombing of the UN mission in Baghdad in 2003 were representative. An example was Nadia Younes. Born in Egypt, Ms. Younes earned a bachelor of arts degree at Cairo University and a master's degree in international relations from New York University. She began her UN career at the age of 24 in the Office of General Services. Later she moved to the Department of Public Affairs, and then for a number of years was UN Chief of Protocol. From 1999 to early 2001, she was in charge of information and communication for the UN Mission in Kosovo. She then became executive director for external relations at the World Health Organization. At the time of her death, she was the chief of staff for Special Representative Vieira de Mello. She had served the Secretariat for a third of a century.[15]

Despite its impartial and international character, the Secretariat has at times been the target of suspicion and criticism by member governments. At the height of the cold war, both the United States and the Soviet Union accused the Secretariat of serving as a tool for the other side; in 1953, by the U.S. government of harboring American employees with Communist sympathies; and in 1960, by the Soviets of being led by a secretary-general overly supportive of Western policies. During the 1980s and 1990s, the most serious charges were that the Secretariat was too large, inefficient, and wasteful. Secretary-General Boutros Boutros-Ghali tried, unsuccessfully, to quiet the critics, particularly in the United States, by freezing the budget and announcing reforms. His successor, Kofi Annan, presented his extensive reform and reorganization plans in 1997, consolidating and regrouping some twenty-four agencies into five divisions and creating a new position—deputy secretary-general—to preside over the streamlined bureaucracy. When the General Assembly approved the first package of proposed reforms, the savings amounted to about $123 million. One consequence was that the U.S. Congress finally passed an appropriation of $819 million to repay some of the $1 billion in back dues the United States owed.

On March 2, 1998, Louise Fréchette became the UN's first deputy secretary-general (DSG). The duties of the DSG are to act for the secretary-general (SG) at UN headquarters when the SG is absent, to enhance coherence and cooperation among UN bodies, to provide leadership in UN economic and social activities, to represent the SG at conferences and official functions, and to "undertake such assignments as may be determined by the secretary-general." The deputy secretary-general serves only during the term of the secretary-general who appoints him or her. As the first occupant of the office, Fréchette defined, by her actions and assigned duties, the initial parameters of the position. Fréchette served on the Senior Management Group and other Secretariat committees. As the first deputy secretary-general, she gave the post a public legitimacy that made the DSG more than just another senior member of the UN Secretariat.

International Court of Justice

The International Court of Justice (ICJ) is the UN's principal judicial organ. It was established in 1945 in the Charter (Chapter XIV) as the successor to the Permanent Court of International Justice (PCIJ). While the court functions as the UN's legal arm, it is an independent institution. Its governing document—the Statute of the International Court of Justice—accentuates this independence. The statute is a part of, and usually appended to, any published copy of the UN Charter. It is based on the 1922 Statute of the Permanent Court of International Justice. The statute details the organization, procedures, and jurisdiction of the court. The ICJ, like the predecessor PCIJ, is often called the *World Court*.

The outbreak of world war in 1939 damaged the reputation not only of the League of Nations, but also of the PCIJ, which met for the last time on December 4, 1939. In 1942 U.S. secretary of state Cordell Hull and the foreign minister of the United Kingdom, Anthony Eden, declared their support for postwar reestablishment of an international court. In early 1943 the United Kingdom invited a number of experts to London to discuss the subject. Forming the Inter-Allied Committee, under the chairmanship of Sir William Malkin, the group held nineteen meetings and published a report on February 10, 1944. The committee suggested, among other recommendations, that the statute of any new court be based on that of the PCIJ. Later that year, at the Dumbarton Oaks Conference, the four attending powers agreed on including an international court of justice in the emerging structure of the United Nations. In April 1945 a meeting of jurists from forty-four nations convened in Washington, D.C. Chaired by G. H. Hackworth of the United States, the committee composed a draft statute for the new court, which was then submitted to the UN's organizing conference in San Francisco. To retain a sensible continuity with evolving international law, the authors of the UN Charter made clear in Article 92 that the ICJ statute was based on that of the PCIJ. The old court convened in October 1945 to dissolve itself and transfer its archives to the new court. The sixth and last president of the PCIJ, Judge J. Gustavo Guerrero, became the first elected president of the new International Court of Justice.

The ICJ is the only principal organ of the United Nations not based in New York City. The seat of the court is at the Peace Palace in The Hague, the Netherlands. The ICJ may hold sessions elsewhere if it so determines, but as of 2005 it had never done so. Its first session took place

April 18, 1946. Since then the ICJ has been considered in continuous session. The court determines its own rules of procedure, elects its own president and vice president, and appoints a registrar (with the equivalent rank of a UN assistant secretary-general) and other registry staff and officers. The ICJ Registry maintains all court records, makes available court publications, communicates with outside organizations, acts as a press office, and maintains a Web site. Appointees to the registry must know both French and English, the official languages of the court.

The World Court should not be confused with the International Criminal Court (ICC), which is located in the same city. The ICC is a relatively new creation, established by the Rome Treaty, to try war criminals. It applies laws of humanity, as authorized by its contracting states, to individuals who are accused of particularly heinous crimes such as genocide. In contrast, the ICJ hears only cases between states that are voluntarily brought to it by one of the adversaries, or it delivers advisory opinions at the request of UN bodies. States are not bound by the ICJ's opinions, nor are they subject to penalties imposed by the court, whereas convicted defendants before the ICC may be incarcerated.

All UN members are parties to the ICJ's statute. Fifteen judges are on the court, elected by the General Assembly and the Security Council for nine-year terms. The procedure of nominating and electing candidates for judgeships on the court is complex and is detailed in Article 4 of the statute (see Appendix D). All nation-states party to the ICJ statute are allowed to put forward candidates, although the nominations are made not by the government, but by a group of four members from the Permanent Court of Arbitration (initiated by The Hague Conference of 1899) who are from the nominating state. If a country is not represented on the Permanent Court of Arbitration, it may still make a nomination through a similar national group of legal experts that would clearly qualify to serve on the arbitration tribunal. Each group can propose as many as four candidates, not more than two of its own nationality. The names are then forwarded to the UN secretary-general, who submits the names to the General Assembly and the Security Council for vote. For this election the permanent members of the Security Council retain no right of veto; the required majority vote for a judge in that body is eight. Both the General Assembly and the Security Council vote simultaneously but separately. To be elected, a candidate must obtain an absolute majority in both chambers. Consequently, several votes must often be taken before an election is decided. The elections are almost always held—in three-year cycles—at UN headquarters in New York during the annual fall session of the General Assembly.

The term of office begins on February 6 of the next year. Judges may be reelected, but no two from the same country may serve simultaneously. (If two candidates of the same nationality are elected at the same time, the elder one receives the appointment.) According to Article 16 of the ICJ statute, judges on the court may not engage in other political or administrative employment or in any other professional occupation. Members of the court are independent; they do not represent their governments. Still, they must be qualified for appointment to the highest judicial offices in their respective countries or be recognized as experts in international law. No judge may be dismissed except by the unanimous decision of the other judges. The United Nations has always tried to apportion the judgeships on an equitable geographic basis. (In 2005 the allocation of seats on the court was two Africans, two Latin Americans, two Asians, two Middle Easterners, two Eastern Europeans, four Western Europeans, and one North American.) There is no entitlement to membership, but normally the court has always had judges from the permanent members of the Security Council, except for China.

The court deals only with disputes between sovereign states; no private party may present a case. The court is not expected to resolve all international conflicts, but only specific legal disputes brought before it. It has compulsory jurisdiction in cases involving countries that have signed optional clause 36 (paragraphs 2 and 3) of the ICJ's statute, which allows the court to adjudicate legal disputes concerning (a) the interpretation of a treaty, (b) any question of international law, (c) the existence of any fact that may constitute a breach of an international obligation, or (d) the nature and extent of a reparation for such a breach. The two affected states must usually agree to bring the case, and no state may be sued before the court unless it consents to such an action. In fact, the effectiveness and the jurisdiction of the court depend on the consent of the states affected.

Cases are normally initiated either by the disputants—who notify the court of a special agreement reached by each to seek court action—or by the initiation of one party, which acknowledges that the opposing party has not recognized the court's jurisdiction, but asks it to do so. Nation-states have no permanent official representatives at the ICJ. Usually, a nation's foreign minister or ambassador to the Netherlands communicates with the court's registrar. Litigants before the court are not required to pay fees or administrative expenses; these costs fall to the United Nations.

Proceedings before the court consist of a written phase, when the parties file and exchange pleadings, and an oral stage, when public hearings are conducted and counsels address the court. The court may hear witnesses and authorize investigations by commissions of experts. The court deliberates in private, but all judgments—arrived at by majority vote—are made public in court chambers. A judge in the minority may file a dissenting opinion, although majority judgments are final; no appeal may be made. The court has no power of enforcement. Article 94 of the UN Charter provides recourse to the Security Council for a successful disputant unhappy at noncompliance with a decision. The council may then forward recommendations or take measures to effect the judgment. In fact, however, given the reality of a world of sovereign nations, the court's verdicts depend wholly on the litigants' compliance. Nonetheless, as of 2005 in only two recorded instances had a party disappointed with a decision failed to comply with the court. The first ICJ decision, in the Corfu Channel case of 1946, was rebuffed by Albania when it failed to pay the United Kingdom the £843,947 mandated by the court as compensation for damages suffered. In the second case, the United States, reacting to the 1984 case of *Nicaragua v. U.S.A.,* in which Nicaragua charged the U.S. government with violating international law by mining the harbor at Minagua, refused for two years to accept prior compulsory jurisdiction of the court in matters relating to Central America. Following the court's insistence (by a 12–3 majority) that the United States had violated international law and should pay reparations to Nicaragua, Washington blocked any appeal to the Security Council. Bear in mind, also, that on several occasions, by request of one of the litigants, cases have been removed from the court's list before a judgment was rendered.

Under the provisions of Article 26 of the ICJ statute, the court may establish a special chamber composed of three or more judges, either at the request of the parties in an individual case or to deal with particular categories of cases. Such a procedure was used for the first time in 1982 and has been used infrequently since (once in 1985 and twice in both 1987 and 2002). In July 1993 the court set up a special seven-member chamber to deal with environmental cases falling within its jurisdiction.

Article 65 of the statute also authorizes the court to deliver **advisory opinions** if requested by another principal UN organ or by a specialized agency. On receiving such a request, the court seeks relevant information and collects written and oral statements on the issue. Otherwise, the procedures for dealing with advisory opinions and the legal sources used are the same as for adversarial cases. Advisory opinions are consultative in nature and thus not binding. A nation may simply disregard an advisory opinion, as happened, for example, when in 1948 the court advised the General Assembly that the Soviet Union could not use its veto to deny UN membership to the states of Italy and Finland. Moscow ignored the decision and ultimately struck a compromise with Western nations that resulted in the admittance of the two countries, along with several other nations. As of summer 2005 the court had rendered twenty-five advisory opinions concerning various topics, including issues of UN membership, reparation for injuries sustained during service in the United Nations, the territorial status of Namibia and Western Sahara, expenses of various UN operations, the status of human rights special rapporteurs, the legality of the threat or use of nuclear weapons, and the permissibility under international law for Israel to build a wall separating Israeli and Palestinian communities on the West Bank.

From 1946 to 2005, about one hundred contentious cases were referred to the court, although several were later removed from the court's list or were considered still pending. (The court had delivered eighty-nine judgments as of 2005.) Of the seventy-five countries that had been litigants in these cases, the United States was involved most often (about twenty times); the United Kingdom and the former Yugoslavia ranked second and third.

Three specific cases provide examples of the court's workings. In its first case, the Corfu Channel case (*United Kingdom v. Albania*), the court tendered three judgments. On March 25, 1948, it asserted its jurisdiction over the case—involving a British grievance against Albania for explosions in the Corfu Channel in 1946 that had damaged a British warship and killed crew members. Then, on April 9, 1949, it found Albania responsible, under international law, for the explosions. Finally, on December 15, 1949, the court assessed Albania a reparation payment to be paid to the United Kingdom. However, as noted previously, Albania refused to observe the judgment.

In the second example, in 1979 the United States requested that the court take the U.S. Diplomatic and Consular Staff in Tehran case (*U.S.A. v. Iran*). Washington brought the case after Iranian militants occupied the U.S. embassy on November 4, 1979, and took its diplomatic and consular staff hostage. The court immediately held that no requirement for international relations was more fundamental than the inviolability of diplomatic envoys and embassies. In a May 24, 1980, judgment, the court found that Iran had violated obligations to the United States according to international law and under existing conventions. However, the court was not called on to deliver any further judgment on reparation, and, on May 12, 1981, the case was removed from the court's list. Ultimately, negotiations between Iran and the United States took place to resolve outstanding grievances on both sides. The result was the establishment of the Iran-U.S. Claims Tribunal to handle claims by nationals of either country. By the end of the century, the tribunal had dealt with more than thirty-nine hundred cases.

The third example is the LaGrand case (*Germany v. United States of America*), decided on June 27, 2001. Citing Article 36 of the statute (explained previously), the court determined that the United States had violated international law when it failed to grant consular services to two German brothers executed in Arizona in 1999. Also, the court found that the United States had ignored an ICJ order to stay one of the executions. The two brothers were charged with murder in a 1982 holdup. During the proceedings, Washington conceded that it had neglected the 1963 Vienna Convention on Consular Relations when prosecuting the LaGrand brothers without informing diplomats from their homeland, but insisted that the brothers had received a fair trial and that the verdicts would have been unaffected by consular intervention. However, ICJ president Gilbert Guillaume, speaking for the court's overwhelming majority, reprimanded the United States for denying defendants their international rights regardless of the likely outcome of a trial. The ruling was also noteworthy because it pronounced, for the first time in the court's history, that ICJ provisional orders, such as the ignored injunction against Walter LaGrand's execution, were legally binding.

As these cases demonstrate, the court considers itself an organ of and a contributor to international law. It decides disputes consistent with international law, the sources of which, according to Article 38 of the statute, are international conventions, international custom, general principles of law recognized by civilized nations, judicial decisions, and teachings of the most qualified publicists on the topic. By the twenty-first century, the ICJ had become part of a remarkably transformed global legal system, featuring a permanent multilateral framework for the resolution of disputes; the preservation of peace; the rules of war; the establishment of war crimes tribunals; financial, economic, environmental, and technological cooperation; and even the promulgation of individual and human rights.

SPECIALIZED AGENCIES, PROGRAMMES AND FUNDS, AND OTHER GROUPS

In addition to the UN's six principal organs, other UN-related groups and activities have contributed to the mutable and evolving character of the world organization. We begin our look at these not-so-distant relatives by first examining **specialized agencies, programmes,** and **funds.** A listing of these groups can be found in the figure of the UN System that appears at the beginning of this chapter.

Specialized Agencies

Specialized agencies are autonomous, self-governing entities that, nonetheless, fall under the general rubric of the United Nations; they are specifically mentioned in Articles 57, 63, and 64 of the UN Charter. At some point in time, specialized agencies formally established a contractual relationship with the broader organization, subjecting themselves to the administrative and budgetary rules of the United Nations. They must report to the world body on all aspects of their work and organization. As noted previously, their conduit to the larger organization is the Economic and Social Council, which is authorized to coordinate the work of specialized agencies and to solicit regular reports from them. However, ECOSOC's "consultations" with and "recommendations" to the agencies—some with overlapping missions—are less ordered than those in some other UN linkages, because each agency is independent. Thus ECOSOC's oversight is generally limited to making broad suggestions and highlighting certain issues. Still, as of 2005, fifteen specialized agencies reported to ECOSOC annually.

Article 57 of the UN Charter explains that specialized agencies are separately chartered, independent organizations. They act in a particular or technical area of international concern, and each has, according to Article 57, "wide international responsibilities . . . in economic, cultural, educational, health and related fields." Such agencies have come into being when the international community has determined that a particular problem or issue required collaborative action or regulation. The General Assembly created a few of these specialized agencies, and UN-sponsored conferences established others. Some came into existence long before the United Nations did. For example, the Universal Postal Union dates from the nineteenth century. The League of Nations originated others, many of which the United Nations ultimately endorsed.

A statute or treaty typically governs a specialized agency, specifying its functions, duties, mandate, voting method, and organizational structure. Specialized agencies are intergovernmental organizations (IGOs) composed of member states. A nation becomes a member by signing and ratifying the relevant treaty. Therefore, not all UN members are ipso facto members of all specialized agencies. Specialized agencies also have their own budgets, which are funded by assessment of members or, often, by members' voluntary contributions.

Each agency has an independent governing body, structure, and method of functioning. Usually, a general conference of the agency's members elects the governing body, which includes day-to-day administrative officers (sometimes called a *secretariat*). Whereas decision

UN SPECIALIZED AGENCY LOCATIONS AROUND THE WORLD

AUSTRIA
Vienna
UN Industrial Development Organization (UNIDO)

CANADA
Montreal
International Civil Aviation Organization (ICAO)

FRANCE
Paris
UN Educational, Scientific and Cultural Organization (UNESCO)

ITALY
Rome
Food and Agriculture Organization (FAO)
International Fund for Agricultural Development (IFAD)

Trieste
International Centre for Science and High Technology (ICS) [under the aegis of UNIDO]

Turin
International Training Center (ILO/ITC) [the training arm of ILO]

SPAIN
Madrid
World Tourism Organization

SWITZERLAND
Berne
Universal Postal Union (UPU)

Geneva
International Labour Organization (ILO)
International Telecommunication Union (ITU)
World Health Organization (WHO)
World Intellectual Property Organization (WIPO)
World Meteorological Organization (WMO)

UNITED KINGDOM
London
International Maritime Organization (IMO)

UNITED STATES OF AMERICA
Washington, D.C.
International Monetary Fund (IMF)
World Bank Group (WBG)
    International Bank for Reconstruction and Development (IBRD) [called the *World Bank*]
    International Development Association (IDA)
    International Finance Corporation (IFC)
    Multilateral Investment Guarantee Agency (MIGA)
    International Centre for the Settlement of Investment Disputes (ICSID)

making in some agencies conforms to basic democratic procedures (one member, one vote), some agencies depart from this standard. Key exceptions are the International Monetary Fund (IMF) and the World Bank, where weighted voting, based on member states' contributions, determines policy (the IMF and the World Bank are discussed in more detail later in this chapter). Likewise, representatives of government, employers, and labor organizations from each member nation have a vote in the International Labour Organization. Some specialized agencies (e.g., the International Civil Aviation Organization, or ICAO) require nations important to the agency's subject matter (e.g., nations with the largest air carriers) to hold seats on the agency's governing body (e.g., the ICAO council). Other specialized agencies may require general conferences to approve decisions made by governing boards or committees of the agency, although in several, governing boards have considerable leeway in determining rules and making general decisions. Also, specialized agencies may draft treaties or conventions to submit to their member states. Often the General Assembly and ECOSOC will endorse and urge ratification of these international agreements.

Finally, of the growing number of nongovernmental organizations that continue to dot the international landscape, many seek to have an influence on the specialized agencies because the latter deal with matters that NGOs consider vital. Specialized agencies even sometimes need the kind of expertise NGOs offer (comparable to that provided by the perhaps unfairly maligned "interest groups" and lobbyists in congressional or parliamentary systems of government). For example, involved closely with the World Health Organization and other health-related agencies, Médecins Sans Frontières (MSF, "Doctors Without Borders") has developed an ongoing partnership. Its experience and that of other long-standing NGOs have encouraged new organizations to form and quickly seek a voice in agency activities. On the basis of MSF's success, in 2001 sociologists who were committed to advancing human rights, particularly in the developing world, met in Madrid and created Sociologists Without Borders. It directed its first efforts toward the UN Educational, Scientific and Cultural Organization, communicating its criticisms of U.S. human rights policy around the world.

Each specialized agency has established its own mandate and mission. Some of the agencies are chiefly rule-making entities that bring international regulatory norms to common practices—such as the ICAO, the Universal Postal Union, the International Telecommunication Union, and the International Maritime Organization. Several of the specialized agencies make use of technical experts, who, though appointed by specific member governments, are expected to act without political motivation. Some agencies concentrate on economic and financial matters (the World Bank and the International Monetary Fund), the rights of labor (the International Labour Organization), world food and health issues (the Food and Agriculture Organization and the World Health Organization), social and economic development (the International Fund for Agricultural Development and the UN Industrial Development Organization), stimulation and sharing of scientific advances and preservation of cultural landmarks (UN Educational, Scientific and Cultural Organization), and common cross-national challenges involving weather, the environment, and the climate, and protection of intellectual property rights (the World Meteorological Organization and the World Intellectual Property Organization). All of them are part of the growing functionalist agenda that is central to the United Nations in the twenty-first century.

Programmes and Funds

Of the many other organizations connected with UN pursuits, programmes and funds hold a singular place. Although confusion about the differences between specialized agencies on the one hand and programmes and funds on the other (e.g., the International Monetary *Fund* and the International *Fund* for Agricultural Development are specialized agencies) can exist, the two can easily be distinguished. Specialized agencies are independent bodies, created by distinct treaties; they maintain their own separate administrative boards. In contrast, the General Assembly has expressly established certain programmes and funds to supervise activities central to UN Charter mandates. While ECOSOC requests annual reports from specialized agencies, UN programmes and funds, as the handiwork of the GA, must report to both the General Assembly and ECOSOC. One similarity is that both specialized agencies, and programmes and funds often rely for their funding, for the most part, on members' voluntary contributions and, in some instances, on private organizations and corporations (thus the moniker *fund*).

As of 2005 ten UN programmes or funds were operating. Among the most visible and popular of these—and the only UN body to deal exclusively with children's issues—is the UN Children's Fund (UNICEF), established in 1946 and widely recognized for its sales of greeting cards during the holiday season late each year. The UN Relief and Works Agency for Palestine Refugees in the Near East (UNRWA), another of the earliest UN offices, was established in 1949. It provides assistance to Palestinians displaced during the several Middle East wars that transpired since 1948.

By the second decade of its existence, the United Nations had turned a considerable amount of attention to development issues, and this concentration was mirrored in the GA's initiation of related programs. The UN Conference on Trade and Development (UNCTAD), begun in 1964, became the GA's chief organ for carrying out intertwined aims in development, including in the areas of finance, technology, investment, and sustainable development. UNCTAD also promotes and represents the interests of developing nations in international trade negotiations. Not to be confused with UNCTAD is the UN Development Programme (UNDP), started a year later, which provides technical assistance to developing countries.

Three other entities are related to development matters. The UN Population Fund (UNFPA), established in 1969, is the largest multilateral organization offering assistance to developing countries by instituting population policies. Concomitantly, UNFPA supports improved reproductive health for women and encourages family planning. The UN Environment Programme (UNEP), originating in 1972 as a response to the UN Conference on the Human Environment held in Stockholm that year, is the principal UN body involved in attempts to protect the world's environment. The World Food Programme (WFP), dating from 1962, extends food assistance to people living in poverty and, when called on, delivers emergency relief to countries and areas affected by disasters.

In 1993, reacting to the crisis of escalating numbers of refugees resulting from conflicts, the General Assembly created the Office of the UN High Commissioner for Refugees (UNHCR). With some five thousand personnel scattered around the world, UNHCR is a noticeable addition to UN efforts to aid refugees and protect their rights. In addition, UNHCR coordinates the efforts of more than 450 nongovernmental organizations whose chief concern is to provide aid to refugees.

Finally, the UN International Drug Control Programme (UNDCP), founded in 1991, is now part of the expanded province of the Office for Drug Control and Crime Prevention. Working with about one thousand NGOs, UNDCP engages in educational and informational efforts to counter drug use and trafficking.

Other Groups

The plethora of activities we have surveyed seems immense but is, nonetheless, an incomplete look at the UN System. Before we leave the topic, we should note a few other entities that do not fit precisely into the specialized agencies, and programmes and funds groupings just detailed.

Among these are the **research and training institutes**—that is, specialized research organizations that engage in consistent research undertakings in their areas of expertise, publish reports, and make available to all nations cutting-edge information about current issues of concern to the UN family. The UN Institute for Training and Research (UNITAR) administers training seminars for new UN staff personnel and concentrates on training individuals from developing countries who aspire to international public service or diplomatic careers. The other institutes are more focused. They include the International Research and Training Institute for the Advancement of Women (INSTRAW), the UN Institute for Disarmament Research (UNIDIR), the UN Interregional Crime and Justice Research Institute (UNICJRI), and the UN Research Institute for Social Development (UNRISD).

Still other groups are associated with the United Nations, some more firmly than others. The International Atomic Energy Agency (IAEA) is one of the more recognizable of what the United Nations calls **related organizations.** Related organizations are completely independent of UN administrative requirements. The IAEA is an intergovernmental forum dedicated to the peaceful uses of nuclear technology. The General Assembly established it as an autonomous entity in 1957 in response to President Eisenhower's proposal in his 1953 "Atoms for Peace" address before the assembly. Headquartered in Vienna, the IAEA had a membership of 138 nations in 2005, and it had become the primary UN organ for monitoring compliance with the Nuclear Non-Proliferation Treaty. The IAEA is covered in more detail in Chapter 5.

Among other related organizations deserving at least a brief mention is the World Tourism Organization, which succeeded several international nongovernmental tourism agencies dating to 1925. In 1976 it became the implementing body for the UN Development Programme's efforts to promote world tourism. Its headquarters is in Madrid. In addition, the Comprehensive Nuclear-Test-Ban Treaty Organization and the Organization for the Prohibition of Chemical Weapons are administrative units specifically designed to detect possible violations of existing treaties within their competence and to strive to coordinate efforts to uphold these treaties. Last of the related organizations—and most loosely related to the United Nations—is the World Trade Organization, the successor organization to the General Agreement on Tariffs and Trade (GATT), which tries to provide a forum for extensive multilateral negotiation among its 148 members (as of 2005) to lower barriers to international trade. The WTO is examined in more detail later in this chapter.

Finally, the GA established what might be called **other UN entities,** each of which provides a specific service to the world community. Three such entities were created. One, the UN Office for Project Services (UNOPS), was originated in 1995 to provide harmonized management for UN programmes and funds. Unique among UN agencies, UNOPS must raise its own revenues by marketing its services, and it provides no funding to its clients and partners. A second entity, the UN Centre for Human Settlements, GA—created in 1978 to coordinate UN activities in this field, was merged with the Commission on Human Settlements in 2002 to bring about the UN Programme on Human Settlements (UN-HABITAT). The GA brought the third entity, the UN High Commissioner for Human Rights (UNHCHR), into being in 1993 in response to the Vienna Declaration on Human Rights issued that year. UNHCHR, whose head the secretary-general chooses, serves as the secretariat for all treaty bodies involving human rights. Two renowned commissioners were Mary Robinson, former president of Ireland, and her successor, the late Sergio Vieira de Mello.

The surfeit of group names listed in the foregoing sections can induce bafflement; some seem to overlap, while others would, reasonably, appear to fall under a different rubric. Accordingly, your best recourse may be to revisit the highlighted categories we used under which to subsume these various organs and, at the same time, to take a look at the figure at the beginning of this chapter showing the UN System. There, you will find these organizations placed, by UN preference, under the same labels we used in the preceding descriptions. Finally, having followed the first two suggestions, you may want to think of the United Nations in its newest formulation as a network of IGOs and special bodies that qualitatively marks the emergence of a "new" United Nations, significantly different from that described in the UN Charter.

NEW STRUCTURES ON THE GLOBAL STAGE

Inevitably, new structures surface to complement the work of the various UN groups, as well as to attend to fresh challenges unanticipated by the UN's founders. You have seen the resonance of this generalization in several places in this and previous chapters, including in the elaboration of the evolution of international law in Chapter 3. These diplomatic innovations have been undertaken as pragmatic experiments, often with the result that they have become formal instruments of UN action. Next, we briefly appraise some of these new structures.

World Conferences

World conferences are UN-sponsored international gatherings attended by thousands of individuals representing themselves, governments, international organizations, UN bodies, the media, nongovernmental organizations, and the international scientific and technical community. Although the UN Charter does not specifically authorize the United Nations to convene these conferences, the world body has used the directive in Article 1 of the Charter, calling on it to be a "centre for harmonizing the actions of nations" as the basis for sponsoring conferences. Held at UN headquarters in New York, in other UN venues, and in cities around the world, these meetings have grown in number, size, and topics covered. The first world conference was held in Havana, Cuba, in 1947–1948 and focused on trade and employment. Meetings held prior to the 1960s were small and infrequent. The UN Conference on Trade and Development (UNCTAD), convened in Geneva in 1964, was the first to attract worldwide attention and to lead to the formation of a formal UN organ, called, appropriately, *UNCTAD*. Since then, UNCTAD meetings have been held quadrennially; UNCTAD XI met in June 2004 in São Paolo, Brazil.

Starting with the 1972 Stockholm Conference on the Human Environment, UN world conferences have attracted the involvement of private international interest groups. More than four hundred groups were accredited to the Stockholm meeting. They presented statements to the conference, lobbied delegations, played a critical role in garnering public support for the aims of the conference, and provided important expertise related to the environment.

World conferences have often been defining events in the development of international legal practices and global agendas. The United Nations has used world conferences to concentrate world attention on a number of themes, including the problems and opportunities associated with the issues of human rights, the environment, women, development, human settlements, racism, ozone depletion, natural disasters, education, disarmament, children, population policy, desertification, society, and sustainable development. A parallel "people's forum" has accompanied each conference held since 1992; this forum allows nongovernmental groups to present their discrete views and try to mold public opinion. In some past cases, the sponsoring UN body authorized NGOs to participate actively in the conference. Forty-seven thousand people attended the 1992 Earth Summit in Rio de Janeiro, fifty thousand attended the Fourth World Conference on Women in Beijing in 1995, and thirty thousand were accredited to the 1996 Istanbul Second World Conference on Human Settlements (HABITAT II). Heads of state and of government also began active participation in world conference sessions, starting with the 1990 World Summit for Children held in New York City.

Both the costs associated with convening the world community to address an important international issue and the usual outcome of world meetings—vague consensual statements—have raised debate between supporters and critics of conferences. The cost to the United Nations for meetings in the 1990s was typically $1.8 to $3.4 million each, although the most expensive was the UN Conference on Environment and Development in 1992, costing more than $10 million. In addition, world conference expenditures have not included outlays of host countries, which often rival UN spending. Conference opponents have argued that the money could have been better spent ameliorating the problems rather than talking about them. Critics have also insisted that the meetings were often duplications of efforts then being undertaken by specialized agencies or private groups and that the conferences diverted world attention from more serious problems, produced diplomatic compromises with limited commitments of resources, and "politicized" issues that required humanitarian or scientific responses. In contrast, defenders of world conferences, including many nations in the developing world, consider the meetings opportunities to mobilize national, local, and nongovernmental activities to address major global problems, to create international standards that rich and powerful nations cannot ignore, to serve as fertile ground for new ideas and strategies, and to cut through UN bureaucracy and world lethargy.

As the new century began, the momentum for convening world conferences had not seemed to slacken. Just between 1999 and 2002, the United Nations sponsored seven world conferences. Secretary-General Kofi Annan, an advocate of more such meetings, had conceived and convened the highly publicized Millennium Summit at the New York headquarters in the fall of 2000. States vied for the right to host future sessions. As a result, for example, South Africa then hosted two world conferences in 2001–2002: the World Conference against Racism, Racial Discrimination, Xenophobia and Related Intolerance (August 31–September 7, 2001) in Durban, and the World Summit on Sustainable Development (September 2–11, 2002) in Johannesburg.[16]

The Global Compact

As you know, the United Nations is an international organization of sovereign nations that serves as a forum for interstate diplomacy and collective action. However, as the new millennium approached, the organization expanded its involvement with the private sector and with nongovernmental organizations. In the area of development, a new UN engagement with private corporations and NGOs emerged (see Chapter 7 for more on this trend). Decreases in donor-state funding made this partnership a necessity. The UN's focus on private actors in the international arena also reflected recognition by the organization's leadership that a more robust international civil society could have an impact on the success or failure of UN initiatives. Within this context, Secretary-General Kofi Annan proposed a "Global Compact" between the United Nations and multinational corporations to protect human rights, international labor standards, and the global environment. Speaking on January 31, 1999, to the World Economic Forum in Davos, Switzerland, Annan urged corporations to work with the world body, bypassing national governments, to fulfill nine principles established in the Rio Declaration of the Earth Summit, the International Labour Organization's Fundamental Principles on Rights of Work, and the Universal Declaration of Human Rights. Subsequently, a tenth principle—to combat corruption—was added to the list. By summer 2005 more than two thousand companies and other stakeholders worldwide had joined this voluntary, international corporate citizenship initiative.

Special Rapporteurs

Although the word *rapporteur* derives from Old French, its meaning can be discerned from the English word *report*. A *rapporteur* compiles reports and presents them to a supervising body. A UN *special rapporteur,* or independent expert, should be distinguished from a special representative of the secretary-general (SRSG), who is chosen by and acts on behalf of, or in place of, the secretary-general. A special rapporteur is commissioned by a UN body through a resolution and is charged with preparing a comprehensive report on an area of concern to that body. The report is normally extensive and consists of an explanation of the commission's mandates and methods; historical background; economic, social, political, and demographic information; assessment of the current situation; information received from relevant countries; reports of field or site visits; and recommendations for UN action. The United Nations may provide these reports to affected countries for guidance. Special rapporteurs are experts in the field about which they are chosen to report, and they are often well-respected scholars or professors. In addition, they almost always speak more than one language. Despite the extraordinary service special rapporteurs provide, they receive little UN Secretariat assistance. They are unpaid volunteers with limited funds and usually no support staff. As the century turned, more than two dozen special rapporteurs were covering a broad range of topics and inspecting specific countries.

Human Rights Tribunals

Among other new UN structures are the recently initiated courts founded to deal with tragic human rights violations. These courts are discussed in detail in Chapter 7. For now, we simply mention the two special courts set up to handle cases arising from civil wars in the 1990s and the International Criminal Court, whose jurisdiction is more general. The Security Council created the two geographic-specific courts: the International Criminal Tribunal for the Former Yugoslavia and the International Criminal Tribunal for Rwanda. The former was the first institution of international criminal prosecution since the end of World War II. The latter materialized on November 8, 1994, deriving from SC Resolution 955. The International Criminal Court (ICC) is a product of the so-called Rome Statute of 1998. It was designed to bring to justice individuals, not countries, who commit the most serious crimes of concern to the international community. As of May 2005, ninety-nine nations were parties to the Rome Statute, which, in fact, had acquired its jurisdiction by July 1, 2002, with the requisite sixty-six ratifications. However, foreboding holdouts included China, Israel, and the United States.

GLOBALIZATION, BRETTON WOODS INSTITUTIONS, AND THE UNITED NATIONS

At the end of World War II, diplomats and political leaders, along with financiers and economists, determined to elude the financial and economic policies of economic nationalism that they thought had helped bring on the interwar challenges of economic ruin and international collapse, as well as world war itself in 1939. Starting at Bretton Woods, the world finance conference held in New Hampshire in 1944, these leaders created institutions to encourage freer movement of goods, money, and labor; international rules to effect economic liberalization; transparency in economic and financial dealings; the ability to locate and rectify sudden economic troubles in specific areas of the world; and mechanisms to provide necessary capital assistance to nations requiring development financing. The founders of this multilateral, cooperative economic regime saw their efforts as complementary to the simultaneous launching of the United Nations. That is, postwar planners aimed to bring the world closer together in economic, financial, political, cultural, and social realms, thinking that nationalist and provincial policies—including high protective tariffs—had spawned the collapse of international order in the 1930s. As the world economy grew substantially during the later twentieth century, these efforts appeared to be remarkably successful.

With the end of the cold war, more and more of the world's nations evinced a keen interest in joining the expanding, less encumbered economy that until then had characterized chiefly the First World only. These nations had good reasons for such interest. Whereas in 1970 about 3 percent of all manufactured goods were produced in the world's developing nations, by the early 1990s their share was 18 percent, and this percentage rose during the next decade as the mechanisms of international economic and financial integration matured. From 1990 to 1998 the thirteen poor countries with the largest populations realized an impressive average economic growth rate of 7.3 percent, higher than in any prior corresponding time.[17] In 2002 *Foreign Policy Magazine* reported a study indicating that the world's most "globalized" countries had achieved greater income equality.[18]

Still, by 1998, according to the World Bank, some 1.2 billion people lived on less than a dollar a day at 1993 prices. While the occurrence of absolute poverty in the most impoverished areas of the world decreased slightly between 1987 and 1998, the total number of the poor remained about the same, with numbers rising in Africa, parts of Europe and Central Asia, and Latin America and the Caribbean, but falling in East Asia.

Meanwhile, during the 1990s, the World Bank, the International Monetary Fund (IMF), and the World Trade Organization (WTO) became controversial. They were seen by some socialists, labor activists, environmentalists, government-subsidized businesses, and strong nationalists as promoters of unwelcome globalization that, detractors charged, benefited only large corporations in the richest capitalist nations at the expense of developing countries, laboring people, distinctive native cultures, and the environment. Critics also insisted that self-interested bankers and financiers, not representatives democratically selected by governments, made the key decisions for the World Bank, the IMF, and the WTO. Defenders insisted that these institutions—by bringing the rule of law to the world economy; providing banking resources for troubled economies; establishing transparent rules of trade among ever more nations; and lowering barriers to trade, travel, and investment—offered the best antidote to persistent poverty and the most sensible stimulus to economic growth worldwide.

Bretton Woods Conference

You may recall from Chapter 2 that the UN Monetary and Financial Conference convened in Bretton Woods, New Hampshire, from July 1 to 22, 1944. At the conference, agreements were drafted establishing three institutions meant to create a postwar global free trade system: the International Monetary Fund (IMF), the International Bank for Reconstruction and Development (IBRD; better known as the *World Bank*), and the General Agreement on Tariffs and Trade (GATT). The last of these was supposed to be an "interim" agreement until an International Trade Organization (ITO)—which would provide a more ambitious regulatory framework for world trade—could be established. GATT, however, remained in place until January 1, 1995, when it was superseded by the **World Trade Organization.**

Sponsored by the United States, the Bretton Woods Conference and its negotiated agreements were intended to establish a new international monetary and trade regime that was stable and predictable. Soon after the Bretton Woods institutions came into being, Washington pegged the dollar to gold at thirty-five dollars an ounce, enacted large foreign aid programs to pump liquidity into the international economic system, and made the largest subscription of funds of any IBRD member to the assets of the World Bank. The IMF, GATT, and the World Bank, while independently administered institutions, initially and since their origin, have been considered part of the UN System.

World Bank

The World Bank is a group of five financial institutions headquartered in Washington, D.C. These institutions are the International Bank for Reconstruction and Development (IBRD; the original "World Bank"), the International Finance Corporation (IFC), the International Development Association (IDA), the Multilateral Investment Guarantee Agency (MIGA), and the International Centre for the Settlement of Investment Disputes (ICSID).

The International Bank for Reconstruction and Development, established in 1945, began operations in 1946 with a mandate to aid the reconstruction of nations ravaged by World War II and to further the flow of capital around the world. The IBRD and the other institutions in the World Bank Group often find themselves working in close cooperation with the International Monetary Fund. Since its founding, the World Bank has expanded its activities in ways that have made it even more important but also increasingly controversial. From the initial objective of restoring war-devastated nations, the World Bank Group has broadened its goals to include reducing poverty worldwide, strengthening the economies of poor nations, improving living standards, and promoting economic growth and development. The IBRD is like a global financial cooperative. That is, its member countries effectively own it. Each of its 184 member states (as of 2005) holds shares in the bank based on the size of the country's economy relative to the world's economy. Thus, although all bank members are represented on the board of executive directors in Washington (and developing nations together could count close to half the votes in 2003), the richest nations (the *Group of 7:* The United States, the United Kingdom, France, Germany, Japan, Italy, and Canada) account for about 45 percent of the shares and therefore have considerable influence over the bank's policies. The United States, with slightly more than 16 percent of the shares in 2003, held a power of veto over any changes in the bank's articles or policies, because according to the 1944 articles of agreement, 85 percent of the shares are needed to effect such changes.

The bank does not make grants. It lends money to countries—almost always poorer countries that need capital, technical assistance, and sometimes financial and economic policy advice. The loans are repaid. Two types of lending are characteristic of the bank. The first is for developing countries that have an ability to pay market interest rates for the loan. The money for these loans comes from investors around the world who buy bonds issued by the bank. A second type of loan goes to the neediest countries that are unable to pay market interest rates. Because the bank cannot issue bonds to raise money for these loans, lending is done by means of the affiliate International Development Association (IDA), the World Bank Group's "concessional" lending body. The IDA's articles of agreement became effective in 1960. The IDA shares the same staff as the IBRD and the same headquarters, reports to the same president (Paul Wolfowitz in 2005), uses the same financial standards in evaluating projects, and, in 2005 had 165 members. The IDA, taking advantage of some thirty countries that provide money needed to extend "credits" to the poorest borrowers, makes loans free of interest. These loans carry a low administrative charge (recently 0.75 percent annually), are long term, and include ten years' grace.

Established in 1956, the International Finance Corporation (IFC) is the largest multilateral source of loan and equity financing for private-sector projects in the Third World. It promotes sustainable private-sector development. In 2005 it had a membership of 178 nations, all of whom must be IBRD members. IFC members appoint representatives to a board of governors that can delegate powers to a board of directors, composed of the IBRD's executive directors. Although the organization has its own articles of agreement, its president is the same as that for the IBRD.

The Multilateral Investment Guarantee Agency (MIGA), created in 1988, advances foreign direct investment into emerging economies to reduce poverty and seek improvement of life in the world's poorer areas. MIGA offers political risk insurance to investors and lenders to attract investment into developing countries. In 2005 MIGA had a membership of 165 nations. Membership is open to all World Bank members. It is administered by a council of governors and receives some of its operating capital from the IBRD.

The International Centre for the Settlement of Investment Disputes (ICSID) was established in 1966 under the Convention on the Settlement of Investment Disputes between States and Nationals of Other States. ICSID is an autonomous, international organization with close links to the World Bank. Through arbitration, it mediates when investment disputes arise between private foreign investors and governments. World Bank national representatives sit as ex officio members of ICSID's administrative council, and the bank finances the ICSID secretariat, although the parties involved bear the costs of specific mediations.

The World Bank Group is one of the largest sources of development assistance in the world.[19] In 2003 it provided more than $18.5 billion in grants and loans and was involved in more than one hundred developing economies. Since its education funding began in 1963, through 2003 it provided more than $31 billion in loans and credits and, as of 2005, was financing 147 educational projects in eighty-six countries. The bank is also a cosponsor of the Joint UN Programme on HIV/AIDS (UNAIDS), having committed by 2003 more than $1.7 billion to curbing the spread of the disease. In fact, the bank is the world's largest external funder of educational programs and of efforts to combat HIV/AIDS. By the turn of the century, the bank was providing an average of $1.3 billion in new lending every year for health, nutrition, and population projects in developing countries.

Although critics continue to fault the bank for ignoring challenges such as the environment, distinctive native cultures, the role of civil society, and more, other people find that the bank has added too much to its mandate. In recent years the bank has expanded its role into social and environmental issues. To ensure that the bank is not working at cross-purposes with other UN bodies, the director sits as a member—along with the directors of both the IMF and the WTO—on the chief executives board of the UN System, chaired by the secretary-general. From reconstruction efforts in the Balkans to educational programs for young girls in Islamic countries, to the struggle against AIDS, the bank's mission, former managing director Jessica Einhorn warns, has become unwieldy.[20] The bank, it seems to contrary perspectives, is doing either too much or not enough.

International Monetary Fund

Also created at the Bretton Woods Conference in 1944, the International Monetary Fund (IMF) is a UN specialized agency designed to promote international monetary cooperation; facilitate economic expansion, world trade, high employment, and income growth; promote stability and eliminate restrictions in international money exchange; and assist its members with temporary financial resources to solve balance-of-payment problems and other financial difficulties. The IMF, also headquartered in Washington, D.C., often finds itself collaborating with the World Bank Group. The economists, financiers, diplomats, and political leaders who forged the post–World War II global structure wanted, in addition to encouraging freer movement of goods, money, ideas, and labor, to avoid the economic and financial pitfalls they believed had helped cause the collapse of international order leading to global conflict. Thus, while seeking transparency in economic and financial arrangements, they also wanted to construct an international ability to locate and rectify sudden economic troubles in discrete areas of the world so as to prevent the spread of such problems. By the end of the twentieth century, the IMF became a particularly clear target of antiglobalization criticisms because of its role in financing debt-ridden nations and imposing stringent conditions on them in order for them to receive help. Financial crises in Mexico (1995), throughout Asia (1997–1998), and in Argentina (2001) led to IMF actions opposed by some national governments, nongovernmental organizations, other international institutions, and citizens' groups. Critics faulted the IMF for operating in secret, with its decision-making process undemocratically controlled by government finance ministries and large banking interests.

The IMF has tried to combine several roles that in their complexity, and possible incompatibility, make the institution controversial. It has taken on the role of an international bank, an insurance company, a regulator, and a charity. To begin with, you should think of the IMF exactly as it is entitled: That is, it is a *fund*. The member countries of the IMF (184 as of 2005) grant an assessed quota to the fund much as individuals deposit money into a bank or a credit union. The quota is based on each member's relative size in the world economy. These quotas determine voting power in the IMF. So, richer nations wield more voting power in IMF decisions. Members pay 25 percent of their quota subscription in international reserve assets (U.S. dollars, euros, Japanese yen, British pound sterling, or so-called special drawing rights, which are defined subsequently). The remaining 75 percent is in the country's own currency. As with a bank or a credit union, members may draw from the general resources of the fund, which are derived from these quota subscriptions. Members with "structural maladjustments" (an inability to meet payments, an accelerating public debt, a dangerously fluctuating currency, a balance-of-trade problem, and so on) may enter into extended arrangements with the IMF. The fund can supplement its resources by borrowing from member countries that have strong economies. Such borrowing may occur when the IMF needs added capital to deal with an immediate problem that threatens international financial stability. Finally, under the "Structural Adjustment Facility" of the "Special Disbursement Account," funds may be made available on "concessional" terms to low-income countries at lower interest rates. Often these developing countries are engaged in structural reform of their economies. During the late twentieth century, such structural readjustment normally meant moving from a command-style, socialist economy in which outside trade was restricted by protectionist policies, to a free market economy emphasizing private enterprise, freer trade, and an internationally convertible currency. Such "structural readjustments" were typically the conditions the IMF imposed on the borrowing countries, whose citizens, accustomed to government sustenance, sometimes suffered at least temporary discomfort.

The member states govern the IMF. A board of governors is composed of one representative from each member, and an equal number of alternate governors. A governor is almost always the minister of finance or the head of the central bank of his or her country. Thus, governors represent their governments. They gather at annual meetings. Otherwise, the governors stay in touch with the IMF executive board stationed at the Washington headquarters. Twenty-four executive directors meet at least three times a week and carry out the policies of the board of governors. In 2005, five executive directors represented individual countries: France, Germany, Japan, the United Kingdom, and the United States. The nineteen remaining directors represented geographic groupings of the other member states. The executive board often makes decisions on the basis of consensus rather than majority vote. Besides its staff of about twenty-five hundred, the fund has a managing director, who is also chair of the executive board.

So-called special drawing rights (SDRs) are a novel creation of the IMF. The term implies that they can be "drawn" by a member state, much as you would "draw" a loan from a bank in which you had deposits. The IMF's board of directors invented SDRs in 1967. By 1969 enough members had ratified the new system to bring it into practice. In international finance, SDRs initially replaced more traditional reserves such as gold. The value of IMF SDRs is measured against a "basket" of a few strong currencies (dollar, yen, pound sterling, and euro) and is based on current market exchange rates. Countries are accorded SDR allotments in the IMF. These SDRs represent the countries' assets within the fund. Technically a paper reserve, SDRs have many of the characteristics of money. For example, SDRs are interest-bearing assets, and interest can be charged on IMF loans made in SDRs. In effect, SDRs represent a movement away from using the dollar, implicit in the Bretton Woods system, as the world's reserve currency.

The IMF engages in several activities. It conducts "surveillance," which means that it constantly monitors, appraises, and reports its members' exchange rates to ensure that they remain stable. It can offer financial assistance, including credits and loans, to members. As of February 2005, the fund had loans outstanding to eighty-two countries for about $90 billion; fifty-nine of these were on concessional terms. It also provides technical assistance to its members to help with fiscal and monetary policy and structural reforms.

The IMF does not lend for specific purposes or projects as regional multilateral development banks (MDBs) do. Reserve assets that a member borrows are normally deposited in the borrowing country's central bank and are available to the country as any other international reserves would be. When lending, the IMF provides reserve assets (in accepted foreign currencies and SDRs) taken from other fund members. A borrower uses its own currency to "purchase" these assets from the fund. To repay, the borrower "repurchases" its own currency with international reserve assets. So, from an accounting perspective, the fund's total resources do not vary. However, financial aid is often linked to specific conditions that the borrowing country must meet. This situation was the case with Mexico and afflicted Asian countries in the mid-1990s, and with Argentina in 2001. In each instance, because the world's richer nations—most important, the United States—held the controlling voting power in the IMF and feared instability in world financial markets, the fund determined to avert a serious world financial crisis, voted to provide "bailout" loans. In August 2001, for example, the IMF arranged a complex eight-billion-dollar loan to troubled Argentina.

In September 2003, as the U.S. occupation of Iraq caused an uncomfortable beginning to the UN's fifty-eighth annual session, and as world trade talks broke down in Cancun, Mexico, the IMF met in a much more serene Dubai, United Arab Emirates, with the World Bank in the organizations' annual get-together. There, in tandem, the institutions' leaders endorsed the bank's earlier report urging a narrowing of the divide between rich and poor nations. While the urging was welcome to less affluent nations, the latter, nonetheless, demanded greater voting rights in the IMF and the World Bank. IMF managing director Horst Koehler said the two financial institutions "very much hope that the shareholders from advanced countries have listened."[21]

World Trade Organization

Joined with the World Bank and the International Monetary Fund, the World Trade Organization (WTO), headquartered in Geneva, completes the triad of multilateral bodies overseeing the international economy as first projected at Bretton Woods. The WTO is a member-directed negotiating regime that establishes and then administers the rules governing world trade. These rules are designed to facilitate the uninhibited, fair, and predictable flow of international commerce. The WTO was created in 1995 as the result of the so-called Uruguay Round of Multilateral Trade Negotiations (originating in Uruguay and occurring in continuous negotiations during 1986–1994). It acquired authority beyond that of its antecedent General Agreement on Tariffs and Trade (GATT; founded in 1948) so that it could better contend with an increasingly complicated system of trade rules. Growing world trade since 1945, assisted by the international rules of first GATT and then the WTO, had been, by the early twenty-first century, one of the main engines of economic development and had contributed, at least according to reliable statistics,[22] to growth in world income and the reduction of poverty.

The WTO's Ministerial Conference, comprising trade ministers or their equivalents from all member countries, meets at least once every two years—as it did at the ill-fated meetings in Seattle in 1999 and in Cancun in 2003—and is the organization's supreme decision-making body. It sets the WTO's strategic direction. A General Council, made up of ambassadors and heads of delegation in Geneva, convenes regularly to make the necessary day-to-day decisions. The General Council also meets as the Trade Policy Review Body and the Dispute Settlement Body (DSB). The Goods Council, Services Council, and Trade-Related Aspects of Intellectual Property Rights (TRIPS) Council report to the General Council. In addition, specialized committees, working groups, and working parties are set up to deal with special issues. A director general is the administrative head of the organization and usually serves a six-year term. However, in 2005, former Thai deputy prime minister Supachai Panitchpakdi was filling out New Zealander Michael Moore's term. This unusual term-sharing arrangement resolved an impasse between the United States and an Asian bloc of countries, led by Japan, over WTO leadership.

The WTO has six main functions:

1. Making available a forum for trade negotiations among all its members
2. Administering the trade agreements thus negotiated
3. Managing specific trade disputes
4. Monitoring national trade policies
5. Providing technical assistance and training on trade policy for developing countries
6. Cooperating with other international organizations on trade issues

The organization has a modest staff of about 630 and had a parsimonious budget of $135 million in 2005.

Between 1947 and 1995, eight rounds of trade negotiations under GATT set up a complex web of some sixty agreements governing world trade. GATT itself, with annexes covering distinct sectors such as agriculture and textiles, and discrete issues such as state trading, product standards, subsidies, and antidumping policies, became the world's umbrella arrangement supporting nondiscrimination in the exchange of goods. A General Agreement on Trade in Services (GATS), which contained both a framework and specific commitments for opening up what are called *service sectors* (insurance, finance, securities management, and banking) to foreign competition, did the same for services. An Agreement on Trade-Related Aspects of Intellectual Property Rights provided protection in international commerce to "intellectual property" such as patents, copyrights, and trademarks. In addition, by a Dispute Settlement Understanding, GATT established procedures for resolving trade disputes through panels and appeals, with the intent of avoiding disruptive unilateral actions. The creation of the Dispute Settlement Board to adjudicate trade complaints among members was, along with crafting the WTO, the major accomplishment of the Uruguay Round, and an advance over the previous GATT dispute resolution process. With the creation of the more broadly empowered WTO, hopes were high for even more progress in world trade relations.

The WTO had 148 member countries as of 2005, accounting for more than 90 percent of world trade. Formerly Maoist China's joining in 2001 was a particularly significant breakthrough, although, as of 2005, neither Russia nor Saudi Arabia, both desirous of membership, had yet been admitted, and the request for membership by Taiwan—an important economic player in Asia—remained doubtful because of China's juridical assertion of sovereignty over the country.

The world trading system epitomized by the WTO—along with its World Bank and IMF associates—has been assailed in recent years by protest groups representing a congeries of interests (sometimes on opposite ideological waves), including protected businesses (particularly in agriculture), environmentalists (who believe that the expanding trade regimes ignore the environment in favor of economic growth), labor groups (who fear their members will be replaced by cheaper overseas workers), nationalists (who favor nationalist economic policies), human rights advocates (who anguish over workers' rights in developing countries), socialist-oriented economists (who prefer command to laissez-faire economic strategies), some ethnic groups (who worry about displacement of their language and culture by more economically dominant cultures), and some political activists (who believe that all the advantages from a more open economy extend only to rich capitalist enterprises). The large demonstrations that disrupted the ill-fated third WTO ministerial meeting held in Seattle in November 1999 received worldwide media coverage and underlined the popular resistance to trade liberalization.

The round of multilateral trade negotiations that was supposed to be launched at Seattle never occurred. More than the protests, however, the main reasons for this failure were disagreements among the United States, the European Union, and Japan over agriculture policies; dissatisfaction among developing countries over the implementation of the previous Uruguay Round WTO agreements; and differing opinions on the use of trade sanctions to enforce labor standards.

The 2001 ministerial meeting in Doha, Qatar (initiating the so-called Doha Round of negotiations), set a goal of January 2005 to complete a further liberalization and boost trade prospects for the world's poorest countries. Prior to the next ministerial gathering—in September 2003 in Cancun—which was to further these efforts, the WTO realized some solid accomplishments: It presided over an agreement that more easily allowed impoverished nations to obtain generic medicines for HIV and other diseases, and, by the time of the September meeting, anticipated the imminent accession of Nepal and Cambodia, two of the world's most destitute nations, to membership.

However, by mid-September 2003, the Cancun talks had ended in disarray. The more affluent nations resolved to concentrate initially on issues of cross-border transportation procedures, rules regarding foreign investment and competition, and transparency in awarding government contracts, while the developing nations insisted just as firmly that the first priority was for the wealthier countries to agree to cut their agricultural subsidy programs and thus entertain freer import trade from poorer areas of the world. Led by a new bloc—the "Group of 21," as the media dubbed it—Third World nations were resolute that their ideas be given equal billing. The diplomatic standoff could not be bridged, and the conference ended with no progress made toward the Doha goals. The Group of 21, led by Brazil (one of the world's largest agricultural producers), insisted, as Brazilian president Luiz Inacio Lula da Silva said, on a level playing field. The aggrieved negotiators pointed out that while *they* were seeking more liberal international trade, the United States, the European Union, and Japan continued agricultural subsidization for their farmers and disallowed virtually any importation from the Third World. For example, the United States and the European Union were lavishing more than $150 billion annually on support for their farmers. As a single case in point, Washington provided about $3 billion in 2002 for twenty-five thousand cotton farmers, which made cotton producers, in Africa, for example, unable to sell their products in the United States. Further clouding the picture, in 2002 the administration of George W. Bush had—in a decidedly "antiglobalization" maneuver—raised tariff protection for the politically sensitive U.S. steel industry.

An odd confluence of forces met in Cancun that reflected the confusing differences of opinion about where the world was headed and where it should go. Nudged by security forces into the distance, away from the negotiations, so as not to disrupt the talks as in Seattle, were the vocal protesters, almost all of whom welcomed the failure of the Cancun meeting. Inside, however, all sides spoke favorably about trade liberalization, or "globalization." Only, seeking their own perceived interests as of the first order, none seemed prepared to compromise to accomplish something rather than nothing at all. Each group desired the benefits of liberalization but found surrendering customary protections for domestic interests extraordinarily difficult. Yet, virtually all participants, poor and rich countries alike, rued the outcome, and most voiced hope that renewed negotiations could get the Doha Round back on track. Secretary-General Kofi Annan, presiding in New York over a tense opening of the fall UN season, captured the prevailing mood when he opined about Cancun: "I hope that is not the end of the road and that the parties will go back, and reflect, and then come back in a determined fashion to try and fashion an agreement."[23] Annan, and many others, had a point, because, as a World Bank study had shown, a liberalized trade agreement such as that envisioned at Doha could lift as many as 144 million people out of poverty by 2015.[24]

SUMMARY

By the first decade of the third millennium, actors within and observers without the UN System spoke out on the need to reform the entire system. In New York City, Secretary-General Annan worried aloud about the impact on the organization of the inability of its majority and the indispensable, powerful United States to see eye to eye on the challenge of Iraq. In Washington, D.C., war hawks persisted in dismissing the United Nations while a growing chorus of U.S. critics embraced the idea of cooperation with the organization. Suggestions for improving the Security Council abounded. Debate on peacekeeping methods persisted. Trade talks broke down, but new hope always recommended. What seemed obvious from an objective distance was that the United Nations was a focus of the news, appearing as a lead story more often than not. It had not yet been relegated to an obscure limbo in contemporary discourse as had happened to the League of Nations two-thirds of a century earlier. The complicated entity called the *UN System* had, during almost three score years, bent but not broken. This endurance, doubtless, was due in large part to the sure adaptation of the system to real-world, and frequently novel, challenges. The UN's many institutions, at least most of them, had evolved, and if the patter of mid decade meant anything, it told of future evolution as well. As it had for sixty years, maybe the UN System could consistently renew itself. Most of the world seemed to hope so.

NOTES

1. Karen A. Mingst and Margaret P. Karns, *The United Nations in the Post–Cold War Era* (Boulder, CO: Westview Press, 1995), 56.

2. UN General Assembly, *Report of the International Atomic Energy Agency* and *Necessity of Ending the Economic, Commercial and Financial Embargo Imposed by the United States of America against Cuba*, A/RES/58/7 and A/RES/58/8, respectively, November 4, 2003.

3. See John Allphin Moore, Jr., and Jerry Pubantz, *To Create a New World? American Presidents and the United Nations* (New York: Peter Lang, 1999), 199–203.

4. United Nations, "Voting," in *Charter of the United Nations* (New York: United Nations, 1945), art. 18, para. 2.

5. United Nations, "Press statement on Baghdad bombing by Security Council president," press release, SC/7847, IK/374, August 19, 2003, http://www.un.org/News/Press/docs/2003/sc7847.doc.httm.

6. Shashi Tharoor, "Why America Still Needs the United Nations," *Foreign Affairs* 82, no. 5 (2003): 71.

7. See the extended discussion on peacekeeping in Chapter 6.

8. The distinction is elaborated on in Chapter 5; in the current context, *peacekeeping* would typically occur in an area where parties in dispute have agreed to invite the peacekeepers; in contrast, *peacemaking,* a much more recent and controversial idea, would result when forces are placed in a violent and still-contentious situation, with the aim of imposing peace before being able to keep it.

9. International Court of Justice, "Chapter I: Organization of the Court," in *Statute of the International Court of Justice* (The Hague, the Netherlands: International Court of Justice, n.d.), art. 4, para. 1.

10. John G. Stoessinger, *The United Nations and the Superpowers,* 4th ed. (New York: Random House, 1977), 3–25.

11. Security Council Resolution 1511, regarding Iraq's future, passed unanimously on October 16, 2003, can be found at http://www.un.org/ News/Press/docs/2003/sc7898.doc.htm. Extensive commentary on the intricate and difficult negotiations leading to this resolution are available in Felicity Barringer and Kirk Semple, "Security Council Adopts U.S. Plan for Iraq in 15–0 Vote," *New York Times,* October 16, 2003; and Felicity Barringer, "Unanimous Vote by U.N.'s Council Adopts Iraq Plan," *New York Times,* October 17, 2003.

12. The official names and acronyms of the five commissions are as follows: Economic Commission for Africa (ECA), Economic Commission for Europe (ECE), Economic Commission for Latin America and the Caribbean (ECLAC), Economic and Social Commission for Asia and the Pacific (ESCAP), and Economic and Social Commission for Western Asia (ESCWA).

13. See Chapter 8 for a comprehensive discussion of *development.*

14. As of 2005, the United Nations had had seven secretaries-general. See Appendix E for the complete list and a brief biography of each.

15. See http://www.un.org/staff/condolence/inmemoriam.html.

16. For more detailed commentary on specific world conferences, see Chapters 7 and 8, and relevant entries in John Allphin Moore, Jr., and Jerry Pubantz, *Encyclopedia of the United Nations* (New York: Facts on File, 2002); and United Nations, *The World Conferences: Developing Priorities for the 21st Century* (New York: United Nations, 1997).

17. J. R. Mandle, "Globalization and Its Critics," *Historically Speaking,* September 2002.

18. A. T. Kearney, "Globalization's Last Hurrah?" *Foreign Policy Magazine,* January/February 2002, 128.

19. For updated statistics, see the World Bank Web site: http://www.worldbank.org.

20. Jessica Einhorn, "The World Bank's Mission Creep," *Foreign Affairs* 80, no. 5 (2001): 22–35.

21. Associated Press, "Global money summit draws to end in Dubai," news release, September 25, 2003.

22. World Bank, *World Development Report 2003: Sustainable Development in a Dynamic World: Transforming Institutions, Growth, and Quality of Life* (New York: Oxford University Press, 2002), Chap. 1.

23. "WTO Reeling from Trade Defeat in Cancun," *New York Times,* September 18, 2003.

24. Evelyn Iritani, "WTO Talks Could Derail in Cancun," *Los Angeles Times,* September 7, 2003.

KEY TERMS

Advisory Opinions (page 141)
Caucus Groups (page 125)
Chapter VI½ Provisions
    (page 130)
Chief Executives Board (CEB)
    for Coordination (page 118)
Double Veto (page 128)
ECOSOC Functional
    Commissions (page 134)
Funds (page 143)
GA Fifth Committee (page 122)

GA First Committee (page 122)
GA Fourth Committee
    (page 122)
GA Second Committee
    (page 122)
GA Sixth Committee (page 122)
GA Third Committee (page 122)
General Committee (page 124)
Other UN Entities (page 147)
P5 (page 127)
Programmes (page 143)

Related Organizations (page
    147)
Research and Training Institutes
    (page 147)
Secretariat (page 137)
Specialized Agencies (page 143)
Special Sessions (page 122)
UN System (page 118)
World Conferences (page 148)
World Trade Organization
    (page 151)

RESOURCES FOR FURTHER RESEARCH
Relevant Web Sites

International Court of Justice (www.icj-cij.org/)

International Monetary Fund (www.imf.org)

Secretariat Senior Management Group (www.un. org/News/ossg/sg/pages/seniorstaff.html)

University of Chicago Law School Library (www.lib.uchicago.edu/~llou/forintlaw)

World Bank Group (www.worldbank.org)

World Trade Organization (www.wto.org)

Books, Articles, and Documents

Bailey, Sydney D., and Sam Daws. *The Procedure of the UN Security Council.* 3rd ed. New York: Oxford University Press, 1998.

Beck, Robert J., and Robert D. Vander Lugt, eds. *International Rules: Approaches from International Law and International Relations.* New York: Oxford University Press, 1996.

Fassbender, Bodo. *UN Security Council Reform and the Right of Veto.* The Hague, The Netherlands: Kluwer Law International, 1998.

Grady, Patrick, and Kathleen Macmillan. *Seattle and Beyond: The WTO Millennium Round.* Ottawa, Canada: Global Economics, 1999.

Mingst, Karen A., and Margaret P. Karns. *The United Nations in the Post–Cold War Era.* Boulder, CO: Westview Press, 1995.

Muldoon, James P., Jr., JoAnn Fagot Aviel, Earl Sullivan, and Richard Reitano, eds. *Multilateral Diplomacy and the United Nations Today.* 2nd ed. Boulder, CO: Westview Press, 2005.

O'Brien, Robert, Anne Marie Goetz, Jan Aart Scholte, Marc Williams, Steve Smith, Thomas Biersteker, Chris Brown et al., eds. *Contesting Global Governance: Multilateral Economic Institutions and Global Social Movements.* New York: Cambridge University Press, 2000.

Peterson, M. J. *The General Assembly in World Politics.* Boston: Allen & Unwin, 1986.

Wade, Robert. "Winners and Losers." *The Economist,* April 26, 2001.

Chapter 5

Maintenance of International Peace and Security

Before 1919, maintaining international peace and security was predicated on the world's countries' maintaining a balance of power, forming alliances, and engaging in individual self-defense. However, after World War I, the Treaty of Versailles introduced the novel notion of **collective security,** which the new League of Nations was to enforce. After World War II, upon the League's failure, another group of nations gathered in 1945 and determined, among other things, "to *unite our strength* to *maintain international peace and security*" and "to take effective *collective measures* for the prevention and removal of threats to the peace."[1] These principles would initially define the United Nations and later reshape it. In this chapter, we discuss the concept of collective security: its evolution as a principle, its role in the United Nations, the effect of the cold war on it, and its current, expanding definition.

HISTORICAL PERSPECTIVE ON INTERNATIONAL PEACE AND SECURITY

Throughout history, human beings and their communities have sought means to improve their mutual relations and to impose order when resorting to force and violence would otherwise be the norm. During the Westphalian era of international politics—so named for its origins in the Treaty of Westphalia (1648), which ended the religious conflict known as the *Thirty Years' War*—the balance of power among sovereign states was the chief means of maintaining peace. Nation-states pursued peace conferences, treaties, alliances, spheres of influence, military deterrence, conventions, bilateral and multilateral negotiations, third-party diplomacy, and even imperial dominion. This approach to peace lasted well into the twentieth century.

In the midst of this era, during the first part of the nineteenth century, war devastated Europe. Napoleon Bonaparte's soldiers conquered most of the continent. Although a traditionally forged "balance-of-power" alliance finally defeated the French leader, the victorious allies determined at the Congress of Vienna (1814–1815) to restructure Europe and modernize its diplomatic practices in a way that would prevent another such conflict. This congress marked an important step in international efforts to achieve peace through permanent organizational vigilance by the great powers; therefore, it was a distant harbinger of the United Nations. The major leaders at Vienna committed their governments to meeting regularly to consult on what to do when disruptive crises arose.

In what was dubbed the *Concert of Europe,* the major powers held successive meetings into the 1820s and authorized the use of force to sustain the governments restored after the fall of Napoleon against the growing challenge of liberal revolutionaries.[2] The Concert maintained the conservative status quo in the face of liberal principles unleashed by the American, French, and Industrial Revolutions. More than an alliance against a common enemy, it intervened in the internal affairs of European states, defending "legitimate" governments against insurgencies that might bring revolutionary regimes to power, which in turn might threaten international peace as Napoleon's government—a legacy of the French Revolution—had done. The Concert was under regular ideological attack, and it was tested by numerous small wars. Nevertheless, it kept Europe from yet another cataclysmic upheaval for a full century.

The Concert of Europe fully collapsed during the Great War of 1914–1918 (otherwise known as *World War I*). That conflict and the even greater carnage of World War II (1939–1945) convinced many leaders, such as U.S. presidents Woodrow Wilson and Franklin Delano Roosevelt, that the traditional diplomatic methods used to avoid or limit war were no longer sufficient. Even great-power collective action could preserve the peace for only so long. European powers and the United States became convinced of the need for a world organization to avert such conflicts. While not abandoning the older approaches to peace and security, they sought to maintain international order through new, universal collective security systems, creating first the League of Nations (1919), then the United Nations (1945). Creating international organizations such as these—permanent organizations dedicated to resolving crises among their member states and eliminating or greatly diminishing the perceived need to resort to war—emerged as a unique twentieth-century phenomenon.

THE CONCEPT OF COLLECTIVE SECURITY

Alliances and collective defense arrangements are directed outwardly against potential external aggressors who might threaten a group of states. A collective security system also intends to keep the peace internally among its members. It attempts to guarantee each state's security by considering an attack on one as an attack on all. It obligates each member state first to renounce the use of force against any other member and second to resist aggression by conforming with the rules and procedures of the collective security organization. It works on the assumption that no state would use force against any member of the collective security system because any aggression—since it would be met by overwhelming international force—would be fruitless. Because a collective security system is both internally and externally directed, it subsumes for its members traditional self-help techniques, such as individual and collective self-defense, alliance creation, and declarations of war against an enemy, which states have used independently in the past to protect their sovereign independence. Members become "state citizens" of a rule-based organization that theoretically defends their legitimate interests against any aggressor.

Keeping world peace through collective security was a revolutionary strategy introduced in the 1919 Treaty of Versailles. This treaty established a League of Nations, the Covenant of which committed its members to foreswear resorting to war to resolve disputes, to reduce their national armed forces "to the lowest point consistent with national defense,"[3] and to act collectively to resist aggression by any state, whether it had joined the League or not. Articles 10, 11, and 16 of the Covenant established the principle of collective security and created enforcement

LEGAL BASIS FOR COLLECTIVE SECURITY: THE COVENANT OF THE LEAGUE OF NATIONS

Article 10
The Members of the League undertake to respect and preserve as against external aggression the territorial integrity and existing political independence of all Members of the League. In case of any such aggression or in case of any threat or danger of such aggression the Council [of the League] shall advise upon the means by which this obligation shall be fulfilled.

Article 11, paragraph 1
Any war or threat of war, whether immediately affecting any of the Members of the League or not, is hereby declared a matter of concern to the whole League, and the League shall take any action that may be deemed wise and effectual to safeguard the peace of nations.

Article 16, paragraph 1
Should any Member of the League resort to war in disregard of its covenants under Articles 12, 13 or 15, it shall ipso facto be deemed to have committed an act of war against all other Members of the League, which hereby undertake immediately to subject it to the severance of all trade or financial relations, the prohibition of all intercourse between their nationals and the nationals of the covenant-breaking State, and the prevention of all financial, commercial or personal intercourse between the nationals of the covenant-breaking State and the nationals of any other State, whether a member of the League or not.

mechanisms. (Compare the provisions listed in the figure titled "Legal Basis for Collective Security: The Covenant of the League of Nations" with those listed in the figure titled "Legal Basis for Collective Security: Charter of the United Nations" later in this chapter. The latter provisions were written twenty-six years after the former.)

The most controversial provisions of the League's Covenant were Articles 10 and 16 because they respectively raised the thorny issues of naming an aggressor and imposing nondiscretionary mandatory sanctions on a "covenant-breaking" state. Coupled with the requirement for unanimity in the League council before enforcement measures could be taken, these articles made identifying an aggressor difficult and meant the League was unlikely to address serious challenges to the peace.

The Covenant provided no legal or political definition of *aggression*. Neither did the UN Charter when it was drafted in 1945. Since then, although critical to a collective security system, reaching agreement on a meaningful definition has proved elusive. All nations agree that the unjustified or improper use of force against another nation constitutes aggression, yet one party can always claim the use of force was provoked by another party's actions. Despite widespread agreement that aggression is wrong, nations engaged in armed conflict consistently contend that they act in self-defense. Even Adolph Hitler claimed that Poland attacked Germany at the start of World War II, in 1939. Often when it is obvious which state attacked another nation, it is still unclear whether the initiation of armed conflict was naked aggression or preemptive defense against an imminent attack. The latter was the justification Israel claimed when it initiated hostilities against its Arab neighbors in 1967. Finally, the opening of military operations in any conflict is usually shrouded in secrecy and confusion, which makes identifying the aggressor and the victim difficult. In the late 1980s, the world community was able to pressure Iran and Iraq to end their unimaginably bloody seven-year war only by, among other things, establishing a commission to investigate who had started the fight. Only twice has the UN Security Council, under the provisions of Article 39 of the Charter, identified an aggressor and then used force to halt the aggression. The first was North Korea in 1950. The second was Iraq in 1990, after that country invaded Kuwait. Argentina was also designated an aggressor in 1982 because of its invasion of the Falkland Islands—called the *Malvinas* by Argentina—off the Argentinian coast, but the United Kingdom, not the United Nations, reacted with force in this case.

Shortly after its creation, the General Assembly established a commission to define the term *aggression*. After almost thirty years, it produced five hundred words of ambiguous language implying that any state that was the first to use force against another state inconsistent with the rules of the UN Charter was an aggressor. However, the definition also described several uses of force that did not constitute aggression, such as acts meant to achieve self-determination from colonial rule. As a practical matter, the definition left each member state to reach its own conclusion about what constituted aggression and effectively left the United Nations the task of reaching a determination on a case-by-case basis. The United Nations—like the League of Nations in the interwar period—to this day has no working definition of *aggression* that is binding under international law.

Much of the problem for international organizations, under the League then, and the United Nations now, lay with the concept of collective security in a world of sovereign states. If collective security is defined narrowly—for example, in terms of immediately confronting an aggressor state that has crossed an internationally recognized border with military force—and if the definition requires a global response without much regard for individual states' national interests at that moment, successful collective action is likely only in limited circumstances.

A collective security system is built on the presumption that the common interest supersedes, or is at least in harmony with, its members' national interests. The sense of *common interest* might seem obvious and overwhelming in the wake of a great conflict such as either of the twentieth-century world wars, or it might be quite real in an alliance in which the members face an extremely dangerous external enemy. For example, from 1949 to 1989 the North Atlantic Treaty Organization (NATO) not only served as a vehicle for confronting the Soviet military threat in Europe, but also—because the threat was immediate and real—provided a mechanism for shading over differences among its European members and between the European allies and the United States. However, once the Soviet Union collapsed, the apparent solidarity in the alliance began to fray as national interests once again asserted themselves. Because a collective security system is also inward looking, trying to maintain peace *among* its members, national interests will often be paramount to its members and asserted against the common interest when the two are no longer seen as synonymous.

The assumption underlying the concept of collective security is the existence of a community of nations in which each has reasonable trust that the other members of the community will play by the international rules and will use the system to resolves disputes. A community such as this presumes the transformation of independent actors formerly part of an anarchic international environment into partners, or even citizens, operating in a framework of international law, democratic procedures, and legitimizing institutions. In this sense, collective security mechanisms work best when an overarching sense of government exists, such as you would find in a domestic society. These preconditions did not exist between the wars, which made the creation of an effective collective security system unrealistic.

Notwithstanding the absence of the necessary conditions for collective security as it was understood in the 1930s, however, the concept can be imagined in broader terms than simply stopping an aggressor at its border, or punishing it once it crosses the border. In fact, many of the threats to international peace and security since the end of World War II have taken a guise significantly different than the traditional scenario in which one nation attacks another. Certainly the latter has occurred, such as in the wars between Israel and surrounding states, between India and Pakistan, and on the Korean peninsula. However, the rise of ethnic and sectarian conflict, civil instability, terrorism, and even pandemic disease has produced a broader, if more ambiguous, understanding of collective security. Rather than a static legal theory, collective security is a "mental construction"[4] that implies a changing meaning as the threats to the community change. Fortunately, the UN Charter does not use the term *collective security*, which has prevented its meaning from becoming ossified in a particular legal definition.

With the creation of the United Nations in 1945, and its evolutionary efforts to maintain or restore peace and security during the succeeding sixty years, the meaning of collective security changed dramatically to include "preventive" diplomacy (meant to preclude aggression before it happened), the defense of community values (including human rights, economic well-being, social justice, and a livable environment), peacekeeping and state building, and authorization of selected community members to act in the name of all. Its meaning was expanded to include terrorism the day after the September 11, 2001, attacks on the World Trade Center towers in New York City and the Pentagon outside Washington, D.C., and the hijacking of Flight 93. The Security Council passed Resolution 1368, declaring acts of terrorism to be threats to international peace and security. The council applied the same judgment to financing terrorist groups, requiring all member states to take mandatory steps to halt the flow of resources both domestically and internationally for this purpose. In terms of disease, beginning in January 2000 the Security Council held regular sessions on the AIDS epidemic in Africa, finding it to be a threat that, under Chapter VII, the council should address. AIDS became the first health issue discussed by the council as a danger to collective security.

Although the League was a model for the later United Nations, the two organizations differ in important respects. As you know from the comparisons between the League and the United Nations in Chapter 2, for example, the founding of the United Nations was purposely separated from peace agreements ending World War II, unlike the League, which was incorporated in the Treaty of Versailles. In this chapter you need simply recognize that, in some ways, the UN Charter retreated from the League's more robust vision of collective security, as in the following two examples: (a) The League's Covenant disallowed parties to a dispute to vote on how to deal with that dispute, while, bending before power politics, the UN Charter contains no such limitation. (b) A permanent member of the Security Council can block UN action with the veto. The veto did not exist in the League's Covenant.

Unlike the League, the United Nations is a "universal" collective security system.[5] With the admission of Switzerland in 2002, all the world's states, except the Vatican, have become members. Consequently, collective security is completely an "internal" matter; no external aggressors are left to confront. Precisely because of the inherent tension caused by the inward orientation of collective security in a world of sovereign states, the UN has had difficulty fulfilling its collective security obligations. For example, member states have never met their obligations under Article 43 of the Charter "to make available to the Security Council . . . in accordance with a

U.S. Permanent Representative Richard Holbrooke, President of the Security Council, Chairing a Debate on AIDS (the First Discussion of a Health Issue as a Threat to Peace and Security). (UN/DPI Photo by Evan Schneider. Reproduced by permission from the United Nations.)

special agreement or agreements, armed forces . . . for the purpose of maintaining international peace and security." The Security Council has had to depend on voluntary contributions of personnel, supplies, and funds through agreements with individual contributing states in order to undertake peace maintenance or restoration missions. Furthermore, all such actions authorized by the United Nations are subject to the veto power. During the cold war this limitation meant that the concept of collective security had to be exercised through reinterpretations of the original meaning of the Charter and extra-Charter devices.

COLLECTIVE SECURITY PROVISIONS OF THE UN CHARTER

Article 2, paragraph 4, of the UN Charter stipulates, "All members shall refrain in their international relations from the threat or use of force against the territorial integrity or political independence of any state, or any other manner inconsistent with the Purposes of the United Nations." The nonuse of force by member states, except as they are authorized to do so as part of a UN operation, is a central tenet of the Charter. Although Article 51 grants members "the inherent right of individual or collective self-defense" against an armed attack, this concession to the fundamental duty of sovereign states to protect their populations and territory, and to regional organizations and military alliances, lasts only until the Security Council can undertake sufficient steps to restore peace. The Charter wording also limits this grant of autonomy by asserting the council's right to investigate and take action on any threat to the peace, even if the states involved in a dispute are opposed to UN involvement.

The Security Council is the body charged with putting the UN's collective security system into practice. Within the UN structure, the founders made the council the repository of great-power resolve to maintain peace—the body comprising the "policemen" of the system. The General Assembly (GA), while it may discuss any dispute in international affairs, is formally barred from making recommendations to resolve an issue while the council is "seized with the matter." This restriction on the GA means that when the council is addressing an issue on its agenda, its members have decided that the matter is of such critical importance to future peace that resolution of the issue falls solely within the Security Council's jurisdiction under Chapter VII of the UN Charter.

Any state may bring "any dispute or any situation" that is likely to endanger the maintenance of international peace and security to the council's attention (Article 35). Although the council is not obligated to discuss or act on every complaint brought to it, appeals by nation-states have been one of the usual means by which international conflicts have been placed on its agenda. For this purpose, each Security Council member has representatives in New York City so that the council may act within twenty-four hours of a request. Iran's complaint in 1946 that, in the aftermath of World War II, Soviet troops still occupied its northernmost province was the first appeal to the council under Article 35. In Africa, states often appealed to the council to end colonialism or to resolve conflicts between neighboring states. Great powers have also used the procedure to obtain UN endorsement for collective or unilateral action against another state. The United States requested sessions of the council at the time of the North Korean invasion of South Korea (1950), the Cuban Missile Crisis (1962), and the Iraqi invasion of Kuwait (1990). Smaller states have appealed to the Security Council to rebuke the actions of major powers. Guatemala in 1954 and Cuba in 1960 used this procedure against the United States, alleging aggression in each case. Since 1948, both Israel and neighboring Arab states have brought complaints about suspected aggression by the other side on many occasions.

The centrality of the Security Council to the collective security system established by the Charter has given the body a unique position in world affairs. It serves as the "legitimizer" or "delegitimizer" for the use of force internationally. Inis Claude, a renowned scholar on the United Nations, noted this emerging function as early as 1966.[6] The cold war obscured this legitimizing role as it was used in events such as the Korean War, the wars in the Middle East (1948–1987), and the Cuban Missile Crisis. However, with the end of the East-West confrontation, the council's imprimatur of legitimacy was recognized as critical in the effort to achieve broad support for the use of force. The two Gulf Wars (1991 and 2003), the 1992 use of force in Somalia, and the international efforts in the Balkans during the 1990s all provide evidence of this phenomenon.

In the case of the U.S. invasion of Iraq in 2003, support for the assault, even for participation by other great powers and states in the region, in principle (and, in most instances, in practice) depended on Security Council endorsement. The United States' inability to gain this endorsement not only made the invasion more difficult, but also undercut the succeeding occupation and reconstruction of Iraq. The legitimacy of an institution, according to Ian Hurd, is the "subjective feeling on the part of the actors that leads them to behave differently than they otherwise would because they believe the institution requires them to."[7] Arab governments, in particular, have looked to the Security Council to provide legitimacy in the eyes of their own populations when determining their foreign policies in the Gulf region and toward the Israeli-Palestinian dispute. Although none of the permanent members of the Security Council are Middle Eastern, Arab, or Muslim, and three—the United States, Great Britain, and France—are perceived as Western neocolonialist powers in the region, Arab governments have been willing to support actions these powers have undertaken with council endorsement that they would not have supported if the actions had been carried out unilaterally.

LEGAL AUTHORITY FOR COLLECTIVE SECURITY: UN CHARTER CHAPTERS VI AND VII

To read the Charter of the United Nations is to envision an institution with revolutionary powers and authority in international affairs. The organization is granted not only the traditional instruments of diplomatic intercourse, but also the authority to impose crushing sanctions, to use military force, and to require nation-states to put their troops at the institution's disposal. Chapters VI and VII of the Charter provide the legal foundation for these sweeping powers. Technically, Chapter VII contains the primary mechanisms for collective security, allowing the organization to undertake all necessary **enforcement measures,** whereas Chapter VI provides for only the traditional means of diplomacy to achieve **pacific settlement** of disputes. However, the distortion of world politics imposed by the cold war made the use of Chapter VII nearly impossible, because its use required the unanimity of the permanent members of the Security Council. Consequently, from 1945 to the late 1980s, collective efforts to sustain the peace had to be fashioned out of reinterpretations of Chapter VII provisions or creative uses of Chapter VI.

Chapter VII provides more far-reaching powers than those in the ill-fated Covenant of the League of Nations. Article 39 of the Charter gives the Security Council the authority under international law to "determine the existence of any threat to the peace, breach of the peace, or act of aggression" and to "decide what measures shall be taken" to halt the threat or punish the aggressor. Given that the council is the sole defining power determining whether international peace and security have been breached, it has broad latitude. According to Article 2, paragraph 7, which prohibits UN intervention in the internal affairs of states, "peace" in Chapter VII is understood as "international peace."[8] For this reason, actions contemplated by the Security Council must be weighed against the sovereignty of the states that such actions would affect. Not until the turn of the century was the council willing to declare anything other than the use of force by one state against another to be a threat to "international peace and security," the litmus test established in Articles 39, 42, and 43 for collective action. So far, only North Korea in 1950, Argentina in 1982, and Iraq in 1990 have been identified as "aggressors," or rather invaders or attackers, and in 1960 an aggression was identified in the Congo, but Belgium—the exiting colonial power—was not mentioned as the perpetrator.

Chapter VII articulates a number of actions that the Security Council may pursue if it determines that a threat to international peace exists. Article 40 empowers it to take provisional measures to prevent an escalation or aggravation of a dispute. Such actions may include calls for a cease-fire or an armistice, or for the withdrawal of troops. If these recommendations are ignored, coercive nonmilitary or military actions may be taken. In July 1987, the Soviet Union and the United States for the first time joined in a resolution on the Middle East under the provisions of Chapter VII. In Resolution 598 they demanded that Iran and Iraq "observe an immediate cease-fire" in their ongoing war, "discontinue all military actions on land, sea and in the air, and withdraw all forces to the internationally recognized boundaries without delay." Citing Article 40, the council decided "to consider further steps to ensure compliance" if either party refused to accept the UN's demands.

Article 41 enumerates steps that do not involve the use of weapons, such as the cessation of diplomatic relations, economic sanctions up to a blockade, and the full or partial disruption of communications between the outside world and the states responsible for the breach of the

LEGAL BASIS FOR COLLECTIVE SECURITY: CHARTER OF THE UNITED NATIONS

Article 25

The Members of the United Nations agree to accept and carry out the decisions of the Security Council in accordance with the present Charter.

Article 39

The Security Council shall determine the existence of any threat to the peace, breach of the peace, or act of aggression and shall make recommendations, or decide what measures shall be taken in accordance with Articles 41 and 42, to maintain or restore international peace and security.

Article 40

In order to prevent an aggravation of the situation, the Security Council may, before making the recommendations or deciding upon the measures provided for in Article 39, call upon the parties concerned to comply with such provisional measures as it deems necessary or desirable. Such provisional measures shall be without prejudice to the rights, claims, or position of the parties concerned. The Security Council shall duly take account of failure to comply with such provisional measures.

Article 41

The Security Council may decide what measures not involving the use of armed force are to be employed to give effect to its decisions, and it may call upon the Members of the United Nations to apply such measures. These may include complete or partial interruption of economic relations and of rail, sea, air, postal, telegraphic, radio, and other means of communication, and the severance of diplomatic relations.

Article 42

Should the Security Council consider that measures provided for in Article 41 would be inadequate or have proved to be inadequate, it may take such action by air, sea, or land forces as may be necessary to maintain or restore international peace and security. Such action may include demonstrations, blockade, and other operations by air, sea, or land forces of Members of the United Nations.

Article 43

1. All Members of the United Nations, in order to contribute to the maintenance of international peace and security, undertake to make available to the Security Council, on its call and in accordance with a special agreement or agreements, armed forces, assistance, and facilities, including rights of passage, necessary for the purpose of maintaining international peace and security.

Article 45

In order to enable the United Nations to take urgent military measures, Members shall hold immediately available national air-force contingents for combined international enforcement action. The strength and degree of readiness of these contingents and plans for their combined action shall be determined, within the limits laid down in the special agreement or agreements referred to in Article 43, by the Security Council with the assistance of the Military Staff Committee.

Article 46

Plans for the application of armed force shall be made by the Security Council with the assistance of the Military Staff Committee.

peace. If the Security Council believes these measures would be inadequate, it may enforce its decisions with military "air, land, and sea forces" of UN member states, and it may also impose embargoes or any other measures deemed necessary.

Sanctions and embargoes have been used in only a few cases—for example, against Iraq after the Gulf War and in the civil wars of the former Yugoslavia. You can find a full discussion of the use of sanctions—especially "smart sanctions"—later in this chapter, but for now you should note that their effectiveness in general remains in dispute. Should sanctions or embargoes not be adequate, Article 42 provides for even harsher measures because it authorizes the United Nations to take military action.

According to the original conception of the United Nations as the guarantor of international peace—as the founders intended—the organization was expected to command military forces under the Security Council's authority and direction and with the help of a Military Staff Committee. All member states, as charged by the letter of Articles 43 and 44, were obliged to contribute troops and equipment to these UN-led operations. The Military Staff Committee, consisting of the military chiefs of staff of the council's permanent members, would "advise and assist" the council when it decided to use force. The Military Staff Committee provision was a realization of the wartime Allies' expectation that the great powers would have the responsibility and authority to act militarily through UN machinery to preserve peace in the postwar period. By Article 26, the drafters of the Charter also contemplated the committee's playing a role in the development of UN disarmament programs.

Despite the founders' intentions in 1945, the Military Staff Committee quickly fell into disuse, largely ignored after 1946. Charged with "the strategic direction of any armed forces placed at the disposal of the Security Council," the committee became an early victim of the cold war.[9] The permanent members were unable to agree on the kind of forces required or the number each should contribute to the committee's command. Article 43 calls on member states to negotiate agreements with the United Nations on the provision of national forces and military facilities to the world organization, but no agreements were ever achieved, which left the Military Staff Committee without troops to command. In 1950, while the USSR was boycotting the Security Council, the committee met briefly to discuss the response to North Korea's invasion of South Korea. The council branded North Korea the aggressor and authorized a military response. Thus, the only military action ever undertaken *under the UN flag* (although with U.S. command) occurred during the Korean War. However, once the Soviet delegate returned with the weapon of the veto, military action had to be taken by individual member states, at best authorized by pertinent Security Council resolutions or by the recommendations of the General Assembly acting in accordance with the Uniting for Peace Resolution, which is discussed later in this chapter.

Given the impracticality of mounting a UN military force under the direction of cooperating great powers in the Security Council during the cold war, a more common practice emerged: The council empowered individual states or other organizations or regional groups to take such action, usually in the form of ad hoc "coalitions of the willing." In this context, the council's role of legitimation is critical. It allows for what Bruno Simma called "another kind of collective security"[10] than the original plan of the Charter. Using Article 48, which requires member states, "or some of them," to "carry out the decisions of the Security Council," the body has regularly authorized coalitions "to use all necessary means" to restore peace and stability. The 1991 Gulf War against Iraq was an authorized UN enforcement operation, conducted by a U.S.-led coalition of member states on the basis of Articles 42 and 48. So, too, actions in Somalia, Rwanda, Bosnia and Herzegovina, East Timor, Liberia, Afghanistan, and the Central African Republic were first undertaken under the authorization rubric. However, when the United States invaded Iraq in March 2003 (and in 1999 led NATO forces into Kosovo), it did so without the kind of authorization other actors had received in the examples just cited. That is, non-UN forces, including those from the United States (as in Korea in 1950 and Iraq in 1991), had, in Security Council–authorized situations, represented the UN's wishes. Such was not the case in 2003 in Iraq, which raised a question about the "legitimacy" of the U.S.-led operation.

On paper, Chapter VII worked a revolution in international politics. The cold war, however, made this revolution more theory than practice. With the Security Council locked in a superpower stalemate, Chapter VII provisions generally could not be implemented when conflicts arose. Instead, council members and the General Assembly were forced to rely on the more traditional methods outlined in Chapter VI in hopes of resolving a dispute or ending hostilities. Chapter VI, comprising Articles 33 through 38 of the UN Charter, describes noncoercive measures for settling disputes between nations peacefully. It provides rules for the implementation of one of the overriding aims of the United Nations as described in Article 1: eliminating threats to global peace and ensuring the settlement or adjustment of potential conflicts that could develop into a threat to international peace and security.

Acting under Chapter VI, the Security Council can decide to investigate a dispute or a situation that could lead to a dispute to ascertain whether it is likely to develop into a threat to international peace and security (Article 34). A member state, as noted previously, may, under Article 35, bring a case to the council's attention. Although the issue under review has normally been of an international nature, in some instances—such as the control of Rhodesia by a racist minority government after 1966, human rights abuses in collapsing states (e.g., Yugoslavia and Rwanda), and the HIV/AIDS crisis—the Security Council has dealt with problems that did not immediately augur open international violence but were instead internal to a state. Also, the secretary-general can alert the Security Council to such a case under Article 99. The Secretariat implements Chapter VI decisions, usually with a mandate but no clear plan from the Security Council.

Once the council establishes that a threat exists, the following options are available for action. First are the measures mentioned in Article 33, paragraph 1: negotiation, mediation, conciliation, arbitration, and judicial decisions, as well as the use of regional institutions and other peaceful means for resolving the threat. The United Nations urges the parties to avail themselves of these options (Article 33, paragraph 2) and encourages the parties to settle the dispute peacefully themselves by direct bilateral negotiations. Mediation would include a third party, such as the United Nations, to serve as a facilitator. A judicial resolution would require the parties to take the dispute to the International Court of Justice. Second, according to Articles 36, paragraph 1, and 37, paragraph 2, respectively, the council can make recommendations about the procedure or method of adjustments and the terms of settlement for disputes. Finally, it can also make more general recommendations if the parties request them (Article 38).

The goal of Chapter VI is not establishing good and amicable relations between nations, only preventing war. Its instruments for doing so are limited and extend slightly beyond the diplomatic techniques of the previous two centuries. Thus, alone, Chapter VI provides the council little more than international public persuasion to end disputes. Yet, without the far-reaching remedies of Chapter VII at their disposal, the Security Council and the General Assembly have often turned to broad interpretations of Chapter VI to end a particular conflict. Through this process of reinterpretation, the devices of peacekeeping and observer missions—phenomena not listed in the Charter as part of the UN's arsenal—have come about. For example, in June 1948, the Security Council created the UN Truce Supervision Organization (UNTSO), the UN's first observer mission. UNTSO was directed to assist the UN mediator in his efforts to stabilize a cease-fire in the Arab-Israeli War of that spring.

The uneasy peace following the 1948 war lasted until the invasion and occupation of Egypt's Suez Canal by Great Britain, France, and Israel in 1956. An emergency special session of the General Assembly urged a cease-fire, withdrawal of invading forces, and reopening of the canal. Canada's UN representative, Lester Pearson, proposed to the assembly that it replace foreign forces along the canal with a UN force. On November 4, the assembly approved Resolution 998 (ES-1), directing Secretary-General Dag Hammarskjöld to submit a plan "for the setting up, with the consent of the nations concerned, of an emergency international United Nations force (later known as UNEF) to secure and supervise the cessation of hostilities." The intent of the operation was to place a neutral force between the combatants and to monitor the cease-fire. Thus, on November 5, 1956, the UN's first peacekeeping operation was born.

UN peacekeeping is detailed in Chapter 6, but for now you should note that this fairly common UN device for restoring peace cannot be found in Chapter VI or VII of the Charter. Secretary-General Hammarskjöld coined the term **Chapter VI½** to designate the Charter-based authority for peacekeeping and observer operations. These operations were developed as an action more intrusive than the peaceful settlement provisions of Chapter VI, yet short of Chapter VII provisions authorizing member states to use force. A new "gray area" of UN action emerged somewhat between the two chapters, keeping UN involvement relevant to the resolution of disputes in ways neither the Charter formally established nor earlier practice by the League of Nations contemplated.

COLLECTIVE SECURITY UNDER COLD WAR CONDITIONS

With the promise of continuing postwar superpower cooperation largely nonexistent by 1946, the UN's ability to respond to international crises depended on its leaders' ingenuity and the great powers' willingness to accept innovations in the application of the Charter. Despite the Charter provisions, UN efforts to secure peace depended on circuitous methods, enhanced roles for the General Assembly and the Secretariat, and expansive interpretations of Chapter VI. Even open aggression could not be addressed through council agreement, as the world discovered in the **Korean War** experience of 1950.

On June 25, 1950, North Korean military forces invaded South Korea. The peninsula had been a source of tension since the end of World War II, with a Communist regime in the north supported by the Soviet Union and the People's Republic of China, and the Republic of Korea (ROK) in the south recognized by the UN General Assembly as the only legitimate government of the Korean people. North Korean aggression was an open challenge to the new United Nations. The United States called for an emergency session of the Security Council, seeking the military defense of the ROK. On June 27 the council determined that a "breach of the peace" had occurred and called on all states, under the authority of Chapter VII of the Charter, "to furnish such assistance . . . as may be necessary to repel the armed attack and to restore peace and security in the area . . . [and to] render every assistance to the United Nations in the execution of this resolution." The council also granted the United States permission to appoint the commander of UN forces. President Truman appointed General Douglas MacArthur to the post. Ultimately, fifteen nations joined the UN coalition, but the bulk of the forces, the strategy, the funding, and the political decisions emanated from Washington, D.C. This operation was to be under the UN flag, but also authorized a single great power—the United States—to defend South Korea.

In contrast to the League's response to the dictators' aggressive actions in the interwar period, the United Nations proceeded decisively. President Truman saw the crisis as a test of the new organization's ability to sustain collective security.[11] However, the ability of the United States and its allies to achieve a strong UN response to North Korean aggression was possible only because of a quirk of UN history: At the time, the Soviet Union was boycotting Security Council meetings in protest of the continuing representation of China on the council by the Nationalist government on Taiwan. Mao Zedong's success in toppling the American-allied government, and the installation in Beijing of a Communist regime, had led the United States to veto resolutions to change China's Security Council seat. With the Soviet ambassador absent, the USSR could not veto the resolution authorizing force to resist North Korea's aggression. Consequently, Chapter VII "worked" only because the unanimity of the permanent council members was not needed.

The war went badly for UN forces in the initial months of combat. However, MacArthur launched spectacular counterassaults in the fall, and Seoul—the capital of South Korea—was liberated on September 28. The United Nations, led by U.S. forces, drove North Korean troops back across the demarcation line (the thirty-eighth parallel) between the two Koreas, and the Security Council approved the forcible reunification of the peninsula on October 7.

Uniting for Peace Resolution

The return of the Soviet ambassador to Security Council sessions made any further council endorsement of allied operations impossible. Deadlock in the council could now mean a UN military failure in Korea, particularly as Chinese "volunteers" entered the battle on the side of the North Koreans. Anticipating an ineffective Security Council, the United States attempted to shift discussion and authority for measures in Korea to the General Assembly. The USSR argued that such a maneuver violated Article 12 of the Charter, which prohibits the General Assembly from making any recommendations concerning a dispute while the Security Council is deliberating on the matter. With its large working majority in the body, however, the United States easily secured passage of the Uniting for Peace Resolution: Fifty-two states voted in favor, five (all from the Soviet bloc) voted against, and two abstained.

The **Uniting for Peace Resolution** (passed on November 3, 1950) "stretched" the Charter, constituting an informal amendment of the document. It gave the General Assembly the authority to discuss a threat to the peace, a breach of the peace, or an act of aggression, and to make recommendations for collective measures whenever "the Security Council, because of lack of unanimity of the permanent members, fails to exercise its primary responsibility for the maintenance of international peace and security." The resolution provided a mechanism to circumvent the anticipated use of the veto—at the time by the Soviet Union, later by other permanent members—to ensure the UN's ability to undertake action to restore the peace. The resolution shifted authority for enforcement measures from the exclusive control of the Security Council to a shared position with the assembly, which now had some legal authority to recommend "the use of armed force when necessary."

Emergency Special Sessions of the General Assembly

The Uniting for Peace Resolution allowed for **emergency special sessions of the General Assembly** to consider recommendations within twenty-four hours of a request by any seven members of the Security Council (nine members after the Charter revisions of 1965). The emergency special session could also be convened at the request of a majority of the assembly's members. The resolution established a Peace Observation Committee and a Collective Measures Committee, and it called on all states to designate and train troops to be on call by either the General Assembly or the Security Council. The resolution opened up a new avenue for maintaining peace or responding to an aggressor when conflict between Washington and Moscow threatened to make the United Nations helpless. Thus, the Uniting for Peace innovation represented part of a general shift in UN activity during the cold war from the council to the larger body, where simple majorities and the absence of the veto made action possible.

The convocation of emergency special sessions would become an accepted procedure. Ironically, the USSR was the first country to use the provisions of the resolution, joining with Yugoslavia to call for an emergency General Assembly session in 1956 on the Suez Crisis. It used the stratagem again following the so-called Six-Day War in 1967 between Israel and an Arab coalition. In the Suez case, the United Kingdom and France had vetoed Security Council measures calling on them to end their invasion of the canal region. The General Assembly then insisted on an immediate cease-fire and withdrawal of forces from the area. It also directed Secretary-General Dag Hammarskjöld to report within forty-eight hours on the preparation and dispatch of a UN Emergency Force (UNEF) to separate the parties. The end of the crisis and the apparent effectiveness of the UN's first peacekeeping operation seemed to demonstrate the worth of the resolution.

Emergency Special Sessions of the UN General Assembly
Authorized by the Uniting for Peace Resolution

Emergency Special Session	Topic	Date of Session
First	Suez Crisis	November 1–10, 1956
Second	Hungarian Crisis	November 4–10, 1956
Third	Lebanon and Jordan	August 8–21, 1958
Fourth	Congo Question	September 17–19, 1960
Fifth	Middle East War of 1967	June 17–September 18, 1967
Sixth	Afghanistan	January 10–14, 1980
Seventh	Palestine	July 22–29, 1980; April 20–28, June 25–26, August 16–19, September 24, 1982
Eighth	Namibia	September 3–14, 1981
Ninth	Occupied Arab Territories	January 29–February 5, 1982
Tenth	Occupied East Jerusalem and the Rest of the Occupied Palestinian Territories	April 24–25, July 15, November 13, 1997; March 17, 1998; February 5, 8, and 9, 1999; October 18–20, 2000; December 20, 2001; May 7, August 5, 2002; September 19, October 20–21, December 3, 2003

In 1956 a second emergency special session convened to consider the crisis in Hungary and the Soviet invasion of that country. Unfortunately, the session demonstrated one of the two most serious weaknesses of the procedure. In this case the offender was one of the two superpowers. The General Assembly soon learned that nothing it might do would force the Soviets to change course. A similar impasse occurred in January 1980, when the assembly held its sixth emergency session, this time to consider the Soviet invasion of Afghanistan. All the assembly could do was "deplore" the invasion, call on the USSR to withdraw, and urge the Security Council to find ways to implement the assembly's resolution. Such UN action had little discernible impact on Soviet foreign policy.

Recommendations by the assembly on matters originally thought to be within the sole jurisdiction of the Security Council also raised constitutional concerns for some UN members; as a result, they were unwilling to pay for or support UN actions that flowed from such recommendations. Following the fourth emergency special session (1960) on the Congolese civil war, both Russia and France refused to pay their assessments for peacekeeping operations that the General Assembly had recommended. The result was a financial crisis that brought the world body to the verge of bankruptcy. The Congolese experience made the Uniting for Peace Resolution far less appealing to UN members. It was not invoked again until 1980.

By the beginning of 2005, the General Assembly had convened ten emergency special sessions, half of them concerning Middle East conflicts. The more recent sessions demonstrated an evolution in the use of the device. During the cold war, one or more permanent members of the Security Council would usually organize the necessary majority to convene the General Assembly, hoping to find support in the face of a veto by one of the other P5. However, in the 1990s a more common occurrence was for groups of smaller states to call an emergency special session. The tenth emergency session, first convened in April 1997 to address Israeli occupation of East Jerusalem, the Gaza Strip, and the West Bank, met several times during the next six years at the behest of the Arab and nonaligned caucuses in the General Assembly. In most cases it met in response to a U.S. veto of a proposed Security Council resolution criticizing particular Israeli actions.

In the fall of 2003, representatives to the General Assembly reopened the tenth emergency special session to discuss two provocative decisions by the government in Tel Aviv. The first was a cabinet vote to favor "in principle" the forcible removal of Yasser Arafat, president of the Palestine Authority, from the occupied territories. The assembly demanded that Israel not deport Arafat or threaten his safety. The second was Israel's decision to build a security wall between Israeli and Palestinian communities in the West Bank, and between Israel proper and the occupied territories. The professed motive for construction of the barrier was protection of the civilian population from terrorist attacks. Following a report from Secretary-General Kofi Annan that Israel had ignored a past General Assembly request to halt construction, Arab nations called for a vote condemning the wall. The emergency session took the unusual step of referring the matter to the International Court of Justice (ICJ) in The Hague for an advisory opinion on the legality of the barrier. The court agreed to hear arguments beginning in February 2004 and delivered its opinion in July. By a vote of 14 to 1, the judges of the ICJ held that the wall was illegal under international law and must be removed. The court called on the General Assembly and the Security Council to "consider what further action is required to bring to an end the illegal situation resulting from the construction of the wall and the associated regime."[12] Days later, the General Assembly, by a vote of 150 to 6, with 10 abstentions, urged all member states to acknowledge the illegality of the wall and to render no aid to the Israeli project.

In its opinion, the court held that it had jurisdiction in the case because the General Assembly had authority to request an advisory opinion, even though the Security Council remained seized with the matter. The ICJ noted,[13]

> There has been an increasing tendency over time for the General Assembly and the Security Council to deal in parallel with the same matter concerning the maintenance of international peace and security (see, for example, the matters involving Cyprus, South Africa, Angola, Southern Rhodesia, and more recently Bosnia and Herzegovina and Somalia).

At least according to one observer, the court's decision opened up another avenue to circumvent a veto by a permanent member of the Security Council—that is, by court decision declaring an act in violation of international law and a threat to international peace and security.[14]

Peacekeeping and Military Observer Groups

Conflict in the Middle East has been not only the UN's longest-running challenge to collective security, but also the cauldron in which the world organization has had to devise its most important innovation to preserve peace and stability. As we noted previously, the 1948 war between the new state of Israel and several Arab states led to the creation of the UN's first observer mission (UNTSO), and the 1956 Suez Crisis brought about the first peacekeeping force (UNEF).

As would be the case for nearly all early UN peacekeeping efforts, the placement of the emergency force along the Sinai in November 1956 was contingent on approval by the sovereign state involved, in this case Egypt. UNEF patrolled the border and monitored the cease-fire until 1967.

In the spring of that year, Egyptian incursions in the Gaza Strip and Sharm el Sheikh, plus moves by other Arab states, convinced the Israelis that an attack was imminent. Of particular moment was Egyptian president Nasser's insistence that the UN "Blue Helmets" (i.e., the UNEF group) be removed in order to open the Sinai for any projected attack. Secretary-General U Thant withdrew the force. Shortly thereafter, the Middle East War of 1967 broke out. Following the war, UNEF II patrolled a new cease-fire. By the time of its termination in 1979, the effort had resulted in the loss of thirty-six peacekeepers' lives from hostile action.

Generally subsumed under the nomenclature of **peacekeeping,** a term not found in the UN Charter, the insertion of outside personnel under UN command to separate warring parties, to monitor a cease-fire, or to provide neutral administration has become a hallmark of the UN's role in world affairs. During the latter half of the twentieth century, the distinctive blue helmets UN peacekeepers wore became a vital symbol of the international security system: the Blue Helmets provided an important mechanism for preserving the global order, ensuring the survival of small states, and protecting human rights. Peacekeeping is a concept that has evolved through the years, and the resulting changes in various peacekeeping missions account for many of the difficulties encountered by these efforts, for much of the misunderstanding about the United Nations, and for both criticism and plaudits of the organization.

DISARMAMENT AND ARMS CONTROL

Peacekeeping was an innovation created to restore peace when the other mechanisms provided by the UN Charter were unavailable because of a deadlock in the Security Council. UN officials, such as Dag Hammarskjöld, Lester Pearson, Ralph Bunche, and Brian Urquhart, with the tacit support of the great powers, cobbled together a case-by-case response to individual conflicts. Far more central to the notion of collective security than peacekeeping, however, was the belief that conflict and general war could be eliminated only by a vast reduction in the world's military arsenals. While the UN Charter says nothing about peacekeeping, it specifically cites "disarmament and the regulation of armaments" as one of the "general principles" on which international peace and security are based.[15] It also charges the Security Council with proposing plans for arms control.[16] Therefore, from its earliest days, the United Nations sought to facilitate the reduction and control of the most destructive weapons. This effort was given an urgency by the dawning of the nuclear age just as the United Nations was coming into being.

One point to note is that disarmament is neither a requirement of nor a necessary condition for collective security. A case can be made that international peace and security require the maintenance of sufficient military force to repel any aggressor or to enforce the world community's decisions. Nonetheless, beginning with World War I, leaders like U.S. president Woodrow Wilson, who hoped to build an international political architecture to maintain the future peace, believed collective security could succeed only if it was accompanied by deep reductions in, and even the elimination of, national military arsenals. Arms races were perceived as inherently destabilizing. Both the Covenant of the League of Nations and the UN Charter committed their respective organizations to the promotion of world disarmament. The rise of military dictatorships in Europe and Asia in the 1930s only reinforced the belief that the reduction of armaments was crucial to the maintenance of peace and to the replacement of the use of force with the rule of law.

During the cold war the UN's preoccupation was with weapons of mass destruction (WMDs) owned by the world's major powers. The proximity of events in 1945 made this preoccupation inevitable. The conclusion of the San Francisco Conference in June of that year, the immediate submission of the Charter to the U.S. Senate for ratification with the public belief that the new world body would be able to address the most serious problems, and, only two months later, the American detonation of the world's first atomic bomb over Hiroshima, Japan, put extraordinary pressure on the United States and other major powers to place atomic energy under UN control. The General Assembly's first resolution, passed on January 24, 1946, created the UN Atomic Energy Commission (UNAEC) to make recommendations to the Security Council on methods to "deal with the problems raised by the discovery of atomic energy." The Security Council members, plus Canada when it was not a council member, were appointed to the commission.

At the inaugural meeting of UNAEC, the United States submitted a proposal to place all uranium mines, processing facilities, and fissionable materials worldwide under UN ownership in a new agency called the *Atomic Development Authority (ADA)*. The ADA would then distribute "denatured" nuclear materials to national governments for peaceful uses. The United States envisioned the transfer of American, Soviet, and all other national nuclear assets to the United Nations in a phased process. The U.S. representative to UNAEC, Bernard Baruch, put forward the *Baruch Plan,* calling for penalties against states that violated ADA authority. The United States promised to destroy its stockpile of weapons and to turn over its scientific information to the ADA once a system of inspections and controls was put in place. The proposal met immediate Soviet opposition, which demonstrated that the emerging cold war antagonisms between Washington and Moscow were likely to make UN progress on disarmament extremely difficult. The USSR argued that the U.S. initiative was simply an attempt by the United States to maintain its nuclear advantage. The Soviets insisted that the U.S. nuclear arsenal had to be destroyed before any controls or UN ownership could be set up. While the commission approved the U.S. plan by 10 to 0 in December 1946, the Soviet Union abstained, which made any practical creation of a UN agency with the designated powers impossible.

In December 1953, President Dwight Eisenhower revised the U.S. position, calling on nuclear powers to transfer a small percentage of their nuclear materials to a new International Atomic Energy Agency (IAEA) under the ultimate authority of the United Nations but largely independent of its control. In the intervening years between the Baruch Plan and Eisenhower's proposal, the Soviet Union detonated its first atomic device (1949) and moved rapidly to catch up with U.S. nuclear efforts. The United States, for its part, had decided to establish a nuclear arsenal and delivery systems capable of guaranteeing deterrence based on a credible second-strike capability against any surprise attack. The arms race had begun, and it had become a centerpiece of the East-West confrontation. Eisenhower's proposal was directed at slowing this arms buildup and easing East-West tensions. He offered to transfer U.S. stockpiles at a rate of 5 to 1 of that turned over by the USSR. Although the Soviet Union rejected the proposal, Eisenhower's initiative led to the creation of the IAEA in 1957. At this point you may want to turn to Chapter 1 to review the organization and work of the agency. Of particular note for this discussion of the UN's role in disarmament was the creation of the IAEA's safeguards inspection system, which was meant to guarantee that nations without nuclear weapons are not diverting nuclear energy materials intended for peaceful purposes to weapons use.

The UN's impact on disarmament in the 1950s was negligible. In 1952 the Atomic Energy Commission and the UN's Commission on Conventional Armaments were merged into the UN Disarmament Commission. However, this forum served as little more than a setting for Soviet and U.S. propaganda bombasts, the former power calling for "general and complete disarmament," the latter insisting on verifiable and intrusive inspection as part of any disarmament plan. Neither state expected its proposals to be accepted by the other side. Serious discussions within the Disarmament Commission occurred only in the Subcommittee on Disarmament, created in 1954 and made up of the United States, the Soviet Union, the United Kingdom, France, and Canada. These states conducted their talks in secret. Otherwise, the commission was reduced to debating proposals by nonnuclear states. To be sure, the growing number of new UN members from the Third World and the desire to maintain influence in these countries led the superpowers to make organizational concessions to the UN membership, but the nuclear powers still monopolized the substantive issues.

In August 1959 the subcommittee was enlarged, becoming the Ten Nation Disarmament Committee with the addition of Bulgaria, Czechoslovakia, Poland, and Romania from the Warsaw Pact, and Italy from the North Atlantic Treaty Organization. Eight nonaligned nations were added in 1961, which resulted in the Eighteen-Nation Disarmament Committee (ENDC). The only serious negotiations, however, were conducted in bilateral contacts between Washington and Moscow.

A number of agreements were concluded in the 1960s and early 1970s as a result of U.S.-USSR talks. Following the dangerous confrontation in the Cuban Missile Crisis, the two sides agreed to the 1963 Partial Test Ban Treaty and a communications hotline between the two capitals to ensure no misunderstandings on the deployment or use of weapons and personnel. In 1972 they reached agreement on the Anti-Ballistic Missile Treaty.

UN negotiations were relegated to what were then seen as peripheral matters. Two topics dominated UN diplomacy: nuclear weapons–free zones (NFZs) and nuclear nonproliferation. The Antarctic Treaty of 1959 was the first agreement to ban nuclear weapons on a regional basis. The treaty prohibited weapons or weapons testing on the Antarctic continent. Signatories pledged to demilitarize Antarctica. To protect the environment, the treaty banned the dumping of radioactive wastes. NFZ agreements were also achieved for Latin America (Treaty of Tlatlelolco, 1976), Africa (Treaty of Pelindaba, 1996), Southeast Asia (Treaty of Bangkok, 1995), and the South Pacific (Treaty of Rarotonga, 1985). In 1979, following successful negotiations, the United Nations effected the prohibition of weapons on the moon and other celestial bodies.

The UN's single greatest achievement in restraining the nuclear arms race was the Treaty on the Non-Proliferation of Nuclear Weapons, usually referred to as the **Nuclear Non-Proliferation Treaty (NPT)**. This treaty was opened for signature on July 1, 1968, and entered into force in 1970. It grew out of negotiations in the Eighteen-Nation Disarmament Committee. In August 1967, for the first time, the United States and the Soviet Union submitted a joint draft agreement. The superpowers hoped to halt the spread of nuclear weapons by convincing states without such weapons to foreswear their acquisition and to bar existing nuclear weapons states from transferring these weapons to any nonnuclear state or assisting any nonnuclear state in manufacturing them. A state adhering to the NPT was obligated to subject its entire peaceful nuclear program to the International Atomic Energy Agency's safeguards inspection regimen and to pledge to acquire nuclear materials and equipment only for peaceful purposes.

Many of the nonnuclear states balked at the U.S.-Soviet draft because it appeared to cement the world power structure permanently, with the nuclear states—at the time the five permanent members of the Security Council only—in a position to dominate world affairs indefinitely. Several ENDC delegations, led by Nigeria and Brazil, indicated that they would not freeze their nuclear development programs while the superpowers continued to stockpile and modernize their weapon systems. These delegations insisted that the United States and the USSR move toward ending their "vertical" proliferation before nonnuclear states commit to halting the "horizontal" proliferation of these weapons around the world.

Without the signatures of the states that were on the threshold of developing nuclear weapons, the NPT would have been worthless. Recognizing this, the superpowers added an article to the draft treaty that committed them to "pursue negotiations in good faith on effective measures relating to the cessation of the nuclear arms race at an early date and to nuclear disarmament" (Article VI). Disarmament was no longer simply an East-West issue but also a North-South issue; the Third World was using its political clout to pressure the superpowers into concessions. The commitments made in the NPT meant that U.S.-USSR negotiations on arms control would have to show some progress or critical nonnuclear states would not sign the treaty. This incentive encouraged the opening of Strategic Arms Limitation Talks (SALT) between Moscow and Washington. These negotiations resulted in the SALT agreements of 1972: the five-year Interim Agreement on Certain Measures With Respect to the Limitation of Strategic Offensive Arms, which curtailed the growth of missile delivery systems on both sides, and the Treaty on the Limitation of Anti-Ballistic Missile Systems (ABM Treaty). The latter limited the number of defensive systems each side could maintain.[17] Thus, the UN negotiations on nonproliferation had contributed to slowing the superpower arms race.

The NPT called for five-year review conferences and for a conference twenty-five years from entry into force to determine whether the treaty should be extended indefinitely or for a defined period. That conference, held at UN headquarters in 1995, reached a consensus: The majority of the parties wanted to extend the NPT indefinitely. The parties also agreed to an "enhanced" review process to hold all governments "accountable" for their NPT obligations. The nuclear weapons states moreover committed to achieve a Comprehensive Nuclear-Test-Ban Treaty (CTBT). During the 1990s, adherence to the NPT accelerated as longtime holdouts like France (1992), China (1992), and South Africa (1991) signed and ratified the treaty. By 2004, only four states stood outside the framework of the treaty: Cuba, India, Pakistan, and Israel.

Following the adoption of the NPT, the General Assembly expanded the ENDC to include all UN members, changing the name to the Conference of the Committee on Disarmament (CCD). The CCD, in turn, was replaced by the Conference on Disarmament (CD) in 1978 on the recommendation of the UN General Assembly's first special session on disarmament. This conference became the world's principal multilateral disarmament negotiating forum. By 2005, the CD had expanded from its original thirty-eight member states to sixty-six. Its set agenda, known as the *Decalogue,* established ten broad areas of disarmament for annual review. However, the size of the conference, coupled with the centrality of nuclear weapons to the strategic interests of the major powers, meant that this Geneva-based body had a diminishing impact on disarmament efforts. As you may recall from Chapter 1, the year 2003 marked the seventh consecutive year that the CD was unable to agree on a program of work.

When the Conference on Disarmament negotiates a specific topic, as it did successfully with the Chemical Weapons Convention (1992) and the Comprehensive Nuclear-Test-Ban Treaty (1996), it usually creates an ad hoc committee with a negotiating mandate to establish the provisions of the treaty. Even this approach has been circumvented on occasion, however. For example, the Landmines Convention of 1997 (officially titled the "1997 Convention on the Prohibition of the Use, Stockpiling, Production and Transfer of Anti-Personnel Mines and on Their Destruction") was debated, negotiated, and adopted for ratification outside the CD in a "fast-track" set of negotiations known as the *Ottawa Process*. The stalemate inside the CD and events outside the CD led to widespread speculation among experts about the need either to maintain the status quo at the commission, to change the CD's rules and procedures, or to endorse the establishment of alternative negotiating forums to address disarmament questions.

The plight of the Conference on Disarmament was emblematic of the difficulty a universal international organization dedicated to collective security has in addressing an issue such as disarmament when such an issue touches on matters critical to the most powerful states' national security interests. These states are unlikely to relinquish their control over the negotiating process or to subject their armaments to international regulation without clearly controllable benefits to themselves. In the United Nations this dilemma meant that the Security Council was unable to put forward a meaningful disarmament program during the cold war, and the General Assembly was relegated to admonishing the nuclear powers about their responsibilities and to creating structures and initiatives to exhort world public opinion on the merits of disarmament.

The General Assembly convened three special sessions on disarmament (1978, 1982, and 1988) prior to the end of the century and committed to a fourth gathering once an agenda and format could be agreed on. These meetings were the first global general conferences on disarmament since the World Disarmament Conference sponsored by the League of Nations in 1932.[18] They were meant to mobilize public sentiment in favor of deep cuts in nuclear stockpiles. The 1978 special session tried to revive the Disarmament Commission, which had been largely ignored since the superpowers took control of the arms-control negotiating process in the 1950s. All UN members were given membership on the commission, but it was eclipsed by both the Conference on Disarmament and the General Assembly's First Committee in New York, which historically has discussed disarmament issues to the exclusion of all other matters.

The 1978 special session also created the UN Institute for Disarmament Research (UNIDIR), which began operations in 1980 as an autonomous intergovernmental organization within the UN System. The institute's small, permanent staff is located in Geneva, Switzerland. UNIDIR is funded by voluntary contributions and the regular UN budget. Its purpose is to provide the international community with data on and analyses of problems related to the arms race, particularly in the nuclear field. It also promotes and assists ongoing disarmament negotiations.

Changing Disarmament Priorities

Nuclear Weapons

The United States and the Soviet Union signed the Intermediate Nuclear Forces Agreement in 1987. It was the first arms-control agreement between the two sides to reduce and dismantle nuclear weapon delivery systems. It was made possible by the deep fissures developing in the frozen antagonistic superpower relationship. Mikhail Gorbachev had succeeded to the leadership of the Soviet Communist Party in March 1985, promising a restructuring of the Soviet economic system and "new thinking" in foreign policy. He moved quickly to repair relations with the West, cut Soviet assistance to client regimes around the world, and opened serious arms negotiations with Washington.

The permanent thaw in U.S.-USSR relations and then the collapse of the Soviet empire by the end of 1991 opened the way to new arms accords between Washington and Moscow. It also shuffled the world community's disarmament priorities. Issues that had been secondary to the superpower strategic buildup—such as proliferation, nonnuclear weapons of mass destruction, arms trafficking, and conventional weapons—now took on new importance. By the turn of the millennium, a virtually unlimited supply of even the most modern weapons in the hands of large and small states, ethnic groups, and terrorist organizations meant that all wars held the potential to endanger the lives of millions. Forty-seven of the forty-nine conflicts waged during the 1990s were fought mainly with small arms, killing nearly four million people.[19] Faced with an estimated five hundred million small arms in circulation worldwide, and new types of WMDs, the United Nations turned its attention to a broader weapons agenda.

Chemical Weapons

The use of chemical weapons by Iraq against the Iraqi Kurds (in Halabja in 1988) and during the Iran-Iraq War revived old images of World War I gas warfare. On November 30, 1992, the UN General Assembly adopted the Convention on the Prohibition of the Development, Production, Stockpiling and Use of Chemical Weapons and on Their Destruction (Chemical Weapons Convention, or CWC). As of 2005, 164 states had become or were in the process of becoming parties to the convention. This international disarmament agreement was the first with the goal of eliminating an entire category of WMDs.

To enforce its provisions, the convention established the Organisation for the Prohibition of Chemical Weapons (OPCW) and gave it the authority to conduct surprise inspections. Each government signing the agreement obligated itself to destroying all chemical weapons it owned or any that it had abandoned in another country, as well as any facilities used to produce these weapons. The OPCW was authorized to carry out surprise inspections, with trained experts, not only of suspected chemical weapons sites, but also of industrial facilities. The dual-use nature of chemicals and the ease of their production, however, made the exclusion of chemical weapons from the world's arsenals nearly impossible. The convention also could not diminish the danger of chemical attacks by terrorist or nonstate groups, such as the sarin chemical attack on the Tokyo subway in 1995.

Still, in a promising breakthrough, Libya joined the OPCW in February 2004 and in March disclosed that it had stockpiled twenty-two tons of mustard gas. It agreed to eliminate all such weapons. This new and welcome cooperative policy led Libya to work with IAEA inspectors to fully dismantle the nation's nuclear arms program.

Biological Weapons

The United Nations also took a renewed interest in biological weapons. This interest was reinforced by the emergence of highly organized and well-financed terrorist groups at the turn of the century. Biological weapons are living organisms, most commonly bacteria and viruses, deliberately disseminated to cause death or disease in humans, animals, or plants. They are considered weapons of mass destruction because they have a potential to destroy life equaled only by nuclear weapons. Deaths in the United States from anthrax sent through the postal system shortly after the terrorist assaults on New York City and Washington, D.C., in 2001 demonstrated the panic and destruction that a coordinated biological attack could cause.

The 1925 Geneva Protocol prohibited the use of biological weapons in warfare. The 1972 Convention on the Prohibition of the Development, Production and Stockpiling of Bacteriological (Biological) and Toxin Weapons and on Their Destruction (Biological Weapons Convention, or BWC) went further by prohibiting their development and possession. The UN secretary-general has authority under the treaty to investigate the alleged use of biological weapons, ascertain facts about such alleged use, and report the findings to member states. A number of countries, however, violated their obligations under the BWC by initiating or continuing to develop and produce biological weapons after the convention entered into force.

Concerns about these types of weapons grew dramatically following the 1991 Gulf War. Persuasive evidence indicated that Saddam Hussein's Iraqi regime had developed an offensive biological weapons capability. After the war the Security Council required the unconditional destruction of Iraq's biological arsenal and the capacity to produce it. Until their forced departure from Iraq in 1998, UN inspectors regularly cataloged and destroyed facilities and munitions. In 2002, upon the return of a UN inspection team headed by Dr. Hans Blix, the search for these weapons was renewed. By the time the United States and Great Britain invaded Iraq in March 2003, the Blix mission had found no evidence of a continuing biological program, but individual national intelligence services continued to assert an Iraqi biological capability, including mobile labs and weaponized missiles. The possibility also remained that Iraq and other states with these weapons could transfer them to terrorist groups.

The continuing danger demonstrated the most serious weakness in the Biological Weapons Convention: the absence of a binding verification regime that could assure countries that suspected producers were not building stockpiles. At a special conference held in April 1994, the parties to the convention established an ad hoc working group to draft an inspection protocol. By the end of the convention's fifth review conference in November 2002, no protocol had been achieved, much to the consternation of states from the nonaligned caucus. The Western group of nations expressed satisfaction that negotiations would continue, but little concern that a protocol seemed no closer to promulgation. The United States, in particular, opposed the verification regime under consideration by the ad hoc group. The conference decided to begin a new process of negotiation through an annual meeting of experts, but with little prospect of early success.

Conventional Weapons

The expanded use of conventional weapons such as land mines and small arms in the post–cold war context of growing sectarian violence in Africa, Asia, and Eastern Europe caused heightened concern at the United Nations. It also generated a strong response by the nongovernmental community, and many nongovernmental organizations (NGOs) began to pressure their governments and the world organization to address the humanitarian disaster these weapons caused.

Since the 1970s, the United Nations had been involved in the movement to ban land mines. In 1980, it negotiated the Convention on Certain Conventional Weapons (CCW). However, frustration with the slow pace of developing a specific land-mine agreement in the Conference on Disarmament led several states and NGOs to pursue negotiations outside the UN structure. In October 1996, Canada and Belgium launched the Ottawa Process. The International Campaign to Ban Landmines (ICBL) led the nongovernmental community, and it was joined by such organizations as Doctors Without Borders and the International Committee of the Red Cross. During the succeeding year, a land-mines convention was hammered out. It prohibited in all circumstances any use of antipersonnel land mines. It also required the destruction of stockpiles within four years after the treaty entered into force and mandated that mines already in the ground be destroyed within ten years. As of June 2005, 152 states had signed or acceded to the convention. In support of the treaty, the United Nations made demining one of its important functions in peacekeeping operations.

Among the states notably absent from the list of signatories were the United States, Israel, and the Russian Federation. However, in a reversal of policy, the U.S. government announced in

February 2004 that it would end the production and use of "persistent" antipersonnel and antitank mines after 2010. The United States committed to use only land mines that would render themselves inert within days of their deployment. Washington also promised to produce only land mines that are detectable by metal detectors. It also increased its budget to assist in mine detection and removal by 50 percent.

Conflicts in the post–cold war era have been fought almost exclusively with light or small arms. The civil wars of Africa and Latin America, the secessionist efforts in southeast Europe, and the ethnic struggles in both Asia and Africa have been between peoples and governments with limited resources. They have obtained their weapons largely from clandestine arms brokers in the growing weapons black market, or from states anxious for revenues from arms sales. The disintegration of states and the weakening of central control over national arsenals have also produced a huge dispersion of these armaments. The United Nations estimated in 2004 that more than six hundred million small arms and light weapons (SALW) were in circulation worldwide.[20]

In 2001 the United Nations convened a world conference to address the spread and use of such weapons, but participating states could not arrive at a consensus on how to cut small-arms quantities or how to regulate their movement. The conference did draw up a plan of action to combat illicit trade in these weapons. The General Assembly endorsed the plan, and it was nurtured by the UN's Department for Disarmament Affairs through convention of a "Meeting of States" in 2003. However, at best, the world community could take only incremental, practical steps, given the diffusion and nongovernmental control of these weapons. In the late 1990s the General Assembly adopted, by consensus, a resolution calling for "practical disarmament measures" (PDMs). These measures included provisions for the destruction of SALW and of ammunition and explosives, as well as the demobilization of forces in civil conflicts with concurrent disarmament of armed personnel, pilot projects for voluntary weapons collection, demining, and harmonization of national legislation on illicit arms traffic. In addition, the United Nations inaugurated the Register of Conventional Arms to contribute to confidence building and transparency. These actions were nevertheless recognized as limited steps for dealing with a disquieting challenge that was likely to grow.

POST–COLD WAR COLLECTIVE SECURITY

During the last decade of the twentieth century, the United Nations faced both the opportunity and the burden of meeting threats to collective security through the original provisions laid down in the Charter. The collective action taken against Iraq in 1991 marked the first use of Chapter VII enforcement measures since the "police action" in the Korean War (1950–1953), and it went much further than any previous peacekeeping effort. Between August—when Iraqi forces invaded and occupied Kuwait—and November, the Security Council passed ten resolutions meant to isolate Iraq and to prepare the legal groundwork for collective military action. Among the most important were Resolutions 660 (a condemnation of the invasion), 661 (the imposition of mandatory economic sanctions), 662 (a declaration that the annexation of Kuwait was null and void), and 678 (which gave Iraq forty-eight days to withdraw from Kuwait or face military retaliation).

As in the case of Korea, the United Nations did not put its own forces in the field under Security Council command. Instead, it authorized a coalition of states led by the United States to use "all necessary means . . . to restore peace and security in the area." However, unlike Korea's police action, in this case the troops did not fight under the UN flag. In practical terms, the United Nations "subcontracted" its collective security duties to an international coalition. The procedure of **subcontracting**—authorizing a state or group of states to act on behalf of the world community to restore peace and stability—became a regular feature of Security Council action at the turn of the millennium. It would be used again in Somalia, Rwanda, Bosnia, Kosovo, and East Timor. Several of these episodes were presented in Chapter 1 as part of our discussion on another UN innovation: second-generation peacekeeping and nation building.

The rapid success of coalition forces in the 1991 war and the subsequent imposition of near-mandate conditions on Iraq seemed to augur a new time of promise for the United Nations. U.S. president George H. W. Bush opined that maybe now, in the wake of the cold war stalemate, the United Nations could live up to its founders' vision of its being the "last best hope for peace."[21] Bush and the leaders of the other permanent Security Council members worked assiduously to maintain unanimity not only on the Iraq crisis but also on other challenges to collective security.

In January 1992 the Security Council encouraged Secretary-General Boutros Boutros-Ghali to draft proposals on "ways of strengthening and making more efficient within the framework and provisions of the Charter the capacity of the UN for preventive diplomacy, for peacemaking and for peacekeeping."[22] The secretary-general outlined his recommendations in *An Agenda for Peace*. He encouraged the council to act early to assist "states at risk." He also urged member states to earmark military contingents for quick UN activation. The report outlined problems in the less developed countries and the need for a humanitarian, political, economic, and military response by the United Nations.

The secretary-general's report contained an unspoken yet tacit assumption that collective security implied something more than the absence of war between two recognized nation-states. Therefore, collective security could not be ensured solely by separating combatants or, in the worst case, driving back an aggressor to its antebellum borders. The definition of the UN's purpose in this regard now included addressing traditionally internal domestic issues, previously thought to be beyond the Charter's reach. As suggested previously, collective security is an intellectual construct, undefined by the Charter. As such, in the new world of post–cold war politics, and in the conception of the post–Gulf War Security Council membership, collective security required innovations and a revision of UN mechanisms.

Immediately affected by the new understanding of collective security was the forty-year-old practice of peacekeeping. As a result of Secretary-General Boutros-Ghali's *An Agenda for Peace*, three new terms—*preventive diplomacy, peacemaking,* and *postconflict peace building*—entered the UN lexicon. **Preventive diplomacy** attempts either to resolve intra- and interstate conflicts before violence erupts or to limit the spread of violence; it is intended to be proactive peacekeeping. **Peacemaking** seeks to bring hostile parties to agreement through negotiation and mediation before or after the intervention of UN peacekeeping forces. **Peace building** aims to construct an environment that sustains durable peace, often by UN administration or facilitation of domestic political functions. It also includes addressing the economic, social, cultural, and humanitarian problems that underpin violent conflict. Taken together and coupled with the long-standing UN practice of peacekeeping, preventive diplomacy, peacemaking, and peace building amount to a UN effort at sustaining and rebuilding nations torn apart by internal violence or governmental collapse. Critics of Boutros-Ghali's report suggested that an expansion of the UN role in these ways was first and foremost beyond the UN's financial and political capabilities and, second, a form of international neocolonialism reminiscent of the League's old mandate system. (A full description of what came to be called *second-generation peacekeeping* is provided in Chapter 6.)

Smart Sanctions

Shortly after the turn of the century, the Security Council addressed the weaknesses of another instrument of collective security: international sanctions that could be used against a state that threatens world peace and security. Article 41 of the UN Charter authorizes the Security Council to impose mandatory sanctions, including "complete or partial interruption of economic relations and of rail, sea, air, postal, . . . and other means of communication, and the severance of diplomatic ties." All member states are obligated to enforce the Security Council's decision. The tradition of using these Draconian measures short of the use of force in order to punish a state and change its behavior dates from the League's Covenant, which went even further and automatically imposed such sanctions when a member was found to have violated the League's principles. Since 1919 the imposition of sanctions has been promoted as a step short of war that will penalize the wrongdoer sufficiently for it to alter its policy.

Unfortunately, little evidence indicates that sanctions—economic, military, or diplomatic—have produced the desired result. Often, enforcing imposed sanctions is difficult because individual states sometimes find the economic incentives to continue trade with the offending government more in their national interest than maintaining solidarity with the rest of the world community. States under sanction have generally pursued policies that have other motivations than those that would be amenable to change under international economic pressure. Their governments, as well, can make the case to the domestic population that any hardships currently experienced are the product of "unjust" international sanctions, not the product of the government's policies. Often the effect of sanctions is to worsen the humanitarian situation while imposing no hardships on the leadership that the sanctions are meant to punish. For several of these reasons, the League of Nations' record on the successful use of sanctions was dismal. As early as the Japanese invasion of Manchuria in 1931, the League could not mold sufficient international unity to impose sanctions. Then, in 1935, Mussolini's Fascist Italy invaded Ethiopia and all that the League could muster were "voluntary" economic sanctions against the invader. They had no effect on Rome's policy.

The UN record has been only slightly better. The ability to impose sanctions is limited by the veto in the Security Council, and, conversely, the power to end them is also restricted by the right of one of the P5 to block such action. Thus, sanctions are never used against a major power. The Security Council imposed mandatory economic sanctions for the first time in November 1965 against the racist regime of the self-declared independent state of Rhodesia. Nearly three years later the council needed to make the sanctions "comprehensive" because they had had little apparent effect on the regime. Sanctions were also imposed on Iran following the 1979 hostage taking of diplomatic personnel at the U.S. embassy in Tehran. The crisis was not resolved until 1981, with little evidence that UN sanctions had played an effective role in the release of the hostages.

The case of sanctions against the South African government meant to end its practice of apartheid is often cited as perhaps the only successful operation of this kind. South Africa's racial policies were first debated in the UN General Assembly in 1946. From that time forward, South Africa rejected any UN debate or resolution on the subject as an unjustified interference in its domestic affairs, in violation of Article 2 of the UN Charter. Under South Africa's apartheid laws, formal and severe racial segregation was mandated, and the minority white population was in control of the government and all important institutions and economic activities. The black majority had limited rights of movement, exercised few political rights, and lived in significant poverty. In 1960 the General Assembly declared apartheid "reprehensible and repugnant to human dignity."

In 1962 the General Assembly placed voluntary sanctions on South Africa, including breaking diplomatic relations, boycotting South African goods, and refusing landing rights to South African aircraft. Six years later it discouraged immigration into the country and advocated the end of economic links with the outside world. Though voluntary, these sanctions heightened South Africa's ostracism from the global community. Yet, the Security Council continued to reject mandatory economic sanctions. The United States, Great Britain, and France refused to support sanctions, citing cold war concerns. The global attention on South Africa's policy, however, did lead to private corporate and individual government decisions that hurt the country's economy and may have hastened the release of Nelson Mandela and the transfer of power from the white minority government.

The growing consensus among the permanent members of the council in the 1990s, coupled with the outbreak of serious ethnic and religious conflict in many parts of the world, produced a new interest in sanctions. Short of military intervention, economic penalties seemed a reasonable first step to punish a violator of contemporary collective security, whether it was a government that violated the human rights of its citizens, carried out genocide, tried to halt legitimate self-determination, or actually committed a cross-border transgression, or it was a nonstate actor that did not live up to its agreements or committed an international atrocity, such as al-Qaeda did in the terrorist attacks on New York City and Washington, D.C. The Security Council, at various times and for a variety of reasons, imposed economic sanctions on Sierra Leone, Iraq, former Yugoslavia, Libya, Haiti, Liberia, Afghanistan, Ethiopia, Sudan, and Rwanda.

The most severe sanctions were imposed on Iraq after the 1991 Gulf War and included both economic and military restrictions. U.S. administrations and their allies in the Security Council insisted that these sanctions were necessary to prevent Saddam Hussein from replenishing his arsenal of weapons of mass destruction. As such, the United States refused to allow the Security Council to revisit the resolution that imposed the sanctions, despite the hardship they caused ordinary Iraqi citizens. Hussein used the unpopularity of the sanctions to maintain his grip on power in Iraq. Faced with growing public criticism and no apparent progress on removing Hussein from office, the council adjusted the sanctions, creating the "oil-for-food" program to allow the sale of Iraq's most important resource in order to purchase needed humanitarian supplies. The sanctions, however, remained unpopular with many governments. As a consequence, black market and government-sponsored violations of the sanctions occurred without a way to penalize the violators.

In April 2000 the Security Council established a working group to consider the troublesome issues surrounding the use of sanctions. The product of these deliberations and of a series of separate expert conferences hosted by Switzerland, Germany, and Sweden was the creation of **smart sanctions.** These sanctions were tailored to "have a high probability of directly hurting those responsible for the targeted policies while sparing the general population."[23] They include freezing the financial assets of the nation's leaders and blocking the transfer of such assets, restricting the leadership's travel outside the country, and embargoing key commodities needed to carry out the objectionable activities. As an example, in July 2000 the Security Council banned the importation of diamonds from Sierra Leone that were not certified by the government. The production and sale of "conflict diamonds"—diamonds sold to finance military operations by rebel or separatist groups—had become a serious problem throughout sub-Saharan Africa.[24] Illicit diamond trade particularly damaged the chances for restoring peace in war-torn Sierra Leone and most of West Africa.

Smart sanctions allow humanitarian assistance and limited trade to continue. Of importance, they carry sunset provisions so that sanctions cannot be frozen in place well beyond their usefulness by the continuing objection of one or more of the Security Council's permanent members. This issue became serious in the first decade of the twenty-first century as the United States and Great Britain refused to lift sanctions against Iraq. France in turn indicated it would not support other sanction regimes, including first a proposed arms embargo against Ethiopia and Eritrea in May 2000, without a declared end to any future sanctions regime.

Important difficulties with the new type of sanctions remain that may not make them much more effective than those attempted since the 1920s. Freezing assets requires nations other than the targeted country to change national legislation, alter import and export policies, and subject their domestic laws to the Security Council's diktats. Since the council cannot force such revisions, smart sanctions, even if "mandatory," require voluntary acquiescence by the UN's member states.

THE UN'S LONGEST COLLECTIVE SECURITY CRISIS: THE ARAB-ISRAELI DISPUTE

The British government first handed the Middle East crisis to the United Nations when it announced in 1947 that it would end its administration of Palestine the following year. The United Nations established the UN Special Commission on Palestine (UNSCOP) to find a solution to the growing conflict between the indigenous Palestinian population and the large number of Zionist Jews who had sought their own state in the former British Mandate for Palestine (1920–1946). UNSCOP recommended partitioning Palestine into Jewish and Arab states and placing Jerusalem under international administration. The General Assembly accepted this formula in Resolution 181,[25] which the Security Council endorsed. Zionist leaders accepted the plan, but Palestinians and regional Arab leaders rejected it as the "theft" of Palestinian land.

On May 14, 1948, Zionist leaders declared the independence of Israel within the borders assigned by Resolution 181. The Arab states of Egypt, Transjordan, Iraq, and Syria responded with military intervention. Despite their overwhelming advantage in numbers, the Arab militaries proved no match for the determined Israelis. During the summer, the United Nations attempted to establish a cease-fire through the diplomacy of its mediator, Swedish Count Folke Bernadotte. His mission met with only temporary success. In June the Security Council created the UN Truce Supervision Organization. Tragically, Bernadotte was assassinated in Jerusalem on September 17 by Israeli ultranationalists. His successor, Ralph Bunche, finally achieved an armistice in the spring of 1949. By the time the fighting ended, Israel's forces were in control of nearly all of Palestine, except East Jerusalem, the West Bank of the Jordan River, parts of the Golan Heights, and the Gaza Strip.

After successive wars in 1948, in 1956 during the Suez Crisis, and in June 1967, the United Nations served as the locus of negotiations for repeated cease-fires and for the provision of peacekeeping forces to separate combatants. Equally important, it responded to the huge flows of Palestinian refugees, who numbered nearly seven hundred thousand in 1948. The General Assembly created UN Relief for Palestine Refugees (UNRPR) in that year, sought twenty-five million dollars in voluntary contributions for it, and gave the effort nine months to assist the refugees. When the assembly realized that refugee assistance would have to extend well into the future, it replaced UNRPR with the UN Relief and Works Agency for Palestine Refugees in the Near East (UNRWA), which continued its work of providing education and work projects in addition to humanitarian assistance into 2005.

The uneasy peace following the 1948 war lasted until 1956, when the nationalist Egyptian leader, Gamal Abdul Nasser, announced his intentions to nationalize the Suez Canal. As noted previously, the October invasion of the Canal Zone by Great Britain, France, and Israel brought about the UN General Assembly's first emergency special session and the creation of UNEF (the UN Emergency Force). UNEF's presence on Egyptian soil ended direct conflict between Israel and its most important Arab neighbor. The next decade witnessed violent terrorist attacks, bombings, and brief border skirmishes. The Arab states sponsored new Palestinian organizations. Nasser made the Palestinian cause a central tenet of his efforts to mobilize a pan-Arab movement in the Middle East. He took the lead in the creation of the Palestine Liberation Organization (PLO) in 1964. With Arab support, Palestinian groups such as al-Fatah launched increasingly severe assaults on Israeli domestic sites.

Hostilities reached a critical point between Israel and two of its foes, Egypt and Syria, in the spring of 1967. Armed Israeli-Syrian clashes took place in April. On May 16 Nasser asked UN secretary-general U Thant to remove UNEF from the Sinai. Thant acceded, much to the consternation of many world leaders. On May 22 Egypt closed the Strait of Tiran and the Gulf of Aqaba, which put a death grip on Israel's economy. Israel responded with a preemptive attack on Egypt, Iraq, Jordan, and Syria. Israeli forces seized the Sinai Peninsula, Syrian territory in the Golan Heights, and the land designated by the 1947 UN partition plan as the space for the Arab state in Palestine—most important, the West Bank and East Jerusalem. The fighting ended in a cease-fire on June 10. Not until November was the Security Council able to arrive at a resolution acceptable to all the parties. **Resolution 242,** adopted unanimously on November 22, called for a withdrawal of Israel's forces from occupied territories to safe and secure borders, a termination of the state of belligerency, and mutual recognition, freedom of navigation, and a settlement of the refugee problem. The resolution was premised on the idea of "land for peace." Later, the parties would spar over the meaning of Resolution 242, specifically concerning whether it required the Israelis to withdraw from all occupied territories or from only those that would not jeopardize Israel's security. Nevertheless, this resolution became the cornerstone for all subsequent peace negotiations.

In 1970 Egyptian president Nasser died and was succeeded by Anwar Sadat. Because of his inability to secure sufficient military assistance from Egypt's erstwhile patron, the Soviet Union, Sadat decided that the return of the Sinai depended on a shift in Cairo's diplomatic alliances, which would lead to a new and positive relationship with the United States. This relationship, in turn, depended on an Egyptian demonstration that it could defeat Israel on the battlefield.

More and more, the growing Third World majority at the United Nations saw Israel as the aggressor and an illegal occupier of Arab lands. The world body steadily shifted toward support for the Palestinian cause, which culminated in recognition of the PLO as the "legitimate representative of the Palestinian people" in 1974 and its achievement of "observer status" at the United Nations. Anti-Israeli sentiment peaked with the passage of a resolution in November 1975 equating Zionism with racism. The pro-Palestinian tilt of the United Nations convinced the most powerful member of the body—the United States—that the United Nations was aggravating the Arab-Israeli crisis. Once the Nixon administration came to power in 1969, Washington sought to exclude UN participation from Middle East diplomacy.

The hesitant peace after the 1967 war lasted only until October 6, 1973. On Yom Kippur, the Day of Atonement in the Jewish calendar, Syria and Egypt opened two fronts against Israel, seeking to liberate lands captured in the previous conflict. Egypt established a line across the Suez Canal, which allowed President Sadat to claim a rare Arab victory against Israeli forces. Within ten days, however, the balance of forces had shifted, and both Syria and Egypt were in retreat. At the United Nations the USSR offered a draft Security Council resolution, and after lengthy negotiations between the Soviet and U.S. governments, the Security Council called for a return to the original cease-fire lines. Following a meeting in the Sinai between Israeli and Egyptian negotiators, under UN auspices, a cease-fire was restored.

SECURITY COUNCIL RESOLUTION 242

[UN Security Council Resolution 242 was adopted unanimously on November 22, 1967, following the cessation of the Middle East War of 1967 (June 5–10). It was the most significant, albeit belated, UN response to the war.]

The Security Council,

Expressing its continuing concern with the grave situation in the Middle East,

Emphasizing the inadmissibility of the acquisition of territory by war and the need to work for a just and lasting peace in which every State in the area can live in security,

Emphasizing further that all Member States in their acceptance of the Charter of the United Nations have undertaken a commitment to act in accordance with Article 2 of the Charter,

1. *Affirms* that the fulfillment of Charter principles requires the establishment of a just and lasting peace in the Middle East which should include the application of both the following principles:

(i) Withdrawal of Israel[i] armed forces from territories occupied in the recent conflict;

(ii) Termination of all claims or states of belligerency and respect for and acknowledgement of the sovereignty, territorial integrity and political independence of every State in the area and their right to live in peace within secure and recognized boundaries free from threats or acts of force;

2. *Affirms further* the necessity

(a) For guaranteeing freedom of navigation through international waterways in the area;

(b) For achieving a just settlement of the refugee problem;

(c) For guaranteeing the territorial inviolability and political independence of every State in the area, through measures including the establishment of demilitarized zones;

3. *Requests* the Secretary-General to designate a Special Representative to proceed to the Middle East to establish and maintain contacts with the States concerned in order to promote agreement and assist efforts to achieve a peaceful and accepted settlement in accordance with the provisions and principles in this resolution;

4. *Requests,* the Secretary-General to report to the Security Council on the progress of the efforts of the Special Representative as soon as possible.

Adopted unanimously at the 1382nd meeting.

The war marked the last time the United Nations would serve as the arena for Arab-Israeli peace initiatives until the turn of the century. U.S. administrations after 1973 used their diplomatic resources to monopolize the peace process. Nixon's secretary of state, Henry Kissinger, launched "Shuttle Diplomacy," hurrying among Middle East capitals, offering American "good offices" and brokering several interim peace arrangements. By the time Kissinger left office in 1977, he had engineered a military disengagement between the Egyptians and the Israelis on the Sinai Peninsula (January 1974) and a similar agreement between the Israelis and the Syrians on the Golan Heights (May 1974). As part of that accord, the United Nations acquired the limited role of placing military observers between the two sides in the Golan Heights (UN Disengagement Observer Force, or UNDOF). U.S. domination of international efforts to resolve the Arab-Israeli dispute continued into Jimmy Carter's presidency. Carter played the central role in the negotiation of the Camp David Accords, which included a "Framework for Peace" between Israelis and Palestinians and a draft peace treaty between Israel and Egypt.

The Carter-negotiated framework, based on UN Resolutions 242 and 338, outlined procedures to complete a comprehensive peace for the region. It recognized the right of Palestinian representatives to participate in negotiations aimed at establishing a Palestinian self-governing entity in the West Bank and Gaza. The framework called on the UN Security Council to ensure that its provisions were carried out.

Attempting to disrupt the Camp David Accords, the PLO stepped up guerrilla attacks on Israel from southern Lebanon and from Syrian territory. In June 1982 the Israeli government conducted a full-scale invasion of Lebanon and headed to Beirut to rout the Palestinians. In response, the UN Security Council passed Resolution 509, demanding that "Israel withdraw all its military forces forthwith and unconditionally to the internationally recognized boundaries of Lebanon." Ignoring the UN action, Israeli forces, within a few days, advanced to the outskirts of Beirut. The UNIFIL (UN Interim Force in Lebanon) forces that had been in the country since 1978 could do little but stand aside and report to New York on the invasion.

The United States regularly vetoed Security Council resolutions that condemned Israeli actions in Lebanon and in the occupied territories. On the ground in the Middle East, those Israeli policies, coupled with no sign of progress in the peace process, produced the 1987 *intifada*, a persistent, spontaneous, and widely supported uprising by Palestinians under occupation. Fearing the loss of allegiance from Palestinians in the territories, the PLO indicated its readiness to accept the legitimacy of, and to negotiate directly with, Israel. At the end of July 1988, King Hussein announced that Jordan would cut all legal and administrative ties to the West Bank. By late summer, considerable activity centered around the Israeli-Palestinian issue, much of which seemed to suggest the possibility of positive movement. Added to this activity was the new friendliness between the Soviet Union and the United States, which made any continuing interpretation of the Middle East problem as part of the cold war senseless.

The U.S.-orchestrated peace process was given a boost by the allied victory over Saddam Hussein in the 1991 Gulf War. Secretary of State James Baker shuttled between capitals in hopes of a breakthrough, an effort culminating in the Madrid Conference in 1991. PLO representatives from the occupied territories joined Israeli government officials and representatives of the Arab states at the negotiating table with President George H.W. Bush and Soviet president Mikhail Gorbachev. The United Nations was granted a meager "observer" status. Of importance, the Madrid Conference provided the umbrella structure for secret talks between the PLO and the Israeli government. These talks led to the **Oslo Accords** of 1993, which formally accepted the long-endorsed UN principle of partition in Palestine. The accords were signed, however, on the White House lawn without the slightest verbal or ceremonial nod to the United Nations.

As part of the accords, the PLO conceded Israel's right to exist and Israel recognized the Palestine Liberation Organization as the representative of the Palestinian people. The Declaration of Principles established a Palestine Authority in the Gaza Strip and in the West Bank city of Jericho, where Arafat then established his new government. The accords contemplated the eventual transfer of most of the occupied territories to Palestinian control.

The peace process sustained a severe blow when a fanatical Jewish religious nationalist assassinated Israel's prime minister Yitzhak Rabin on November 4, 1995. While the interim government of Shimon Peres attempted to move ahead with the accords, Israeli elections brought to power Benjamin Netanyahu, who opposed any more concessions to the Palestine Authority. The new government emphasized security and settlements in the territories, the latter of which the UN General Assembly regularly declared illegal. In the spring of 1997, the United States vetoed a Security Council resolution condemning the construction of an Israeli settlement at Har Homa. President Clinton went to great lengths to explain the veto, arguing that the insertion of the United Nations into the issue could jeopardize the ongoing peace negotiations between the Israelis and the Palestinians.

Clinton convened a second Camp David Summit in the summer of 2000, bringing together Arafat and Ehud Barak, Netanyahu's successor. All three leaders had conveyed optimism that a final agreement resolving all the remaining Arab-Israeli issues could be reached. Unfortunately, the meeting ended in failure. While Barak made major concessions on land and Palestinian control over the Holy Sites, Arafat refused to accept an agreement that did not recognize the refugees' right of return and did not grant full sovereignty in Jerusalem. The collapse of the summit contributed to the inauguration of a second intifada in the fall. Sparked by Israeli politician Ariel Sharon's untimely appearance in September atop the holiest (and most contentious) site in Jerusalem—the Temple Mount, or Al-Haram al-Sharif—Palestinians took to the streets and attacked Israeli security forces and settlers. Israel responded with heavy military force.

As hostilities grew in the streets of the West Bank, for the first time since 1973 a U.S. administration sought the active leadership of the UN secretary-general. Kofi Annan, who had been shuttling among Jerusalem, Tel Aviv, and Gaza City, and traveling elsewhere in the Middle East in a quest to ease tensions, stepped into the U.S.-Israeli-Palestinian standoff. He persuaded Barak, Arafat, and Egyptian president Hosni Mubarak to convene a summit at Sharm El-Sheik on October 14, 2000. The Israeli government had come to trust Annan, partly because of his expression of regret for the tone of past UN resolutions. Annan particularly expressed satisfaction at the General Assembly's 1991 repeal of the 1975 "Zionism is Racism" resolution.

At Sharm El-Sheik, Barak agreed to withdraw Israeli military forces to positions held before the beginning of the unrest, to lift the closure of the West Bank and Gaza, and to reopen the Gaza airport. Security forces from both sides agreed to resume a dialogue that had been interrupted by the crisis. President Clinton appointed a U.S.-controlled fact-finding committee (the Mitchell Commission, named for its chair, former U.S. senator George Mitchell) after consulting with the parties and Annan. The text of the commission's report, then, was to be shown to Annan and UN officials before publication, and the United States was to make the final decision on the wording of the report. A new triangulation had emerged among the White House, UN headquarters, and Middle East leaders.

The partnership opened tantalizing prospects for a comprehensive peace in the region, but nothing seemed able to stop the "popular diplomacy" of street violence and retaliatory Israeli security measures. Faced with opposition from within Palestinian ranks, and with no evidence that his commitments at Sharm El-Sheik could halt protests in the streets, Arafat demonstrated his political sense by proposing a UN peacekeeping presence in the territories. He sought two thousand

UN peacekeepers to separate the parties on the West Bank and particularly in Gaza, and to limit police actions by the Israeli occupation forces. Tel Aviv immediately declared the proposal unacceptable, but many states, including several European powers, thought the idea worth pursuing. A nonstarter previously, Arafat's suggestion now took on the image of sensibility given the new legitimacy U.S. policy had given the United Nations. Just before Christmas and the Jewish Holy Days of 2000, the UN Security Council took one of its most dramatic actions on the Palestinian-Israeli confrontation in more than two decades. On December 18, the council came extremely close (within one vote of a majority) to approving a force of military and police observers for the occupied territories, an action that would have simultaneously handed Palestine Authority president Arafat a huge diplomatic success and triggered a U.S. veto on behalf of the embattled government of Ehud Barak.[26]

Annan's cooperation with the United States, and vice versa, continued into the early days of President George W. Bush's new administration. The Mitchell Commission issued its report, calling for an end to the violence and a halt to the Israeli construction of settlements in the territories. Both UN and U.S. officials endorsed the commission's recommendations. President Bush sent Secretary of State Colin Powell to the region. On June 28, 2001, he announced a change in U.S. policy, endorsing the placement of an observer mission to monitor a cooling-off period until peace negotiations could resume.

Despite concerted UN and U.S. diplomacy, violence escalated during the summer. Deadly suicide bombings orchestrated by Palestinian groups and reprisal military assassinations of Palestinian leaders on the West Bank and the Gaza Strip by the Sharon government became the norm. The terrorist attack on the World Trade Center in New York City on September 11, 2001, and the strong U.S. response against terrorist organizations in Afghanistan, encouraged the Israeli government to move military forces into territories controlled by the Palestine Authority. Prime Minister Sharon claimed that President Arafat was responsible for terrorism against Israeli civilians and could no longer be a partner in the peace process. Sharon's contention was reinforced in January 2002 by the interception of a large arms shipment to the Palestinians, ostensibly supplied from Iran. Israeli forces surrounded Arafat's headquarters on the West Bank, barring his freedom of movement. Israel announced that the government would attempt to create "buffer zones" between Palestinian and Israeli communities, which would effectively segregate the warring sides. The expressed intention to build a wall permanently separating Israel and its settlements from the Palestinian territories incensed Arab nations, who introduced a Security Council resolution condemning Israeli actions. The council instead passed Resolution 1397, calling for an end to the violence and the creation of two side-by-side states.

Palestinian claims of genocide by Israeli forces in Jenin led the secretary-general to propose sending a fact-finding commission. The United States did not veto Security Council Resolution 1405, which encouraged Annan's initiative, but it did not press the Israeli government to accept the investigation. Instead, it undertook a campaign of criticism against the leadership of President Arafat, indicating that no peace was possible while he remained in power. Washington urged Israeli withdrawal from Palestinian communities, but it pointedly saw little wisdom in including the secretary-general's initiative as part of a return to the peace process. With diminished U.S. support, the secretary-general had to withdraw his proposal. The UN's collective security role in the Palestinian-Israeli confrontation still depended heavily on U.S. support.

When Washington then sent its special representative, Anthony Zinni, to the region to declare Arafat no longer acceptable as a peace partner, Arab states responded angrily at the United Nations with a series of proposed resolutions. In December the United States cast a lone veto in the Security Council,[27] which defeated a resolution sponsored by Egypt and Tunisia that would have condemned Israeli occupation of Palestinian towns and the excessive use of force and would have established a UN "monitoring mechanism" in the territories in accordance with Mitchell Commission recommendations.

While Iraq consumed the world's attention in 2002 and 2003, the news from Great Britain's former Palestine Mandate was a story of revenge and reprisal. Bus bombings and suicide attacks by Hamas, radical units of al-Fatah, and other Palestinian groups—followed by Israeli retaliatory raids and an announced Israeli policy of planned assassination attacks on Palestinian leaders—put pressure on the world community to make progress on the peace process. In June 2002, President Bush announced his support for a Palestinian state living side by side with Israel, and he expressed America's interest in developing a "Road Map" to bring about a final resolution. Working with the United Nations, the European Union, and Russia, the United States joined **"The Quartet,"** which produced a "performance-based roadmap to a permanent two state solution," made public on September 18. The Road Map called for a series of parallel steps by both sides toward the vision of creating two independent states by 2005. It called on the Palestine Authority to curb all terrorist activity originating from its territory and for Israel to withdraw forces in a staged process from the West Bank and Gaza. It also called for an end to Israeli settlement activity.

While the toppling of Saddam Hussein in Iraq and the new clout of the United States in the region were expected to lead to a reasonable chance for the success of the road map, by autumn 2004 peace seemed as elusive as ever. In Israel, growing consternation over the continuing terrorist attacks undermined support for the road map and led to calls for the expulsion of Arafat from the territories altogether. The Palestinians protested Israel's construction of a 625-mile security fence. Much of the world saw the fence as a new form of apartheid. As we noted previously, the General Assembly took the unusual step of seeking an advisory opinion from the International Court of Justice on the legality of the barrier. A court decision declaring the wall illegal and condemnations of its construction in the United Nations, however, fell on deaf ears in Tel Aviv.

Then, in November 2004, President Arafat died. By early January 2005 moderate Palestinian Mahmoud Abbas had been elected president of the Palestine National Authority in an open election. These events seemed to alter the situation significantly. By spring, Abbas had visited a genial President Bush at the White House, and what seemed to be serious negotiations were taking place between Abbas and Israeli prime minister Sharon. For his part, Sharon faced more serious challenges, first, from Israeli settlers who balked at the prime minister's plan to withdraw unilaterally from the Gaza Strip and, second, from the Bush administration, which wanted him to halt new settlement activity.

After almost six decades of UN engagement with the conflict, uncertainty remained as to whether the collective security apparatus was sufficient to produce a resolution acceptable to both sides, to regional actors, or to the great powers. However, as is always the case with the United Nations in the Middle East, hope prevailed.

SUMMARY

Universal collective security is the principle on which the United Nations is founded. It was meant to replace the older and more traditional methods—the balance of power, alliances, and individual self-defense—for keeping the peace and avoiding another war like the two that so traumatized the world in the twentieth century. However, collective security presumes a group of citizen states committed to defending the community against any violator of its rules. In the cold war this environment did not exist. The United Nations had to develop substitutes for the Charter's collective security provisions or face the same fate as that of the League of Nations in an earlier time. It responded with peacekeeping and Chapter VI½ innovations. Only the new United Nations of the post–cold war era has been able to approach its founders' intent.

In this new era, as well, collective security has come to mean something more than simply the defense of the community against an internal or external aggressor. Defined by Security Council actions, collective security in the twenty-first century challenges the bedrock principle of state sovereignty, defining violations of human rights, domestic oppression, terrorism, disease, and other nontraditional phenomena of the international order as threats to international peace and security. The extent to which this expanding definition can serve the world community depends now on the commitment of the UN's members, particularly that of its most powerful states, to use the United Nations as the central legitimizing institution for the use of force or its prohibition.

NOTES

1. United Nations, "Preamble" and "Chapter I: Purposes and Principles," in *Charter of the United Nations* (New York: United Nations, 1945), art. 1, para. 1 (italics added).

2. See Paul W. Schroeder, *The Transformation of European Politics, 1763–1848* (Oxford, UK: Clarendon Press, 1994).

3. League of Nations, *The Covenant of the League of Nations* (Geneva, Switzerland: League of Nations, 1919), art. 8.

4. Brian Frederking, "Constructing Post–Cold War Collective Security," *American Political Science Review* 97, no. 3 (2003): 363.

5. The League reached nearly universal membership during its lifetime, having a minimum of sixty members at any one time and a maximum of sixty-three.

6. Inis Claude, "Collective Legitimation as a Political Function of the UN," *International Organization* 20, no. 3 (1966): 367–79.

7. Ian Hurd, "Legitimacy, Power and the Symbolic Life of the Security Council," *Global Governance* 8, no. 1 (2002): 38.

8. Bruno Simma, ed., *The Charter of the United Nations: A Commentary* (Munich, Germany: C. H. Beck, 1995), 572.

9. The final debate among the permanent members about the creation of a UN force occurred in August 1948. After that, the representatives of each country's chief of staff met biweekly for five to fifteen minutes, ceremonially marking the existence of the committee. Only once, at the time of the Iraqi invasion of Kuwait, was a meeting of the full Military Staff Committee held in which serious discussions took place about military operations. However, no actions ensued from those discussions.

10. Simma, *The Charter,* 575, note 25.

11. John Allphin Moore, Jr., and Jerry Pubantz, *To Create a New World? American Presidents and the United Nations* (New York: Peter Lang, 1999), 71–73.

12. International Court of Justice, "The court finds that the construction by Israel of a wall in the occupied Palestinian Territory and its associated régime are contrary to international law," press release, 2004/28, July 9, 2004.

13. International Court of Justice, *Legal Consequences of the Construction of a Wall in the Occupied Palestinian Territory,* General list no. 131, advisory opinion, July 9, 2004, para. 27.

14. Gregory Khalil, "Just Say No to Vetoes," *New York Times,* July 19, 2004.

15. United Nations, "Chapter IV: The General Assembly," in *Charter of the United Nations* (New York: United Nations, 1945), art. 11, para. 1.

16. Ibid., "Chapter V: The Security Council," art. 26.

17. Jerry Pubantz, "Strategic Arms Limitation Talks," in *The Modern Encyclopedia of Russian and Soviet History,* ed. George N. Rhyne and Joseph L. Wieczynski (Gulf Breeze, FL: Academic International Press, 1984), 37:173.

18. A. LeRoy Bennett, *International Organizations: Principles and Issues,* 4th ed. (Upper Saddle River, NJ: Prentice Hall, 1988), 322.

19. See the UN Web site on conventional arms: http://disarmament2.un.org/cab/salw.html.

20. Ibid.

21. Moore and Pubantz, *To Create a New World,* 296–97, 304–305.

22. Boutros Boutros-Ghali, *An Agenda for Peace,* UN document A/47/277-S/2411 (New York: United Nations, June 17, 1992), para. 1, http://www.un.org/Docs/SG/agpeace.html.

23. Michael Brzoska, "From Dumb to Smart? Recent Reforms of UN Sanctions," *Global Governance* 9, no. 4 (2003): 522.

24. See the UN Web site on conflict diamonds: http://www.un.org/peace/africa/Diamond.html.

25. UN General Assembly, *Resolution 181 (II). Future Government of Palestine,* A/RES/181(II), November 29, 1947.

26. UN Security Council, "Security Council fails to adopt draft resolution on observer mission for occupied Palestinian territories," press release, SC/6976, December 18, 2000, http://www.un.org/News/Press/docs/2000/sc6976.doc.htm.

27. Twelve nations voted in favor; Norway and the United Kingdom abstained.

KEY TERMS

Chapter VI½ (page 172)
Collective Security (page 161)
Emergency Special Sessions of the General Assembly (page 173)
Enforcement Measures (page 168)
Korean War (page 172)

Nuclear Non-Proliferation Treaty (NPT) (page 178)
Oslo Accords (page 190)
Pacific Settlement (page 168)
Peace Building (page 184)
Peacekeeping (page 176)
Peacemaking (page 184)
Preventive Diplomacy (page 184)

"The Quartet" (page 193)
Resolution 242 (page 188)
Smart Sanctions (page 186)
Subcontracting (page 183)
Uniting for Peace Resolution (page 173)

RESOURCES FOR FURTHER RESEARCH
Relevant Web Sites

International Atomic Energy Agency (www.iaea.org)

Organisation for the Prohibition of Chemical Weapons (www.opcw.org)

Preparatory Commission for the Comprehensive Nuclear-Test-Ban Treaty Organization (http://pws.ctbto.org)

UN Department for Disarmament Affairs (http://disarmament2.un.org)

UN Institute for Disarmament Research (www.unidir.org)

UN Mine Action Service (www.mineaction.org/index.cfm)

UN Security Council (www.un.org/Docs/sc/)

Books, Articles, and Documents

Butler, Richard. *Iraq, Weapons of Mass Destruction, and the Growing Crisis of Global Security.* New York: Public Affairs, 2000.

Chemical Disarmament: Basic Facts. The Hague, the Netherlands: Organization for the Prohibition of Chemical Weapons, 2000.

Claude, Inis. *Swords into Plowshares: The Problems and Promise of International Organization.* 2nd ed. New York: Random House, 1959.

Conlon, Paul. *United Nations Sanctions Management: A Case Study of the Iraq Sanctions Committee, 1990–1994.* Ardsley, NY: Transnational, 2000.

Cortright, David. *The Sanctions Decade: Assessing UN Strategies in the 1990s.* Boulder, CO: Lynne Rienner, 2000.

Lepgold, Joseph, and Thomas G. Weiss, eds. *Collective Conflict Management and Changing World Politics.* Albany: State University of New York Press, 1998.

Simma, Bruno, ed. *The Charter of the United Nations: A Commentary.* Munich, Germany: C. H. Beck, 1995.

Tucker, Jonathan B., ed. *Toxic Terror: Assessing Terrorist Use of Chemical and Biological Weapons.* Cambridge, MA: MIT Press, 2000.

Chapter 6

Peacekeeping and Nation Building

When you think of the United Nations today, you probably envision an organization engaged in peacekeeping and nation-building operations. Many twentieth- and twenty-first-century UN missions in countries around the world have been devoted to these objectives. The ramifications of such change have been enormous and have resulted in a redefinition of the entire UN organization. In this chapter, we discuss many of the peacekeeping and nation-building missions that have contributed to the evolution of the UN's role in the world.

THE ORIGINATION OF PEACEKEEPING IN THE UNITED NATIONS

The founders of the United Nations did not envisage anything like peacekeeping. The idea of using a neutral international force to facilitate peace was a novel innovation, requiring the development of an entirely new method of operation without the benefit of previous precedents that normally govern international activity. Yet, by the summer of 2005, more than sixty-six thousand peacekeepers from one-hundred-five countries were serving in multinational missions around the world. Sixty operations had been undertaken since 1948, costing more than two thousand fatalities among the peacekeeper contingents. Of the total operations, forty-seven had been established after 1988. At its peak in 1993, the United Nations deployed more than seventy thousand personnel. The nature of these missions evolved dramatically from their initial character to include, by the end of the century, humanitarian assistance, civil administration, combatant separation, truce observation, peacemaking, refugee repatriation, election administration, disarmament, and nation building.

As initially conceived in 1948 and 1949—and practiced for the first forty years of the United Nations—peacekeeping was a narrowly focused process with limited and specific purposes. During the cold war, peacekeeping operated according to fairly clear rules. **Ralph Bunche,** under-secretary-general for special political affairs and the highest-ranking American in the UN administration, developed most of these rules in the 1950s. Peacekeeping normally involved an international effort to end a war between states by offering to place UN-authorized observers or military personnel into a conflict region as part of an agreement to end hostilities. It was always carried out with the express permission of both sides to the conflict. Only military from small or relatively neutral states were included in the peacekeeping force. Neither the superpowers nor any of the other permanent members of the Security Council contributed personnel. Authorized by a Security Council resolution or an emergency special session of the General Assembly, a peacekeeping operation was supervised by the secretary-general or his designee. Peacekeepers arrived after both parties had negotiated a settlement. The peacekeepers then positioned themselves between the combatants. The sole purpose of early peacekeeping efforts was to supervise the implementation of truce agreements and specifically to verify that both sides took appropriate actions to carry out the agreements already reached. Although military personnel were involved, they carried no more than light arms. Peacekeepers had no enforcement powers and were directed to use force just to defend themselves. Peacekeepers were sent only after the UN Secretariat negotiated a **Status of Forces Agreement (SOFA),** by which the host state—since it remained a sovereign nation—granted permission to use its territory. The agreement also defined the peacekeepers' powers, their access to facilities, and the specific territory in which they would operate.

Beginning with the UN Emergency Force (UNEF) in 1956, the United Nations found that the most serious administrative problem to solve with regard to putting a peacekeeping force in the field was obtaining the financial resources to support it. Dispatched as part of the resolution of the Suez Crisis, UNEF was placed along the Suez Canal on Egyptian territory, replacing British, French, and Israeli troops that had invaded the area. At that time, Secretary-General Hammarskjöld proposed that the expenses be paid out of the regular UN budget, citing Article 17 of the Charter, which obligates member states to pay "the expenses of the Organization." This type of payment had already been made in the case of the UN Truce Supervision Organization (UNTSO) in 1948. The Soviet Union and several Arab states objected, demanding that the "aggressors"—Great Britain, France, and Israel—pay the costs. In 1960, when the General Assembly authorized a peacekeeping force to intervene in the Congolese civil war, France joined the states refusing to pay assessments associated with the operation. The French argued that only the Security Council, under Chapter VII of the Charter, could obligate the organization and its members to fund such operations. Despite an advisory opinion from the International Court of Justice in July 1962 that peacekeeping expenses are expenses of the organization within the meaning of the Charter, raising sufficient funding for these operations remained problematic. By 1964, member states' neglect in paying their peacekeeping assessments put the United Nations in the first of its periodic financial crises.

As a result, stopgap measures were instituted to pay for peacekeeping.[1] Although a peacekeeping budget was established as one of the "regular" budgets of the organization, the United Nations depended heavily on voluntary contributions. At various times it also floated bond issues to cover expenses. With fluctuating annual costs reaching more than three and a half billion dollars at different times during the 1990s and arrears in assessed contributions topping one and a half billion dollars, the organization was often unable to reimburse governments that contributed troops and equipment.

IMPORTANT COLD WAR PEACEKEEPING MISSIONS

UN Military Observer Group in India and Pakistan

Just seven months after establishing UNTSO to monitor the cease-fire in the 1948 Arab-Israeli War, the United Nations sought to sustain a cease-fire between the newly independent Asian states of Pakistan and India. Controversy between the two states over claims to the territory of Kashmir and Jammu dated from the partition of the subcontinent and the departure of British rule.

The 1947 partition plan allowed the disputed region to join either state. Following its accession to India, an act Pakistan disputed, fighting broke out between the Muslim and Hindu nations. In January 1948 India and Pakistan accepted UN observers to monitor a cease-fire. UN Military Observer Group in India and Pakistan (UNMOGIP) personnel arrived in January 1949. UNMOGIP continued its presence even during outbreaks of hostility in 1965 and 1971, which demonstrated the fecklessness of early peacekeeping missions to halt open warfare. In July 1972 the two sides agreed to a "line of control" in Jammu and Kashmir that approximately corresponded to the cease-fire line established in 1949. With this agreement, India then argued that the UN mission was no longer needed, and New Delhi thus opposed its continuation. Succeeding UN secretaries-general, nonetheless, took the position that only the Security Council could terminate the operation, which it had not done by the summer of 2005.

Total UNMOGIP costs have exceeded $100 million, paid out of its own UN special account. The budget for 2003 alone was $9.2 million. In June 2005 the operation had an authorized strength of forty-four military observers, twenty-four international civilian personnel, and forty-six local civilian staff. Its commander, Major General Guido Palmieri from Italy, oversaw personnel from his home country and from Belgium, Chile, Denmark, Croatia, Finland, South Korea, Sweden, and Uruguay.

UN Operation in the Congo

The United Nations first became involved in the Congo when the Belgian colony achieved independence in July 1960. On July 4 the Armée Nationale Congolaise (ANC) mutinied against its Belgian officers and began attacking European civilians. Against the Congolese government's wishes, Belgium sent ten thousand paratroopers to restore order. On July 10 Congolese prime minister Patrice Lumumba asked UN secretary-general Dag Hammarskjöld for assistance to restore order. The next day, the mineral-rich Katanga Province seceded. Heavy fighting between Belgian and Congolese troops led both Lumumba and the Belgians to request the dispatch of UN peacekeepers. Foreshadowing what would become an initiative to expand on the peacekeeping role developed so far by the UN Secretariat, the secretary-general invoked Article 99 of the Charter to bring the crisis to the Security Council's attention. The council established the UN Operation in the Congo (ONUC) to replace the Belgian troops and to support the central government against rebel and secessionist challenges.

The United Nations became more involved in the civil war after a constitutional crisis emerged in late 1960 and Lumumba was murdered. On February 15, 1961, Hammarskjöld declared that ONUC could act to investigate the assassination, protect civilians, prevent clashes between armed units, reorganize the army, and remove Belgians from Katanga. The Security Council authorized the use of force, if necessary, to prevent civil war. In response to an increasingly radical and violent secessionist movement, the council extended ONUC's authorization to detain and apprehend mercenaries and confiscate their arms. In December 1961 the Katangans attacked the Elisabethville airport, and ONUC retaliated, killing fifty civilians.

In the Congo, the United Nations attempted to expand the meaning of peacekeeping by going beyond simply separating two independent states and monitoring an armistice or a cease-fire. The original model of peacekeeping could be rationalized as an extension of collective security because it was intended to secure the peace between UN member states when Chapter VII measures were not available as a result of divisions in the Security Council. However, in this case, Secretary-General Hammarskjöld's forces were inserting themselves into an internal dispute and taking sides, albeit the central government's side.

Some UN member states criticized ONUC's operations as inappropriate because the Security Council had not authorized them. The French adopted this position, which led Paris to refuse to pay its assessment for the mission. Given that the costs of the operation exceeded the rest of the UN budget at the time, nonpayment by France and other states created a financial crisis for the United Nations from which it did not recover during the twentieth century. Nations in the Soviet bloc, led by the USSR, objected to the operation altogether. Soviet leaders contended that UN actions were little more than operations in support of U.S. interests in the Congo. ONUC thus became a matter of contention between Washington and Moscow, which jeopardized the UN's effectiveness and legitimacy in general. Even mild Soviet support for UN policy reached a breaking point when the Soviet-sponsored Congolese leader Lumumba was assassinated after being released from UN protective custody. The Soviet UN delegation refused to have any further working relationship with the secretary-general and stepped up its efforts to replace him with a *troika*—a constitutional revision of the Charter that would have replaced the secretary-general with a committee of three secretaries, two representing the paramount ideological blocs in the cold war and the remaining one representing the neutral states. (To refresh your understanding of the troika, you can review Chapter 2.)

Dag Hammarskjöld died in a 1961 plane crash in a remote part of Northern Rhodesia (now Zambia) while on an inspection trip to the Congo. His successor, U Thant, continued to mediate peace talks between the Congolese government and Katanga throughout 1962. In response to a UN budgetary crisis in 1963, the Congolese government sought bilateral military aid from Belgium, Israel, Italy, and the United States to counter the rebellion. On June 30, 1964, ONUC forces left the Congo. From 1960 to 1964, more than ninety-three thousand troops served in ONUC; twenty thousand were present at any one time. The total cost of military operations was $402 million. In the 1990s UN forces would return to the Congo with a different type of mission reflecting novel post–cold war requirements. This changed form of UN peacekeeping operation is described as part of our subsequent discussion on "second-generation" peacekeeping in the wake of the cold war.

The initial Congo mission raised constitutional questions about peacekeeping and military enforcement under Chapters VI and VII of the UN Charter as well as about the role of the secretary-general in peace and security issues. The mission was generally perceived as a UN failure because it entangled the United Nations in the cold war rivalry of the time, it cost far too much, and it was too ambitious in its goals. This mission turned into an early experiment in nation building—an undertaking that went beyond the existing understanding of the Charter. However, the effort did introduce some elements of *future* peacekeeping missions, many of which remained dormant until cold war hostilities receded. For instance, for the first time, UN civilian police contingents were introduced into a peacekeeping mission. By the turn of the century, many peacekeeping missions would have far more police personnel than military troops. The preeminent role of the secretary-general and his staff, challenged by the Soviet bloc at the time, increasingly became a hallmark of later missions, and the insertion of UN forces in a *domestic* conflict became an accepted mechanism by the 1990s.

UN Peacekeeping Force in Cyprus

The last legacy of the Congo effort was soon replicated on the island of Cyprus. Controlled by the Turkish Ottoman Empire from the sixteenth century, Cyprus, the third largest island in the Mediterranean Sea, was annexed by Great Britain during World War I. For centuries the majority ethnic Greek population considered Greece the mother country. Cyprus became independent in

1960, and full rights were promised to its minority Turkish population. In 1964 communal clashes occurred between Greek and Turkish Cypriots, and a temporary UN peacekeeping force—the UN Peacekeeping Force in Cyprus (UNFICYP)—was sent to the island to help end the dispute.

In 1974 Archbishop Makarios, the Cypriot president, was overthrown by a military coup apparently seeking to merge with Greece. Turkey responded with an invasion to protect the Turkish minority. The United Nations augmented UNFICYP to supervise a buffer zone (ranging from a few yards to several miles cutting completely across the island) between the Greek Cypriot National Guard and Turkish forces. Turkey controlled about 40 percent of the country and in 1983 proclaimed a separate "Turkish" republic. The Security Council declared this action invalid, and the secretary-general and his special adviser on the island tried to draw the opposing forces into direct discussions to end the long stalemate and initiate meaningful negotiations leading to a comprehensive settlement. The lengthy presence of UNFICYP, which separated the two communities (extended by the Security Council in October 2004 for another year), had the ironic consequence of lessening incentives for reunification.

Talks aimed at reunification resumed in 1999. Driven by Cypriot interests in joining the European Union (EU) and the EU's acceptance of Cyprus conditioned on progress toward reunification of the island, a peacemaking impetus emerged early in the twenty-first century. Secretary-General Annan put forward the *Annan Plan* in 2003, based on his provision of "good offices" in talks conducted between the two sides. The plan called for a referendum on reunification under a federal arrangement. It urged territorial adjustments, a new property regime, and the creation of a reconciliation commission. After additional negotiations, Annan was authorized, on his own, to make adjustments in the plan and to submit it for a referendum.[2] When he did so in April 2004, Turkish voters approved the plan, but the Greek Cypriots rejected it by 3 to 1. Annan opined that "another missed opportunity" had occurred in Cyprus and reunification would have to await a change in Greek attitudes. By summer 2005 a new UN effort was under way to initiate further reunification talks.

Partly driving Annan's personal attempt to bring final resolution to the Cypriot crisis was the mounting cost of the status quo for UNFICYP. Through the years, the mission had added humanitarian and policing functions to its tasks. It created bureaucratic subdivisions to cover public information duties, civil affairs, and even emergency helicopter services, such as medical evacuations.[3] Voluntary contributions financed much of this activity. With the seemingly unending UN financial crisis, however, UN headquarters was unable to reimburse contributing countries. The deficit produced by mission costs exceeding voluntary contributions surpassed $250 million by the close of the century. This financial problem led countries such as Sweden and Finland to withdraw from the force. The Danes, British, Canadians, and Austrians also reduced their contingents. The Security Council was compelled not only to restructure the force to make it leaner, but also to cover any revenue shortfalls with funds from the regular UN budget. The shift to nation-building functions by UNFICYP, along with Annan's direct involvement in the negotiations between Turkish and Greek communities on the island, brought about an evolution in the nature of the UN operation. Increasingly it moved from a *peacekeeping endeavor* to a *peacemaking initiative.*

UN Disengagement Observer Force

In October 1973 war broke out between Israel and Egypt in the Sinai and between Israel and Syria in the Golan Heights, a barrier range—and, at the time, a Syrian territory—between the two states. With the achievement of a cease-fire in the war, the Security Council hurriedly returned

UNEF to the Suez Canal region. By May 1974 Israel and Syria reached a disengagement agreement that included a provision for the insertion of a UN military observer force. For the first time a UN force was used to maintain an area of separation between two warring nations. For three decades UN Disengagement Observer Force (UNDOF) forces were the only military presence allowed in a region of the Golan stretching more than fifty miles long and varying between one and seven miles wide. The observer force established permanently manned installations, turned back any incursions by personnel from either side, conducted mine clearing, and inspected "areas of limitation" outside the separation zone for illegal armaments or military activity. At the end of 2003, UNDOF still had a force of more than one thousand. It was commanded by a Polish major general and included military personnel from Austria, Canada, Japan, and the Slovak Republic. In essence, the force served as a trip wire against either combatant's launching a surprise attack and as a guarantee against an accidental reigniting of the Syrian-Israeli conflict.

UN Interim Force in Lebanon

Established by the Security Council on March 19, 1978, the UN Interim Force in Lebanon (UNIFIL) was sent to the Middle East to confirm withdrawal of Israeli forces that had invaded southern Lebanon in response to an earlier Palestinian commando attack. UNIFIL's mandate included restoration of peace and security in the area and assistance to the Lebanese government in returning its effective authority to its southern region. The force, still in that country in 2005, seemed less and less "interim" as troubled Lebanon remained embedded in the Arab-Israeli dispute.

In the early 1970s the delicate balance that had been maintained among Lebanese ethnic and religious groups deteriorated. Between March 1975 and November 1976, an estimated forty thousand Lebanese were killed in civil strife, which ended only when a Syrian force intervened. Palestinian guerrillas in southern Lebanon proceeded to stage raids on Israel, dragging the country into the wider regional conflict. In March 1978 commandos, in a cross-boundary attack, killed and wounded many Israelis. Israeli forces responded with an invasion and within days occupied the southern part of the country. Beirut appealed to the Security Council, insisting that it had no connection with the Palestinian raid and protesting the invasion. The council adopted two resolutions, 425 and 426, the first calling on Israel to halt its military action and withdraw its forces and the latter establishing UNIFIL.

In June 1978 Israel withdrew. However, because of the activities of the various, virtually autonomous militias in the country, and because of conflict between Syrian forces and Lebanese Christians as well as Israeli air raids in the Beirut region, the central government appeared powerless. Then, on June 6, 1982, Israel invaded again, this time driving all the way to Beirut. The following three years witnessed a massacre by Israeli-allied Christian forces in Palestinian refugee camps in a Beirut suburb; the short-lived intrusion of a multinational force from the United States, the United Kingdom, France, and Italy; and the departure of the Palestine Liberation Organization (PLO), whose center of operations had been in Lebanon's capital. UNIFIL found itself behind Israeli lines and limited to providing humanitarian assistance.

In April 2000 the Israeli government of Prime Minister Ehud Barak notified Secretary-General Kofi Annan of its intention to withdraw all forces from Lebanon by July "in full accordance with Security Council Resolutions 425 and 426." By June 16 the secretary-general reported to the Security Council that the withdrawal had been completed. Nevertheless, challenges lingered. Mine clearance was an acute problem. Numerous minor violations of the line of withdrawal (the so-called Blue Line) took place on both sides. Well into late 2001 the Lebanese central government took the position that as long as no comprehensive peace with Israel existed, its army would not act as a border guard in the south. As a consequence, the Islamic guerrilla group Hizbollah was left to control the area. For all these reasons, Secretary-General Annan recommended to the Security Council that UNIFIL remain in Lebanon. Finally, in July 2003, Annan reported nearly six months of calm in southern Lebanon; he asserted such peace despite repeated Israeli violations of Lebanese airspace and Hizbollah's firing antiaircraft missiles. The council decided at that time to extend UNIFIL's mission through July 2004, in hopes that a comprehensive peace could be achieved in the region by then. However, heightened instability led the council to extend the operation's mandate into summer 2005.

UNIFIL's force, headquartered at Naqoura in southern Lebanon, had varied in number through the years but was about two thousand in November 2003, supplemented by more than four hundred international and local civilian staff and fifty military observers from the UN Truce Supervision Organization. Troop totals were reduced from more than four thousand in 2001 as UNIFIL was reconfigured as solely an observer mission in the wake of the Israeli withdrawal. Personnel for UNIFIL came from Finland, France, Ghana, India, Ireland, Italy, Poland, and Ukraine. During its twenty-six years in the country, the force had sustained 248 fatalities; one of the most recent was a Ghanaian peacekeeper shot to death on February 21, 2004. He was murdered by an Iraqi Kurdish migrant, one of several dozen who had crossed illegally from Lebanon into Israel and had been returned to southern Lebanon by the Israeli army. The UN mission had been able to repatriate several of the Kurds to Iraq, but others refused to return. They continued to harass UN facilities and personnel during the succeeding months. The shooting fatality of the peacekeeper was the most tragic event to date in the series of Kurdish-UN confrontations. The death demonstrated the persistent danger in which UNIFIL worked and reflected the changing nature of its mission.

In its mandated lifetime UNIFIL, like UNFICYP, bridged the eras of international politics that dominated the last half of the twentieth century. Children of the cold war, both peacekeeping missions had to evolve in the post–cold war era as politics at the United Nations and in the world shifted. A partial solution to serious conflicts in an atmosphere of superpower competition, each mission faced review, restructuring, and possible elimination at the turn of the millennium. As discussed next, the end of the cold war brought a metamorphosis in peacekeeping—the introduction of "second-generation" missions—that made these earlier efforts in some ways relics of a time when the United Nations could not live up to its obligation to maintain peace and security in the world.

SECOND-GENERATION PEACEKEEPING

The 1990s saw the launching of almost three times as many peacekeeping missions as were initiated during the previous forty years. This growing number reflected increasing security crises and greater reliance on the United Nations to address domestic upheavals. The new missions were significantly different in their mandates and in their day-to-day operations, constituting what came to be known as *robust peacekeeping,* or **second-generation peacekeeping.** Only thirteen peacekeeping missions were authorized prior to 1988. From 1988 through 2000, more than thirty-six operations were undertaken. Merely raising the necessary troops and funding the costs of that many operations became major concerns, in addition to conducting the missions. As noted in Chapter 3, the financial burden of robust peacekeeping was one of the factors pressing the United Nations toward significant internal reform. In 1988 fewer than ten thousand peacekeepers were on duty, costing the organization $364 million annually.[4] By 1993 the number was approaching eighty thousand personnel, and the peacekeeping budget had risen to $4 billion. Other

ONGOING PEACEKEEPING MISSIONS (SEE APPENDIX G)

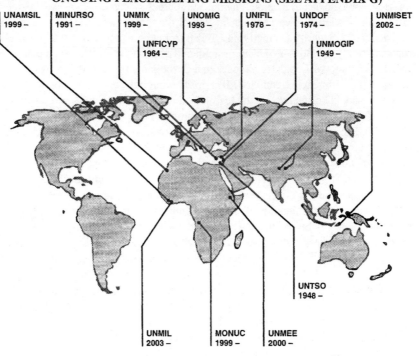

Department of Public Information
Cartographic Section

(Map No. 4000(E), Rev. 23 United Nations, October 2003. Reproduced by permission from the UN Cartographic Section.)

challenges included providing adequate training, and equipping and transporting troops pledged by various nations.

UN Department of Peacekeeping Operations

To manage the escalating mission and size of UN peacekeeping, the Department of Peacekeeping Operations (DPKO) was created in 1992 as an integral part of the executive office of the UN secretary-general. Prior to then the under-secretary-general (USG) for special political affairs controlled missions authorized by the Security Council or the General Assembly. The department has administrative, managerial, planning, and preparation responsibilities for all peacekeeping missions. It is headed by the USG for peacekeeping and has divisions for operations, planning and support, training and evaluation, and assessment of past operations. The General Assembly established the Training and Evaluation Office to coordinate and standardize training for national peacekeeping units. It provides courses, publications, and training exercises for member states that contribute forces to peacekeeping operations.

Following apparent peacekeeping successes in Angola and Namibia, which are described later in this chapter, the world was confident that the United Nations could intervene effectively in disintegrating states, not only to restore peace but also to undertake state building. However, failures in Somalia (1993) and Rwanda (1994) induced strong pressures for an evaluation of DPKO operations and the UN peacekeeping function in general. The department struggled with inadequate resources, trying to meet new mandates that went far beyond the original idea of peacekeeping. The United States, in particular, urged an overhaul of DPKO, including the creation of a rapidly deployable headquarters team, the maintenance of a database of available forces, and a modest airlift capability. An initial response to these recommendations was the creation of the Lessons Learned Unit in April 1995, which was mandated to study past peacekeeping operations, discover the strengths and weaknesses of these efforts, and make recommendations for administrative improvement. In 2001 this unit was merged with the department's Policy and Analysis Unit and renamed the *Peacekeeping Best Practices Unit (PBPU)*. Among its other activities, PBPU sponsored seminars on peace building, reconstruction efforts, and conflict resolution, and it published guidelines for future operations.

Early Nation-Building Missions

The conflicts brought to the United Nations after 1988 mainly involved domestic turmoil—that is, internal civil wars, several disputing the legitimacy of an existing government or assaulting ethnic, religious, and minority groups. Although these conflicts often affected, or potentially affected, international peace and security, they were outside the UN's original scope, which dealt only with international disputes and interstate warfare. Consequently, UN intervention in the guise of peacekeeping necessarily involved the world organization in domestic administration, the provision of humanitarian assistance, and the reconstruction of civil society.

The new collection of activities now the responsibility of the UN operation was reminiscent of the old mandate system of the League of Nations, although state administration was now internationalized and the United Nations was becoming something equivalent to the League's mandatory power. This UN role amounted to **nation building**. It challenged the bedrock international principle of national sovereignty. In so doing, it reinterpreted the UN Charter, which does not provide explicit authority for the United Nations to act contrary to the full sovereignty of a member state. Originally, UN intervention in a state's internal affairs was considered acceptable only with that government's permission. This premise seemed to follow the intent of the Charter language in Article 2, paragraph 7: "Nothing contained in the present Charter shall authorize the United Nations to intervene in matters which are essentially within the domestic jurisdiction of any state." However, the same paragraph contains a delicate caveat: "but this principle shall not prejudice the application of enforcement measures under Chapter VII." Furthermore, because at least one of the parties involved in these new disputes was likely a rebel movement, the United Nations (specifically the Security Council, which is authorized to act under Chapter VII of the Charter) found itself in nearly every case intervening without the approval of all parties to the dispute, which violated one of the "rules" of peacekeeping operations established in the earliest UN missions. Thus, nation building meant entering entirely new legal ground.

Modern warfare also changed; civilians increasingly became the targets of rebels using unconventional warfare methods. Peacekeepers were often asked to protect refugees and guard the delivery of humanitarian aid, as well as to investigate and seek to prevent violations of the human rights of the populace. Once peacekeepers attempted to protect victims or segments of the population, the neutrality on which their actions had previously been based was compromised, and they could be perceived as parties to the conflict by at least one side. Efforts to protect civilians involved unprecedented cooperation of peacekeeping forces with specialized agencies and nongovernmental organizations, requiring complex coordination. In addition, the new mandates often involved lengthy deployments that included not merely troops but also police officers and legal officials, economic advisers, and humanitarian workers.

Three early second-generation peacekeeping missions—in Namibia, Angola, and Cambodia—are worthy of comment. They produced varied results but also provided models for later, more comprehensive operations.

Namibia

Namibia, known until 1968 as *South-West Africa,* became a colony of Germany in 1884. With Germany's defeat in World War I, Namibia was classified under Article 22 of the League of Nations Covenant as a class "C" mandate, administered by the Republic of South Africa. In 1946 the UN General Assembly encouraged all mandatory states to end their trusteeship agreements. South Africa refused to end its control. Despite a series of General Assembly resolutions adverse to South African supervision and legal proceedings in the International Court of Justice, the region remained under Pretoria's domination into the 1980s.

During the last twenty years of South African control, the ruling authorities faced a UN-recognized rebel organization known as the *South-West Africa People's Organisation (SWAPO).* In response to rebel operations, South African forces increased repression in Namibia and invaded Angola to destroy SWAPO bases there. In response, Angola requested military support from Cuba. As violence in the region escalated in the late 1970s, the Security Council passed two resolutions: Resolution 385 (1976), which called for a cease-fire and withdrawal of all forces to their bases, and Resolution 435 (1978), which called for Namibia's independence and for free elections based on universal suffrage. Cold war politics enabled South Africa to stall Namibian independence for more than a decade. However, by 1988 the high human and monetary costs of war and the changing relationship between the United States and the USSR led the parties to reach an agreement on a cease-fire and on South African and Cuban withdrawals from Namibia and Angola. They also agreed to free elections in Namibia.

The Security Council designed the UN Transition Assistance Group (UNTAG) to assist with the independence process. UNTAG educated and registered voters, oversaw the 1989 elections for a constituent assembly, assisted in Namibian refugee repatriation, and confirmed that troops were confined to bases. UNTAG deployed 1,500 police monitors, 2,000 civilian administrators, and 4,650 military personnel. It declared the elections—in which 96 percent of eligible Namibians voted and SWAPO won a majority—to be free and fair. On March 21, 1990, Namibia achieved full independence and UNTAG left the country. Independent Namibia became a UN member in April 1990. With a total cost of $368 million, UNTAG was seen as a harbinger of a new and vital role for the United Nations in a world of disintegrating states.

Angola

The success in Namibia was not repeated in Angola, however. Angola gained independence from Portugal in 1975 but from the beginning was wracked by an ethnic civil war that also had the overlay of cold war competition in Africa. In the long-ensuing struggle, the two major contenders for power, the MPLA (Movimento Popular de Libertação de Angola) and UNITA (União Nacional para a Independência Total de Angola), were supported by the Soviet Union and the United States, respectively. The MPLA managed to achieve power in November 1975 and established the first independent government in Angola. This event did not end the civil war, however: UNITA, under the leadership of Jonas Savimbi, continued the struggle with assistance from Washington and from South Africa.

The agreements on Namibia, particularly those requiring the withdrawal of Cuban troops, opened an important opportunity to realize peace in Angola as well. In 1991 the MPLA and UNITA negotiated a set of peace accords that were intended to lead to national reconciliation and democratic elections. Elections were finally held in 1992, under UN observation; however, Savimbi alleged widespread electoral fraud and refused to accept the results, which clearly favored the MPLA over UNITA.

Between 1988 and 1999, the United Nations initiated three "verification" missions to the country (UN Angola Verification Missions I, II, and III, or UNAVEM I, II, and III) and one observer mission (UN Observer Mission in Angola, or MONUA). At best, these operations provided short buffer periods between intensified conflict. UNAVEM I provided a military observer group to verify the withdrawal of fifty thousand Cuban troops from Angolan soil. This mission was concluded successfully in May 1991, and UNAVEM I was judged to be a successful example of a traditional UN peacekeeping operation. Following the completion of this mission, the Angolan government asked the United Nations to send a second force to verify implementation of the Namibian agreements as they applied to Angolan territory. By March 1992, again at the Angolan government's request, the mandate for UNAVEM II was extended to include observation of the 1992 Angolan general elections. With Savimbi's rejection of the electoral outcome, the country returned to a state of civil war. Given the deteriorating security conditions, Secretary-General Boutros-Ghali soon decided to decrease the strength of the mission.

In February 1995 the secretary-general recommended the establishment of UNAVEM III to assist the Angolan government and UNITA in restoring peace and achieving national reconciliation. UNAVEM III had a maximum strength of seven thousand troops and military support personnel. It officially ended on June 30, 1997, as the Security Council authorized an observer mission (UN Observer Mission in Angola, or MONUA) beginning on July 1. However, at the close of the term for UNAVEM III progress toward peace was clearly being thwarted by UNITA's failure to adhere to the elements of previous peace accords.

The mandate for MONUA was to verify the neutrality of the Angolan national police force, monitor the collection and destruction of weapons, and oversee the security of UNITA leaders. The Security Council originally anticipated that the mission would be completed by February 1998. As the security situation deteriorated, the Security Council extended the mission several times, finally to February 1999. During the last week of 1998, rebel forces shot down two MONUA airplanes, killing more than twenty passengers and crew. When UN officials were denied access to the crash site, the Security Council condemned the rebel actions, "deplored the incomprehensible lack of cooperation," and ordered all UN workers out of the country. UNAVEM and MONUA cost the United Nations one and a half billion dollars and the loss of sixty staff members in a failed attempt to bring peace to the country.

Cambodia

Cambodia was left in internal chaos following the U.S. debacle in Vietnam. In 1975 the particularly vicious government of the Khmer Rouge, a Communist guerrilla movement led by Pol Pot, came to power. It carried out a massive genocide of whole classes in Cambodian society and imposed totalitarian rule, closing the country off from the outside world.[5] Vietnam invaded Cambodia in December 1978 and replaced the Pol Pot government with the Heng Samrin–Hun Sen regime. Three Cambodian factions opposing the Hun Sen regime quickly emerged, including the remnants of the Khmer Rouge movement.

The United Nations was involved early in seeking a political settlement of the conflict that followed the installation of the Hun Sen government. The General Assembly convened an international conference in 1981, but it failed to achieve concrete results. A significant UN role became possible only in August 1990, when the Security Council's permanent members reached agreement on a framework for a political settlement. In September the Cambodian parties accepted the framework. The Security Council created the UN Transitional Authority in Cambodia (UNTAC) to impose the UN plan. UNTAC took on an unprecedented set of responsibilities. It managed daily administration of Cambodian foreign and defense policy, provided domestic government services, and stationed more than twenty thousand UN personnel in the country.

Elections took place in May 1993 under UNTAC supervision and were declared free and fair. UNTAC withdrew from Cambodia, but several UN agencies remained in the country to support reconstruction and development. Secretary-General Boutros-Ghali appointed a special representative to assist the government in promoting and protecting human rights, strengthening civil society, and building democratic institutions and legal structures.

Despite the elections and the UN's further efforts, differences among the various Cambodian factions lingered. In 1997 Hun Sen executed a coup, removing his opponents from the power-sharing arrangement then in place. Intricate internal negotiations ensued, and in July 1998, again with international monitors present, another controversial election took place, won by Hun Sen. The United Nations also provided technical assistance for municipal and parliamentary elections in 2002–2003. However, early in the twenty-first century, Cambodia remained unstable and ill equipped to come to grips with the reality of the one and a half million Cambodians who were executed or who died from starvation and disease during Khmer Rouge rule.

Results of the Early Nation-Building Missions

These early transitional peacekeeping missions, despite their checkered record of success, set the stage for several comprehensive second-generation operations during the decade that followed the Gulf War. In Chapter 1 we described the nation-building operations in East Timor and the effort to bring about multiethnic peace in Kosovo as examples of the new approach. Faced with the "return of history" in Eastern Europe, the Middle East, and Africa, the great powers, particularly the United States, looked for multilateral mechanisms to maintain an uneasy peace among warring ethnic and religious communities and to help establish stable governments that could meet international standards for human rights and democracy.[6] Collective security was now recognized to include these domestic conditions, as well as refugee repatriation, humanitarian assistance, and the elimination of weapons of mass destruction. The new missions were all undertaken under the unique powers of the Security Council, which emerged as the "legitimizer"[7] for the practical operating definition of collective security in the new millennium.

Later Second-Generation Peacekeeping Missions

Despite the tentative successes of the early nation-building missions, two particular conflicts in the 1990s tested the limits of what second-generation peacekeeping could achieve. In decaying Yugoslavia, the United Nations was faced with the disintegration of one of its founding members. This disintegration was accompanied by acts of brutality and bloodshed not seen in Europe since the end of World War II. The UN's inability to achieve a peaceful solution and its apparent ineffectiveness even to protect innocent civilians strengthened critics' arguments that the world body was not able to address the major conflicts of the current era. Likewise, in central Africa, the UN's inactivity was blamed for the scope of the genocide that ravaged Rwanda in 1994.

UN Transitional Administration in East Timor (UNTAET)
(UN/DPI Photo by Eskinder Debebe. Reproduced by permission from the United Nations.)

Former Yugoslavia

The state of Yugoslavia emerged after World War I out of Balkan territories of the former Ottoman Empire, bringing together a number of groups of Slavic ethnic peoples, each with its own desire for independent statehood. The new nation was the creation of the powers that drafted the 1919 Treaty of Versailles. Through most of its history, authoritarian governments forcibly united the country. When its Communist leader, Josep Broz Tito, died in 1980, Yugoslavia slowly began to unravel. Its disintegration accelerated in 1987, when Slobodan Milosevic became the leader of the Serbian ultranationalist movement. As Serb dominance of the federal government escalated, restive Yugoslav republics moved toward declarations of independence. Slovenia was the first to do so, followed by Croatia.

Milosevic responded with force, first in Slovenia, then with **ethnic cleansing** in Serb-dominated parts of Croatia. Croats and Serbs had been bitter enemies in World War II. The Croatian Ustache militia had, with the help of the German army, rounded up Serbs and placed them in the Jasenovac concentration camp. This history served as the backdrop for the post–cold war violence in which Serb military units "cleansed" areas of Croats, killing many and driving others into refugee status.

The UN's initial involvement came in September 1991, when the Security Council imposed an arms embargo on Yugoslavia. The secretary-general then appointed a personal envoy, former U.S. secretary of state Cyrus Vance, to coordinate UN cooperation with European Union peace efforts, led by veteran British diplomat Lord Owen. The Vance-Owen Plan concentrated on finding a solution to the brewing Bosnian crisis—the republic under the leadership of Aliya Izetbegovic had declared its intention to hold an independence referendum in the spring of 1992. Bosnia had a Muslim majority with a sizable Serb minority that was adamantly opposed to independence. Milosevic's government in Belgrade supported the Serb minority militarily and financially. The Vance-Owen Plan envisioned the cantonization of Bosnia, dividing the republic among Bosnian Muslim, Bosnian Serb, and Croatian communities. None of the parties was willing to accept the proposed subdivisions, and the mission failed.

Bosnia proved to be the battleground for the most brutal Balkan fighting and the most violent war crimes.[8] Bosnia and Herzegovina declared independence in March 1992 and became a member of the United Nations on May 22, 1992. In ethnically mixed Bosnia, Serb militias moved to drive out Muslims from areas that would then have a Serb majority. These militias, led by General Ratko Mladic, under the political leadership of Radovan Karadzic, killed Muslim men, women, and children; carried out a systematic campaign of rape and terror; and created death and detention centers at Omarska, Trnopolje, and Manjaca. Images of these camps, displayed in the Western media, reminded the international community of Nazi concentration camps and produced demands for intervention.

The United Nations was unsuccessful at ending the violence. The North Atlantic Treaty Organization (NATO) also proved incapable of reaching a consensus on military measures that would halt the Serbian attacks. Bosnian Muslim calls for stronger action were met with international indifference. A peacekeeping force, the UN Protection Force (UNPROFOR)—established by the Security Council in early 1992—was sent to Yugoslavia, but it proved ineffective. The Muslim populations moved from the countryside to UNPROFOR "protected areas," or safe havens, in Mostar, Gorazde, Srebrenica, and elsewhere, believing in the UN promise of protection, only to find the peacekeepers unable to fight off the Serb militias. At Srebrenica, Mladic's forces gathered up men and boys, marched them out of the town as UN peacekeepers were held hostage, and summarily executed the civilians in the surrounding fields.[9]

By 1994 a quarter-million people may have fallen to the war in the Balkans, and more than two and a half million had been displaced. The United Nations had demonstrated, by its ineffectiveness, the limits of the institution in the new post–cold war world. The "promise" that had appeared evident in the afterglow of the Gulf War was dissipating. Although the old veto crisis on the Security Council that had persisted for forty years had disappeared, national interests among the five permanent members (P5) and a determined enemy in the hills of the Balkans made the United Nations a less attractive venue for resolving the conflict.

After a brutal mortar attack on the marketplace in Sarajevo, NATO, pressured intensively by the Clinton administration, bombed Serb positions around the capital in August 1995. However, before the president could achieve a NATO commitment, under rules developed in the Security Council, he had to have the assent of the secretary-general's special representative and head of UNPROFOR. The special representative rejected requests for air strikes on five occasions before authorizing a military response to the Sarajevo massacre, which led the U.S. government to seek action outside the UN framework.

Coupled with a successful Croatian offensive that reclaimed large territories held by the Serbs, the long-awaited NATO action forced Milosevic to the bargaining table. Invited by Clinton to Dayton, Ohio, the leaders of Serbia, Croatia, and Bosnia hammered out an agreement. The Bosnian war ended with the negotiation of the **Dayton Peace Accords** (November 1995), which provided that the United Nations monitor the agreement through the Implementation Force (IFOR) made up of NATO troops, to be replaced later by a Stabilization Force (SFOR).

All parties agreed to establish a permanent cease-fire in Bosnia, repatriate refugees, and create a multiethnic state with a tripartite presidency and autonomous ethnic enclaves. Most important, the accords inserted NATO ground forces in support of a contemplated UN peacekeeping operation. Clinton committed twenty thousand U.S. troops to the multinational force, noting that unlike the UN forces, the new contingent would be heavily armed and ready "to respond immediately . . . with overwhelming force . . . to any violations"[10] of the peace agreement. While the administration had hopes that multilateral diplomacy would bring about "burden sharing" in the new era, Bosnia demonstrated the United States' unique position and role in contemporary international affairs. It also made clear the limitations of UN-sponsored solutions.

As NATO forces arrived in Bosnia, calls were made for them to search out, capture, and send to The Hague the Bosnian Serb leaders who had been charged with war crimes. In 1993 the Security Council had created the International Criminal Tribunal for the Former Yugoslavia (ICTY) as the first institution of international criminal prosecution since the end of the World War II. It was charged with indicting and trying suspected war criminals for crimes against humanity. The ICTY issued its first indictment on November 11, 1994, for Dragan Nikolic, a Bosnian Serb who was allegedly the commander of a small prison camp in eastern Bosnia. In October 2001 the parliament of the Bosnian Serb enclave approved the arrest of individuals under indictment by the international tribunal in The Hague. In July 2004 the parliament of the semiautonomous community directed its own government to hunt for the indicted individuals.[11] As late as the summer of 2005, Mladic, Radovan Karadzic, and other senior leaders remained at large.

The creation of the ICTY and the eventual indictment and trial of Slobodan Milosevic were the few bright highlights in the UN's performance during the Bosnian crisis. (You may recall our description of the proceedings against Milosevic in Chapter 1.) However, even after combined NATO and UN intervention, international administrators experienced little cooperation from local ethnic leaders in pacifying and reconstructing the country. The United Nations was given a minor role in postconflict Bosnia. The Security Council established the UN Mission in Bosnia and Herzegovina (UNMIBH), but its limited responsibilities were to reform the local police and assess the Bosnian judicial system. Real power was placed in the hands of the High Representative, a post created directly by the Dayton Accords. The UN mission completed its job in 2002, turning over police oversight to a European Union police mission, but the High Representative continued the hard work of trying to create a multiethnic and peaceful state among highly distrustful Serb, Muslim, and Croat communities.

Rwanda

In Yugoslavia the United Nations responded ineffectively and late to rising ethnic tensions, allowing Milosevic's forces to carry out horrendous human rights violations that led to the deaths of hundreds of thousands of people. The UN failure in Rwanda at approximately the same time as the Balkan debacle may have been even more regrettable in that UN actions actually contributed to the human suffering and death in that African nation.[12] When ethnic tensions rose dramatically in Rwanda in 1994, Security Council members, particularly the United States, cautioned against UN intervention. The genocide of nearly eight hundred thousand Tutsis ensued, and even more Rwandans (Tutsi and Hutu) fled the country into makeshift refugee camps in the Congo and other surrounding states.

Fighting between the Hutu majority government of Rwanda and Tutsi rebels commenced in 1990. Several cease-fire agreements were reached; the most important was the Arusha Agreement in 1992. To monitor the cease-fire and assist in the creation of a transitional government, the Security Council created UNAMIR—the UN Assistance Mission for Rwanda.

Belgian and Bangladeshi forces—the only contingents offered by the world community—were stationed in Kigali, the nation's capital.

The crisis that sparked the planned genocide of Tutsis by Hutu militia occurred in April 1994 when the presidents of Rwanda and Burundi were killed in a plane crash arriving at Kigali airport. Among those killed in the succeeding slaughter were the Rwandan prime minister, several cabinet members, and Belgian peacekeepers protecting the government officials. The Security Council's immediate response was to reduce UNAMIR's presence from more than 2,500 peacekeepers to 270. Another six months would pass before UN forces in sufficient numbers were introduced into the maelstrom to secure an end to the fighting and restore stability. In the meantime, nearly three and a half million people were killed, and two million fled to refugee camps outside Rwanda.

In April 1998, Secretary-General Annan traveled to Rwanda. Before that country's parliament, he sought to repair an abiding ill will by acknowledging the UN's delinquency in responding to the horrific Tutsi massacre. A year later the secretary-general appointed an independent commission to look into UN actions at the time of the Rwandan disaster. The inquiry found that "the failure by the United Nations to prevent, and subsequently, to stop the genocide in Rwanda was a failure by the United Nations System as a whole."[13] It cited a lack of resources and political will on the part of the major powers on the Security Council as contributory factors to the high death toll. It noted that the Nigerian president rightly assessed the situation when he suggested the council "risked becoming the laughing stock of the world"[14] if it did not act. The secretary-general was also criticized: The commission asserted that "he could have done more."[15] The inquiry's members recommended a number of reforms in UN peacekeeping operations and said that the United Nations had to take partial responsibility for the breadth of the massacre.

Brahimi Report

In March 2000, Secretary-General Annan appointed a panel of experts to study the new challenges facing UN peacekeeping. After the disaster in the Balkans and UN disregard in Rwanda, he thought a wise move would be to respond to the expectations created by the Rwanda inquiry criticisms. He hoped the new panel would provide useful advice on ways to manage the growing number and variety of UN missions. It would also blunt political attacks on UN peacekeeping as unresponsive to its past perceived failures. He appointed former Algerian foreign minister Lakhdar Brahimi to chair the group. Brahimi had previously served as Annan's special representative to Afghanistan and would return to that role following the overthrow of the Taliban government in 2001. The secretary-general asked Brahimi to prepare frank and specific recommendations that would narrow the gap between the UN's burgeoning peacekeeping responsibilities and its limited financial and organizational resources.

In August the Panel on UN Peace Operations published a seventy-page report calling for dramatic reform of the UN's peacekeeping missions, its Department of Peacekeeping Operations, the process by which the Security Council and the secretary-general implemented decisions to intervene in conflicts, and the funding mechanisms for peacekeeping efforts.[16] The panel recommended formalizing the UN's peacekeeping activities, ending ad hoc deployments, and creating a new information-gathering and analysis office within the United Nations to act as a professional policy-planning staff for DPKO. Coming on the eve of the Millennium Summit, the Brahimi Report recommendations elicited the most earnest and sustained discussion among the attending heads of government.

The report consisted of nearly sixty proposals. One of the most significant recommendations in the report was to establish for each mission an integrated task force combining political analysis, military operations, civilian police, electoral assistance, aid to refugees, finance, logistics, public information, and streamlined procurement procedures. The panel also urged that definitions of *self-defense* be stretched to allow UN peacekeeping missions to take a more offensive posture in dangerous situations. It proposed that traditional UN "impartiality" between combatants in a conflict not be allowed to "amount to complicity with evil." According to the panel, the credibility of UN peacekeeping depended on being able "to distinguish victim from aggressor."[17]

Although the Brahimi Report did not call for a standing UN army, it advocated reform of the UN Standby Arrangements System (UNSAS) to ensure that the United Nations could fully deploy a peacekeeping force within thirty days of a Security Council decision to do so. The panel recommended that to fund rapid deployment, the secretary-general be authorized to commit as much as fifty million dollars in advance of a contemplated Security Council decision to undertake a new operation. The panel encouraged "a substantial increase in resources for Headquarters support of peacekeeping operations" and called on Annan to submit a financing proposal to the General Assembly, as well as a plan for implementation of the other recommendations in the report.

Annan welcomed the panel's findings and directed Deputy Secretary-General Louise Fréchette to proceed with implementation. He requested that the General Assembly authorize the expenditure of twenty-two million dollars to carry out all the recommendations. In January 2001 the assembly granted a first installment of nine and a half million dollars for this purpose. The General Assembly's willingness to fund the reforms was due in part to a fall review by the Security Council's Special Committee on Peacekeeping Operations that had endorsed them and to Annan's steps toward implementation. Initial reaction to the report among developing states, however, was cool; they feared the new rules for peacekeeping might amount to a form of UN "colonialism" at the behest of U.S. foreign policy. Among the permanent Security Council members, this concern was initially reflected by the demur of Chinese president Jiang Zemin and Russian president Vladimir Putin. A vigorous public relations effort by Annan and Brahimi, combined with the promise of U.S. funding if the recommendations were accepted, ended this opposition. By the spring of 2001, most national leaders supported the activist peacekeeping vision of Secretary-General Annan and Ambassador Brahimi.

Peace Building

Even in a promising new era, the UN's options remain limited with regard to ending conflict or preventing the outbreak of war. Its dependence on subcontracting the use of force confirms this assessment. Second-generation peacekeeping and nation building, although far more intrusive than earlier UN operations, are implicit acknowledgments that much more is required than simply restoring peace if the world community wants to ensure that a fissured domestic society will not fall back into a state of anarchy and violence. Yet, the UN Charter provides no guidelines or directives on how to prevent a return to war.

The United Nations has attempted to lessen the chances of a regress to the conditions that brought on conflict in the first place by creating "peace-building" and political support offices, not only where peacekeeping missions are under way, but also in states and regions where a likely threat of violent instability exists. In his 2003 report to the General Assembly, Secretary-General Annan noted that "even when apparently successful in repairing war-torn States, the international community can ill-afford to declare 'victory' prematurely."[18] Usually these offices are headed by the special representative of the secretary-general (SRSG), who will normally head the peacekeeping operation as well. By the twenty-first century more than four dozen peace-building, political, nation-building, and second-generation peacekeeping operations had been undertaken. They could be found on every populated continent except North America.

Second-Generation Peacekeeping, Nation-Building, Political, and Peace-Building Operations in the New Era

Area	Missions	Dates of Operation
Africa		
Angola	UN Angola Verification Mission I (UNAVEM I)	December 1988–May 1991
	UN Angola Verification Mission II (UNAVEM II)	May 1991–February 1995
	UN Angola Verification Mission III (UNAVEM III)	February 1995–June 1997
	UN Observer Mission in Angola (MONUA)	June 1997–February 1999
	UN Office in Angola (UNOA)	October 1999–August 2002
	UN Mission in Angola (UNMA)	August 2002–February 2003
Burundi	UN Office in Burundi (UNOB)	October 1993–May 2004
	UN Operation in Burundi (ONUB)	June 2004–
Central African Republic	UN Mission in the Central African Republic (MINURCA)	April 1998–February 2000
	UN Office in the Central African Africa (BONUCA)	February 2000–
Côte d'Ivoire	UN Mission in Côte d'Ivoire (MINUCI)	May 2003–April 2004
	UN Operation in Côte d'Ivoire (UNOCI)	April 2004–
Democratic Republic of the Congo	UN Organization Mission in the Democratic Republic of the Congo (MONUC)	December 1999–
Ethiopia/Eritrea	UN Mission in Ethiopia and Eritrea (UNMEE)	July 2000–
Great Lakes Region	Office of the Special Representative of the Secretary-General for the Great Lakes Region	January 1997–
Guinea-Bissau	UN Peace-Building Support Office in Guinea-Bissau (UNOGBIS)	March 1999–
Liberia	Observer Mission in Liberia (UNOMIL)	September 1993– September 1997
	UN Peace-Building Support Office in Liberia (UNOL)	November 1997–August 2003
	UN Mission in Liberia (UNMIL)	September 2003–
Mozambique	UN Operation in Mozambique (ONUMOZ)	December 1992–December 1994
Namibia	UN Transition Assistance Group (UNTAG)	April 1989–March 1990
Rwanda	UN Assistance Mission for Rwanda (UNAMIR)	October 1993–March 1996
Rwanda/ Uganda	UN Observer Mission for Uganda-Rwanda (UNOMUR)	June 1993–September 1994
Sierra Leone	UN Observer Mission in Sierra Leone (UNOMSIL)	July 1998–October 1999

Area	Missions	Dates of Operation
	UN Assistance Mission in Sierra Leone (UNAMSIL)	October 1999–
Somalia	UN Operation in Somalia I (UNOSOM I)	April 1992–March 1993
	UN Operation in Somalia II (UNOSOM II)	March 1993–March 1995
	UN Political Office for Somalia (UNPOS)	April 1995–
Sudan	UN Mission in the Sudan (UNMIS)	March 2005–
West Africa	UN Office for West Africa (UNOWA)	March 2002–
Western Sahara	UN Mission for the Referendum in Western Sahara (MINURSO)	April 1991–

Latin America and the Caribbean

Area	Missions	Dates of Operation
Central America	UN Observer Group in Central America (ONUCA)	November 1989–January 1992
El Salvador	UN Observer Mission in El Salvador (ONUSAL)	July 1991–April 1995
Guatemala	UN Verification Mission in Guatemala (MINUGUA)	January 1997–November 2004
Haiti	UN Mission in Haiti (UNMIH)	September 1993–June 1996
	UN Support Mission in Haiti (UNSMIH)	July 1996–July 1997
	UN Transition Mission in Haiti (UNTMIH)	August–November 1997
	UN Civilian Police Mission in Haiti (MIPONUH)	December 1997–March 2000
	UN Civilian Support Mission in Haiti (MICAH)	December 1999–February 2004
	Multinational Interim Force (MIF)	February 2004–June 2004
	UN Stabilization Mission in Haiti (MINUSTAH)	June 2004–

Asia

Area	Missions	Dates of Operation
Afghanistan	UN Assistance Mission in Afghanistan (UNAMA)	March 2002–
Afghanistan/ Pakistan	UN Good Offices Mission in Afghanistan and Pakistan (UNGOMAP)	March 1988–March 1990
	UN Special Mission to Afghanistan (UNSMA)	December 1993–February 2004
Cambodia	UN Advance Mission in Cambodia (UNAMIC)	October 1991–March 1992
	UN Transitional Authority in Cambodia (UNTAC)	March 1992–September 1993
East Timor	UN Mission in East Timor (UNAMET)	June–October 1999
	UN Transitional Administration in East Timor (UNTAET)	October 1999–May 2002
	UN Mission of Support in East Timor (UNMISET)	May 2002–May 2005
	UN Office in Timor-Leste (UNOTIL)	April 2005–

(continued)

Area	Missions	Dates of Operation
Georgia	UN Observer Mission in Georgia (UNOMIG)	August 1993–
	UN Office for the Protection and Promotion of Human Rights in Abkhazia, Georgia (HROAG)	December 1996–
Papua New Guinea	UN Political Office in Bougainville (UNPOB)	June 1998–December 2003
	UN Observer Mission (UNOMB)	January 2004–June 2005
Tajikistan	UN Mission of Observers in Tajikistan (UNMOT)	December 1994–May 2000
	UN Tajikistan Office of Peace-Building (UNTOP)	June 2000–
Europe		
Bosnia and Herzegovina	UN Mission in Bosnia and Herzegovina (UNMIBH)	December 1995–December 2002
	UN Mission of Observers in Prevlaka (UNMOP)	February 1996–December 2002
Croatia	UN Confidence Restoration Operation (UNCRO)	March 1995–January 1996
	UN Transitional Authority in Eastern Slavonia, Baranja, and Western Sirmium (UNTAES)	January 1996–January 1998
	UN Civilian Police Support Group (UNPSG)	January 1998–October 1998
Cyprus	UN Peacekeeping Force in Cyprus (UNFICYP)	March 1964–
Former Yugoslav Republic of Macedonia	UN Preventive Deployment Force in the Former Yugoslav Republic of Macedonia (UNPREDEP)	March 1995–February 1999
Former Yugoslavia	UN Protection Force (UNPROFOR)	February 1992–March 1995
	UN Interim Administration Mission in Kosovo (UNMIK)	June 1999–
Middle East		
Iraq	UN Assistance Mission for Iraq (UNAMI)	August 2003–
Israel/ Occupied Territories	Office of the UN Special Coordinator for the Middle East Peace Process and Personal Representative of the Secretary-General to the Palestine Liberation Organization and the Palestinian Authority (UNSCO)	September 1999–

Often the political and peace-building offices are in distant corners of the globe that have gained little world attention but could easily find their way to the front pages of the world's press with the outbreak of internal violence. Bougainville is a fair example. An island in the southwestern Pacific Ocean, Bougainville is a province of Papua New Guinea. A former French, then

German, then Australian colony, it was merged with Papua New Guinea against much of the local population's wishes. By the late 1980s, separatists had formed the Bougainville Revolutionary Army and were attacking the central government's defense forces and non-Bougainvillean economic interests on the island. Meanwhile, anti-independence Bougainvilleans formed their own army to attack the rebels, which led to a three-way battle and the general destruction of life in Bougainville. In 1989 the UN secretary-general opened the UN Political Office in Bougainville (UNPOB) with a mandate to encourage a peace process, to help implement agreements reached between the warring groups, to restore services and the economy in Bougainville, and to achieve an agreement among the groups on holding elections under a new constitution. The UN operation contributed to the signing of several peace agreements and the imposition of a regional peace-monitoring group including personnel from Fiji, New Zealand, Australia, and Vanuatu. UNPOB and an observer mission created by the Security Council directed the disposal of weapons used in prior conflicts, which diminished the chances of a revival of open warfare. On June 15, 2005, a new autonomous Bougainville government was inaugurated.

Political and peace-building offices similar to UNPOB were established in Côte d'Ivoire, Angola, Burundi, and the Great Lakes Region on the African continent. Elsewhere, they could be found in Afghanistan, the Palestinian territories, Haiti, and Tajikistan. The mission in Afghanistan (UN Assistance Mission in Afghanistan, or UNAMA), brought into being March 28, 2002, by Security Council Resolution 1401, and the mission initially established in 1994 by the secretary-general in the midst of the Israeli-Palestinian conflict (Office of the United Nations Special Coordinator for the Middle East Peace Process and Personal Representative of the Secretary-General to the Palestine Liberation Organization and the Palestinian Authority, or UNSCO) are particularly noteworthy. The Security Council created UNAMA following the U.S.-led invasion of Afghanistan. The United States toppled the Taliban government in Kabul and attacked installations of the al-Qaeda terrorist network. The Security Council action amounted to a tacit approval of the U.S. action and an internationalization of the postwar political and economic reconstruction of Afghanistan.

Secretary-General Annan sent the reliable Lahkdar Brahimi as his special representative to head UNAMA, with a mandate to coordinate all UN activities in the country and to work with indigenous political groups and the occupying forces to establish a viable working democracy in Afghanistan. The mission also worked with the International Security Assistance Force (ISAF), the multinational military operation in the country put in place after the invasion. In this regard, the operation reflected the UN's growing willingness to work closely with regional and military organizations. ISAF, first under rotating national commands, was placed under NATO leadership at the end of 2003. Likewise, in Liberia and Sierra Leone on the African continent, UN activities supported the politicomilitary intervention of ECOWAS (Economic Community of West African States).

Attempting to "rebuild" Afghanistan, the United Nations sponsored the Bonn Conference in 2002 to indicate to Afghans the international community's commitment to reforming the political process in the country, to encouraging warlords to submit to central authority, and to writing a new Afghan constitution (which was put in place in January 2004). Meanwhile, the international Tokyo Conference raised pledges of economic assistance. UNAMA worked to implement the will that emerged from these gatherings. UNAMA also coordinated much of the NGO assistance in the country, addressed human rights issues left by the previous fundamentalist regime, and created civil society institutions that were meant to undergird democracy and the rule of law. Despite UNAMA's progress, its work was hampered by a deteriorating security environment. Elections scheduled for September 2004 had to be postponed, and NGOs, such as Doctors Without Borders, withdrew from the country in increasing numbers to protect their workers. Afghanistan demonstrated that peace-building operations could be effective only where general, if fragile, domestic tranquility existed.

ONGOING POLITICAL AND PEACE-BUILDING MISSIONS (SEE APPENDIX G)

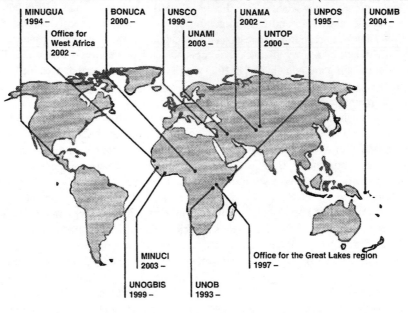

(Map No. 4147(E) Rev. 9, United Nations, January 2004. Reproduced by permission from the UN Cartographic Section.)

In the Middle East the creation of UNSCO emerged from the events put in train by the 1993 Oslo Accords between Israel and the Palestine Liberation Organization. The accords established a process by which a final settlement would ostensibly be reached between the two sides. In September 1999, Secretary-General Annan decided to appoint a personal representative to co-ordinate UN activities in the occupied territories, to handle socioeconomic aspects of the peace process, and to provide "good offices" to both sides. This last function grew in importance when the United Nations joined the "Quartet"—the United Nations, Russia, the European Union, and the United States—that put forward the "Road Map" for peace in April 2003.

Political and peace-building operations are part of a sliding scale of UN involvement. In some cases, such as Bougainville, they can lead to the apparent restoration of a legitimate central government and the resolution of internal conflicts, which allows the United Nations to withdraw its mission. However, if the political office is unsuccessful, the Security Council must consider increasing direct UN involvement. In 2004 this situation occurred in Côte d'Ivoire, where rebel forces and the government had been engaged in fighting for the previous seventeen months. A small UN political mission, accompanied by ECOWAS and French troops, worked to keep the warring factions apart, to provide assistance to a half million internally displaced refugees, and to negotiate a resolution.

In January 2003 the parties reached a tentative peace agreement that called for a power-sharing transitional government in anticipation of internationally administered elections. This agreement in turn led to a cease-fire accord in May. To assist the newly created Government of National Reconciliation's efforts to carry out the "DDR (disarmament, demobilization, reintegration and repatriation) Programme" agreed to by all sides, the Security Council replaced the existing

UN office of fewer than 50 personnel with a full-fledged peacekeeping operation. Named the *UN Operation in Côte d'Ivoire (UNOCI)*, the mission included a 6,240-member force.[19] With no assurance of final success, given that what Secretary-General Annan called "hard-line elements" were continuing to perpetrate acts of violence, the council initiated an operation that was expected to add $303 million to UN expenses in its first six months.[20] Coupled with other operations in Africa, UNOCI highlighted the world community's concern over the escalating instability on the continent and the need to contain it.

AFRICA

Collective security is a legacy of great European wars, both those fought on the continent in the eighteenth, nineteenth, and twentieth centuries and those fought around the world by European powers. Europe has been a dangerous continent ever since the nation-state system was born. In the twentieth century alone, the continent absorbed the most violent and deadly wars in history. Coupled with war is European colonization and imperialism. At the end of World War II, in response to conflict, instability, and colonialism, the great powers sought a new formula for peace through the concept of collective security established first in the League of Nations.

The irony in the new millennium is that Europe is generally at peace and the devices created half a century ago to keep the peace, now implemented by the United Nations, are mostly directed elsewhere, particularly toward Asia and Africa. In his 2003 report to the General Assembly, Secretary-General Annan made special note of Africa's problems and the need for the world to address them:[21]

> Africa's development . . . continues to be hampered by war. Many of the continent's recent conflicts have been characterized by extreme acts of violence perpetrated against civilians, including brutal acts of torture, rape, mutilation, harassment and executions. Children are routinely subject to abduction and forced militarization, perpetuating a youth culture of alienation and violence.

The problems of grinding poverty, disease, sectarian strife in postcolonial multiethnic states, artificial borders imposed by colonial powers, religious division, and authoritarianism have made sub-Saharan Africa the focal point of world conflict and will probably keep it in upheaval for years to come. Many UN second-generation peacekeeping and peace-building operations have been established in Africa in hopes of ameliorating human suffering and ensuring that Africa does not become the new "tinderbox" for wider conflagration.

Somalia

In December 1992 Security Council members found the instability in Somalia to be a threat to international peace and authorized intervention under U.S. leadership. After long-time dictator Siad Barre was deposed in 1991, civil war erupted between Somalia's different clans and factions. In addition to attacking each other, private armies harassed UN and NGO relief efforts. To help ease the suffering of the population, the Security Council established the first UN Operation in Somalia (UNOSOM I) in April 1992. The council hoped that the warring factions would respect UN peacekeepers as they attempted to deliver critical food and humanitarian assistance, but even food warehouses in the capital, Mogadishu, came under regular attack. In the fall, Secretary-General Boutros-Ghali wrote to President George H. W. Bush, asking for U.S. military assistance. The president agreed to act and requested a Security Council resolution authorizing U.S. military intervention. On December 3 the council passed Resolution 794, invoking Chapter VII and accepting the offer "by a member state" to put together an international coalition (UNITAF, or

Unified Task Force) to protect the distribution of humanitarian supplies. For the first time, the United Nations had expressly subcontracted a peacekeeping operation.

Although the deployment of UNITAF did much to pacify the situation and make humanitarian assistance by the United Nations and other groups possible (the level of malnutrition and starvation decreased considerably in many areas), the needed "secure environment" could not be established. Somalia remained without a functioning and effective central government. In early 1993 the Security Council set up a second mission—UNOSOM II. Its mandate included disarming the warring factions, demining, assisting in the reconstruction of the Somali economy and political institutions, repatriating refugees, and building the social infrastructure of the country. UNOSOM II undertook no less than the salvation of a "failed" state. The Security Council committed twenty-eight thousand military and police personnel to the task.

The enhanced UN presence did not end the violence. In June 1993, 25 Pakistani peacekeepers were killed, and on October 18, U.S. soldiers perished when two helicopters were shot down. The political process also did not make much progress. The Security Council revised the mandate for UNOSOM II in February 1994, reducing force levels to 22,000 and prohibiting the use of coercive measures such as attempts to arrest Somali warlords or to disarm private militia. The council authorized the mission to carry out humanitarian tasks only. UNOSOM II left in early March 1995, having sustained 147 casualties during the two years of the mission, at a cost of $1.6 billion.

The experience in Somalia demonstrated the limits of robust peacekeeping. It could not succeed where indigenous clans sought to undermine national reconciliation. The departure of UNOSOM II did not end the UN's political involvement, however. The secretary-general established the UN Political Office for Somalia (UNPOS) in April 1995. One sign of how little progress the United Nations had made was that UNPOS had to be headquartered outside the country, in Nairobi, Kenya. In February 2000 the United Nations facilitated a peace conference in Djibouti that led to the election of a new Somali president and national assembly and to the creation of a transitional national government in August.

The years after UNOSOM II marked a transition from peacekeeping to UN peace building in Somalia. The UN specialized agencies and programmes increased their presence to address humanitarian needs. Among them were the Food and Agriculture Organization; the UN Development Programme; the UN Educational, Scientific and Cultural Organization; the UN High Commissioner for Refugees; the UN Children's Fund; the UN Development Fund for Women; the World Health Organization; and the World Food Programme. UNPOS encouraged the reconciliation process and worked closely with the Kenyan government and the Intergovernmental Authority on Development (IGAD), the cosponsors of the Somali National Reconciliation Conference.

In October 2002 the conference reached agreement on a declaration of principles—known as the *Eldoret Declaration*—to guide the cessation of hostilities and the continuing reconciliation process. This declaration was followed by an agreement among the most important clan leaders and the transitional national government about the restoration of peace in Mogadishu. Unfortunately, these positive signs were regularly undermined by violent outbreaks in the cities of Somalia, many of them fueled by the flow of illegal weapons and ammunition into the country. On December 16, 2003, the Security Council, acting under Chapter VII, unanimously established a monitoring group to investigate violations of the mandatory arms embargo in Somalia. The council threatened to impose "possible future measures" against states and groups that violated the embargo.[22] Despite thirteen years of UN involvement, Somalia remained a land with devastating humanitarian problems and little prospect for a stable, peaceful government in the foreseeable future.

The Congo

The second period of UN involvement in the Congo was precipitated by the 1994 Rwandan genocide and the consequent exodus of one million primarily Hutu ethnic refugees into temporary camps in eastern Congo (then called *Zaire*). These camps became staging grounds from which Hutu extremists attacked Rwanda and Uganda. Zaire's long-time dictator, Mobutu Sese Seko, was unable to control the camps and faced rebel movements in eastern Zaire. With the help of outside forces, Laurent Kabila's Alliance of Democratic Forces for the Liberation of Congo (ADFL) overthrew President Mobutu in May 1997. In the process, ADFL forces attacked the refugee camps and killed more than two hundred thousand people.

A month before Kabila's victory, the UN Commission on Human Rights (CHR), with the support of the Security Council, established a mission headed by Roberto Garretón (a UN diplomat from Chile) to investigate alleged human rights abuses. For almost a year UN officials were detained, threatened, and denied access to the sites where refugees were massacred. On April 17, 1998, Secretary-General Annan announced the permanent withdrawal of the UN investigators because of the lack of cooperation from the Kabila government.

Kabila proved to be no more popular than his predecessor. His government also faced opposition from neighboring countries that in turn aided anti-Kabila rebel groups. Past allies of Kabila, Rwanda and Uganda were disappointed that the new president had not secured the borders of eastern Congo. Angola, Zimbabwe, and Namibia sent troops to aid Kabila, and Chad and Sudan sent military advisers, which created Africa's "first war." In April 1999 the UN secretary-general appointed a special envoy to assist in peace negotiations. The Security Council called for an immediate cease-fire and condemned the foreign intervention in the Democratic Republic of the Congo (DRC). In Lusaka, Zambia, on July 10, 1999, the DRC, Angola, Namibia, Rwanda, Uganda, and Zimbabwe signed a cease-fire agreement. The **Lusaka Agreement** called for an inter-Congolese dialogue on the country's future, normalization of the DRC border, militia disarmament, and the establishment of a Joint Military Commission (JMC) of two representatives from each party under a neutral chair. The Security Council welcomed the Lusaka Agreement and authorized the deployment of a 90-person UN liaison group to the capitals of signatory states and the JMC provisional headquarters. After a recommendation by the secretary-general, the council extended the mandate of the UN liaisons until January 15, 2000 (Resolution 1973) and then decided that these personnel would constitute the UN Organization Mission in the DRC (MONUC). The council authorized the expansion of the mission to 5,537 military personnel. By 2005 troop strength had grown to more than 16,700 under the command of Senegalese Lieutenant General Babacar Gaye and Special Representative of the Secretary-General William Swing from the United States.

MONUC was directed to work with the JMC to monitor the cease-fire, to facilitate humanitarian assistance, to verify the disengagement of the contending parties' forces, and to protect civilians. It was also authorized to deploy infantry battalions in order to take all necessary action to protect civilians and UN staff who might be under imminent threat of physical harm. This last charge became more important as the civil war devolved into regional separatism and internecine fighting. The secretary-general expressed his concerns for human rights violations, the limited progress on the inter-Congolese dialogue, and the uncertain environment in which to deploy UN troops. In spring 2000 fighting also erupted between Ugandan and Rwandan forces near Kisangani. More than two hundred Congolese were killed and a thousand were injured. In response, the Security Council called for the immediate withdrawal of Rwanda and Uganda from the DRC.

The assassination of President Laurent Kabila and the succession of his son Joseph in January 2001 opened another chapter in the war. The new government responded favorably to a

South African diplomatic initiative to mediate among the parties. By April 2003 the South African government had negotiated a peace accord between the DRC and outside countries as well as among the internal factions to the war. Under the agreements, Kabila accepted terms for a transitional government that would share power with rebel parties, and he agreed to elections by 2005.

MONUC placed its full resources behind the agreements, pressuring Kabila to move more quickly than he seemed inclined to do to appoint representatives of competing groups to his government. It also used its military forces to combat ethnic rebel groups, particularly in the northeast part of the country. The city of Bunia in the Ituri District had become a center of rebel activity. As many as fifty thousand civilians may have lost their lives during the fighting in the region. It was also the site of ethnic massacres; one of the most brutal was reported in mid-January 2004, when a local militia rounded up men and boys in the village of Gobi, just north of Bunia. At least one hundred were systematically executed. In Bunia itself, foreigners and UN forces were regularly attacked. MONUC used both infantry and helicopter gunships to attack enemy positions.

The commitment of MONUC to use its forces on behalf of the central government, the peace process, and a particular outcome to the civil war was made clear by Special Representative Swing. He criticized all attacks on UN assets and on the civilian population. He said, "We are going to use all the necessary means in our possession to protect the populations, our helicopters and troops. That is what the [UN Charter's] Chapter VII is about."[23] Forty years earlier, a UN peacekeeping mission to the Congo had also tried to expand its mandate beyond simply supervising a cease-fire to include nation building in a civil war. It had proved a disaster both for the Congo and for the UN's peacekeeping role in the world. MONUC's efforts would test how much world affairs had changed in the intervening period as well as the limits of the new robust peacekeeping. As of January 2004 at least two and a half million Congolese had died of disease, malnutrition, and violence in the civil war.

MONUC also worked to prevent Congolese turmoil from endangering regional stability in surrounding states. In particular, arms trafficking, refugee flows, and assistance to rebel groups in neighboring Burundi undermined the national reconciliation process sponsored by the African Union in that country. To support this process and reinforce transboundary efforts by MONUC, the Security Council established a peacekeeping mission in Burundi in June 2004. Known by the acronym ONUB, the UN Operation in Burundi was authorized to put as many as 5,650 military and civilian personnel in the field. Upgrading an eleven-year UN presence in Burundi from a political office to a full-blown peacekeeping operation, the council hoped to disarm warring groups, report on human rights abuses, and prepare the country for elections in the fall.

Sierra Leone and Liberia

Situated on the west coast of Africa, between Guinea and Liberia, Sierra Leone had gone relatively unnoticed in the three decades following its independence from Great Britain in 1961. It came to the public's attention because of a ruinous civil war in 1991. The country had suffered under the one-party dictatorship of Siaka Stevens and his successor, Joseph Momoh. The regime was a classic example of inept economic stewardship and political repression on the African continent. By the close of the 1980s, the International Monetary Fund had declared Sierra Leone in a state of economic emergency and ineligible for further IMF lending.

This economic disaster was met by domestic calls for a return to democratic elections. The country was further weakened in 1991 when armed rebels attacked, initiating the civil war that ravaged Sierra Leone and destabilized neighboring Liberia. The rebels, known as the *Revolutionary United Front (RUF)*, were led by Foday Sankoh and supported by Liberian president Charles

Taylor. As in the case of other African conflicts, such as in Angola, the RUF capitalized on Sierra Leone's vast resources of alluvial diamonds to fund its activities.

In 1992 dissatisfied members of the Sierra Leone army carried out a coup. Although it initially enjoyed popular support, by 1994 the people were demanding a return to civilian government. In 1995, Secretary-General Boutros-Ghali appointed Mr. Berhanu Dinka as his special envoy to aid negotiations that would lead to democratic elections. Mr. Dinka worked closely with both the Organization of African Unity (OAU-renamed the *African Union, or AU*, in 2001) and the Economic Community of West African States to facilitate a return to civilian rule. Elections were held in 1996, and Ahmed Tejan Kabbah was elected president. However, in the spring of 1997, this time in collaboration with the RUF, the military ousted the Kabbah government.

In response to the coup, the UN Security Council imposed an arms and oil embargo. It authorized ECOWAS to administer the sanctions through its own peacekeeping force, ECOMOG (the ECOWAS Monitoring Group), comprising mostly Nigerian troops. The council's decision to work with ECOWAS reflected the new UN premise of regionalizing peacekeeping responsibilities: Collective security need not be imposed directly from UN headquarters, but can be approached by subcontracting international authority to a regional organization. The council also pursued this strategy in Bosnia and Herzegovina, where the UN operation worked closely with NATO, and in Georgia, where the corresponding organizations were the OSCE (Organization for Security and Cooperation in Europe) and the Commonwealth of Independent States (CIS).

President Kabbah successfully regained power in the spring of 1998, and in June the Security Council authorized the UN Observer Mission in Sierra Leone (UNOMSIL) to encourage disarmament, to report on human rights violations, and to restructure Sierra Leone's security forces. Subsequently, a joint UN–ECOWAS–Sierra Leone government coordination mechanism was established for conflict management in Sierra Leone.

The RUF and the government of Sierra Leone reached a comprehensive peace accord (known as the **Lomé Agreement**) in July 1999. It established the legal provisions for the RUF to become a political party in Sierra Leone and for its members to hold important cabinet positions within the government. UNOMSIL was replaced by the UN Assistance Mission in Sierra Leone (UNAMSIL), which included the deployment of 11,500 armed forces (with a maximum authorization of 17,500). Its primary purpose was to assist the central government in restoring peace and security. During the war, nearly 700,000 people were displaced, 75,000 died, and thousands were purposefully maimed through brutal amputations conducted by the RUF.

Peace and reconciliation seemed to be within reach with the Lomé Agreement; however, the RUF failed to comply with the terms of the agreement, and intermittent fighting and terrorist acts were still too common as the century turned. Parts of Sierra Leone continued to be under rebel control. In June 2000, to address the perceived illegal intervention in Sierra Leonean affairs by the Taylor government of Liberia, as well as the human rights abuses perpetrated by the RUF, President Kabbah asked Secretary-General Annan to establish a tribunal to try suspected war criminals. He hoped for an international tribunal like the tribunals established for Rwanda and the former Yugoslavia. In January 2002 the Special Court for Sierra Leone was established, with a mixed composition of international and Sierra Leonean jurists. This special court is discussed in more detail in Chapter 7. The court indicted, among other people, Liberia's Charles Taylor for his support of the RUF.

The interconnections between Sierra Leone and Liberia at the turn of the century ran deeper than simply Taylor's involvement in Sierra Leone's civil war. At times the future stability of all West African nations appeared to depend on how these two countries' troubled histories, in tandem, would evolve. For this reason ECOWAS took the lead in promoting the peace process, working closely with the United Nations, even introducing regional troops into both states. In the case of Liberia, ECOWAS first introduced military observers in 1990. It also negotiated the first peace agreement in the ongoing civil war in 1993, which led to the introduction of the UN Observer Mission in Liberia (UNOMIL). This UN peacekeeping operation was the first to be undertaken in cooperation with a peacekeeping mission already established by another organization.

Civil conflict in Liberia began in 1989. UNOMIL and ECOMOG worked together to implement a 1993 peace agreement, which ultimately brought Charles Taylor to power. With the agreement, the United Nations believed it could diminish its role in the country, replacing UNOMIL with a peace-building operation (named *UN Peace-Building Support Office in Liberia,* or *UNOL*). However, national reconciliation lasted only until the late 1990s. As the Taylor regime became increasingly oppressive and human rights abuses mounted, new rebel movements emerged. Both sides funded their military operations with the illegal sales of "conflict diamonds." The escalating bloodshed took as many as one hundred thousand civilian lives.

In July 2003, Secretary-General Annan urged the Security Council to deploy a multinational force to restore order in Liberia. The council agreed and created UNMIL (UN Mission in Liberia), authorizing a force of fifteen thousand troops for deployment on October 1. President Taylor was also under broad international pressure to resign, which he did on August 11. ECOWAS peacekeepers serving in Liberia were "rehatted" as UN peacekeepers in October. These forces came from eight West African countries. Additional personnel were soon added from other African states and from all the permanent Security Council members except Russia. Peacekeepers were deployed out of the capital of Monrovia to disparate parts of the country with their first task: disarming the warring groups. Politically, the hope was that UNMIL could help the new transitional government restore normal services and civil society.

SUMMARY

The term *peacekeeping,* like *collective security,* cannot be found in the UN Charter. Yet, during the past fifty years, peacekeeping operations have been the most visible expression of the UN's commitment to maintaining peace and security. Created as a pragmatic innovation existing legally somewhere between Chapters VI and VII of the Charter, peacekeeping has evolved from the placement of a neutral force between consenting combatant governments to a comprehensive project meant to reconstruct failed states. The Security Council and the General Assembly have authorized operations, or subcontracted missions to member states, first in the Middle East, then in Latin America, Asia, and most recently Africa, in hopes of ending violent conflicts.

By its nature, peacekeeping in the new millennium is significantly different from the missions created during the cold war. Second-generation peacekeeping challenges the fundamental principle of state sovereignty on which the United Nations was originally built. It places the new United Nations directly in the internal affairs of disintegrating nations, engaging it in the processes of peacemaking and nation building. In so doing, peacekeeping has become one of the UN's most important successes, but also its largest financial and administrative burden. It has also risked the UN's credibility, albeit for a worthy cause. It has forced the world body and its members to reconsider and expand the definition of collective security to include the defense of citizens' rights and well-being within their own nation. Consequently, it has contributed to a redefinition of the organization from solely an intergovernmental organization to, as well, a central institution in the construction of domestic societies.

NOTES

1. See A. LeRoy Bennett, *International Organization: Principles and Issues,* 4th ed. (Upper Saddle River, NJ: Prentice Hall, 1988), 94–97; United Nations, *Basic Facts About the United Nations* (New York: United Nations, 2004), 19–20; and Diana Ayton-Shenker, ed., *A Global Agenda: Issues Before the 57th General Assembly of the United Nations* (Lanham, MD: Rowman & Littlefield, 2002), 277.

2. Kofi Annan, press conference on Cyprus, February 13, 2004, http://www.hri.org/news/world/undh/2004/04-02-13.undh.html.

3. See http://www.unficyp.org/Facts+figures/facts+fig.htm.

4. Senate Committee on Foreign Relations, *Reform of the United Nations Peacekeeping Operations: A Mandate for Change* (Washington, D.C.: U.S. Government Printing Office, 1993), viii.

5. Samantha Power, *"A Problem from Hell": America and the Age of Genocide* (New York: Basic Books, 2002), 107–27.

6. Brian Frederking, "Constructing Post–Cold War Collective Security," *American Political Science Review* 97, no. 3 (2003): 374–75.

7. Ian Hurd, "Legitimacy, Power and the Symbolic Life of the Security Council," *Global Governance* 8, no. 1 (2002): 38.

8. For a full discussion of the war in Bosnia and the UN's role in its resolution, see, among other works, Jasminka Udovicki and James Ridgeway, eds., *Burn This House: The Making and Unmaking of Yugoslavia,* rev. and exp. ed. (Durham, NC: Duke University Press, 2000); Richard Holbrooke, *To End a War* (New York: Random House, 1998); and Power, *"A Problem from Hell."*

9. This discussion of events in Bosnia is drawn in large measure from two other works by the authors. See John Allphin Moore, Jr., and Jerry Pubantz, *Encyclopedia of the United Nations* (New York: Facts on File, 2002), 30–31, 114–17; and John Allphin Moore, Jr., and Jerry Pubantz, *To Create a New World? American*

Presidents and the United Nations (New York: Peter Lang, 1999), 321–24.

10. "Address to the Nation on Implementation of the Peace Agreement in Bosnia-Herzegovina," November 27, 1995, *Public Papers of the Presidents of the United States.*

11. Reuters, "Bosnia Serb Parliament Urges Karadzic to Surrender," July 20, 2004.

12. United Nations, *Report of the Independent Inquiry into the Actions of the United Nations during the 1994 Genocide in Rwanda,* UN document S/1999/1257 (New York: United Nations, December 16, 1999), 3, 21, 23, 35.

13. Ibid., 3.

14. Ibid., 23.

15. Ibid., 37.

16. The full Brahimi Report can be found at http://www.un.org/peace/reports/peace_operations/.

17. Ibid., ix.

18. UN General Assembly, *Implementation of the United Nations Millennium Declaration: Report of the Secretary-General,* UN document A/58/323 (New York: United Nations, September 2, 2003), para. 42.

19. UN News Centre, "Security Council Authorizes Full Peacekeeping Operation in Cote d'Ivoire," February 27, 2004.

20. UN News Centre, "Cote d'Ivoire: UN Peacekeeping Mission Would Cost $303 Million for 6 Months," February 26, 2004, http://www.un.org/apps/news/story.asp?NewsID=9897&Cr=ivoire&Cr1=.

21. UN General Assembly, *Implementation of the United Nations Millennium Declaration,* para. 8.

22. UN Security Council, "Security Council requests establishment of monitoring group to investigate violations of arms embargo on Somalia," press release, SC/7957, December 16, 2003, http://www.un.org/News/Press/docs/2003/sc7957.doc.htm.

23. UN Organization Mission in the Democratic Republic of the Congo (MONUC), press release, January 19, 2004, http://www.un.org/Depts/dpko/missions/monuc/.

KEY TERMS

Ralph Bunche (page 197)
Dayton Peace Accords (page 210)
Ethnic Cleansing (page 209)
Lomé Agreement (page 223)

Lusaka Agreement (page 221)
Nation Building (page 205)
Second-Generation Peacekeeping (page 203)
Status of Forces Agreement (SOFA) (page 198)

RESOURCES FOR FURTHER RESEARCH
Relevant Web Sites

An Agenda for Peace: Preventive diplomacy, peacemaking and peace-keeping (www.un.org/Docs/SG/agpeace.html)

Report of the Panel on United Nations Peace Operations (www.un.org/peace/reports/peace_operations)

UN Department of Peacekeeping Operations (www.un.org/Depts/dpko/dpko/index.asp)

UN Department of Peacekeeping Operations Best Practices Unit (www.un.org/depts/dpko/lessons/)

Books, Articles, and Documents

Boulden, Jane. *The United Nations Experience in Congo, Somalia, and Bosnia.* Westport, CT: Praeger, 2001.

Boutros-Ghali, Boutros. *Supplement to An Agenda for Peace.* New York: United Nations, 1995.

Hirsch, John L., and Robert B. Oakley. *Somalia and Operation Restore Hope.* Washington, D.C.: United States Institute of Peace Press, 1995.

UN Department of Public Information. *The Blue Helmets: A Review of United Nations Peacekeeping.* 3rd ed. New York: United Nations, 1996.

———. *UN Peacekeeping: 50 Years, 1948–1998.* New York: United Nations, 1998.

———. *The UN and Somalia: 1992–96.* Vol. 3. UN Blue Book Series. New York: United Nations, 1996.

Chapter 7

Making Global Public Policy: Promoting Civil Society, Human Rights, and Women's Empowerment

Besides maintaining international peace and security, the United Nations, by virtue of its Charter, is authorized to protect human rights. Increasingly, it has found itself creating, promoting, and enforcing public policy on various human rights topics. Only states may be UN members, yet with increasing frequency and depth of participation, private actors are taking part in UN policy-making. The UN's use of these vehicles for ensuring human rights is yet another indicator that the organization has become a *transnational* body. In this chapter, we cover how the United Nations has been responding to thematic issues, such as human rights, and in the process has become a central policymaker in the lives of people around the world.

THE EMERGENCE OF THEMATIC DIPLOMACY

The UN Charter commits the United Nations to international cooperation "in solving international problems of an economic, social, cultural, or humanitarian character, and in promoting and encouraging respect for human rights and for fundamental freedoms for all" (Article 1). At the San Francisco Conference in 1945, delegations from newly independent nations, as well as from Latin America and the United States, urged a mandate for the United Nations that would be wider than solely the immediate preservation of international peace and security through the imposition of Security Council enforcement measures. The delegations argued that only by addressing the underlying social and economic problems facing the world's populations could long-term peace be achieved. Their success in including this broader mandate became particularly meaningful as cold war deadlock between the superpowers materialized in the council. The General Assembly, with its growing membership from the developing world, increasingly found itself focusing on economic development and the human challenges in the Third World.

In the decades following 1960, a **thematic diplomacy** emerged that emphasized international cooperation to solve human problems of a global character. These problems might be of a domestic intrastate nature as much as they might be the basis for disputes between states. Often dubbed the *Other United Nations* during the cold war—because it addressed "soft," or "peripheral," issues—thematic diplomacy emerged by the close of the millennium as a central mission of the world body. The Charter also identified some thematic areas critical to world peace such as disarmament, decolonization, international law, and human rights. Furthermore, many intergovernmental organizations (IGOs) that were founded long before the United Nations was formed took as their missions the amelioration of human suffering and the betterment of living conditions. As you learned in Chapter 4, many of these IGOs were brought into the UN System as UN specialized agencies.

After the cold war ended, the United Nations expanded its role in developing global public policies by providing the framework, initiative, and resources needed to address a broad range of human issues. The election of Kofi Annan as secretary-general accelerated the process. His efforts at UN reform included a new, inclusive approach to the private sector. By the time of the UN's Millennium Summit in 2000, Annan could report the "forging of global partnerships that would hardly have been conceivable a decade ago."[1] These partnerships included ties to the business community, civil society organizations, and philanthropic foundations. Coordinated through the UN Fund for International Partnerships (UNFIP), collaborative arrangements were struck with a wide range of organizations, including the Rockefeller Foundation, the Bill and Melinda Gates Foundation, the Coca-Cola Company, Cisco Systems, United Way International, and Ericsson Corporation. Secretary-General Annan pursued a "stakeholder" strategy, attempting to engage three broad categories of nonstate participants: nongovernmental organizations (NGOs); civil society members, including private individuals and subnational organizations; and the world business community.

Together, these three components create a strong advocacy group for addressing thematic issues in the world community. They also mark an evolution in the UN's role as an intergovernmental organization. This change in organizational character has the salutary effect of bringing the United Nations into a closer working relationship with international civil society. It also generates the risk that UN leaders and agencies may misjudge the willingness of governments to dilute their monopoly on the policy process. In the end, the United Nations can involve private entities in its work only to the extent that member states—particularly those that are large and powerful—are willing to allow it.

THE AGE OF THE NONGOVERNMENTAL ORGANIZATION

The growing inclusion of nonstate actors in the work of UN bodies has contributed to the UN's augmented role in shaping thematic policy and has provided conduits beyond traditional member state agencies for implementing this policy. Article 71 of the Charter allows **nongovernmental organizations** to establish "consultative status" with the Economic and Social Council (ECOSOC). Starting in the late 1980s, NGO participation in the United Nations changed in quantity and quality. The statistics on nongovernmental organizations granted consultative status are telling: 41 in 1948; 377 in 1968; 1,200 in 1997; 2,200 in 2003; and 2,613 in June 2005. By 1990 the United Nations maintained ninety-three offices in eighteen cities around the world to accommodate NGO activities.[2] The growth in numbers and participation has led UN bodies to identify NGOs as recognized entities of emerging international "civil society." They have become

NONGOVERNMENTAL ORGANIZATION PARTICIPATION IN THE UN SYSTEM

"The United Nations system, including international finance and development agencies, and all intergovernmental organizations and forums should . . . take measures to . . . review and report on ways of enhancing existing procedures and mechanisms by which non-governmental organizations contribute to policy design, decision-making, implementation and evaluation at the individual agency level, in inter-agency discussions and in United Nations conferences."

—United Nations, "Strengthening the Role of Non-Governmental Organisations:
Partners for Sustainable Development," in *The Earth Summit 1992: Agenda 21*
(New York: United Nations, 1992), Chap. 27, para. 27.9.

"citizen organizations" within the UN System, advocating particular goals and mobilizing support for and against UN initiatives.

In 1996 ECOSOC enhanced the role NGOs could play in its work (Resolution 31), designating some as eligible to propose items for its agenda. Those granted "general" consultative status were allowed to designate representatives to sit as observers at ECOSOC meetings and to submit written statements to both the council and subsidiary bodies. As of 1997 NGOs could address the council on subjects of interest, a step that reflects the democratization of UN procedures.

The ECOSOC decision was part of an expanding acceptance of NGOs in the daily work of UN bodies, conferences, and agencies, and it accelerated their participation in other sectors of the UN System. Nearly all General Assembly committees have procedures for NGO participation, including the First Committee (Disarmament) and the Sixth Committee (Legal), which have historically been dominated by government representatives protecting the highest state interests. In the latter case, nongovernmental organizations played a critical role in the negotiations leading to the creation of the International Criminal Court (ICC). NGOs also provide participants for panels of experts; serve on agencies such as the Joint UN Programme on HIV/AIDS (UNAIDS); and develop program proposals for disease control, poverty eradication, and other social improvements in poor parts of the globe. In an unprecedented step, representatives of three NGOs—Oxfam, CARE, and Médecins Sans Frontières (Doctors Without Borders)—gave an informal briefing to the Security Council in February 1997 on the humanitarian crisis in Africa. Since then an NGO consultation group has met regularly with the Security Council president to provide advice on council matters.

All UN-sponsored world conferences since the early 1970s have incorporated companion NGO forums in an effort to generate public support for the programs launched by the conferences. At these meetings NGOs have often been allowed to present statements and to lobby delegations. Maurice Strong, secretary-general of the 1972 UN Conference on the Human Environment (UNCHE), held in Stockholm, believed NGO participation to be critical not only to the success of the conference, but also to the implementation of its initiatives. In its final report the conference called on not only states but also "citizens and communities, . . . enterprises and institutions at every level [and] . . . [g]overnments and peoples to exert common efforts for the preservation and improvement of the human environment."[3] By the close of the 1990s, the UN General Assembly routinely required the participation of NGO representatives in the "PrepComms"— preparatory committees—for UN-sponsored global meetings, and in the subsequent plenary sessions. In June 1993, for example, seven thousand participants, including the representatives of more than eight hundred NGOs gathered in Vienna for the Second World Conference on Human Rights to review and debate the status of human rights around the world.

Nongovernmental organizations bring community concerns to UN bodies, monitor global policies and international agreements, provide analysis and expertise, serve as early warning mechanisms, and generally act as interest groups within the UN System. They are critical to the local implementation of UN programs, where subnational and private organizations are best suited to provide the workforce and public support for UN efforts. Often, NGOs and UN agencies partner to undertake joint projects.

NGOs at the United Nations have established several bodies to coordinate their activities, three of which deserve special mention. First, CONGO, the Conference on Non-Governmental Organizations in Consultative Status with the Economic and Social Council, serves as a representative voice of NGOs. Its aims are to ensure that NGOs enjoy the fullest opportunities and appropriate facilities for performing their consultative functions, to provide a forum on the consultative process, and to convene meetings of member organizations to exchange views on matters of common interest. Second, the NGO community elects an executive committee to act in an advisory and liaison capacity to channel information and represent its interests in the UN's Department of Public Information (DPI). Each year the committee and the DPI stage the largest NGO conference convened by the world body. In 2002 it attracted more than 2,000 people from 760 NGOs in 70 countries. Finally, the UN Non-Governmental Liaison Service (NGLS) assists NGOs working on development issues to coordinate their efforts with UN agencies, providing, among other services, the organization of meetings between relevant private groups and UN offices.

Of the three NGO bodies, CONGO has proved the most active and contentious, advocating increased NGO access and influence in all aspects of UN operations. With major offices in New York City, Vienna, and Geneva, CONGO brings together members of the UN Secretariat, national delegations, and NGOs to serve on thematic committees in the hope of developing consensus on critical issues. The committee agendas present issues ranging from aging, the status of women, and freedom of religion to narcotics trafficking, mental health concerns, social development, and disarmament. Despite its presence in many UN settings, the organization regularly expresses consternation that NGO access to UN agencies and policymakers is too limited.

Although Article 71 links NGOs to only the Economic and Social Council, other principal UN organs and most specialized agencies have followed the pattern ECOSOC established and have created consultative status for relevant private groups. Among the agencies to have done so are the International Labour Organization (ILO), the UN Conference on Trade and Development (UNCTAD), the World Intellectual Property Organization (WIPO), the International Telecommunication Union (ITU), the World Health Organization (WHO), the Food and Agriculture Organization (FAO), and the International Maritime Organization (IMO). As in all public policy settings, NGOs associated with these bodies bargain for enhanced power and influence, criticize agency policies, publicize perceived organization failures, create alliances with like-minded interest groups and sympathetic UN officials, and lobby individual national delegations on behalf of desired policies. When NGOs are not successful in one UN setting, they often seek other avenues to influence the world community. They add complexity to international policy and UN policymaking, but they also ensure broader consensus for adopted policies than would otherwise be expected.

The first intergovernmental organization to incorporate popular participation in decision making was the International Labour Organization. This post–World War I agency grants each member state four representatives, only two of which are government delegates. The other delegation members are employer and worker representatives. Delegation members are not required to speak or vote with one national voice, but they may and do cast differing votes on issues brought before the organization. UNAIDS was the first UN "programme" to welcome NGO representatives to full membership on its coordinating board. The board includes delegates from twenty-two governments from all regions of the world, seven representatives from participating agencies, and five representatives from NGOs, which include associations of people living with AIDS. The UN Children's Fund (UNICEF), the UN High Commissioner for Refugees, the UN Population Fund, and the World Food Programme also make extensive use of NGOs. Their operational competence, flexibility, and knowledge of local conditions, as well as the complementary resources that they bring to humanitarian programs, make NGOs key operational partners and implementing agents. In April 2003, for example, the UN Development Programme (UNDP) entered into a global partnership with the WWF (formerly known as the World Wildlife Fund) to combat environmental problems such as deforestation, climate change, and desertification. With more than twenty-eight national organizations, twenty-four program offices, and a history of investing more than $1 billion in 130 nations since 1985, the WWF was in a particularly strong position to assist the UNDP, and, conversely, affect the agency's agenda and policies. In a particular partnership project, UNDP and the WWF signed an agreement with Bhutan to protect that nation's "green corridor" of forest and mountain ecosystems. The $1.8 million price tag was to be paid by the World Bank's Global Environment Facility (GEF), Bhutan, and the WWF.

In cases when IGOs have failed to follow the UN lead, they have often faced demands for "democratization" of their institutions and procedures. The most dramatic expression of these "people's demands" has come in connection with the internal decision-making processes of the World Trade Organization (WTO) and the World Bank. The Marrakesh Agreement replacing GATT with the WTO makes specific reference to NGOs. However, neither the WTO nor the World Bank has been as proactive as other parts of the UN System in co-opting nongovernmental organizations, which has produced broad criticism of these two institutions and demands for greater private participation. Anger at the closed methods the Bretton Woods institutions use has spilled over into street protests and petitions for greater inclusion.

SPECIAL RAPPORTEURS

Private individuals and NGO representatives have also been inducted into the UN decision-making process. They serve as individuals on important committees and are given access to UN officials and agencies. In fact, they are often appointed as UN **special rapporteurs.** The UN Commission on Human Rights (CHR) makes the most extensive use of special rapporteurs. In 1967 ECOSOC authorized the commission to move beyond general discussions on human rights and to deliberate on violations of rights in specific countries and in specific categories. Since then, the commission has appointed special rapporteurs to examine human rights in particular countries and to investigate common practices that threaten human rights in many parts of the world.

Usually a well-known expert in the field, the special rapporteur often visits sites, gathers information from affected individuals, and makes recommendations for action. As of May 2003, the UN Commission on Human Rights was sponsoring twenty-seven rapporteurs who were working simultaneously on different projects.[4] These rapporteurs were charged with investigating thematic issues, such as torture, violence against women, arbitrary detention, child prostitution and pornography, involuntary disappearances, the use of mercenaries, summary executions, racial discrimination, and even the "right" to food. Special rapporteurs, when asked to investigate suspected human rights abuses in particular countries, have publicized violations in Afghanistan, Sri Lanka,

Bosnia and Herzegovina, Haiti, Iran, Nigeria, Sudan, Rwanda, Somalia, Burundi, Cambodia, the former Zaire, the former Yugoslavia, Equitorial Guinea, Iraq, and Myanmar.

Often these *country mechanisms*—the lifeless term the United Nations uses to designate special rapporteurs—have also provided the most up-to-date information on human rights abuses that is available to the world community. Regularly, one rapporteur, upon his or her resignation, will be succeeded by another expert who will continue monitoring questionable activities of the government under investigation. In the case of Afghanistan, three individuals were appointed between 1984 and 2000. The special rapporteurs' periodic reports on the situation in Afghanistan provided the most important, up-to-date, and substantive information for UN organs and member states as they determined their policies toward successive Afghan governments. With a rapporteur's report in hand, ECOSOC, the Commission on Human Rights, the General Assembly, or the secretary-general—whichever body sponsored the rapporteur's work—is both in a better position and under greater public pressure to respond to identified problems.

In May 1994 the UN High Commissioner for Human Rights (UNHCHR) convened a special meeting of rapporteurs and independent experts in Vienna. These individuals summarized the benefits of their work and noted the many challenges they faced within the UN System. They called for more assistance not only from UN agencies, but also from NGOs with expertise on the topic or country that the rapporteur was investigating. The participants asserted their right to conduct their work with complete independence and noninterference or intimidation by national governments or international agencies.

Special rapporteurs' findings can be critical to the prevention of future human rights violations and threats to international security. In April 1993 the special rapporteur on summary executions warned the United Nations that genocide was imminent in Rwanda. Unfortunately, his report went unattended outside the CHR, which left the world body unprepared for the massacres that occurred a year later. Fortunately, the report of Roberto Garretón, special rapporteur on human rights in the Democratic Republic of the Congo, faired better. In January 2000 Mr. Garretón was invited to brief the Security Council as it addressed the deteriorating situation in that country. Using the **Arria formula**—a procedure by which the Security Council hears from nonstate representatives—the special rapporteur reported to the council on three occasions. Other experts, such as the special rapporteur on Burundi, also provided briefings to the council as it contemplated peacekeeping operations in troubled regions of the globe.[5]

THE GLOBAL COMPACT

In January 1999, Secretary-General Annan proposed a distinctively different partnership for the United Nations: a close working relationship with multinational and domestic businesses. As we described in Chapter 4, the secretary-general asked these corporations to join a **Global Compact** based on nine principles, later increased to ten. Companies joining the compact agree to do the following:

1. Respect human rights within their corporations and within the sphere of influence their market provides
2. Ensure that they are not complicit in human rights abuses
3. Uphold freedom of association and the right to collective bargaining
4. Promote the elimination of all forms of forced and compulsory labor
5. Work for the abolition of child labor
6. Support the elimination of discrimination with respect to employment and occupation

7. Take a precautionary approach to environmental challenges
8. Promote environmental responsibility in every way
9. Develop environmentally friendly technologies
10. Combat corruption

The program requires the chief executive officers of participating corporations to submit a letter to the executive office of the secretary-general committing the corporation to these ten principles and agreeing to post them on the premises of the enterprise. Other private organizations, ranging from chambers of commerce and labor organizations to activist environmental and human rights NGOs, are also allowed to join the Global Compact.

Companion efforts to engage the private sector in UN development initiatives have accompanied the Global Compact. For example, the World Bank and UNDP sponsor the Money Matters Institute (MMI), a forum in which private companies, international organizations, and Third World policymakers can exchange ideas on the effective use of private capital in the development process. This approach is a revolutionary shift from the UN's antipathy to corporate investment in the developing world, which was expressed forcefully in the 1960s and 1970s by General Assembly resolutions and by efforts to impose regulatory restraints on transnational corporations (TNCs).

Within his executive office Annan established a Global Compact office that began operations on July 26, 2000, with a seventeen-member advisory council. Six sponsoring organizations support the work of the new office: the UN Environment Programme (UNEP), the UN Development Programme, the International Labour Organization, the Office of the UN High Commissioner for Human Rights, UN Office on Drugs and Crime (UNODC), and the UN Industrial Development Organization (UNIDO). The last of these—UNIDO—became a core agency of the compact in May 2003. The Secretariat sought its expertise in meeting the specific needs of small and medium enterprises (SMEs). Of the approximately nine hundred companies that are members of the Global Compact, one-third are SMEs. UNIDO also maintains special programs on investment and technology, training, and business partnerships.

The Global Compact set as its overall goals the promotion of international corporate citizenship, social responsibility, and the establishment of corporate "good practices." Rejecting the regulatory approach advocated by developing states in the 1974 proposal of a New International Economic Order (NIEO), the compact employs a learning model that entices corporations to join a global consensus on methods to achieve these goals.[6] The Global Compact office stages policy dialogues that bring together corporate officers, policy specialists from the private sector, NGO leaders, and labor representatives. During its first operating years, the compact sponsored forums on the role of the private sector in zones of conflict (business leaders from thirty countries participated) and on transparency, voluntary initiatives, and revenue-sharing agreements. In October 2001 the United Nations launched the Global Compact Learning Forum, an online service for sharing experiences and discussing lessons learned in private corporate efforts. Corporations are also urged to submit case studies demonstrating how they have met the compact's ten principles. The studies are then discussed and often put into a learning bank for emulation by other enterprises. The Global Compact's most ambitious meeting came in June 2004. More than four hundred representatives gathered in New York City with Kofi Annan and members of his senior staff. It was the largest meeting of business, labor, and civil society leaders ever held at UN headquarters.[7] Specific pledges were made to implement the compact's principles in business supply chains, to defend human rights in zones of conflict, to ensure decent working conditions, to invest in clean technologies, to implement no-bribe policies, to combat diseases such as AIDS, and to create and expand small businesses in the least developed countries.

The Global Compact has not been without controversy. Given the profit motive that drives every private business, many other actors in the UN System have questioned the wisdom of a UN-corporate partnership. Many NGOs and national governments blame transnational corporations for creating the most serious development and environmental problems in the underdeveloped world. They suggest that the compact gives UN endorsement to capitalist globalization, which negates the UN's authority to speak out against labor, human rights, financial, and environmental abuses caused by corporations. The United Nations, however, cannot regulate all enterprises on a global scale, nor do member states always agree on what form such regulation should take. By including national and international labor organizations and critical NGOs such as Amnesty International, the WWF, the World Conservation Union (IUCN), and Human Rights Watch, among others, as members of the Global Compact, the United Nations has attempted to address these concerns. The Global Compact creates a transnational network of nonstate actors that both supports the expansion of private investment and challenges perceived abuses by investing companies. The hope is that, through the process of negotiation, dialogue, and consensus formation, common global policy will emerge voluntarily.

GLOBAL CIVIL SOCIETY

What you can see in Secretary-General Annan's creation of the Global Compact, the UN's use of special rapporteurs, and its extensive involvement with nongovernmental organizations are examples of the new United Nations acting transnationally, going beyond its traditional membership of nation-states to engage private entities in its work. Begun as an intergovernmental organization, the United Nations has, in truth, become a *transnational* body, with a large part of its budget and institutional structure committed to addressing policy issues in cooperation with nonstate actors. Mindful consideration of the private sector in the international arena is a recognition by the UN leadership that an emerging international civil society exists and that it will have a significant impact on the success or failure of UN initiatives. With limited resources, the United Nations has extended its reach by including private components of the international community. Among the benefits of such inclusion is one of special note: the world body has been allowed to extend its reach through **subsidiarity**—a concept of governance that places responsibility for policymaking and implementation at the lowest and most decentralized level commensurate with the ability to perform assignments effectively and efficiently. Subsidiarity allows for burden sharing between UN agencies and private entities. It encourages expansive relationships among sovereignty-free actors, civil society, regional and transregional organizations, UN specialized agencies, and principal UN organs. Such burden sharing can protect the United Nations from overload, and it attracts support for UN policies by lowering the locus of decision making to the level where the costs and benefits of decisions are most immediately experienced.

As part of international civil society, the United Nations has taken on specific functions within the world community. Thematic diplomacy, which we described at the beginning of this chapter, has opened the door for a comprehensive global policy process with the United Nations as a central actor in it. This process also includes national governments, other international organizations, world markets, NGOs, and individuals. The United Nations not only employs and interacts with these entities, but also is deeply affected by them. Nonstate actors have many centers of policymaking within the UN System that they can target in their effort to influence global policy. The General Assembly, the Security Council, the Economic and Social Council, specialized agencies, regional economic commissions, the World Bank and the WTO, UN world conferences, and development programs all provide entry points into policymaking. The result is a comprehensive international public policy process in which the United Nations serves as both arena and actor, producing with time global policy on some of the most important thematic issues of the twenty-first century. We look at several of these policy areas in this chapter as well as in Chapter 8.

HUMAN RIGHTS

The Policy Process

Tuesday, April 29, 2003: Slobodan Milosevic, former dictator of Yugoslavia, sat in Trial Chamber III. Judge Richard George May was presiding as Milosevic prepared, as he had done many times in the previous six months, to cross-examine a witness testifying against him. Milosevic stood accused of war crimes and genocide against the peoples of Croatia and Bosnia. He was being tried in the International Criminal Tribunal for the Former Yugoslavia (ICTY) in The Hague. He was the ultimate "prize," the person everyone, except for ultranationalist Serbs, wanted to see tried for the heinous Balkan barbarism of the previous decade. The session had begun at 9:03 that morning with witness C-048. The prosecutor had brought the witness to the stand to inquire about killings ordered by the Yugoslav security services, of which C-048 had knowledge. Milosevic was representing himself and contesting the right of the court to try him, firmly believing that because the actions for which he was indicted had been carried out when he was president of a sovereign state, the charges were unwarranted. Thus, he aggressively challenged all the witness's contentions. At one point the following exchange occurred:[8]

Milosevic:	All right. You're claiming that in the former Yugoslavia, in the Socialist Federal Republic of Yugoslavia, in fact, when it existed that a decision could be made at the meeting of the federal minister and of his republican ministers to kill somebody. Is that what you're claiming?
C-048:	Yes, of course.
Milosevic:	Fine. Now, who gave instructions? Who gave the order? . . . Who gave instructions in March 1990 for this killing, the killing that you're talking about? Who gave the order? You must know that, if you know that an order was given by the service as you say.
C-048:	Well, I know that the order was given by the service. . . .
Milosevic:	So who gave the order?
C-048:	[My informant] didn't mention that.
Milosevic:	Ah. He didn't mention a name. Right. . . .

The world had not seen such drama since the Nazi war crimes trials at Nuremberg in 1945. Security Council Resolution 827, in May 1993, had established The Hague tribunal to indict, try, and punish individuals responsible for a long list of war crimes that had occurred during the bloody breakup of Yugoslavia. Soon thereafter, the United Nations created an equivalent court to try human rights abuses committed during the 1994 civil war in Rwanda.

Although the Rwandan and Yugoslav tribunals emerged only in the wake of the cold war, human rights have been a concern of the United Nations since its founding. Before World War II, human rights were rarely addressed in international relations. Only a few international human rights agreements had been realized, such as the Slavery Convention of 1926 and The Hague Convention of 1907, which dealt with a government's treatment of foreign nationals. However, nothing had been said about a nation's treatment of its citizens. Under the principle of sovereignty, the relations between a government and its people were considered an internal matter.

The preamble of the UN Charter, however, raises international concern for human rights to a new level of significance. It declares that one of the organization's purposes is "to reaffirm faith in fundamental human rights, in the dignity and worth of the human person, in the equal rights of men and women and of nations large and small." The Charter contains several references to human rights (Articles 13, 55, 56, 62, 68, and 76) but does not define the term.

Authorized by the Charter, the Economic and Social Council created the **Commission on Human Rights** in 1946. At its initial session the commission established a small drafting group to prepare the **Universal Declaration of Human Rights (UDHR).** Eleanor Roosevelt, widow of U.S. president Franklin D. Roosevelt, chaired the drafting committee. On December 10, 1948, the General Assembly adopted the Universal Declaration as "a common standard of achievement." Reflecting the predominantly Western membership of the United Nations in 1948, twenty-two of the declaration's thirty articles deal with individual, civil, and political rights, and only six articles deal with economic, social, and cultural rights. The declaration stresses the "inherent dignity" of the individual; the principle of equality; and the three interrelated fundamental rights of life, liberty, and the security of the person. The declaration accepts the principle that states can limit human rights only when such laws are "solely for the purpose of securing due recognition

Eleanor Roosevelt and *The Universal Declaration of Human Rights.* (UN/DPI Photo. Reproduced by permission from the United Nations.)

and respect for the rights" of others and establishing "the just requirements of morality, public order and the general welfare in a democratic society."

The Universal Declaration set the direction for all later agreements in the field of human rights. However, it required elaborate negotiations spanning another eighteen years to produce the other two documents that, with the Universal Declaration, compose the composite **International Bill of Human Rights.** The General Assembly adopted the much more specific **International Covenant on Civil and Political Rights (ICCPR)** and the **International Covenant on Economic, Social and Cultural Rights (ICESCR)** much later, in 1966. These two covenants are written in the form of treaties, requiring ratification by the member states and consequently creating legally binding obligations. The ICCPR details the freedoms of speech, press, worship, and assembly; the security of person and property; free political participation; and procedural due process, protecting the individual against arbitrary and unreasonable government action. Each state assumes the obligation to submit regular reports to a new UN Human Rights Committee, which reviews them in detail and makes recommendations to governments for improvement and additional legislation. The ICESCR provides guarantees of "the right of everyone to the enjoyment of an adequate standard of living for himself and his family, including adequate food, clothing, and housing, and to the continuous improvement of living conditions." It also guarantees access to adequate education, social security, medical care, employment, shelter, mental health, and leisure, requiring an expansion of governmental functions. At the insistence of the developing nations, which by 1966 made up a majority of UN membership, both documents recognize the right of self-determination. By the end of the century, about two-thirds of the UN member states had ratified the covenants.

The effort to produce these agreements was arduous because of differing views among countries over what constitutes a human right. On the one hand, Western states and their citizens, drawing on a tradition of democratic politics that accentuates the primacy of the individual, place strong emphasis on civil and political rights. That is, they stress the rights of the person and view human rights as protecting the individual from actions by the state. They emphasize protection of minority groups against majority power. This viewpoint advocates the use of the judicial process to protect human rights. Such an outlook emphasizes rights such as free speech, freedom of religion, freedom of assembly, specific rights of the accused, and the right to organize. On the other hand, developing nations emphasize economic, social, and cultural rights, considering them prerequisite to the exercise of political rights. Western nations object to the inclusion of these elements, contending they are "goals" rather than "rights." In part, the Third World viewpoint is based on living conditions and the culture in these states. Theirs is a collective outlook that holds that societies, as groups, have rights and that the rights of the group as a whole supercede individual rights. This approach requires government action to provide citizens with the conditions and facilities essential for the full realization of rights. Developing nations view economic rights, particularly the right to development, as creating obligations for the international system as well, including the provision of needed resources for development. Developing nations have emphasized the primacy of rights such as adequate food, tolerable living standards, and requisite shelter. The developed world has resisted elevating economic rights to a position of primacy because it views doing so as an effort to redistribute wealth to its disadvantage.

Despite the difference in outlook by member states, the United Nations has negotiated and adopted a long list of conventions and declarations that have sought to extend and clarify the meaning of *human rights.* The Commission on Human Rights drafted some, other bodies drafted some, and several resulted from UN conferences or came from specialized agencies. Among the principal documents on the long list are the conventions on the Prevention and Punishment of the

Crime of Genocide (1948), the Elimination of All Forms of Racial Discrimination (1965), the Suppression and Punishment of the Crime of Apartheid (1973), the Political Rights of Women (1952), the Elimination of All Forms of Discrimination against Women (1979), the Suppression of the Traffic in Persons and of the Exploitation of the Prostitution of Others (1949), the Status of Refugees (1951), the Status of Stateless Persons (1954), Torture and Other Cruel, Inhuman or Degrading Treatment or Punishment (1984), the Rights of the Child (1989), and the Protection of the Rights of All Migrant Workers and Members of Their Families (1990). Declarations have dealt with the Eradication of Hunger and Malnutrition (1974), the Protection of Women and Children in Emergency and Armed Conflict (1974), the Rights of Disabled Persons (1975), the Right to Development (1986), and the Rights of Persons Belonging to National or Ethnic, Religious and Linguistic Minorities (1992). Additional protocols have been added to several of the existing covenants. Many agencies and organizations within the UN System have also negotiated agreements relating to human rights. The International Labour Organization has formulated several treaties regarding the rights of labor, including the right to organize. Other agencies that have drafted and approved agreements include the UN Children's Fund, the UN Commission on the Status of Women (CSW), and the UN High Commissioner for Refugees (UNHCR). All set standards and require reporting by governments. Together these agreements and conventions constitute a body of growing international law on human rights.

LANDMARKS IN THE DEVELOPMENT OF HUMAN RIGHTS INTERNATIONAL LAW

International Bill of Human Rights

The Universal Declaration of Human Rights	December 10, 1948
International Covenant on Civil and Political Rights	December 16, 1966
International Covenant on Economic, Social and Cultural Rights	December 16, 1966

Important UN Human Rights Instruments

Convention on the Prevention and Punishment of the Crime of Genocide	December 9, 1948
Convention on the Political Rights of Women	December 20, 1952
International Convention on the Elimination of All Forms of Racial Discrimination	December 21, 1965
Convention on the Elimination of All Forms of Discrimination against Women	December 18, 1979
Convention against Torture and Other Cruel, Inhuman or Degrading Treatment or Punishment	December 10, 1984
Declaration on the Right to Development	December 4, 1986
Convention on the Rights of the Child	November 20, 1989
International Criminal Tribunal for the Former Yugoslavia	May 25, 1993
Vienna Declaration on Human Rights	June 25, 1993
UN High Commissioner for Human Rights	December 20, 1993
International Criminal Tribunal for Rwanda	November 8, 1994
Rome Statute of the International Criminal Court	July 17, 1998
International Criminal Court	July 1, 2002

The UN institutional structure within which these agreements and the international human rights regime have been negotiated consists of the Commission on Human Rights and the Human Rights Committee mentioned previously, as well as five other committees established to monitor the implementation of the more important conventions. They are the Committee against Torture; the Committee on the Elimination of Racial Discrimination; the Economic, Social and Cultural Rights Committee; the Committee on the Elimination of Discrimination against Women; and the Committee on the Rights of the Child. The Commission on Human Rights, however, holds the greatest authority. Although the Universal Declaration may be its most important accomplishment, the CHR has a long record of proposing new conventions, declarations, and conferences attending to specific human rights issues or to the rights of specific vulnerable groups. Each year it passes more than eighty resolutions on these matters.

The CHR has steadily increased in size, growing from eighteen members in 1946 to fifty-three states at the turn of the century. Its membership and activities have not been without controversy, particularly because some members that have been elected have had questionable human rights records. The chorus of criticism led to Secretary-General Annan's proposal that the commission be replaced by a smaller but more respected human rights council, its members elected at large by two-thirds vote of the member states in the General Assembly.

The CHR members are elected by ECOSOC and are chosen in part on the basis of geographic distribution. The United States, having provided the first chairperson of the commission in Eleanor Roosevelt, has held membership on the body continuously except for 2001–2003, joining Russia and India as the longest-serving members. During 2001–2003, irritated by U.S. foreign policy and Bush administration criticisms of the United Nations, a coalition of states prevented the United States from holding the seat available for the Western European and Other States bloc. The United States, however, was elected again to the CHR in 2003.

The CHR has created working groups on arbitrary detention, forced disappearances, a draft optional clause to the Convention against Torture, indigenous peoples, and "Human Rights Situations." This last group decides whether to refer a particular human rights abuse or concern to the full commission. Most important, the CHR has established the Sub-Commission on the Promotion and Protection of Human Rights. The subcommission is composed of twenty-six experts who act in their personal capacity and meet annually in Geneva. They undertake studies on discrimination and individual freedoms and make recommendations to the full commission on steps it should take to strengthen human rights protections. The subcommission is an important access point in the policy process for NGOs, other intergovernmental organizations, and national representatives.

The membership of the five treaty committees varies from ten to twenty-four individuals, who are selected by the states that are parties to the specific convention. Often the state membership that makes up a committee is criticized because it includes nations that are regularly cited for human rights violations. However, in most cases the individuals who serve are nationals selected for their expertise, commitment to human rights, and high moral standing. Moreover, their activity and voting on the committee are not governed by state policy because they serve as individuals, not as government representatives.

The committees solicit "country reports" from governments that have signed the relevant convention. They then review these reports and often hear individual and NGO complaints about national human rights violations. Committees can request special reports or appoint country rapporteurs when specific human rights issues come to light. On rare occasions the committee may make an official visit to a country that has given its permission. More regularly, individual committee members travel to states to observe a human rights situation at the request of a nongovernmental organization.

In 1967 ECOSOC authorized the Commission on Human Rights to move beyond general discussion and to consider human rights violations in individual countries. It was allowed to entertain specific complaints by individuals against their own government. Although no enforcement is possible, both the commission and the General Assembly pass resolutions condemning the worst abuses on a country-specific basis each year. In 1979–1980 the commission expanded its efforts by establishing special procedures to enable investigations, which led to the appointment of special rapporteurs to investigate and compile reports for the commission. This procedure ensures discussion of the specific abuses and often leads to resolutions criticizing the offending state. The commission's approach has been replicated by most of the human rights monitoring bodies.

The critical stages in the human rights review process are the committee's "dialogue" with government representatives of the state under review and the issuance of its public report. Since the committees cannot impose formal penalties, their strongest weapon is public visibility and subsequent international pressure to change the country's policies. In the dialogue-report process, the committee becomes the nexus for national governments, NGOs, the committee's secretariat, and UN agencies in the development of human rights norms. The state under review is given time to present its human rights record in a positive light, to challenge past criticisms by other actors, and to answer committee members' questions. While government delegations may attempt to avoid answering embarrassing questions, states will often submit follow-up written responses. In the preparation of their final reports, committees consult other UN bodies and specialized agencies. Regular participants in this process that generally have a significant impact on the final outcome of committee decision making are the ILO, UNDP, WHO, FAO, UNICEF, UNAIDS, UN High Commissioner for Refugees, and UN Educational, Scientific and Cultural Organization (UNESCO).

UN human rights bodies are assisted by a large number of nongovernmental organizations that serve as advocates of human rights and work to protect these rights. At times the NGOs intervene to protect individuals who are denied their rights. These NGOs monitor the situation in each of the world's nations and submit informative reports to the various monitoring bodies. While functioning separately, they therefore are indirectly a part of the global monitoring system for human rights. The issue of human rights is an area of concern for one of the largest blocs of nongovernmental organizations. Among the most influential in the UN policy process are Amnesty International and Human Rights Watch. Nearly all UN human rights committees actively solicit NGO participation. Materials submitted by nongovernmental organizations are regularly distributed to committee members. Each committee, depending on its specific rules of procedure, allows NGOs to address the plenary session, working groups, or informal sessions of the body. Private representatives also lobby members between sessions and throughout the year. In many ways these private international interest groups set the general human rights agenda for the world community to address through UN structures.[9]

In 1993 the United Nations convened the World Conference on Human Rights, known as the **Vienna Conference.** Its charge was to conduct a global review of human rights and UN efforts in this area. The Vienna Declaration and Program of Action, adopted by the participants, who represented 171 nations, highlighted the links among development, democracy, and the promotion of human rights, bridging the differing interpretations of the West and the developing nations. It emphasized the universality, indivisibility, and interdependence of civil, cultural, economic, political, and social rights, declaring all to be the responsibility of governments and requiring governments to promote all human rights and fundamental freedoms. The declaration reaffirmed the right to development as a universal, inalienable, integral, and fundamental part of human rights. The signatories of the Vienna Declaration agreed that the development of the poorest nations was the collective responsibility of the international community. The final document asserted that extreme poverty and social exclusion constituted a "violation of human dignity." The declaration emphasized the rights of all vulnerable groups, especially women, and extended this protection to indigenous peoples.

The Vienna Declaration also recommended the creation of the position of **UN High Commissioner for Human Rights (UNHCHR),** a new office to advocate human rights and to coordinate UN programs, agencies, and offices involved in this field. The creation of a central office for UN human rights efforts had become a necessity by 1993. With a plethora of institutions and a vibrant NGO community involved in the policy process, as well with a new realization that human rights protection was a critical aspect of maintaining international peace in a world of growing ethnic and religious separatism, the General Assembly acceded to the conference proposal. The High Commissioner serves as the focal point for all UN human rights activities and acts as the secretariat for all treaty bodies monitoring compliance with human rights covenants and agreements. The Centre for Human Rights is part of the Office of the High Commissioner. Located in Geneva, the centre conducts studies and provides recommendations, information, and analysis to all UN organs dealing with human rights issues. The UNHCHR carries out its mission by promoting international agreements that set standards and then urges member states to report on their progress. The United Nations supplies information and assists nations in meeting human rights standards through technical missions and by developing model codes and programs. The Office of the High Commissioner sponsors training programs for police, legal, and military personnel; establishes field offices in conflict zones; and directs necessary world attention to particularly egregious cases of human rights violations. UN secretaries-general have given high visibility to the post, encouraging and receiving direct reports from the high commissioner. Particularly with the appointment in 1997 of Mary Robinson, the former president of Ireland, who traveled widely to conflict areas and made public indictments of rights violators, the UNHCHR became an independent voice in the policy arena. This trend continued under Robinson's successor, Sergio Vieira de Mello, whom Secretary-General Annan also appointed his special representative to postwar Iraq in 2003.

The Judicial Process

During the past seventy years, society has witnessed a growing acceptance of the idea that individuals may be held criminally responsible for what had previously been considered acts of state. Since the days of royal absolutism and the acceptance of state sovereignty in the seventeenth century, public leaders could cite their role as political figures and have little fear that they would face legal prosecution for their acts. However, after World War II, the Allies successfully tried the German and Japanese leadership for war crimes. The tribunals at Nuremberg and Tokyo included a new charge: "crimes against humanity." For the first time, the international community asserted that an individual leader could be tried in an international court for crimes committed against the domestic population. At Nuremberg, the four victorious powers—the United States, the United Kingdom, France, and the Soviet Union—served as judges. The highest leaders under indictment received the death penalty from both tribunals. Each court cooperated with the UN War Crimes Commission, but the trials were military rather than UN trials.

In the course of developing human rights treaties, the United Nations adopted the Nuremberg Tribunal Charter. This charter defined *crimes against humanity* as crimes of "murder, extermination, enslavement, deportation, and other inhumane acts committed against any civilian population, before or during a war . . . whether or not in violation of the domestic law of the country where perpetrated." In so doing, the United Nations established an inherent tension between its commitment not "to intervene in matters which are essentially within the domestic jurisdiction of any state or [to] require the Members to submit such matters" for settlement (Article 2, paragraph 7) and the promotion of human rights and fundamental freedoms, which was also part of the UN's mission listed in its Charter (Articles 1, 13, and 55).

As we noted previously in this chapter and in Chapter 4, in the 1990s the United Nations established judicial bodies to deal with this type of crime: the International Criminal Tribunal for the Former Yugoslavia, in The Hague, and the International Criminal Tribunal for Rwanda (ICTR), with headquarters in Arusha, Tanzania. Each had jurisdiction involving only the specified country, and, in the Rwandan case, for Rwandan citizens who may have committed war crimes in neighboring states. The creation of these tribunals was an expression of the wide-reaching horror at the genocide practiced in both crises. The relative success of the two tribunals encouraged authorities in Sierra Leone to request a similar UN court for persons charged with crimes in that country's ongoing civil war and with violations of international humanitarian law against UN personnel in the country. After negotiations between the government and the UN Secretariat, the Special Court for Sierra Leone was established in the fall of 2000. These three tribunals responded to particular atrocities occurring in specific civil conflicts. However, their ad hoc nature left many governments with the conclusion that the long-term response to human rights crimes should be a permanent court to which suspected violators could be remanded for trial. Although an old idea, it was given a new impetus by the encouragement of U.S. president Bill Clinton. In 1998 a conference of one hundred countries approved the Rome Statute of the **International Criminal Court,** establishing a permanent body to investigate and decide cases involving individuals responsible for the most serious crimes of concern to the international community. The Rome Statute extended the court's jurisdiction to genocide, war crimes, and crimes against humanity, and it provided definitions for these crimes. The statute however, did not authorize the court to hear cases involving alleged terrorism.

Article 1 of the ICTY statute states, "The International Tribunal shall have the power to prosecute persons responsible for serious violations of international humanitarian law committed in the territory of the former Yugoslavia since 1991" until the UN Security Council decides to withdraw its mandate. The crimes it was specifically empowered to prosecute were grave breaches of the 1949 Geneva Convention, violations of the laws and customs of war, genocide, and crimes against humanity. The ICTY could also prosecute persons already under accusation in a national court if the accused was charged only with an "ordinary" offense (i.e., not a war crime) or if the national trial had not been impartial.

The Security Council, upon recommendation of the secretary-general, selected the judges and the lead prosecutor for the tribunal. The council was careful to include broad multinational representation among the judges and prosecutors. The International Criminal Tribunal for the Former Yugoslavia could not try defendants in absentia, but a Rule 61 proceeding allowed the prosecutor to present evidence publicly and to call witnesses. The stated purpose for this allowance was to reconfirm the indictment against the defendant and to permit the judges to issue an international arrest warrant. Thus, the tribunal could publicly air the charges against the individual being sought, and increased pressure was placed on alleged war criminals, who subsequently would not be able to travel out of the country without fear of detention by a UN member.

Although the indictment, arrest, and trial of Slobodan Milosevic may have marked the high point of the tribunal's activities, during its first decade 88 accused persons appeared before the court. The ICTY issued its first indictment on November 11, 1994, for Dragan Nikolic, a Bosnian

Serb who was alleged to have been the commander of a small prison camp in eastern Bosnia. The first conviction was Dusko Tadic, who was convicted of every count established by the statute except genocide. Other notable indictments included Bosnian Serb leaders Radovan Karadzic and General Ratko Mladic. As of June 2005, the tribunal had publicly indicted 162 individuals and conducted sixty-five trials; 37 persons had been convicted. Of those found guilty, Radislav Krstic (chief of staff of Bosnian Serb forces that attacked civilians and UN personnel in the safe haven of Srebrenica) received the most severe sentence. The ICTY sentenced him to forty-six years' imprisonment for genocide, crimes against humanity, and violations of the laws of war.

The ICTY relied on other institutions, most notably the North Atlantic Treaty Organization (NATO), to apprehend and extradite indicted individuals. It could give a maximum punishment of life in prison. Once sentenced, defendants would serve their terms in nations that volunteered prison space and were approved by the tribunal. Of the first ten individuals convicted by the tribunal and sentenced to serve active sentences, all were placed in European prison systems.

The UN Security Council created the International Criminal Tribunal for Rwanda on November 8, 1994 (Resolution 955). Article 1 of its statute authorized the court "to prosecute persons responsible for serious violations of international humanitarian law committed in the territory of Rwanda and Rwandan citizens responsible for such violations committed in the territory of neighbouring States between 1 January 1994 and 31 December 1994." As such, the ICTR had a limited time jurisdiction, but its mandate extended beyond the borders of Rwanda to incorporate crimes against Rwandans in refugee camps in the Republic of the Congo and in Burundi. The crimes it was empowered to prosecute were much the same as those before the Yugoslav tribunal, as were its structure and procedures. The two tribunals shared the judges of the appeals chamber as well as the lead prosecutor—the Swiss jurist Carla Del Ponte—through the summer of 2003, when the Security Council decided to appoint a separate prosecutor for the Rwandan court.

The ICTR issued its first indictments, charging eight persons, on November 28, 1995. The tribunal also charged Jean-Paul Akayesu, a high government official, with inciting other persons to commit rape—the first time in history this offense was recognized as a "war crime." Former Rwandan prime minister Jean Kambanda was tried and convicted in September 1998. The first head of government to be convicted for such crimes, Kambanda was sentenced to life imprisonment. The convictions of Akayesu and Kambanda were the first ever rendered by an international court for genocide. Despite these convictions, many nongovernmental organizations—among them the Lawyers Committee for Human Rights (now called *Human Rights First*), Human Rights Watch, War Criminal Watch, Africa South of the Sahara, and the International Commission of Jurists— criticized the court for the slow pace of the trials and its apparent leniency toward many individuals who were charged.

By July 2004 the tribunal had secured the arrest of sixty-seven individuals accused of involvement in the 1994 Rwandan massacre. These people included the former Rwandan ministers of defense, interior, and finance, as well as the chief of staff of the army and the president of the national assembly. Private citizens were not immune from charges; religious leaders, businesspeople, and students were also detained. Mali was the first country to provide prison facilities for the enforcement of the tribunal's sentences. Benin, Swaziland, Belgium, Denmark, and Norway also indicated their willingness to incarcerate convicted persons. The ICTR was authorized to give a maximum punishment of life in prison, but no death penalty.

The apparent success of the tribunals for Yugoslavia and Rwanda strengthened the case for a permanent criminal court and led to the consideration of additional ad hoc panels in countries where conflict had produced human rights abuses. By 2000 **judicial diplomacy** had emerged as a reasonable way for the world community to punish political leaders who violated their citizens' rights and to dissuade others with the sure expectation of criminal responsibility. Sierra Leone provided such a venue. Wracked by civil war from 1991 onward despite two fragile peace agreements between the central government and the Revolutionary United Front (RUF), Sierra Leonean president Alhaji Ahmad Tejan Kabbah asked the international community to establish a tribunal to try suspected war criminals. After considering a letter Kabbah sent to Secretary-General Annan in June 2000, the Security Council directed Annan to negotiate the terms of a court for this purpose. An agreement was reached in January 2002.

Unlike the international tribunals in The Hague and Arusha, the Special Court for Sierra Leone was not a subsidiary organ of the United Nations, but rather a treaty-based court of mixed composition and jurisdiction—both national and international. Created by agreement between the United Nations and the national government, this court was charged with prosecuting "persons who bear the greatest responsibility for serious violations of international humanitarian law and Sierra Leonean law committed in the territory of Sierra Leone since 30 November 1996." The court's jurisdiction extended to the following:[10]

> The most egregious practices of mass killing, extrajudicial executions, widespread mutilation, in particular amputation of hands, arms, legs, lips, . . . sexual slavery, abduction of thousands of children and adults, . . . forced recruitment into armed groups, looting and setting fire to large urban dwellings and villages.

During its first years of operation, the court indicted several prominent politicians, including Brima "Bazzy" Kamara, the commander of the military junta that seized power in 1997. Kamara was charged with terrorizing civilians, attacking UN personnel, and sexual violence. However, the June 2003 indictment of Liberian president Charles Taylor for his support of the RUF demonstrated the limits of using judicial process to end conflicts and discourage human rights abuses. At the time of his indictment and the issuance of an international arrest warrant, President Taylor was in Ghana, participating in delicate peace negotiations to end the violence then under way in Liberia. Instead of arresting Taylor, Ghanaian and UN officials let him leave the country. The court's chief prosecutor expressed outrage. Kofi Annan's spokesman indicated that the secretary-general supported the work of the court but also attached "great importance to the peace process" in Liberia, and implied that Taylor was not arrested because of the political need to keep Taylor engaged with that process. Peace diplomacy trumped human rights proceedings, which demonstrated the fine distinctions that so often must be made in pursuing the desired, complex, but not always complementary goals of the international community.[11]

While the Yugoslav, Rwandan, and Sierra Leonean courts were distinct responses to specific crises, a milestone in human rights policy was reached on July 17, 1998, with the adoption of the Rome Statute, which established the permanent International Criminal Court. The ICC began operations in the summer of 2002 and was charged with investigating and bringing to justice individuals, not countries, who commit the most serious crimes of concern to the international community, such as aggression, genocide, war crimes, and crimes against humanity—including widespread murder of civilians, torture, and mass rape. Unlike the International Court of Justice, the ICC supercedes the usual limitations of sovereignty by having persons, not states, before it and by bringing cases against involuntary parties. Its jurisdiction complements national legal systems by taking cases that states refuse or are unwilling to undertake against their own nationals. Cases may be referred to the ICC by the Security Council under Chapter VII of the Charter, by one of the parties to the Rome

Statute, or by the chief prosecutor with the approval of three judges. The court has no restrictions in terms of geography or time, which remedies a weakness in the existing tribunals.

As early as October 1946, participants in international legal meetings discussed the possibility of a permanent war crimes tribunal to sustain the momentum created at Nuremberg and Tokyo. In 1948 the International Law Commission of the United Nations began discussions for the creation of a criminal court, and this sentiment was given greater momentum with the signing of the Geneva Conventions on December 9, 1948. The issue remained on the commission's agenda throughout the cold war.

One hundred sixty countries participated in the UN Diplomatic Conference of Plenipotentiaries on the Establishment of an International Criminal Court (June 15–July 17, 1998), along with 124 NGOs, 17 intergovernmental organizations, and 14 UN specialized agencies and funds. By April 2002 the sixty ratifications necessary to bring the court into existence had been achieved. However, creation of the court did not occur without controversy. In particular, the United States objected to the court's jurisdiction, fearing U.S. military personnel and peacekeepers could be subject to unwarranted charges and hauled before the international forum. The United States not only declared that it would ratify the statute only if its jurisdiction were limited to cases referred to it by the UN Security Council, but also brought considerable pressure to bear on governments specifically to exempt U.S. personnel. The statute, as opened for signature in 1998, had no such provisions and claimed universal jurisdiction on the basis of international law. U.S. president Bill Clinton signed the Rome Statute but noted the need for amendments to it. Clinton's successor, President George W. Bush, withdrew the statute from Senate consideration for ratification until Washington's concerns were met. Within the Security Council, the United States pressed for and achieved yearly exemptions from the court's jurisdiction over UN peacekeepers. It was successful because of support from Russia and China, each of whom had not ratified the Rome Statute as of 2004. In the summer of that year, however, the United States dropped its effort to renew its exemption, when, faced with the scandal of U.S. abuse of prisoners in occupied Iraq and the strong objection of Secretary-General Annan, other council members made clear they would accept no language that gave special treatment to U.S. military personnel.

Although the United Nations shepherded the creation of the court, the ICC is not a subordinate agency. It is an independent international organization with a diplomatic agreement on the modalities of its relationship with the United Nations. Its eighteen judges are elected to nine-year terms by the Assembly of the Statute's state parties; no two judges come from the same country. The assembly also elects the chief prosecutor. The judges elect the president of the court. The ICC has pretrial, trial, and appeals divisions. The court may impose fines, forced compensation to victims, or imprisonment. It may not impose the death penalty. During its first year in operation, the ICC received more than two hundred complaints seeking court action.

The International Criminal Court breaks new ground in international law. Not only does it limit claims of state sovereignty and make persons, not states, the subjects of international legal standing, but for the first time in history it allows the direct participation of alleged victims. Victims may make written submissions to the court, participate at every stage of the criminal proceedings, be represented by counsel of their own choosing before the court, and seek compensation for the human rights abuses they have suffered. For the first time in history, an international court has the authority to order an individual to compensate another individual. It may do so to provide restitution, indemnification, or rehabilitation. Ordered compensation is paid through the Victims Trust Fund established in the Rome Statute. The fund can be augmented further by contributions from nation-states, private individuals, and other international organizations.

WOMEN'S RIGHTS

Securing Group Rights through Public Mobilization

In the Western philosophical tradition, human rights have been considered primarily individual rights. They arise from the "self-evident" condition of equality. The persistence of inequality, however, means that identifiable groups of human beings are often mistreated, exist in a condition of second-class citizenship, or are unable to share in the full benefits of society as others do. Certainly, the largest "minority" to experience unequal treatment in nearly all societies is women, who, in fact, make up a majority of the human population. In 1945 the UN Charter became the first international document in history to acknowledge the role of women in the world and to accentuate gender equality as a fundamental human right. One of the UN's first acts was to create the Commission on the Status of Women (CSW) in 1946 as the first functional commission of ECOSOC. Many of the UN's strategies, first employed on behalf of women, have also been used to improve the lives of children, the elderly, indigenous peoples, and ethnic minorities. In so doing, the United Nations has elevated "group" rights to comparable status with individual human rights.

The lengthy history of efforts on behalf of human rights and the successes of these UN initiatives, have necessarily generated global policy affecting particular groups within the universal human family. The promotion of legal standards through binding conventions and treaties, the judicial defense of personal rights against human rights abuses, and the growing endorsement of personal sovereignty as a limitation on state sovereignty in international civil society have provided a rationale for group rights. In the UN endeavor to secure these rights, however, the organization has not stressed primarily legalist and judicial policymaking strategies. This fact is particularly true with regard to the creation of international gender policy that has been directed toward enhancing women's rights and power. The United Nations has employed three additional strategies that have generally eclipsed the "judicial diplomacy" used in the defense of individual rights: mobilization of public opinion through world conferences and public forums; enhancement of research on women, with the goal of permanent empowerment; and provision of assistance for women in areas traditionally underfunded or ignored by national governments, such as health, child rearing, education, development, and environmental safety. These strategies cumulatively constitute a "campaign" on behalf of women, organized and promoted by the United Nations. In addition to providing legitimacy and an institutional arena in the global effort to achieve gender equality, the United Nations is cheerleader, interest group, and fund-raiser, with a particular set of goals—some of them controversial—that it has pursued with member states, nongovernmental organizations, and other IGOs.

To be sure, the United Nations has created several legal instruments intended to enhance the status of women. These documents address a number of issues, including prostitution (Convention for the Suppression of the Traffic in Persons and of the Exploitation of the Prostitution of Others, 1949), equal pay for men and women for work of equal value (International Labour Organization Convention Concerning Equal Remuneration for Men and Women Workers for Work of Equal Value, 1951), the ability to vote and hold public office (Convention on the Political Rights of Women, 1952), marital rights (Convention on Consent to Marriage, Minimum Age for Marriage and Registration of Marriages, 1962), the right to equal education (UNESCO Convention against Discrimination in Education, 1960), and the end to gender discrimination (UN Convention on the Elimination of All Forms of Discrimination against Women, or CEDAW, 1979). Most recently, the United Nations, at the urging of the Commission on the Status of Women, has taken up the cause of ending violence against women, including pernicious practices such as the honor killings and trafficking of women regularly found in the Middle East and Asia. These efforts have grown out of the UN Declaration on the Elimination of Violence against Women adopted in 1993.

The campaign on behalf of women's rights, however, has been far more a media and public opinion effort than an exercise in international law formation. Beginning with the UN Decade for Women (1976–1985), which encouraged governments, nongovernmental organizations, and UN units to focus on women's conditions in various parts of the world, the United Nations has directed media attention toward women's issues. It has also hosted four major world conferences on women (Mexico City, 1975; Copenhagen, 1980; Nairobi, 1985; and Beijing, 1995) and a follow-up General Assembly special session (Beijing +5, 2000) to outline the challenges to gender equality and the actions needed to remove these barriers. These conferences served to mobilize other actors both internationally and domestically and to raise awareness about the conditions of women and girls around the world. Other UN conferences, such as the 1993 World Conference on Human Rights and the 1995 World Social Summit in Copenhagen, emphasized the critical needs and roles of women in their societies.

CHRONOLOGY OF UN EFFORTS ON BEHALF OF WOMEN

June 26, 1945	UN Charter signed in San Francisco
June 21, 1946	Commission on the Status of Women created
Dec. 20, 1952	Convention on the Political Rights of Women adopted
Nov. 7, 1967	UN Declaration on the Elimination of Discrimination against Women
June 19–July 2, 1975	First World Conference on Women (Mexico City)
Dec. 18, 1979	Convention on the Elimination of All Forms of Discrimination against Women (CEDAW) adopted
Summer 1980	Second World Conference on Women (Copenhagen)
Apr. 6, 1982	CEDAW Committee created
Aug. 11, 1983	International Research and Training Institute for the Advancement of Women (INSTRAW) opens
Dec. 14, 1984	UN Development Fund for Women (UNIFEM) created
July 15–27, 1985	Third World Conference on Women (Nairobi)
Apr. 20, 1987	Nafis Sadik becomes the first woman to head a major UN program—UN Population Fund
Dec. 21, 1990	Secretariat sets 1995 targets for the employment of women: 25 percent in senior posts
Feb. 7, 1992	Margaret Joan Anstee becomes first woman to head a peacekeeping mission and to be appointed a special representative of the secretary-general (to Angola)
Dec. 20, 1993	UN Declaration on the Elimination of Violence against Women
July 12, 1995	Rosalyn Higgins is elected the first woman judge to the International Court of Justice
Sept. 4–17, 1995	Fourth World Conference on Women (Beijing)
Mar. 2, 1998	Louise Fréchette becomes the first deputy secretary-general
June 5–19, 2000	Beijing +5 special session convenes in New York
Apr. 26, 2002	Secretary-general appoints M. Patricia Durrant the first ombudsman

Delegations from 133 governments took part in the first world conference on women held in Mexico City in 1975. Organized by the CSW, the conference debated and then adopted a World Plan of Action for addressing the issues of equality, development, and peace. The momentum of this meeting led to the creation of the Voluntary Fund for development projects related to women, later known as the *UN Development Fund for Women (UNIFEM)*. Also, a special UN research agency known as *INSTRAW (International Research and Training Institute for the Advancement of Women)* was established. We describe these agencies' work later in this chapter. In Copenhagen four years later, 145 governments participated and nearly eight thousand individuals attended a concurrent NGO forum. A redefined Plan of Action was adopted that drew attention to problems of employment, health, and education.

The first two conferences highlighted a normal characteristic of policymaking: debate over priorities and methods for achieving accepted goals. In Mexico City and Copenhagen, differences emerged between countries of the North and those of the South; the developing world suggested that the important issues for women were those imposed by the economic and political neocolonialism of the developed states. Representatives from developed states emphasized challenges to women in the workplace and the political arena.[12] This debate carried over to the third world conference, held in Nairobi, Kenya, in 1985. There, attention was once again given to themes of equality, peace, and development. The final document of the conference, known as the **Nairobi Forward-Looking Strategies for the Advancement of Women,** called for new recognition that women and children are often the groups most harmed by poverty, drought, armed conflict, family violence, and marginalization caused by refugee, migrant, or ethnic minority status. Strategies were devised to accelerate fulfillment of women's rights issues during the last fifteen years of the twentieth century. According to the United Nations, in the last ten years of the century, approximately 120 governments reported progress in meeting the targets established at Nairobi.

In 1995 a fourth World Conference on Women was held, in Beijing. Representatives of 189 governments attended the meeting, and a new five-year global action plan affirming the themes of equality, peace, and development was adopted. The **Beijing Declaration** and **Platform for Action (PFA)** identified twelve critical areas of concern for women's advancement and empowerment: poverty, education and training, health, violence, armed conflict, economy, decision making, institutional mechanisms, human rights, media, environment, and the girl child. Five years after the Beijing conference, a special session held in June 2000, known as *Beijing +5,* gave government representatives and NGOs an opportunity to assess progress on the platform.

At Beijing a new rift in the world community's approach to gender issues became evident. Conservative religious forces, particularly right-to-life NGOs, the Vatican, Islamic delegations, and nations with sizable Roman Catholic populations, opposed any language in the final conference statement that might imply endorsement of abortion or that might disrupt traditional national custom and law concerning the role of women in society. Using compromise language, the Beijing Platform for Action affirmed "the right of men and women to be informed and to have access to safe, effective, affordable and acceptable methods of family planning of their choice, as well as other methods of their choice for the regulation of fertility *which are not against the law.*"

The clash between secularists and traditionalists had first caught the public's attention at the UN's International Conference on Population and Development (ICPD) in Cairo in September 1994. Attended by 179 government participants and 4,200 representatives of 1,500 NGOs, the Cairo meeting was the fifth global conference on population, but the first to end in strong ethical controversy. It endorsed the rights of all people to reproductive freedom, and it encouraged policies that would slow population growth, including the empowerment of women, expanded educational opportunities, gender equality, and poverty reduction. This stance was a significant shift from the usual conference goals of setting targets for demographic growth and reflected the persuasive influence of moderate women's NGOs arrayed between conservative forces represented by Catholic and Islamic groups on one side and radical feminist groups at the other end of the spectrum.[13] With regard to abortion and family planning, all the conference could do was endorse ambiguous compromise language. It urged governments "to deal with the health impact of unsafe abortion as a major public health concern and to reduce the recourse to abortion through expanded and improved family planning services." It also declared that "in no case should abortion be promoted as a method of family planning."

In addition to the Beijing women's conference and the Cairo meeting on population, the World Summit on Social Development (WSSD; March 1995) emphasized the importance of women in the development process and the need to create equity between men and women in all aspects of social life. Despite differences between developed and developing states, and between religious and secular forces, the UN sessions that convened in the mid-1990s created the agenda for progress on women's issues. Women's NGOs played the critical role of "framing" these issues for subsequent UN action. As a result the General Assembly was able to set benchmarks for measuring progress through 2015. It recommended, among other goals, that the 1990 illiteracy rate for women and girls be halved by 2005, that the primary school enrollment ratio for all children be increased to 90 percent by 2010, and that 100 percent of all family planning facilities offer comprehensive services by 2015.

Research on Women

The United Nations collects statistics on women. Few countries keep separate records on women or attempt any statistical analysis of women's lives and work. Since the late 1970s, the UN Statistical Office, INSTRAW, and the ILO have created methodologies appropriate for studying women. Two key studies, *The World's Women 1970–1990* and *The World's Women 1995,* provide data on and analysis of women's experiences around the globe. These studies highlight the effects of long-term inequalities and encourage governments as well as the United Nations to take action to prevent them. In the 1990s, UN advocacy for women fostered training programs and development projects all aimed at raising awareness and improving women's lives.

The Economic and Social Council created the International Research and Training Institute for the Advancement of Women in 1976 as the primary agency for data collection and dissemination of information on women. INSTRAW is an autonomous institute within the UN System framework, joining the Division for the Advancement of Women (DAW) and the UN Development Fund for Women (UNIFEM) as one of the three UN entities committed solely to promoting the advancement of women. In 1983 INSTRAW accepted the Dominican Republic's offer of facilities for its permanent headquarters, which situated it within the developing world, the arena of most of its efforts.

A board of ten directors selected on the basis of equitable geographic distribution governs the institute. Nominated by ECOSOC member states and appointed by the council to three-year terms, the directors are individuals with international reputations and expertise in gender-equity issues. The board meets annually to review the work of the staff, headed by a director appointed by the UN secretary-general. It also approves the institute's program, activities, and budget. The institute's training, research, and information-dissemination programs are funded completely by voluntary contributions from governments, nongovernmental organizations, and private contributors. However, INSTRAW has had significant difficulty raising sufficient resources to finance its programs. In September 2003 it had income of little more than $1 million, including a grant of $250,000 by the General Assembly.[14] A year later the assembly had to subsidize the institute with $500,000 from the UN's regular budget. INSTRAW was under strong pressure to revise its operations, increase fund-raising, and live within its limited budget.

The General Assembly had earlier approved a new working method for INSTRAW that allowed it to make maximum use of information technology systems. Its Gender Awareness Information and Networking System (GAINS) served as a "virtual workshop," producing and distributing information about women. GAINS also provided a mechanism for interactive research and training projects. INSTRAW directed much of its effort at not only the opportunities that globalization raises for women, but also the threats it can pose. Besides addressing other research agenda aims, INSTRAW undertook a study of the increasing role the Internet plays in the migration of women as "e-mail order brides" worldwide, as well as research on the role of gender in the cycles of conflict the world has witnessed since the end of the cold war. INSTRAW also sponsored conferences on critical issues involving women and gender equity.

The Division for the Advancement of Women has existed within the UN Secretariat in one form or another since 1946. In 1995 it served as the substantive secretariat for the world conference in Beijing, and since then it has prepared analytical studies on the priority areas identified in the Beijing Declaration. Its Gender Analysis Section organizes panels of experts and workshops on emerging women's issues. The division encourages a gender perspective in the intergovernmental organizations with which it works, and it collaborates with nongovernmental organizations on ways to reach the goals set at both Beijing and Nairobi.

Assistance to Women

The United Nations provides assistance to women in areas such as health, education, family planning, investment, combating gender violence, and the environment. Many of these initiatives are implemented through the UN specialized agencies. Prominently, the UN Children's Fund, the World Food Programme, and the World Health Organization have provided assistance to women and girls in most countries of the world. In the case of WHO, the organization has made a special effort to focus international attention on the effects of AIDS on women and girls.

Since the Beijing conference, the central agency for UN assistance programs has been the UN Development Fund for Women. As mentioned previously, UNIFEM is an outgrowth of the 1976 Voluntary Fund established after the Mexico City world conference. In 1985 this fund officially became a separate agency in autonomous association with the UN Development Programme. The primary source for UNIFEM's income is voluntary contributions from UN member states—more than twenty million dollars in 2003. Unlike INSTRAW, the organization has had little problem raising funds. Member states with consistently high donations to UNIFEM include The Netherlands, Norway, Italy, the United Kingdom, and the United States. However, additional funding comes from UNIFEM's national committees, other international women's organizations, foundations, corporations, and private citizens. In recent years Ford, Cisco, MacArthur, Conrad Hilton, and Noel Foundations have made significant contributions. UNIFEM, in conjunction with UNDP, gives direct financial and technical support to development projects for women mostly in developing countries.

According to the General Assembly resolution creating UNIFEM, the organization has three purposes:

1. To support innovative development projects benefiting women
2. To serve as a catalyst for encouraging the inclusion of women in decision-making processes associated with mainstream development activities
3. To serve as a liaison for women in the UN's overall system of development cooperation

Despite being an arm of an intergovernmental organization, UNIFEM has developed close working relationships with activist NGOs, particularly in Africa and Latin America, to achieve these goals. One of its core strategies in the new millennium is forging "new partnerships among women's organizations, governments, the UN System and the private sector."[15] The organization first made use of NGOs as implementing agencies for its projects in the 1980s, a practice UNDP and other UN development bodies soon followed. In 2001 it maintained an NGO committee of thirty-nine organizations in "consultative status" with the organization. Many of these nongovernmental organizations pressed an agenda that UN member states often found problematic.

UNIFEM supports many projects promoting the political, social, and economic empowerment of women within developing regions of the world. These projects range from small grassroots enterprises that improve working conditions for women to widespread public education campaigns about AIDS and preventing violence against women. Since 1978 UNIFEM has funded projects in more than one hundred developing countries with an average cost of $130,000 per project. In the mid-1990s UNIFEM adopted a tripartite strategy aimed at strengthening women's economic capacity as entrepreneurs and producers, enhancing their role in governance and leadership within their societies, and advocating for women's human rights. Its program mirrored the broader public policy debate under way in the United Nations. Its engagement with NGOs in its programs also reflected UN involvement with international civil society in the policy process.

SUMMARY

The United Nations was founded as an intergovernmental organization of sovereign member states primarily dedicated to keeping the peace through collective security measures. Its Charter, however, authorizes it to protect human rights and to better the lives of people around the world. During the past sixty years, the effort to respond to thematic issues relevant to individuals' lives has led the United Nations into a central policymaking role separate from the immediate causes of peace and war, and into a complex relationship with nonstate actors of all types. As such, the United Nations has become a key player on the international, national, and subnational levels of the public policy process. In this chapter we discussed how the United Nations has been central to the judicial and legal definition and enforcement of the world's conception of human rights and how it has mobilized public opinion on behalf of an international women's agenda. In Chapter 8 we look at international economic development and global environmental policy, respectively, and explain that the United Nations also serves as a conduit for particular states' objectives for the international community and as the initiator of public policy processes that go beyond the institution itself to involve other multilateral forums.

NOTES

1. UN General Assembly, *Report of the Secretary-General on the Work of the Organization,* UN document A/55/1 (New York: United Nations, 2000).

2. Chadwick Alger, "The Emerging Roles of NGOs in the UN System: From Article 71 to a People's Millennium Assembly," *Global Governance* 8, no. 1 (2002): 103.

3. UN Environment Programme, *Declaration of the United Nations Conference on the Human Environment* (Geneva, Switzerland: UN Environment Programme, June 16, 1972), preamble, para. 7.

4. For the most current list of special rapporteurs and independent experts, see the Web site for the UN Office of the High Commissioner for Human Rights (UNHCHR):http://www.ohchr.org/english/bodies/chr/special/themes.htm. Also see http://www.ohchr.org/english/bodies/chr/special/countries.htm.

5. UN Economic and Social Council, *Report of the United Nations High Commissioner for Human*

Rights and Follow-Up to the World Conference on Human Rights: Effective Functioning of Human Rights Mechanisms, UN document E/CN.4/2002/14 (New York: United Nations, September 11, 2001).

6. John Gerard Ruggie, "global _ governance.net: The Global Compact as Learning Network," *Global Governance* 7, no. 4 (2001): 371–78.

7. United Nations, "Global Compact Summit concludes with emphasis on need to fight corruption," press release, ECO/70, June 24, 2004, http://www.un.org/News/Press/docs/2004/eco70.doc.htm.

8. The exchange can be found at http://mitglied.lycos.de/desarea/Apr292003.html, the Web site for the trial of Slobodan Milosevic at the International Criminal Tribunal for the Former Yugoslavia.

9. NGOs have been particularly persuasive in establishing the UN agenda on women's human rights issues. See Jutta Joachim, "Framing Issues and Seizing Opportunities: The UN, NGOs, and Women's Rights," *International Studies Quarterly* no. 47 (2003): 247–74.

10. UN Security Council, *Report of the Secretary-General on the Establishment of a Special Court for Sierra Leone,* UN Document S/2000/915 (New York: United Nations, October 4, 2000), 1.

11. Michael P. Scharf, "The Special Court for Sierra Leone," *International Peacekeeping* (July–December 2000): 156–58.

12. Joachim, "Framing Issues," 256.

13. Ibid., 247, 268.

14. UN General Assembly, *Report of the Secretary-General on the Financial Situation of the International Research and Training Institute for the Advancement of Women,* UN document A/58/426 (New York: United Nations, October 10, 2003), 4.

15. UN Development Fund for Women, *UNIFEM Annual Report 2001* (New York: UN Development Fund for Women, 2002).

KEY TERMS

Arria Formula (page 232)

Beijing Declaration (page 248)

Commission on Human Rights (page 236)

Global Compact (page 232)

International Bill of Human Rights (page 237)

International Covenant on Civil and Political Rights (ICCPR) (page 237)

International Covenant on Economic, Social and

Cultural Rights (ICESCR) (page 237)

International Criminal Court (page 242)

Judicial Diplomacy (page 243)

Nairobi Forward-Looking Strategies for the Advancement of Women (page 248)

Nongovernmental Organizations (page 228)

Platform for Action (PFA) (page 248)

Special Rapporteurs (page 231)

Subsidiarity (page 234)

Thematic Diplomacy (page 228)

UN High Commissioner for Human Rights (UNHCHR) (page 241)

Universal Declaration of Human Rights (UDHR) (page 236)

Vienna Conference (page 240)

RESOURCES FOR FURTHER RESEARCH
Relevant Web Sites

Commission on Human Rights (www.unhchr.ch/html/menu2/2/chr.htm)

International Criminal Court (www.icc-cpi.int)

Office of the UN High Commissioner for Human Rights (www.ohchr.org/english/)

UN Development Fund for Women (www.unifem.org)

UN International Research and Training Institute for the Advancement of Women (www.uninstraw.org/en/index.html)

WomenWatch (www.un.org/womenwatch)

Books, Articles, and Documents

Forsythe, David P. *Human Rights in International Relations*. New York: Cambridge University Press, 2000.

Glendon, Mary Ann. *A World Made New: Eleanor Roosevelt and the Universal Declaration of Human Rights*. New York: Random House, 2001.

Järvinen, Taina. *Human Rights and Post-Conflict Transitional Justice in East Timor: UPI Working Papers 47 (2004)*. Helsinki, Finland: Finnish Institute of International Affairs, 2004.

Jones, John R. W. D. *The Practice of the International Criminal Tribunals for the Former Yugoslavia and Rwanda*. Irvington, NY: Transnational, 1999.

Korey, William. *NGOs and the Universal Declaration of Human Rights: "A Curious Grapevine."* New York: St. Martin's Press, 1998.

Moore, John Allphin, Jr., and Jerry Pubantz. *Encyclopedia of the United Nations*. New York: Facts on File, 2002.

Pietilla, Hilkka, and Jeanne Vickers. *Making Women Matter: The Role of the United Nations*. London: Zed Books, 1996.

Weiss, Thomas G., and Leon Gordenker, eds. *NGOs, the UN and Global Governance*. Boulder, CO: Lynne Rienner, 1996.

Zoelle, Diana. *Globalizing Concern for Women's Human Rights*. New York: St. Martin's Press, 2000.

Chapter 8

Economic Development, the Environment, and Health Policy

Besides making and promoting policy on human rights and women's issues, the United Nations has been actively engaged in creating development policy, examining and addressing economic, environmental, and health issues affecting the world. In this chapter, we discuss mainly economic development in the poorer nations of the world, but also global environmental politics, the battle with HIV/AIDS, and the concepts of *sustainable development* and *sustainable* human *development.*

BACKDROP TO ECONOMIC DEVELOPMENT POLICY

As we noted in the last chapter, the first article of the UN Charter called on the United Nations to address "international problems" of an economic and social character. The UN's founders recognized that challenges to international peace and security could come in forms other than solely military threats. The Charter committed its members to provide "higher standards of living, full employment, and conditions of economic and social progress and development . . . [and] solutions of international economic, social, health, and related problems" as *preconditions* to continuing global "stability and well-being"(Article 55). The following article, Article 56, made a general pledge on behalf of the UN's members to "take joint and separate action" to achieve these ends.

The "idea" of improving people's social and economic lives as a route to international peace was not new when delegates gathered in San Francisco in 1945. It had already been embodied in the initiation of functional international organizations in the nineteenth century to address humanitarian and social needs. Also, Woodrow Wilson's famous 1918 speech laying out "Fourteen Points" to guide the reconstruction of the world in the wake of the Great War implicitly acknowledged that all nations should advance the living standards and human circumstances of their populations. This element of emerging international discourse was embodied in the Covenant of the League of Nations and manifested by the League in its creation of such agencies as the International Labour Organization.

Much of the postwar planning in the 1940s for a new international order following the defeat of the Axis powers included what political scientists would call the "articulation" of economic, social, and human rights interests as critical components of the proposed United Nations.[1] Parallel organizational efforts were being made to aggregate these interests and to develop institutional and policy responses to these perceived needs. Among such efforts were the convening of the Bretton Woods Conference, which led to the creation of the World Bank as a source of financing for development, and the 1943 meeting in Hot Springs, Virginia, that created the Food and Agriculture Organization to meet the overwhelming humanitarian food needs of the time, to enhance living conditions in the world's rural areas, and to elevate agricultural productivity.

The commitment to social and economic development by the authors of the UN Charter was as real as their effort to make peace, self-determination, and human rights central tenets of the new world organization.[2] In 1945, however, long-term amelioration of living conditions was not considered a priority item for UN action; the world looked to the new body to deal with more immediate threats of conflict. Nonetheless, spurred by the initiatives of important member states—particularly the United States—and faced with the abysmal poverty of millions of people in immediate postwar Europe (and for the years following in Africa, Asia, and Latin America), economic development and global social policy became central tasks of the world organization. By the 1960s the UN's newly independent members from the underdeveloped world used their voting majority in the General Assembly to encourage even greater efforts in these areas. The twin pressures of the East-West confrontation during the cold war and North-South tensions then and since served as the primary motivating forces inspiring UN development policies and institutions. Poorer states used the United Nations as their public relations platform to criticize aid policies instituted by the superpowers and other industrialized nations. With a working majority, they were able to launch UN initiatives and expand the parameters of the global development debate. In the give-and-take between donor and recipient nations, major UN development agencies were created, policy terminology and direction were set, and the world economic development agenda was established. Today myriad UN specialized agencies, "programmes," and "funds" are headquartered in New York City, Geneva, Nairobi, and many cities in the underdeveloped world, providing a comprehensive global system of economic and social development aid for the world's poor.

In the spring of 1949, U.S. president Harry Truman delivered his State of the Union Address to the U.S. Congress, and in it he made a direct appeal for funds to improve the lives and economies of peoples in the impoverished nations of Africa, Asia, and Latin America. Called the **Point Four Program,** Truman's plan proposed that the resources be administered through the United Nations.[3] The president rationalized his proposal to Congress by avowing that it would blunt the growing threat of worldwide Communism; however, it also reflected the U.S. commitment to bolster the process of self-determination then under way in the collapsing colonial empires. Congress provided the funds by June, and within a year the UN Economic and Social Council, with new prospective funding, was able to establish the Expanded Program of Technical Assistance (EPTA). Financed by voluntary contributions—60 percent of its twenty-million-dollar budget coming from the United States—EPTA was the largest UN program at the time.

Truman's immediate successors in the White House, Dwight Eisenhower and John Kennedy, also urged greater economic development efforts in the "Third World" under UN auspices. The motive for their encouragement turned to the U.S. desire to diminish Soviet influence in developing countries. President Eisenhower also couched U.S. proposals for expanded aid in the context of the nuclear arms race. In what came to be known as his *Chance for Peace* speech, delivered to a group of newspaper editors in April 1953, Eisenhower called on Soviet leaders to accept a broad reduction in armaments on both sides. He argued that the resources saved from reduced military budgets of the superpowers by an agreed arms-control regime could then be put to the task of meeting the human needs of people in the poorest parts of the world. With a passion that would seem uncharacteristic of later presidents, Eisenhower made his point: "Every gun that is made, every warship launched, every rocket fired signifies in the final sense, a theft from those who hunger and are not fed, those who are cold and are not clothed."[4] While the president saw the value to a U.S. foreign policy of providing bilateral aid directly from Washington to less affluent states, he regularly promoted UN administration of disarmament savings on behalf of the "700 million people . . . who have won full independence since World War II."[5]

The American call for greater economic assistance to the developing world and the creation of the EPTA met with enthusiasm among the postcolonial member states of the United Nations. However, the EPTA focused mostly on providing technical assistance and experts rather than on shifting capital from the industrialized states to poor countries.[6] To encourage the latter, the General Assembly established the Special UN Fund for Economic Development (SUNFED) in 1957. Marking the first confrontation in what would become the **North-South debate,** the developing states of the Third World, located mostly in the Southern Hemisphere, hoped SUNFED would attract $250 million in contributions from the wealthier states of the Northern Hemisphere. Many governments demanded that the industrialized states give as much as 1 percent of their gross national product to the fund, citing the need to build roads, schools, hospitals, electrical power plants, and other essential infrastructure for further economic development.

The financial response by rich nations was tepid. Several European countries contributed a few million dollars, and the United States agreed to match two-thirds of the total amount collected, but SUNFED never achieved its funding goals. In part, this failure was due to the continuing East-West competition between the United States and the Soviet Union. Each was suspicious of UN development projects and investments that might be intended to curry favor by its opponent. Such suspicion was particularly the case once Nikita Khrushchev took over the undisputed reins of Soviet leadership in 1956. He reversed Stalin's policy of Soviet noninvolvement in Third World politics, agreeing to provide significant bilateral aid to "nonaligned" nations in Asia, the Middle East, and Africa. Aid programs to India and Egypt in particular were seen in the West as attempts to spread the Communist influence. In the early 1960s the United States, under President John Kennedy, countered the Soviet initiative with expanded aid programs—military and economic—of its own. Kennedy suggested that the struggle between the "free" world and Communism would be won or lost largely through foreign aid to impoverished places in Africa, Latin America, and Asia.

Superpower foreign aid competition poured funds into the developing world, but these resources did not fully address the conditions or meet the recipient states' desired needs. Tied to specific terms of trade, and largely given to advance U.S. or Soviet foreign policy goals, the aid was often spent inefficiently with little long-term stimulus to economic improvement. Developing countries preferred that assistance come through the United Nations, where their growing numbers would ensure multilateral coordination and little direct influence from donor nations in the administration of the aid.

Once the deadlock on UN membership expansion was broken in 1955, Third World states were quickly admitted to the organization, and by the early 1960s they had become a majority in the General Assembly. With the focus of UN activity shifting from the Security Council—because of continuing confrontation between the United States and the USSR—to the assembly, these new members used the forum to highlight North-South differences over economic development. They criticized aid and trade policies controlled by the prosperous nations of the North and urged a new global economic system in which "fair" trade and the redistribution of global wealth to the developing world would be hallmarks. In essence, the South was demanding an overhaul of the Bretton Woods system.

Beginning in 1961 the General Assembly established four consecutive **Development Decades** to bring attention to the plight of poor countries. These decades gave visibility to UN efforts to assist the least developed countries (LDCs) and to inspire increased foreign assistance. Central to the message of the Development Decades was the perennial demand that the developed world transfer a larger percentage of its GDP to the Third World. Particularly during the Second and Third Decades (1971–1990), the General Assembly made a concerted effort to promote the agenda of the confrontational New International Economic Order (NIEO), which we describe later in this chapter.

In the Third Development Decade, the United Nations adopted the Substantial New Programme of Action (SNPA) for least developed countries and the New Industrial Development Strategy. These programs marked a shift in Third World tactics by encouraging LDCs to move toward economic liberalization, to end corruption, and to provide greater transparency and consistency in economic policies. The confrontation with the richer North having produced little improvement in their economic fortunes, poor nations sought global assistance to bring their economies into the process of globalization and to end pernicious debt owed to world financial institutions and donor states.

UN CONFERENCE ON TRADE AND DEVELOPMENT

During the First Development Decade, the UN majority initiated two structural innovations that dominated development policy for the rest of the century: the convocation of the **UN Conference on Trade and Development (UNCTAD)** and the creation of the UN Development Programme (UNDP). The initiative for a conference on trade and development first came from the **Non-Aligned Movement (NAM),** a group of states self-characterized as neutral in the East-West conflict. NAM originated with a conference of Asian and African nations in Bandung, Indonesia, in 1955. Later, partly in response to NAM's urging, the UN Economic and Social Council voted to convene a world conference. UNCTAD met in Geneva from March 23 to June 16, 1964. It would meet regularly every four years after that in a different city of the world—the next three convening in cities of the global South: New Delhi, India; Santiago, Chile; and Nairobi, Kenya.[7]

The first UNCTAD meeting was expected to be only a conference, but at that meeting delegates recommended making it a permanent organization within the UN System, with Raúl Prebisch of Argentina as its first secretary-general. The General Assembly followed suit and established UNCTAD as one of its subsidiary organs, with headquarters in Geneva.

With a universal membership, UNCTAD is an intergovernmental organization (IGO) committed to ameliorating the economic problems of underdevelopment in the global South by negotiating with the industrialized nations of the North, particularly on trade issues. It expends an annual budget of fifty million dollars and another twenty-five million dollars in technical assistance funds helping governments to understand and deal with foreign direct investment; the connections among foreign investment, trade, technology, and development; and problems related to economic globalization. UNCTAD assists needy countries in attracting investors by means of reliable and transparent financial information at the corporate level. It has also undertaken extensive responsibilities for the implementation of the UN's sustainable development program in the Third World.

UNCTAD's relatively nonpolitical character in the new millennium represents a shift in image and policy since the confrontational era of the 1960s and 1970s. Raúl Prebisch, in contrast to other heads of UN organs, was an activist on behalf of the developing nations of the South. The major initiatives undertaken during his tenure included the creation of commodity agreements and the establishment of a General System of Preferences (GSP) to open the markets of developed states to goods from developing countries. *Commodity agreements* are arrangements among producing nations, sometimes including consuming nations, to cooperate in marketing raw materials. The objective of these agreements is to stabilize prices. An alternative approach is for the producing nations to establish marketing quotas that limit the amount of a given product in world trade, which would thus prevent prices from falling below the cost of production. Prebisch's UNCTAD secretariat also promoted establishment of the Common Fund, which would support price stabilization.

Prebisch had broad support among the LDCs participating in UNCTAD. Most important, a Third World caucus known as the **Group of 77 (G-77)** coalesced around Prebisch's leadership and put together a set of consensus demands. During the next thirty-five years, the G-77 grew to 133 nations, finding in their cohesion the voting strength to dominate UNCTAD's agenda. Success in passing resolutions, however, does not automatically translate into new policy in an intergovernmental organization. In this case it would require convincing the sovereign donor states and stakeholders in the Bretton Woods system to alter policy. The G-77 regularly found that it could not overcome the opposition of the United States and other capitalist member states to policies they saw as restrictive of a free market world economy.

One of the most controversial proposals the G-77 and UNCTAD put forward was known as the **New International Economic Order,** a plan to radically reform and even replace large components of the world trade system put in place at the close of World War II, and to require the world's industrialized states and multinational corporations to conform their aid and investment policies to UN-approved guidelines. The Group of 77 proposed the NIEO as a way to redress global trade imbalances, which it perceived as unfair to the developing states. The plan was based on Prebisch's **theory of "dependency,"** which asserted that the industrialized nations had manipulated the rules to keep less fortunate nations permanently impoverished and "dependent" on developed nations for goods and support.

The NIEO was approved at a 1974 special session of the General Assembly. The NIEO called for a radical reform of the world trade system with a new set of rules, including more favorable terms of trade for primary commodities, the transfer of technology to developing countries, a charter establishing the economic rights and duties of states in the international system, more-liberal aid policies, and a code of conduct for multinational corporations. The overall goal of the NIEO was a global redistribution of wealth, believed by its advocates to be the only hope for LDCs to escape poverty.

The New International Economic Order found little support in developed countries. It was criticized as an inappropriate regulation of international free trade, likely to limit, not encourage, foreign direct investment. Despite special sessions of the General Assembly convened in 1975, 1980, and 1986 to deal with development issues, and despite recurring calls for the implementation of NIEO at UNCTAD gatherings, wealthy nations made few concessions beyond granting preferences for imports from specific LDCs.

By the 1980s the NIEO agenda was politically dead, superceded by a new concern for the growing debt levels maintained by developing states. In May 2003 UNCTAD became co-owner with the World Bank of the Debt Management and Financial Analysis System (DMFAS), which gave it the ability to work with sixty-one low- and middle-income states on lowering and managing their debt levels. These states accounted for 40 percent of the world's outstanding publicly owned long-term debt. The NIEO's recommendations were also becoming irrelevant as a result of the rapid expansion of free markets as the cold war came to an end.

The collapse in commodity prices worldwide early in the 1980s likewise limited the effectiveness of NIEO-endorsed commodity agreements. Increasingly, governments in LDCs sought foreign investment and debt reduction or forgiveness, jettisoning the more radical NIEO proposals. However, they still demanded tariff exemptions, protection for newly created domestic industries, development assistance, export diversification, and guaranteed access to the markets of industrialized countries. That is, the G-77 became more practical, diplomatic, and pragmatic in its proposed solutions to the problems of development.

Although the success of neoliberal free market policies undermined the initial thrust of UNCTAD, the relative decline of developing countries' economies during the 1990s revived interest in the role of the organization. In 1996, at UNCTAD IX, held in Midrand, South Africa, the organization adopted a number of reforms to its structure and procedures and committed itself to helping less fortunate nations deal with the challenges presented by globalization. Issues of particular importance to UNCTAD included the plight of least developed, landlocked, and island countries; development and poverty alleviation in Africa; empowerment of women; and economic cooperation among developing nations. It also encouraged the growing trend by transnational corporations to transfer their regional and global headquarters to developing countries.

The acceptance of globalization as a fait accompli did not prevent UNCTAD from being critical of the World Bank and donor states for neglecting the continuing "unfair" aspects of world trade. At the Midrand meeting many delegations noted the inequities imposed by globalization in the developing world and the many states that had not benefited from the liberalization of trade. In particular the World Trade Organization was criticized for ignoring the development concerns of LDCs and other poor nations. Delegates urged greater inclusion of the developing world in the decision-making processes of international financial organizations.[8] UNCTAD also criticized the International Monetary Fund (IMF) and the World Bank for changing their structural adjustment requirements on conditional lending to poor countries, by giving new emphasis to domestic poverty reduction strategies in those states.[9] True to its ideological origins, UNCTAD called on financial institutions to correct inequities in the world trading system, newly exacerbated by global economic liberalization.

UN DEVELOPMENT PROGRAMME

The General Assembly replaced the Special UN Fund for Economic Development and the Expanded Program of Technical Assistance with a new organization—the **UN Development Programme**—in 1965. Like UNCTAD, UNDP is an outcome of the First Development Decade and a subsidiary organ of the General Assembly. Headquartered in New York City, it serves as the lead agency for all UN development efforts. It maintains a network of national and regional offices in more than 170 countries and territories. About 90 percent of UNDP's resources—derived primarily from voluntary contributions and amounting to the largest item in the UN budget—go to about 65 nations with nearly 90 percent of the world's poorest people. More than 80 percent of all UNDP staff are assigned to local offices in developing countries. The offices work closely with the national governments and civil societies of these countries and often function as the local contact and coordination office for the entire UN System. UNDP prepares publications, among them the annual *Human Development Report*. This report is a compilation of statistics based on comparative country data that provides information on specific countries as well as on world and regional trends.

Following the 1992 Earth Summit (the **UN Conference on Environment and Development**), UNDP took on expanded responsibilities for implementing many of the new UN initiatives directed at sustainable development. The conference's Agenda 21 called for UNDP to join with the UN Environment Programme, the World Bank, UNCTAD, the Global Environment

Facility (GEF), the International Development Association (IDA), and regional development banks to carry out more than one thousand specific recommendations. In fulfilling its new tasks, UNDP has come to play a coordination role among these UN agencies, and particularly between recipient nations and the Bretton Woods financial institutions. It distributes most of the technical assistance resources provided by the UN System.

With its new responsibilities, UNDP expanded its mission statement in the early 1990s to encompass humanitarian assistance and social development. UNDP has become increasingly active in diverse fields—from establishing solar power energy supply systems and natural disaster management to supporting elections in transitional states. To attain the larger goal of sustainable *human* development, UNDP has focused on poverty eradication, democratic governance projects, information and communications technology, energy and the environment, and crisis

UN DEVELOPMENT PROGRAMME AT A GLANCE

Origin	Created in 1965 by General Assembly Resolution 2029; subsumed the Expanded Program on Technical Assistance and the Special UN Fund for Economic Development
Headquarters	New York City
Administrator	Mark Malloch Brown (April 15, 2003: elected to a second four-year term); member of secretary-general's Senior Management Group
Governing Body	Executive board of thirty-six members; also governs the UN Population Fund (eight African states, seven Asian states, five Latin American and Caribbean states, twelve Western and Other States)
Voluntary Contributions (2003)	$770 million
Thematic Trust Funds	Crisis Prevention and Recovery Democratic Governance Energy & Environment HIV/AIDS
Offices	In 166 nations
Oversees	UN Development Fund for Women UN Capital Development Fund Special Unit/Technical Cooperation Among Developing Countries (SU/TCDC) UN Volunteers
Implementation Responsibilities	Global Environment Facility Agenda 21 Sustainable Development Global Programme to Combat HIV/AIDS
Publications	*Human Development Report* (annual)

prevention and recovery. To move the development process forward as expeditiously as possible, UNDP has sponsored a "roundtable process" that brings together governments that receive assistance with the donor community in order to address the priority items on the agency's agenda. In its efforts to eliminate duplication in UN work, UNDP manages a number of associated funded projects, including the UN Development Fund for Women (UNIFEM).

In all its work, UNDP has given special emphasis to full equality between men and women and to enhancing the power of women in their countries. It joined with UNIFEM and UNCTAD in July 2003 to create a special UN task force on "gender and trade," hoping to "sensitize" policymakers to issues of international trade that affect women's lives and their roles in the development process.[10] The task force found that increased trade and investment in the labor-intensive sectors of developing countries expand employment opportunities for women. It also warned that economic liberalization, particularly of a country's service sector, worsens inequities in women's access to basic resources and services. It called for global attention to the needs of women in the workplace and to the creation of employment conditions that ensure gender equality.[11]

UNDP is also responsible for the UN Volunteers (UNV); the UN Capital Development Fund (UNCDF), which provides credit for the poor in LDCs and encourages sustainable uses of natural resources; the UN Fund for Science and Technology for Development (UNFSDT); the UN Revolving Fund for Natural Resources (UNRFNRE); and the UN Sudano-Sahelian Office (UNSO), which spearheads efforts to reverse the spread of desertification and drought. UNDP has formed partnerships with other UN programs and specialized agencies to address specific issues such as HIV/AIDS and environmental degradation. It has placed the fight against HIV/AIDS at the center of its work with governments in the developing world, serving as one of the implementing agencies of the Global Programme to Combat HIV/AIDS.

THE RIGHT TO DEVELOPMENT AND THE LEAST DEVELOPED COUNTRIES

The creation of UNCTAD and UNDP were significant victories for states residing mostly in the Southern Hemisphere, but these organizations did not produce immediate or meaningful changes in the development policies of donor states. Developed nations often criticized UN development efforts to the extent that they were bound up with the proposals of the New International Economic Order, violated free trade principles, or seemed to be politicized by the overlapping confrontation between the capitalist West and the socialist bloc. In the view of major Western nations, any moral claim to resources from the industrialized North by the postcolonial world was specious. Economic development could best be achieved by full participation in the world trade system and the creation of free market economies at home. Some Western European states also expressed concern that unfettered industrial development in the Third World could do irreversible damage to the environment.

In December 1986 the General Assembly declared development to be[12]

> an inalienable human right by virtue of which each person and all peoples are entitled to participate in, contribute to and enjoy economic, social, cultural and political development in which all human rights and fundamental freedoms can be fully realized.

Several world conferences subsequently reaffirmed the principle in their final documents. Among them, the most important were the Rio Declaration (Principle 3) of the 1992 Earth Summit, the 1993 Vienna Declaration and Programme of Action at the World Conference on Human Rights, and the Declaration of the Third UN Conference on the Least Developed Countries in 2001.

Declared principles require policy initiatives to make them meaningful. After four years of deliberation, the General Assembly, in June 1997, adopted the Agenda for Development. The idea for an agenda emerged in 1992 in response to Secretary-General Boutros Boutros-Ghali's elaboration of *An Agenda for Peace.* At that time, many nations in the global South worried that the international community was downgrading development concerns in favor of concentrating on the traditional issues of peace and security. Poorer nations believed in a continued need to assert the UN's primacy in the area of economic progress for less privileged peoples. Fearing that UN agencies had become marginalized by the Bretton Woods institutions, they saw the core thrust of the agenda as reaffirming the importance of development and resituating the world organization's central role in that process. The agenda addressed the familiar components of development—such as economic growth, trade, finance, science and technology, poverty eradication, employment, and human resource development—but also placed new emphasis on the role of democracy, human rights, popular participation, good governance, and the empowerment of women.

Between 1980 and 2001 the United Nations convened three world conferences on the plight of least developed countries, acknowledging at each meeting that the many international efforts to lift impoverished countries out of the depths of privation had largely failed. Conference declarations noted that poor countries were marginalized in the world economy; in fact, in many cases these countries' per capita incomes were decreasing, even in absolute terms. The growing international debt crisis of the 1980s aggravated their plight. Each conference called for new types of aid and for economic reforms in LDCs that would make these states more competitive in world trade and more efficient at home.

The first UN Conference on Least Developed Countries (UNLDC-I) occurred in Paris in 1981. The conference adopted the "Substantial New Programme of Action" noted previously which emphasized the decentralization of LDCs' economies, political democratization, and financial transparency. When UNLDC-II convened nine years later in Paris, little evidence indicated that SNPA had halted the slide into extreme poverty. LDCs had declined in all areas of per capita measurement. They had also taken on huge debt burdens that eliminated resources for investment and discouraged foreign direct investment. The 150 governments attending the second world conference approved the Paris Declaration. It established as its basic principle "shared responsibility and strengthened partnership" between LDCs and all other groups—developed states, NGOs, other developing states, international financial institutions, and the private sector. The conference charged UNCTAD with the implementation of the conference's recommendations and called on the World Bank and UNDP to monitor and encourage country-level efforts.

Although economic conditions did not improve noticeably in the least developed states during the 1990s (only one LDC—Botswana—"graduated" from the official list of forty-nine nations in this category), signs could be seen that the UN's attention had generated new international and domestic initiatives to solve their problems. Lending states evinced a new interest in debt relief, as evidenced by the World Bank's and IMF's creation of the Heavily Indebted Poor Country (HIPC) Initiative in 1996. Faced with the reality that many poor countries spend several times more funds on servicing accumulated international debt than on the problems facing their people, the initiative sought to achieve "debt sustainability" in these states and overall poverty reduction. A nation that is declared an "HIPC" and is willing to implement economic reform programs aimed at reducing poverty receives special assistance and debt relief from the world community. HIPC efforts have been reinforced by additional funding and concessions from the major economic powers, known as the *G-8.*[13] Assistance was given to more than two dozen states, with long-term commitments of more than thirty-five billion dollars.[14] In April 2002 the International Monetary Fund added another two billion dollars to HIPC resources.[15] In June

2005 the G-8 reached agreement on a forty-billion-dollar write-off of debt owed by eighteen of the world's poorest countries and owed mostly to the International Monetary Fund, the World Bank, and the African Development Bank.

In addition to the World Bank Group institutions, the four UN regional development banks have contributed financial support and expertise to economic development activities in the Third World. Along with the World Bank, subregional banks, and Multilateral Financial Institutions (MFIs), these banks make up a complex lending structure directed at development. They are the African Development Bank, created in 1964; the Asian Development Bank (1966); the Inter-American Development Bank (1959); and the newest of the four, the European Bank for Reconstruction and Development, established in 1991. Each bank has its own mandate, board of directors, and independent status but is part of the UN System. The banks have overlapping members, including both borrowing countries and developed states that invest in the institutions, and work closely with other multilateral financial institutions, the most important of which are the European Investment Bank, the International Fund for Agricultural Development, the Islamic Bank, the Nordic Development Fund, the Nordic Investment Bank, and the OPEC (Organization of Petroleum Exporting Countries) Fund for International Development. The banks are also closely associated with regional organizations in their area. For example, the African Development Bank and the Islamic Development Bank entered into an agreement with the Economic Community of West African States (ECOWAS) to finance projects both for regional and nonregional entrepreneurs and for microenterprises. Each regional bank provides several types of assistance: long-term loans to developing countries in their region at market rates, very long term loans—referred to as *credits*—at interest rates well below those in the international market, and grants. The regional banks also use donor contributions to make loans that are not financially viable in the market. Loans and credits made in the late 1990s totaled one to five billion dollars annually for each bank.

As in the case of the African and Islamic banks' association with ECOWAS, multilateral financial institutions work closely with the regional economic commissions established by the United Nations during the past sixty years. ECOSOC created the first two of these commissions—the Economic Commission for Europe (ECE) and the Economic Commission for Asia and the Far East—in 1947. The latter was renamed, in 1974, the *Economic and Social Commission for Asia and the Pacific (ESCAP)*. These mechanisms were used to encourage regional cooperation in postwar reconstruction. Pressed by Latin American states to acknowledge that economic development was equally important in all parts of the world, the United Nations created the Economic Commission for Latin America in 1948, redesignating it in 1984 the *Economic Commission for Latin America and the Caribbean (ECLAC)*. ECOSOC created the Economic Commission for Africa (ECA) in 1958 and the Economic Commission for Western Asia (ECWA) in 1974, renamed the *Economic and Social Commission for Western Asia (ESCWA)* in 1985. The five regional commissions include countries within their respective regions and work with the regional multilateral banks, other regional organizations, the World Bank Group, and nongovernmental organizations in an effort to develop regional responses to economic and social challenges. The commissions are funded by the regular UN budget. They provide technical expertise, planning services, and sponsorship of regional development agencies.

Despite the new sense of cooperation among the various actors in the development effort, between 1990 and 1998 the GDP in the least developed countries grew by only 3.2 percent, compared with 3.4 percent for the more fortunate developing countries. Much of the LDC growth is explained by one state's progress—namely, Bangladesh. According to successive annual *Human Development Report* editions issued by UNDP, this growth rate was insufficient for LDCs to make any headway on ending crushing poverty and its attendant social problems. In this context,

Secretary-General Kofi Annan opened the third UN Conference on Least Developed Countries on May 14, 2001, in Brussels. Charged with developing "measures for the sustainable development of the least developed countries and their progressive integration into the world economy," the conference set a goal of having rich countries provide development assistance equal to 0.15–0.20 percent of developed states' gross national income (GNI); the United Nations later endorsed this goal as part of the Millennium Development Goals.[16] The assistance target in this case varied from the traditional UN target of 0.7 percent aid to "developing countries."[17] As of 1998, only five states had achieved the target: Denmark, the Netherlands, Sweden, Norway, and Luxembourg. Four years later, only one other nation—Ireland—could be added to that list of donors.[18] When these states' contributions were coupled with a decrease in development assistance from several countries, notably the United Kingdom, the world ratio of development assistance to GNI fell between 2001 and 2002 from 0.12 percent to 0.07 percent.[19]

The conference also set the following objectives: to halve the proportion of people living in extreme poverty and suffering from hunger by 2015, to increase LDCs' growth rates to 7 percent per annum (with a rate of investment to GDP of 25 percent), and to encourage public-private cooperation among North-South and South-South countries. Among the priority issues to be addressed, according to the conference report, were poverty eradication, gender equality, national governance, the environmental goals established in the Rio Declaration of the Earth Summit, and the reduction of HIV infection rates by 25 percent in the most affected countries. Finally, the conference called for the accession of the least developed states to the World Trade Organization, with the goal of achieving duty-free and quota-free access to the developed countries' markets.

This collection of recommendations reflected the merger of an evolving policy consensus on two fronts—economic development strategy and a global environmental policy that had been gestating for nearly thirty years. Secretary-General Annan highlighted the development strategy at the **Millennium Summit.** Noting that in the new century the United Nations must serve not only the states that are its members but the world's people as well, Annan called on the summit participants to end extreme poverty wherever it existed, calling such poverty "an affront to our common humanity."[20] He pointed out,[21]

> Nearly half the world's population still make do on less than $2 per day. Approximately 1.2 billion people—500 million in South Asia and 300 million in Africa—struggled on less than $1 . . . [and] people living in Africa south of the Sahara are almost as poor today as they were 20 years ago.

He laid out an ambitious set of **Millennium Development Goals (MDGs)** and targets to be achieved by 2015.

Millennium Development Goals and Targets

Goal 1	**Eradicate Extreme Poverty and Hunger**
Target 1	Halve by 2015* the proportion of people whose income is less than one dollar a day
Target 2	Halve by 2015 the proportion of people who suffer from hunger
Goal 2	**Achieve Universal Primary Education**
Target 3	Ensure that by 2015 children everywhere, boys and girls alike, will be able to complete a full course of primary schooling

Goal 3	**Promote Gender Equality and Empower Women**
Target 4	Eliminate gender disparity in primary and secondary education, preferably by 2005, and to all levels of education no later than 2015
Goal 4	**Reduce Child Mortality**
Target 5	By 2015 reduce by two-thirds the under-five mortality rate
Goal 5	**Improve Maternal Health**
Target 6	By 2015 reduce by three-quarters the maternal mortality ratio
Goal 6	**Combat HIV/AIDS, Malaria, and Other Diseases**
Target 7	Have halted by 2015 and begun to reverse the spread of HIV/AIDS
Target 8	Have halted by 2015 and begun to reverse the incidence of malaria and other major diseases
Goal 7	**Ensure Environmental Sustainability**
Target 9	Integrate the principles of sustainable development into country policies and programs and reverse the loss of environmental resources
Target 10	Halve by 2015 the proportion of people without sustainable access to safe drinking water
Target 11	By 2020 achieve a significant improvement in the lives of at least one hundred million slum dwellers
Goal 8	**Build a Global Partnership for Development**
Target 12	Develop further an open, rule-based, predictable, nondiscriminatory trading and financial system [includes a commitment to good governance, development, and poverty reduction—both nationally and internationally]
Target 13	Address the special needs of the least developed countries [includes tariff- and quota-free access for LDC exports, an enhanced program of debt relief for Heavily Indebted Poor Countries and cancellation of official bilateral debt, and more generous Official Development Assistance (ODA) for countries committed to poverty reduction]
Target 14	Address the special needs of landlocked countries and small island developing states (through the Programme of Action for Sustainable Development of Small Island Developing States and the outcome of the twenty-second special session of the General Assembly)
Target 15	Deal comprehensively with the debt problems of developing countries through national and international measures to make debts sustainable in the long term
Target 16	In cooperation with developing countries, develop and implement strategies for decent and productive work for youth
Target 17	In cooperation with pharmaceutical companies, provide access to affordable, essential drugs in developing countries
Target 18	In cooperation with the private sector, make available the benefits of new technologies, especially information and communications

*Proportional targets for 2015 are in relation to 1990 base data.

Immediately following the summit, the General Assembly adopted the **Millennium Declaration** (see the text in Appendix F), which enshrined these goals and eighteen specific development targets. Among them were commitments to cut in half the number of people who had an income of less than a dollar a day (at least 1.2 billion individuals in 2003, one in five people on Earth) or who were in extreme hunger. The assembly also targeted massive improvements in primary education, housing, and health.

The official development goals of the world community in 2000 were a far cry from the New International Economic Order and the South's persistent demands on a recalcitrant North that dominated development debate in the 1960s and 1970s. The end of the cold war, along with the economic realities of world debt and globalization, brought about a much more cooperative atmosphere. As the Millennium Declaration asserted, a generally common strategy emerged with the United Nations—"as the most universal and most representative organization in the world"— playing "the central role." This situation did not mean, however, that policy differences no longer remained between developed and developing states. In fact, the latter continued to emphasize the structural impediments built into the Bretton Woods system, the need to overcome the economic inequalities between the two groups, and the elimination of debt as a precondition to economic development. Conversely, rich nations focused on the MDGs that called for better governance in LDCs, market liberalization, domestic responsibilities for education and health goals, and the impact of unbridled development on the global environment. Nonetheless, the Millennium Goals and the commitment to "sustainable development" marked cooperative progress on the economic problems facing a large proportion of the world's population.

THE ENVIRONMENT AND SUSTAINABLE DEVELOPMENT

In his report to the Millennium Summit, Secretary-General Annan acknowledged the negative consequences that economic development practices were having on the global environment: "In rich countries, the by-products of industrial and agribusiness production poison soils and waterways. In the developing countries, massive deforestation, harmful farming practices and uncontrolled urbanization are major causes of environmental degradation."[22] He warned that without a strong global response, ecosystems and the ozone layer would continue to degrade, drinkable water would be difficult to find, biodiversity would diminish, and the benefits provided by the environment would be damaged to the point at which "the freedom of future generations to sustain their lives on this planet" would be in jeopardy. His message reflected a growing consensus among environmental NGOs, scientists, and many governments, particularly in the developed world. It also reflected a new UN concern, not contemplated by the institution's founders, and one with significant ramifications for UN development policy.

Nothing in the UN Charter specifically authorizes the organization to deal with environmental issues. In 1945 such issues were perceived to be matters for national governments and for organizations outside the UN structure. Yet, beginning in the 1970s the United Nations became the initiator and primary sponsor of global efforts to protect the environment from detrimental human activities and to ensure that its protection was compatible with social and economic development. The United Nations sponsored world conferences, panels of experts, international conventions, and the creation of new environmental law and concepts, all of which came to define the international regime of environmental politics by the end of the century.

UN-sponsored world conferences have often been defining events in the creation of international legal regimes and policies. They are an innovation without specific authorization in the Charter. Article 1, however, commits the organization to serving as the "centre for harmonizing the actions of nations." Under this rubric the world body has regularly convened delegates in ever-larger international meetings to address social, economic, environmental, and legal problems. The UN Conference on Trade and Development in 1964 was the first such meeting to garner broad international attention. The four international conferences on women held so far have demonstrated the effectiveness of this strategy to galvanize world opinion and private organizations on behalf of a particular cause. Likewise, in the actual formation of international policy, no area has seen a more adept use of the world conference approach by the United Nations than the environment has.

The 1972 UN Conference on the Human Environment (UNCHE), held in Stockholm, was the world body's first global conference on the topic. Earlier meetings sponsored by private groups and by some of the UN's specialized agencies—particularly the 1968 Biosphere Conference convened by the UN Educational, Scientific and Cultural Organization (UNESCO)—had put pressure on the General Assembly to convene a world conference focused on natural resource conservation. Also, at the 1968 U.S.-Soviet Summit meeting in Glassboro, NJ, the two superpowers called for international cooperation on environmental matters as a way to promote cooperation in East-West diplomacy. Finally, growing European concerns that unrestricted development in the Third World would damage the global commons and, consequently, the quality of life in the developed world led the United Nations to accept a Swedish invitation to host the Stockholm Conference.

UNCHE concentrated on conservation and pollution issues, seeing the natural environment as fundamentally under threat from economic development. The conference issued the "Stockholm Declaration," outlining the environmental obligations and duties of states, and a Plan of Action with 109 recommendations. The conference documents suggested that development and environmental protection were laudable movements that unfortunately required trade-offs between the two. Environmental issues are inherently global concerns. National borders do not restrict the deleterious effects of bad environmental practices. Any efforts to limit these effects require the international community to direct its attention to the internal practices of nation-states. Consequently, sovereignty, the bedrock principle of the international system, must give way to some extent if the environment is to be protected. Methods to safeguard the environment sometimes seem to run contrary to development strategies put in place by developing states. These strategies, in turn, may cause environmental problems, or the effort to accommodate them to environmentally friendly techniques may be too costly. Thus, poorer nations at the conference viewed the demand that states alter their development programs to meet international environmental standards as an unwarranted and counterproductive intrusion into their internal affairs.

The apparent conflict between environmental conservation and development pitted the developed states of the North with their concern for "quality-of-life" issues against developing states that wanted to protect their right to raise their people's standard of living through economic strategies unfettered by environmental regulation. Neither group of states wanted to undermine the fundamental principle of sovereignty. The Stockholm meeting attempted to balance the conflicting interests in the final declaration. **Principle 21** asserted,

> States have . . . a sovereign right to exploit their own resources pursuant to their own environmental policies . . . [but States also have] the responsibility to ensure that activities within their jurisdiction or control do not cause damage to the environment of other States, or of areas beyond the limits of national jurisdiction.

In addition, the conference established the "Polluter Pays Principle" (PPP) and the "Precautionary Approach" for all states. PPP obligated states to pay for pollution prevention. As a corollary, the conference asserted that a state was responsible for pollution emanating from it into areas beyond its borders. The Precautionary Approach required states, even when science had not yet fully proved the damaging environmental effects of various development activities, to take precautionary measures to avoid degrading the environment.

UN ENVIRONMENT PROGRAMME

The most important institutional outcome of the Stockholm meeting was the establishment of a new environmental agency. In December 1972 the General Assembly created the UN Environment Programme (UNEP). Its expenses were to be paid through a voluntary fund, and its headquarters was located in Nairobi to ease concerns in the developing world that UNEP might represent Northern nations' desires to limit development policies. During its first decade UNEP became an effective and visible actor in promoting environmental awareness and in attracting major contributions from the industrialized states to international environmental projects.

On several occasions UN conferences and meetings have identified UNEP as the lead agency for international efforts to save the environment. However, unlike UNDP, which plays an equivalent role in the area of development, UNEP vies for leadership with other organizations and faces more limited funding in its endeavors to effect global environmental policy. Its success has been due in part (a) to the political talents of its successive directors—only three in its first 30 years of existence: Maurice Strong (Canada), Mostapha Tolba (Egypt), and Klaus Töpfer (Germany); (b) to the organization's mobilization of scientists, civil society organizations, and environmental NGOs on behalf of particular environmental initiatives; and (c) to the scientific expertise it has developed in a number of monitoring and information-sharing programs. UNEP also serves as the secretariat for several of the international environmental conventions member states have signed since its inception, including both the Basel Convention on the Movement of Hazardous Wastes and the Montreal Protocol on substances that deplete the ozone in our atmosphere. This last agreement grew out of the 1985 Vienna Convention for the Protection of the Ozone Layer, itself the culmination of four years of negotiation initiated by UNEP.

On the tenth anniversary of the Stockholm Conference, seventy government representatives met at UNEP headquarters in Nairobi to assess the progress that had been made on environmental matters. However, an impasse remained between poor nations' push for development on the one hand and efforts to conserve the environment on the other hand. Progress on either front seemed to undercut success on the other. The Nairobi meeting concluded that a reinvigorated international effort was needed. In 1983 the General Assembly established the World Commission on Environment and Development (WCED), with Norwegian prime minister Gro Harlem Brundtland as the commission's chairperson. Secretary-General Javier Pérez de Cuéllar charged the commission with establishing "a global agenda for change."

The twenty-one-member commission and its panel of experts held hearings and interviewed thousands of individuals and groups during a two-year period. The commission's final report, entitled **Our Common Future,** proved to be one of the UN's most widely read and influential publications. It concluded that further progress could be made only if the legitimate claims of both camps were recognized. *Our Common Future* encouraged the world community to develop legally binding rights and obligations for states that recognized the direct links between development and the environment. It introduced the concept of **sustainable development,** defined as "development that meets the needs of the present without compromising the ability of future generations to meet their own needs." Sustainable development became the popular mantra for all future UN efforts to address global environmental challenges. The United Nations created new agencies and reformed old ones to enshrine this concept as a central responsibility of national governments and international organizations. While imprecisely defined, sustainable development appealed to political leaders in states with environmental concerns because it seemed to put a natural limit on economic development strategies. For developing countries it officially recognized the legitimate claim to development.

The WCED called on the United Nations to convene another world conference, this one with the expressed purpose of drafting an international convention on the rights and duties of states in terms of sustainable development. The result was the UN Conference on Environment and Development (UNCED), also known as the *Earth Summit,* which convened in Rio de Janeiro in 1992. UNCED was the largest, most expensive, and most widely covered UN meeting in history. One hundred seventy-eight national delegations and two-thirds of the world's heads of government attended. More than 140 nongovernmental organizations, with UN blessing, staged a Global Forum in tandem with the conference that attracted thirty thousand participants.

UNCED produced three important international agreements—the Rio Declaration, Agenda 21, and the Statement of Forest Principles—and served as the venue for the signing of the Framework Convention on Climate Change (UNFCCC) and the Convention on Biological Diversity (CBD). These documents attempted to balance the concerns of developed states for greater environmental protection—and their desire to avoid huge new financial responsibilities associated with the proposed global commitments—with the developing countries' desire to protect their sovereignty and pursue unrestrained national economic policies.

The *Rio Declaration* asserted twenty-seven "principles" that reflected the existing consensus on sustainable development. The first principle proclaimed that "human beings are at the centre of concerns for sustainable development," shifting the emphasis away from the prior (Stockholm's) emphasis on "nature" and environmental conservation. It elevated the right of development to equal status with environmental protection. It called on developed states to increase aid to poor nations to support the latter's efforts to meet the goals of the declaration, which, as operationalized in Agenda 21, were likely to impose huge new costs on involved governments. The declaration reasserted Stockholm's "Polluter Pays Principle"as well as Principle 21 of the Stockholm Declaration, which stated that governments, although free to develop their domestic resources as they wanted, were accountable for practices that injured the environment beyond their borders.

Agenda 21, an eight-hundred page document, filled with more than one thousand specific recommendations to achieve a "comprehensive plan for global action in all areas of sustainable development," set international and national objectives and provided programmatic suggestions on how to fulfill the objectives. The areas designated for remedial progress included world trade, poverty eradication, population, cities, atmospheric pollution, deforestation, drought, desertification, marine resource management, waste management, agriculture, biodiversity, and the transfer of technology. Agenda 21 identified many UN agencies, including UNEP, UNDP, the World Bank and its Global Environment Facility (GEF), the regional development banks, and UNCTAD, as actors with central responsibility for making sustainable development a reality. It encouraged broad participation by NGOs, individuals, subnational jurisdictions, business, labor, and the intellectual community. While reasserting sovereignty as an element of sustainable development, Agenda 21 sought to democratize diplomacy and remove it from the sole purview of national governments.

UNCED also issued the *Non-legally Binding Authoritative Statement of Principles for a Global Consensus on the Management, Conservation and Sustainable Development of All Types of Forests (Statement of Forest Principles).* This document fell far short of the world convention on forests that developed states and NGOs sought. Developing states that profited from the export of lumber products (such as Brazil and Indonesia) resisted international restrictions on the use of forests. With no possibility of an agreement between developing and developed states, the Statement of Forest Principles simply called for the protection of forests but recognized the right of states to use their forests as they wanted. After the Earth Summit, international negotiations continued within UN-sponsored bodies, culminating in the creation of the UN Forum on Forests (UNFF) by ECOSOC in October 2000. The new forum became a "subsidiary body" of ECOSOC, joining the council's other ad hoc working groups and convened yearly after that, regularly recommending steps governments could take to protect their forests.

More than 150 nations and the European Union took the occasion of the Earth Summit to sign the UN Framework Convention on Climate Change and the Convention on Biological Diversity, which provided much of the perceived "success" of the Rio conference. Global media coverage, particularly of the climate change agreement, created an impetus for many national governments to establish domestic environmental programs and agencies. It also encouraged the General Assembly to endorse the negotiation of additional environmental conventions.

The most lasting product of UNCED's work was the recommendation that the General Assembly create a permanent commission to oversee the implementation of the conference's decisions. Accordingly, the assembly established the Commission on Sustainable Development (CSD) as a functional body of the Economic and Social Council. At the time, it was seen as a possible alternative center of environmental decision making to the long-standing UN Environment Programme. In addition, with its membership of fifty-three states dominated by developing states, it was expected to pressure rich nations for the resources needed to cover extra costs in the Third World imposed by environmentally friendly development policies. The forty-seventh session of the General Assembly directed nongovernmental organizations, other UN bodies, and intergovernmental economic organizations, on both global and regional levels, to participate in the commission's work. NGOs were authorized to submit written reports and to address the commission, as well as to conduct "consultations" with its members at the invitation of the chair or the UN secretary-general. More than one thousand NGOs gained accreditation to CSD.

However, two overriding, perennial dilemmas plagued CSD: the apparent conflict between environmental protection and economic development, and the intrusiveness of international efforts to preserve the environment on the one hand and the inviolability of sovereignty on the other. Faced with these countervailing pressures, the Commission on Sustainable Development had limited success in implementing Agenda 21 objectives, which left UNEP as the dominant UN agency in environmental policymaking. Between 1994 and 1996 CSD reviewed each area identified by Agenda 21. In 1997 the Earth Summit +5 Special Session of the General Assembly directed CSD to begin work on identifying "indicators of sustainable development" that could be used to measure progress toward the goals established at Rio, which it thereafter completed.

Although the commission was charged with the primary responsibility for ensuring sustainable development, all UN agencies after 1992 premised their activities on its attainment. The World Bank's Global Environment Facility, the WTO, and UNCTAD took on primary responsibility for enhancing financial and trade assistance to the Third World to help states reach self-sustaining development. As part of this effort, UNCTAD decided to make sustainable development the central theme of its third Conference on Least Developed Countries. At the national and subnational levels, UNDP and Habitat assisted with the capacity building and infrastructure necessary for a social and economic order that could maintain the principle. UNDP launched a *sustainable development network (SDN)* to foster dialogue among citizens and policymakers and to provide the latest technical information related to the topic. Even relatively independent agencies such as the World Health Organization (WHO) undertook its promotion. In fact, WHO underwent a structural reorganization to make "sustainable development and healthy environment" one of its primary "clusters" of activity after Gro Harlem Brundtland, the former chair of the World Commission on Environment and Development, took over as WHO's director general in July 1998.

The WHO experience demonstrated that by the turn of the century sustainable development had metamorphosed from solely a development and environmental construct. It had been adapted to other areas of UN concern. UNEP executive director Klaus Töpfer told the world community in July 2000 that "the most toxic element in the environment is poverty."[23] He and other UN officials began talking about sustainable *human* development (SHD).

While sustainable development was enshrined at the 1992 Earth Summit as the overarching aspiration for all UN environmental activities, the Rio gathering additionally gave impetus to five areas of environmental policy that would then be pursued in UN and other IGO settings. They were as follows:

The atmosphere and climate change
Water pollution and marine resources
Biodiversity and natural resources
Deforestation and desertification
International financing of environmental initiatives

Atmosphere and Climate Change

In the 1980s and 1990s, the World Meteorological Organization (WMO) and UNEP played the central roles in trying to halt the interrelated problems of ozone-layer depletion and global warming. Under their sponsorship a number of countries agreed to the Vienna Convention for the Protection of the Ozone Layer. This convention made a general commitment to protect the ozone layer by reducing ozone-depleting chemical compounds in the atmosphere. At meetings following the inauguration of the convention in 1985, the signatories amended it several times. The most important elaboration was the Montreal Protocol in 1987, which set specific production and consumption limits on refrigerant and industrial substances known as *chlorofluorocarbons,* or *CFCs.*

UNEP and WMO created the Intergovernmental Panel on Climate Change (IPCC) in 1988 to study the phenomenon of climate change, its causes, its rapidity, and its consequences. The IPCC comprised more than one thousand scientists, policymakers, legal experts, and climate specialists from more than sixty nations. The work of the panel led to the UN Framework Convention on Climate Change (UNFCCC). This convention, opened for signature at the Earth Summit, took effect in March 1994. It set an "ultimate objective" of stabilizing greenhouse gases at a level that would prevent dangerous human-induced interference with the climate system. These criteria proved difficult to define and elusive of agreement among the 185 ratifying nations. The UNFCCC, however, established a process for succeeding negotiation and the promulgation of amendments, or "protocols," that would establish specific targets that parties to the agreement would have to meet. The most important was the Kyoto Protocol. Adopted in 1997, the protocol set specific greenhouse gas (GHG) emission targets for industrialized states to meet by 2012. The goal was to lower overall emissions of carbon dioxide, nitrous oxide, methane, hydrofluorocarbons, perfluorocarbons, and sulphur hexafluoride 5 percent below 1990 levels.

One group of greenhouse gases the Kyoto Protocol did not cover was chlorofluorocarbons (CFCs). These gases had already been addressed in the 1987 Montreal Protocol on substances that deplete the ozone in the atmosphere. The Montreal Protocol, amended five times in the 1990s, eventually covered ninety-six substances. Schedules were established to reduce emission

CHRONOLOGY OF UN POLICY ON THE ENVIRONMENT

June 5–16, 1972	UN Conference on the Human Environment convenes (Stockholm)
Oct. 2, 1973	United Nations Environment Programme begins its work
Mar. 22, 1985	Vienna Convention for the Protection of the Ozone Layer opened for signature
Oct. 19, 1987	*Our Common Future* submitted to the General Assembly
Jan. 1, 1989	Montreal Protocol on the Depletion of the Ozone Layer enters into force
Mar. 14, 1991	Global Environment Facility Trust Fund created
June 3–14, 1992	Earth Summit (Rio de Janeiro)
June 4, 1992	UN Framework Convention on Climate Change opened for signature
June 5, 1992	Convention on Biological Diversity opened for signature
Feb. 12,1993	Commission on Sustainable Development established
Oct. 14, 1994	Convention to Combat Desertification opened for signature
June 23–27, 1997	Earth Summit +5 convenes (New York)
July 25, 1997	Intergovernmental Forum on Forests established
Dec. 11, 1997	Kyoto Protocol adopted
Apr. 1–3, 1998	First Assembly of the Global Environment Facility (GEF) convenes (New Delhi)
Sept. 6–8, 2000	Millennium Summit (New York City)
Aug. 7, 2002	Single largest replenishment in GEF history made to the Global Environment Facility ($2.92 billion)
Sept. 11, 2003	Cartagena Protocol of the Convention on Biological Diversity enters into force
Feb. 16, 2005	Kyoto Protocol enters into force

levels gradually to the amounts produced or consumed in a particular year (1986 was the earliest base year) and then to eliminate these substances completely. For major producing nations, the protocol required immediate 50 percent cuts, followed by decreasing use until they emitted none of these. To help finance projects by developing countries meant to phase out ozone-depleting substances, a Multilateral Fund for the Montreal Protocol was established. By 2003 it had dispersed more than $1.4 billion to eliminate CFCs.

The provisions of the Kyoto Protocol were directed at the industrialized states, which produced the overwhelming bulk of effluents responsible both for global warming and for ozone depletion. Annex I to the protocol specifically identified these nations. Annex I states committed themselves to legally binding emissions targets that were expected to reduce collective emissions of six key greenhouse gases by at least 5 percent. The protocol required each country to achieve its target—for example, 8 percent by Switzerland, the European Union, and most central and east European states; 7 percent by the United States; and 6 percent by Canada, Japan, Poland, and Hungary—by the 2008–2012 period. Each state was also expected to make "demonstrable progress" by 2005.

For the protocol to go into effect, it had to be ratified by fifty-five states that were parties to the UNFCCC and it had to be ratified by sufficient Annex I countries to account for 55 percent of carbon dioxide (CO_2) emissions in 1990. The United States produced more than one-third of the world's annual CO_2 emissions in 2004. European Union countries accounted for another 24 percent. To reach the overall targets, U.S. and European negotiators agreed to cut emissions by 8 percent and 7 percent, respectively. Without ratification of the agreement by the United States and European countries, including Russia (accounting for 17.4 percent of emissions), the protocol would be stillborn. Developing states were not required to cut emissions in the first phase of the protocol's implementation. The Kyoto agreement recognized "common but differentiated responsibilities" among developed and developing states, holding the states that produced the largest amounts of greenhouse gases initially responsible for addressing the problem. Developing countries were encouraged to report on their emissions and to take measures to cut them, contingent on the receipt of financial assistance and technology transfers.[24]

To provide flexibility to the agreement and to counter criticism that Kyoto imposed "unequal" conditions on industrial and developing countries, the protocol provided several innovative ways that Annex I states could meet their targets without huge cuts in domestic emissions and without causing unacceptable distress to industries that produced greenhouse gases. The protocol included a "clean development mechanism" that gave developed states a number of ways to earn emission credits, including financing sustainable development projects in the developing world that reduce emissions in the recipient country. States could also offset their own emissions of greenhouse gases by increasing the use of what are called carbon *sinks*. These sinks included approved programs of reforestation, cropland management, revegetation, or other activities that help take CO_2 out of the atmosphere. They could be used as "credits" against emission totals as a state sought to meet Kyoto's assigned target. "Emission trading" was also sanctioned. To the extent that a country stayed below its target, it could "trade"—that is, "sell"—the difference to another Annex I country that was having difficulty meeting its target.

Post-Kyoto meetings sought to develop operational plans for implementing the protocol. The most important of these occurred at Marrakesh in 2001. The Marrakesh Accords established two special funds to aid LDCs and developing states meet the goals of Kyoto, and they expanded the scope of activities that would be eligible for funding from the World Bank's Global Environment Facility.

On May 31, 2002, the European Union presented its member nations' ratifications of the Kyoto Protocol to UN secretary-general Annan in New York. He lauded the European states' decisions and expressed the hope that "others will follow suit."[25] His reference was directed at several major states that had not ratified, including chiefly the United States and Australia, whose governments had indicated that they did not support the agreement. With Canada's and Poland's ratification in December 2002, the second "trigger" was within reach, as industrialized countries accounting for 44 percent of CO_2 emissions had agreed to the provisions of the protocol. However, without either the United States or the Russian Federation signing on, it could not go into effect. The Bush administration in Washington expressed unaltered opposition to the arrangement, citing its "unfairness" by not including mandated cuts in emissions for developing states and its costs to U.S. producers in difficult economic times. In 2002 President Putin of Russia committed to submit the protocol to the Duma for ratification, but delayed submission once influential advisers urged him not to participate. They suggested that additional global warming might even be economically beneficial to Russia by warming areas that are now inhospitable for agricultural production.[26] Their objections were overcome when it became clear that Russia would actually profit from implementation of the protocol, given its weakened economy had already lowered pollution levels below the targets set by the accord. The Duma ratified the protocol and it went into force in February 2005.

Water Pollution and Marine Resources

The 1972 Stockholm Declaration emphasized protecting the marine environment. Consequently, its successor organization, the UN Environment Programme, developed a number of programs to improve marine fish stocks, ocean and freshwater bodies, and transboundary waterways. Under UNEP auspices, efforts to protect the world's oceans resulted in a number of regional seas agreements. Nine were signed in the 1970s, beginning with an agreement among countries bordering the Mediterranean Sea. Six more agreements were signed in the 1980s. In addition to UNEP, the Economic Commission for Europe played a critical role in developing the 1992 Convention on the Protection and Use of Transboundary Watercourses and International Lakes.

Central to the UN's activity to protect the world's oceans was the Law of the Sea Convention, adopted in 1982. Part XII of the convention dealt specifically with the protection of the marine environment. By the time of the convention, serious concern had been expressed that the long-standing custom of "freedom of the seas" had contributed to overexploitation of oceanic fish stocks by expanded distant fishing fleets, had damaged the marine environment as a consequence of the uncontrolled acquisition of natural resources (especially oil and natural gas), and had caused further harm by tolerating increasing numbers of oil tanker spills. The agreement was augmented in 1995 with a global commitment to protect highly migratory fish stocks. The effort to build on the Law of the Sea Convention to enhance marine protection became a priority of the Commission on Sustainable Development.

The Law of the Sea Convention created its own international tribunal to adjudicate cases that arose among parties to the agreement. These cases could involve matters related to the environmental clauses in the convention. In the fall of 2001, Ireland brought a case to the tribunal against the United Kingdom's operation of a nuclear reprocessing facility on its west coast. Fearful that waste dumping or a terrorist attack could pollute the Irish Sea between Dublin and the plant, Ireland sought an injunction until an arbitration panel could settle the matter.[27] Although the tribunal did not issue the injunction, it did note that Part XII of the convention requires cooperation among the parties. The tribunal ordered Ireland and Great Britain to exchange information on the possible threat presented by the plant to the Irish Sea, to monitor the continuing risks, and to devise measures to prevent pollution of the marine environment.[28]

As critical as marine life and resources are to the world's population, sustainable development depends even more heavily on access to freshwater sources. In 2003 more than two billion people lacked sufficient safe drinking water. The Millennium Development Goals set a target of cutting this number in half by 2015. The Johannesburg World Summit on Sustainable Development, the tenth anniversary follow-up conference to the meeting in Rio, also committed the world to cut in half the number of people without access to minimal sanitation. UNEP was assigned primary responsibility for achieving both goals. The United Nations declared 2003 the International Year of Fresh Water, and UNEP launched the World Water Assessment Programme (WWAP), which published the first *UN World Water Development Report*. Taking advantage of the visibility afforded by the international year, the environment program also scheduled an International Fresh Water Forum for Dushanbe, Tajikistan, in August.

UNEP's assessment program provides freshwater data collection and dissemination for national governments, IGOs, and nongovernmental organizations. Funded by a voluntary trust fund,

WWAP, with its secretariat at UNESCO headquarters in Paris, serves as the "umbrella" for coordinating existing UN freshwater programs in other agencies and thus has created a global water information network.[29] It develops recommendations for capacity building in water-strapped states and seeks to find ways to improve the conservation of clean water from unnecessary pollution.

UN clean water programs arose not only through the commitments of the various environmental gatherings that convened during the previous thirty years, but also through a separate conference process on this specific topic. In 1977 the United Nations convened a conference on water at Mar del Plata, Argentina, that led to the declaration of an International Drinking Water and Sanitation Decade beginning in 1981. The conference set goals for the decade, but few were met. Along with these unmet goals came the realization that solving clean water problems would take far more time and funds than had been contemplated. In 1990 both the "global consultation" on safe water and sanitation held in New Delhi, India, and the World Summit on Children called for renewed international efforts. The momentum from these meetings culminated in the International Conference on Water and the Environment, meeting in Dublin, Ireland, during the same year as the Earth Summit. This conference issued the Dublin Statement on Water and Sustainable Development, establishing consensus principles on the protection and management of freshwater. The statement declared, among other principles, that water was an economic good and urged that its development and management be based on a participatory approach involving users, planners, and policymakers.

All the social and environmental UN conferences of the 1990s (UNCED, the UN Conference on Population and Development, the Fourth World Conference on Women, HABITAT II, and the World Food Summit) found room in their declarations and plans of action to include recommendations on the conservation and provision of freshwater. As a lead-up to the Millennium Summit, a World Water Forum convened in The Hague. It identified seven challenges (meeting basic needs, securing a food supply, protecting ecosystems, sharing water resources, managing risks, valuing water, and governing water wisely) that the world needed to address.[30] Thus, Kofi Annan's call at the millennium gathering for halving the number of people without water was not unexpected. However, a bonus of the focus on freshwater was the formation of a separate World Water Council. Created in 1997 with its headquarters in Marseilles, France, this council is a hybrid organization including not only UN agencies such as UNDP, the World Bank, and UNESCO, but also private and public firms, foundations, national government agencies, NGOs, banks, and academic and research institutes. The council organized the March 2000 world forum, which fifty-seven hundred participants attended.

Biodiversity and Natural Resources

Pressed to do so by many environmental NGOs, UNEP sponsored negotiations, beginning in 1987, on a convention to protect biological diversity. These negotiations resulted in the Convention on Biological Diversity, opened for signature at the Earth Summit. The convention sought to conserve biodiversity and to provide fair and equitable sharing of genetic resources and technology. Under the terms of the convention, nations were required to take national inventories of biodiversity, develop national plans for the sustainable use of biodiversity, restore degraded ecosystems, and regulate the release of genetically modified organisms. The convention established a Conference of the Parties (COP) to implement and enhance the pact through continuing negotiations. Within a decade of its signing, nearly all nation-states had ratified the agreement and joined the COP.

The most significant accomplishment of COP meetings was the promulgation of the Cartagena Protocol in January 2000, which created a regulatory system for the safe transfer, handling, and use of genetically modified organisms. At Cartagena the parties made specific reference to Principle 15 of the Rio Declaration, which required all states to take a precautionary approach when dealing with highly sensitive, and possibly dangerous, genetic materials.[31] The protocol set standards primarily on genetically altered farm products for human consumption and animal feed. It set up a Biosafety Clearing-House to make scientific risk assessments. With Palau's ratification of the protocol in June 2003, enough states had agreed to it to bring the protocol into effect by the following fall.[32] The success of the protocol depended, however, on the financial ability of developing states to participate. To this end, UNEP, with the assistance of the Global Environment Facility, pumped more than thirty-eight million dollars into one hundred countries.

The Cartagena Protocol was critically needed to manage the burgeoning private trade in genetically modified living organisms. In 1996 UNCTAD had launched its Biotrade Initiative, which was meant to stimulate trade and investment in biological resources in the developing world. UNCTAD then established biotrade country programs to help governments identify opportunities for sustainable resource development. On the basis of the 1997 Memorandum of Understanding between the Convention on Biological Diversity secretariat and UNCTAD, the two organs identified partnerships that could be developed among governments, NGOs, and international agencies that had the potential to turn the protection of biodiversity into a development asset for LDCs.

Desertification and Deforestation

Although economic development and environmental protection have frequently been incompatible, one area in which the two reinforce each other is slowing land degradation. In Africa the steady growth of the Sahara Desert has diminished arable land and, thus, undercut agricultural production and lowered the standard of living. The misuse of arid and semiarid land and the overgrazing of livestock have dramatically increased both deforestation and desertification. More than one hundred countries, mostly in the developing world, are affected by these phenomena. By 2000, 44 percent of sub-Saharan Africa was at high risk of devastating drought. In the new millennium, estimates put 135 million people at risk from desertification directly, or from mass exodus and conflict in the dryland regions.

Led by states in the Sahel region during the 1980s, African nations pressed for international action. The Earth Summit recommended that the United Nations create a negotiating committee to draft a convention on the problem of desertification. The Convention to Combat Desertification (CCD) opened for signature in Paris in October 1994 and entered into force in December 1996. The CCD established its secretariat in Bonn, Germany.

The convention radically departed from the traditional approaches to desertification in its strong emphasis on a "bottom-up" approach with strong local participation in decision making. That is, the convention put local officials on an equal footing with other actors in the development process. Communities and their leaders, as well as nongovernmental organizations, experts, and government personnel, were invited to make proposals for new programs and to participate actively in implementation efforts. By 2003 more than 650 NGOs were accredited with observer status for COP meetings. NGOs not only played a prominent role in the convention process, but also raised public awareness of the convention and lobbied governments on behalf of desertification projects.

Activities recommended by the convention required extensive new funding, which proved difficult to raise. Unlike the biodiversity and climate change conventions that had funding mechanisms through the Global Environment Facility, the CCD had to set up its own funding structure. It did so through the International Fund for Agricultural Development (IFAD) in Rome. Its funds, never large under the IFAD arrangement, were directed at reducing poverty in arid and semiarid areas in the belief that poverty led to agricultural practices that exacerbated desertification. In August 2002 the convention's executive secretary asked the World Summit on Social Development (WSSD) to recommend GEF as the future funding mechanism for desertification projects. The conference did so, and the GEF council approved desertification and deforestation as a central area of its work. The convention's signatories could now apply directly to the facility for funding of national projects.

At the time of the Earth Summit, the positive connections between environmentally sound policies concerning forests and economic development in the underdeveloped world were not as clear as they were in the area of desertification. Industrialized states had become concerned by reports of significant damage to the rain forests and to tropical stands of timber as the result of land clearing, the sale of mahogany and other precious lumber, and development practices that threatened this part of the global commons. While deforestation produced land degradation, often in the form of erosion, LDCs argued that this practice was necessary if, first, land was to be made available for agricultural and industrial development and, second, forest products were going to be part of the nation's export production. As we commented previously in this chapter, this conflict limited the outcome of the Earth Summit to a vague Statement of Forest Principles.

The failure of the Rio meeting to reach agreement on proposals for preserving the world's forests was a harbinger of future negotiations. As one scholar on the subject said, compared with global efforts to address ozone problems, the attempt to create an international legal regime on forest management proved to be "a resounding failure."[33] The inability to demonstrate transborder dangers from forest degradation, the general perception that forests are a domestic resource beyond international control, and the belief that forest problems can usually be solved unilaterally by governments all diminished incentives toward reaching a binding treaty. In addition, no group of countries stepped forward with offers to finance international initiatives in this area.

The UN Commission on Sustainable Development established an Intergovernmental Panel on Forests (1995–1997) and an Intergovernmental Forum on Forests (1997–2000), which collectively put forward more than 270 proposals for action. These proposals "encouraged" countries to take a wide array of steps to protect their forests. Given the acknowledgment that states had the right to use their forest resources as they wanted for development purposes, the panels did not mandate international norms or action. However, the promulgation of the Kyoto Protocol in 1997 gave new impetus to international discussions about forest preservation. The incentives created by the protocol's "sinks" provisions would reward states for planting and restoring forests. This opportunity demonstrated that progress in one area of environmental policy could open up avenues for sound environmental progress in another. The UN Forum on Forests (UNFF) continued to work on this possibility and hoped to establish a funding mechanism to emulate Kyoto's incentives.

The UNFF issued a ministerial declaration in 2002 endorsing the intergovernmental panel proposals just noted and called for "sustainable forest management."[34] By the time of its fourth session, meeting in May 2004 in Geneva, UNFF was directing its attention to means of implementing this standard through the transfer of environmentally sound technologies, new financing, and capacity building in individual countries.[35] Yet, real progress depended on a consensus among the negotiating states on the merits of a binding treaty. While many nations from both the developing and developed worlds supported an agreement, the antitreaty coalition included the United States, Brazil, Japan, Mexico, India, and Indonesia, among others.[36] As long as this group refused to accede to an agreement, forest preservation would have to be left to national governments, NGOs, subnational citizens' groups, and the private sector.

International Financing

The inclusion of desertification as one of six focal areas for financing in the Global Environment Facility—the others being climate change, international waters, biodiversity, persistent organic pollutants, and the ozone layer—completed the emergence of GEF as the central financial institution for UN environmental initiatives. Created in 1991 as an experimental project of the World Bank to meet the Brundtland Commission's concerns about insufficient international financing of environmentally friendly development projects, GEF soon acquired significant donor assets for its projects. At the conclusion of UNCED, the conference secretariat estimated that $125 billion in foreign assistance to developing countries would be needed to implement all the Agenda 21 recommendations. This cost was nearly ten times the 1992 level of global aid. Yet no large contributions to a "Green Fund" were made at the conference by the major industrialized states. Given the newness of GEF and its ties to the World Bank, LDCs urged the creation of the Commission on Sustainable Development as an alternative body to seek financial aid for Agenda 21 projects. When the fact that the rich nations were not going to provide any significant new funds through CSD became clear, the world community fell back on using GEF as an interim mechanism. In 1994 the facility was restructured and became the central institution of international environmental financing.

The primary purpose of the Global Environment Facility is to provide grants to developing countries for environment-related projects and to facilitate networking and cooperation among donors. In addition to the grants it has made, GEF has leveraged another twelve billion dollars in cofinancing. The funds have been spent in more than 140 countries on more than a thousand projects. The World Bank is the trustee of the GEF fund. It acts as one of the facility's three implementing agencies, along with UNDP and UNEP. In addition, the four regional development banks and several other UN specialized agencies can access GEF funds as "executing" bodies. GEF operations are directed by an assembly composed of its 175 member states, which meets every three years, and a council, which functions as a board of directors. GEF assets come from donor members; more than 35 nations had contributed in excess of seven billion dollars during the 1990s.

Any individual or group may propose a project to the facility. The project must meet two key criteria: It must improve or reduce risks to the environment, and it must reflect national or regional priorities, with the support of the country or countries involved. GEF project ideas may be proposed directly to any of its implementing agencies. Developing countries that have ratified the relevant convention are eligible to propose projects within the confines of that agreement. Other countries, primarily those with economies in transition, are eligible if the country is a party to the appropriate treaty and is eligible to borrow from the World Bank or receives technical assistance grants from UNDP. The facility is particularly welcoming of private and NGO participation. More than 150 GEF-financed projects have been managed by NGOs. Much of the investment by GEF in the private sector has been directed at power generation, but additional monies have gone to private companies to reduce greenhouse gas emissions, for renewable energy projects, and for biodiversity protection. Between 1991 and 1999 GEF provided $991 million in grants for biological diversity projects, and $884 million for climate change projects, as well as $1.5 billion and $4.7 billion in cofinancing in these same areas, respectively. It also allocated $360 million to international water initiatives and $155 million to projects to phase out ozone-depleting substances. By the end of its first decade, GEF had provided more than $4.2 billion in direct financing.

The regional development banks complemented GEF financing. They first worked with the World Bank on the Committee of International Development Institutions on the Environment (CIDIE), created in the 1980s, to resolve the competing interests between development in the poorest countries and the global environmental initiatives launched at the 1972 Stockholm Conference. The Earth Summit encouraged the development banks to take a greater role in financing sustainable development. Each bank set up an environmental department to support methods of development that protect environmental interests. The decision to bring the banks within the restructured GEF organizational plan in 1994 made them key executing bodies for environmentally friendly development in their respective regions. For the last decade the banks have worked within a cohesive and unified financing structure coordinated by the facility.

SUSTAINABLE *HUMAN* DEVELOPMENT: THE FIGHT AGAINST HIV/AIDS

> HIV/AIDS pushes people deeper into poverty as households lose their breadwinners, livelihoods are compromised and savings are consumed by the cost of health care. The pandemic also adds to the strain on national institutions and resources, and undermines the social systems that help people to cope with adversity. In the most severely affected settings there is already evidence that HIV/AIDS is eroding human security and productivity, undermining economic development, and threatening social cohesion.
>
> —World Health Organization, *Global Health Sector Strategy for HIV/AIDS: 2003–2007*, p. 3

If human beings are at the center of the concern for sustainable development as the Rio Declaration asserted, then sustainable *human* development is the ultimate goal of UN efforts in the new millennium. In particular, poverty eradication has been identified by UN agencies and the Millennium Summit as a critical step in providing healthier, safer, and more productive lives for the world's population. However, addressing poverty requires solving simultaneously the human afflictions that keep whole societies from economic progress. As the quotation from the World Health Organization's report suggests, widespread and rampant disease in poor parts of the globe not only undermines the prospects for improving standards of living, but also threatens international peace and security.

Disease is not the only social problem that stalemates development. Homelessness, refugee flows, human rights violations, narcotics, crime, and corruption all make sustainable development difficult. However, the presence of diseases such as measles and tuberculosis in the LDCs—long controlled in the richer nations of the world—and the quick spread of viruses in recent years due to globalization and human migration have focused the UN's attention on disease as a primary threat to development. At the beginning of the new millennium, the world community identified three diseases—HIV/AIDS, tuberculosis, and malaria—as the triple threat to poverty reduction and launched the Global Fund to fight them, with support from all UN agencies, the major economic world powers, and the nongovernmental community. In view of an estimated three hundred million cases of malaria worldwide each year, the United Nations undertook a global partnership—"Roll Back Malaria"—to halve that number by 2010. Tuberculosis cases increased 6 percent between 1997 and 1999.[37] The most significant increases occurred in African states affected by the HIV/AIDS crisis. "Stop TB" was launched as a global partnership to halt the incidence of the disease, particularly in twenty-two heavily affected states.

Vaccination in the Congo
(UN/DPI Photo by B. Zarov. Reproduced by permission from the United Nations.)

The pandemic of HIV (human immunodeficiency virus) and AIDS (acquired immunode-ficiency syndrome), with an estimated forty-two million people infected by 2002,[38] raises a par-ticularly dire threat to all international efforts to achieve sustainable human development. The UN effort to mobilize world resources in the fight against HIV/AIDS has included the usual methods of world meetings; a General Assembly special session; and cooperative ventures with governments, NGOs, and the private sector.[39] The UN Security Council has also recognized the potentially destabilizing force of HIV/AIDS, particularly among communities ravaged by con-flicts and warfare. Through a number of resolutions, and four sessions on the topic by January 2001, the council had identified the disease as the first health issue to be considered a threat to global peace and security. Particular attention focused on the links between regional conflicts in sub-Saharan Africa and the incidence of HIV/AIDS. The council expressed a particular concern about the epidemic's spread to peacekeepers participating in UN operations.

However, unlike the campaign for sustainable development, much of the UN campaign against HIV/AIDS has been made through its specialized agencies, particularly the World Health Organization. In 1985 WHO drafted a global strategy for the prevention and control of the dis-ease; two years later it set up its Special Programme on AIDS, renamed the *Global Programme on AIDS (GPA)* in 1987. From that point forward WHO became the lead agency in the UN re-sponse to the crisis. The agency gave high priority to stopping the accelerated spread of the dis-ease. In 2003 it established the "Three by Five" goal: to provide three million people in the developing world with the antiretroviral drugs they need by 2005. This effort was to be coupled with a new Global Health Sector Strategy covering the period through 2007, in which WHO would work closely with national health ministries to slow the infection rate.

Despite interagency agreements under the leadership of the World Health Organization, co-ordinating policies, strategies, and support activities remained problematic. In response to rising difficulties and to the growing awareness that HIV/AIDS was not only a medical problem but also an epidemic with social, economic, and political complexities, a new UN program, the **Joint UN Programme on HIV/AIDS (UNAIDS),** was created in 1986. With eight agencies (the UN Children's Fund, UNDP, the UN Population Fund, WHO, UNESCO, the World Bank, the International Labour Organization, and the UN Drug Control Programme) operating under the leadership of a program secretariat, UNAIDS filled the need for greater coordination to combat the increasingly complex nature of this global scourge. An important element of the UNAIDS program design was cooperation with the numerous NGOs active in HIV prevention worldwide, as well as the active participation of national HIV/AIDS agencies, including the U.S. Centers for Disease Control. A "Country Response Monitoring Project" was just one of the UN's initiatives, in collaboration with national governments and NGOs, to provide the latest information on the epidemic in specific countries.

The goal of UNAIDS is to strengthen and orchestrate the expertise, resources, and influence that each constituent organization offers. The agency fosters expanded national responses to HIV/AIDS, particularly in developing countries, and identifies, develops, and advocates international "best practices" for HIV prevention. UNAIDS is governed by its Programme Coordinating Board, comprising government delegates, envoys from the participating UN agencies, and representatives from nongovernmental organizations, which include associations of people living with AIDS. As such, UNAIDS is the first UN programme to include NGOs in its governing body. Its secretariat, based in Geneva, operates on behalf of the participating agencies to provide policy development and research, technical support, advocacy, and coordination. In the developing nations, where more than 95 percent of the world's infected population is found, UNAIDS operates through the UN Theme Group on AIDS, consisting of representatives of the participating UN agencies. The representatives work with national government agencies as well as NGOs to support the host governments' efforts to develop a comprehensive response to HIV/AIDS.

The United States has been the largest contributor to UNAIDS programs. In 2002 it gave the organization eighteen million dollars. Other major contributors include Japan, the Netherlands, and Scandinavian countries. The UNAIDS annual budget reached nearly one hundred million dollars in the new millennium. The constituent agencies have also separately spent large sums on battling the disease. Since 1986 the World Bank, for example, has spent more than two billion dollars in sixty-four countries, and has launched multicountry programs, such as a one-billion-dollar initiative for Africa and the Caribbean.

The General Assembly's special session on the disease in 1987 issued its Declaration of Commitment, recognizing HIV/AIDS as a problem that creates political challenges as well as human rights and economic threats to the world community. This declaration called for an increased emphasis on prevention, noting the particular vulnerability of women to HIV disease. The General Assembly set as its target for 2005 to reduce HIV infection among young people aged 15 to 24 by 25 percent in the most affected countries, and the proportion of infants infected by 20 percent. Globally it sought a reduction in these two categories of 25 percent and 50 percent, respectively, by 2010. The special session also called for the immediate implementation of the Heavily Indebted Poor Country Initiative and cancellation of all bilateral debts of HIPC countries heavily impacted by HIV/AIDS.

Despite the injection of significant international funds, most LDC government health programs are incapable of providing the necessary drugs and infrastructure to deal with AIDS. Secretary-General Annan met with and called on pharmaceutical companies to provide antiretroviral drugs at steeply reduced prices. His efforts, and those of AIDS activists, achieved some success, and other private companies with employees in the developing world responded with funds and treatment programs.

Recognizing the strain on the poorer countries facing the devastation of AIDS, Annan and the General Assembly called for a global AIDS fund to generate between $8 and $10 billion annually. The G-8 industrial countries promptly endorsed the idea, and the Global Fund to Fight AIDS, Tuberculosis and Malaria took form. Financial commitments flowed immediately into its coffers. Through 2004, $2.6 billion were pledged, with another $2.1 billion pledged through 2008. During its first 18 months of existence the Global Fund was able to make grants worth $1.5 billion to more than 150 programs in 92 countries.[40] UNAIDS signed a Memorandum of Understanding with the fund, recognizing the latter as a "critical financing mechanism" in the fight against AIDS. The memorandum assigned UNAIDS the key tasks of strategic analysis, policy advice, and provision of technical expertise.[41]

Within two years of its inception, the Global Fund took on much of the same role that the Global Environment Facility served in environmental matters. Like the GEF, the fund provided grants for public, private, and nongovernmental projects directed at prevention or treatment of the disease, or the care of AIDS patients. Its emergence marked a specialization of labor in the UN fight against HIV/AIDS that was the product of a maturing policy process at the international level.

The fund's governing board makes decisions about the allocation of resources. In 2003 the board included among its voting members an unusual combination of personages: government ministers, a representative of the Bill and Melinda Gates Foundation, a representative of a private corporation, NGO delegates, doctors, and a professor expert in the fight against AIDS. Among the ex officio nonvoting members were representatives of UNAIDS, WHO, and the World Bank. In the United Nations of the twenty-first century, the fight against HIV/AIDS merged private and public in seamless ways, which produced a consensus global policy. This policy-making mode is significantly different from that contemplated by the UN founders or practiced in the field of development fifty years earlier.

SUMMARY

UN development policy has been made in many ways during the last half century. It has been the product of particular states' objectives in the international community and the outcome of conflicts among those states. UN efforts to meet the Charter's commitment to raise the standards of living and the social conditions of the world's poorest populations have been buffeted by both the East-West and the North-South struggles. These struggles have shaped development policy, using the architecture of the United Nations as the policy arena. However, the United Nations has also sought to make economic and social policy by mobilizing the world on behalf of particular agendas and strategies. Through many types of multilateral forums—world conferences, panels of experts, media events, General Assembly special sessions, and public campaigns—the United Nations has wedded environmental concerns to the search for economic progress in the underdeveloped world, producing with time a new conception of economic development as "sustainable" development. Through its worldwide system of programs, funds, specialized agencies, and offices, the United Nations has also addressed policymaking in such personally human fields as health, and individual rights and dignity, for sustainable development is possible only where sustainable *human* development is achieved. In its efforts to end the scourge of AIDS, the United Nations has moved most dramatically toward a "people-centered" institution that sees its mission not only in terms of protecting the interests of the states that are its members. The whole UN System has gravitated to the center of global policymaking, public and private, on human challenges previously thought peripheral to international politics.

NOTES

1. See John Allphin Moore, Jr., and Jerry Pubantz, *To Create a New World? American Presidents and the United Nations* (New York: Peter Lang, 1999), 46–53.
2. For a comprehensive discussion on the "idea" of economic and social development embodied in the United Nations and its work, see Louis Emmerij, Richard Jolly, and Thomas Weiss, *Ahead of the Curve? UN Ideas and Global Challenges* (Bloomington: Indiana University Press, 2001).
3. Office of the Federal Register, National Archives and Records Administration, *Public Papers of the Presidents of the United States, 1949* (Washington, D.C.: Office of the Federal Register, National Archives and Records Administration, 1949), 113.
4. ———, *Public Papers of the Presidents of the United States, 1953* (Washington, D.C.: Office of the Federal Register, National Archives and Records Administration, 1953), 179.
5. ———, *Public Papers of the Presidents of the United States, 1956* (Washington, D.C.: Office of the Federal Register, National Archives and Records Administration, 1956), 1072–73. Also see Moore and Pubantz, *To Create a New World?* 93.
6. Whereas poor nations in the underdeveloped world are often referred to as *less developed countries,* the United Nations has devised a nomenclature that distinguishes among these states on the basis of per capita gross domestic product (GDP). In general, these states are differentiated from the rich nations of the world by the term *developing countries* and then divided into four income groups: high income, middle income, low income, and least developed countries (LDCs). High-income states have a per capita GDP of more than four thousand U.S. dollars as of 1995. Forty-eight states carried this designation in 2002. Middle-income states have a per capita GDP between eight hundred and four thousand dollars (seventy-two countries in 2002). Low-income states have a per capita GDP of less than eight hundred dollars (sixty-six states in 2002). LDCs have less than an eight-hundred-dollar per capita GDP as well, but they must meet other specific criteria to be designated as an LDC. In 2002 forty-nine nations were declared LDCs.
7. Following the 1976 meeting in Nairobi, UNCTAD convened in Manila (1979), Belgrade (1983), Geneva (1987), Cartagena (1992), Midrand (1996), Bangkok (2002), and São Paolo (2004).
8. Eco' Diagnostic, *International Geneva Yearbook 2000–2001* (Geneva, Switzerland: United Nations, 2000), 234–35.
9. Diana Ayton-Shenker and John Tessitore, eds., *A Global Agenda: Issues Before the 56th General Assembly of the United Nations* (Lanham, MD: Rowman & Littlefield, 2002), 137.
10. UN Conference on Trade and Development, "Gender & trade task force begins work," press release, UNCTAD/PRESS/IN/2003/59, July 22, 2003, http://www.unctad.org/Templates/Webflyer.asp?docID=3771&intItemID=2068&lang=1.
11. United Nations, *Trade and Gender: Opportunities, Challenges and the Policy Dimension,* UN document TD/392 (New York: United Nations, April 4, 2004).
12. General Assembly Resolution 128; see UN General Assembly, *Declaration on the Right to Development,* UN document A/RES/41/128, December 4, 1986, http://www.un.org/documents/ga/res/41/a41r128.htm.

13. The "G-8" are Germany, the United States, the Russian Federation, France, the United Kingdom, Italy, Japan, and Canada.

14. Diana Ayton-Shenker, ed., *A Global Agenda: Issues Before the 57th General Assembly of the United Nations* (Lanham, MD: Rowman & Littlefield, 2002), 162.

15. United Nations, *United Nations Handbook 2002*, 40th ed. (Wellington: New Zealand Ministry of Foreign Affairs and Trade, 2002), 313.

16. For the program of action resulting from the third UN Conference on Least Developed Countries, held May 20, 2001, see UN General Assembly, *Programme of Action for the Least Developed Countries,* UN document A/CONF.191/11 (New York: United Nations, June 8, 2001), 51. See also UN Conference on Trade and Development (UNCTAD), *The Least Developed Countries Report 2004* (Geneva, Switzerland: UN Conference on Trade and Development, May 27, 2004), pt. I, Chap. 1, 20.

17. See, for example, United Nations, *Ministerial Declaration and Message from the United Nations Forum on Forests to the World Summit on Sustainable Development,* UN document A/CONF.199/PC/8 (New York: United Nations, March 19, 2002).

18. UNCTAD, *The Least Developed Countries Report,* 20.

19. Ibid.

20. Kofi Annan, *We the Peoples: The Role of the United Nations in the 21st Century* (New York: United Nations, 2000), 19.

21. Ibid.

22. Ibid., 53.

23. UN Environment Programme, "Foreward," in *Global Environment Outlook 2000* (New York: UN Environment Programme, 2000).

24. For a full discussion of the requirements imposed by the Kyoto Protocol and the structure and procedures created by the UN Framework Convention on Climate Change (UNFCCC), see Climate Change Secretariat, *A Guide to the Climate Change Convention Process,* prelim. 2nd ed. (Bonn, Germany: UNFCCC Secretariat, 2002).

25. UN Information Service, "Secretary-general welcomes European Union ratification of Kyoto Protocol," press release, SG/SM/8251, May 31, 2002, http://www.unis.unvienna.org/unis/pressrels/2002/sgsm8251.html.

26. Paul Brown, "Russia Urged to Rescue Kyoto Pact," *The Guardian,* February 26, 2003, http://www.guardian.co.uk/climatechange/story/0,12374,903094,00.html.

27. International Tribunal for the Law of the Sea (ITLOS), "Order in the MOX Plant case (*Ireland v. United Kingdom),*" press release 62, December 3, 2001, http://www.itlos.org/cgi-bin/cases/case_detail.pl?id=10&lang=en.

28. Ayton-Shenker and Tessitore, *Global Agenda: 56th General Assembly,* 272–73.

29. UN Educational, Scientific and Cultural Organization, *World Water Development Report: Water for People, Water for Life* (Paris: UN Educational, Scientific and Cultural Organization, March 2003), 3.

30. Ibid., 5.

31. Ayton-Shenker, *Global Agenda: 47th General Assembly,* 222.

32. UN Environment Programme, "Treaty on international trade in GMOs to become law," press release, June 13, 2003, http://www.unep.org/Documents.Multilingual/Default.asp?DocumentID=321&ArticleID=4039&1=en.

33. Radoslav S. Dimitrov, "Knowledge, Power, and Interests in Environmental Regime Formation," *International Studies Quarterly* 47 (March 2002): 134.

34. United Nations, *Ministerial Declaration.*

35. For the agenda of the fourth UNFF session, see http: //www.un.org/esa/forests/documents-unff.html#4.

36. Dimitrov, 136.

37. Ayton-Shenker and Tessitore, *Global Agenda: 56th General Assembly,* 222.

38. World Health Organization, *Global Health Sector Strategies for HIV/AIDS, 2003–2007* (Geneva, Switzerland: World Health Organization, 2003), 3. Note that other authoritative sources placed the estimate as high as seventy million people in 2002.

39. In addition to engaging in their own activities, key UN agencies have served as cosponsors of the annual International AIDS Conference, along with national governments, NGOs, and pharmaceutical and other private corporations.

The fifteenth annual conference was held in Bangkok, Thailand, in July 2004.

40. The Global Fund to Fight AIDS, Tuberculosis and Malaria, "UNAIDS and Global Fund sign Memorandum of Understanding," press release, August 4, 2003, http://www.theglobalfund.org/en/media_center/press/pr_030804.asp.

41. Ibid.

KEY TERMS

Development Decades (page 257)

Group of 77 (G-77) (page 258)

Joint UN Programme on HIV/ AIDS (UNAIDS) (page 281)

Millennium Declaration (page 266)

Millennium Development Goals (MDGs) (page 264)

Millennium Summit (page 264)

New International Economic Order (page 258)

Non-Aligned Movement (NAM) (page 257)

North–South Debate (page 256)

Our Common Future (page 268)

Point Four Program (page 255)

Principle 21 (page 267)

Sustainable Development (page 268)

Theory of "Dependency" (page 258)

UN Conference on Environment and Development (page 259)

UN Conference on Trade and Development (UNCTAD) (page 257)

UN Development Programme (UNDP) (page 259)

RESOURCES FOR FURTHER RESEARCH
Relevant Web Sites

Commission on Sustainable Development (www.un.org/esa/sustdev/index.html)

Group of 77 (www.g77.org)

Millennium Development Goals (www.un.org/millenniumgoals)

UN Conference on Trade and Development (www.unctad.org)

UN Development Programme (www.undp.org)

UN Environment Programme (www.unep.org)

UN Framework Convention on Climate Change (UNFCCC) and Kyoto Protocol (www.unfccc.int/2860.php)

Books, Articles, and Documents

Bastos, Cristiana. *Global Responses to AIDS: Science in Emergency*. Bloomington: Indiana University Press, 1999.

Bergesen, Helge Ole, Goerg Parmann, and Oystein B. Thommessen. *Yearbook of International Cooperation on Environment and Development, 1999/2000*. London: Earthscan Publications, 1999.

Chasek, Pamela S. *The Global Environment in the Twenty-First Century: Prospects for International Cooperation*. New York: United Nations University Press, 2000.

Elliott, Lorraine. *The Global Politics of the Environment*. New York: New York University Press, 1998.

Smith, Raymond. *Encyclopedia of AIDS: A Social, Political, Cultural, and Scientific Record of the HIV Epidemic*. Chicago: Fitzroy Dearborn, 2000.

UN Conference on Trade and Development. *The Least Developed Countries Report*. New York and Geneva: United Nations, issued annually.

Upton, Barbara. *The Multilateral Development Banks: Improving U.S. Leadership*. Washington, D.C.: Center for Strategic and International Studies, 2000.

Werksman, Jacob. *Greening International Institutions*. London: Earthscan Publications, 1996.

World Commission on Environment and Development. *Our Common Future*. New York: Oxford University Press, 1987.

Epilogue

Having now surveyed the United Nations from top to bottom and situated it in the political and theoretical traditions of modern international relations and organization, we are obliged to conclude by briefly addressing a common query: Is the United Nations worthwhile, given that it seems unable on many occasions to enforce its decisions or carry out its resolutions? During the lead-up to the U.S. invasion of Iraq in 2003, Washington advanced the equally commonplace grumble that the United Nations had demonstrated its "irrelevancy" in modern world politics. You may sense that the complex answer to the query and the grouse rests within the pages preceding this epilogue. So, although a thorough response would hearken back to the full text, we recognize that these familiar comments require a reasonable final parry.

To assess the UN's merits requires a preliminary recognition of its weaknesses. First, virtually all organizations that span geographic, population, and political realms—national and local governments, military alliances, universities, labor unions, chambers of commerce, and more—can at times seem irrelevant and incapable of effecting stated policies and goals. The United Nations is not immune and may even be unusually susceptible to this caveat. Second, the United Nations, like U.S. national and state governments, has developed a large bureaucracy and a confusing budget that sometimes appear to have lives of their own apart from the UN's advertised intentions (in Chapter 3 we detailed the UN's attempts to reform both). Third, as the Charter makes clear, the United Nations is unable to claim sovereign authority over its members the way a nation-state can make such a claim over its citizens. Rather, the United Nations is an international organization, one we have characterized as more like a "confederacy" (made up of theoretically coequal nations) than a "unitary" or "federal" government (the most familiar forms of sovereign nation-state polities). Consequently, the UN's ability to enforce its decisions is contingent on its members' actions.

This fact is most obvious in the Security Council, the only UN organ that can claim an enforcement entitlement. For this reason, the Security Council is most often in the spotlight when complaints surface about the UN's inability to act. However, when a majority of the council, along with all the permanent veto-wielding members, *does* agree, it has been able to act. To underscore this point, we recommend that you compare our discussion in Chapter 6 of the genocide crisis in Rwanda in 1993, when the Security Council *did not act,* with the converse posture toward Iraq in 1991 and in East Timor in the late 1990s. In East Timor, UN intervention eventually brought peace and a democratic election to a poor, distraught, new nation. These cases demonstrate that the United Nations pursues its decisions and is effective only when its members provide sufficient support. No supranational enforcer governs these nation-states. The UN's members—including, above all, the powerful permanent five—would not accede to such a reform. Nonetheless, as we pointed out, the world's nations—including even the United States within a year of its invasion of Iraq without Security Council approval—often seek the legitimacy that only the United Nations, and particularly the Security Council, can bestow.

Other than the Security Council, most of the other UN organs are best understood as places where virtually all nations in the world can find a place to convene, defend their policies, try to persuade others to accept their viewpoint, insert crucial new issues into the global conversation, verbally assail adversaries, seek out friends, and attempt to craft common approaches to the planet's challenges. The United Nations provides a permanent site—actually a multitude of sites—at which to engage in what some people see as irksome international *politics;* however, bear in mind that one of the pre-UN options was international *conflict.* In addition, the United Nations has been the umbrella organization shepherding a halting, certainly incomplete, but interesting development in the domain of international law. Finally, we must say again, as we often do in this text, that both a traditional "old" and an emergent "new" UN exist, comprehending within the full UN System the broadest spectrum of global activities.

Still, the assessment we just made may seem too obvious, maybe too precious. So we next propose to address the question differently. Let us consider a "theoretical" methodology that professional historians occasionally use: counterfactual history. Some scholars, by taking real-world data, ask, "What might have been?" under altered, but imaginable circumstances.[1] You can easily understand how such analysis is conducted. For example, we can ask the following precise counterfactual, but reasonable, question: Who would have been the victor in the 2000 U.S. presidential election if Ralph Nader had not been a third-party candidate in Florida? Although the question is counterfactual because Nader *did* run, the undeniable answer seems to be that Al Gore would have won the election over George W. Bush. A more problematic, outsized, but suggestive question might be: What would have been the consequences had the South won the U.S. Civil War? World history from that time onward would have been considerably different.

Falling somewhere between an explicit and a wide-ranging counterfactual inquiry is a question most germane to this text: What if a United Nations had never existed? Would the state of affairs be the same as it is today or different? If different, can we speculate on the nature and quality of that difference? We should think hard about this question. Serious problems face the world now just as they have in the past. However, we can say some things with clarity. No world organization like the United Nations existed in the late nineteenth century; World War I occurred. The League of Nations collapsed during the interwar period; World War II occurred. The United Nations came into existence following World War II; we have not had World War III. We cannot assume an automatic one-to-one correspondence between these facts and possible outcomes. However, in this stark way, we can raise the critical concern about potential alternative realities. The United Nations is more than sixty years old. Simply in terms of its longevity and its universal membership, it is the most successful international organization in history. Without it, would the world be the same? better? worse?

Counterfactual history allows us to elevate human action (sometimes called *human "agency"*) as important, even decisive, in history, which deflects the notion that events occur inevitably and that history is "determined" apart from what humans actually do or do not do. The United Nations is a creature of human agency. In this sense it is imperfect because all human-contrived institutions are imperfect. However, this defect does not suggest that without the United Nations the world would be more peaceful and just. Whether the United Nations works properly or not may depend less on it as an abstraction and more on what the world's people do with it.

---

[1] See Martin Bunzl, "Counterfactual History: A User's Guide," *American Historical Review,* June 2004, 845–58; and Robert Cowley, ed., *What If? 2: Eminent Historians Imagine What Might Have Been: Essays* (New York: Putnam, 2001). Cowley has edited four volumes of *What If* books; the others were published in 1999, 2002, and 2003.

Some of the answer to the query about the UN's value may be found in what people and governments have already done with it. They have decided *against* treating it as a static entity created in the 1940s to respond only to the unique problems of that time. The United Nations has evolved *by choice*, not by a grand design or external undeterrable forces. The result is a different United Nations today than its founders or its cold war participants imagined it would be. This kind of evolution—often imposed on the world body because of frustration with its apparent ineffectiveness—is evidence of its vitality and usefulness in the eyes of the people and groups who have the final word on its survival. We trust that the foregoing pages supply you with key factual and analytical information so that you can join the world's peoples in determining what in fact to do next with this *old* and *new* organization.

Appendix A

Charter of the
United Nations

PREAMBLE

We the Peoples of the United Nations Determined

to save succeeding generations from the scourge of war, which twice in our lifetime has brought untold sorrow to mankind, and

to reaffirm faith in fundamental human rights, in the dignity and worth of the human person, in the equal rights of men and women and of nations large and small, and

to establish conditions under which justice and respect for the obligations arising from treaties and other sources of international law can be maintained, and

to promote social progress and better standards of life in larger freedom,

And for These Ends

to practice tolerance and live together in peace with one another as good neighbours, and

to unite our strength to maintain international peace and security, and

to ensure, by the acceptance of principles and the institution of methods, that armed force shall not be used, save in the common interest, and

to employ international machinery for the promotion of the economic and social advancement of all peoples,

Have Resolved to Combine our Efforts to Accomplish These Aims

Accordingly, our respective Governments, through representatives assembled in the city of San Francisco, who have exhibited their full powers found to be in good and due form, have agreed to the present Charter of the United Nations and do hereby establish an international organization to be known as the United Nations.

CHAPTER 1: PURPOSES AND PRINCIPLES

Article 1

The Purposes of the United Nations are:

1. To maintain international peace and security, and to that end: to take effective collective measures for the prevention and removal of threats to the peace, and for the suppression of acts of aggression or other breaches of the peace, and to bring about by peaceful means, and in conformity with the principles of justice and international law, adjustment or settlement of international disputes or situations which might lead to a breach of the peace;

2. To develop friendly relations among nations based on respect for the principle of equal rights and self-determination of peoples, and to take other appropriate measures to strengthen universal peace;

3. To achieve international co-operation in solving international problems of an economic, social, cultural, or humanitarian character, and in promoting and encouraging respect for human rights and for fundamental freedoms for all without distinction as to race, sex, language, or religion; and

4. To be a centre for harmonizing the actions of nations in the attainment of these common ends.

Article 2

The Organization and its Members, in pursuit of the Purposes stated in Article 1, shall act in accordance with the following Principles.

1. The Organization is based on the principle of the sovereign equality of all its Members.

2. All Members, in order to ensure to all of them the rights and benefits resulting from membership, shall fulfill in good faith the obligations assumed by them in accordance with the present Charter.

3. All Members shall settle their international disputes by peaceful means in such a manner that international peace and security, and justice, are not endangered.

4. All Members shall refrain in their international relations from the threat or use of force against the territorial integrity or political independence of any state, or in any other manner inconsistent with the Purposes of the United Nations.

5. All Members shall give the United Nations every assistance in any action it takes in accordance with the present Charter, and shall refrain from giving assistance to any state against which the United Nations is taking preventive or enforcement action.

6. The Organization shall ensure that states which are not Members of the United Nations act in accordance with these Principles so far as may be necessary for the maintenance of international peace and security.

7. Nothing contained in the present Charter shall authorize the United Nations to intervene in matters which are essentially within the domestic jurisdiction of any state or shall require the Members to submit such matters to settlement under the present Charter; but this principle shall not prejudice the application of enforcement measures under Chapter VII.

CHAPTER 2: MEMBERSHIP

Article 3

The original Members of the United Nations shall be the states which, having participated in the United Nations Conference on International Organization at San Francisco, or having previously signed the Declaration by United Nations of 1 January 1942, sign the present Charter and ratify it in accordance with Article 110.

Article 4

1. Membership in the United Nations is open to all other peace-loving states which accept the obligations contained in the present Charter and, in the judgment of the Organization, are able and willing to carry out these obligations.
2. The admission of any such state to membership in the United Nations will be effected by a decision of the General Assembly upon the recommendation of the Security Council.

Article 5

A Member of the United Nations against which preventive or enforcement action has been taken by the Security Council may be suspended from the exercise of the rights and privileges of membership by the General Assembly upon the recommendation of the Security Council. The exercise of these rights and privileges may be restored by the Security Council.

Article 6

A Member of the United Nations which has persistently violated the Principles contained in the present Charter may be expelled from the Organization by the General Assembly upon the recommendation of the Security Council.

CHAPTER 3: ORGANS

Article 7

1. There are established as the principal organs of the United Nations: a General Assembly, a Security Council, an Economic and Social Council, a Trusteeship Council, an International Court of Justice, and a Secretariat.
2. Such subsidiary organs as may be found necessary may be established in accordance with the present Charter.

Article 8

The United Nations shall place no restrictions on the eligibility of men and women to participate in any capacity and under conditions of equality in its principal and subsidiary organs.

CHAPTER 4: THE GENERAL ASSEMBLY

COMPOSITION

Article 9

1. The General Assembly shall consist of all the Members of the United Nations.
2. Each Member shall have not more than five representatives in the General Assembly.

FUNCTIONS AND POWERS

Article 10

The General Assembly may discuss any questions or any matters within the scope of the present Charter or relating to the powers and functions of any organs provided for in the present Charter, and, except as provided in Article 12, may make recommendations to the Members of the United Nations or to the Security Council or to both on any such questions or matters.

Article 11

1. The General Assembly may consider the general principles of co-operation in the maintenance of international peace and security, including the principles governing disarmament and the regulation of armaments, and may make recommendations with regard to such principles to the Members or to the Security Council or to both.
2. The General Assembly may discuss any questions relating to the maintenance of international peace and security brought before it by any Member of the United Nations, or by the Security Council, or by a state which is not a Member of the United Nations in accordance with Article 35, paragraph 2, and, except as provided in Article 12, may make recommendations with regard to any such questions to the state or states concerned or to the Security Council or to both. Any such question on which action is necessary shall be referred to the Security Council by the General Assembly either before or after discussion.
3. The General Assembly may call the attention of the Security Council to situations which are likely to endanger international peace and security.
4. The powers of the General Assembly set forth in this Article shall not limit the general scope of Article 10.

Article 12

1. While the Security Council is exercising in respect of any dispute or situation the functions assigned to it in the present Charter, the General Assembly shall not make any recommendation with regard to that dispute or situation unless the Security Council so requests.
2. The Secretary-General, with the consent of the Security Council, shall notify the General Assembly at each session of any matters relative to the maintenance of international peace and security which are being dealt with by the Security Council and shall similarly notify the General Assembly, or the Members of the United Nations if the General Assembly is not in session, immediately the Security Council ceases to deal with such matters.

Article 13

1. The General Assembly shall initiate studies and make recommendations for the purpose of:
   a. promoting international co-operation in the political field and encouraging the progressive development of international law and its codification;
   b. promoting international co-operation in the economic, social, cultural, educational, and health fields, and assisting in the realization of human rights and fundamental freedoms for all without distinction as to race, sex, language, or religion.
2. The further responsibilities, functions and powers of the General Assembly with respect to matters mentioned in paragraph 1 (b) above are set forth in Chapters IX and X.

Article 14

Subject to the provisions of Article 12, the General Assembly may recommend measures for the peaceful adjustment of any situation, regardless of origin, which it deems likely to impair the general welfare or friendly relations among nations, including situations resulting from a violation of the provisions of the present Charter setting forth the Purposes and Principles of the United Nations.

Article 15

1. The General Assembly shall receive and consider annual and special reports from the Security Council; these reports shall include an account of the measures that the Security Council has decided upon or taken to maintain international peace and security.
2. The General Assembly shall receive and consider reports from the other organs of the United Nations.

Article 16

The General Assembly shall perform such functions with respect to the international trusteeship system as are assigned to it under Chapters XII and XIII, including the approval of the trusteeship agreements for areas not designated as strategic.

Article 17

1. The General Assembly shall consider and approve the budget of the Organization.
2. The expenses of the Organization shall be borne by the Members as apportioned by the General Assembly.
3. The Assembly shall consider and approve any financial and budgetary arrangements with specialized agencies referred to in Article 57 and shall examine the administrative budgets of such specialized agencies with a view to making recommendations to the agencies concerned.

VOTING

Article 18

1. Each member of the General Assembly shall have one vote.

2. Decisions of the General Assembly on important questions shall be made by a two-thirds majority of the members present and voting. These questions shall include: recommendations with respect to the maintenance of international peace and security, the election of the non-permanent members of the Security Council, the election of the members of the Economic and Social Council, the election of members of the Trusteeship Council in accordance with paragraph 1 of Article 86, the admission of new Members to the United Nations, the suspension of the rights and privileges of membership, the expulsion of Members, questions relating to the operation of the trusteeship system, and budgetary questions.

3. Decisions on other questions, including the determination of additional categories of questions to be decided by a two-thirds majority, shall be made by a majority of the members present and voting.

Article 19

A Member of the United Nations which is in arrears in the payment of its financial contributions to the Organization shall have no vote in the General Assembly if the amount of its arrears equals or exceeds the amount of the contributions due from it for the preceding two full years. The General Assembly may, nevertheless, permit such a Member to vote if it is satisfied that the failure to pay is due to conditions beyond the control of the Member.

PROCEDURE

Article 20

The General Assembly shall meet in regular annual sessions and in such special sessions as occasion may require. Special sessions shall be convoked by the Secretary-General at the request of the Security Council or of a majority of the Members of the United Nations.

Article 21

The General Assembly shall adopt its own rules of procedure. It shall elect its President for each session.

Article 22

The General Assembly may establish such subsidiary organs as it deems necessary for the performance of its functions.

CHAPTER 5: THE SECURITY COUNCIL

COMPOSITION

Article 23

1. The Security Council shall consist of fifteen Members of the United Nations. The Republic of China, France, the Union of Soviet Socialist Republics, the United Kingdom of Great Britain and Northern Ireland, and the United States of America

shall be permanent members of the Security Council. The General Assembly shall elect ten other Members of the United Nations to be non-permanent members of the Security Council, due regard being specially paid, in the first instance to the contribution of Members of the United Nations to the maintenance of international peace and security and to the other purposes of the Organization, and also to equitable geographical distribution.

2. The non-permanent members of the Security Council shall be elected for a term of two years. In the first election of the non-permanent members after the increase of the membership of the Security Council from eleven to fifteen, two of the four additional members shall be chosen for a term of one year. A retiring member shall not be eligible for immediate re-election.

3. Each member of the Security Council shall have one representative.

FUNCTIONS AND POWERS

Article 24

1. In order to ensure prompt and effective action by the United Nations, its Members confer on the Security Council primary responsibility for the maintenance of international peace and security, and agree that in carrying out its duties under this responsibility the Security Council acts on their behalf.

2. In discharging these duties the Security Council shall act in accordance with the Purposes and Principles of the United Nations. The specific powers granted to the Security Council for the discharge of these duties are laid down in Chapters VI, VII, VIII, and XII.

3. The Security Council shall submit annual and, when necessary, special reports to the General Assembly for its consideration.

Article 25

The Members of the United Nations agree to accept and carry out the decisions of the Security Council in accordance with the present Charter.

Article 26

In order to promote the establishment and maintenance of international peace and security with the least diversion for armaments of the world's human and economic resources, the Security Council shall be responsible for formulating, with the assistance of the Military Staff Committee referred to in Article 47, plans to be submitted to the Members of the United Nations for the establishment of a system for the regulation of armaments.

VOTING

Article 27

1. Each member of the Security Council shall have one vote.

2. Decisions of the Security Council on procedural matters shall be made by an affirmative vote of nine members.

3. Decisions of the Security Council on all other matters shall be made by an affirmative vote of nine members including the concurring votes of the permanent members; provided that, in decisions under Chapter VI, and under paragraph 3 of Article 52, a party to a dispute shall abstain from voting.

PROCEDURE

Article 28

1. The Security Council shall be so organized as to be able to function continuously. Each member of the Security Council shall for this purpose be represented at all times at the seat of the Organization.
2. The Security Council shall hold meetings at which each of its members may, if it so desires, be represented by a member of the government or by some other specially designated representative.
3. The Security Council may hold meetings at such places other than the seat of the Organization as in its judgment will best facilitate its work.

Article 29

The Security Council may establish such subsidiary organs as it deems necessary for the performance of its functions.

Article 30

The Security Council shall adopt its own rules of procedure, including the method of selecting its President.

Article 31

Any Member of the United Nations which is not a member of the Security Council may participate, without vote, in the discussion of any question brought before the Security Council whenever the latter considers that the interests of that Member are specially affected.

Article 32

Any Member of the United Nations which is not a member of the Security Council or any state which is not a Member of the United Nations, if it is a party to a dispute under consideration by the Security Council, shall be invited to participate, without vote, in the discussion relating to the dispute. The Security Council shall lay down such conditions as it deems just for the participation of a state which is not a Member of the United Nations.

CHAPTER 6: PACIFIC SETTLEMENT OF DISPUTES

Article 33

1. The parties to any dispute, the continuance of which is likely to endanger the maintenance of international peace and security, shall, first of all, seek a solution by negotiation,

enquiry, mediation, conciliation, arbitration, judicial settlement, resort to regional agencies or arrangements, or other peaceful means of their own choice.

2. The Security Council shall, when it deems necessary, call upon the parties to settle their dispute by such means.

Article 34

The Security Council may investigate any dispute, or any situation which might lead to international friction or give rise to a dispute, in order to determine whether the continuance of the dispute or situation is likely to endanger the maintenance of international peace and security.

Article 35

1. Any Member of the United Nations may bring any dispute, or any situation of the nature referred to in Article 34, to the attention of the Security Council or of the General Assembly.

2. A state which is not a Member of the United Nations may bring to the attention of the Security Council or of the General Assembly any dispute to which it is a party if it accepts in advance, for the purposes of the dispute, the obligations of pacific settlement provided in the present Charter.

3. The proceedings of the General Assembly in respect of matters brought to its attention under this Article will be subject to the provisions of Articles 11 and 12.

Article 36

1. The Security Council may, at any stage of a dispute of the nature referred to in Article 33 or of a situation of like nature, recommend appropriate procedures or methods of adjustment.

2. The Security Council should take into consideration any procedures for the settlement of the dispute which have already been adopted by the parties.

3. In making recommendations under this Article the Security Council should also take into consideration that legal disputes should as a general rule be referred by the parties to the International Court of Justice in accordance with the provisions of the Statute of the Court.

Article 37

1. Should the parties to a dispute of the nature referred to in Article 33 fail to settle it by the means indicated in that Article, they shall refer it to the Security Council.

2. If the Security Council deems that the continuance of the dispute is in fact likely to endanger the maintenance of international peace and security, it shall decide whether to take action under Article 36 or to recommend such terms of settlement as it may consider appropriate.

Article 38

Without prejudice to the provisions of Articles 33 to 37, the Security Council may, if all the parties to any dispute so request, make recommendations to the parties with a view to a pacific settlement of the dispute.

CHAPTER 7: ACTION WITH RESPECT TO THREATS TO THE PEACE, BREACHES OF THE PEACE, AND ACTS OF AGGRESSION

Article 39

The Security Council shall determine the existence of any threat to the peace, breach of the peace, or act of aggression and shall make recommendations, or decide what measures shall be taken in accordance with Articles 41 and 42, to maintain or restore international peace and security.

Article 40

In order to prevent an aggravation of the situation, the Security Council may, before making the recommendations or deciding upon the measures provided for in Article 39, call upon the parties concerned to comply with such provisional measures as it deems necessary or desirable. Such provisional measures shall be without prejudice to the rights, claims, or position of the parties concerned. The Security Council shall duly take account of failure to comply with such provisional measures.

Article 41

The Security Council may decide what measures not involving the use of armed force are to be employed to give effect to its decisions, and it may call upon the Members of the United Nations to apply such measures. These may include complete or partial interruption of economic relations and of rail, sea, air, postal, telegraphic, radio, and other means of communication, and the severance of diplomatic relations.

Article 42

Should the Security Council consider that measures provided for in Article 41 would be inadequate or have proved to be inadequate, it may take such action by air, sea, or land forces as may be necessary to maintain or restore international peace and security. Such action may include demonstrations, blockade, and other operations by air, sea, or land forces of Members of the United Nations.

Article 43

1. All Members of the United Nations, in order to contribute to the maintenance of international peace and security, undertake to make available to the Security Council, on its call and in accordance with a special agreement or agreements, armed forces, assistance, and facilities, including rights of passage, necessary for the purpose of maintaining international peace and security.
2. Such agreement or agreements shall govern the numbers and types of forces, their degree of readiness and general location, and the nature of the facilities and assistance to be provided.

3. The agreement or agreements shall be negotiated as soon as possible on the initiative of the Security Council. They shall be concluded between the Security Council and Members or between the Security Council and groups of Members and shall be subject to ratification by the signatory states in accordance with their respective constitutional processes.

Article 44

When the Security Council has decided to use force it shall, before calling upon a Member not represented on it to provide armed forces in fulfilment of the obligations assumed under Article 43, invite that Member, if the Member so desires, to participate in the decisions of the Security Council concerning the employment of contingents of that Member's armed forces.

Article 45

In order to enable the United Nations to take urgent military measures, Members shall hold immediately available national air-force contingents for combined international enforcement action. The strength and degree of readiness of these contingents and plans for their combined action shall be determined, within the limits laid down in the special agreement or agreements referred to in Article 43, by the Security Council with the assistance of the Military Staff Committee.

Article 46

Plans for the application of armed force shall be made by the Security Council with the assistance of the Military Staff Committee.

Article 47

1. There shall be established a Military Staff Committee to advise and assist the Security Council on questions relating to the Security Council's military requirements for the maintenance of international peace and security, the employment and command of forces placed at its disposal, the regulation of armaments, and possible disarmament.
2. The Military Staff Committee shall consist of the Chiefs of Staff of the permanent members of the Security Council or their representatives. Any Member of the United Nations not permanently represented on the Committee shall be invited by the Committee to be associated with it when the efficient discharge of the Committee's responsibilities requires the participation of that Member in its work.
3. The Military Staff Committee shall be responsible under the Security Council for the strategic direction of any armed forces placed at the disposal of the Security Council. Questions relating to the command of such forces shall be worked out subsequently.
4. The Military Staff Committee, with the authorization of the Security Council after consultation with appropriate regional agencies, may establish regional sub-committees.

Article 48

1. The action required to carry out the decisions of the Security Council for the maintenance of international peace and security shall be taken by all the Members of the United Nations or by some of them, as the Security Council may determine.

2. Such decisions shall be carried out by the Members of the United Nations directly and through their action in the appropriate international agencies of which they are members.

Article 49

The Members of the United Nations shall join in affording mutual assistance in carrying out the measures decided upon by the Security Council.

Article 50

If preventive or enforcement measures against any state are taken by the Security Council, any other state, whether a Member of the United Nations or not, which finds itself confronted with special economic problems arising from the carrying out of those measures shall have the right to consult the Security Council with regard to a solution of those problems.

Article 51

Nothing in the present Charter shall impair the inherent right of individual or collective self-defence if an armed attack occurs against a Member of the United Nations, until the Security Council has taken measures necessary to maintain international peace and security. Measures taken by Members in the exercise of this right of self-defence shall be immediately reported to the Security Council and shall not in any way affect the authority and responsibility of the Security Council under the present Charter to take at any time such action as it deems necessary in order to maintain or restore international peace and security.

CHAPTER 8: REGIONAL ARRANGEMENTS

Article 52

1. Nothing in the present Charter precludes the existence of regional arrangements or agencies for dealing with such matters relating to the maintenance of international peace and security as are appropriate for regional action, provided that such arrangements or agencies and their activities are consistent with the Purposes and Principles of the United Nations.
2. The Members of the United Nations entering into such arrangements or constituting such agencies shall make every effort to achieve pacific settlement of local disputes through such regional arrangements or by such regional agencies before referring them to the Security Council.
3. The Security Council shall encourage the development of pacific settlement of local disputes through such regional arrangements or by such regional agencies either on the initiative of the states concerned or by reference from the Security Council.
4. This Article in no way impairs the application of Articles 34 and 35.

Article 53

1. The Security Council shall, where appropriate, utilize such regional arrangements or agencies for enforcement action under its authority. But no enforcement action shall be taken under regional arrangements or by regional agencies without the authorization

of the Security Council, with the exception of measures against any enemy state, as defined in paragraph 2 of this Article, provided for pursuant to Article 107 or in regional arrangements directed against renewal of aggressive policy on the part of any such state, until such time as the Organization may, on request of the Governments concerned, be charged with the responsibility for preventing further aggression by such a state.

2. The term enemy state as used in paragraph 1 of this Article applies to any state which during the Second World War has been an enemy of any signatory of the present Charter.

Article 54

The Security Council shall at all times be kept fully informed of activities undertaken or in contemplation under regional arrangements or by regional agencies for the maintenance of international peace and security.

CHAPTER 9: INTERNATIONAL ECONOMIC AND SOCIAL CO-OPERATION

Article 55

With a view to the creation of conditions of stability and well-being which are necessary for peaceful and friendly relations among nations based on respect for the principle of equal rights and self-determination of peoples, the United Nations shall promote:

a. higher standards of living, full employment, and conditions of economic and social progress and development;
b. solutions of international economic, social, health, and related problems; and international cultural and educational co-operation; and
c. universal respect for, and observance of, human rights and fundamental freedoms for all without distinction as to race, sex, language, or religion.

Article 56

All Members pledge themselves to take joint and separate action in co-operation with the Organization for the achievement of the purposes set forth in Article 55.

Article 57

1. The various specialized agencies, established by intergovernmental agreement and having wide international responsibilities, as defined in their basic instruments, in economic, social, cultural, educational, health, and related fields, shall be brought into relationship with the United Nations in accordance with the provisions of Article 63.
2. Such agencies thus brought into relationship with the United Nations are hereinafter referred to as specialized agencies.

Article 58

The Organization shall make recommendations for the co-ordination of the policies and activities of the specialized agencies.

Article 59

The Organization shall, where appropriate, initiate negotiations among the states concerned for the creation of any new specialized agencies required for the accomplishment of the purposes set forth in Article 55.

Article 60

Responsibility for the discharge of the functions of the Organization set forth in this Chapter shall be vested in the General Assembly and, under the authority of the General Assembly, in the Economic and Social Council, which shall have for this purpose the powers set forth in Chapter X.

CHAPTER 10: THE ECONOMIC AND SOCIAL COUNCIL

COMPOSITION

Article 61

1. The Economic and Social Council shall consist of fifty-four Members of the United Nations elected by the General Assembly.
2. Subject to the provisions of paragraph 3, eighteen members of the Economic and Social Council shall be elected each year for a term of three years. A retiring member shall be eligible for immediate re-election.
3. At the first election after the increase in the membership of the Economic and Social Council from twenty-seven to fifty-four members, in addition to the members elected in place of the nine members whose term of office expires at the end of that year, twenty-seven additional members shall be elected. Of these twenty-seven additional members, the term of office of nine members so elected shall expire at the end of one year, and of nine other members at the end of two years, in accordance with arrangements made by the General Assembly.
4. Each member of the Economic and Social Council shall have one representative.

FUNCTIONS AND POWERS

Article 62

1. The Economic and Social Council may make or initiate studies and reports with respect to international economic, social, cultural, educational, health, and related matters and may make recommendations with respect to any such matters to the General Assembly, to the Members of the United Nations, and to the specialized agencies concerned.
2. It may make recommendations for the purpose of promoting respect for, and observance of, human rights and fundamental freedoms for all.
3. It may prepare draft conventions for submission to the General Assembly, with respect to matters falling within its competence.

4. It may call, in accordance with the rules prescribed by the United Nations, international conferences on matters falling within its competence.

Article 63

1. The Economic and Social Council may enter into agreements with any of the agencies referred to in Article 57, defining the terms on which the agency concerned shall be brought into relationship with the United Nations. Such agreements shall be subject to approval by the General Assembly.
2. It may co-ordinate the activities of the specialized agencies through consultation with and recommendations to such agencies and through recommendations to the General Assembly and to the Members of the United Nations.

Article 64

1. The Economic and Social Council may take appropriate steps to obtain regular reports from the specialized agencies. It may make arrangements with the Members of the United Nations and with the specialized agencies to obtain reports on the steps taken to give effect to its own recommendations and to recommendations on matters falling within its competence made by the General Assembly.
2. It may communicate its observations on these reports to the General Assembly.

Article 65

The Economic and Social Council may furnish information to the Security Council and shall assist the Security Council upon its request.

Article 66

1. The Economic and Social Council shall perform such functions as fall within its competence in connexion with the carrying out of the recommendations of the General Assembly.
2. It may, with the approval of the General Assembly, perform services at the request of Members of the United Nations and at the request of specialized agencies.
3. It shall perform such other functions as are specified elsewhere in the present Charter or as may be assigned to it by the General Assembly.

VOTING

Article 67

1. Each member of the Economic and Social Council shall have one vote.
2. Decisions of the Economic and Social Council shall be made by a majority of the members present and voting.

PROCEDURE

Article 68

The Economic and Social Council shall set up commissions in economic and social fields and for the promotion of human rights, and such other commissions as may be required for the performance of its functions.

Article 69

The Economic and Social Council shall invite any Member of the United Nations to participate, without vote, in its deliberations on any matter of particular concern to that Member.

Article 70

The Economic and Social Council may make arrangements for representatives of the specialized agencies to participate, without vote, in its deliberations and in those of the commissions established by it, and for its representatives to participate in the deliberations of the specialized agencies.

Article 71

The Economic and Social Council may make suitable arrangements for consultation with non-governmental organizations which are concerned with matters within its competence. Such arrangements may be made with international organizations and, where appropriate, with national organizations after consultation with the Member of the United Nations concerned.

Article 72

1. The Economic and Social Council shall adopt its own rules of procedure, including the method of selecting its President.
2. The Economic and Social Council shall meet as required in accordance with its rules, which shall include provision for the convening of meetings on the request of a majority of its members.

CHAPTER 11: DECLARATION REGARDING NON-SELF-GOVERNING TERRITORIES

Article 73

Members of the United Nations which have or assume responsibilities for the administration of territories whose peoples have not yet attained a full measure of self-government recognize the principle that the interests of the inhabitants of these territories are paramount, and accept as a sacred trust the obligation to promote to the utmost, within the system of international peace and security established by the present Charter, the well-being of the inhabitants of these territories, and, to this end:

    a. to ensure, with due respect for the culture of the peoples concerned, their political, economic, social, and educational advancement, their just treatment, and their protection against abuses;

b. to develop self-government, to take due account of the political aspirations of the peoples, and to assist them in the progressive development of their free political institutions, according to the particular circumstances of each territory and its peoples and their varying stages of advancement;

c. to further international peace and security;

d. to promote constructive measures of development, to encourage research, and to cooperate with one another and, when and where appropriate, with specialized international bodies with a view to the practical achievement of the social, economic, and scientific purposes set forth in this Article; and

e. to transmit regularly to the Secretary-General for information purposes, subject to such limitation as security and constitutional considerations may require, statistical and other information of a technical nature relating to economic, social, and educational conditions in the territories for which they are respectively responsible other than those territories to which Chapters XII and XIII apply.

Article 74

Members of the United Nations also agree that their policy in respect of the territiories to which this Chapter applies, no less than in respect of their metropolitan areas, must be based on the general principle of good-neighbourliness, due account being taken of the interests and well-being of the rest of the world, in social, economic, and commercial matters.

CHAPTER 12: INTERNATIONAL TRUSTEESHIP SYSTEM

Article 75

The United Nations shall establish under its authority an international trusteeship system for the administration and supervision of such territories as may be placed thereunder by subsequent individual agreements. These territories are hereinafter referred to as trust territories.

Article 76

The basic objectives of the trusteeship system, in accordance with the Purposes of the United Nations laid down in Article 1 of the present Charter, shall be:

a. to further international peace and security;

b. to promote the political, economic, social, and educational advancement of the inhabitants of the trust territories, and their progressive development towards self-government or independence as may be appropriate to the particular circumstances of each territory and its peoples and the freely expressed wishes of the peoples concerned, and as may be provided by the terms of each trusteeship agreement;

c. to encourage respect for human rights and for fundamental freedoms for all without distinction as to race, sex, language, or religion, and to encourage recognition of the interdependence of the peoples of the world; and

d. to ensure equal treatment in social, economic, and commercial matters for all Members of the United Nations and their nationals, and also equal treatment for the latter in the administration of justice, without prejudice to the attainment of the foregoing objectives and subject to the provisions of Article 80.

Article 77

1. The trusteeship system shall apply to such territories in the following categories as may be placed thereunder by means of trusteeship agreements:
   a. territories now held under mandate;
   b. territories which may be detached from enemy states as a result of the Second World War; and
   c. territories voluntarily placed under the system by states responsible for their administration.
2. It will be a matter for subsequent agreement as to which territories in the foregoing categories will be brought under the trusteeship system and upon what terms.

Article 78

The trusteeship system shall not apply to territories which have become Members of the United Nations, relationship among which shall be based on respect for the principle of sovereign equality.

Article 79

The terms of trusteeship for each territory to be placed under the trusteeship system, including any alteration or amendment, shall be agreed upon by the states directly concerned, including the mandatory power in the case of territories held under mandate by a Member of the United Nations, and shall be approved as provided for in Articles 83 and 85.

Article 80

1. Except as may be agreed upon in individual trusteeship agreements, made under Articles 77, 79, and 81, placing each territory under the trusteeship system, and until such agreements have been concluded, nothing in this Chapter shall be construed in or of itself to alter in any manner the rights whatsoever of any states or any peoples or the terms of existing international instruments to which Members of the United Nations may respectively be parties.
2. Paragraph 1 of this Article shall not be interpreted as giving grounds for delay or postponement of the negotiation and conclusion of agreements for placing mandated and other territories under the trusteeship system as provided for in Article 77.

Article 81

The trusteeship agreement shall in each case include the terms under which the trust territory will be administered and designate the authority which will exercise the administration of the trust territory. Such authority, hereinafter called the administering authority, may be one or more states or the Organization itself.

Article 82

There may be designated, in any trusteeship agreement, a strategic area or areas which may include part or all of the trust territory to which the agreement applies, without prejudice to any special agreement or agreements made under Article 43.

Article 83

1. All functions of the United Nations relating to strategic areas, including the approval of the terms of the trusteeship agreements and of their alteration or amendment, shall be exercised by the Security Council.
2. The basic objectives set forth in Article 76 shall be applicable to the people of each strategic area.
3. The Security Council shall, subject to the provisions of the trusteeship agreements and without prejudice to security considerations, avail itself of the assistance of the Trusteeship Council to perform those functions of the United Nations under the trusteeship system relating to political, economic, social, and educational matters in the strategic areas.

Article 84

It shall be the duty of the administering authority to ensure that the trust territory shall play its part in the maintenance of international peace and security. To this end the administering authority may make use of volunteer forces, facilities, and assistance from the trust territory in carrying out the obligations towards the Security Council undertaken in this regard by the administering authority, as well as for local defence and the maintenance of law and order within the trust territory.

Article 85

1. The functions of the United Nations with regard to trusteeship agreements for all areas not designated as strategic, including the approval of the terms of the trusteeship agreements and of their alteration or amendment, shall be exercised by the General Assembly.
2. The Trusteeship Council, operating under the authority of the General Assembly, shall assist the General Assembly in carrying out these functions.

CHAPTER 13: THE TRUSTEESHIP COUNCIL

COMPOSITION

Article 86

1. The Trusteeship Council shall consist of the following Members of the United Nations:
    a. those Members administering trust territories;
    b. such of those Members mentioned by name in Article 23 as are not administering trust territories; and
    c. as many other Members elected for three-year terms by the General Assembly as may be necessary to ensure that the total number of members of the Trusteeship Council is equally divided between those Members of the United Nations which administer trust territories and those which do not.
2. Each member of the Trusteeship Council shall designate one specially qualified person to represent it therein.

FUNCTIONS AND POWERS

Article 87

The General Assembly and, under its authority, the Trusteeship Council, in carrying out their functions, may:

a. consider reports submitted by the administering authority;
b. accept petitions and examine them in consultation with the administering authority;
c. provide for periodic visits to the respective trust territories at times agreed upon with the administering authority; and
d. take these and other actions in conformity with the terms of the trusteeship agreements.

Article 88

The Trusteeship Council shall formulate a questionnaire on the political, economic, social, and educational advancement of the inhabitants of each trust territory, and the administering authority for each trust territory within the competence of the General Assembly shall make an annual report to the General Assembly upon the basis of such questionnaire.

VOTING

Article 89

1. Each member of the Trusteeship Council shall have one vote.
2. Decisions of the Trusteeship Council shall be made by a majority of the members present and voting.

PROCEDURE

Article 90

1. The Trusteeship Council shall adopt its own rules of procedure, including the method of selecting its President.
2. The Trusteeship Council shall meet as required in accordance with its rules, which shall include provision for the convening of meetings on the request of a majority of its members.

Article 91

The Trusteeship Council shall, when appropriate, avail itself of the assistance of the Economic and Social Council and of the specialized agencies in regard to matters with which they are respectively concerned.

CHAPTER 14: THE INTERNATIONAL COURT OF JUSTICE

Article 92

The International Court of Justice shall be the principal judicial organ of the United Nations. It shall function in accordance with the annexed Statute, which is based upon the Statute of the Permanent Court of International Justice and forms an integral part of the present Charter.

Article 93

1. All Members of the United Nations are ipso facto parties to the Statute of the International Court of Justice.
2. A state which is not a member of the United Nations may become a party to the Statute of the International Court of Justice on conditions to be determined in each case by the General Assembly upon the recommendation of the Security Council.

Article 94

1. Each Member of the United Nations undertakes to comply with the decision of the International Court of Justice in any case to which it is a party.
2. If any party to a case fails to perform the obligations incumbent upon it under a judgment rendered by the Court, the other party may have recourse to the Security Council, which may, if it deems necessary, make recommendations or decide upon measures to be taken to give effect to the judgment.

Article 95

Nothing in the present Charter shall prevent Members of the United Nations from entrusting the solution of their differences to other tribunals by virtue of agreements already in existence or which may be concluded in the future.

Article 96

1. The General Assembly or the Security Council may request the International Court of Justice to give an advisory opinion on any legal question.
2. Other organs of the United Nations and specialized agencies, which may at any time be so authorized by the General Assembly, may also request advisory opinions of the Court on legal questions arising within the scope of their activities.

CHAPTER 15: THE SECRETARIAT

Article 97

The Secretariat shall comprise a Secretary-General and such staff as the Organization may require. The Secretary-General shall be appointed by the General Assembly upon the recommendation of the Security Council. He shall be the chief administrative officer of the Organization.

Article 98

The Secretary-General shall act in that capacity in all meetings of the General Assembly, of the Security Council, of the Economic and Social Council, and of the Trusteeship Council, and shall perform such other functions as are entrusted to him by these organs. The Secretary-General shall make an annual report to the General Assembly on the work of the Organization.

Article 99

The Secretary-General may bring to the attention of the Security Council any matter which in his opinion may threaten the maintenance of international peace and security.

Article 100

1. In the performance of their duties the Secretary-General and the staff shall not seek or receive instructions from any government or from any other authority external to the Organization. They shall refrain from any action which might reflect on their position as international officials responsible only to the Organization.
2. Each Member of the United Nations undertakes to respect the exclusively international character of the responsibilities of the Secretary-General and the staff and not to seek to influence them in the discharge of their responsibilities.

Article 101

1. The staff shall be appointed by the Secretary-General under regulations established by the General Assembly.
2. Appropriate staffs shall be permanently assigned to the Economic and Social Council, the Trusteeship Council, and, as required, to other organs of the United Nations. These staffs shall form a part of the Secretariat.
3. The paramount consideration in the employment of the staff and in the determination of the conditions of service shall be the necessity of securing the highest standards of efficiency, competence, and integrity. Due regard shall be paid to the importance of recruiting the staff on as wide a geographical basis as possible.

CHAPTER 16: MISCELLANEOUS PROVISIONS

Article 102

1. Every treaty and every international agreement entered into by any Member of the United Nations after the present Charter comes into force shall as soon as possible be registered with the Secretariat and published by it.
2. No party to any such treaty or international agreement which has not been registered in accordance with the provisions of paragraph I of this Article may invoke that treaty or agreement before any organ of the United Nations.

Article 103

In the event of a conflict between the obligations of the Members of the United Nations under the present Charter and their obligations under any other international agreement, their obligations under the present Charter shall prevail.

Article 104

The Organization shall enjoy in the territory of each of its Members such legal capacity as may be necessary for the exercise of its functions and the fulfilment of its purposes.

Article 105

1. The Organization shall enjoy in the territory of each of its Members such privileges and immunities as are necessary for the fulfilment of its purposes.
2. Representatives of the Members of the United Nations and officials of the Organization shall similarly enjoy such privileges and immunities as are necessary for the independent exercise of their functions in connexion with the Organization.
3. The General Assembly may make recommendations with a view to determining the details of the application of paragraphs 1 and 2 of this Article or may propose conventions to the Members of the United Nations for this purpose.

CHAPTER 17: TRANSITIONAL SECURITY ARRANGEMENTS

Article 106

Pending the coming into force of such special agreements referred to in Article 43 as in the opinion of the Security Council enable it to begin the exercise of its responsibilities under Article 42, the parties to the Four-Nation Declaration, signed at Moscow, 30 October 1943, and France, shall, in accordance with the provisions of paragraph 5 of that Declaration, consult with one another and as occasion requires with other Members of the United Nations with a view to such joint action on behalf of the Organization as may be necessary for the purpose of maintaining international peace and security.

Article 107

Nothing in the present Charter shall invalidate or preclude action, in relation to any state which during the Second World War has been an enemy of any signatory to the present Charter, taken or authorized as a result of that war by the Governments having responsibility for such action.

CHAPTER 18: AMENDMENTS

Article 108

Amendments to the present Charter shall come into force for all Members of the United Nations when they have been adopted by a vote of two thirds of the members of the General Assembly and ratified in accordance with their respective constitutional processes by two thirds of the Members of the United Nations, including all the permanent members of the Security Council.

Article 109

1. A General Conference of the Members of the United Nations for the purpose of reviewing the present Charter may be held at a date and place to be fixed by a two-thirds vote of the members of the General Assembly and by a vote of any nine members of the Security Council. Each Member of the United Nations shall have one vote in the conference.

2. Any alteration of the present Charter recommended by a two-thirds vote of the conference shall take effect when ratified in accordance with their respective constitutional processes by two thirds of the Members of the United Nations including all the permanent members of the Security Council.
3. If such a conference has not been held before the tenth annual session of the General Assembly following the coming into force of the present Charter, the proposal to call such a conference shall be placed on the agenda of that session of the General Assembly, and the conference shall be held if so decided by a majority vote of the members of the General Assembly and by a vote of any seven members of the Security Council.

CHAPTER 19: RATIFICATION AND SIGNATURE

Article 110

1. The present Charter shall be ratified by the signatory states in accordance with their respective constitutional processes.
2. The ratifications shall be deposited with the Government of the United States of America, which shall notify all the signatory states of each deposit as well as the Secretary-General of the Organization when he has been appointed.
3. The present Charter shall come into force upon the deposit of ratifications by the Republic of China, France, the Union of Soviet Socialist Republics, the United Kingdom of Great Britain and Northern Ireland, and the United States of America, and by a majority of the other signatory states. A protocol of the ratifications deposited shall thereupon be drawn up by the Government of the United States of America which shall communicate copies thereof to all the signatory states.
4. The states signatory to the present Charter which ratify it after it has come into force will become original Members of the United Nations on the date of the deposit of their respective ratifications.

Article 111

The present Charter, of which the Chinese, French, Russian, English, and Spanish texts are equally authentic, shall remain deposited in the archives of the Government of the United States of America. Duly certified copies thereof shall be transmitted by that Government to the Governments of the other signatory states.

IN FAITH WHEREOF the representatives of the Governments of the United Nations have signed the present Charter.

DONE at the city of San Francisco the twenty-sixth day of June, one thousand nine hundred and forty-five.

Appendix B

Universal Declaration of Human Rights

PREAMBLE

Whereas recognition of the inherent dignity and of the equal and inalienable rights of all members of the human family is the foundation of freedom, justice and peace in the world,

Whereas disregard and contempt for human rights have resulted in barbarous acts which have outraged the conscience of mankind, and the advent of a world in which human beings shall enjoy freedom of speech and belief and freedom from fear and want has been proclaimed as the highest aspiration of the common people,

Whereas it is essential, if man is not to be compelled to have recourse, as a last resort, to rebellion against tyranny and oppression, that human rights should be protected by the rule of law,

Whereas it is essential to promote the development of friendly relations between nations,

Whereas the peoples of the United Nations have in the Charter reaffirmed their faith in fundamental human rights, in the dignity and worth of the human person and in the equal rights of men and women and have determined to promote social progress and better standards of life in larger freedom,

Whereas Member States have pledged themselves to achieve, in co-operation with the United Nations, the promotion of universal respect for and observance of human rights and fundamental freedoms,

Whereas a common understanding of these rights and freedoms is of the greatest importance for the full realization of this pledge,

Now, Therefore THE GENERAL ASSEMBLY proclaims THIS UNIVERSAL DECLARATION OF HUMAN RIGHTS as a common standard of achievement for all peoples and all nations, to the end that every individual and every organ of society, keeping this Declaration constantly in mind, shall strive by teaching and education to promote respect for these rights and freedoms and by progressive measures, national and international, to secure their universal and effective recognition and observance, both among the peoples of Member States themselves and among the peoples of territories under their jurisdiction.

Article 1

All human beings are born free and equal in dignity and rights. They are endowed with reason and conscience and should act towards one another in a spirit of brotherhood.

Article 2

Everyone is entitled to all the rights and freedoms set forth in this Declaration, without distinction of any kind, such as race, colour, sex, language, religion, political or other opinion, national or social origin, property, birth or other status. Furthermore, no distinction shall be made on the basis of the political, jurisdictional or international status of the country or territory to which a person belongs, whether it be independent, trust, non-self-governing or under any other limitation of sovereignty.

Article 3

Everyone has the right to life, liberty and security of person.

Article 4

No one shall be held in slavery or servitude; slavery and the slave trade shall be prohibited in all their forms.

Article 5

No one shall be subjected to torture or to cruel, inhuman or degrading treatment or punishment.

Article 6

Everyone has the right to recognition everywhere as a person before the law.

Article 7

All are equal before the law and are entitled without any discrimination to equal protection of the law. All are entitled to equal protection against any discrimination in violation of this Declaration and against any incitement to such discrimination.

Article 8

Everyone has the right to an effective remedy by the competent national tribunals for acts violating the fundamental rights granted him by the constitution or by law.

Article 9

No one shall be subjected to arbitrary arrest, detention or exile.

Article 10

Everyone is entitled in full equality to a fair and public hearing by an independent and impartial tribunal, in the determination of his rights and obligations and of any criminal charge against him.

Article 11

1. Everyone charged with a penal offence has the right to be presumed innocent until proved guilty according to law in a public trial at which he has had all the guarantees necessary for his defence.
2. No one shall be held guilty of any penal offence on account of any act or omission which did not constitute a penal offence, under national or international law, at the time when it was committed. Nor shall a heavier penalty be imposed than the one that was applicable at the time the penal offence was committed.

Article 12

No one shall be subjected to arbitrary interference with his privacy, family, home or correspondence, nor to attacks upon his honour and reputation. Everyone has the right to the protection of the law against such interference or attacks.

Article 13

1. Everyone has the right to freedom of movement and residence within the borders of each state.
2. Everyone has the right to leave any country, including his own, and to return to his country.

Article 14

1. Everyone has the right to seek and to enjoy in other countries asylum from persecution.
2. This right may not be invoked in the case of prosecutions genuinely arising from non-political crimes or from acts contrary to the purposes and principles of the United Nations.

Article 15

1. Everyone has the right to a nationality.
2. No one shall be arbitrarily deprived of his nationality nor denied the right to change his nationality.

Article 16

1. Men and women of full age, without any limitation due to race, nationality or religion, have the right to marry and to found a family. They are entitled to equal rights as to marriage, during marriage and at its dissolution.
2. Marriage shall be entered into only with the free and full consent of the intending spouses.
3. The family is the natural and fundamental group unit of society and is entitled to protection by society and the State.

Article 17

1. Everyone has the right to own property alone as well as in association with others.
2. No one shall be arbitrarily deprived of his property.

Article 18

Everyone has the right to freedom of thought, conscience and religion; this right includes freedom to change his religion or belief, and freedom, either alone or in community with others and in public or private, to manifest his religion or belief in teaching, practice, worship and observance.

Article 19

Everyone has the right to freedom of opinion and expression; this right includes freedom to hold opinions without interference and to seek, receive and impart information and ideas through any media and regardless of frontiers.

Article 20

1. Everyone has the right to freedom of peaceful assembly and association.
2. No one may be compelled to belong to an association.

Article 21

1. Everyone has the right to take part in the government of his country, directly or through freely chosen representatives.
2. Everyone has the right of equal access to public service in his country.
3. The will of the people shall be the basis of the authority of government; this will shall be expressed in periodic and genuine elections which shall be by universal and equal suffrage and shall be held by secret vote or by equivalent free voting procedures.

Article 22

Everyone, as a member of society, has the right to social security and is entitled to realization, through national effort and international co-operation and in accordance with the organization and resources of each State, of the economic, social and cultural rights indispensable for his dignity and the free development of his personality.

Article 23

1. Everyone has the right to work, to free choice of employment, to just and favourable conditions of work and to protection against unemployment.
2. Everyone, without any discrimination, has the right to equal pay for equal work.
3. Everyone who works has the right to just and favourable remuneration ensuring for himself and his family an existence worthy of human dignity, and supplemented, if necessary, by other means of social protection.
4. Everyone has the right to form and to join trade unions for the protection of his interests.

Article 24

Everyone has the right to rest and leisure, including reasonable limitation of working hours and periodic holidays with pay.

Article 25

1. Everyone has the right to a standard of living adequate for the health and well-being of himself and of his family, including food, clothing, housing and medical care and necessary social services, and the right to security in the event of unemployment, sickness, disability, widowhood, old age or other lack of livelihood in circumstances beyond his control.
2. Motherhood and childhood are entitled to special care and assistance. All children, whether born in or out of wedlock, shall enjoy the same social protection.

Article 26

1. Everyone has the right to education. Education shall be free, at least in the elementary and fundamental stages. Elementary education shall be compulsory. Technical and professional education shall be made generally available and higher education shall be equally accessible to all on the basis of merit.
2. Education shall be directed to the full development of the human personality and to the strengthening of respect for human rights and fundamental freedoms. It shall promote understanding, tolerance and friendship among all nations, racial or religious groups, and shall further the activities of the United Nations for the maintenance of peace.
3. Parents have a prior right to choose the kind of education that shall be given to their children.

Article 27

1. Everyone has the right freely to participate in the cultural life of the community, to enjoy the arts and to share in scientific advancement and its benefits.
2. Everyone has the right to the protection of the moral and material interests resulting from any scientific, literary or artistic production of which he is the author.

Article 28

Everyone is entitled to a social and international order in which the rights and freedoms set forth in this Declaration can be fully realized.

Article 29

1. Everyone has duties to the community in which alone the free and full development of his personality is possible.
2. In the exercise of his rights and freedoms, everyone shall be subject only to such limitations as are determined by law solely for the purpose of securing due recognition

and respect for the rights and freedoms of others and of meeting the just requirements of morality, public order and the general welfare in a democratic society.

3. These rights and freedoms may in no case be exercised contrary to the purposes and principles of the United Nations.

Article 30

Nothing in this Declaration may be interpreted as implying for any State, group or person any right to engage in any activity or to perform any act aimed at the destruction of any of the rights and freedoms set forth herein.

Appendix C

UN Member States
(June 2005)

Member	Date of Admission	Member	Date of Admission
Afghanistan	November 19, 1946	Burundi	September 18, 1962
Albania	December 14, 1955	Cambodia	December 14, 1955
Algeria	October 8, 1962	Cameroon	September 20, 1960
Andorra	July 28, 1993	Canada	November 9, 1945
Angola	December 1, 1976	Cape Verde	September 16, 1975
Antigua and		Central African	
Barbuda	November 11, 1981	Republic	September 20, 1960
Argentina	October 24, 1945	Chad	September 20, 1960
Armenia	March 2, 1992	Chile	October 24, 1945
Australia	November 17, 1945	China	October 24, 1945
Austria	December 14, 1955	Colombia	November 5, 1945
Azerbaijan	March 9, 1992	Comoros	November 12, 1975
Bahamas	September 18, 1973	Congo	September 20, 1960
Bahrain	September 21, 1971	Costa Rica	November 2, 1945
Bangladesh	September 17, 1974	Côte d'Ivoire	September 20, 1960
Barbados	December 9, 1966	Croatia	May 22, 1992
Belarus	October 24, 1945	Cuba	October 24, 1945
Belgium	December 27, 1945	Cyprus	September 20, 1960
Belize	September 25, 1981	Czech Republic	January 19, 1993*
Benin	September 20, 1960	Democratic Republic	
Bhutan	September 21, 1971	of the Congo	September 20, 1960
Bolivia	November 14, 1945	Denmark	October 24, 1945
Bosnia and			
Herzegovina	May 22, 1992		
Botswana	October 17, 1966		
Brazil	October 24, 1945		
Brunei Darussalam	September 21, 1984		
Bulgaria	December 14, 1955		
Burkina Faso	September 20, 1960		

*The Czech Republic is one of two successor states to Czechoslovakia, which was an original member of the United Nations. Czechoslovakia ceased to exist on December 31, 1992. The other successor state is the Slovak Federal Republic, which was also admitted to the United Nations.

Member	Date of Admission	Member	Date of Admission
Djibouti	September 20, 1977	Kiribati	September 14, 1999
Dominica	December 18, 1978	Korea, North	September 17, 1991
Dominican Republic	October 24, 1945	Korea, South	September 17, 1991
Ecuador	December 21, 1945	Kuwait	May 14, 1963
Egypt	October 24, 1945	Kyrgyzstan	March 2, 1992
El Salvador	October 24, 1945	Laos	December 14, 1955
Equatorial Guinea	November 12, 1968	Latvia	September 17, 1991
Eritrea	May 28, 1993	Lebanon	October 24, 1945
Estonia	September 17, 1991	Lesotho	October 17, 1966
Ethiopia	November 13, 1945	Liberia	November 2, 1945
Fiji	October 13, 1970	Libya	December 14, 1955
Finland	December 14, 1955	Liechtenstein	September 18, 1990
France	October 24, 1945	Lithuania	September 17, 1991
Gabon	September 20, 1960	Luxembourg	October 24, 1945
Gambia	September 21, 1965	Macedonia	April 8, 1993
Georgia	July 31, 1992	Madagascar	September 20, 1960
Germany	September 18, 1973†	Malawi	December 1, 1964
Ghana	March 8, 1957	Malaysia	September 17, 1957
Greece	October 25, 1945	Maldives	September 21, 1965
Grenada	September 17, 1974	Mali	September 28, 1960
Guatemala	November 21, 1945	Malta	December 1, 1964
Guinea	December 12, 1958	Marshall Islands	September 17, 1991
Guinea-Bissau	September 17, 1974	Mauritania	October 7, 1961
Guyana	September 20, 1966	Mauritius	April 24, 1968
Haiti	October 24, 1945	Mexico	November 7, 1945
Honduras	December 17, 1945	Micronesia	September 17, 1991
Hungary	December 14, 1955	Moldova	March 2, 1992
Iceland	November 19, 1946	Monaco	May 28, 1993
India	October 30, 1945	Mongolia	October 27, 1961
Indonesia	September 28, 1950	Morocco	November 12, 1956
Iran	October 24, 1945	Mozambique	September 16, 1975
Iraq	December 21, 1945	Myanmar	April 19, 1948
Ireland	December 14, 1955	Namibia	April 23, 1990
Israel	May 11, 1949	Nauru	September 14, 1999
Italy	December 14, 1955	Nepal	December 14, 1955
Jamaica	September 18, 1962	The Netherlands	December 10, 1945
Japan	December 18, 1956	New Zealand	October 24, 1945
Jordan	December 14, 1955	Nicaragua	October 24, 1945
Kazakhstan	March 2, 1992	Niger	September 20, 1960
Kenya	December 16, 1963	Nigeria	October 7, 1960
		Norway	November 27, 1945
		Oman	October 7, 1971
		Pakistan	September 30, 1947
		Palau	December 15, 1994
		Panama	November 13, 1945
		Papua New Guinea	October 10, 1975

†On September 18, 1973, both the Federal Republic of Germany (FRG) and the German Democratic Republic (GDR) were admitted to UN membership. The absorption of the GDR by the FRG in 1990 united the two entities into one state.

Member	Date of Admission	Member	Date of Admission
Paraguay	October 24, 1945	Swaziland	September 24, 1968
Peru	October 31, 1945	Sweden	November 19, 1946
Philippines	October 24, 1945	Switzerland	September 10, 2002
Poland	October 24, 1945	Syria	October 24, 1945
Portugal	December 14, 1955	Tajikistan	March 2, 1992
Qatar	September 21, 1971	Tanzania	December 14, 1961**
Romania	December 14, 1955	Thailand	December 16, 1946
Russian		Timor-Leste	September 27, 2002
Federation	October 24, 1945‡	Togo	September 20, 1960
Rwanda	September 18, 1962	Tonga	September 14, 1999
Saint Kitts and		Trinidad and	
Nevis	September 23, 1983	Tobago	September 18, 1962
Saint Lucia	September 18, 1979	Tunisia	November 12, 1956
Saint Vincent and		Turkey	October 24, 1945
the Grenadines	September 16, 1980	Turkmenistan	March 2, 1992
Samoa	December 15, 1976	Tuvalu	September 5, 2000
San Marino	March 2, 1992	Uganda	October 25, 1962
São Tomé and		Ukraine	October 24, 1945
Príncipe	September 16, 1975	United Arab	
Saudi Arabia	October 24, 1945	Emirates	December 9, 1971
Senegal	September 28, 1960	United Kingdom	October 24, 1945
Seychelles	September 21, 1976	United States	
Sierra Leone	September 27, 1961	of America	October 24, 1945
Singapore	September 21, 1965	Uruguay	December 18, 1945
Slovakia	January 19, 1993§	Uzbekistan	March 2, 1992
Slovenia	May 22, 1992	Vanuatu	September 15, 1981
Solomon Islands	September 19, 1978	Venezuela	November 15, 1945
Somalia	September 20, 1960	Vietnam	September 20, 1971
South Africa	November 7, 1945	Yemen	September 30, 1947††
Spain	December 14, 1955	Yugoslavia	October 24, 1945‡‡
Sri Lanka	December 14, 1955	Zambia	December 1, 1964
Sudan	November 12, 1956	Zimbabwe	August 25, 1980
Suriname	December 4, 1975		

‡On December 24, 1991, the Russian Federation took over the seat of the Union of Soviet Socialist Republics (USSR) in all the UN organs. The USSR had ceased to exist.

§The Slovak Federal Republic is one of two successor states to Czechoslovakia, which was an original member of the United Nations. Czechoslovakia ceased to exist on December 31, 1992. The other successor state is the Czech Republic, which was also admitted to the United Nations.

**Tanganyika became a member of the United Nations on December 14, 1961. Its union with Zanzibar, which had been a member of the organization as well, on April 26, 1964, led to a change in the name of the country to the United Republic of Tanzania.

††On May 22, 1990, Yemen merged with Democratic Yemen, which was also a member state of the United Nations. Since then the two entities have been represented as one member with the name Yemen.

‡‡The Federal Republic of Yugoslavia, the successor state to the founding member state, was admitted as a member of the United Nations by General Assembly Resolution A/RES/55/12 on November 1, 2000.

Appendix D

Statute of the International Court of Justice

Article 1

The International Court of Justice established by the Charter of the United Nations as the principal judicial organ of the United Nations shall be constituted and shall function in accordance with the provisions of the present Statute.

CHAPTER I: ORGANIZATION OF THE COURT

Article 2

The Court shall be composed of a body of independent judges, elected regardless of their nationality from among persons of high moral character, who possess the qualifications required in their respective countries for appointment to the highest judicial offices, or are jurisconsults of recognized competence in international law.

Article 3

1. The Court shall consist of fifteen members, no two of whom may be nationals of the same state.
2. A person who for the purposes of membership in the Court could be regarded as a national of more than one state shall be deemed to be a national of the one in which he ordinarily exercises civil and political rights.

Article 4

1. The members of the Court shall be elected by the General Assembly and by the Security Council from a list of persons nominated by the national groups in the Permanent Court of Arbitration, in accordance with the following provisions.
2. In the case of Members of the United Nations not represented in the Permanent Court of Arbitration, candidates shall be nominated by national groups appointed for this purpose by their governments under the same conditions as those prescribed for members

of the Permanent Court of Arbitration by Article 44 of the Convention of The Hague of 1907 for the pacific settlement of international disputes.

3. The conditions under which a state which is a party to the present Statute but is not a Member of the United Nations may participate in electing the members of the Court shall, in the absence of a special agreement, be laid down by the General Assembly upon recommendation of the Security Council.

Article 5

1. At least three months before the date of the election, the Secretary-General of the United Nations shall address a written request to the members of the Permanent Court of Arbitration belonging to the states which are parties to the present Statute, and to the members of the national groups appointed under Article 4, paragraph 2, inviting them to undertake, within a given time, by national groups, the nomination of persons in a position to accept the duties of a member of the Court.

2. No group may nominate more than four persons, not more than two of whom shall be of their own nationality. In no case may the number of candidates nominated by a group be more than double the number of seats to be filled.

Article 6

Before making these nominations, each national group is recommended to consult its highest court of justice, its legal faculties and schools of law, and its national academies and national sections of international academies devoted to the study of law.

Article 7

1. The Secretary-General shall prepare a list in alphabetical order of all the persons thus nominated. Save as provided in Article 12, paragraph 2, these shall be the only persons eligible.

2. The Secretary-General shall submit this list to the General Assembly and to the Security Council.

Article 8

The General Assembly and the Security Council shall proceed independently of one another to elect the members of the Court.

Article 9

At every election, the electors shall bear in mind not only that the persons to be elected should individually possess the qualifications required, but also that in the body as a whole the representation of the main forms of civilization and of the principal legal systems of the world should be assured.

Article 10

1. Those candidates who obtain an absolute majority of votes in the General Assembly and in the Security Council shall be considered as elected.

2. Any vote of the Security Council, whether for the election of judges or for the appointment of members of the conference envisaged in Article 12, shall be taken without any distinction between permanent and non-permanent members of the Security Council.

3. In the event of more than one national of the same state obtaining an absolute majority of the votes both of the General Assembly and of the Security Council, the eldest of these only shall be considered as elected.

Article 11

If, after the first meeting held for the purpose of the election, one or more seats remain to be filled, a second and, if necessary, a third meeting shall take place.

Article 12

1. If, after the third meeting, one or more seats still remain unfilled, a joint conference consisting of six members, three appointed by the General Assembly and three by the Security Council, may be formed at any time at the request of either the General Assembly or the Security Council, for the purpose of choosing by the vote of an absolute majority one name for each seat still vacant, to submit to the General Assembly and the Security Council for their respective acceptance.

2. If the joint conference is unanimously agreed upon any person who fulfills the required conditions, he may be included in its list, even though he was not included in the list of nominations referred to in Article 7.

3. If the joint conference is satisfied that it will not be successful in procuring an election, those members of the Court who have already been elected shall, within a period to be fixed by the Security Council, proceed to fill the vacant seats by selection from among those candidates who have obtained votes either in the General Assembly or in the Security Council.

4. In the event of an equality of votes among the judges, the eldest judge shall have a casting vote.

Article 13

1. The members of the Court shall be elected for nine years and may be re-elected; provided, however, that of the judges elected at the first election, the terms of five judges shall expire at the end of three years and the terms of five more judges shall expire at the end of six years.

2. The judges whose terms are to expire at the end of the above-mentioned initial periods of three and six years shall be chosen by lot to be drawn by the Secretary-General immediately after the first election has been completed.

3. The members of the Court shall continue to discharge their duties until their places have been filled. Though replaced, they shall finish any cases which they may have begun.

4. In the case of the resignation of a member of the Court, the resignation shall be addressed to the President of the Court for transmission to the Secretary-General. This last notification makes the place vacant.

Article 14

Vacancies shall be filled by the same method as that laid down for the first election subject to the following provision: the Secretary-General shall, within one month of the occurrence of the vacancy, proceed to issue the invitations provided for in Article 5, and the date of the election shall be fixed by the Security Council.

Article 15

A member of the Court elected to replace a member whose term of office has not expired shall hold office for the remainder of his predecessor's term.

Article 16

1. No member of the Court may exercise any political or administrative function, or engage in any other occupation of a professional nature.
2. Any doubt on this point shall be settled by the decision of the Court.

Article 17

1. No member of the Court may act as agent, counsel, or advocate in any case.
2. No member may participate in the decision of any case in which he has previously taken part as agent, counsel, or advocate for one of the parties, or as a member of a national or international court, or of a commission of enquiry, or in any other capacity.
3. Any doubt on this point shall be settled by the decision of the Court.

Article 18

1. No member of the Court can be dismissed unless, in the unanimous opinion of the other members, he has ceased to fulfill the required conditions.
2. Formal notification thereof shall be made to the Secretary-General by the Registrar.
3. This notification makes the place vacant.

Article 19

The members of the Court, when engaged on the business of the Court, shall enjoy diplomatic privileges and immunities.

Article 20

Every member of the Court shall, before taking up his duties, make a solemn declaration in open court that he will exercise his powers impartially and conscientiously.

Article 21

1. The Court shall elect its President and Vice-President for three years; they may be reelected.

2. The Court shall appoint its Registrar and may provide for the appointment of such other officers as may be necessary.

Article 22

1. The seat of the Court shall be established at The Hague. This, however, shall not prevent the Court from sitting and exercising its functions elsewhere whenever the Court considers it desirable.
2. The President and the Registrar shall reside at the seat of the Court.

Article 23

1. The Court shall remain permanently in session, except during the judicial vacations, the dates and duration of which shall be fixed by the Court.
2. Members of the Court are entitled to periodic leave, the dates and duration of which shall be fixed by the Court, having in mind the distance between The Hague and the home of each judge.
3. Members of the Court shall be bound, unless they are on leave or prevented from attending by illness or other serious reasons duly explained to the President, to hold themselves permanently at the disposal of the Court.

Article 24

1. If, for some special reason, a member of the Court considers that he should not take part in the decision of a particular case, he shall so inform the President.
2. If the President considers that for some special reason one of the members of the Court should not sit in a particular case, he shall give him notice accordingly.
3. If in any such case the member Court and the President disagree, the matter shall be settled by the decision of the Court.

Article 25

1. The full Court shall sit except when it is expressly provided otherwise in the present Statute.
2. Subject to the condition that the number of judges available to constitute the Court is not thereby reduced below eleven, the Rules of the Court may provide for allowing one or more judges, according to circumstances and in rotation, to be dispensed from sitting.
3. A quorum of nine judges shall suffice to constitute the Court.

Article 26

1. The Court may from time to time form one or more chambers, composed of three or more judges as the Court may determine, for dealing with particular categories of cases; for example, labour cases and cases relating to transit and communications.
2. The Court may at any time form a chamber for dealing with a particular case. The number of judges to constitute such a chamber shall be determined by the Court with the approval of the parties.
3. Cases shall be heard and determined by the chambers provided for in this article if the parties so request.

Article 27

A judgment given by any of the chambers provided for in Articles 26 and 29 shall be considered as rendered by the Court.

Article 28

The chambers provided for in Articles 26 and 29 may, with the consent of the parties, sit and exercise their functions elsewhere than at The Hague.

Article 29

With a view to the speedy dispatch of business, the Court shall form annually a chamber composed of five judges which, at the request of the parties, may hear and determine cases by summary procedure. In addition, two judges shall be selected for the purpose of replacing judges who find it impossible to sit.

Article 30

1. The Court shall frame rules for carrying out its functions. In particular, it shall lay down rules of procedure.
2. The Rules of the Court may provide for assessors to sit with the Court or with any of its chambers, without the right to vote.

Article 31

1. Judges of the nationality of each of the parties shall retain their right to sit in the case before the Court.
2. If the Court includes upon the Bench a judge of the nationality of one of the parties, any other party may choose a person to sit as judge. Such person shall be chosen preferably from among those persons who have been nominated as candidates as provided in Articles 4 and 5.
3. If the Court includes upon the Bench no judge of the nationality of the parties, each of these parties may proceed to choose a judge as provided in paragraph 2 of this Article.
4. The provisions of this Article shall apply to the case of Articles 26 and 29. In such cases, the President shall request one or, if necessary, two of the members of the Court forming the chamber to give place to the members of the Court of the nationality of the parties concerned, and, failing such, or if they are unable to be present, to the judges specially chosen by the parties.
5. Should there be several parties in the same interest, they shall, for the purpose of the preceding provisions, be reckoned as one party only. Any doubt upon this point shall be settled by the decision of the Court.
6. Judges chosen as laid down in paragraphs 2, 3, and 4 of this Article shall fulfill the conditions required by Articles 2, 17 (paragraph 2), 20, and 24 of the present Statute. They shall take part in the decision on terms of complete equality with their colleagues.

Article 32

1. Each member of the Court shall receive an annual salary.
2. The President shall receive a special annual allowance.
3. The Vice-President shall receive a special allowance for every day on which he acts as President.
4. The judges chosen under Article 31, other than members of the Court, shall receive compensation for each day on which they exercise their functions.
5. These salaries, allowances, and compensation shall be fixed by the General Assembly. They may not be decreased during the term of office.
6. The salary of the Registrar shall be fixed by the General Assembly on the proposal of the Court.
7. Regulations made by the General Assembly shall fix the conditions under which retirement pensions may be given to members of the Court and to the Registrar, and the conditions under which members of the Court and the Registrar shall have their travelling expenses refunded.
8. The above salaries, allowances, and compensation shall be free of all taxation.

Article 33

The expenses of the Court shall be borne by the United Nations in such a manner as shall be decided by the General Assembly.

CHAPTER II: COMPETENCE OF THE COURT

Article 34

1. Only states may be parties in cases before the Court.
2. The Court, subject to and in conformity with its Rules, may request of public international organizations information relevant to cases before it, and shall receive such information presented by such organizations on their own initiative.
3. Whenever the construction of the constituent instrument of a public international organization or of an international convention adopted thereunder is in question in a case before the Court, the Registrar shall so notify the public international organization concerned and shall communicate to it copies of all the written proceedings.

Article 35

1. The Court shall be open to the states parties to the present Statute.
2. The conditions under which the Court shall be open to other states shall, subject to the special provisions contained in treaties in force, be laid down by the Security Council, but in no case shall such conditions place the parties in a position of inequality before the Court.
3. When a state which is not a Member of the United Nations is a party to a case, the Court shall fix the amount which that party is to contribute towards the expenses of the Court. This provision shall not apply if such state is bearing a share of the expenses of the Court.

Article 36

1. The jurisdiction of the Court comprises all cases which the parties refer to it and all matters specially provided for in the Charter of the United Nations or in treaties and conventions in force.

2. The states parties to the present Statute may at any time declare that they recognize as compulsory ipso facto and without special agreement, in relation to any other state accepting the same obligation, the jurisdiction of the Court in all legal disputes concerning:

   a. the interpretation of a treaty;

   b. any question of international law;

   c. the existence of any fact which, if established, would constitute a breach of an international obligation;

   d. the nature or extent of the reparation to be made for the breach of an international obligation.

3. The declarations referred to above may be made unconditionally or on condition of reciprocity on the part of several or certain states, or for a certain time.

4. Such declarations shall be deposited with the Secretary-General of the United Nations, who shall transmit copies thereof to the parties to the Statute and to the Registrar of the Court.

5. Declarations made under Article 36 of the Statute of the Permanent Court of International Justice and which are still in force shall be deemed, as between the parties to the present Statute, to be acceptances of the compulsory jurisdiction of the International Court of Justice for the period which they still have to run and in accordance with their terms.

6. In the event of a dispute as to whether the Court has jurisdiction, the matter shall be settled by the decision of the Court.

Article 37

Whenever a treaty or convention in force provides for reference of a matter to a tribunal to have been instituted by the League of Nations, or to the Permanent Court of International Justice, the matter shall, as between the parties to the present Statute, be referred to the International Court of Justice.

Article 38

1. The Court, whose function is to decide in accordance with international law such disputes as are submitted to it, shall apply:

   a. international conventions, whether general or particular, establishing rules expressly recognized by the contesting states;

   b. international custom, as evidence of a general practice accepted as law;

   c. the general principles of law recognized by civilized nations;

   d. subject to the provisions of Article 59, judicial decisions and the teachings of the most highly qualified publicists of the various nations, as subsidiary means for the determination of rules of law.

2. This provision shall not prejudice the power of the Court to decide a case *ex aequo et bono,* if the parties agree thereto.

CHAPTER III: PROCEDURE

Article 39

1. The official languages of the Court shall be French and English. If the parties agree that the case shall be conducted in French, the judgment shall be delivered in French. If the parties agree that the case shall be conducted in English, the judgment shall be delivered in English.
2. In the absence of an agreement as to which language shall be employed, each party may, in the pleadings, use the language which it prefers; the decision of the Court shall be given in French and English. In this case the Court shall at the same time determine which of the two texts shall be considered as authoritative.
3. The Court shall, at the request of any party, authorize a language other than French or English to be used by that party.

Article 40

1. Cases are brought before the Court, as the case may be, either by the notification of the special agreement or by a written application addressed to the Registrar. In either case the subject of the dispute and the parties shall be indicated.
2. The Registrar shall forthwith communicate the application to all concerned.
3. He shall also notify the Members of the United Nations through the Secretary-General, and also any other states entitled to appear before the Court.

Article 41

1. The Court shall have the power to indicate, if it considers that circumstances so require, any provisional measures which ought to be taken to preserve the respective rights of either party.
2. Pending the final decision, notice of the measures suggested shall forthwith be given to the parties and to the Security Council.

Article 42

1. The parties shall be represented by agents.
2. They may have the assistance of counsel or advocates before the Court.
3. The agents, counsel, and advocates of parties before the Court shall enjoy the privileges and immunities necessary to the independent exercise of their duties.

Article 43

1. The procedure shall consist of two parts: written and oral.
2. The written proceedings shall consist of the communication to the Court and to the parties of memorials, counter-memorials and, if necessary, replies; also all papers and documents in support.
3. These communications shall be made through the Registrar, in the order and within the time fixed by the Court.

4. A certified copy of every document produced by one party shall be communicated to the other party.
5. The oral proceedings shall consist of the hearing by the Court of witnesses, experts, agents, counsel, and advocates.

Article 44

1. For the service of all notices upon persons other than the agents, counsel, and advocates, the Court shall apply direct to the government of the state upon whose territory the notice has to be served.
2. The same provision shall apply whenever steps are to be taken to procure evidence on the spot.

Article 45

The hearing shall be under the control of the President or, if he is unable to preside, of the Vice-President; if neither is able to preside, the senior judge present shall preside.

Article 46

The hearing in Court shall be public, unless the Court shall decide otherwise, or unless the parties demand that the public be not admitted.

Article 47

1. Minutes shall be made at each hearing and signed by the Registrar and the President.
2. These minutes alone shall be authentic.

Article 48

The Court shall make orders for the conduct of the case, shall decide the form and time in which each party must conclude its arguments, and make all arrangements connected with the taking of evidence.

Article 49

The Court may, even before the hearing begins, call upon the agents to produce any document or to supply any explanations. Formal note shall be taken of any refusal.

Article 50

The Court may, at any time, entrust any individual, body, bureau, commission, or other organization that it may select, with the task of carrying out an enquiry or giving an expert opinion.

Article 51

During the hearing any relevant questions are to be put to the witnesses and experts under the conditions laid down by the Court in the rules of procedure referred to in Article 30.

Article 52

After the Court has received the proofs and evidence within the time specified for the purpose, it may refuse to accept any further oral or written evidence that one party may desire to present unless the other side consents.

Article 53

1. Whenever one of the parties does not appear before the Court, or fails to defend its case, the other party may call upon the Court to decide in favour of its claim.
2. The Court must, before doing so, satisfy itself, not only that it has jurisdiction in accordance with Articles 36 and 37, but also that the claim is well founded in fact and law.

Article 54

1. When, subject to the control of the Court, the agents, counsel, and advocates have completed their presentation of the case, the President shall declare the hearing closed.
2. The Court shall withdraw to consider the judgment.
3. The deliberations of the Court shall take place in private and remain secret.

Article 55

1. All questions shall be decided by a majority of the judges present.
2. In the event of an equality of votes, the President or the judge who acts in his place shall have a casting vote.

Article 56

1. The judgment shall state the reasons on which it is based.
2. It shall contain the names of the judges who have taken part in the decision.

Article 57

If the judgment does not represent in whole or in part the unanimous opinion of the judges, any judge shall be entitled to deliver a separate opinion.

Article 58

The judgment shall be signed by the President and by the Registrar. It shall be read in open court, due notice having been given to the agents.

Article 59

The decision of the Court has no binding force except between the parties and in respect of that particular case.

Article 60

The judgment is final and without appeal. In the event of dispute as to the meaning or scope of the judgment, the Court shall construe it upon the request of any party.

Article 61

1. An application for revision of a judgment may be made only when it is based upon the discovery of some fact of such a nature as to be a decisive factor, which fact was, when the judgment was given, unknown to the Court and also to the party claiming revision, always provided that such ignorance was not due to negligence.
2. The proceedings for revision shall be opened by a judgment of the Court expressly recording the existence of the new fact, recognizing that it has such a character as to lay the case open to revision, and declaring the application admissible on this ground.
3. The Court may require previous compliance with the terms of the judgment before it admits proceedings in revision.
4. The application for revision must be made at latest within six months of the discovery of the new fact.
5. No application for revision may be made after the lapse of ten years from the date of the judgment.

Article 62

1. Should a state consider that it has an interest of a legal nature which may be affected by the decision in the case, it may submit a request to the Court to be permitted to intervene.
2. It shall be for the Court to decide upon this request.

Article 63

1. Whenever the construction of a convention to which states other than those concerned in the case are parties is in question, the Registrar shall notify all such states forthwith.
2. Every state so notified has the right to intervene in the proceedings; but if it uses this right, the construction given by the judgment will be equally binding upon it.

Article 64

Unless otherwise decided by the Court, each party shall bear its own costs.

CHAPTER IV: ADVISORY OPINIONS

Article 65

1. The Court may give an advisory opinion on any legal question at the request of whatever body may be authorized by or in accordance with the Charter of the United Nations to make such a request.
2. Questions upon which the advisory opinion of the Court is asked shall be laid before the Court by means of a written request containing an exact statement of the question upon which an opinion is required, and accompanied by all documents likely to throw light upon the question.

Article 66

1. The Registrar shall forthwith give notice of the request for an advisory opinion to all states entitled to appear before the Court.
2. The Registrar shall also, by means of a special and direct communication, notify any state entitled to appear before the Court or international organization considered by the Court, or, should it not be sitting, by the President, as likely to be able to furnish information on the question, that the Court will be prepared to receive, within a time limit to be fixed by the President, written statements, or to hear, at a public sitting to be held for the purpose, oral statements relating to the question.
3. Should any such state entitled to appear before the Court have failed to receive the special communication referred to in paragraph 2 of this Article, such state may express a desire to submit a written statement or to be heard; and the Court will decide.
4. States and organizations having presented written or oral statements or both shall be permitted to comment on the statements made by other states or organizations in the form, to the extent, and within the time limits which the Court, or, should it not be sitting, the President, shall decide in each particular case. Accordingly, the Registrar shall in due time communicate any such written statements to states and organizations having submitted similar statements.

Article 67

The Court shall deliver its advisory opinions in open court, notice having been given to the Secretary-General and to the representatives of Members of the United Nations, of other states and of international organizations immediately concerned.

Article 68

In the exercise of its advisory functions the Court shall further be guided by the provisions of the present Statute which apply in contentious cases to the extent to which it recognizes them to be applicable.

CHAPTER V: AMENDMENT

Article 69

Amendments to the present Statute shall be effected by the same procedure as is provided by the Charter of the United Nations for amendments to that Charter, subject however to any provisions which the General Assembly upon recommendation of the Security Council may adopt concerning the participation of states which are parties to the present Statute but are not Members of the United Nations.

Article 70

The Court shall have power to propose such amendments to the present Statute as it may deem necessary, through written communications to the Secretary-General, for consideration in conformity with the provisions of Article 69.

Appendix E

Secretaries-General of the United Nations

ORDER OF SERVICE

Trygve Lie	Norway	1946–1952
Dag Hammarskjöld	Sweden	1953–1961
U Thant	Burma	1961–1971
Kurt Waldheim	Austria	1972–1981
Javier Pérez de Cuéllar	Peru	1982–1991
Boutros Boutros-Ghali	Egypt	1992–1996
Kofi Annan	Ghana	1997–

BRIEF BIOGRAPHIES

Trygve Halvdan Lie (1896–1968)

The first secretary-general of the United Nations was born in Oslo, Norway, in 1896. He studied law at Oslo University and later served as minister of justice in a labor government. He fled Norway during World War II and acted as foreign minister for his homeland's exiled government in London. Trygve Lie was head of the Norwegian delegation to the San Francisco UN organizing conference in April 1945, where he played a prominent role in drafting the Security Council provisions in the new Charter. He headed the Norwegian delegation to the General Assembly meeting in London in early 1946 and was elected the UN's first secretary-general on February 1, 1946.

Lie considered the job of secretary-general to be one of energetic leadership. During the crisis of the Korean War, his support of UN prosecution of the war annoyed the Soviet Union, which perceived him as a tool of U.S. foreign policy. During the McCarthy era of the early 1950s, Secretary-General Lie's willingness to fire U.S. employees of the Secretariat who came under suspicion as Communist infiltrators reinforced the Soviet view.

At the close of his term in 1951, the USSR indicated it would veto his reelection. The U.S. government responded that it would support no other candidate. The impasse was finessed by the General Assembly, which decided by a vote of 46-5-8 to "continue in office" the secretary-general

335

for another three years. The Soviet delegation considered the vote illegitimate and subsequently refused to work with Lie, which hastened his early retirement. In 1953 he returned to Norway, where, before his death in 1968, he continued an active political and diplomatic life.

Dag Hjalmar Agne Carl Hammarskjöld (1905–1961)

The second secretary-general served from April 10, 1953, until his untimely death on September 18, 1961, while on a peace mission to the recently independent Congo. Dag Hammarskjöld was born in 1905 in Jönköping, Sweden. At the university in Uppsala, he studied French literature, political economy, and law, and in 1934 he completed a doctorate degree in economics at the university in Stockholm. He joined the Swedish civil service and after World War II entered the foreign service. From 1951 to 1953 he represented Sweden at the sixth and seventh General Assembly sessions held, consecutively, in Paris and New York. In early April 1953, on the recommendation of the Security Council, the assembly unanimously appointed Hammarskjöld to the position from which Secretary-General Lie had resigned five months earlier. Hammarskjöld was unanimously reelected in 1957.

Hammarskjöld's term as secretary-general was marked by considerable activity. On several occasions he criticized the superpowers for disregarding the UN's role in the maintenance of collective security and its responsibility for disarmament negotiations. He traveled extensively, including two highly visible trips to the war-torn Middle East, in his attempt to lessen tensions in the world. In an effort to resolve the Suez Crisis of 1956, he guided the launching of the UN Emergency Force, the UN's first peacekeeping mission. However, the greatest challenge confronting the secretary-general, the one that would result in his death, emerged from the center of Africa.

The Belgian Congo became the independent country of the Congo on June 30, 1960, and almost immediately civil strife broke out between various factions, some eventually associated with the major cold war competitors. The secretary-general, fearful that Washington and Moscow might once again circumvent the United Nations, quickly assumed an active role in the crisis. He convened an emergency night session of the Security Council on July 13, which immediately called on Belgian forces to withdraw and opposed the secession of Katanga Province. Hammarskjöld then helped craft the UN Force in the Congo and personally made four trips to the area in connection with UN operations there. The United States gave its full support to Hammarskjöld's efforts to shore up the central government. Moscow denounced Hammarskjöld, believing him a tool of the Americans, and demanded that he be replaced by a three-person board (the Troika Proposal), equally representing the West, Soviet bloc nations, and neutral countries. Nevertheless, Hammarskjöld, with Western support, persisted in his efforts. On September 12, 1961, he began what would be the last trip of his unusually vigorous diplomatic career. He was on his way to urge secessionist leader Moise Tshombe of the breakaway province of Katanga to pursue peace and to drop his challenge to the central government. Hammarskjöld died on September 18, when his plane crashed in a remote area of Northern Rhodesia (now Zambia).

U Thant (1909–1974)

U Thant began serving following the death of Hammarskjöld in 1961, and he continued in the post until 1971. Thant was born in 1909 in Pantanaw, Burma (now Myanmar). He was educated at the University of Rangoon (Yangon) and then the Arts and Science University. After World War II (when Japan occupied Burma), the Anti-Fascist People's Freedom League recruited him for government service. In 1955 he became executive secretary of Burma's Economic and Social Board.

He joined the Burmese delegation to the General Assembly in 1952 and was serving as ambassador from his country when he was named to complete Hammarskjöld's unexpired term. He proved acceptable enough to the cold war competitors to receive their endorsement for a full term in November 1962 and a second term beginning in 1966. Thant inclined toward neutralism. He could be critical of both the East and the West when he believed their national purposes and actions threatened international comity.

At times during his tenure, Thant played an important part in critical international events. In 1962 U.S. ambassador to the United Nations, Adlai Stevenson, privately sounded out the secretary-general as a possible intermediary during the Cuban Missile Crisis, and Nikita Khrushchev even publicly suggested that Thant be the principal mediator to resolve the dispute. In the end, the United Nations played a secondary role in ending the standoff. During his first term, the secretary-general was involved in the transfer of Irian Barat (Western New Guinea) to Indonesia in 1962, a resolution of the civil war in the Congo in 1963, and the establishment of a peacekeeping force on Cyprus in 1964. In 1965, following the outbreak of hostilities between India and Pakistan over their ongoing territorial disputes, the United Nations declared a ceasefire, and Thant, on his own authority, created a new peacekeeping operation: the UN India-Pakistan Observation Mission (UNIPOM).

The action for which the secretary-general received perhaps the most criticism occurred in spring 1967, when Egyptian president Gamal Abdul Nasser insisted that Thant withdraw UN peacekeepers from the Sinai and the Gaza Strip, where they had been since the armistice of 1956. Believing the lives of UN troops to be in danger and sensitive to the sovereign right of Egypt to demand removal of outside forces from her land, the secretary-general withdrew the UN forces. Nasser closed the Gulf of Aqaba, Israel set in motion a preemptive strike, and by June of that year a new Israeli-Arab war broke out, which resulted in Israeli occupation of the Sinai, as well as the Gaza Strip, the West Bank of the Jordan River, East Jerusalem, and the Golan Heights. Critics believed that the vacuum left when the United Nations withdrew paved the way for the territorial disruptions of the Middle East that international diplomacy tried to resolve for the next decades.

During Thant's years in New York, the United Nations substantially increased its involvement in social and economic development in the Third World, but he could not find a solution to the growing problem of financing UN operations. Thant retired on January 1, 1972, and continued to live in New York, where he died of cancer in November 1974.

Kurt Waldheim (1918–)

Kurt Waldheim was born in Sankt Andrä-Wördern, Austria, near Vienna, in 1918. He served as a volunteer in the Austrian army from 1936 to 1937, and, following the *Anschluss* that merged Germany and Austria, he was conscripted into the German army. He served on the Russian front until he was wounded in 1941. Although he later claimed to have spent the remainder of the war studying law, documents uncovered in 1986 indicated that he had been a German army staff officer in the Balkans from about 1942 to the end of the war. He received a doctorate of jurisprudence from the University of Vienna in 1944. He had also graduated from the Vienna Consular Academy, and in 1945 he joined the Austrian diplomatic service. In 1955 he became Permanent Observer for Austria to the United Nations. Later that same year, when Austria was admitted to the world organization, he became head of the mission and, in 1964, permanent Austrian representative. He left New York for a two-year stint as his nation's foreign minister (1968–1970), then returned to the United Nations.

Waldheim was the first candidate for secretary-general to openly seek the post, which he did on three occasions. He began his term in January 1972 and was reelected in 1976, despite opposition from some Third World countries. He was blocked from a third term by a veto from the Chinese government.

Waldheim traveled widely and was constantly engaged in trying to resolve, or help resolve, major international problems, including the 1971 India-Pakistan dispute, the Middle East War of 1973, the Vietnamese invasion of Cambodia, the decade-long Iran-Iraq War, and the ripple effects of the Iranian Revolution of 1979. Waldheim also oversaw large relief efforts in Bangladesh, Cambodia, Nicaragua, and Guatemala, and peacekeeping operations in Cyprus, the two Yemens, Angola, and Guinea, as well as in the Middle East. He became a point person in efforts to gain the release of U.S. hostages held by the revolutionary Iranian government from November 1979 to January 1981, but he could not resolve the crisis.

Waldheim left office in 1981 and became active in Austrian politics. He was elected Austrian president in 1986. His presidency, however, was clouded by revelations about his wartime service with the German army. Documents showed that he had been an interpreter and intelligence officer for the Germans who were engaged in reprisals against Yugoslav partisans and civilians, and that he had been responsible for sending much of the Jewish population of Salonika, Greece, to concentration camps. Waldheim admitted his earlier lack of candor but denied knowledge or participation in wartime atrocities. An international investigation cleared him of complicity, but his reputation had been severely tarnished.

Javier Pérez de Cuéllar (1920–)

Javier Pérez de Cuéllar was the first Latin American to become secretary-general, serving two terms. He was born in Lima, Peru, in 1920 to a family descended from Spanish nobility. Educated early in life in Roman Catholic schools, Pérez de Cuéllar developed a keen interest in Hispanic art, culture, and literature. While studying law at Catholic University in Lima, he took a position in the Peruvian foreign ministry as a clerk, which commenced a long diplomatic career. In 1946 he became a member of Peru's delegation to the first General Assembly session. In 1971 he became Peru's permanent representative to the United Nations. Secretary-General Waldheim twice named Pérez de Cuéllar as his special representative—to Cyprus in 1975 and to Afghanistan in 1981—and in early 1979 he became under-secretary-general for special political affairs.

In 1981, at the age of 61, Pérez de Cuéllar intended to retire from his long and active diplomatic career, but events would conspire to delay his leaving the world stage. For six weeks the Security Council deadlocked on the nomination of a new secretary-general while either the United States or China vetoed opposing candidates. On December 11, 1981, the council went into closed session for an arduous half day to consider nine candidates. By the end of the session, only one of the candidates proved acceptable to all the permanent members: Javier Pérez de Cuéllar. Most likely, since he was 61, no one thought he would serve more than one term. Yet he would be reelected and would serve a full ten years.

His first major challenge was a military confrontation between Great Britain and Argentina over the Falkland Islands, called the *Malvines* by the Argentineans, who invaded and claimed the islands in April 1982. Although his efforts at mediation came to naught—by June 1982 Great Britain had defeated the Argentine army and reestablished control over the island—he was widely praised in the international community for his labors. He continued with other personal initiatives—in Russian-occupied Afghanistan, in South Africa–occupied Namibia, in Lebanon (plagued by Israeli invasion and internal civil strife), and in the Guyana-Venezuela border dispute—in the event continuing to win praise for his mediation efforts and enhancing his growing reputation as an impartial negotiator. He also initiated a program to bring relief to Ethiopia during a devastating famine in the late 1980s.

The new post–cold war era brought opportunities for the United Nations and the need for additional financial resources and more personnel. Pérez de Cuéllar expanded the UN bureaucracy and lobbied for increased funding. Unfortunately, his efforts encountered growing hostility from the United States, historically the UN's most important supporter. Demanding reforms at the United Nations, President Reagan limited annual assessment payments, demanded a 15 percent reduction in the UN staff, and withdrew from UNESCO (United Nations Educational, Scientific and Cultural Organization).

Pérez de Cuéllar oversaw the conclusion of the most devastating war in the post–World War II period. The Iran-Iraq War, begun in 1980, ended in 1988, when both sides accepted UN Resolution 598, which called for a cease-fire and withdrawal of forces to prewar boundaries. The resolution, a product, in part, of Pérez de Cuéllar's active participation, was historic: For the first time, the United States and the Soviet Union jointly sponsored a Security Council resolution on the Middle East.

Boutros Boutros-Ghali (1922–)

Boutros Boutros-Ghali was the first Arab and first African to become secretary-general. He was born in Cairo, Egypt, in 1922 into a distinguished Coptic Christian family. His grandfather had been prime minister of Egypt and his father finance minister. Boutros-Ghali studied political science, economics, and law at Cairo University, where he received a bachelor of law degree in 1946. In 1949 he earned a doctorate degree in international law from the University of Paris (Sorbonne). He then held professorships at Cairo University, wrote numerous scholarly books and articles, and lectured on international affairs at several universities throughout the world.

Appointed as minister of state for foreign affairs in 1977, Boutros-Ghali accompanied Egyptian president Anwar Sadat that year on the historic trip to Jerusalem and is considered one of the main architects of the Camp David Accords of 1978, which led to the Egyptian-Israeli peace treaty the following year. He openly campaigned for secretary-general in 1991, knowing that he had the advantages of appealing to both African states and Arab states and of being acceptable to Israel (and the United States) because of his work on the Egyptian-Israeli peace. In November 1991 the Security Council chose him on the first ballot.

Within a few months of his assuming the office, Boutros-Ghali authored *An Agenda for Peace*—which introduced into UN affairs the concepts of *peace enforcement* and *peace building,* as distinct from *peacekeeping.* He also proposed that military forces be placed at the UN's disposal for rapid action in times of crisis. At his urging, U.S. president George H. W. Bush sent forces, authorized by the Security Council, into Somalia in December 1992. They were inserted to secure food supplies and to restore order. The Americans soon became enmeshed in a nasty civil conflict between rival warlords. On October 3, 1993, the new Clinton administration was confronted with front-page news stories of eighteen U.S. soldiers trapped in a firefight and killed, along with a lurid photograph of one of them being dragged through the streets of Mogadishu. U.S. support for more vigorous UN peacekeeping efforts then waned, troops were home within the year, and criticism mounted that the United Nations was incapable of ordering the internal affairs of any country.

The 1994 off-year congressional elections in the United States, bringing Republicans into a majority in both houses for the first time in almost half a century, brought the secretary-general, and his ideas about an invigorated United Nations, into direct conflict with the world's most powerful nation. In response to growing criticism about UN bureaucratic wastefulness, Boutros-Ghali froze the UN budget and took a number of other steps to allay concerns, particularly those expressed in Washington. By 1993 U.S. arrears to the organization reached one billion dollars. In hopes of ending the freeze on U.S. contributions to the United Nations, Boutros-Ghali appointed Richard Thornburgh, a former U.S. attorney general, as under-secretary-general for administration and management. He gave Thornburgh carte blanche to review all operations in the world body. The Thornburgh Report, issued within the year, called for tighter quality control of the UN staff; budgetary reforms; and the appointment of an inspector general to root out fraud, waste, and abuse. In tandem, a Ford Foundation report (commissioned by Thornburgh) called for a unified peacekeeping budget. Boutros-Ghali indicated that he would take steps to implement many of the recommendations. However, the secretary-general could not stem the crescendoing criticism from conservative U.S. senators, who saw the United Nations as inefficient, inept, yet bent on gaining too much power at the expense of U.S. sovereignty. The Clinton administration in turn indicated that it would not support the secretary-general's reelection.

Having entered office at a high point of optimism regarding the possibilities of the international organization, Boutros Boutros-Ghali, the victim of a spate of uncontrollable in-state collapses and the decline of UN financing, left office in 1997 after one tumultuous term.

Kofi Atta Annan (1938–)

Kofi Annan was the first person to be elected secretary-general from the ranks of the UN career staff, the first black, and the first from sub-Saharan Africa. Born in Kumasi, Ghana, in 1938, he studied at the University of Science and Technology at Kumasi and then, in 1961, completed a bachelor's degree in economics at Macalester College in St. Paul, Minnesota. He pursued graduate studies at the Institut Universitaire de Hautes Études Internationales (Graduate Institute of International Studies) in Geneva, and from 1971–1972 he was a Sloan Fellow at the Massachusetts Institute of Technology, where he earned a master of science degree in management. Annan spent much of his early professional life with the United Nations in Europe, Africa, and New York.

Secretary-General Boutros-Ghali appointed him to a special assignment to negotiate safe passage for some half-million stranded Asian workers and the release of hostages during the Gulf War of 1990–1991. In 1993 Annan became assistant secretary-general for peacekeeping operations and then, in early 1994, under-secretary-general. He also supervised the removal of UN forces from Somalia in 1995 and served as Boutros-Ghali's special representative to the former Yugoslavia.

Annan's reputation and acceptability to conservative forces in the United States (led by North Carolina senator Jesse Helms, chair of the Senate Foreign Relations Committee) gained him the Clinton administration's firm support as a replacement for Boutros-Ghali and made him the consensus favorite in the Security Council. After election by the General Assembly, Annan assumed the post on January 1, 1997.

The secretary-general's first major initiative was his reform plan, *Renewing the United Nations.* Unveiled in July 1997, the plan called for restructuring and pruning the UN's bureaucracy. In response, the U.S. Congress passed budget legislation in November 1999 appropriating $819 million for partial repayment of the $1 billion back dues owed by Washington.

By early 1998 the issue of weapons inspections in Iraq brought the threat of confrontation between Baghdad and the United States. Annan was able to gain from the Iraqi leader the Memo of Understanding of February 22, 1998, whereby Iraq accepted all previous Security Council resolutions pertaining to the issue and agreed to "unconditional and unrestricted" inspections. As a consequence the Security Council lifted the annual limit on Iraqi oil sales, on condition that the extra income be used to buy food and medicine and to pay for repairs to the country's infrastructure. However, in August 1998 Saddam Hussein again halted inspections, and the unresolved standoff persisted.

In March 1998 the secretary-general visited the Middle East. Speaking to the Palestinian Legislative Council in Gaza City, he urged nonviolence and patience regarding peace talks with Israel; then he spoke to the Israeli Foreign Relations Council in Jerusalem, where he apologized for past unfair UN actions toward Israel but criticized settlements in Palestinian areas and undue hardships imposed on Palestinians. When the peace process collapsed in the Middle East in October 2000, Annan led a feverish diplomatic shuttle among the parties and brokered an emergency summit at Sharm el-Sheik, Egypt, where he brought together Israeli prime minister Ehud Barak, Palestinian Authority chairman Yasser Arafat, U.S. president Bill Clinton, and Egyptian president Hosni Mubarak.

In April 1998 the secretary-general traveled to Rwanda. Before that country's parliament, he sought to repair an abiding ill will by acknowledging the delinquency of the United Nations in responding to the horrific massacre of Tutsis during disturbances in 1994, a time when he was under-secretary-general. This and other problems related to the challenge of disintegrating states led the secretary-general to support and build on certain ideas about peacekeeping that were associated with his predecessor, Boutros Boutros-Ghali. In September 1998, at the opening of the General Assembly, he recommended intervention in the escalating conflict between Serbs and Albanians in Kosovo. By June 1999 the Security Council approved the NATO-led peacekeeping force in Kosovo, and the UN Interim Administration Mission in Kosovo (UNMIK) acquired the difficult responsibility of forming a multinational police force, setting up a justice system, and restoring order in the province. When, in the fall of 1999, East Timor voted to secede from Indonesia, Annan negotiated with the Indonesian government to allow UN forces to enter the province. Eventually a UN-sanctioned force, led by Australians, did begin to restore order, and UN-monitored elections brought independence and peace to East Timor.

In August 2000 the United Nations issued a report, drawn from an international panel of experts, headed by Lakhdar Brahimi, that the secretary-general had appointed. The Brahimi Report reflected Annan's vision for peacekeeping and included a number of reform proposals.

The secretary-general convened the Millennium Summit in September 2000. The largest gathering of world leaders in history and Annan's brainchild, this meeting entertained some 200 speeches from about 150 prime ministers, presidents, and potentates from most of the world's countries. These individuals addressed many of the greatest challenges to the world, including reforming peacekeeping, eliminating poverty, reversing the spread of AIDS, promoting disarmament, advancing the Middle East peace process, ensuring that economic globalization left no one behind, and more.

The following June 27, six months before his first term was to end, the Security Council unanimously renominated Annan and forwarded his name to the General Assembly, where, on June 29, 2001, he was reelected to his post by acclamation. Annan's early reelection broke UN tradition. Later that year, the secretary-general and the United Nations garnered the Nobel Peace Prize.

Annan's second term was plagued by crises generated from the terrorist attacks in the United States on September 11, 2001. By the end of that year a Security Council coalition had invaded Afghanistan, seeking to root out Al Qaeda terrorists. In 2002–2003, however, the coalition collapsed as the United States decided to go to war with Iraq and toppled Saddam Hussein's regime. The United States did so on the basis of a new foreign policy doctrine—preemption—which challenged the underlying UN principle of collective security. Secretary-General Annan worried that the UN's effectiveness was in jeopardy. In addition, scandals associated with the "oil-for-food" program in Iraq tarnished Annan's reputation with member governments. Independent investigations showed that his son had benefited financially from the program and persons close to the secretary-general may have been involved in criminal conduct. Annan was accused of lax leadership, which led to calls by critics of the United Nations for his resignation. He insisted that he would serve out his term of office. In a demonstration of his commitment to remain, in 2005 he put forward sweeping reform proposals, urging an expansion of the Security Council, the abolition of the Trusteeship Council, the replacement of the Commission on Human Rights with a smaller, more authoritative Human Rights Council elected by the General Assembly, and other programmatic changes.

Appendix F

Selected UN Resolutions

SECURITY COUNCIL RESOLUTION 678

S/RES/678 (1990)

[Invoking the enforcement provisions of Chapter VII for only the second time in its history, the Security Council authorized member states "to use all necessary means" in the liberation of Kuwait from Iraqi occupation. The resolution provided the legal basis for the military operations subsequently conducted by a coalition of states led by United States.]

The Security Council,

Recalling and reaffirming its resolutions 660 (1990) of 2 August 1990, 661 (1990) of 6 August 1990, 662 (1990) of 9 August 1990, 664 (1990) of 18 August 1990, 665 (1990) of 25 August 1990, 666 (1990) of 13 September 1990, 667 (1990) of 16 September 1990, 669 (1990) of 24 September 1990, 670 (1990) of 25 September 1990, 674 (1990) of 29 October 1990 and 677 (1990) of 28 November 1990,

Noting that, despite all efforts by the United Nations, Iraq refuses to comply with its obligation to implement resolution 660 (1990) and the above-mentioned subsequent relevant resolutions in flagrant contempt of the Security Council,

Mindful of its duties and responsibilities under the charter of the United Nations for the maintenance and preservation of international peace and security,

Determined to secure full compliance with its decisions,

Acting under Chapter VII of the Charter,

1. *Demands* that Iraq comply fully with resolution 660 (1990) and all subsequent relevant resolutions, and decides, while maintaining all its decisions, to allow Iraq one final opportunity, as a pause of goodwill, to do so;
2. *Authorizes* Member States co-operating with the Government of Kuwait, unless Iraq on or before 15 January 1991 fully implements, as set forth in paragraph 1 above, the above-mentioned resolutions, to use all necessary means to uphold and implement resolution 660 (1990) and all subsequent relevant resolutions and to restore international peace and security in the area;
3. *Requests* all States to provide appropriate support for the actions undertaken in pursuance of paragraph 2 above;

4. *Requests* the States concerned to keep the Security Council regularly informed on the progress of actions undertaken pursuant to paragraphs 2 and 3 above;

5. *Decides* to remain seized of the matter.

Adopted at the 2963rd meeting by 12 votes to 2 (Cuba and Yemen), with one abstention (China).
29 November 1990

SECURITY COUNCIL RESOLUTION 1368

S/RES/1368 (2001)

[The Security Council unanimously adopted Resolution 1368 on September 12, 2001, one day after terrorists killed thousands of people by crashing civilian jetliners into both towers of the World Trade Center in New York City and into the Pentagon near Washington, D.C. Another commandeered airplane crashed in Pennsylvania. Council members departed from tradition and stood to adopt Resolution 1368. In the text, the council held that any act of international terrorism was a threat to international peace and security.]

The Security Council,

Reaffirming the principles and purposes of the Charter of the United Nations,

Determined to combat by all means threats to international peace and security caused by terrorist acts,

Recognizing the inherent right of individual or collective self-defence in accordance with the Charter,

1. *Unequivocally condemns* in the strongest terms the horrifying terrorist attacks which took place on 11 September 2001 in New York, Washington (D.C.) and Pennsylvania and *regards* such acts, like any act of international terrorism, as a threat to international peace and security;

2. *Expresses* its deepest sympathy and condolences to the victims and their families and to the People and Government of the United States of America;

3. *Calls* on all States to work together urgently to bring to justice the perpetrators, organizers and sponsors of these terrorist attacks and stresses that those responsible for aiding, supporting or harbouring the perpetrators, organizers and sponsors of these acts will be held accountable;

4. *Calls also* on the international community to redouble their efforts to prevent and suppress terrorist acts including by increased cooperation and full implementation of the relevant international anti-terrorist conventions and Security Council resolutions, in particular resolution 1269 of 19 October 1999;

5. *Expresses* its readiness to take all necessary steps to respond to the terrorist attacks of 11 September 2001, and to combat all forms of terrorism, in accordance with its responsibilities under the Charter of the United Nations;

6. *Decides* to remain seized of the matter.

Adopted unanimously at the 4370th meeting.

UNITED NATIONS MILLENNIUM DECLARATION
A/RES/55/2 (18 September 2000)

The General Assembly

Adopts the following Declaration:

United Nations Millennium Declaration

I. Values and principles

1. We, heads of State and Government, have gathered at United Nations Headquarters in New York from 6 to 8 September 2000, at the dawn of a new millennium, to reaffirm our faith in the Organization and its Charter as indispensable foundations of a more peaceful, prosperous and just world.

2. We recognize that, in addition to our separate responsibilities to our individual societies, we have a collective responsibility to uphold the principles of human dignity, equality and equity at the global level. As leaders we have a duty therefore to all the world's people, especially the most vulnerable and, in particular, the children of the world, to whom the future belongs.

3. We reaffirm our commitment to the purposes and principles of the Charter of the United Nations, which have proved timeless and universal. Indeed, their relevance and capacity to inspire have increased, as nations and peoples have become increasingly interconnected and interdependent.

4. We are determined to establish a just and lasting peace all over the world in accordance with the purposes and principles of the Charter. We rededicate ourselves to support all efforts to uphold the sovereign equality of all States, respect for their territorial integrity and political independence, resolution of disputes by peaceful means and in conformity with the principles of justice and international law, the right to self-determination of peoples which remain under colonial domination and foreign occupation, non-interference in the internal affairs of States, respect for human rights and fundamental freedoms, respect for the equal rights of all without distinction as to race, sex, language or religion and international cooperation in solving international problems of an economic, social, cultural or humanitarian character.

5. We believe that the central challenge we face today is to ensure that globalization becomes a positive force for all the world's people. For while globalization offers great opportunities, at present its benefits are very unevenly shared, while its costs are unevenly distributed. We recognize that developing countries and countries with economies in transition face special difficulties in responding to this central challenge. Thus, only through broad and sustained efforts to create a shared future, based upon our common humanity in all its diversity, can globalization be made fully inclusive and equitable. These efforts must include policies and measures, at the global level, which correspond to the needs of developing countries and economies in transition and are formulated and implemented with their effective participation.

6. We consider certain fundamental values to be essential to international relations in the twenty-first century. These include:

   • **Freedom.**   Men and women have the right to live their lives and raise their children in dignity, free from hunger and from the fear of violence, oppression or injustice. Democratic and participatory governance based on the will of the people best assures these rights.

- **Equality.** No individual and no nation must be denied the opportunity to benefit from development. The equal rights and opportunities of women and men must be assured.
- **Solidarity.** Global challenges must be managed in a way that distributes the costs and burdens fairly in accordance with basic principles of equity and social justice. Those who suffer or who benefit least deserve help from those who benefit most.
- **Tolerance.** Human beings must respect one other, in all their diversity of belief, culture and language. Differences within and between societies should be neither feared nor repressed, but cherished as a precious asset of humanity. A culture of peace and dialogue among all civilizations should be actively promoted.
- **Respect for nature.** Prudence must be shown in the management of all living species and natural resources, in accordance with the precepts of sustainable development. Only in this way can the immeasurable riches provided to us by nature be preserved and passed on to our descendants. The current unsustainable patterns of production and consumption must be changed in the interest of our future welfare and that of our descendants.
- **Shared responsibility.** Responsibility for managing worldwide economic and social development, as well as threats to international peace and security, must be shared among the nations of the world and should be exercised multilaterally. As the most universal and most representative organization in the world, the United Nations must play the central role.

7. In order to translate these shared values into actions, we have identified key objectives to which we assign special significance.

II. Peace, security and disarmament

8. We will spare no effort to free our peoples from the scourge of war, whether within or between States, which has claimed more than 5 million lives in the past decade. We will also seek to eliminate the dangers posed by weapons of mass destruction.
9. We resolve therefore:

- To strengthen respect for the rule of law in international as in national affairs and, in particular, to ensure compliance by Member States with the decisions of the International Court of Justice, in compliance with the Charter of the United Nations, in cases to which they are parties.
- To make the United Nations more effective in maintaining peace and security by giving it the resources and tools it needs for conflict prevention, peaceful resolution of disputes, peacekeeping, post-conflict peace-building and reconstruction. In this context, we take note of the report of the Panel on United Nations Peace Operations and request the General Assembly to consider its recommendations expeditiously.
- To strengthen cooperation between the United Nations and regional organizations, in accordance with the provisions of Chapter VIII of the Charter.
- To ensure the implementation, by States Parties, of treaties in areas such as arms control and disarmament and of international humanitarian law and human rights

law, and call upon all States to consider signing and ratifying the Rome Statute of the International Criminal Court.

- To take concerted action against international terrorism, and to accede as soon as possible to all the relevant international conventions.
- To redouble our efforts to implement our commitment to counter the world drug problem.
- To intensify our efforts to fight transnational crime in all its dimensions, including trafficking as well as smuggling in human beings and money laundering.
- To minimize the adverse effects of United Nations economic sanctions on innocent populations, to subject such sanctions regimes to regular reviews and to eliminate the adverse effects of sanctions on third parties.
- To strive for the elimination of weapons of mass destruction, particularly nuclear weapons, and to keep all options open for achieving this aim, including the possibility of convening an international conference to identify ways of eliminating nuclear dangers.
- To take concerted action to end illicit traffic in small arms and light weapons, especially by making arms transfers more transparent and supporting regional disarmament measures, taking account of all the recommendations of the forthcoming United Nations Conference on Illicit Trade in Small Arms and Light Weapons.
- To call on all States to consider acceding to the Convention on the Prohibition of the Use, Stockpiling, Production and Transfer of Anti-personnel Mines and on Their Destruction, as well as the amended mines protocol to the Convention on conventional weapons.

10. We urge Member States to observe the Olympic Truce, individually and collectively, now and in the future, and to support the International Olympic Committee in its efforts to promote peace and human understanding through sport and the Olympic Ideal.

III. Development and poverty eradication

11. We will spare no effort to free our fellow men, women and children from the abject and dehumanizing conditions of extreme poverty, to which more than a billion of them are currently subjected. We are committed to making the right to development a reality for everyone and to freeing the entire human race from want.

12. We resolve therefore to create an environment—at the national and global levels alike—which is conducive to development and to the elimination of poverty.

13. Success in meeting these objectives depends, inter alia, on good governance within each country. It also depends on good governance at the international level and on transparency in the financial, monetary and trading systems. We are committed to an open, equitable, rule-based, predictable and non-discriminatory multilateral trading and financial system.

14. We are concerned about the obstacles developing countries face in mobilizing the resources needed to finance their sustained development. We will therefore make every effort to ensure the success of the High-level International and Intergovernmental Event on Financing for Development, to be held in 2001.

15. We also undertake to address the special needs of the least developed countries. In this context, we welcome the Third United Nations Conference on the Least Developed

Countries to be held in May 2001 and will endeavour to ensure its success. We call on the industrialized countries:

- To adopt, preferably by the time of that Conference, a policy of duty- and quota-free access for essentially all exports from the least developed countries;
- To implement the enhanced programme of debt relief for the heavily indebted poor countries without further delay and to agree to cancel all official bilateral debts of those countries in return for their making demonstrable commitments to poverty reduction; and
- To grant more generous development assistance, especially to countries that are genuinely making an effort to apply their resources to poverty reduction.

16. We are also determined to deal comprehensively and effectively with the debt problems of low- and middle-income developing countries, through various national and international measures designed to make their debt sustainable in the long term.

17. We also resolve to address the special needs of small island developing States, by implementing the Barbados Programme of Action and the outcome of the twenty-second special session of the General Assembly rapidly and in full. We urge the international community to ensure that, in the development of a vulnerability index, the special needs of small island developing States are taken into account.

18. We recognize the special needs and problems of the landlocked developing countries, and urge both bilateral and multilateral donors to increase financial and technical assistance to this group of countries to meet their special development needs and to help them overcome the impediments of geography by improving their transit transport systems.

19. We resolve further:

- To halve, by the year 2015, the proportion of the world's people whose income is less than one dollar a day and the proportion of people who suffer from hunger and, by the same date, to halve the proportion of people who are unable to reach or to afford safe drinking water.
- To ensure that, by the same date, children everywhere, boys and girls alike, will be able to complete a full course of primary schooling and that girls and boys will have equal access to all levels of education.
- By the same date, to have reduced maternal mortality by three quarters, and under-five child mortality by two thirds, of their current rates.
- To have, by then, halted, and begun to reverse, the spread of HIV/AIDS, the scourge of malaria and other major diseases that afflict humanity.
- To provide special assistance to children orphaned by HIV/AIDS.
- By 2020, to have achieved a significant improvement in the lives of at least 100 million slum dwellers as proposed in the "Cities Without Slums" initiative.

20. We also resolve:

- To promote gender equality and the empowerment of women as effective ways to combat poverty, hunger and disease and to stimulate development that is truly sustainable.
- To develop and implement strategies that give young people everywhere a real chance to find decent and productive work.

- To encourage the pharmaceutical industry to make essential drugs more widely available and affordable by all who need them in developing countries.
- To develop strong partnerships with the private sector and with civil society organizations in pursuit of development and poverty eradication.
- To ensure that the benefits of new technologies, especially information and communication technologies, in conformity with recommendations contained in the ECOSOC 2000 Ministerial Declaration, are available to all.

IV. Protecting our common environment

21. We must spare no effort to free all of humanity, and above all our children and grandchildren, from the threat of living on a planet irredeemably spoilt by human activities, and whose resources would no longer be sufficient for their needs.

22. We reaffirm our support for the principles of sustainable development, including those set out in Agenda 21, agreed upon at the United Nations Conference on Environment and Development.

23. We resolve therefore to adopt in all our environmental actions a new ethic of conservation and stewardship and, as first steps, we resolve:

- To make every effort to ensure the entry into force of the Kyoto Protocol, preferably by the tenth anniversary of the United Nations Conference on Environment and Development in 2002, and to embark on the required reduction in emissions of greenhouse gases.
- To intensify our collective efforts for the management, conservation and sustainable development of all types of forests.
- To press for the full implementation of the Convention on Biological Diversity and the Convention to Combat Desertification in those Countries Experiencing Serious Drought and/or Desertification, particularly in Africa.
- To stop the unsustainable exploitation of water resources by developing water management strategies at the regional, national and local levels, which promote both equitable access and adequate supplies.
- To intensify cooperation to reduce the number and effects of natural and man-made disasters.
- To ensure free access to information on the human genome sequence.

V. Human rights, democracy and good governance

24. We will spare no effort to promote democracy and strengthen the rule of law, as well as respect for all internationally recognized human rights and fundamental freedoms, including the right to development.

25. We resolve therefore:

- To respect fully and uphold the Universal Declaration of Human Rights.
- To strive for the full protection and promotion in all our countries of civil, political, economic, social and cultural rights for all.
- To strengthen the capacity of all our countries to implement the principles and practices of democracy and respect for human rights, including minority rights.
- To combat all forms of violence against women and to implement the Convention on the Elimination of All Forms of Discrimination against Women.

- To take measures to ensure respect for and protection of the human rights of migrants, migrant workers and their families, to eliminate the increasing acts of racism and xenophobia in many societies and to promote greater harmony and tolerance in all societies.
- To work collectively for more inclusive political processes, allowing genuine participation by all citizens in all our countries.
- To ensure the freedom of the media to perform their essential role and the right of the public to have access to information.

VI. Protecting the vulnerable

26. We will spare no effort to ensure that children and all civilian populations that suffer disproportionately the consequences of natural disasters, genocide, armed conflicts and other humanitarian emergencies are given every assistance and protection so that they can resume normal life as soon as possible.

We resolve therefore:

- To expand and strengthen the protection of civilians in complex emergencies, in conformity with international humanitarian law.
- To strengthen international cooperation, including burden sharing in, and the coordination of humanitarian assistance to, countries hosting refugees and to help all refugees and displaced persons to return voluntarily to their homes, in safety and dignity and to be smoothly reintegrated into their societies.
- To encourage the ratification and full implementation of the Convention on the Rights of the Child and its optional protocols on the involvement of children in armed conflict and on the sale of children, child prostitution and child pornography.

VII. Meeting the special needs of Africa

27. We will support the consolidation of democracy in Africa and assist Africans in their struggle for lasting peace, poverty eradication and sustainable development, thereby bringing Africa into the mainstream of the world economy.

28. We resolve therefore:

- To give full support to the political and institutional structures of emerging democracies in Africa.
- To encourage and sustain regional and subregional mechanisms for preventing conflict and promoting political stability, and to ensure a reliable flow of resources for peacekeeping operations on the continent.
- To take special measures to address the challenges of poverty eradication and sustainable development in Africa, including debt cancellation, improved market access, enhanced Official Development Assistance and increased flows of Foreign Direct Investment, as well as transfers of technology.
- To help Africa build up its capacity to tackle the spread of the HIV/AIDS pandemic and other infectious diseases.

VIII. Strengthening the United Nations

29. We will spare no effort to make the United Nations a more effective instrument for pursuing all of these priorities: the fight for development for all the peoples of the world, the fight against poverty, ignorance and disease; the fight against injustice; the fight against violence, terror and crime; and the fight against the degradation and destruction of our common home.

30. We resolve therefore:

- To reaffirm the central position of the General Assembly as the chief deliberative, policy-making and representative organ of the United Nations, and to enable it to play that role effectively.
- To intensify our efforts to achieve a comprehensive reform of the Security Council in all its aspects.
- To strengthen further the Economic and Social Council, building on its recent achievements, to help it fulfil the role ascribed to it in the Charter.
- To strengthen the International Court of Justice, in order to ensure justice and the rule of law in international affairs.
- To encourage regular consultations and coordination among the principal organs of the United Nations in pursuit of their functions.
- To ensure that the Organization is provided on a timely and predictable basis with the resources it needs to carry out its mandates.
- To urge the Secretariat to make the best use of those resources, in accordance with clear rules and procedures agreed by the General Assembly, in the interests of all Member States, by adopting the best management practices and technologies available and by concentrating on those tasks that reflect the agreed priorities of Member States.
- To promote adherence to the Convention on the Safety of United Nations and Associated Personnel.
- To ensure greater policy coherence and better cooperation between the United Nations, its agencies, the Bretton Woods Institutions and the World Trade Organization, as well as other multilateral bodies, with a view to achieving a fully coordinated approach to the problems of peace and development.
- To strengthen further cooperation between the United Nations and national parliaments through their world organization, the Inter-Parliamentary Union, in various fields, including peace and security, economic and social development, international law and human rights and democracy and gender issues.
- To give greater opportunities to the private sector, non-governmental organizations and civil society, in general, to contribute to the realization of the Organization's goals and programmes.

31. We request the General Assembly to review on a regular basis the progress made in implementing the provisions of this Declaration, and ask the Secretary-General to issue periodic reports for consideration by the General Assembly and as a basis for further action.

32. We solemnly reaffirm, on this historic occasion, that the United Nations is the indispensable common house of the entire human family, through which we will seek to realize our universal aspirations for peace, cooperation and development. We therefore pledge our unstinting support for these common objectives and our determination to achieve them.

Appendix G

Acronyms and Abbreviations

ABM	Anti-Ballistic Missile	CBD	Convention on Biological Diversity
ACABQ	Advisory Committee on Administrative and Budgetary Questions	CCD	Conference of the Committee on Disarmament; Convention to Combat Desertification
ACC	Administrative Committee on Coordination	CCW	Convention on Certain Conventional Weapons
ADA	Atomic Development Authority	CD	Conference on Disarmament
ADFL	Alliance of Democratic Forces for the Liberation of Congo	CEB	(UN System) Chief Executives Board for Coordination
ANC	Armée Nationale Congolaise	CEDAW	Convention on the Elimination of All Forms of Discrimination against Women
APEC	Asian Pacific Economic Cooperation Organization		
ASEAN	Association of Southeast Asian Nations	CFCs	Chlorofluorocarbons
AU	African Union	CHR	UN Commission on Human Rights
BONUCA	UN Peace-Building Office in the Central African Africa	CIDIE	Committee of International Development Institutions on the Environment
BWC	Convention on the Prohibition of the Development, Production and Stockpiling of Bacteriological (Biological) and Toxin Weapons and on Their Destruction (Biological Weapons Convention)	CIS	Commonwealth of Independent States
		CITES	Convention on International Trade in Endangered Species
		CONGO	Conference on Non-Governmental Organizations in Consultative Status with the Economic and Social Council
CARICOM	Caribbean Community		

COP	Conference of the Parties	ECE	Economic Commission for Europe
CPR	Committee of Permanent Representatives	ECLAC	Economic Commission for Latin America and the Caribbean
CSD	Commission on Sustainable Development	ECOFIN	Economic and Financial Committee (GA Second Committee)
CSW	UN Commission on the Status of Women		
CTBT	Comprehensive Nuclear-Test-Ban Treaty	ECOMOG	ECOWAS Monitoring Group
CTBTO	Comprehensive Nuclear-Test-Ban Treaty Organization	ECOSOC	Economic and Social Council
		ECOWAS	Economic Community of West African States
CWC	Convention on the Prohibition of the Development, Production, Stockpiling and Use of Chemical Weapons and on Their Destruction (Chemical Weapons Convention)	ECWA	Economic Commission for Western Africa
		ENDC	Eighteen-Nation Disarmament Committee
		EPTA	Expanded Program of Technical Assistance
DAW	Division for the Advancement of Women	ESCAP	Economic and Social Commission for Asia and the Pacific
DDA	Department for Disarmament Affairs	ESCWA	Economic and Social Commission for Western Asia
DDR	Disarmament, demobiliza-tion, reintegration and repatriation	EU	European Union
		FAO	Food and Agriculture Organization
DESA	Department of Economic and Social Affairs	FBI	Federal Bureau of Investigation
DGAACS	Department for General Assembly Affairs and Conference Services	FRG	Federal Republic of Germany
		G-8	Group of 8
DM	Department of Management	G-77	Group of 77
DMFAS	Debt Management and Financial Analysis System	GA	General Assembly
		GAINS	Gender Awareness Information and Networking System
DPA	Department of Political Affairs		
DPI	Department of Public Information	GAO	General Accounting Office (U.S.)
DPKO	Department of Peacekeeping Operations	GATS	General Agreement on Trade in Services
DRC	Democratic Republic of the Congo	GATT	General Agreement on Tariffs and Trade
DSB	Dispute Settlement Body (WTO)	GDP	Gross domestic product
		GDR	German Democratic Republic
DSG	Deputy secretary-general	GEF	Global Environment Facility
ECA	Economic Commission for Africa	GEMS	Global Environment Monitoring System

GHG	Greenhouse gas	IDA	International Development Association
GNI	Gross national income		
GPA	Global Programme on AIDS	IFAD	International Fund for Agricultural Development
GRID	Global Resource Information Database		
		IFC	International Finance Corporation
GSP	General System of Preferences		
		IFOR	Implementation Force
HABITAT II	Second World Conference on Human Settlements	IGAD	Intergovernmental Authority on Development
HIPC	Heavily Indebted Poor Country	IGOs	Intergovernmental organizations
HROAG	UN Office for the Protection and Promotion of Human Rights in Abkhazia, Georgia	ILO	International Labour Organization
		ILO/ITC	International Training Center
IADA	International Atomic Development Authority	IMF	International Monetary Fund
		IMO	International Maritime Organization
IAEA	International Atomic Energy Agency		
		INSTRAW	International Research and Training Institute for the Advancement of Women
IBE	International Bureau of Education		
IBRD	International Bank for Reconstruction and Development [World Bank]	IPCC	Intergovernmental Panel on Climate Change
		ISAF	International Security Assistance Force
ICAO	International Civil Aviation Organization		
		ITC	International Trade Centre; International Training Centre
ICBL	International Campaign to Ban Landmines		
		ITLOS	International Tribunal for the Law of the Sea
ICC	International Criminal Court		
ICCPR	International Covenant on Civil and Political Rights	ITO	International Trade Organization
ICESCR	International Covenant on Economic, Social, and Cultural Rights	ITU	International Telecommunication Union
		IUCN	World Conservation Union
ICJ	International Court of Justice	JIU	Joint Inspection Unit
ICPD	International Conference on Population and Development	JMC	Joint Military Commission
		KFOR	UN Kosovo Force
		LDCs	Least developed countries
ICS	International Centre for Science and High Technology	MDB	Multilateral Development Bank
ICSID	International Centre for the Settlement of Investment Disputes	MDGs	Millennium Development Goals
		MFIs	Multilateral Financial Institutions
ICTR	International Criminal Tribunal for Rwanda	MICAH	UN Civilian Support Mission in Haiti
ICTY	International Criminal Tribunal for the Former Yugoslavia	MIF	Multilateral Interim Force (Haiti)

MIGA	Multilateral Investment Guarantee Agency	ODCCP	Office for Drug Control and Crime Prevention
MINUCI	UN Mission in Côte d'Ivoire	OHCHR	Office of the UN High Commissioner for Human Rights
MINUGUA	UN Verification Mission in Guatemala		
MINURCA	UN Mission in the Central African Republic	OHRLLS	Office of the High Representative for the Least Developed Countries, Landlocked Developing Countries and Small Island Developing States
MINURSO	UN Mission for the Referendum in Western Sahara		
MINUSTAH	UN Stabilization Mission in Haiti		
MIPONUH	UN Civilian Police Mission in Haiti	OIOS	Office of Internal Oversight Services
		OLA	Office of Legal Affairs
MMI	Money Matters Institute	ONUB	UN Operation in Burundi
MONUA	UN Observer Mission in Angola	ONUC	UN Operation in the Congo
		ONUCA	UN Observer Group in Central America
MONUC	UN Organization Mission in the Democratic Republic of the Congo	ONUMOZ	UN Operation in Mozambique
MPLA	Movimento Popular de Libertação de Angola	ONUSAL	UN Observer Mission in El Salvador
MSF	Médecins Sans Frontières	OPCW	Organisation for the Prohibition of Chemical Weapons
NAFTA	North American Free Trade Association		
NAM	Non-Aligned Movement	OPEC	Organization of Petroleum Exporting Countries
NATO	North Atlantic Treaty Organization	OSCE	Organization for Security and Cooperation in Europe
NEPAD	New Partnership for Africa's Development	P5	Five permanent members
NFZs	Nuclear weapons–free zones	PBPU	Peacekeeping Best Practices Unit
NGLS	(UN) Non-Governmental Liaison Service	PCIJ	Permanent Court of International Justice
NGOs	Nongovernmental organizations	PDD-25	Presidential Decision Directive 25
NIEO	New International Economic Order	PDMs	Practical disarmament measures
NPT	Treaty on the Non-Proliferation of Nuclear Weapons (Nuclear Non-Proliferation Treaty)	PFA	Platform for Action (UN Fourth World Conference on Women)
OAU	Organization of African Unity	PLO	Palestine Liberation Organization
OCHA	Office for the Coordination of Humanitarian Affairs	PPP	Polluter Pays Principle
		PRC	People's Republic of China
ODA	Official Development Assistance	ROK	Republic of Korea
		RUF	Revolutionary United Front

SALT	Strategic Arms Limitation Talks	UNAMIC	UN Advance Mission in Cambodia
SALW	Small arms and light weapons	UNAMIR	UN Assistance Mission for Rwanda
SC	Security Council	UNAMSIL	UN Assistance Mission in Sierra Leone
SDN	Sustainable development network	UNAVEM	UN Angola Verification Mission
SDRs	Special drawing rights		
SFOR	Stabilization Force	UNC	UN Command in Korea
SG	Secretary-general	UNCC	UN Compensation Commission
SHD	Sustainable human development	UNCDF	UN Capital Development Fund
SMEs	Small and medium enterprises		
SMG	Senior Management Group	UNCED	UN Conference on Environment and Development
SNPA	Substantial New Programme of Action		
SOCHUM	Social, Humanitarian and Cultural Committee (GA Third Committee)	UNCETDG/GHS	UN Committee of Experts on the Transportation of Dangerous Goods and on the Globally Harmonized System of Classification and Labelling of Chemicals
SOFA	Status of Forces Agreement		
SRSG	Special representative of the secretary-general		
SU/TCDC	Special Unit/Technical Cooperation among Developing Countries	UNCHE	UN Conference on the Human Environment
		UNCHS	UN Centre for Human Settlements
SUNFED	Special UN Fund for Economic Development	UNCIO	United Nations Conference on International Organization
SWAPO	South-West Africa People's Organisation	UNCITRAL	UN Commission on International Trade Law
TICAD	Tokyo International Conference for African Development	UNCLOS	UN Conference on the Law of the Sea
TNCs	Transnational corporations	UNCRO	UN Confidence Restoration Operation
TRIPS	Trade-Related Aspects of Intellectual Property Rights	UNCTAD	UN Conference on Trade and Development
UDHR	Universal Declaration of Human Rights	UNDCP	UN International Drug Control Programme
UN	United Nations		
UNAEC	UN Atomic Energy Commission	UNDOF	UN Disengagement Observer Force
UNAIDS	Joint UN Programme on HIV/AIDS	UNDP	UN Development Programme
		UNECE	UN Economic Commission for Europe
UNAMA	UN Assistance Mission in Afghanistan	UNEF	UN Emergency Force
UNAMET	UN Mission in East Timor	UNEP	UN Environment Programme
UNAMI	UN Assistance Mission for Iraq	UNESCO	UN Educational, Scientific and Cultural Organization

UNFCCC	UN Framework Convention on Climate Change	UNMIS	UN Mission in the Sudan
UNFF	UN Forum on Forests	UNMISET	UN Mission of Support in East Timor
UNFICYP	UN Peacekeeping Force in Cyprus	UNMOGIP	UN Military Observer Group in India and Pakistan
UNFIP	UN Fund for International Partnerships	UNMOP	UN Mission of Observers in Prevlaka
UNFPA	UN Population Fund	UNMOT	UN Mission of Observers in Tajikistan
UNFSDT	UN Fund for Science and Technology for Development	UNMOVIC	UN Monitoring, Verification and Inspection Commission
UNGOMAP	UN Good Offices Mission in Afghanistan and Pakistan	UNOA	UN Office in Angola
UN-HABITAT	UN Human Settlements Programme	UNOB	UN Office in Burundi
		UNOCI	UN Operation in Côte d'Ivoire
UNHCHR	UN High Commissioner for Human Rights	UNODC	UN Office on Drugs and Crime
UNHCR	UN High Commissioner for Refugees	UNOG	UN Office at Geneva
UNICEF	UN Children's Fund	UNOGBIS	UN Peace-Building Support Office in Guinea-Bissau
UNICJRI	UN Interregional Crime and Justice Research Institute	UNOL	UN Peace-Building Support Office in Liberia
UNIDIR	UN Institute for Disarmament Research	UNOMB	UN Observer Mission in Bougainville
UNIDO	UN Industrial Development Organization	UNOMIG	UN Observer Mission in Georgia
UNIFEM	UN Development Fund for Women	UNOMIL	UN Observer Mission in Liberia
UNIFIL	UN Interim Force in Lebanon	UNOMSIL	UN Observer Mission in Sierra Leone
UNIPOM	UN India-Pakistan Observer Mission	UNOMUR	UN Observer Mission for Uganda-Rwanda
UNITA	União Nacional para a Independência Total de Angola	UNON	UN Office in Nairobi
UNITAF	Unified Task Force	UNOPS	UN Office for Project Services
UNITAR	UN Institute for Training and Research	UNOSOM	UN Operation in Somalia
		UNOTIL	UN Office in Timor-Leste
UNLDC	UN Conference on Least Developed Countries	UNOWA	UN Office for West Africa
		UNPOB	UN Political Office in Bougainville
UNMA	UN Mission in Angola		
UNMEE	UN Mission in Ethiopia and Eritrea	UNPOS	UN Political Office for Somalia
UNMIBH	UN Mission in Bosnia and Herzegovina	UNPREDEP	UN Preventive Deployment Force in the Former Yugoslav Republic of Macedonia
UNMIH	UN Mission in Haiti		
UNMIK	UN Interim Administration Mission in Kosovo	UNPROFOR	UN Protection Force
		UNPSG	UN Civilian Police Support Group
UNMIL	UN Mission in Liberia		

UNRFNRE	UN Revolving Fund for Natural Resources	UNTAG	UN Transition Assistance Group
UNRISD	UN Research Institute for Social Development	UNTCOK	UN Temporary Commission on Korea
UNRPR	UN Relief for Palestine Refugees	UNTMIH	UN Transition Mission in Haiti
UNRWA	UN Relief and Works Agency for Palestine Refugees in the Near East	UNTOP	UN Tajikistan Office of Peace-building
UNSAS	UN Standby Arrangements System	UNTSO	UN Truce Supervision Organization
UNSCO	Office of the UN Special Coordinator for the Middle East Peace Process and Personal Representative of the Secretary-General to the Palestine Liberation Organization and the Palestinian Authority	UNU	UN University
		UNV	UN Volunteers
		UPOV	International Union for the Protection of New Varieties of Plants
		UPU	Universal Postal Union
		USG	Under-secretary-general
		WBG	World Bank Group
		WCED	World Commission on Environment and Development
UNSCOM	UN Special Commission on Iraq		
UNSCOP	UN Special Commission on Palestine	WFP	World Food Programme
		WHO	World Health Organization
UNSMA	UN Special Mission to Afghanistan	WIPO	World Intellectual Property Organization
UNSMIH	UN Support Mission in Haiti	WMDs	Weapons of mass destruction
UNSO	UN Sudano-Sahelian Office	WMO	World Meteorological Organization
UNTAC	UN Transitional Authority in Cambodia		
UNTAES	UN Transitional Authority in Eastern Slavonia, Baranja, and Western Sirmium	WSSD	World Summit on Social Development
		WTO	World Trade Organization
		WWAP	World Water Assessment Programme
UNTAET	UN Transitional Administration in East Timor	WWF	World Wildlife Fund

Index

Abbas, Mahmoud, 193
Acheson, Dean, 95, 96
ADA. *See* Atomic Development Authority
Administrative Committee on Coordination (ACC), 103, 118
Administrative reform, 98, 101, 103–104
Advisory opinions, 89, 91, 140, 141, 142
Afghanistan
  food program, 27
  health care program, 15
  loss of General Assembly vote, 92
  rebuilding, 215, 217
  Soviet invasion of, 67, 82, 174, 175
  special rapporteurs, 231, 232
  terrorists, war against, 12, 71
  UN membership, 319
Africa
  cold war effects, 66–67
  Congo, 112–113, 221–222, 280, 336
  Congo crisis, 66–67, 81, 91, 92, 168, 174, 175, 198, 199–200
  desertification, 276, 349
  formation of UN, attitude toward, 57–58
  HIV/AIDS crisis, 165, 279, 350
  loss of General Assembly vote, 92
  regional development bank, 263
  Rwanda, 99, 105, 211–212, 243
  Sierra Leone and Liberia, 222–224
  Somalia, 98–99, 105, 219–220
  UN membership, 319, 320, 321
Agencies. *See* Specialized agencies
Agenda, General Assembly, 123–124
Agenda 21, 229, 259, 260, 269, 270, 278
Agenda for Peace, An, 98, 105, 184, 262, 339
Aggression, 163–165, 168, 169, 172–173
AIDS programs. *See* HIV/AIDS programs
Akayesu, Jean-Paul, 243
Alabama claims arbitration, 87
Al Qaeda, 71, 72, 186
Amendments
  Charter, 55, 79–81, 311–312
  to International Court of Justice Statute, 334
  Kassebaum, 97
ANC. *See* Armée Nationale Congalaise
Angell, Norman, 39
Angola, 206–207, 319
Annan, Kofi
  on Africa, 219
  biography, 340–342
  on budget crisis, 95
  Cyprus, 9, 201
  economic development, 264
  executive committees created by, 102
  Global Compact, 149, 233
  human rights and sovereignty, 80
  on international gatherings, 149
  Israeli wall construction report, 175
  Lebanon, 202–203
  Millennium Development Goals, 106–107, 264–265
  on "new" United Nations mission, 29–30, 213
  reform proposals, 32, 100–112, 137, 139
  Rwanda, 212
  Security Council, summoning to Geneva, 128
  thematic diplomacy, 228
  U.S. invasion of Iraq, conflict over, 11, 19, 73
  World Trade Organization, 158
Annan, Kojo, 113
Annual meeting, General Assembly, 121, 122–123
Antarctic Treaty of 1959, 178
Anti-Ballistic Missile Treaty, 178
Arab-Israeli dispute, 187–193, 201–202
Arafat, Yasser, 84, 175, 191–192, 341

Argentina, 164, 168, 319, 338
Armée Nationale Congalaise (ANC), 199
Arms control. *See* Disarmament and arms control
Arms races, 63, 177, 180
Arria formula, 232
Asia
  formation of UN, attitude about, 57–58
  growing UN membership, 79
  regional development bank, 263
Assertive multilateralism, 70
Assessments
  budget crisis, 92–95
  nonpayment, 93, 95–97
  peacekeeping, refusal to pay, 175
Atlantic Charter, 42–43, 49, 55
Atlantic Conference, 44
Atmospheric change, 271–274
Atomic Development Authority (ADA), 177
Austria, 64, 319
Baker, James, 190
Balance of power theory, 38
Bangladesh, 263–264, 319
Barak, Ehud, 191, 202
Barre, Siad, 219
Baruch, Bernard, 177
Beijing Declaration, 248, 250
Belgium
  Congo independence, 168, 199, 336
  conventional weapons, 182
  UN membership, 319
Bentham, Jeremy, 85
Berlin Wall, 68
Berne, Switzerland, offices, 25
Berne Convention for the Protection of Literary and Artistic Works, 39
Bhutan, 231, 319
Biodiversity, 270, 275–276
Biological weapons, 181–182
Biotrade Initiative, 276
Blix, Hans, 70, 71, 182
Bolivia, 40, 319
Bolshevik Revolution, 41, 48
Bolton, John, 73
Bosnia-Herzegovina, 131, 209–211, 319
Botswana, 262, 319
Bougainville, 216–217
Bourgeois, Léon, 39
Boutros-Ghali, Boutros
  Angola, 207
  biography, 339–340
  economic development, 262
  preemptive security, 184
  programmatic reform, 105
  reforms, 97–100
  Secretariat controversy, 138–139
  Somalia, 219
Brahimi, Lakhdar, 71, 73, 212–213, 217
Brahimi Report
  adoption, 127
  human rights and sovereignty, 80
  peacekeeping, 212–213
  publication, 109
Brazil, 56, 319
Bretton Woods Conference
  described, 53
  drawbacks, 266
  end of system, 83–84
  institutions, end of, 33
  international monetary and trade regime, 151–152
  UN agencies, marginalization of, 262
British Empire, 38, 58

Budget, UN
  assessments, 92–95
  control, 57
  reforms, 340
  U.S. nonpayment of dues, 68, 93, 95–97, 101–102
Bunche, Ralph, 66, 176, 187, 197
Burundi, 222, 319
Bush, George H. W., 98, 184, 193, 219, 339
Bush, George W.
  antiterrorism campaign, 70–71
  Arab-Israeli dispute, 192–193
  doctrine of preemption, 72, 73, 108
  human rights, international, 245
  Iraq war, 11, 71–73
  Kyoto Protocol, 273–274
  policies toward specialized agencies, 93
  Somalia peacekeeping mission, 98–99
  World Trade Organization, 158
Byzantium, 37
Cairo, Egypt, 248–249
Cambodia, 8, 207–208, 311
Camp David Accords/Summit, 8, 190, 191
Canada
  budget contributions, 95
  conventional weapons agreement, 182
  Disarmament Commission, 178
  indigenous children, rights of, 16
  International Bank for Reconstruction and Development (IBRD), 152
  Kyoto Protocol, 272, 273
  Montreal, agencies and meetings in, 23, 24, 25, 26, 144
  Ottawa Process, 180, 182
  role at the San Francisco Conference, 56
  UN Atomic Energy Commission, 177, 178
  UN membership, 319
Cancun trade talks, 157–158
Carbon dioxide, 273
Cardoso, Fernando Henrique, 107
Cardoso Report, 107, 109
Cartagena Protocol, 275–276
Carter, Jimmy, 95, 190
Cassin, René, 90
Caucus groups, 125
CCD. *See* Conference of the Committee on Disarmament;
  Convention to Combat Desertification
CCW. *See* Convention on Certain Conventional Weapons
CD. *See* Conference on Disarmament
CEB. *See* Chief Executive Board
Cecil, Lord Robert, 39
CFCs. *See* Chlorofluorocarbons
Chaco War, 40
Chang, Peng-chung, 90
Chapter VI ½, 81, 130, 172
Charter of the UN
  administrative reform, 101–104
  amendments, 55, 79–81, 311–312
  Annan reforms, 100–112
  budget crisis, 92–97
  cold war, 81–82
  and collective security, 166–172
  contents, 77–79, 289–312
  Dumbarton Oaks proposals, 51
  economic and social co-operation, international, 301–302
  Economic and Social Council, 133, 302–304
  financial crisis, 91–92
  General Assembly, 292–294
  International Court of Justice, 139, 309
  international law, evolving, 85–91
  international peace and security, 166–172
  international trusteeship system, 305–307
  membership, 82, 291
  national liberation, 84
  nation building, 205
  Non-Aligned Movement, 84–85
  non-self-governing territories, declaration regarding, 304–305
  North-South relations, 83–84
  organs, 291
  Pacific Settlement of Disputes, 296–298

  peacekeeping, 176, 184, 198
  Pérez de Cuéllar and Boutros-Ghali reforms, 97–100
  personal sovereignty, 106–107
  preamble, 289
  principal organs created by, 14
  programmatic reform, 104–108
  purposes and principles, 290
  ratification and signature, 55, 312
  reform, 100–102, 127–139, 342
  regional arrangements, 300–301
  registration of international agreements, 79, 310
  sanctions, 185
  Secretariat, 309–310
  security, collective, 168–172
  Security Council, 129–130, 294–296
  structural reform, 108–112
  threats to the peace, breaches of peace, and acts of aggression, 298–300
  transitional security arrangements, 311
  Trusteeship Council, 136–137, 307–308
  Uniting for Peace Resolution, 173
  weaknesses, 286
  world conferences, 148
Chemical weapons, 181
Chemical Weapons Convention (CWC), 181
Chiang Kai-shek, 52
Chief Executive Board (CEB), 103, 118
China. *See* People's Republic of China; Republic of China
Chirac, Jacques, 11
Chlorofluorocarbons (CFCs), 271–272
CHR. *See* Commission on Human Rights
Churchill, Winston
  Atlantic Conference, 44
  British Empire, preserving, 58
  UN, creation of, 46–48
  Yalta Conference, 43
Civil society, 32, 107
Climate change, 269, 270, 271–274
Clinton, Bill
  Bosnia, 211
  human rights, international, 242, 245
  Iraq policy, 70
  Kosovo, 27–28
  Palestine Liberation Organization–Israeli talks, 191
  Somalia peacekeeping mission, 98–99
  UN reform and budget assessment, 97, 98
Coalitions, military
  Afghanistan, 341
  Iraq war, 183–184, 341–342
  Korean War, 172–173
  as Security Council activity, 170–171
Cold war
  Charter and, 81–82
  collective security and, 172–176
  Cuban Missile Crisis, 67
  disarmament and arms control and, 177–182
  General Assembly emergency sessions and, 173–176
  history of, 63–69
  Korea, 64–65
  least developed countries and, 256–257
  North-South relations and, 83–85
  peacekeeping and, 92, 176, 197–198
  Secretariat, controversy over, and, 138–139
  troika proposal and, 66–67, 336
  UN reform and, 8, 111
Collective security
  cold war background, 172–173
  defined, 161, 342
  evolution, 162–166
  legal basis for, 163, 168–172
  Un Charter provisions for, 166–168
Colombia, 27, 319
Colonialism, end of
  charter provisions, 78
  empires' attempt to stop, 58
  national liberation, 84
  new members, 82–83

Commission on Human Rights (CHR)
  Annan's reform proposals, 342
  Eleanor Roosevelt and the Universal Declaration of Human
    Rights, 32, 60, 90, 236–237
  organizational structure, duties, and activities, 221, 239
  use of special rapporteurs, 231–232
Commission on the Status of Women (CSW), 238, 246, 247, 248
Commission on Sustainable Development (CSD), 270
Committee on the Peaceful Uses of Outer Space, 89
Committee on the Rights of the Child, 16
Committees
  advisory opinions, International Court of Justice, 141
  Economic and Social, standing, 14, 55, 59, 60, 61, 62, 78, 83, 90,
    102, 110–111, 122, 133–136, 143, 228–229, 231–232, 239,
    240, 246, 249, 263
  executive, listed, 102
  General Assembly, main, 122
  General Assembly, procedural, 122, 294
  human rights, 239
  nongovernmental organizations, work with, 229
  Security Council, standing, 129
Commodity agreements, 258–259
Communism. See Cold war
Comprehensive Nuclear-Test-Ban Treaty (CTBT), 179
Comte, Auguste, 2
Concert of Europe, 38–39, 162
Confederation, 124
Conference of the Committee on Disarmament (CCD), 179–180
Conference on Disarmament (CD), 18, 19, 179, 180
Conference on Non-Governmental Organizations in Consultative
    Status with the Economic and Social Council (CONGO), 230
Conflict of laws, 85
Confucianism, 37
CONGO. See Conference on Non-Governmental Organizations in
    Consultative Status with the Economic and Social Council
Congo. See also Africa, Congo; Africa, Congo crisis
  aggression, identified, 168
  Hammarskjöld and, 336
  peacekeeping, 66, 81, 91–92, 175, 198, 199–200
  scandals, 112–113
  UN membership, 319
Constructivism, 5
Consultations, 128
Convention on Certain Conventional Weapons (CCW), 182
Convention to Combat Desertification (CCD), 276–277
Convention on the Prohibition of the Development, Production and
    Stockpiling of Bacteriological (Biological) and Toxin Weapons
    and on Their Destruction (Biological Weapons Convention, or
    BWC), 181–182
Convention on the Prohibition of the Development, Production,
    Stockpiling and Use of Chemical Weapons and on Their
    Destruction (Chemical Weapons Convention, or CWC), 181
Convention to Combat Desertification (CCD), 276–277
Conventional weapons treaties, 182–183
Corfu Channel case, 142
Cotecna, 113
Court. See International Court of Justice; International Criminal
    Court
Covenant of the League of Nations, 39–40
Cox, James M., 43
Crimean War, 86–87
Crimes against humanity, 12, 24, 86, 90–91, 106, 140, 150, 211,
    241–244
Critical theory, 5
Croatia, 209, 319
CSD. See Commission on Sustainable Development
CSW. See Commission on the Status of Women
CTBT. See Comprehensive Nuclear-Test-Ban Treaty
CTBTO. See Preparatory Commission for the Comprehensive
    Nuclear-Test-Ban Treaty Organization
Cuban Missile Crisis, 67, 81, 337
CWC. See Chemical Weapons Convention
Cyprus
  Annan Plan, 9, 201
  UN membership, 319
  UN Peacekeeping Force in Cyprus (UNFICYP), 175, 200–201,
    216, 337, 338

Czechoslovakia, 40, 49
Darfur. See Sudan
Dayton Peace Accords, 9, 210, 211
Debt, international, 154, 262, 281
Debt Management and Financial Analysis System (DMFAS), 258
Declaration of Paris, 86–87
Declaration by United Nations, 47, 55
Deforestation, 276–278
Democratic Republic of the Congo (DRC), 221, 319
Democratization, 32, 106, 108
Department of Peacekeeping Operations (DPKO), 14, 104–105,
    204–205
Department of Public Information (DPI), 62, 102, 138, 230
Dependency theory, 6, 258
Desertification, 276–278, 349
Development Decades, 257
Dili, Timor-Leste, offices, 27–29
Dinka, Berhanu, 223
Disarmament and arms control. See also Conference on
    Disarmament
  biological weapons, 181–182
  chemical weapons, 181
  conventional weapons, 182–183
  Covenant of the League of Nations, 39
  International Atomic Energy Agency (IAEA), 177–178
  1950s, 176–178
  1960s and 1970s agreements, 178–180
  1980s agreements, 180–181
Disarmament Commission, 178, 180
DMFAS. See Debt Management and Financial Analysis System
Double veto, 128
DPI. See Department of Public Information
DPKO. See Department of Peacekeeping Operations
DRC. See Democratic Republic of the Congo
Drug trafficking, 23
Drummond, Sir James Eric, 40
Dulles, John Foster, 54
Dumbarton Oaks Conference, 43, 45, 50–51, 54, 55
Durrant, M. Patricia, 103
Dzhugashvili, Iosif Vissarionovich. See Stalin, Joseph
Earth Summit. See UN Conference on Environment and
    Development (UNCED)
Earthwatch, 21
Eastern Europe, cold war politics, 63–64, 65–66
East Germany, 64
East Timor, 9, 12, 27, 208, 209, 286
Economic development
  early UN history, 254–257
  environment and sustainable development, 266–268
  executive committees, listed, 102
  goals, 106
  HIV/AIDS programs, 279–282
  In Larger Freedom, 109, 110–112
  North-South relations, 83–84
  right to development and least developed countries, 261–266
  UN Conference on Trade and Development (UNCTAD),
    257–259
  UN Development Programme (UNDP), 259–261
  World Food Programme (WFP), 27
  women, role of, 250–251
Economic and Social Council (ECOSOC)
  agencies, coordinating, 61
  caucus groups, 83
  Charter provision, 14, 55, 59, 78
  Commission on Human Rights (CHR), 239, 240
  Commission on the Status of Women (CSW), 246
  consultations and recommendations to other agencies, 143
  Eleanor Roosevelt and, 60, 90
  network, 135–136
  nongovernmental organizations (NGOs), 228–229
  reform proposals, 110–111
  regional development banks, 263
  responsibilities, 133–136
  special rapporteurs, 231–232
  sustainable development, 62
  women, role of, 249
Eden, Anthony, 47–48, 55, 56, 139

Egypt
  Israel, 1973 war with, 201–202
  peacekeeping troops, 337
  Suez Canal invasion and occupation, 172, 174, 176, 187–188, 198
  UN membership, 320
Eisenhower, Dwight
  cold war, 66
  nuclear regulations, 147, 177–178
  world economic development, 255–256
El Baradei, Mohamed, 22, 71
Eldoret Declaration, 220
Election monitoring, 132
Eleventh Air Navigation Conference, 26
El Salvador, 9, 56, 320
Embargoes, 168–170, 223
Emergency Sex and Other Desperate Measures: A True Story from Hell on Earth, 112
Emergency special sessions of General Assembly, 173–176
Empires. *See also* Colonialism, end of
  demise of, 38
  diplomacy among, 37
Enforcement measures, 168
Enlightenment period, 6–7, 37
Environment
  agencies, 22
  climate change, 269, 270, 271–274, 276, 278
  conference on, 21
  international law, 89–90
  sustainable development and, 266–268
  as thematic policy, 31
  UN Environment Programme (UNEP), 20, 21–22, 30, 31, 136, 146, 233, 268–279, 285
Environment and Natural Resources Information Networking program, 21
EPTA. *See* Expanded Program of Technical Assistance
Ethiopia, 185, 320
Ethnic cleansing, 209
European Union (EU), 201
Evatt, Herbert, 60
Executive committees
  listed, 102
  thematic, 109
Expanded Program of Technical Assistance (EPTA), 259
Falkland Islands, 338
Feminism, 5–6, 88
Fifth Committee, GA, 93, 98, 122
Financial crisis
  Charter, 91–92
  debt-ridden nations, 154
First Committee, GA, 122, 180, 229
"Five Ambassadors" Proposal, 19
Food and Agriculture Organization (FAO), 26–27
Food programs, 27
Ford Foundation study on administrative reform, 98
Forests, 269–270, 277
"Four Policemen" proposal, 44, 47
Fourth Committtee, GA, 122
France
  attitude about U.S. invasion of Iraq, 11, 131
  Middle East role, 167
  peacekeeping, objections to assessments for, 198
  Ruhr Valley occupation, 40
  sanctions, votes against, 186–187
  Suez Canal invasion and occupation, 172, 187–188, 198
  UN creation, concerns about, 58
  UN membership, 320
Fréchette, Louise, 139, 213
French Revolution, 38
Functional commissions, 134
Functionalism, 30
GAINS. *See* Gender Awareness Information and Networking System
Garretón, Roberto, 232
GATS. *See* General Agreement on Trade in Services
GATT. *See* General Agreement on Tariffs and Trade
Gaye, Babacar, 221
GEF. *See* Global Environment Facility
GEMS. *See* Global Environmental Monitoring System

Gender Awareness Information and Networking System (GAINS), 250
General Agreement on Tariffs and Trade (GATT), 33, 53, 89, 156, 231
General Agreement on Trade in Services (GATS), 156
General Assembly (GA)
  agenda. *See* Agenda, General Assembly
  amendments, adopting, 79
  annual meeting. *See* Annual meeting, General Assembly
  emergency special sessions, 173–176
  functions, 119–126
  hall, 119
  main, 122
  meetings, 10, 12, 17–18, 60, 66, 68, 70, 72, 83, 108, 119, 122–123, 124, 140, 172, 173–176, 179–180, 187, 247, 248, 249, 258, 265, 279, 281, 294, 312, 348
  powers, expansion during creation of UN, 57
  procedural, 122, 294
  reform proposals, 111, 112
  restriction on security matters, 167
General Debate, 10–11
Genetically modified organisms, 276
Geneva, Switzerland
  Conference on Disarmament (CD), 18, 19, 179–180
  League of Nations, 40
  specialized agencies, 25
Geneva Protocol (1925), 181–182
Germany
  attitude about U.S. invasion of Iraq, 9, 11–12, 17
  cold war, 64
  East and West, uniting, 82
  UN membership, 320
  war crimes trials, 90
  World War II, outbreak of, 41
  Yalta Conference, 51–52
Gigiri compound, 20
Global civil society, 108, 109, 234–235, 246–249
  mobilization, public, 246–249
Global Compact, 31, 109, 149, 232–234
Global Environmental Monitoring System (GEMS), 21
Global Environment Facility (GEF), 277, 278
Global Environment Outlook, 21
Global Fund to Fight AIDS, Tuberculosis and Malaria, 282
Globalization, 5, 23, 31, 37, 108, 136, 150–151, 158, 234, 257, 259, 266, 279, 345
Global public policy
  global civil society, 234–235, 246–249
  Global Compact, 232–234
  human rights, 235–245
  nongovernmental organizations (NGOs), 228–231
  special rapporteurs, 231–232
  thematic diplomacy, emerging, 227–228
  women's rights, 246–251
Global Resource Information Database (GRID), 21
Golan Heights. *See* UN Disengagement Observer Force, Middle East
Goldberg Reservation, 92, 96–97
Gorbachev, Mikhail, 68, 180, 190
Great Britain. *See* United Kingdom
Greece, 26, 63, 320
GRID. *See* Global Resource Information Database
Grotius, Hugo, 38, 86
Group of 7, 152
Group of 18, 109
Group of 21, 157
Group of 77 (G-77), 83, 84–85, 258
Guatemala, 9, 320
Guerrero, J. Gustavo, 139
Gulf War
  biological weapons and, 182
  collective security and, 9, 183–184
  George H. W. Bush and, 98, 184
  and peace process in the Middle East, 190
  relevant UN resolutions, 9, 72
  Saddam Hussein and, 22, 69–70, 182
  sanctions after, 170, 186
  Security Council and, 68, 130, 167
  UN Compensation Commission (UNCC), 18–19
Hackworth, G. H., 139
The Hague, the Netherlands, offices, 23–24

The Hague Peace Conferences, 39
Haig, Alexander, 96
Haiti, 92, 135, 186, 215, 217, 232, 320, 354, 355, 357, 358
Hammarskjöld, Dag, 91–92, 172, 174, 176, 198
  biography, 335, 336
  cold war, 66, 92
  and Congo, 66, 198, 199, 200, 336
  early nation building, 8
Harding, Warren G., 43
Heavily Indebted Poor Country (HIPC) Initiative, 262–263
Helms, Jesse, 99–100, 101–102
Heritage Foundation, 96
High-level Panel on Threats, Challenges and Change, 108–109
High-Level Segment, ECOSOC, 134
HIPC. See Heavily Indebted Poor Country Initiative
Hitler, Adolf, 40, 46–47, 163
HIV/AIDS programs, 15, 18, 62, 102, 122, 123, 136, 157, 171, 229, 261, 348, 350
  economic development, 260, 264, 265, 279–282
  as thematic policy, 31, 63, 106
  World Bank funding, 152–153
Holbrooke, Richard, 166
Holkeri, Harri, 28
Hoover, Herbert, 43
Hopkins, Harry, 57
House, Edward, 39
Hull, Cordell, 43–45, 49, 139
Human rights
  bill of rights, 60, 237, 238
  charter provisions, 58–59, 80
  conventions and treaties related to, 51, 90, 235, 237–239
  Global Compact, 149, 232–234
  international law, 90–91
  judicial process, 241–245
  policy process, 235–241
  special rapporteurs investigating, 231–232
  as thematic policy, 31, 106
  tribunals, 150
  UN High Commissioner for Human Rights (UNHCHR), 16, 18, 102, 103, 131, 147, 233, 238, 241, 252
  Universal Declaration of Human Rights, 31, 32, 59–60, 80, 90, 149, 236–237, 238, 349
Human Rights Council, 111
Hungary, 174, 320
Hunte, Julian, 10–11, 14, 107
Hurd, Ian, 167
Hussein, King of Jordan, 190
Hussein, Saddam
  biological weapons, 182
  Kuwait, Iraqi invasion of, 69–70
  oil-for-food program, 112
  sanctions, fighting, 186
Hutu, 211–212
IAEA. See International Atomic Energy Agency
ICBL. See Land mines
IBRD. See International Bank for Reconstruction and Development
ICAO. See International Civil Aviation Organization
ICC. See International Criminal Court
ICCPR. See International Covenant on Civil and Political Rights
ICESCR. See International Covenant on Economic, Social and Cultural Rights
ICJ. See International Court of Justice
ICPD. See International Conference on Population and Development
ICSID. See International Centre for the Settlement of Investment Disputes
ICTR. See International Criminal Tribunal for Rwanda
ICTY. See International Criminal Tribunal for the Former Yugoslavia
IDA. See International Development Association
Idealism theory of international relations, 3–4, 95–96
IFAD. See International Fund for Agricultural Development
IFC. See International Finance Corporation
IGO. See Intergovernmental organization
IMF. See International Monetary Fund
IMO. See International Maritime Organization

India, 239, 257, 275
  in British Empire, 38
  deforestation treaty, 277
  and Kashmir, 198–199
  Non-Aligned Movement, 84
  Nuclear Non-Proliferation Treaty (NPT), 179
  and Pakistan, 165, 198–199
  reform proposals, 110
  role in the creation of the Security Council, 56
  UN membership, 320
Indigenous people, rights of, 16
Indonesia, 28–29, 320
Industry and Development Office, UNEP, 21
Infoterra, 21
In Larger Freedom (UN report), 109, 110–112
INSTRAW. See International Research and Training Institute for the Advancement of Women
Intergovernmental organization (IGO)
  described, 2, 230–231
  early efforts to establish, 228
  Eleanor Roosevelt, 61
  evolution of the UN as an IGO, 14, 32, 148
  founding of UN, 14, 29–30
  in Geneva, Switzerland, 17, 19
  International Atomic Energy Agency (IAEA), 22
  joining UN, 228
  in Nairobi, Kenya, 20
  popular participation in, 230–231
  specialized agencies, 17, 19, 22, 24, 143, 257
Intermediate Nuclear Forces Agreement, 180
International anarchy, 37–38
International Atomic Energy Agency (IAEA)
  Baruch Plan, 65
  disarmament and arms control, 177–178
  Dwight D. Eisenhower, 147, 177–178
  Iran, 22, 23
  Iraq, 71–72
  as related organization, 147
  in Vienna, Austria, 22
International Bank for Reconstruction and Development (IBRD), 53, 152
International Bill of Human Rights, 237, 238
International Centre for the Settlement of Investment Disputes (ICSID), 153
International Civil Aviation Organization (ICAO), 24, 26
International Code of Conduct on the Distribution and Use of Pesticides, 22
International Conference on Population and Development (ICPD), 248–249
International Convention to Ban Landmines (ICBL). See Land mines
International Court of Justice (ICJ)
  advisory opinions, 333–334
  amendment, 334
  Charter provisions, 78
  competence, 328–329
  creation of, 31–32
  described, 139–143
  in The Hague, 23–24, 88
  Israeli security wall case, 175
  organization, 322–328
  peacekeeping assessments, opinion on, 198
  procedure, 330–333
  Statute of the, 322–334
  threats, mediating, 171
International Covenant on Civil and Political Rights (ICCPR), 237, 252
International Covenant on Economic, Social and Cultural Rights (ICESCR), 237, 252
International Criminal Court (ICC), 32, 140, 150, 229, 244–245
International Criminal Tribunal for Rwanda (ICTR), 129, 242, 243
International Criminal Tribunal for the Former Yugoslavia (ICTY), 24, 211, 235
International Decade of the World's Indigenous People, 16
International Development Association (IDA), 152
International Finance Corporation (IFC), 152–153
International financing of environmental projects. See World Bank
International Fund for Agricultural Development (IFAD), 26, 27, 277

International law
  evolving, 85–91
  human rights, 38
  law of the sea, 22, 274
  Security Council resolutions, binding nature of, 129
International Law Commission of the United Nations, 245
International Maritime Organization (IMO), 25, 30, 89, 144, 230
International Monetary Fund (IMF), 25, 30, 144
  Bretton Woods Conference, 53, 151, 152
  controversy, 151
  economic development, 157, 222, 259, 262
  HIV/AIDS funding, 153–155
  organization and procedures, 151, 153–155
  role, increasing, 8, 145
International organization
  Concert of Europe, 38–39
  defined, 2
  early efforts to establish, 36
  League of Nations, 39–42
  pre–twentieth century, 37–38
  U.S. and allies view, 42–50
International peace and security
  Arab-Israeli dispute, 187–193
  cold war conditions, 172–176
  collective security concept, 162–166
  disarmament and arms control, 176–183
  history, 161–162
  post–cold war, 183–187
  UN Charter provisions, 166–172
International Red Cross, 38, 182
International Register for Potentially Toxic Chemicals, 22
International relations theory, 2–7, 37
International Research and Training Institute for the Advancement
    of Women (INSTRAW), 136, 247, 249
International Telegraph Union, 38, 87
Intifada, 190, 191
Investigating disputes, 171
Iran
  Iraq, war with, 78, 168, 339
  nuclear weapons activity, 22
  Soviet occupation, 64, 167
  UN membership, 320
  U.S. hostages, 142
Iraq
  aggressor, identification as, 168
  biological weapons, concern about, 182
  chemical weapons, use of, 181
  Gulf War (Kuwait, invasion of), 9, 18–19, 69–70, 130,
    183–184, 190
  Iran, war with, 78, 168, 339
  nuclear weapons, discussion of, 22
  oil-for-food program, 112
  sanctions, 186
  Security Council debate over U.S. attack, 128, 131–132
  after September 11, 2001, 71–73
  UN membership, 320
  UN workers killed in, 11
  U.S. invasion, 9, 11–12, 171
  weapons inspections, 340–341
Irian Barat, 337
Iron Curtain, 65–66
Israel
  Arab dispute, collective security and, 67, 165, 187–193
  creation, 8
  Egypt and Syria, wars with, 187–188, 201–202
  Lebanon, invasion into, 202–203
  occupied territories, 175, 190, 192–193, 216, 337
  Palestine Liberation Organization (PLO), 84, 192–193, 218
  Resolution 242, 67
  Road Map for peace, 12, 193
  security wall constructed, 142, 175
  settlements policy, 191–192, 341
  Suez Canal invasion and occupation, 91, 172, 174, 187–188, 198
  UN membership, 320
  war of 1967, 164, 176, 337
  war of 1973, 188
  "Zionism is Racism" resolution, 188, 191

Italy, 14, 25, 26–27, 33, 39, 40, 64, 141, 144, 152, 178, 185, 202,
    203, 320
Izetbegovic, Aliya, 210
Japan
  Manchuria, invasion of, 40, 185
  reform proposals for the Security Council, 94, 110
  UN budget assessment, 94
  UN membership, 320
  war crimes trials, 90
Jay Treaty, 87
Jiang Zemin, 213
Joint Four-Nation Declaration, 45
Joint UN Programme on HIV/AIDS (UNAIDS), 15,
    153, 281
Jordan, 190, 320
Judicial diplomacy, 243–244
Judicial process, 241–245
Kabbah, Alhaji Ahmad Tejan, 244
Kabila, Joseph, 221–222
Kabila, Laurent, 221
Kamara, Brima "Bazzy," 244
Kambanda, Jean, 243
Kant, Immanuel, 3, 37, 39
Karzai, Hamid, 71
Kassebaum Amendment, 97
Kay, David, 72
Kennan, George, 64
Kennedy, John F., 67, 255
Kenya, 14, 20–21, 220, 248, 257, 320
Khmer Rouge, 207–208
Khrushchev, Nikita, 66, 67, 337
Kirkpatrick, Jeane, 96
Kissinger, Henry, 3, 87, 95, 190
Korea
  Cold War and, 64–65
  Soviet Union, finessing veto power, 111
  UN membership, 320
  war endorsed by Security Council, 130, 172–173
Kosovo, 9, 24, 27–29, 68, 132, 138, 171, 184, 208,
    216, 341
Krstic, Radislav, 243
Kurds, 69–70, 181
Kuwait, 9, 19, 68, 69, 130, 320
Kyoto Protocol, 90, 271–274
LaGrand case, 142
Land mines
  International Campaign to Ban Landmines
    (ICBL), 182
  land-mines agreement, 180, 182–183
  use as a conventional weapon, 182
Latin America, 56, 57–58
Law of nations, 85
Law of the Sea Convention, 274
League of Nations
  activities, 39–42
  agencies surviving, 61
  collective security, 40, 163, 168
  Covenant compared with UN Charter, 79
  economic development policy, 254
  establishment, 162–163
  international law, 87
  international organization, 36
  as model for UN, 165
  offices, 16
  parliamentary diplomacy, 13
  sanctions, 185
Least developed countries (LDCs)
  budget assessment, lowering, 94
  conferences about, 259, 261–262, 264, 270, 348
  focus on, 134
  HIV/AIDS crisis, 281–282
  human rights agreements, view of, 237–238
  Office of the High Representative for the Least Developed
    Countries, Landlocked Developing Countries and Small Island
    Developing States (OHRLLS), 14
  right to development, 261–266
  UN membership, 256–257

Lebanon
  Palestine Liberation Organization attacks, 190, 202
  peacekeeping, 202–203
  UN membership, 320
Lenin, Vladimir, 48
Liberal democratic nationalism, 37
Liberal internationalism, 3
Liberia, 12, 27, 222–224, 320
Lichenstein, Charles M., 96
Lie, Trygve Halvdan, 65, 66, 335–336
Lodge, Henry Cabot, 41
Lomé Agreement, 223
London, UK, agencies, 25
Lula da Silva, Luiz Inacio, 157
Lumumba, Patrice, 199
Lusaka Agreement, 221
MacArthur, Douglas, 172, 173
Makarios, Archbishop of Cyprus (Michael Mouskos), 201
Malaria, 63, 106, 265, 279, 282, 345
Mali, 243, 320
Mao Zedong, 67
Marx, Karl, 4, 5, 6, 7, 48
Marxism as a theory of international relations, 4–5
McCarthyism, 66
MDGs. See Millennium Development Goals
Médecins Sans Frontières, 145
Mediation, 171
Mekdad, Fayssal, 128
Membership, UN, 319–321
  Charter chapter, 77
  growth, 79, 82
Member states, listed, 319–321
Middle East
  Arab-Israeli dispute, 187–193, 218–219
  assessment, budget, 94
  authority of UN, 72
  General Assembly, emergency special sessions of, 174, 175
  Gulf War, 9, 18–19, 69–70, 130, 183–184, 190
  Iran, 22, 64, 78, 142, 167, 168, 339
  Iraq, 9, 11–12, 18–19, 22, 69–73, 78, 112, 128, 130–132, 168, 171, 181–184, 186, 190, 339–341
  Lebanon, 190, 202–203
  regional development bank, 263
  "Road Map" for peace, 12, 193
  Security Council role, 167
  Suez Canal invasion and occupation, 172
  West Bank, 142, 175, 187–188, 190–192, 193, 337
MIGA. See Multilateral Investment Guarantee Agency
Military coalitions
  Afghanistan, 341
  coalitions of the willing, 170
  Iraq war, 183–184, 341–342
  Korean War, 172–173
  North Atlantic Treaty Organization (NATO), 2, 9, 28, 64, 68, 71, 164, 171, 210–211, 217, 223, 243, 341
  as Security Council activity, 170–171
Military observer groups, 176
Military Staff Committee, 110, 129, 170
Millennium Declaration
  adoption, 109
  Africa, meeting special needs of, 350
  development and poverty eradication, 347–349
  environment, protecting common, 349
  human rights, democracy and good governance, 349–350
  peace, security and disarmament, 346–347
  protection of vulnerable populations, 350
  strengthening United Nations, 350–351
  sustainable development, 266
  values and principles, 345–346
Millennium Development Goals (MDGs), 20, 26, 62–63, 106–107, 108, 264–265, 274
Millennium Summit
  described, 149, 341
  nongovernmental organizations (NGOs), 228
  peacekeeping operations, importance of, 68–69, 105–106
  vision, 11, 29–30
Milosevic, Slobodan, 24, 209, 211, 235

Mitchell, George, 191
Mladic, Ratko, 210
MMI. See Money Matters Institute
Modern liberal democratic nationalism, 37
Molotov, Vyacheslav I., 54, 55, 56
Molotov-Ribbentrop agreement, 49
Money Matters Institute (MMI), 233
Montreal, Canada, offices, 24, 25, 26
Montreal Protocol, 271–272
MONUC. See UN Organization Mission in the DRC
Moore, Michael, 156
Moscow Conference of Foreign Ministers, 45, 55
Movimento Popular de Libertação de Angola (MPLA), 206–207
Multilateral Investment Guarantee Agency (MIGA), 153
Nair, Dileep, 113
Nairobi, Kenya, offices, 20–22, 268
Nairobi Forward-Looking Strategies for the Advancement of Women, 248
Namibia
  Angolan territory, 207
  nation building, early, 8, 206
  UN membership, 320
Napoleon Bonaparte, 38, 86, 161–162
Nasser, Gamal Abdul, 187, 188, 337
Nation building
  Afghanistan, 29, 215, 217
  Angola, 104, 206–207, 214, 217
  Cambodia, 104, 207–208
  Charter, 81
  described, 205–206
  East Timor, 29, 208, 215
  Kosovo, 9, 28, 208, 216
  Namibia, 104, 206
  programmatic reform proposals, 99–100, 105
  second-generation peacekeeping, 106, 110, 214–215
  Somalia, 105, 219–220
National liberation, 79, 84
National sovereignty, 37–38, 205
NATO. See North Atlantic Treaty Organization
Naturalist school of international law, 86
Nazi Germany, 49
New International Economic Order (NIEO), 83, 233, 258, 266
"New" United Nations, 29–33
New York City, 10–16, 126, 128
NGOs. See Nongovernmental organizations
Nicaragua, 9, 320
NIEO. See New International Economic Order
Nikolic, Dragan, 211, 242
Nixon, Richard, 96
Non-Aligned Movement, 84–85, 125, 257
Nongovernmental organizations (NGOs)
  conventional weapons, concern about, 182
  environmental projects, funding, 278–279
  food programs, 27
  global public policy, 228–231
  human rights, 239
  international criminal court, criticism of, 243
  organization of, 61–62
  role, increasing, 107–108, 145
  thematic diplomacy, growth of, 31
  UN Population Fund, 15
  women's rights, 248–249
  world conferences, 148–149
Noninterference, 80
Non-Proliferation of Nuclear Weapons, Treaty on the (Nuclear Non-Proliferation Treaty, or NPT), 22, 178–179
Normative international relations, 2–3
North Atlantic Treaty Organization (NATO)
  Afghanistan, 71
  Argentina, 164
  Herzegovina, 210
  human rights, 243
  Kosovo, 28
North Korea
  aggressor, identification as, 168, 170, 172
  nuclear weapons activity, 22
  UN membership, 320

North-South relations, 83–84, 125, 179, 255, 256, 264
Nuclear Non-Proliferation Treaty (NPT), 22, 178–179
Nuclear weapons
  arms-limitation talks, 81
  Cold War, 65
  treaties, 178–181
  treaty, suspected violations of, 22–23
Obaid, Thoraya Ahmed, 15
Oceans, protection of, 22
Office for Drug Control and Crime Prevention (ODCCP), 23, 136
Office of the High Representative for the Least Developed
    Countries, Landlocked Developing Countries and Small Island
    Developing States (OHRLLS), 14, 30
Office of Internal Oversight Services (OIOS), 98, 109, 113, 138
Oil-for-food program, 112, 113, 186
OIOS. *See* Office of Internal Oversight Services
Olympic Games (2004), 26
Ombudsman, 103, 109
Organisation for the Prohibition of Chemical Weapons (OPCW),
    147, 181
Oslo Accords, 190
Ottawa Process, 180, 182
Ottoman Empire, 37
Our Common Future, 268, 272
P5. *See* Permanent members of Security Council
Pacific settlement of disputes, 168, 296–298
Pakistan, 38, 179, 198–199, 320
Palais de Nations, 16–18, 40
Palau, Micronesia, 110, 136, 320
Palestine, 187, 190
Palestine Liberation Organization (PLO), 84, 188, 190–191
Palestinians
  assaults on Israelis, 188
  humanitarian aid, 187
  intifada, 190, 191
  Israeli security wall, 142, 175
  land, support for, 193
  Oslo Accords, 190
  Resolution 242, 67
  UN Relief and Works Agency for Palestine Refugees in the Near
    East (UNRWA), 30, 136, 146, 187
  Yasser Arafat, 84, 175, 191–192, 341
Palmieri, Guido, 199
Panitchpakdi, Supachai, 156
Panyarachun, Anand, 108
Paraguay, 40, 320
Paris, France, offices, 25
Paris Peace Conference, 36, 39
Parliamentary diplomacy, 13, 55, 80
Partial Test Ban Treaty (1963), 178
Pasvolsky, Leo, 44, 54, 55
PBPU. *See* Peacekeeping Best Practices Unit
PCIJ. *See* Permanent Court of International Justice
PDD-25. *See* Presidential Decision Directive 25
Peace building, 184, 213–218
Peacebuilding Commission, 110–111
Peacekeeping
  assessments, refusal to pay, 175
  Brahimi Report, 212–213
  Charter provisions, 78, 81
  cold war, 176
  Congo, 199–200, 221–222
  Cyprus, 200–201
  Department of Peacekeeping Operations (DPKO), 204–205
  East Timor, 29, 132, 170, 184, 209, 215, 286, 341
  executive committees, 102
  former Yugoslavia, 209–211
  India and Pakistan, military observer group in, 198–199
  Lebanon, Interim Force in, 202–203
  Liberia, 12, 222–224
  nation building, 205–208
  offices, 213–219
  origins, 197–198
  programmatic reform, 104–105
  Rwanda, 211–212, 341
  scandals, 112–113
  second-generation, described, 29, 32, 203–204, 208, 214–216

Security Council actions, 130
Sierra Leone, 222–224
Sinai and Golan Heights Disengagement Observer Force,
    201–202
Somalia, 219–220
Suez Canal, 172
as thematic policy, 31
U.S. limitations, 99–100
Peacekeeping Best Practices Unit (PBPU), 205
Peacemaking, 184
Peace Palace, 23
Pearson, Lester, 172
People's Republic of China (PRC), 67, 172
  accession to the Nuclear Non-Proliferation Treaty, 179
  Cancun trade talks, 157
  cold war, 67
  international law, 88, 245
  Iraq war, 19, 131
  Korean War, 64–65, 172–173
  Kyoto Protocol, 90
  seating of PRC delegation, 64, 67, 96, 125
  women's rights conference, 248
  World Trade Organization (WTO), 156, 157
Pérez de Cuéllar, Javier, 97–100, 338–339
Permanent Court of Arbitration, 39
Permanent Court of International Justice (PCIJ), 139
Permanent members of Security Council (P5)
  organization, 127, 129
  reform proposals, 137
  sanctions, 185
PFA. *See* Platform for Action
Plan for the Establishment of an International Organization for the
    Maintenance of International Peace and Security, 45
Platform for Action (PFA), 248
PLO. *See* Palestine Liberation Organization
Point Four Program, 255
Polluter Pays Principle (PPP), 267–268
Positive international relations, 2
Post–cold war international peace and security, 183–187
Postmodernism, 6–7
Poverty, eradication of, 31, 106
Powell, Colin, 19, 72–73
Powers, Francis Gary, 66
PPP. *See* Polluter Pays Principle
PRC. *See* People's Republic of China
Prebisch, Raúl, 257–258
Preemption foreign policy doctrine, 342
Preparatory Commission for the Comprehensive Nuclear-Test-Ban
    Treaty Organization (CTBTO), 23
Presidency (or President), Security Council, 128, 229
Presidential Decision Directive 25 (PDD-25), 99
Preventive diplomacy, 98, 184
Principal organs, UN, 119–143
Principle 21, 267
Pristina, Serbia-Montenegro (Kosovo Province), 27–29
Private international law, 85
Programmatic reform, 104–108
Programmes and funds, 145–146
Provisional Notification Scheme for Banned and Severely
    Restricted Chemicals, 22
Public international law, 85
Public mobilization, 246–249
Public policy, global
  global civil society, 108, 109, 234–235
  Global Compact, 232–234
  human rights, 235–245
  nongovernmental organizations (NGOs), 228–231
  special rapporteurs, 231–232
  thematic diplomacy, emerging, 227–228
  women's rights, 246–251
Putin, Vladimir, 213, 273
Quadrant Conference, 47
Quartet, The, 193
Rabin, Yitzhak, 191
Rasevic, Mitar, 24
Reagan, Ronald, 68, 96–97, 137
Realism as a theory of international relations, 3, 95

Red Cross. *See* International Red Cross
Related organizations, UN, 147
Renewing the United Nations (UN reform proposals), 101, 104, 109
Republic of China
    Dumbarton Oaks Conference, 51, 55
    "Four Policemen" proposal, 44
    history, 37, 40, 41, 52, 64
    Moscow Conference of Foreign Ministers, 43, 55
    removal from UN membership, 64, 67, 96, 125
    San Francisco Conference, 54
Resolutions
    authorized operations in Liberia (1509), 132
    annexation of Kuwait declared null and void (662), 183
    became legal basis of future settlement of Israeli-Palestinian
        standoff (242), 67, 188
    Brahimi Report (1327), 127
    cease-fire in Egypt-Israeli conflict (338), 8, 190
    condemnation of Iraqi invasion of Kuwait (660), 183
    condemned South African aggression in Namibia (385), 206
    Department of Public Information created (13), 62
    Economic and Social Council (ECOSOC) qualified nongovern-
        mental organizations (NGOs) to promote UN programs (31),
        62, 229
    economic sanctions against Iraq (661), 183
    empowered UN to provide humanitarian relief and help in nation
        building for Iraq (1483), 132
    end of Palestinian-Israeli violence and creation of two states
        (1397), 192
    extended mandate of UN liaisons in Congo (1973), 221
    fact-finding commission to investigate Palestinian claims of
        genocide (1405), 192
    first UN peacekeeping operation born (998), 172
    formula for future government of Palestine (181), 187
    Governing Council of UN Compensation Commission established
        (692), 129
    The Hague tribunal established to punish Yugoslavian war crimes
        (827), 235
    International Criminal Tribunal for Rwanda (ICTR) established
        (955), 129, 150, 243
    International Criminal Tribunal for the former Yugoslavia (ICTY)
        established (808), 129
    international terrorism (1368), 70, 165, 344
    Iran-Iraq War (598), 68, 168, 339
    Iraq deadline to withdraw from Kuwait (678), 183
    Israeli halt of military action in Lebanon (425), 202
    Israeli withdrawal from Lebanon (509), 190
    Israeli withdrawal to safe and secure borders (242), 8, 67, 188,
        189, 190
    Kuwait liberation from Iraq occupation (678), 9, 183, 343–344
    Namibia's independence and elections called for (435), 206
    UN Assistance Mission in Afghanistan (UNAMA) created
        (1401), 217
    UN Development Programme created (2029), 260
    UN Interim Administration Mission in Kosovo (UNMIK)
        created (1244), 28
    UN Interim Force in Lebanon (UNIFIL) established (426), 202
    UN Operation in Somalia I (UNOSOMI) established (751), 98
    Unified Task Force (UNITAF) formed (794), 219
    United Nations Millennium Declaration, 345–351
    Uniting for peace. See Uniting for Peace Resolution of 1950
    WMD disarmament of Iraq (1441), 71, 72
Revolutionary United Front (RUF), 222, 244
Rice, Condoleezza, 73
Rights. *See* Human rights
Rio Declaration, 269, 276, 277, 279
River commissions, early European, 38
Riza, S. Iqbal, 113
Road Map for peace. *See* Arab-Israeli dispute
Robinson, Mary, 147, 241
Roman Empire, 37
Rome, Italy, offices, 25–27
Rome Statute, 150, 244–245
Romulo, Carlos, 58
Roosevelt, Eleanor
    formation of UN, 59–61
    husband's political career, 43
    Millennium Summit goals, 62–63

nongovernmental organizations (NGOs), 61–62
    specialized agencies, 61
    Universal Declaration of Human Rights, 32, 60, 90, 236–237
Roosevelt, Franklin D.
    activities, 48
    Churchill and, 43, 47–48, 49, 50, 51, 52, 55
    Concert of Europe, 162
    Stalin and, 49–50
    UN, creation of, 48
    Yalta Conference, 51, 52
Roosevelt, Theodore, 47
RUF. *See* Revolutionary United Front
Russia. *See also* Soviet Union
    Bolshevik Revolution, 41, 48
    Kyoto Protocol, 273–274
Rwanda
    human rights, warnings about, 232
    International Criminal Tribunal for Rwanda (ICTR), 243
    nation building, early, 208
    peacekeeping, 99, 105, 211–212, 341
    Security Council, 131
    UN membership, 321
    war crimes trials, 31–32
Saar Territory administration, 40–41
Sadat, Anwar, 188
Safire, William, 113
Salim, Ahmed, 137
SALT. *See* Strategic Arms Limitation Talks
Sanctions, 168–170, 184–187
Sanders, Chris, 19
San Francisco Conference. *See* UN Conference on International
    Organization
Sankoh, Foday, 222
Savimbi, Jonas, 206
Scale of assessment, 93–94, 109
Scandal, oil-for-food, 112–113, 342
SDN. *See* Sustainable development network
SDRs. *See* Special drawing rights
Second Committee, GA, 122
Secretariat
    Charter provisions, 14, 78–79, 291, 309–310
    Chief Executives Board (CEB) for Coordination, 103
    departments and structure, 14, 18, 55, 62, 108
    executive committees, 89
    reform proposals, 101, 111, 137–139
    Senior Management Group (SMG), 101, 103
Secretary-general. *See also individual secretaries-general listed by
    name*
    biographies, 335–342
    charter provisions, 78–79
    order of service, 335
    Secretariat and, 137
Security Council
    Belgian Congo emergency session, 336
    cold war, 63–64, 81–82
    creation, 52, 55, 56–57
    deadlock, working around, 176
    emergency special sessions of General Assembly, calling,
        173–174
    expansion, proposed, 110
    HIV/AIDS crisis, 280
    Iraq war, conflict over, 11, 12, 19, 108, 110
    Israeli-Palestinian conflict, 67, 192
    Korean War, 173
    members, blocking, 82
    organization, 127–129
    powers, 78, 129–130
    proposal, 45–46
    reform, call for, 130–132
    report to General Assembly, 122
    responsibilities, 14, 126–127
    secretary-general's relationship, 78–79
    September 11, 2001, attacks, 70
    Timor-Leste (East Timor), creation of, 29
    weaknesses, 286–287
Seko, Mobutu Sese, 221
Selassie, Haile, 40

Senior Management Group (SMG), 101, 103
September 11, 2001
    actions following, 341–342
    General Assembly following, 12
    Iraq following, 70–73
    preventive diplomacy, 165
Serbs, 9, 209
Sexual harassment, UN employees' claim, 112
Sharon, Ariel, 191–193
Shi Jiuyong, 23
Sierra Leone, 222–224, 321
Simma, Bruno, 170
Sixth Committee, GA, 122
Smart sanctions, 184–187
SMG. See Senior Management Group
Smuts, Jan, 39
SOFA. See Status of Forces Agreement
Somalia, 80, 98–99, 105, 129, 167, 170, 175, 184, 205, 215, 219–220,
    225, 226, 232, 321, 339, 340
Soong, T. V., 55
South Africa
    Namibia, control of, 206
    reforms, 8
    sanctions against, 185–186
    UN membership, 321
South-West Africa. See Namibia
South-West Africa People's Organisation (SWAPO), 206
Sovereignty
    national, 38, 80, 86
    personal, 106–107
Soviet Union. See also Cold war; Russia
    Afghanistan, invasion of, 67, 82, 174, 175
    Congo, action in, 200
    disarmament and arms control, 177
    Hungary, invasion of, 174
    Israeli conflict, 188
    Korean War, 172, 173
    League of Nations, 40
    nuclear weapons agreements, 180–181
    opposition to peacekeeping missions, 92
    Roosevelt's view of UN, 44
    Security Council vetoes, 130–131
    Stalin, 48–50
    troika proposal, 66–67, 336
    Trygve Lie, attempt to oust, 335–336
    UN creation, 57
    World War II, outbreak of, 41
Spanish Civil War, 40
Special Commission on Iraq (UNSCOM), 69–70
Special Court for Sierra Leone, 223
Special drawing rights (SDRs), 155
Specialized agencies, 16, 25, 26, 32, 87, 101, 133, 134, 143–145,
    205, 220, 230, 237, 250, 293, 304
    Eleanor Roosevelt and, 61
    in Geneva, Switzerland, 17, 18, 19
    HIV/AIDS campaign, 280–281
    in Montreal, Canada, 24
    scope, 14, 78, 255, 261, 267, 278, 301–303
    U.S. withholding funds from, 93
Special rapporteurs, 150, 231–232
Special representative of the secretary-general (SRSG), 150, 213
Special sessions, General Assembly, 122, 123
Special UN Fund for Economic Development (SUNFED),
    256, 259
Stalin, Joseph
    biography, 48–50
    cold war, 63, 65–66
    UN, attitude toward, 47, 57
    veto, use of, 64
    Yalta Conference, 43, 52
State building, 204. See also Nation building
Status of Forces Agreement (SOFA), 105, 198
Stettinius, Edward
    Atlantic Conference, 44
    Dumbarton Oaks Conference, 54, 55
    Security Council proposal, 45–46, 56
    Yalta Conference, 47

Stevenson, Adlai, 67, 337
Stimson Doctrine, 40
Stockholm Conference. See UN Conference on the Human
    Environment
Stockholm Declaration, 267, 269, 274
Strategic Arms Limitation Talks (SALT), 179
Structural reform, 108–112
Subsidiarity, 234
Sudan, 186, 215, 221, 232, 261, 321
Suez Canal. See Egypt
SUNFED. See Special UN Fund for Economic Development
Sustainable development, 21, 31, 62, 134, 135, 146, 148, 149, 159,
    254, 257, 259, 260, 265–275, 277–280, 349, 350
Sustainable development network (SDN), 270–271
SWAPO. See South-West Africa People's Organisation
Swing, William, 221, 222
Syria
    Israel, clashes with, 188, 201–202
    mandate system and, 58
    Palestine Liberation Organization attacks from, 190
    UN membership, 321
    on U.S. invasion of Iraq, 128
Tadic, Dusko, 243
Taiwan, 64, 67, 157
Taliban, 15, 27, 71, 212, 217
Tanzania, 9, 129, 137, 242, 321
Taylor, Charles, 12, 222–223, 224, 244
Terrorism. See also September 11, 2001
    air navigation, 26
    Iraq war discussion, 11–12
    nuclear weapons and, 23
    Security Council response, 129
Thant, U
    biography, 336–337
    Congo, 200
    Cuban Missile Crisis, 67
    Israel, 188
    troika proposal, 66–67
Thematic diplomacy, emerging, 30, 227–228
Theory of dependency, 83
Third Committee, GA, 122
Third World countries. See Least developed countries
Thirty Years' War, 38
Thornburgh, Richard, 97–98, 340
Thornburgh Report, 97–98, 109, 340
TICAD. See Tokyo International Conference for African
    Development
Timor-Leste (East Timor), 27, 28–29, 209
Tito, Josep Broz, 209
Tokyo International Conference for African Development
    (TICAD), 15
Töpfer, Klaus, 268, 271
Transnational corporations, 233–234
Treaties, registration, 79
Treaty on the Non-Proliferation of Nuclear Weapons (Nuclear Non-
    Proliferation Treaty, or NPT), 22
Treaty of Versailles, 39, 41, 49, 53, 161, 162
Treaty of Westphalia, 36, 38, 53, 86, 161
Trieste, Italy, agencies, 25
Troika proposal, 66–67, 336
Truman, Harry S.
    cold war, 64
    economic development to impoverished nations, 255
    Korean War, 172–173
    UN, creation of, 46, 48, 54, 57, 58, 59, 74, 95
Trusteeship Council, 58, 78, 110, 136–137
Tshombe, Moise, 336
Tuberculosis, 279
Turin, Italy, agencies, 25
Turkey, 26, 63, 201, 321
Tutsis, 211–212, 341
UNAIDS. See Joint UN Programme on HIV/AIDS
UN Atomic Energy Commission (UNAEC), 177
UNCC. See UN Compensation Commission
UN Centre for Human Settlements (UNCHS), 20
UN Charter. See Charter of the UN
UNCHE. See UN Conference on the Human Environment

UN Children's Fund (UNICEF), 16, 93, 146
UNCIO. *See* UN Conference on International Organization
UN Commission on Human Rights (CHR), 231–232
UN Commission on International Trade Law (UNCITRAL), 23, 89
UN Commission on Sustainable Development, 277
UN Compensation Commission (UNCC), 18–19
UN Conference on Environment and Development (UNCED), 107, 123, 148, 149, 259, 261, 264, 269–270, 271, 272, 275, 276, 277, 279
UN Conference on the Human Environment (UNCHE), 148, 267
UN Conference on International Organization (UNCIO), 43, 50, 53–59, 91
UN Conference on Trade and Development (UNCTAD), 146, 148, 257–259, 267
UN Conferences on Least Developed Countries (UNLDC-I and -II), 262
UN Convention on the Law of the Sea, 89
UNDCP. *See* UN International Drug Control Programme
UN Decade for Women, 247
Under-secretary-general (USG), 108, 204
UN Development Fund for Women (UNIFEM), 250–251, 261
UN Development Programme (UNDP), 15, 146, 231, 259–261
UN Diplomatic Conference of Plenipotentiaries on the Establishment of an International Criminal Court, 245
UN Disengagement Observer Force (UNDOF), 190, 201, 202, 204. *See also* Middle East
UNDP. *See* UN Development Programme
UN Educational, Scientific and Cultural Organization (UNESCO), 68, 96, 275
UN Emergency Force (UNEF)
    financial crisis, 91
    financial resources, obtaining, 198
    Ralph Bunche, 66, 176, 187, 197
    Suez Canal invasion and occupation, 174, 188
UN Environment Programme (UNEP)
    atmosphere and climate change, 271–274
    biodiversity and natural resources, 275–276
    desertification and deforestation, 276–278
    development, 268–271
    funding, 146
    international financing, 278–279
    in Nairobi, Kenya, 20, 21–22
    water pollution and marine resources, 274–275
UNESCO. *See* UN Educational, Scientific and Cultural Organization
UNFICYP. *See* UN Peacekeeping Force in Cyprus
UNFIP. *See* UN Fund for International Partnerships
UN Forum on Forests (UNFF), 277–278
UNFPA. *See* UN Population Fund
UN Framework Convention on Climate Change (UNFCCC), 269, 271, 273
UN Fund for International Partnerships (UNFIP), 228
UN-HABITAT. *See* UN Human Settlements Programme
UNHCHR. *See* UN High Commissioner for Human Rights
UNHCR. *See* UN High Commissioner for Refugees
UN High Commissioner for Human Rights (UNHCHR), 16, 18, 102, 103, 131, 147, 233, 238, 241, 252
UN High Commissioner for Refugees (UNHCR), 146
UN Human Settlements Programme (UN-HABITAT), 20
União Nacional para a Independência Total de Angola (UNITA), 206–207
UNICEF. *See* UN Children's Fund
UNIDIR. *See* UN Institute for Disarmament Research
UNIDO. *See* UN Industrial Development Organization
UNIFEM. *See* UN Development Fund for Women
UNIFIL. *See* UN Interim Force in Lebanon
UN Industrial Development Organization (UNIDO), 23
UN Institute for Disarmament Research (UNIDIR), 180
UN Institute for Training and Research (UNITAR), 147
UN Interim Administration Mission in Kosovo (UNMIK), 28, 204, 216, 341
UN Interim Force in Lebanon (UNIFIL), 190, 202–203, 204
UN International Drug Control Programme (UNDCP), 146, 281
UNITA. *See* União Nacional para a Independência Total de Angola
UNITAR. *See* UN Institute for Training and Research

United Kingdom
    empire, 38
    Falkland Islands dispute, 164, 338
    Iraq war, 69, 182
    Middle East role, 167, 193, 202
    Palestine, pull out of, 187
    pollution programs, 274
    role in the Security Council, 49–52, 110, 127, 167, 186
    sanctions, votes against, 186
    Suez Canal invasion and occupation, 172, 174, 187–188, 198
    UN membership, 321
United Nations Millennium Declaration. *See* Millennium Declaration
United States of America. *See also* Cold war
    anthrax deaths, 181
    Arab-Israeli dispute negotiation, 190
    Civil War *Alabama* claims arbitration, 87
    Commission on Human Rights membership, 239
    conservatives' attack on UN, 68, 99
    conventional weapons agreement, 182–183
    Gulf War, 9, 18–19, 69–70, 130, 183–184, 190
    HIV/AIDS funding, 281
    international organization, 42–50
    Iraq, invasion of, 9, 11–12, 171
    Korean War, 172–173
    Middle East role, 167
    nonpayment of dues, 68, 93, 95–97, 101–102
    nuclear weapons agreements, 180–181
    oil-for-food investigation, 113
    sanctions, votes against, 186
    UN membership, 321
    UN reform, 97, 98
Uniting for Peace Resolution of 1950, 81–82, 111, 173, 174, 175
Universal Declaration of Human Rights, 31, 32, 59–60, 236–237, 313–318
Universal Postal Union, 38, 61, 87
UNLDC-I and -II. *See* UN Conferences on Least Developed Countries
UN membership, 319–321
UNMIK. *See* UN Interim Administration Mission in Kosovo
UNMIL. *See* UN Mission in Liberia
UN Military Observer Group in India and Pakistan (UNMOGIP), 199, 204
UNMISET. *See* UN Mission of Support in East Timor
UN Mission in Liberia (UNMIL), 12, 204
UN Mission of Support in East Timor (UNMISET), 29, 204
UNMOGIP. *See* UN Military Observer Group in India and Pakistan
UN Monetary and Financial Conference, 53, 55
UN Monitoring, Verification and Inspection Commission (UNMOVIC), 70
UNOCI. *See* UN Operation in Côte d'Ivoire
UNO-City, 22
UN Office at Geneva (UNOG), 17
UN Office for Project Services (UNOPS), 147
UN Office in Nairobi (UNON), 21
UN offices
    Baghdad, deaths in, 11–12
    Dili, Timor-Leste, 27–29
    expansion, 14–15
    Geneva, Switzerland, 16–20
    The Hague, the Netherlands, 23–24
    Montreal, Canada, 24, 26
    Nairobi, Kenya, 20–22
    New York City, 10–16
    Paris, France, 25
    peacekeeping, 213–219
    Pristina, Serbia-Montenegro (Kosovo Province), 27–29
    Rome, Italy, 26–27
    specialized agencies, 25
    Vienna, Austria, 22–23
UNOG. *See* UN Office at Geneva
UNON. *See* UN Office in Nairobi
UN Operation in Côte d'Ivoire (UNOCI), 219
UN Operation in Somalia I and II (UNOSOM I and II), 215, 219–220
UNOPS. *See* UN Office for Project Services

UN Organization Mission in the DRC (MONUC), 204, 221–222
UNOSOM I and II. *See* UN Operation in Somalia I and II
UN Peacekeeping Force in Cyprus (UNFICYP), 201, 204
UN Population Fund (UNFPA), 15, 16, 30, 93, 94, 136, 146
UN Protection Force (UNPROFOR), 210, 216
UN Relief and Works Agency for Palestine Refugees in the Near East (UNRWA), 30, 136, 146, 187
UN Relief for Palestine Refugees (UNRPR), 187
UNRPR. *See* UN Relief for Palestine Refugees
UNRWA. *See* UN Relief and Works Agency for Palestine Refugees in the Near East
UNSCOM. *See* UN Special Commission on Iraq
UNSCOP. *See* UN Special Commission on Palestine
UN Special Commission on Iraq (UNSCOM), 69–70
UN Special Commission on Palestine (UNSCOP), 187
UN System
  Chief Executives Board (CEB), 103, 118
  civil society and, 32
  coordination, 118
  described, 13
  offices, map of, 30
UN Transitional Authority in Cambodia (UNTAC), 208
UN Transition Assistance Group (UNTAG), 206
UN Truce Supervision Organization (UNTSO), 171, 198, 204
Uruguay Round of Multilateral Trade Negotiations, 156
U.S. *See* United States of America; *see also* Cold war
U.S. Commission on the Status of Women, 59
USG. *See* Under-secretary-general
USSR. *See* Soviet Union
Vaccination programs, 279–280
Vance, Cyrus, 209–210
Vattel, Emmerich de, 38
Versailles, Treaty of, 39, 41, 49, 53, 161, 162
Veto, Security Council
  controversy, 57
  described, 128, 130–131
  drawbacks, 111–112
  Dumbarton Oaks proposals, 51
  Israeli activities, 190
  members, blocking, 82
  Stalin's use of, 64
Vieira de Mello, Sergio, 12, 13, 131–132, 147, 241
Vienna, Austria, offices, 22–23, 25
Vienna Conference of 1814–1815, 36, 53, 86, 240–241
Vienna International Centre, 22–23
Volcker, Paul, 98, 113
Volcker-Ogata report, 98
Waldheim, Kurt, 137, 337–338
War crimes trials
  crimes against humanity, defining, 241–242
  early nation building, 8, 9
  International Criminal Court (ICC), 32, 140, 150, 229, 244–245
  International Criminal Tribunal for Rwanda (ICTR), 129, 242, 243
  International Criminal Tribunal for the Former Yugoslavia (ICTY), 24, 211, 235
  post–World War II, 90
  Rwanda, 31–32
  Special Court for Sierra Leone, 223
  twentieth century, turn of, 90–91
Washington, D.C., agencies, 25
Water pollution and marine resources, 274–275
Weapons of mass destruction (WMDs), 69–72, 177, 181
Welles, Sumner, 44
Westphalia, Treaty of, 36, 38, 53, 86, 161
WFP. *See* World Food Programme
WHO. *See* World Health Organization
Williams, William Appleman, 4
Willkie, Wendell, 45

Wilson, Woodrow
  Concert of Europe, 162
  League of Nations and, 39, 41–42
  reconstruction, post-World War I, 254
WIPO. *See* World Intellectual Property Organization
WMDs. *See* Weapons of mass destruction
WMO. *See* World Meteorological Organization
Women
  assistance to, 250–251
  global public policy concerning, 246–251
  international law on, 90
  public mobilization on behalf of, 246–249
  research about, 249–250
  rights of, 238, 246–251
  sexual harassment, UN employees' claim of, 112
  as thematic policy, 31
  as UN employees, 103–104
World Bank
  Global Environment Facility (GEF), 278
  HIV/AIDS funding, 153
  international financing of environmental projects, 278–279
  Money Matters Institute (MMI), 233
  organization and procedures of, 152–153
  regional development banks and, 263
  UN Conference on Trade and Development (UNCTAD), and, 258
World Conference on the Human Environment, 21, 146, 148, 229, 267, 272
World conferences, 148–149
World Court. *See* International Court of Justice
World Food Programme (WFP), 27, 146
World Health Organization (WHO)
  funding issues, 93
  HIV/AIDS crisis, 279, 280–281
  sustainable development, 270–271
World Intellectual Property Organization (WIPO), 89
World Meteorological Organization (WMO), 271
World Summit on Social Development (WSSD), 249
World Tourism Organization, 147
World Trade Organization (WTO)
  commodity agreements, 259
  controversy, 151
  environment, 89
  HIV/AIDS funding, 155–158
  Seattle protests, 33
  special rapporteurs, 231
World War I, 87
World War II
  Bretton Woods Conference, 53
  Dumbarton Oaks Conference, 50–51
  international law and, 87
  UN, creation of, 42
  Yalta Conference, 51–52
World Water Assessment Programme (WWAP), 274
World Wildlife Fund (WWF) 231
World Without a U.N., A (Heritage Foundation), 96
WSSD. *See* World Summit on Social Development
WTO. *See* World Trade Organization
WWAP. *See* World Water Assessment Programme
WWF. *See* World Wildlife Fund
Yalta Conference, 43, 45, 47, 50, 51–52, 55
Younes, Nadia, 138
Yugoslavia. *See also* Dayton Peace Accords
  cold war, end of, 68
  disintegration, 208, 209–211
  Milosevic war crimes trial, 235–236
  peacekeeping, 31–32, 209–211
  tribunals, 243
  UN membership, 321
Zinni, Anthony, 192
Zionists, 187